- substantial shortfall of CRE funding but man headwinds
against meeting to do '

MW00761192

regulation of rating agencies   Ch 11

# Commercial Mortgage Loans and CMBS: Developments in the European Market

*Second Edition*

# Commercial Mortgage Loans and CMBS: Developments in the European Market

*Second Edition*

Editor
**Andrew V. Petersen**

K&L GATES

**SWEET & MAXWELL**

 THOMSON REUTERS

First Edition     2006     Editor: Andrew V. Petersen
Second Edition     2012     Editor: Andrew V. Petersen

Published in 2012 by Sweet & Maxwell, 100 Avenue Road, London NW3 3PF part of
Thomson Reuters (Professional) UK Limited (Registered in England & Wales, Company No
1679046.
Registered Office and address for service: Aldgate House, 33 Aldgate High Street, London
EC3N 1DL)

For further information on our products and services, visit *www.sweetandmaxwell.co.uk*

Typeset by Letterpart Ltd, Reigate, Surrey

Printed and bound in Great Britain by MPG Books Ltd, Bodmin, Cornwall.

No natural forests were destroyed to make this product; only farmed timber was used and
re-planted.

A CIP catalogue record of this book is available for the British Library.

ISBN: 978-0-414-02558-5

Thomson Reuters and the Thomson Reuters logo are trademarks of Thomson Reuters.

Sweet & Maxwell ® is a registered trademark of Thomson Reuters (Professional) UK
Limited.

Crown copyright material is reproduced with the permission of the Controller of HMSO and
the Queen's Printer for Scotland.

All rights reserved. No part of this publication may be reproduced or transmitted in any
form or by any means, or stored in any retrieval system of any nature without prior written
permission, except for permitted fair dealing under the Copyright, Designs and Patents Act
1988, or in accordance with the terms of a licence issued by the Copyright Licensing Agency
in respect of photocopying and/or reprographic reproduction. Application for permission for
other use of copyright material including permission to reproduce extracts in other published
works shall be made to the publishers. Full acknowledgement of author, publisher and
source must be given.

© 2012 Thomson Reuters (Professional) UK Limited

Central bank support of banks
end in a year? Would cause banks
to unload loans to delever?

# Foreword

The CRE real estate market and the CRE finance market has experienced a tumultuous and remarkable five years since its peak in the summer of 2007. After a ten year period of almost continuous growth in capital values, lowering of financing costs and increases in availability of funding that abruptly ended in 2007, the contrast to today's market and the losses experienced by the industry since the peak are sobering.

The CRE finance market in Europe, which has been dominated by banks, now finds itself faced with a significant funding gap triggered by banks deleveraging due to regulatory pressures and over-exposure to the asset class and weak performance of legacy assets on their balance sheets. In addition, the CMBS new issue market is virtually non-existent.

The CRE property market, while stronger than its post-crisis nadir, has been affected by the constrained financing availability and is still far below the peak of 2007. CRE transaction volumes are muted, concentrated on prime assets in prime locations, and forecasts of CRE values, in line with GDP growth and unemployment rates, do not point to significant improvements over the next few years.

But amidst these undeniably difficult conditions in the CRE finance market, there are some very interesting and promising developments. Banks are delevering and disposing of unwanted assets, new local and international investors and lenders are entering the market, regulations are being fine-tuned and implemented, bid-ask spreads for loans and CRE assets are narrowing and clearing prices are slowly crystallising.

The deleveraging process will eventually lead to a more balanced and healthy CRE finance market, but the path will be long and, for some if not most participants, painful and difficult. A more diversified set of finance and capital providers, including insurance companies, banks, specialty finance companies, private equity, debt funds, pension funds and others, is slowly emerging and providing a wider and more creative range of CRE financing. An active capital markets for CMBS and loan trading should help complement the supply of credit to the market. If there is one certainty in this market it is that such credit is badly needed. It is further hoped that mortgage REITS can also emerge to fill the enormous funding gap?

Amongst the turmoil of the markets, the CREFC Europe has been very active in promoting the CRE finance market liquidity and best practices. Some of the initiatives undertaken by the CREFC Europe include topics like CMBS 2.0, investor reporting (E-IRP 2.0), loan underwriting due diligence, taxes affecting CRE transactions, intercreditor agreements and hedging for CRE finance. These are discussed throughout this book and in its appendices. I would encourage any reader who is not a member of the CREFC Europe to join and be a relevant part of the discussion and shape of our markets going forward.

I would like to commend Andrew Petersen at K&L Gates for his initiative, unrelenting energy and support in driving this second edition to completion. Given the turmoil faced in the markets such a second edition is timely. In addition, I would like to thank all the expert and dedicated contributors who have volunteered and taken the time to share their thoughts in the production of this book.

**Christian Janssen**

*Chair, CREFC Europe*

*Portfolio Manager, Real Estate Finance Fund, Renshaw Bay*

*November, 2012*

# Preface

In the years leading up to 2007, the remarkable and unprecedented explosion in the use of commercial real estate (CRE) debt resulted in investors scrambling for relatively inexpensive financing off the back of rising real estate asset values. The opportunity for yield and returns, for all parties throughout the capital structure, helped propel the meteoric rise in real estate debt and CMBS transactions. The first edition of this book chartered the development of the innovative CMBS product during this time, where, as a result of technological improvements and the lowering of global investment barriers, CMBS proved remarkable in its ability to address the needs of borrowers, loan originators and investors, in a way few would have thought possible. This transformation resulted in an explosion of issuance, as the CMBS market in Europe reached €46 billion (more than double the total for 2004), peaking at €65 billion in 2007. However, the provision of capital, during this boom period, tended to be very capital intensive and in respect of the commercial mortgage loan market, of a longer-term nature, mostly funded by balance sheet banks using relatively shorter-dated funds, thus allowing them larger spreads through effectively taking maturity transformation risk. This position could not continue indefinitely.

Every action has an equal but opposite reaction, and the deterioration that began in the US sub-prime mortgage market in the second half of 2007 became through contagion, interdependence and interconnection a deep crisis for the global securitisation markets, across all asset classes. In 2008, this crisis developed into a global financial crisis on a scale and with such far reaching impact as never seen before, a decrease in leveraged M&A transactions, falling share prices, a weakening of the global economy and the shutting down of the global real estate capital markets, ending the seemingly unstoppable growth of issuance in the European CMBS. As a result, the commercial mortgage loan and CMBS markets are currently unrecognisable to the markets that existed on the publication of the first edition of this book in 2006.

Since 2008, the markets have witnessed seismic structural shifts; many financial institutions with strong histories have failed, consolidated or been nationalised and sovereign states have become effectively bankrupt amongst the chaos of the financial crisis and real estate values across the globe have almost without exception suffered unanticipated catastrophic declines. As a result, there has been an unprecedented level of intervention

vii

by the world's central banks and state bail-outs of the financial and capital markets as well as a new regulatory framework aimed at trying to minimise the risk of these events occurring again. This second edition will consider the CRE debt and CMBS markets in the context of this post- 2008 world. It is hoped that, as with the first edition of the book, this edition, expanded to cover the wider CRE debt markets, will prove a timely and useful publication, as it is the case that real estate remains a tremendously important asset.

After all, one of the most striking developments in the global debt and capital markets over the last decades has been the metamorphosis of real estate from an asset class that had been famously regarded by institutional investors as illiquid and cumbersome outside the US. It is fitting then that Ch.1 begins by considering the legacy markets for CRE financing and CMBS in the post-2008 world, to determine whether the challenges that currently exist in the commercial mortgage markets can be overcome and whether the financing of CRE can continue to adapt and evolve on a journey based on financial innovation.

Chapter 2 explores the development and structure of Europe's CRE lending markets over the past decade first by looking in detail at the structure of the markets in Europe, focusing on bank lending, covered bonds and CMBS. The chapter then goes on to look at deleveraging in the marketplace, attitudes towards lending and explores the near-term outlook for Europe's CRE debt markets, through examining the potential debt funding gap and the ways in which the market is attempting to bridge this gap.

Chapter 3 recognises the vast opportunity that has arisen out of the financial crisis and considers the immense and continuously expanding global pool of private equity capital that is searching for liquid and rewarding investments. Such demand for investments will always result in new and exciting opportunities in real estate across the globe. 2013 and beyond will witness a formidable wave of money (ready to be invested at the correct time and in the correct product) chasing opportunities to take advantage of real estate's relentless globalisation, hopefully aided by greater transparency in domestic markets. This chapter demonstrates opportunities for private equity investors to achieve attractive risk-adjusted returns, when pursuing senior, mezzanine and equity investments thrown up by the financial crisis. Its conclusion that well-capitalised private equity investors with close relationships to borrowers and financial institutions will be well positioned to benefit from the market dynamics and opportunities is an exciting prospect.

Chapter 4 explores some of the key lessons learned since the advent of the financial crisis in relation to the structuring of new CMBS transactions and the many issues that market participants have had to face during the downturn relating to loan defaults and enforcement, consensual extensions

*lessons learned*

and restructurings, availability of information, voting mechanisms and the role of transaction counterparties. Through the initiative to introduce CMBS 2.0, led by organisations such as the CREFC Europe (and the guidelines published by its CMBS 2.0 Committee – see Appendix 3) and publications such as this, together with pressure from new investors, it is hoped that investor appetite for CMBS will be restored. This in turn will have a major impact on the real economy: as the financial crisis exposed the fragility of lenders' balance sheets. The capital markets offer the broadest and deepest potential investor base and should play a much larger role in our new landscape. What shape the new capital markets based debt products will take in coming years is uncertain, but CMBS 2.0, is expected to result in far more robust and more appropriate structures for the European CMBS markets in the future.

Servicing and asset management remain key issues in 2012. Chapters 5, 6 and 7 considers how the role of a facility agent, servicer and special servicer has been transformed since the vintage 2004-2007 originations and how servicers have had to adapt in the post- 2008 world. These chapters conclude that, as liquidity in 2012 in both the commercial mortgage loan and CMBS markets remains relatively stagnant, servicers face challenges to their own businesses as legacy deals begin to run off and the attendant fee income begins to evaporate. Servicers of the future will need to be more than just servicers, reliant on CMBS portfolio instructions; those with real estate experience, experienced asset management platforms and investment teams will be best placed place to profit from the next boom, or indeed the continuing bear, as Chapter 7 concludes.

One of the recurring themes of the restructuring of legacy debt transactions is the issue of swaps and hedging put in place at the time of origination. The hedging techniques referred to in Chapter 8, including the mismatch in loan maturity with loans dated swaps, highlight how the historically poor reputation of over-the-counter (OTC) derivatives, has plumbed to new depths amongst some CRE market participants since the advent of the financial crisis. This will result (quite rightly) in all parties paying much closer attention to the maximum liability that is possible under the hedging strategy that is contemplated at origination.

The book moves into a contemplative section through Chapters 9 to 13 which aim to understand the drivers and the economic conditions of the relatively successful golden era of 1998 to 2007, the structural and secular changes that have surfaced since the financial crisis and how those changes have affected the CRE finance industry and its participants (including lenders, investors, issuers, trustees, rating agencies and those that advise them). This section also considers how different lenders (portfolio lenders as well as debt capital markets orientated lenders), investors, trustees, issuers, and rating agencies operated their businesses during the boom times and how they may operate their businesses going forward. Here there is a message: there is no doubt that the financial crisis will have a lasting legacy on the European debt landscape and many market participants may have to reposition or reinvent themselves and their businesses to create opportunity.

Chapters 14 and 15 consider the world of intercreditor agreements (described in the first edition as a car crash waiting to happen!) and the opportunities for utilising subordinated debt structures going forward. Such structures are likely to be particularly important in the near future as distressed or discounted assets change hands. These chapters also discuss new developments in the high yield arena, in particular, borrower debt buy-backs (with a focus on the impact of a borrower in the debt stack).

European financial markets are currently in the most extensive period of financial regulatory reform in living memory. The two central and interrelated objectives of the global reform agenda are the strengthening of the world's financial institutions and the extension of regulatory oversight. Accordingly, Chapter 16 gives timely consideration to the numerous incentives which are, at the time of writing, under consideration by regulators and governments. It concludes that the challenge for the CRE industry will be to convince the regulators that the financing needs of the CRE market can be met in a way that does not increase systemic risk. It is hoped that, far from ending the innovation which has characterised the CRE and CMBS markets over the years, it will spurn new ways of thinking and transacted.

Given the importance of Germany to the CRE finance markets, it would be remiss of this book not to focus specifically on Germany. Chapter 17, in Part I, considers the continental European commercial mortgage loan and CMBS markets and their outlook, before Part II takes a closer look at the specific legal and regulatory environment framework, and recent developments in, commercial mortgage loans and CMBS in Germany.

CRE has been an increasingly important asset class for Islamic compliant transactions and banks since the publication of the first edition of this book in 2006. During this period, Islamic compliant finance has proven to be an alternative source of funds for investors entering the European CRE market, as highlighted by such high profile London CRE deals, such as the Chelsea Barracks and the Shard of Glass, the tallest building in Europe. These developments are reflected in Chapter 18, which considers the Islamic compliant financing of CRE, a subject which has, for a number of years, attracted a great deal of interest.

Moreover, when discussing real estate the force of globalisation cannot be ignored. The 2008 financial crisis has demonstrated (perhaps for the first time) the myriad ways in which financial markets and economies are inextricably linked and interdependent. Whilst investment in European

CRE has long been regarded as a relative value play for many global investors, North American interest in European CRE has, in particular, proven to be an effective counterweight to the traditional interest of European investors in US CRE opportunities. In recent years, global economic forces affecting world financial markets have been drawing capital inexorably towards European CRE. However, for those investors who understand the intricacies and can accurately price risk and reward, European CRE investments can represent extraordinary opportunities to achieve high yields. The implications behind this are considered in detail in Chapter 19.

The establishment of real estate as a global asset class in its own right is unlikely to be reversed and I have no doubt that real estate will re-emerge as a popular asset class. Given that the continuing credit crisis is, in many respects, as much due to a crisis of confidence as to any other factors, such re-emergence will, be dictated in large part by the confidence in our financial architecture. Any developments or products we can provide to help restore market confidence as well as remove or reduce risk can only be a good thing. Thus Chapter 20, in the challenging and stressed markets witnessed at the time of writing, provides some answers when considering the opportunities and offers some concise thoughts to address the prominent underlying challenge faced by commercial mortgage loan and CMBS markets in 2012: to once again play a role in ensuring smooth capital flow between investor and financier. As the balance of economic power shifts from west to east, participants will need to adapt to seek out the changing pockets of capital in order to overcome the challenges in the commercial mortgage markets. Innovation in adapting to the challenges faced by the sector will continue, as is already seen in the arrival of specialist debt funds and fixed rate products on offer. It concludes that in addition to traditional sources of capital, debt market participants in Europe will need a more global perspective in seeking out capital to allocate to real estate debt. South-East Asia, the Americas, the Middle East, Russia, Japan and importantly China will all have an increased role to play in the European commercial mortgage debt markets of the next decade and beyond.

When conceiving the first edition of this book in 2005, my desire was to produce a book that included a vital mix of business chapters alongside legal chapters: a new generation of textbook spanning the sometimes achingly visible gap between business people and their professional advisors. By bringing together 30 specialist industry professionals in a true collaboration between principals and advisors, this edition embraces this concept again.

On a personal note, I wish to thank my wife Sarah and my daughters, Livia and Isobel, for their infinite patience and continuing understanding in putting up with my absences at weekends and evenings whilst working on this book.

**Andrew V. Petersen**

*November, 2012*

# Acknowledgement

Many people have been involved in bringing this book to fruition. It is hoped that the mentioning of the names below will go some way to thanking those listed for all the time and effort they have contributed.

First and foremost, thanks must be directed at the team of specialist contributors. When I began approaching potential contributors, I was amazed at the depth of expertise we still have in this industry, and indeed new expertise that has developed as a result of the factors at play in the market. Each contributor was enthusiastic and unwavering in producing their respective chapter. Without their selfless undertaking, this volume would have not reached publication.

Acknowledgment is further due to the assistance given in the production process by Justin Joshi of K&L Gates. Justin played an important role assisting in the task of proofing and editing a number of chapters. In addition, thanks are due to Juliette Challenger, James Buncle and Katie Hillier of K&L Gates for their diligent reviews of various chapters.

Ollie Tagg of K&L Gates, together with Justin Joshi, must also be singled out for succeeding in the mammoth task of producing the book's glossary of terms and abbreviations. The glossary will act as a valuable stand alone tool to assist readers wishing to understand this important area. It could be published as a stand alone piece in its own right!

I also want to thank Christian Janssen for contributing the foreword to this volume and the collaboration received in producing this book from the officers and directors of CREFC Europe in particular Carol Wilkie, its London Managing Director. CREFC Europe carries out sterling work promoting the real estate industry in the midst of an incredibly important and difficult time dealing with numerous market initiatives and EC regulatory issues, the outcome of which will shape our industry for years to come. If this book can assist in some small way, alongside their work, then it is only fitting that its current Chair has the first words and its important market initiatives appear in Appendices 1 to 4.

The enthusiasm for the project from within K&L Gates should also be mentioned, especially from Tony Griffiths, the firm's London Administrative Partner and K&L Gates' Chairman Peter Kalis, each for recognising this project as a truly collaborative effort bringing together many lawyers from across our global law firm and for each being truly supportive and permitting the K&L Gates' contributors the time to undertake this work.

Finally, I would like to thank Sweet & Maxwell and in particular our Publisher Nick Bliss, first for helping to make all of this possible with his foresight to commission the book and secondly for his endless encouragement and support in completing it. Also, I am grateful to the editorial team who undertook – with great success – a difficult job and ensured this volume was published efficiently and promptly.

**Andrew V. Petersen**

*November, 2012*

# Contents

1   **The Commercial Mortgage Loan and CMBS Markets: Legacy and current positions**

Andrew V. Petersen

*Partner, K&L Gates LLP*

2   **Commercial mortgage loans, CMBS and its role in the wider real estate debt capital markets**

Hans Vrensen,

*Global Head of Research, DTZ*

Nigel Almond,

*Head of Strategy, Research, DTZ*

**6    Servicing Distressed Legacy Commercial Mortgage Loan and CMBS Loans: Workouts, Enforcements**

Matt Grefsheim,

*Director – Special Servicing, Hatfield Philips*

**7    Servicing Commercial Mortgage Loans and CMBS 2.0: the Legal Issues**

James A. Spencer,

*Senior Associate, K&L Gates LLP*

**8    Derivatives in Legacy Cre Financings and their Role in Future Transactions: How Derivatives Continue to Impact Restructurings and Finance Strategy**

Mark Battistoni,

*Director, Chatham Financial*

Jonathan Lye,

*Senior Hedging Adviser, Chatham Financial*

**15    The Modern Intercreditor Agreement: Terms and Issues**

Diego Shin,
*Senior Associate, K&L Gates LLP*

Philip Moore,
*Principal, DRC Capital*

**16    European CMBS and Regulatory Reform**

Stephen H. Moller,
*Partner, K&L Gates LLP*

**17    Continental European Commercial Mortgage Loans and CMBS**

Dr. Stefan Luthringshauser,
*Director, Capita Asset Services GmbH*

Volker Gattringer and Dr. Christian Büche,
*Partners K&L Gates LLP*

**18    Islamic Compliant Financing of Commercial Real Estate**

Jonathan Lawrence,
*Partner, K&L Gates LLP*

**19    Lost (and Found) in Translation: US Cross-border Investments in European Commercial Mortgage Markets**

Anthony R. G. Nolan,
*Partner, K&L Gates LLP*

Diego Shin,
*Senior Associate, K&L Gates LLP*

20    **Challenges and Opportunities For Commercial Mortgage Loan and CMBS Markets**

Craig B Prosser,
*Landesbank Baden-Württemberg*

**Appendices**

# Abbreviations

A full glossary is provided at Appendix 5.

| | |
|---|---|
| AAOIFI | Accounting and Auditing Organisation for Islamic Financial Institutions |
| ABCP | Asset Backed Commercial Paper |
| ABS | Asset Backed Securities / Securitisation |
| ADR | American Depository Receipts |
| AFC | Available Funds Cap |
| AIF | Authorised Investment Funds |
| AIFM | Alternative Investment Fund Manager |
| AIFMD | Alternative Investment Fund Managers Directive |
| AIM | Alternative Investment Market of the London Stock Exchange |
| ALTA | American Land Title Association |
| AREA | Asian Real Estate Association |
| AUM | Assets under Management |
| AVM | Automated Valuation Models |
| BBA | British Bankers' Association |
| BCO | British Council for Offices |
| BIPRU | FSA's Prudential Sourcebook for Banks, Building Societies and Investment Firms |
| BIS | Bank for International Settlements |
| BOV | Broker's Opinion of Value |
| Bp | Basis Point |
| bppa | Basis Points Per Annum |
| BPF | British Property Federation |
| CAGR | Compound Annual Growth Rate |
| CBO | Collateralised Bond Obligation |
| CCR | Controlling Class Representative |
| CDO | Collateralised Debt Obligation |
| CDO2 | Collateralised Debt Obligation Squared |
| CDS | Credit Default Swaps |
| CFC | Controlling Foreign Company |
| CEBS | Committee of European Banking Supervisors |
| CEE | Central and Eastern Europe |
| CESR | Committee of European Securities Regulators |
| CGT | Capital Gains Tax |

| | |
|---|---|
| CIS | Collective Investment Scheme |
| CLN | Credit Linked Note |
| CLO | Collateralised Loan Obligations |
| CMBS | Commercial Mortgage Backed Securitisation / Securities |
| CMO | Collateralised Mortgage Obligation |
| CMSA | Commercial Mortgage Securities Association |
| CMVM | Portuguese Securities Commission |
| COE | Cost of Equity |
| COMI | Centre of Main Interest |
| CP | Commercial Paper |
| CPR | Constant Prepayment Rates |
| CRA | Credit Rating Agency |
| CRD | Capital Requirements Directive |
| CRD 2 | Capital Requirements Directive 2 |
| CRD 3 | Capital Requirements Directive 3 |
| CRE | Commercial Real Estate |
| CREFC | Commercial Real Estate Financial Council |
| CSA | Collateral Support Agreements |
| CSA | Credit Support Annex |
| CSWA | Capital Structure Weighted Average |
| CVA | Company Voluntary Arrangement |
| CVE | Control Valuation Event |
| DCF | Discounted Cash Flow |
| DOL | Department of Labor (US) |
| DPO | Discounted Pay Off / Discounted Purchase Offer |
| DSCR | Debt Service Coverage Ratio |
| DTAA | Double Taxation Avoidance Agreements |
| EAD | Exposure at Default |
| EBA | European Banking Authority |
| E-IRP | European Investor Reporting Package |
| EC | European Community |
| ECB | European Central Bank |
| EEA | European Economic Area |
| EFTA | European Free Trade Association |
| EIOPA | European Insurance and Occupational Pensions Authority |
| EL | Expected Loss |
| EMEA | Europe, the Middle East and Africa |
| EMIR | European Market Infrastructure Regulations |
| EONIA | Euro OverNight Index Average |
| EPF | European Property Federation |
| EPRA | European Public Real Estate Association |
| ERISA | Employee Retirement Income Security Act 1974 (US) |
| ERV | Estimated Rental Value |
| ESF | European Securitisation Forum |
| ESMA | European Securities and Markets Authority |
| ETF | Exchange Traded Fund |

| | |
|---|---|
| EU | European Union |
| EUIR | European Union Insolvency Regulation |
| EURIBOR | Euro Inter-Bank Offered Rate |
| FATCA | Foreign Account Tax Compliance Act |
| FDI | Foreign Direct Investment |
| FDIC | Federal Deposit Insurance Corporation (US) |
| FFI | Foreign Financial Institution |
| FHCMC | Federal Home Loan Mortgage Corporation (Freddie Mac) |
| FIRREA | Financial Institutions Reform, Recovery and Enforcement Act 1989 (US) |
| FNMA | Federal National Mortgage Association (Fannie Mae) |
| FSA | Financial Services Authority |
| FSB | Financial Stability Board |
| FSF | Financial Stability Forum |
| FSMA | Financial Services and Markets Act 2000 (UK) |
| GAAP | Generally Accepted Accounting Principles |
| GCC | Gulf Cooperation Council |
| GIC | Guaranteed Investment Contract |
| GNMA | Government National Mortgage Association (Ginnie Mae) |
| GOEF | German Open-Ended Funds |
| GSIFIs | Globally Systemically Important Financial Institutions |
| GSE | Government Sponsored Entities (US) |
| HEL | Home Equity Loans |
| HIRE | Hiring Incentives to Restore Employment Act 2010 (US) |
| HMRC | Her Majesty's Revenue & Customs (UK) |
| HNWI | High Net-Worth Individual |
| HVRE | High Volatile Real Estate |
| ICR | Issuer Credit Rating |
| ICR | Interest Cover Ratio |
| IDB | Islamic Development Bank |
| IFRS | International Financial Reporting Standards |
| IFSB | Islamic Financial Services Board |
| IMF | International Monetary Fund |
| INREV | Investors in Non-Listed Real Estate Vehicles |
| IO | Interest-Only |
| IOSCO | International Organisation of Securities Commissions |
| IPD | Interest Payment Date / International Property Databank |
| IPF | Investment Property Forum |
| IPRE | Income Producing Real Estate |
| IRAP | Italian Regional Tax on Productive Activities |
| IRB | Internal Ratings-Based Approach |
| IRES | Italian Corporate Income Tax |
| IRP | Investor Reporting Package |
| IRR | Internal Rate of Return |
| IRS | Internal Revenue Service (US) |
| ISDA | International Swaps and Derivatives Association |

| | |
|---|---|
| ISE | Irish Stock Exchange |
| LGD | Loss Given Default |
| LIBOR | London Inter-Bank Offered Rate |
| LLP | Loan Loss Provision |
| LMA | Loan Market Association |
| LOC | Letter of Credit |
| LP | Limited Partner |
| LPE | Limited Purpose Entity |
| LSE | Luxembourg Stock Exchange |
| LTC | Loan-To-Cost |
| LTV | Loan-To-Value |
| LTRO | Long Term Refinancing Operation |
| M | Effective Maturity |
| M&A | Mergers and Acquisitions |
| MAD | Market Abuse Directive |
| MBMP | Multi-Borrower Multi-Property |
| MBS | Mortgage Backed Securities / Securitisation |
| MCR | Minimum Capital Requirement |
| MFC | French Monetary and Financial Code |
| MFH | Multi-Family Housing |
| MGS | Malaysian Global Sukuk Inc. |
| MiFID | Markets in Financial Instruments Directive |
| MTN | Medium-Term Note |
| NAMA | National Asset Management Agency |
| NAREIT | National Association of Real Estate Investment Trusts (US) |
| NAV | Net Asset Value |
| NCREIF | National Council for Real Estate Investment Fiduciaries (US) |
| NICE | Non Inflationary Consistent Expansion |
| NIM | Net Interest Margin |
| NOCF | Net Operating Cash Flow |
| NOI | Net Operating Income |
| NPL | Non-Performing Loan |
| NRSRO | Nationally Recognized Statistical Rating Organizations |
| NSFR | Net Stable Funding Ratio |
| NSMIA | National Securities Markets Improvement Act 1996 (US) |
| OA | Operating Advisor |
| OC | Offering Circular |
| OECD | Organisation for Economic Co-operation & Development |
| OEIC | Open Ended Investment Company |
| OIC | Organisation of the Islamic Conference |
| OSCRE | Open Standards Consortium for Real Estate |
| OTC | Over-The-Counter |
| OTD | Originate to Distribute |
| PAIF | Property Authorised Investment Fund |
| PFIC | Passive Foreign Investment Company |

| | |
|---|---|
| PIA | Property Industry Alliance |
| PIC | Property Investment Certificate |
| PIC | Property Income Distribution |
| PIIGS | Portugal Ireland Italy Greece Spain |
| PIK | Payment in Kind |
| PLN | Property Linked Note |
| PUT | Property Unit Trust |
| PD | Default Probability |
| PMA | Property Market Analysis |
| PMP | Professional Market Parties |
| QFC | Qualifying Floating Charge |
| QIB | Qualified Institutional Buyer |
| QIS | Qualified Investor Scheme |
| QIV | Qualifying Investment Vehicle |
| QRS | Qualified REIT Subsidiary |
| RAC | Rating Agency Confirmation |
| RBA | Ratings Based Approach |
| RBC | Risk Based Capital |
| RED-SIG | Real Estate Derivatives Special Interest Group |
| REIT | Real Estate Investment Trusts |
| REMIC | Real Estate Mortgage Investment Conduit |
| REO | Real Estate Owned Through Enforcement Action |
| REOC | Real Estate Operating Company |
| RICS | Royal Institution of Chartered Surveyors |
| RIE | Recognised Investment Exchange |
| RIS | Regulatory Information Services |
| RMBS | Residential Mortgage Backed Securities |
| ROC | Return on Capital |
| ROE | Return on Equity |
| RTC | Resolution Trust Corporation (US) |
| RW | Risk Weight |
| RWA | Risk Weight Assets |
| S&L | Savings & Loan |
| SCR | Solvency Capital Requirement |
| SDLT | Stamp Duty Land Tax |
| SEC | Securities and Exchange Commission |
| SF | Supervisory Formula |
| SIV | Structured Investment Vehicle |
| SME | Small and Medium Enterprises |
| SMMEA | Secondary Mortgage Market Enhancement Act 1984 (US) |
| SONIA | Sterling OverNight Index Average |
| SPE | Special Purpose Entity |
| SPV | Special Purpose Vehicle |
| SWF | Sovereign Wealth Fund |
| TALF | Term Asset Backed Securities Loan Facility (US) |
| TARP | Troubled Asset Relief Programme (US) |

| | |
|---|---|
| TIN | Taxpayer Identification Number |
| TMP | Taxable Mortgage Pool |
| TOGC | Transfer of a business as a Going Concern |
| TRS | Total Return Swap |
| UBTI | Unrelated Business Taxable Income |
| UCC | Uniform Commercial Code (US) |
| UCIT | Undertakings for Collective Investment in Transferable Securities |
| UNCITRAL | United Nations Commission on International Trade Law |
| UL | Unexpected Loss |
| VAT | Value Added Tax |
| VATA 1994 | Value Added Tax Act 1994 |
| VRE | Voting Rights Enforcement |
| WAC | Weighted-Average Coupon |
| WAFF | Weighted-Average Foreclosure Frequency |
| WALS | Weighted-Average Loss Severity |
| WAM | Weighted–Average Maturity |
| WAULT | Weighted-Average Unexpired Lease Term |
| WBS | Whole Business Securitisation |

# Chapter 1

# The Commercial Mortgage Loan and CMBS Markets: Legacy and current positions

Andrew V. Petersen

Partner, K&L Gates LLP

## 1.1. Introduction

Commercial real estate (CRE) remains a tremendously important asset, as the content of this book will determine. However, the commercial mortgage loan and commercial mortgage-backed securities (CMBS) markets are, at the time of writing, unrecognisable to the markets that existed on the publication of the first edition of this book, published in 2006. Since then, the markets have witnessed seismic structural shifts. Numerous financial institutions with strong histories have failed, consolidated or been nationalised and, amongst the chaos of the credit crisis, CRE and the CRE capital markets have had a visible presence throughout, with nearly all real estate values across the globe suffering unanticipated catastrophic declines.

The first edition of this book chartered the introduction and development of the innovative CMBS product in Europe up to 2006.[1] During this period, as a result of technological improvements and the lowering of global investment barriers that freed CMBS from the restrictions of US REMIC rules, the development of the product proved remarkable in its ability to address the needs of borrowers, loan originators and investors, in a way few would have thought possible. This transformation resulted in an explosion of issuance, as the CMBS market in Europe reached €46 billion (more than double the total for 2004), peaking at €65 billion in 2007. This issuance came off the back of a boom in CRE financing, fuelled by an overheated CRE market, fostered by the availability of plentiful and cheap funding, coupled with relatively low capital requirements, that established real estate as a global asset class in its own right.

However, the provision of capital to the CRE industry, which tends by definition to be very capital intensive and of a longer-term nature was,

---

[1]    A.V. Petersen, *Commercial Mortgage-Backed Securitisation: Developments in the European Market*, 1st edn (London: Sweet & Maxwell, 2006).

1

during this boom period, mostly funded by balance sheet banks using relatively shorter-dated funds, thus allowing them larger spreads through effectively taking maturity transformation risk. This position could not continue indefinitely. Due in a large part to the deterioration that began in the US sub-prime mortgage market in the second half of 2007, became through contagion, interdependence and interconnection a deep crisis for the global securitisation markets, across all asset classes that developed in 2008 and in the subsequent years quickly morphed into a global liquidity crisis.

The global liquidity crisis in turn gave rise to a deep global financial crisis, a decrease in leveraged M&A transactions, falling share prices, a weakening of the global economy[2] and the shutting down or freezing of the global real estate capital markets, ending the seemingly unstoppable growth of issuance in European and US CMBS markets witnessed prior to the summer of 2007. This development was not a cyclical change, as had occurred in the past, but a major structural change, giving rise to questions over the viability of the CMBS "originate-to-distribute" model, based in part on structural weaknesses revealed in the securities themselves. Such questions will need to be addressed in the coming years, as many believe that the impact of this structural shift may last for a period of up to 10 years.

Given this backdrop, 2008 witnessed an unprecedented level of intervention by the world's central banks and state bail-outs of the financial and capital markets,[3] and this second edition will consider these markets in the context of a post 2008 world.[4] In doing so, this Chapter will consider the legacy markets for CRE financing and CMBS and will examine the impact on the respective markets. In order to do so, it is necessary to go back in time to examine the evolution of the CRE and CMBS markets in an effort to understand and to determine whether CMBS will continue to be an important source of funding and risk diversification tool and resurge from a

---

[2]   The IMF estimates that losses from the financial crisis exceed US $4 trillion.

[3]   In a potted history of events, in a short period that ultimately forever altered the modern financial markets, in September 2008, the US government took control of Freddie Mac and Fannie Mae, government-sponsored entities that were created to generate funding for the US housing market through securitising home loans, in (at the time) the world's largest financial bailout. On September 15, 2008, Lehman Brothers announced it would file for bankruptcy and Bank of America announced that it would acquire Merrill Lynch for US $50 billion. On September 16, 2008, the US Federal Reserve announced it would lend AIG, once the world's largest insurance company with a market value of US $239 billion, US $85 billion in emergency funds. On September 17, 2008, Lloyds Bank announced it would take over HBOS, previously the United Kingdom's largest savings institution, for £12 billion. On September 22, 2008, the remaining US investment banks, Goldman Sachs and Morgan Stanley, were approved by the Federal Reserve to become bank holding companies, a move that subjects them to regulation by the Federal Reserve. The failure of Washington Mutual, the sixth largest US bank, on September 25, 2008 marked the largest bank failure in US history and in the United Kingdom, the government nationalised Bradford & Bingley.

[4]   The terms "subprime" and "credit crunch" were, in mid-2008, recognised as new words in the English language by the *Oxford English Dictionary* providing a constant reminder of how the world and financial markets had developed.

temporary setback witnessed at the time of writing. Thus, when we consider the legacy commercial mortgage loan and CMBS markets that exist at the time of writing, we have to split such analysis up into two separate periods: up to 2007 and post 2007.

## 1.2. The commercial mortgage loan and CMBS markets prior to 2007

The European bank lending sector has traditionally been the key and biggest provider of financing to the CRE market, providing 90–95 per cent of the financing to the sector as banks with significant balance sheet capacity (but not strength, as it turned out) grew their exposure to real estate substantially during the period 1997 to 2007. This was predominantly as a result of falling interest rates which stimulated demand for real estate following the technology market crash and dotcom bust of early 2000s as investors sought solace in longer-term assets that effectively hedged interest rate risk. During the period from 1997 to 2007, given the relatively low development of other forms of financing, CRE financing was one of the fastest growing lending classes for banks, particularly in the United Kingdom and Spain. The largest CRE lenders were made up of UK, German and Irish banks (in each case lending both domestically and internationally). Spanish banks also generated a large CRE exposure, although primarily domestic. Prior to this period, commercial and residential real estate debt was held on the balance sheets of mortgage lenders, such as banks, building societies and insurance companies. To the extent that a secondary market existed for this debt, it was largely a club syndication and participation market. Securitisation through the issuance of CMBS played a small (historically around 10–15 per cent the total outstanding debt in the sector), but meaningful, role in funding European CRE throughout this development and it is important to understand its origins.

### 1.2.1. The birth of commercial mortgage-backed securitisation

Whilst the United States claims to be the birthplace of CMBS, securities, in the form of European mortgage bonds, have existed in Europe for over 200 years. Nonetheless, it is true that CMBS in the modern form ultimately did not become popular in Europe until after the 1980s following the widespread acceptance in the US marketplace where many of the legal structural foundations of the modern CMBS market were put into place, paving the way for the growth of the modern CMBS industry. Such growth was based on the changing dynamics of real estate lending that had its origins in the 1970s, particularly as US government-sponsored enterprises, such as the Federal National Mortgage Association (Fannie Mae) and the Federal Home Loan Mortgage Corporation (Freddie Mac) began to facilitate increasing growth in home ownership by guaranteeing mortgage-backed securities backed by portfolios of US mortgages.

CMBS in the United States received a further catalyst for growth with the advent of the savings and loan crisis of the late 1980s. The crisis led to a seminal event in the development of the modern US CMBS industry, with the passage of the Financial Institutions Reform, Recovery and Enforcement Act (FIRREA) in August, 1989. Among other things, it imposed stricter capital standards on regulated commercial lenders and created the Resolution Trust Corporation (RTC). The RTC was charged with resolving failed thrift institutions and disposing of the assets of these failed institutions. In the early 1990s, the RTC, and later the US Federal Deposit Insurance Corporation (the FDIC), began to reduce the inventory of assets that they had acquired from failed depository institutions during the savings and loan crisis. The biggest portion of the RTC's inventory consisted of a portfolio of mortgage loans, which by August 1990 was estimated to be more than US $34 billion that had been originated and held by depository institutions that the RTC controlled. It was quickly realised that selling those loans one by one was neither efficient, nor, in the final analysis, even achievable. As the market for mortgage-backed securities had developed dramatically up to this time, the RTC, in a significant step in the evolution of the mortgage capital markets, turned to the then novel concept of private-label securitisation of assets that did not conform to the Fannie Mae or Freddie Mac underwriting standards as a way to dispose of this overhang of now publicly owned private debt.[5]

The success of the RTC's CMBS program resulted in private label mortgage conduits bursting forth in the early 1990s as a way of funding and securitising vast pools of commercial and multi-family loans. It is during this period, through financial innovation, that the alchemy of securitisation truly prospered as the "originate-to-distribute" business model took hold where mortgages were originated with the sole intention of distributing them or selling them on in the market shortly after being written, thereby passing the risk of default to another financial institution. Such alchemy allowed risky mortgage assets to be mixed in a melting pot of potions to be turned overnight into highly-rated investment grade assets based on a wide range of investor demand and appetite. Meanwhile, the European securitisation markets, whilst lagging behind the developing market in the United States, slowly metamorphosed into a European securitisation industry based on three types of securitisation methods:

---

[5] See further Ch.1 of the 1st edn. The RTC's famous "Series C" transactions marked the first time that commercial mortgages were packaged and securitised in large volumes. These programs not only helped to resolve the overhang of the savings and loan crisis, but also created standard templates for securitisable- loan terms, securitisation structures, loan servicing conventions, property information reporting templates and the like, paving the way for the growth of a vibrant commercial mortgage conduit securitisation industry. Many of these standards are still in use to date, although see Ch.4 for the development of the market post 2008 and the implementation of new standards surrounding CMBS 2.0.

"On-balance sheet securitisation", such as covered mortgage bonds and *Pfandbrief*- style products;

"Off-balance sheet pass through" securitisation, where assets are transferred to a trustee for the sole purpose of issuing asset-backed securities; and

"Off-balance sheet pay through" securitisation. This development and growth was as a result of the diversity of the European markets in terms of the types of underlying assets, types of security and the applicable taxes, regulations and laws that permeate throughout Europe.

The introduction of the euro currency towards the end of the 1990s resulted in a reduction of the currency translation risks of cross-border transactions, translating into an increase in issuance fuelled by strong investor demand, which formed the basis for the creation of a relatively large European MBS market. A UK-centric, fixed rate market in the late 1990s quickly developed. During this time, CMBS transformed the CRE market. What was initially an isolated, self-contained business funded by domestic (and often geographically local) banks and insurance companies which invested a fixed "real estate" allocation of capital into the CRE markets for portfolio purposes and held those mortgage loans on their balance sheets to maturity, transformed itself into a business funded by the broad global capital markets.

By the late 1990s, fixed income investors invested in rated bonds throughout the capital stack, up and down the risk curve enabling the spread of risk. A growing number of boutique, high-yield real estate players further emerged to invest in the below investment grade segment of the risk curve. CMBS led to an enormous increase in the availability of finance and became a major driver of economic growth, in western markets. However, the Autumn of 1998 witnessed the Russian rouble debt crisis which, whilst shaking the industry to its core, also matured the industry,[6] such that (for a time) there were tightened underwriting standards throughout the early years of the 2000s, a period which also led to a high-yield market for subordinate tranches of CRE loans.[7]

In the United Kingdom, prior to 2004 listed real estate companies or corporates were the major issuers of CMBS as it was mainly used as a financial or capital raising tool, a means for such entities to borrower directly from the capital markets to finance investments more efficiently on longer terms than borrowing directly from banks. CMBS proved attractive as, due to capital efficiencies resultant from the CMBS product, margins offered through a CMBS financing were often lower than through conventional bank debt funding. Thus, a price arbitrage was developing between bank lending and CMBS lending. Then from 2005 to 2007,

---

[6] See further Ch.1 of the 1st edn.
[7] See further Ch.14.

following the birth of banks' conduit programmes (described below), CMBS began lending in increasing amounts direct to highly geared CRE investors, such as private equity funds and property funds, leading to a dramatic shift in the use of CMBS from a long term financing to a shorter term funding method. The loans originated by these programmes were often set up by investment banks or commercial banks, which would then deposit the loans to capital markets issuing entities for packaging and distribution to investors.[8] These investors, broadly speaking, saw bonds backed by commercial mortgage debt, not as an isolated "alternative investment" but simply as one among many core investment opportunities which were pursued with more or less vigour depending upon perceptions of relative value[9]. This led to a range of assets being financed through securitisation conduit programs, such as operating businesses made up of pubs, hotels, nursing homes through to offices, retail properties and industrial properties. With this development, the CMBS industry morphed into a major source of capital with 75 per cent of all outstanding CMBS bonds existing at the time of writing, being issued between 2005 to 2007, mostly all through conduit programmes. Thus through CMBS, CRE and its funding depended, in a very material way, upon direct access to the capital markets. It is worth setting out what exactly the CMBS product consists of for those readers unfamiliar with the product.

### 1.2.2.  Key features of CMBS[10]

CMBS is largely a mechanism for capital transfer based on a methodology of channelling capital into real estate debt based on cash flows generated by separate pools of commercial mortgages through the creation and issuance of securities. This methodology, based on an indirect real estate investment, is a means of providing liquidity to the markets by issuing securities whose payments are backed by illiquid real estate. In essence, illiquid assets are converted into securities that can be sold to investors, through a product, designed to spread risk, through the method of pooling and repackaging of cash-flow producing commercial mortgage loans by mortgage originators, usually in the form of off-balance sheet vehicles in the form of newly formed special purpose vehicles (SPVs). The SPVs issue securities backed by the CRE loans that are then sold to investors in the global capital markets. Instead of requiring the originator to hold all of the credit risk of a CRE loan until maturity, thereby inefficiently trapping capital of the originator, CMBS provides the originator a way of selling the CRE loan upon origination and using the funds received to originate further loans. The process produces fixed income fees for the bank through the creation, sale and underwriting/arranging of the product, and, on occasion, at the same time reducing the mortgage originators' capital requirements/capital relief.

---

[8]  See further Ch.3 of the 1st edn.
[9]  See further Ch.1 of the 1st edn.
[10]  See further Ch.4.

The move in the late 1980s and early 1990s to securitise US mortgage debt effectively remedied one of the primary impediments to real estate becoming a global asset class, that of illiquidity, at the same time serving as a useful credit portfolio risk management tool for CMBS originators. Cash flows from whole loans can be (i) isolated from the individual whole loans and reassembled in a number of ways (based on investor demand) to pay principal and interest (in normal market conditions at a lower amount than the rates received from the borrowers, thereby providing additional income to the CMBS originators), and (ii) stratified by interest rate, risk and duration, thereby boosting the volume of lending available for CRE, via a tradeable security that provides investors with an income stream backed by real assets. Such investor demand drives the value of the sum of the securities to equal or exceed the par amount of the loans backing these securities.[11]

Table 1 provides an overview of a CMBS with a B Loan.[12]

**Table 1: Overview of a Securitisation with a B Loan**

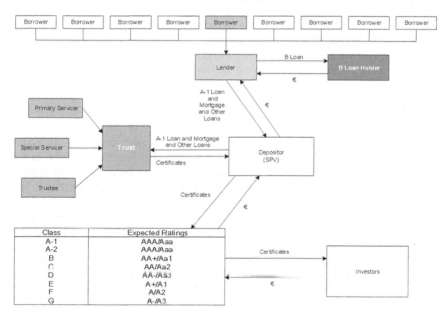

| Class | Expected Ratings |
|-------|------------------|
| A-1 | AAA/Aaa |
| A-2 | AAA/Aaa |
| B | AA+/Aa1 |
| C | AA/Aa2 |
| D | AA-/Aa3 |
| E | A+/A1 |
| F | A/A2 |
| G | A-/A3 |

A very important feature of CMBS is the dispersion of risk through tranching of credit risk based on subordination, so that the pool of mortgage assets (together with any credit enhancement) can effectively be

---

[11] See further Ch.1 of the 1st edn.
[12] See further Chs 14 and 15.

tranched all the way from triple-A rated securities to non-investment grade securities that bear the first loss of risk on the assets in the pool (see Table 1 above). The securities in a CMBS are rated by international credit rating agencies (CRAs),[13] such as Moody's, Standard & Poor's, Fitch Ratings and DBRS, based on a methodology which recognises the different levels of risk, return, order of payment and degree of credit support. The credit ratings proffered by the CRAs became, over time, a crucial indicator of risk as investors relied on such ratings as they themselves were often not in a position to evaluate the quality of, or risk factors associated with, the underlying assets. Indeed often, investment criteria for senior tranche investors were based on the fact that two of the three largest CRAs had provided the same rating and thus an element of reliance of CRAs undertaking the task instead of investors took hold.

By creating tranched capital structures for investments in pools of mortgage debt, CMBS transactions permit investors in senior tranches ranging from triple-A, with the first claim on payments (thus reducing risk but also providing a lower return), to obtain highly-rated exposures to diverse pools of financial assets at a yield greater than that for comparably rated corporate or sovereign debt. Whilst investors in subordinate tranches (the so-called "first loss" piece, as these notes are the first to absorb losses and consequently receive the highest rate of returns), only receive payments once the senior tranches have been paid (i.e. based on a waterfall principle), such investors can obtain leveraged exposures to diverse pools of financial assets without the risk of margin calls.

Such tranching led to the investor base for CMBS becoming highly targeted based on differential risk-return appetites. Treasury departments of banks, structured investment vehicles (SIVs), asset backed commercial paper (ABCP) conduits, insurance companies and pension funds, were the major participants in the most highly-rated tranches, due to many of these entities being required to only hold highly-rated securities, which presents the risk of a forced sale in the event of a rating downgrade of the triple-A notes. The drive for these institutions into senior CMBS tranches was based on the need for a return on a product with triple-A credit ratings. That attracted similar high ratings as compared to government bonds or treasuries, but because interest rates were at historic low levels, offered much lower yields. On the other end of the scale, real estate investors, hedge funds and other opportunistic high yield investors with a high tolerance for risk or a keen understanding of the underlying real estate assets, invested in the most subordinate tranches that provided credit support for the more senior tranches. The participation of SIVs and the ABCP conduits, as leveraged buyers of CMBS, proved controversial, as they engaged in arbitrage by funding their investments through issuing short-term debt, by way of ABCP and repurchase or "repo" agreements or arrangements at low interest rates and then buying CMBS longer-term securities that paid a higher rate

---

[13]   See further Ch.11.

*The tale of SIVs*

of interest. SIVs were thus highly-leveraged vehicles, mainly held and treated as off-balance sheet by banks subject to capital requirements in relation to their balance sheets (as the banks had no direct claim to the bonds). As banks wanted to take on more debt to make the returns that MBS offered, the banks made such investments through SIVs and ABCP conduits. As soon as the ability to raise short-term funding in the market disappeared with the advent of the liquidity crisis, the SIVs were either liquidated (to the extent they were allowed to do so) or brought onto the balance sheet of the banks to protect and preserve the bank's reputation and positions in the market, thereby rendering them unable to purchase CMBS but more importantly still keeping the risk of default within the banking system. This effectively eradicated a large section of the investor base and as buyers for the product disappeared, the CMBS market effectively closed in the second half of 2007.

## 1.3. 2007 to the present day

Since 2007, the CRE market has witnessed a severe cut back from bank lenders due to the uncertainty of value of the assets they had lent against during the boom years. Moreover, regulatory pressures surrounding the banks' capital and its use and a general contraction in the inter-bank lending market, with bank lenders less than enthusiastic to lend to each other, further contributed to such cut back. As a result, banks continued to shrink their balance sheets and the shadow banking sector (discussed below) continued to reduce their exposure to real estate. Further, the value of the assets held on the balance sheet of banks has continued to cause concern, as one important consequence of the examination of such assets in the market that developed post 2007 has been the increasing difficulty of valuing such assets. Such difficulty has also highlighted tensions with international accounting standards, particularly the "fair value" system that requires banks to mark the value of their assets to market price. Post 2007, this has resulted in banks and other holders of real estate debt marking values to a virtually non-existent market. When market value is the price that a fair-minded buyer is willing to pay to a seller that does not need to sell, there is a real question raised as to how one values the assets held on balance sheet that cannot be sold at any price because the market for such assets has effectively closed down?[14] This problem was recognised by the Basel Committee, which in 2009 issued guidelines to banks that allow flexibility in marking asset values to illiquid market valuations, particularly where one or more of the transactions (i.e. asset sales) have occurred at less than expected value due to illiquid market conditions.

Overall, the CRE sector has received a very limited amount of financing from CMBS markets during the period from 2007 to the present day. Most of the CMBS bonds not able to be securitised due to the shutting down of the

---

[14]   See further Ch.4.

CMBS markets have been retained by banks and used to obtain liquidity from the Bank of England (in the United Kingdom) and the European Central Bank (ECB) (throughout Europe). Further, the markets have witnessed a contraction of lending against CRE by other credit providers such as funds, hedge funds and other institutional investors, the so-called "shadow banking" sector. It is estimated that the shadow banking system comprised in excess of 80 per cent of the total credit provided in the US economy prior to the financial crisis of 2007–08. Once the short-term money markets and CMBS markets effectively shut down in 2007–08, the shadow banking system shrank dramatically with important consequences. In particular, the declining profitability of the funds (particularly hedge funds) caused in some cases a dramatic rise in redemption requests from investors. Faced with a large number of redemption requests, some funds were forced to liquidate large portions of their CRE debt portfolios, in many cases through forced sales at well below book value for the assets. This has had a knock-on effect on the broader commercial mortgage loan and CMBS markets by contributing to a general decline in value and liquidity.

To put the level of funding available in the market, at the time of writing, into context, Table 2 (Gross value of annual lending in the UK) illustrates the level of funding available in the United Kingdom between 2007 and 2011.

### 1.3.1. CMBS market since 2008

In the United Kingdom, since 2008, there have been eight CMBS transactions issued. This contrasts with the period from 2004–07 where there were hundreds of new issuances. The most recent transactions (2011 and 2012) are from Deutsche Bank's DECO platform, true sale securitisations of the Chiswick Park and Merry Hill loans and Vitus German Multifamily deal.[15] The other securitisations were from two corporates that have used CMBS to raise funding totalling £3 billion. Tesco Plc brought four CMBS issues to the market, totalling £2.64 billion, backed by rental payments from properties occupied by Tesco Plc. Land Securities Plc issued £360 million of CMBS backed by rental payments from a UK government body. These issuances had several common characteristics that appealed to institutional investors: (i) they were single tranches with no subordinate debt; (ii) they were backed by investment grade credits; (iii) they carried fixed coupons; and (iv) were relatively long dated, with maturity dates ranging from 2027 to 2040. As such, they resembled investment grade corporate bonds and did not represent a true re-opening of the CMBS market, as investors were primarily taking credit risk rather than property risk.[16]

---

[15] See Deco 2011-E5, Deco 2012-MHILL and FLORE 2012–1.
[16] See the Investment Property Forum's Short Paper Series, Paper 12: A review of the current state of the UK CMBS market (February 2011) p.6.

Table 2: Gross value of annual lending in the UK

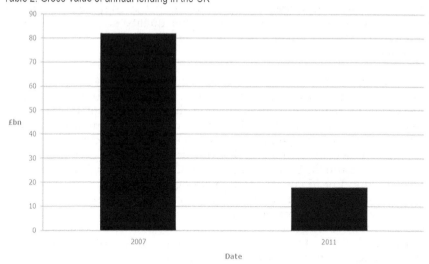

Commercial Real Estate Finance Council
EUROPE

## *1.3.2. Challenges to re-establishing a viable CMBS market*

Re-establishing a sustainable market in CMBS, since the markets have effectively frozen, has proved challenging. This is because CMBS has become associated with a number of disadvantages.

Firstly, because of the insistence of CMBS loans being originated to SPVs, to minimise insolvency and other creditor risk, CMBS noteholders, following a default, have to rely on the underlying cash flow generated by the properties, since there is no guarantee against other funds. This has led to performance issues, with some commentators and regulators branding CMBS as being "toxic" assets, which contributed to the credit crisis. In this regard, it is important to differentiate between the United States and Europe (including the United Kingdom). As discussed above, in the United States, certain products, such as subprime residential mortgage bonds and Collateralised Debt Obligations (CDOs)[17] created from these bonds, have performed poorly through the credit crisis. The delinquency rate of United States subprime loans in 2010 rose above 50 per cent. In Europe, however, these same products were not created and the assets backing most

---

[17] See Ch.11 of the 1st edn.

securitised products, including CMBS, have performed reasonably well since the crisis, with statistics suggesting that the commercial property loans that were securitised may be of higher quality on average than the commercial property loans that were not securitised in the United Kingdom.

Secondly, being off-balance sheet and existing effectively in the shadow banking market, CMBS, have historically, not been subject to banking supervision or regulations, thus creating the possibility of moral hazard based on weakening underwriting standards. As set out above, CMBS allows a CRE loan originator to avoid the individual credit risk of its borrowers, however, it may (it is argued) also reduce the originator's incentive to ensure the borrower has the ability to repay (insisting on higher levels of equity) or to ensure through strong underwriting and loan terms and provisions (for example, trapping of cash; interest reserve war chests) that the real estate will provide for repayment. Thus, this argument, taken to its extreme, would state that where the originator retains no risk and is compensated merely for making CRE loans, regardless of how well those loans are underwritten and without any regard to whether or not that loan will be repaid, there may be no incentive for the originator to maintain strict underwriting standards (so called "covenant light" loans), leading to a shift in focus of the originator from maintaining high credit standards to generating maximum volume of product. As was witnessed with the spread of the contagion from a US sub-prime crisis to a global financial crisis, the ease by which large financial institutions were able to package up loans into securities and sell those securities in the global capital markets allowed the risk of mortgage defaults to spread well beyond traditional mortgage lenders to investors that may or may not have understood real estate and the risk of having an indirect investment in it.

Finally, there is a refinancing risk as witnessed at the time of writing with a considerable amount of overhanging CRE debt in need of refinancing. This is due to the fact that CMBS securities (generally around ten years) are not matched to the underlying loans (typically around five to seven years) raising the risk that borrowers may not be able to obtain refinancing at the time of their loan's maturity dates.

### 1.3.3. Refinancing risk

Given the catastrophic decline in CRE values since 2007, most LTVs on CRE loans have risen in excess of 100 per cent. This has resulted in many borrowers being in negative equity. As most CMBS loans do not amortise (preferring instead a single repayment bullet at maturity), these high LTVs will persist for many years to come. Thus, whilst it remains the case that most UK CMBS and loans continue to out-perform balance sheet loans, it is predicted that there is, at the time of writing, refinancing risk for CMBS of around €75 billion, owing to a gradual maturing of existing CMBS. Based

*[handwritten margin note: Financing shortage of European CRE]*

on a prediction that up to 50 per cent of all UK CRE that requires refinancing may not even be suitable for CMBS origination (not being standardised enough to be trusted by investors) and with an estimated €25 billion of equity capital outflow from real estate markets due to open ended funds terminations, it is predicted that there exists, at the time of writing, a total financing shortage for the European CRE sector of around €400—€700 billion. Of the £56 billion of UK CMBS bonds outstanding, £27 billion is due to be repaid over the next 10 years. These bonds are predominantly of the "conduit" variety, which were issued by investment bank programmes from 2005 to 2007, as described above. Given CRE loans tend to have an average duration of five to seven years, preceding the peak in CMBS bond maturities in 2014, a wave of UK CMBS loans, totalling £19 billion, is due to mature from 2012 to 2014.

*[handwritten margin note: wave of CMBS maturities]*

At the time of writing, debt held against UK commercial property continues to fall from £228.1 billion in 2011 to £212.3 billion in 2012, a drop of 6.8 per cent.[18] The *UK Commercial Property Lending Market* report by De Montfort University *De Montfort Report*), found that "while the overall level of debt was falling and progress had been made in dealing with the distressed legacy debt, there was a long way to go with between £72.5 billion and £100 billion struggling to be refinanced on current market terms when the debt matures as it has a loan-to-value ratio of over 70%." The *De Montfort Report* has further recognised that although progress has been made in addressing the legacy situation, banks still face a significant overhang of pre-recession CRE debt held on their balance sheets, with around £51 billion due to mature in 2012 and £153 billion—72 per cent of outstanding debt—by year-end 2016.

Bright spots in the *De Montfort Report* show loan originations on the increase and new lenders to the market increasing their market share to 8 per cent.[19] However, this is a mere drop in the ocean compared to the level of deleveraging—Morgan Stanley expect €1.6 to €3 trillion of total loan reduction over the next three to five years, as banks endeavour to increase capital, recover funding, improve profitability and generally refocus business models. Morgan Stanley derive this number from the sum of the specific CRE deleveraging plans already announced by some banks

---

[18] See *UK Commercial Property Lending Market Report* by De Montfort University which is the United Kingdom's largest property lending survey (the *De Montfort Report*). The survey of 72 lending teams from 63 banks and other lending organisations said that 2011 started with some optimism for the commercial property lending market, including the first CMBS issue since 2007, but that this changed dramatically during the second half of 2011 as the Eurozone sovereign debt crisis heralded "extremely tough times" to the economy.

[19] In 2012 alone, a number of senior debt funds have been announced as being formed (it is not clear at what stage of the funds raising these funds are at) and current senior lenders, open for business are said to consist of Aeriance AEW, Agfe, AIG, Allianze, Aviva, AXA, BAML, BAWAG, Barclays, BlackRock, Canada Life, CBRE Global Investors, Citibank, Deutsche Bank, Fortress, GE Capital, various German Banks, Goldman Sachs, Henderson, HSBC, ING, JP Morgan, L&G, M&G, Lloyds, MacQuarie, Metlife, PIMCO, Prudential, RBC, Royal Bank of Scotland, Santander, Schroeders, Starwood, UBS and Wells Fargo.

*not refinance*

(approximately €300 billion of loans) and it estimates that up to €300 billion of exposure may not be entirely rolled over as banks retrench and refocus their business, and thus reduce their cross-border loans or simply reduce LTVs. To put this into context, this is equivalent to five times the annual real estate transactions over the last four years in Europe.[20] Bill Maxted, author of the *De Montfort Report*, said: "At the end of 2011, lending organisations were reporting that the Eurozone crisis had created instability in the money markets, leading to rising costs, with many banks managing their capital based on a worst-case scenario both in the Eurozone and the UK" This has led to a significant amount of deleveraging. However, this is typical of when lenders pull back from lending to the sector. Previous cyclical downturns in real estate in the United Kingdom have shown that lenders reduced or unwound their exposure over a five to seven-year period. On the plus side this will create significant opportunities for alternative providers of capital, as will be discussed in Chs 4 and 9, through the resultant increased enforcement actions of "bad banks" and banks' restructuring units, with CMBS special servicers increasingly enforcing against defaulted borrowers, as the maturity profile plays out. In addition, related to banks' divestment needs, the markets continue to witness, at the time of writing, an increasing number of loan portfolios coming to market. With the buyers of these loan portfolios more inclined to sell a loan's property collateral than the seller, given these portfolios are acquired at a discount, the purchaser has a different breakeven level to meet its return target and will often benefit from a quick property sale. These actions of banks, CMBS special servicers and loan purchasers could result in higher investment volumes for secondary and tertiary properties than in the period from 2008 to 2012, facilitating the formation of "real market prices" or recalibrating value in these segments, most likely lower than reported at the time of writing. However, on the down side this presents a significant protracted recovery of the commercial mortgage and CMBS markets. Given the larger scale of the problem and synchronisation across several countries, the interconnection of the markets, and the belief that this time the issue is structural rather than cyclical, deleveraging could affect the CRE sector over an even longer period, with Morgan Stanley estimating up to 10 years.[21]

*headwinds against CRE market returning*

## 1.4.  Conclusion

As stated above, the European CRE and CMBS markets have undergone a dramatic structural shift since 2007 and the central banks that regulate them have faced unprecedented challenges. Such a structural shift has high-lighted (as did the Russian rouble crisis of 1998, the 2007 sub-prime credit crisis and the 2008 (and continuing at the time of writing) liquidity crisis)),

---

[20] See Morgan Stanley's Blue Paper March 15, 2012 "Banks Deleveraging and Real Estate—Implications of a €400–€700 billion Financing Gap" (the *Morgan Stanley Report*) p.17.
[21] *Op cit.*

that in disintermediated credit markets, how such shifts and crises can quickly morph into a global credit crisis, where investors flee to the relative quality of government treasury securities, resulting in situations where subordinate interests cannot be sold for any price. SIVs (a readily available market for CMBS) have largely disappeared, and alongside this shifting investor base, so too have originators' business models changed. Given these changes, it is predicted that CMBS will remain only a marginal provider of CRE capital over the medium term due, in a large part, to the seismic shifts that have brought regulatory challenges such as:

- Basel III,[22] that by increasing the amount of capital financial institutions must hold to ensure solvency during periods of financial stress, in turn makes it more costly for such institutions to hold CMBS;
- Article 122a of the CRD, which came into effect in January 2011, the so called "5% skin in the game"provisions.[23] Bank and insurance investors in all securitisations now need to ensure that the transaction originators retain 5 per cent "skin in the game", meaning that they retain a 5 per cent interest (first loss or vertical) in every CMBS transaction they bring to market. The retention rule has not prevented the resumption of primary issuance in funding-motivated products like prime residential mortgage-backed securities (RMBS) and consumer asset-backed securities (ABS) because originators typically retained an equity interest even before the crisis. However, art.122a has materially altered the economics of CMBS issuance, which was heavily reliant on a conduit "originate to distribute" model. Investment banks were the sponsors of these conduits and retaining 5 per cent exposure in every new transaction over its lifetime translates into a significant drain on capital;[24]

---

[22] Basel III has been introduced due to criticism of Basel II which is based on risk-weighted assets, with the risk weighting given to certain assets based on ratings given by CRAs. The lower the credit rating the greater the riskweighting given to the asset. Unfortunately, the Basel II requirements, which have been widely adopted, resulted in financial institutions across the globe seeking out similar asset classes and similar highly-rated securities that would carry lower risk weighting, as under Basel II, banks were given the opportunity to define the risk weighting of each asset on their balance sheet using their internal risk models, under three methodologies (standardised, foundation or advanced internal ratings based (IRD)), which were characterised by increasing levels of sophistication. The introduction of the Basel II discipline often resulted in banks being able to reduce the risk parameters applied to their assets and thus reduce the level of equity held against them, a move that has since been widely criticised. As a result, falls in the market value of these highly-rated securities have been felt throughout the financial markets and capital adequacy rules designed to improve the stability of individual banks, have instead increased the level of systemic instability.

[23] See further Ch.16. The skin in the game provisions are attempting to combat the cyclicality and thus periodic crises of the CMBS markets by aligning the interests of the issuers and the investors. With a focus on minimising risk and strengthening underwriting standards, originators and those that securitise will be required to retain some of the risk of the loans they originate or package as part of a CMBS.

[24] See the *Morgan Stanley Report*, pp.28–29.

- significant derivatives legislation, with the European Commission's proposed derivatives legislation potentially forcing European commercial property companies and funds to collateralise their interest rate swaps on floating rate loans. In Europe, CRE loans are typically floating rate and swapped to fixed in order to hedge the risk of interest rates increasing. If borrowers were forced to cash collateralise these swaps, the cost of borrowing on a floating rate basis would increase. Chatham Financial estimates that €64.9 billion of working capital could be required across EU Member States to comply with the legislation. If the proposed legislation is passed, borrowers may prefer to use fixed rate loans or to hedge via out of the money caps. Fixed rate loans could be conducive for issuing fixed rate CMBS, as is the norm in the United States. However, European borrowers have traditionally rejected fixed rate loans due to the prepayment penalties that are incurred if the property is sold and the loan prepaid;[25] changes to the IFRS accounting standards; and shifting and conservative rating agency treatment.[26]

### 1.4.1. Challenges to the wider commercial mortgage market

Based on the reasons highlighted throughout this Chapter, it remains the case that, at the time of writing, CRE lending is no longer as attractive for banks as it previously has been. CRE lending has transformed from purely property focussed to a relationship-driven business. Unlike in 2005–07, since 2008, the quality of the sponsor (ultimate equity owner of the property) of the non-recourse CRE loans and the prospects of ancillary business with the sponsor have become more important than ever. As a consequence, quality prime sponsors stand the best chance of obtaining a loan secured by non-prime properties. Such transformation is based on a number of factors. In the *Morgan Stanley Report*, Morgan Stanley attributed the reduced appeal of CRE lending to five factors:

(i) Financing is no longer easy and is getting more expensive, especially for long-term tenures. The boom in CRE financing between 2004 and 2007 was fostered by the availability of plentiful and cheap funding for the banks, coupled with relatively low capital requirements. That is not to say that all long-term lending is dead. Issuance of *Pfandbriefe* covered bonds in Germany, for example, although more expensive than in the past, still provides substantial financing for the industry.[27] However, volumes are greatly reduced, and this will continue to constrain new business. For this reason, Morgan Stanley are seeing signs of more international banks trying to set up legal entities in Germany to take advantage of the cheap and liquid *Pfandbriefe* market;

---

[25] See further Ch.8 and the Investment Property Forum's Short Paper Series, Paper 12: A review of the current state of the UK CMBS market (February 2011) p.11.
[26] See further Ch.11.
[27] See further Ch.2.

(ii)    capital is getting tighter, especially as the markets move towards Basel III. This may mean that banks are no longer able to make a return on CRE lending that covers the cost of equity, and indeed in some cases they may be loss making;

(iii)   CRE relationships are less profitable than corporate client relationships. Ultimately, despite the fact that banks have over-extended their balance sheets to the real estate sector, this is still a marginal activity and one that does not relate to their core client base. Also, compared to corporate lending, it provides lower ancillary revenues;

(iv)    huge cyclicality makes the business less attractive. The peak-to-trough loan loss provisioning in CRE is significantly higher than that of any corporate lending activity; and

(v)     there tends to be more pressure from governments and regulators to keep financing corporates and SMEs in sectors that are more crucial for the real economy.

Further, banks face other issues when trying to deleverage:

- lack of alternative financing is the single biggest issue banks encounter when trying to reduce their loan exposure. If borrowers cannot find alternative sources of funding, they cannot repay, unless they sell the underlying assets;

- falling property prices mean that borrowers find it hard to sell and repay, while quality of exposure declines and LTVs increase. This often makes loan extensions and other forms of restructuring of CRE loans that otherwise would be in breach of LTV covenants more likely; and

- swap transactions linked to loans may also prevent banks from selling down exposure more aggressively. As CRE companies prefer to take loans at fixed rates and banks tend to want to lend at variable rates, banks usually sell an interest rate swap contract to the company that takes the loan. These swap contracts are becoming an issue when banks try to offload the loans, as they may be forced to take losses on the swap, especially if contracts have been put together when interest rates were higher.[28]

Further challenges to the commercial mortgage loan market arise in the process of "slotting", planned at the time of writing to be introduced by the Financial Services Authority (FSA), which would introduce additional regulatory capital requirements to real estate lending, suggesting that the consequences of the changes would be to reduce the volume and increase the cost of business. The FSA's 2012 proposed rule change could make debt even more scarce and may require UK banks to raise up to £40 billion of capital to cover losses from bad property loans. Slotting—a stricter classification of loans and the amount of capital that banks must hold against them—may, if introduced, result in a loan not able to be refinanced on "current market terms" being classified as "weak".

---

[28]   See the *Morgan Stanley Report*, pp.22–26 and Chs 8 and 20.

However, the fragility of the bank's balance sheet during the global credit crisis has highlighted how the CRE market needs CMBS and its access to global capital markets. This means that CMBS certainly has a supporting role to play and may eventually prove to be most competitive in financing yieldly, secondary properties that are not suited for on-balance sheet lending by banks. In other words, CMBS could eventually become the equivalent of the high yield market for CRE finance,[29] with LTV potentially limited to 50–60 per cent and required spreads in excess of 500bp, based on the current capital stack as set out in Table 3.

*the future for European CMBS?*

Table 3: The Capital Stack


**Equity**


**Junior/Preferred Equity**
**(to 85%)**


**Stretched Senior/Enhanced Senior**
**(to 75%)**


**Senior**
**(to 60%)**


**Super Senior**
**(40%)**
**(Pfandbrief)**

Commercial Real Estate Finance Council
EUROPE

---

[29]  See the Morgan Stanley Report, p.29.

Moreover, this Chapter has shown that when discussing European CRE it is clear that globalisation cannot be ignored.[30] The globalisation or internationalisation of capital has played an integral role in the financial crisis, with both benefits and disadvantages. Such globalisation can provide for access to global markets, thus reducing financing costs and allowing for business cycles to be smoothed, but it can also allow for the rapid transmission of economic shocks between economies. As discussed above, investors are able to purchase a wide variety of securities offered on various international markets (by way of example, Swedish farmers had exposure to single parent families in Illinois), which has in turn allowed the impact of the sub-prime crisis in the United States to spread around the world. Further, it also allows for regulatory arbitrage as financial institutions or investors transfer their operations and investments to jurisdictions they perceive as favourable. Regulatory arbitrage results in jurisdictions with inadequate regulation creating risks for other jurisdictions due to the interconnection of economies and markets.

As regards real estate, the 2008 credit crisis highlighted that, whilst real estate remains an essentially local illiquid asset, its financing is not and our real estate finance markets and economies are inextricably linked and interdependent and it is very hard to dislocate the economic forces that they produce. After all, one of the most striking developments in the global debt and capital markets over the last decade has been the powerful journey and metamorphosis of CRE in creating a truly global market for CRE finance, investment and development, an asset class that had been famously regarded by institutional investors as illiquid and cumbersome. However, if the last decade will be remembered for this development, the following decade will be remembered for the creation of the post-2008 banking and financial regulatory landscape that affects real estate (and its financing, investment and development) and still persists at the time of writing.

The establishment of real estate as a separate asset class is unlikely to be reversed and it is undeniable that real estate will (despite the advent of the 2008 global credit crisis) re-emerge in the coming years as a popular asset class. Given that the credit crisis was (and remains at the time of writing) as much due to a crisis of confidence as to any other factors, such re-emergence will, in a large part, be dictated by the confidence in our financial architecture. Any developments or products the CRE market participants can provide to help restore market confidence, such as greater regulation and transparency, improved reporting standards,[31] clarity over servicing standards and servicer responsibilities[32] and more standardised and clear documentation (particularly uniformity surrounding controlling

---

[30] See A.V. Petersen, *Real Estate Finance: Law Regulation & Practice*, (London: LexisNexis, 2008).

[31] See Ch.12 and Appendix 4 where the efforts to create transparency in accessing real estate market data and real estate reporting information are dealt with to examine whether there is a developing arbitrage between investor reporting for CMBS loans as opposed to balance sheet loans thereby placing a more onerous burden on CMBS issuers.

[32] See Chs 5, 6 and 7.

party rights and intercreditor arrangements),[33] that will hopefully reverse credit rationing and soften the impact of widespread de-leveraging, as well as remove or reduce risk to investing in real estate, can only be a good thing. However, the overriding aim must be to strike a balance between market reform (through all of the above) and efficient markets. It is our financial architecture. Markets are essential to human development through economic advancement and human well-being and should not be impeded or innovation suffocated such that they cannot function. Nor should markets be allowed to operate with unintended consequences which sow the seeds for future crises. After all, this Chapter has highlighted that we have been down this road before and whilst this crisis remains structural rather than cyclical, the desire to reform must be accompanied by caution. The remaining Chapters in this book will examine the markets in this light to determine whether the challenges that exist, at the time of writing, in the commercial mortgage markets can be overcome and whether the funding of CRE through commercial mortgage loans and CMBS can continue to adapt and evolve on a journey based on transformational financial innovation.

---

[33] See Chs 14 and 15.

# Chapter 2

# Commercial mortgage loans, CMBS and its role in the wider real estate debt capital markets

Hans Vrensen,

Global Head of Research, DTZ

Nigel Almond,

Head of Strategy, Research, DTZ

## 2.1. Introduction

This Chapter explores the development and structure of Europe's (CRE) lending markets over the past decade and highlights their importance to the financial markets generally. This Chapter first looks in detail at the structure of the CRE market in Europe, focussing on bank lending, covered bonds and CMBS, exploring how Europe's markets differ to those in Asia Pacific and North America. This Chapter then goes on to look at deleveraging in the marketplace and attitudes towards lending, based on survey analysis of the CRE market undertaken by DTZ. It then explores the near-term outlook for Europe's CRE debt markets, through examining the potential debt funding gap and the ways in which the market is attempting to bridge this gap. Finally, this Chapter concludes by looking at predictions for the future of CRE markets in Europe.

### 2.1.1. Importance of lending to commercial real estate

Lending to CRE entities has played, and continues to play, an important role in the functioning of Europe's CRE markets. Since the turn of the 21st century, debt outstanding to CRE vehicles across Europe grew nearly three-fold to €1.9 trillion, equivalent to 59 per cent of the total value of commercial property held for investment purposes. Of this, close to €1.8 trillion is held by banks on their balance sheets, in the form of bank lending and covered bonds. This is equivalent to around 7 per cent of all bank lending to non financial corporations, although in some markets, such as the United Kingdom, lending on CRE is even higher at over 10 per cent of all lending. (See Figure 1).

21

**Figure 1 Growth in outstanding debt to EU CRE**

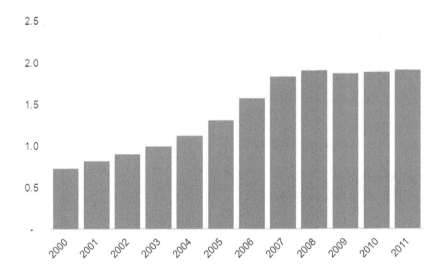

Source: DTZ Research

The availability of cheap debt from banks during the period 2003–07 supported the wider growth in Europe's CRE investment market. By 2007, transaction volumes across Europe rose by 165 per cent from €87 billion in 2003 to €230 billion. In the wake of the financial crisis, growth in outstanding debt slowed, before turning negative in 2009. The lagged response from the peak in values in 2007 reflected the fact that lines of credit agreed towards the peak of the market, were gradually drawn down and hence only recorded as and when facilities were drawn upon. This lag effect is a normal response in the market. The subsequent reduction reflected the fact that redemptions and writedowns on loans were higher than new loan originations for the first time in over a decade. The weakness in new loan originations led to a collapse in transactional activity which reached a decade low of €62 billion in 2009. As liquidity slowly returned to lending markets, there was, from 2010, a strong recovery in transaction volumes. However, current activity remains well below levels at the peak of the market in 2006/07. (See Figure 2).

Figure 2 EU investment activity and change in outstanding debt

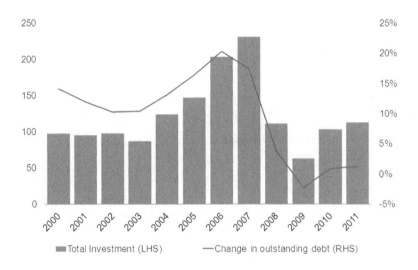

Source: DTZ Research

## 2.2. Structure of Europe's debt markets

Lending towards EU CRE is dominated by bank lending. Of the outstanding debt in this sector, 76 per cent is secured through bank lending. A further 17 per cent is through covered bonds, which are originated through, and remain on the banks' balance sheet. The remainder is secured through CMBS (5 per cent)[1] and Property Company bonds (2 per cent). In this respect, Europe's market is similar to Asia Pacific in the dominance of bank lending for the CRE market. This contrasts with North America, where just 60 per cent of the outstanding amount is secured by banks, where CMBS accounts for a further 22 per cent and institutions a further 12 per cent, providing a more diverse funding base.

The diversity of funding sources in North America is one of the reasons why the region is better placed than Europe to weather the storm thrown up by the financial crisis, as will be set out in para 2.5.4 below. Specifically, in the United States, other financial institutions, comprising 12 per cent,

---

[1]  See Ch.1 for more detail on the CMBS market.

including life insurance companies and CMBS, around 22 per cent, account for a third of historical lending. These differences will be explored below. (See Figure 3).

**Figure 3. Outstanding debt by lender type, 2011**

C/mss 5%     cDms 22%

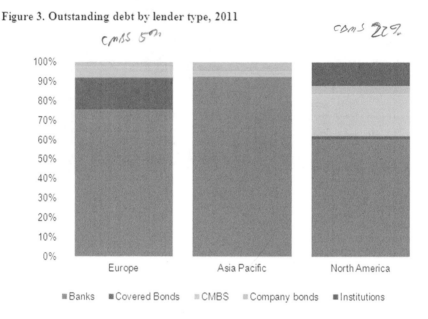

■ Banks  ■ Covered Bonds  ■ CMBS  ■ Company bonds  ■ Institutions

Source: DTZ Research, Standard & Poor's, Verband deutscher Pfandbriefbanken, Bloomberg, ECBC.

Across Europe, the share of bank activity in the CRE sector has remained strong over the past decade, although its share has diminished somewhat, due to increased activity in both covered bond lending and CMBS. Of course, there are variations in the structure of lending sources across markets, so it is worthwhile examining in more detail the key areas of bank lending, covered bonds and CMBS. (See Figure 4).

### 2.2.1. Bank lending

At the beginning of the 21st century, as highlighted in Ch.1, banks accounted for over 80 per cent of lending to CRE across Europe. Whilst the share of total lending has slowly reduced, bank lending still remains the most dominant source of funding, accounting for over three quarters of the total debt outstanding on CRE. Close to half of the outstanding debt, comprising nearly €710 billion, is secured against assets in the United Kingdom, France and Spain. A further 25 per cent is secured against assets

**Figure 4 Outstanding debt by lender type 1999-2011**

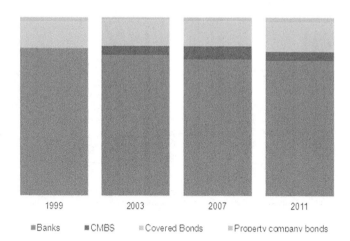

Source: DTZ Research, Standard and Poor's, Verband deutscher Pfandbriefbanken, ECBC

in the Nordics, Italy and Benelux totalling €370 billion. German assets represent just 7 per cent of the outstanding amount to banks. This is just over a third of the value of outstanding bank debt to UK assets, even though the invested stock in Germany is just 25 per cent lower than the United Kingdom. The main reason for the lower value of lending to Germany from banks reflects the greater reliance on the *Pfandbriefe* market, which is Germany's covered bond market, detailed in para 2.2.2 below. (See Figure 5).

Across Europe, investors traditionally focus on lenders as a source of funds. In many established EU markets, it is not just domestic lenders who are active, but also branches of overseas banks. Lending terms are traditionally five years, and will, subject to the type and quality of asset, be based on Libor/Euribor plus a margin.[2] Margins vary through time, and have been elevated in recent years due to the higher funding costs of banks reflecting much higher credit default swaps. Since 2008, these have been rising steadily with a significant gap emerging between different banks. This diversity could offer a competitive advantage to some banks should they wish to be active in the market. (See Figure 6).[3]

---

[2]   The Wheatley Report, published in September 2012, has recommended a complete overhaul of the way Libor is calculated.

[3]   See further Ch. 20 where the opportunities for lenders in this market are addressed.

**Figure 5. Banks' outstanding debt to real estate by geography, 2011**

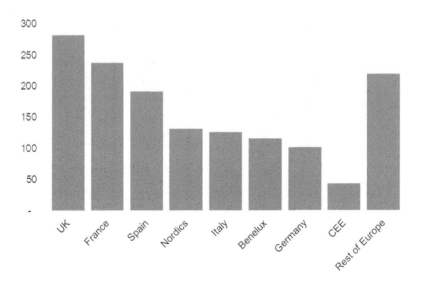

Source: DTZ Research

Lending by institutions other than banks, in the CRE market in Europe, is limited and reliable data is not widely available. Those players who are active have often tended to focus on more niche types of lending such as doctors' surgeries, healthcare and student accommodation. Loans are typically longer in duration, of up to 20 years, where there is limited competition with traditional banks.

### 2.2.2. Covered bonds

The EU covered bond market has grown and developed over recent years, increasing its share of the CRE lending market to 17 per cent, by the end of 2011, and the second largest source of finance against EU real estate after bank lending. However, the market itself is not new and in Germany[4] covered bonds date back to 1769. In Spain,[5] the other major market in Europe for covered bonds, legislation dates more recently to the 1980s. Both these countries now have well established covered bond markets.

---

4   In Germany, the covered bond market is the *Pfandbriefe*.
5   In Spain, the covered bond market is the Cédulas.

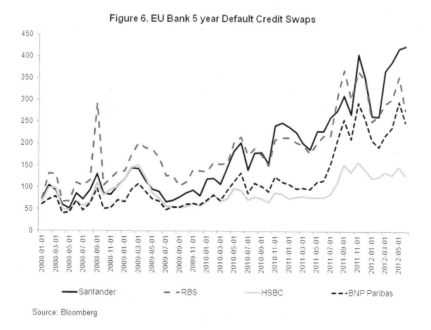

Figure 6. EU Bank 5 year Default Credit Swaps

Source: Bloomberg

Although the funding is effectively provided by banks, covered bonds are secured by a cover pool of mortgage loans to which investors have a preferential claim in the event of default. Unlike other asset backed securities, such as CMBS, these bonds remain on the banks balance sheet and assets can be replaced in the pool. In the case of the German *Pfandbriefe* market, there are also stricter lending regulations compared with terms available from traditional bank lending. For example, property financings may be included in the cover pool only up to 60 per cent of the prudently calculated mortgage lending value. Similar restrictions are also imposed with Spanish Cédulas, although there are some exceptions in the case of construction and residential premises where the limit is raised to 80 per cent.[6] Consequently, covered bonds are seen as a safer source of funding than traditional bank lending, underlined by the fact that there has not been a *Pfandbriefe* default since 1901 and no defaults have been reported on Spanish Cédulas.

As stated above, the majority of collateral secured by EU covered bonds is in Germany, representing 45 per cent of the market. This reflects the dominance of the *Pfandbrief* market. Assets in Spain account for a further 25 per cent of the EU covered bonds market. Overseas lending is permitted in both the German and Spanish regulations with the United Kingdom at 9 per

---

[6]    See *2011 European Covered Bond Fact Book* for more detail.

cent and France at 7 per cent, keys targets. The combination of these four countries, represent over 85 per cent of the collateral in EU covered bonds. (See Figure 7).

**Figure 7. Covered bond outstanding debt to real estate by geography, 2011**

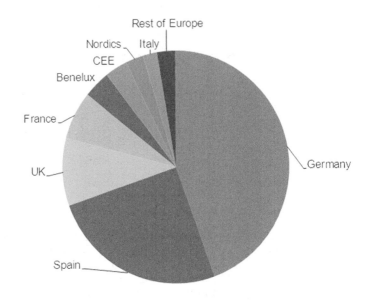

Source: DTZ Research, Verband deutscher Pfandbriefbanken, ECBC

The security offered by covered bonds has also been a benefit in the current financial crisis. Whilst growth in bank lending to real estate slowed markedly in 2007 (12 per cent) and 2008 (1 per cent), the covered bond market remained resilient with growth rates of 45 per cent and 29 per cent, respectively. Those banks which have provided such lending have benefitted from the European Central Bank's (ECB) covered bond purchase programme. The first tranche ended in 2010 with €60 billion purchased. A second programme, launched in November 2011 with a limit of €40 billion, has used €14 billion as at July 17, 2012. These programmes have provided liquidity to those banks partaking in the programme and potentially provided for additional new lending. The programmes have now effectively been superseded by the more recent long term refinancing operation (LTRO), three year term loan facility provided by the ECB.[7]

### 2.2.3. CMBS

The EU CMBS market grew from virtually nothing in 2000, with the amount outstanding reaching a peak of €146 billion in 2007. With the EU CMBS market witnessing a severe cutback since 2007,[8] with little new issuance taking place or predicted, the amount outstanding according to data from Standard and Poor's has fallen back to €100 billion by year end 2011, reflecting redemptions and writedowns. In 2012, at the time of writing, the market represents 5 per cent of the outstanding debt in the EU CRE sector. The majority of assets underlying these bonds are located in the United Kingdom and Germany, which combined, represent over three quarters of the collateral, with the remaining assets mostly located in France, Italy and the Netherlands. (See Figure 8).

As set out in Ch.1, unlike traditional bank lending or covered bonds, CMBS is held off-balance sheet. It grew in popularity in Europe during the mid-2000's enabling banks to repackage loans for sale in the capital markets, thereby removing these assets from their balance sheet and raising fresh capital. In Europe, CMBS has traditionally involved both single high quality assets, and portfolios of loans. Since the onset of the financial crisis, issuance of new CMBS in Europe has been highly limited with just a handful of transactions, and often based on the credit rating of the underlying tenant as evidence by recent Tesco securitisations.[9]

## 2.3.  Deleveraging in the market

Despite the pressures on banks to shrink their balance sheets, the amount of debt outstanding in the EU CRE market remains elevated and at its highest level in over a decade. The scale of debt remaining in the market has been surprising, in particular the growth in outstanding debt during 2011. The rise highlights the delay in deleveraging, in part due to the liquidity supports provided to the banking sector through quantitative easing by central banks, and the most recent rounds of the €1 billion LTRO (long term refinancing operation) three yearterm loan facility, provided by the ECB.[10]

During 2008, many banks chose to roll-over loans with impending maturity dates due to refinance given the liquidity restraints. As the financial crisis continued, those loans that were unable to be refinanced, but were still

---

[7]  See further Ch.20.
[8]  See Ch.1, para 1.3.
[9]  See Ch.1, para 1.3 for further detail on the structure and recent activity in the CMBS market.
[10]  See further Ch.3.

**Figure 8. EU CMBS Outstanding, 2011**

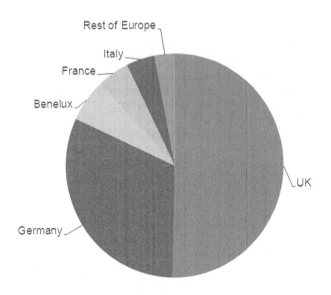

Source: Standard & Poor's

performing, were extended, in some cases up to a period of five years. Maturity date extensions have continued, albeit at a lesser pace in recent years. This behaviour has inevitably delayed the deleveraging process, although market commentators agree a significant reduction in both aggregate bank lending in general and specifically of that to CRE, remains.[11]

Whilst the volume of debt outstanding has been growing, the growth in equity across Europe has remained robust and rising at a faster pace—5 per cent in 2010 and 12 per cent in 2011. This faster growth in equity[12] has therefore helped to drive down overall leverage ratios. There are, inevitably, variations across markets. In a number of core EU markets, such as France, Germany and the United Kingdom, loan to value ratios (LTVs) have been on the decline in the last couple of years, in part reflecting modest declines

---

[11] See Ch.1, para.1.3. for estimates on deleveraging.
[12] Equity refers to refers to the equity proportion of the commercial real estate holdings of for example institutions, private property companies and individuals, unlisted property vehicles and listed property companies including REITs. Debt is stripped out by applying a different gearing ratio for each investor group.

in debt, but mostly as a consequence of rising levels of equity. Whilst this may not be good news for banks, it provides breathing space for borrowers who may have been under water. In some markets, such as Sweden, LTVs have been low and remained below the EU average, reflecting more conservative lending. At the other end of the scale are more troubled markets, such as Ireland and Spain, where capital values have fallen significantly and shown little signs of recovery so far. Both these markets also have high levels of loans towards uncompleted developments and land. These present greater challenges to lenders, as more often than not, there is no income being secured against the asset and in many cases the potential for development, speculative or with a pre-let in place, is limited, given the scale of the economic downturn. In the near term this will have an impact on site values and lead to significant writedowns on these loans. (See Figure 9).

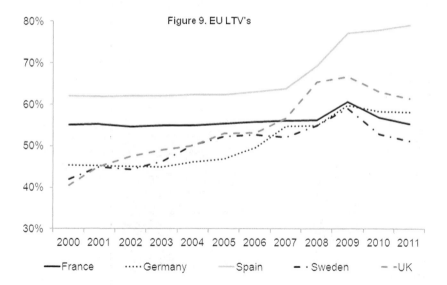

Figure 9. EU LTV's

France ····· Germany ── Spain ─ · Sweden ─ -UK

## 2.4.  Current attitudes towards lending

During the first quarter of 2011, DTZ undertook a survey of lenders and investors to gauge their opinions on current market conditions and their outlook for the market. The surveys represented lenders with an aggregate loan book of close to $400 billion and investors with assets under management in excess of $800 billion. The DTZ lenders' survey aimed to capture details on the current loan book, expected lending intentions in the near term and impact of regulation on lending activity. The DTZ investors' survey was primarily focussed on past and expected investment decisions but also considered the availability of finance both in 2011 and in future years, 2012 to 2013. Both surveys incorporated questions that had been asked in a similar survey undertaken in 2011, allowing a comparison of responses through time.

### 2.4.1. Loan terms and performance

The DTZ 2012 lenders' survey found that existing lenders, predominantly banks, expect that the value of new lending will decrease in 2012 compared with 2011 and that the terms and conditions on loans would also tighten. When compared to the same question in the DTZ 2011 lenders' survey, those expecting lending to increase in 2012 more than halved. (See Figure 10).

**Figure 10. Expectations for new lending and changes in terms and conditions**

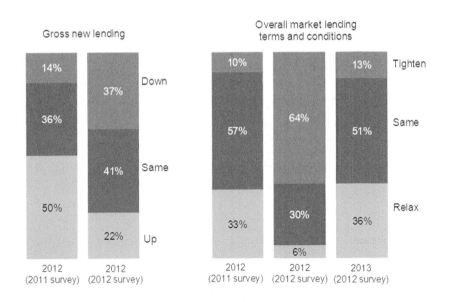

Source: DTZ Research

In addition, 2012 lending terms and conditions deteriorated acutely between the 2011 and 2012 surveys, with a more than six-fold increase in those expecting tighter terms and conditions.[13] Based on responses from the

---

[13] Terms and conditions typically relate to loan duration, finance costs and margins,

DTZ 2012 lenders' survey, the expectation is that terms and conditions will relax in 2013, to a similar level to those expected for 2012.

The DTZ 2012 lenders' survey results also show that lenders also expect loan performance to deteriorate further in 2012. This is in contrast to results from the same question in the 2011 DTZ lenders' survey, when lenders expected all categories of loan performance to improve in 2012. The DTZ 2012 lenders' survey responses indicate an anticipated doubling for defaults, an anticipated tripling of arrears and a predicted near quadrupling of losses, when compared to the 2011 survey expectations for 2012. (See Figure 11).

## Figure 11. Expectations for loan performance

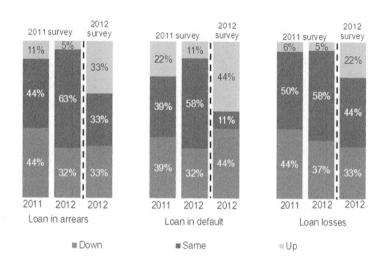

Source: DTZ Research

The DTZ 2012 lenders' survey results further demonstrate that the working out of loans is well underway for prime property. Lenders' views of progress in 2012 are similar to the responses in the same question from the 2011 DTZ lenders' survey. Only 15 per cent state that the prime asset workouts are left to complete, compared to 20 per cent in the 2011 survey. With non-prime property, 43 per cent of the workout has not yet started according to the 2012 DTZ lenders' survey. This is 10 per cent less than the

---

covenants on for example LTVs and interest cover, and any required scheduled amortisation, prepayment, debt service coverage ratios and enforcement.

expectations for 2012, as reported in the DTZ 2011 lenders' survey. In short, the 2012 DTZ lenders' survey shows that more progress has been made on working out non-prime versus prime collateral during 2012. (See Figure 12).

**Figure 12. Lenders' assessment of progress in working out**

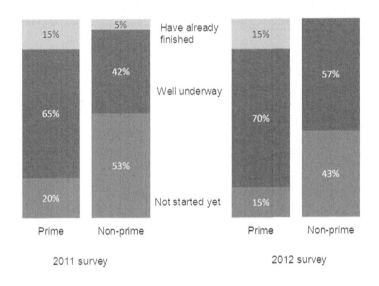

Source: DTZ Research

Half of investors in EMEA countries, and 75 per cent in North America, are in talks with banks in relation to loan amendments and/or extensions according to the 2012 DTZ investors' survey. This contrasts with the Asia Pacific region, where just over a quarter of investors are in a similar position. Additionally, the 2012 DTZ investors' survey indicates that if loans are unable to be refinanced, or extended, then investors continue to favour equity injection as their most preferable solution. Partial loan repayment comes second in ranking, followed by consensual asset sales. (See Figure 13).

The 2012 DTZ investors' survey shows that investors' own involvement in bridging the overall market's financing gap is gradually increasing. 42 per cent of investors acknowledge that they have invested in property loans or engaged in partial equity positions. This is up by over a third from the 31 per cent in the same question conducted in the DTZ 2011 investors' survey.

Figure 13. Investors' exposure to loan workout, 2012

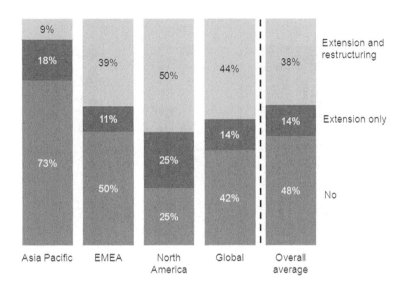

Source: DTZ Research

Among those investors who responded positively, the balance between investment in property loans and in equity positions has now shifted to the former. Further movement of investors into property loans seems a possibility, but may be limited as the proportion of those not involved, but having no capability (as opposed to no interest), has increased. This capacity issue is most likely the result of those investors not having the appropriate teams and skills in place. In 2012 and beyond, investors could team up with existing financiers to create joint ventures to circumvent this problem.[14] (See Figure 14).

The 2012 DTZ lenders' survey indicates that the expectations of lenders, for exposure by asset class, favours prime assets. In aggregate, 64 per cent of lenders plan to increase their lending secured by prime assets, up from the 40 per cent in the 2011 survey. The focus on prime illustrates a continued "flight to quality" in lending where the focus is on ensuring the servicing of the loan, or, in the event of default or voids, the ability to sell or re-let will be much reduced. Non-prime lending shows a mirror image that is consistent with this finding. Close to two-thirds (64 per cent) of lenders want less exposure given that perceived risks are much greater, but may

---

[14] See further Ch.20.

**Figure 14. Investors' exposure to loan and equity positions**

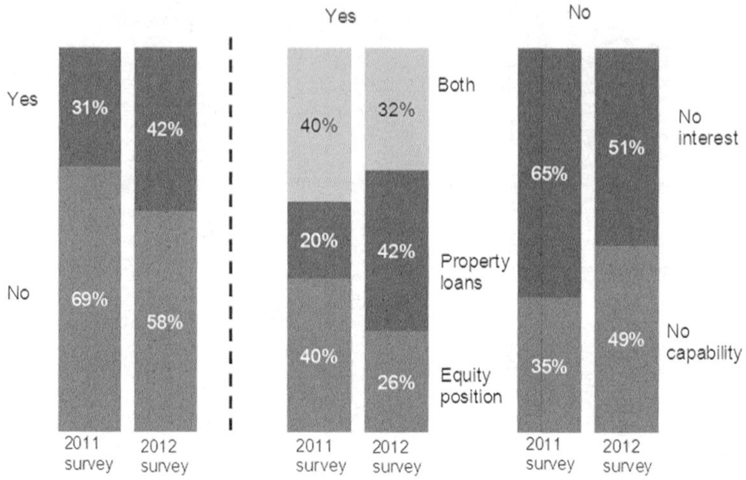

Source: DTZ Research

also be susceptible to falling values, as many banks have yet to work-out their secondary loans and where current pricing levels may not fully reflect the risks.[15] Aversion to lending for speculative development has also grown in the 2012 survey, to 55 per cent. There is very little development finance being made available, and only for pre-let schemes. (See Figure 15).

Looking at the end of 2012 and 2013, there are an increasing number of regulatory reforms being put in place as a response to the global financial crisis. When comparing both the results from the 2012 investors' and lenders' surveys, it is clear that the biggest majority of lenders, comprising 76 per cent of those surveyed, and investors totalling 60 per cent, expect Basel III will have a negative impact among the reforms proposed. A smaller proportion of lenders and investors expect a negative impact from Solvency II and the EBA capital adequacy regulation, but the responses still reflect a broad-based expectation of reduced lending by banks, as a result of these regulatory reforms.[16] (See Figure 16).

Both lenders and investors now expect regulatory reforms to have, on balance, a negative impact on property markets. Compared to the 2011 surveys, both lenders and investors have become more negative. However,

---

[15] See Ch.13 for further comment on secondary markets.
[16] See Ch.16 for more detail on the regulatory environment.

Figure 15. Lender intentions for loan book exposure

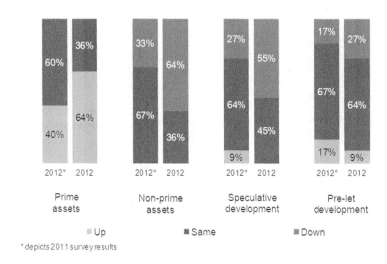

Source: DTZ Research

the data suggest that the outlook of lenders is now nearly twice as negative compared to investors. This is a worrying sign for investors going forward, as it is thought that lenders may be in a better position to assess the impacts of pending regulations, and other regulatory reforms, on lending than investors.

In aggregate, the surveys highlight the challenges facing the CRE market. Lending capacity from banks is reduced and the overall costs of borrowing have increased. Lending that is available is mainly focussed towards prime assets, as banks still have much work to do in working out their secondary loan books. This comes at a time when regulators seek to place greater burdens on lenders, which may have further negative consequences for the market. Paragraph 2.5 below seeks to quantify these impacts across Europe and consider the impact new regulations may have.

## 2.5. Debt funding gap

Between 2012 and 2015, it is estimated that there will be close to €1 trillion of loans outstanding due to be refinanced. This represents more than half of the debt outstanding in the CRE sector. The high level of refinancing, in

**Figure 16. Impact of regulatory reforms on lending, 2012**

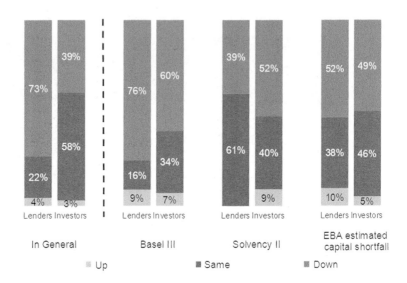

Source: DTZ Research

part, reflects the recent short-term extension of loans which has effectively pushed loan maturities back, in addition to the already high level of refinancing due. Much of this lending was originated or refinanced at the peak of the market in 2007.[17]

The debt funding gap can be defined as the gap between the existing debt balance and the debt available to replace it. The debt funding gap is considered to be the biggest challenge to many international property markets. It is a relevant issue because a lack of funding at maturity is the most likely trigger of a loan event of default. Defaults during the loan term have, and are expected to be, limited as lenders often turn a blind eye to minor covenant breaches where loans continue to perform. Only at loan maturity is the borrower forced to find an alternative refinancing source.

### 2.5.1. Estimating the debt funding gap

One approach to estimating the debt funding gap is undertaken in a six step process that can be explained in the example of a single loan (see Figure 17). In the example below, the gap is calculated for a single loan as follows:

---

[17] See Ch.1 for more information on refinancing risk.

(a)  Loan of EUR 100 million granted in 2006.
(b)  Value of assets financed total EUR 116 million, assuming an LTV of 86 per cent in 2006.
(c)  Loan due to mature in 2011 based on a five year term.
(d)  Based on capital value changes from the IPD index and forecasts prepared by DTZ, it is estimated that capital values will have fallen by 32 per cent (EUR 37 million) over 2006–11.
(e)  The resulting asset value at 2011 is EUR 79 million.
(f)  In 2011 it is estimated that debt of EUR 58 million will be available for refinance based on a 73 per cent LTV.
(g)  The debt funding gap of EUR 42 million is the difference between the value of the original loan (EUR 100 million) and the estimated debt available for refinance (EUR 58 million). (See Figure 17).

**Figure 17. Estimating the debt funding gap**

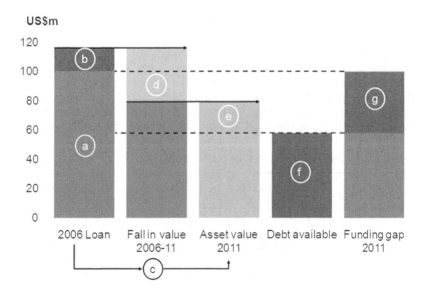

Source: DTZ Research

In reality, a multitude of loans would need to be taken into account, originated in different years and of differing maturities. As it has been common practice, it is prudent in such analysis to account for a proportion of loans to be extended.

The funding gap will vary, depending upon changes in capital values, in both the past and expected future growth. The availability of debt finance will also be a contributing factor. As the sovereign debt crisis in Europe has escalated through 2012, lenders have become increasingly risk averse, leading to more conservative lending terms, and LTVs have subsequently reduced and range between 60–65 per cent. This compares to levels of over 80 per cent at the peak of the market in 2007. Lower LTVs on a reduced asset value increases the risk of a financing gap.

### 2.5.2. Impact of regulation on bank deleveraging

In 2011 and 2012, Europe's banks have been confronted with the EBA's stress testing aimed at restoring stability and confidence to the markets. This required those 65 banks under review, in these tests, to ensure that their core tier 1 capital ratio reached a level of 9 per cent by the end of June 2012. Having met these targets, the EBA has stressed the need for banks to maintain their core tier 1 capital ratio at 9 per cent indefinitely.

In their 2012 report[18] the IMF sets out three policy scenarios and their impact on bank deleveraging. The details of these scenarios are summarised in Table 1, along with the reduction in bank assets. In the case of the current policies scenario, the IMF estimate the total amount of deleveraging required, based on their discussions with a subset of 58 banks. In total, these banks have plans to reduce their assets by $2.6 trillion, or equivalent to a 7 per cent reduction of total assets. In this scenario, it is assumed that systemic risks in the financial system are averted, but strains remain.

*Table 1 Summary of IMF policy responses*

|  | Complete policies | Current policies | Weak policies |
|---|---|---|---|
| Summary of trends | Shift to good equilibrium of funding costs, structural and governance reforms | Systemic risks are averted, but strains remain | Continued implementation of fiscal consolidation |
|  | Smoother deleveraging | Fragile confidence, foreign investors will not increase exposure to peripheral bonds | Credible firewall to stem contagion |

---

[18] See *IMF Global Financial Stability Report*, April 2012.

| | Development of a road map for a pan-euro-area financial stability framework | Responsibility for financial system remains divided | Further progress on bank restructuring and resolution |
|---|---|---|---|
| | Progress towards fiscal sharing | Banks face pressure to shed assets due to funding concerns | Banks exercise appropriate restraint on dividend and remuneration |
| % change in bank assets | | -7% | -10% |

Source: IMF

The scenarios stated above, assumes deleveraging over a period of two years, 2012 to 2013, with a 7 per cent reduction in total bank assets. As there is insufficient data to extract this subset from the data obtained by DTZ, a similar reduction to the whole real estate sector has been assumed. The IMF has also provided detail on the timescale of deleveraging of two years, 2012 to 2013. DTZ had previously made an assumption of deleveraging over three years, 2012 to 2014, but this has now been amended to a two-year analysis.

There are valid arguments for the volume of deleveraging to be higher or lower. CRE lending could be impacted more than other segments given the value of loans tend to be relatively higher. It would therefore be easier for banks to deleverage more quickly through real estate, especially given the current appetite from private equity funds to acquire loan portfolios. Property too, is not high on the political agenda. For example, in the United Kingdom, under Project Merlin,[19] banks are focused on lending to SMEs to create jobs, rather than to SPVs funding real estate. On the other hand, banks may also profit from additional business to these SPVs, therefore it may not be of interest to shrink lending to this sector. Also, the complexity of CRE lending, including additional swaps and hedging,[20] may make such sale more complex. Given there are valid arguments on both sides to either increase or decrease the reduction in assets, DTZ have adopted to keep the current policies estimate of 7 per cent of the outstanding debt and applied across the board.

---

[19] Project Merlin is an agreement between the British Government and four of the major high street banks in the United Kingdom. These banks are Barclays, Lloyds Banking Group, the Royal Bank of Scotland and HSBC. The agreement covers aspects of banking activity, notably lending, pay and bonuses with the intention of promoting lending to businesses, particularly small businesses.
[20] See Ch.8.

To calculate any additional deleverage, DTZ first estimate the total deleveraging required under the new rules. In this example it represents 7 per cent of the total outstanding debt (€361 billion), which equates to €25 billion. With €17 billion of deleveraging already coming through, as estimated in the initial debt funding gap analysis, the residue (€9 billion) reflects the additional deleveraging required under the new rules. Where the debt funding gap figure is higher than the estimated deleveraging, then no additional reduction will be required. (See Figure 18).

**Figure 18. Estimating the impact of the EBA 9% rule, € billion**

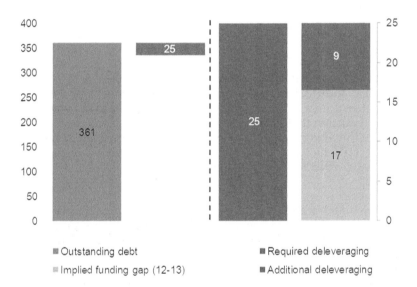

2.5.3.  *EU debt funding gap*

In accounting for the increased deleveraging in the wake of the increased regulation, DTZ estimates that Europe's gross funding gap more than doubles by $107 billion to $182 billion in the next two years. This pushes the global debt funding gap to $216 billion.[21]

Based on DTZ's analysis, the United Kingdom continues to have the highest absolute debt funding gap of $35 billion along with Spain, at $26 billion. Both these markets have relatively limited impacts under the new rules. Ireland, which has been highlighted previously as a market with a relatively

---

[21]  See *DTZ Insight, Global Debt Funding Gap, New non-bank lending offsets EBA impact*, May 11, 2012.

high funding gap, has no impact under the new rules with a gap of $8 billion. Lending on CRE in Germany, totalling $26 billion and lending to France totalling $25 billion, will be the most impacted by the new EBA requirement. Lending to Dutch CRE will also face to a huge increase of its debt funding gap to $10 billion. (See Figure 19).

**Figure 19. EU debt funding gap 2012-13, $ billion**

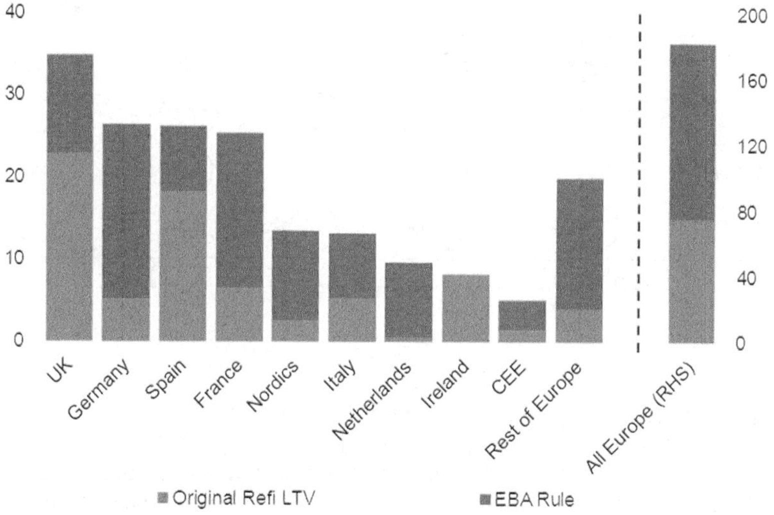

Source:     DTZ Research

### 2.5.4. *Lending terms to reduce funding gap*

Europe's funding gap contrasts with no funding gap in the United States. This partially reflects the structure of the US market. In particular, the United States has on average longer loan terms of around 10 years, compared to five years typically available in Europe. This means the market is less susceptible to short-term volatility in capital values at the point of refinance (see Table 2). For loans maturing in 2012, in Europe and the United Kingdom, the value of these assets could be up to 25 per cent lower than their value at origination. In the United States, the value of assets will typically still be above their level at origination in 2002. This eases the refinancing burden in the United States. (See Table 2).

# Table 2. Capital value index pre and post crisis

| Year | US | Europe (ex UK) | UK | Japan | Asia Pacific (ex Japan) |
|------|-----|------|-----|-------|------|
| 2002 | 56 | 56 | 74 | 48 | 39 |
| 2007 | 100 | 100 | 100 | 100 | 100 |
| 2010 | 70 | 81 | 75 | 57 | 95 |
| 2012 | 77 | 86 | 75 | 58 | 100 |

Source: DTZ Research, IPD, NCREIF TBI

Additionally, as highlighted above,[22] the United States has a more diverse source of finance which supports lending capacity. Of note is the share of activity by institutions that are traditionally more conservative lenders. Whilst institutions tended to be less active at the peak of the market, relative to commercial banks, this meant they were less exposed to the downturn in values and the market, and were thus able to lend at the bottom of the market cycle and increase their market share whilst banks were less active (See Figure 20).

Globally, there remains sufficient equity to plug the debt funding gap over the next three years. This may create an attractive opportunity for private equity investors, but such an opportunity assumes, of course, the equity being targeted matches the debt. With no debt funding gap in North America and only a limited funding gap in Asia Pacific,[23] DTZ sees no issues in these two regions, with more than sufficient equity available (See

---

[22] See Figure 3.

[23] Asia Pacific's debt funding gap is mostly concentrated in Japan which has been most exposed to the crisis due to relatively shorter loans, but also greater volatility in capital values. In the rest of Asia Pacific LTVs have been on average lower than those in Europe. Also the origination of loans in emerging economies such as China and India has been more recent, peaking in 2008/09. Monetary policies have also been more accommodative. Were these markets to be exposed to significant falls in capital values then this could expose them to problems at refinance.

Figure 20. US loan originations index by source

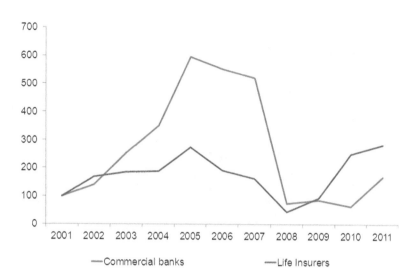

Source: Mortgage Bankers Association

Figure 21). In Europe, there is greater tension. The gross debt funding gap over the next two years of $182 billion is not matched by the $109 billion of equity.

However, there is the potential for the funding gap in Europe to be reduced through additional lending capacity from insurers and other non-bank lenders.[24] Over the next two years DTZ estimate there could be up to $75 billion of new lending capacity in Europe. This would shrink Europe's funding gap to a net $107 billion, reducing a significant amount of the burden imposed by new regulatory requirements. On this basis it is possible, from the DTZ data, to anticipate just sufficient equity to bridge the gap, (See Figures 21 and 22).

During the first half of 2012, a number of banks—including Commerzbank, Societe Generale, DG Hyp, Yorkshire Bank and Clydesdale Bank—have either withdrawn from the market or retreated to their home markets, as a means of reducing their exposure to CRE. In Europe, which is heavily

---

[24]  See further Ch.20.

**Figure 21. Debt Funding Gap and Available Equity 2012-13, $ billion**

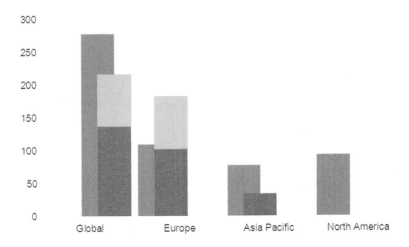

Source:    DTZ Research

reliant on banks for funding, any withdrawal is unwelcome,[25] given the growing level of refinancing, which totals over €1 trillion in the next four years.

Just as there is shrinkage in new lending capacity from traditional bank lenders in Europe, there is also a growing number of insurers and other non-bank lenders seeking to enter or grow their lending across Europe, including a number of overseas organisations, predominantly from the United States. There are already ten life insurers active in the United Kingdom and Continental Europe, including AIG, Allianz, AXA, Aviva, Legal & General, MetLife, M&G and Canada Life. Following Met Life's entry into the UK CRE market, other US insurers, including New York Life and Mass Mutual, are understood to be eyeing entrance to the market, and more may follow given the opportunities available. They come alongside the likes of GE Capital Real Estate and Renshaw Bay who are also seeking opportunities.

---

[25]  In late June 2012 Commerzbank deemed all CRE lending as non-core. With a EU CRE loan book totalling close to €70 billion based on data published in the July 2011 EBA stress tests, it was a significant lender to CRE.

Figure 22. EU Debt Funding Gap and Available Equity in Europe 2012-13 $ billion

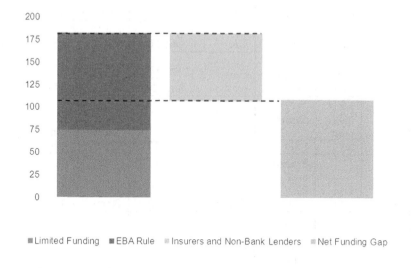

■ Limited Funding    ■ EBA Rule    ■ Insurers and Non-Bank Lenders    ■ Net Funding Gap

Source:    DTZ Research

Over the past year, there has been increasing activity from lenders in working out their loan books, although progress in reducing the outstanding debt remains slow. Of those markets in Europe with bigger problems (notably the United Kingdom, Spain and Ireland), it is only in the United Kingdom where we have seen significant efforts to date to bring about a solution and reduction in overall debt

At the end of 2011, CRE loans had been sold for just over GBP £4 billion in the United Kingdom. Much of this was accounted for in two major transactions by the Royal Bank of Scotland and Lloyds Banking Group. Sales of UK CRE loans by NAMA and the Bank of Ireland also made significant contributions. However, the value of these reflected discounts to face value of loans between 30 per cent and 40 per cent (see Table 3).

*Table 3. Past and pending EU loan sales, May 2012*

| Seller | Buyer | Property/ Loan name | Country/ Region | Date | Face value | Sale price | Dis- count |
|--------|-------|---------------------|-----------------|------|------------|------------|------------|
|        |       |                     |                 |      |            |            |            |

| | | | | | | | |
|---|---|---|---|---|---|---|---|
| Lloyds Bank-ing Group | Lon-estar | UK Loans | UK | Dec-11 | GBP 1.08bn | GBP 0.65bn | 40% |
| RBS | Black stone | Project Isobel | UK | Dec-11 | GBP 1.4bn | GBP 0.98bn | 30% |
| Bun-des-bank | Lon-estar | Excali-bur | Ger-many | Jan-12 | EUR 430m | EUR 279m | 35% |
| NAMA | Mor-gan Stan-ley | Saturn Port-folio | UK | Mar-12 | GBP 220m | GBP 65m | 70% |
| Soci-ete Gen-erale | Lon-estar | France and Ger-many | Europe | Apr-12 | EUR 200m | EUR 116m | 30% |
| RBS | n/a | Max Bahr Port-folio | Ger-many | Pending | EUR 1bn | EUR 0.6bn | 40% |
| Intesa San-paolo | n/a | NPL port-folio | Italy | Pending | EUR 4bn | n/a | n/a |
| Lloyds Bank-ing Group | | Project Harro-gate | UK | Pending | GBP 625m | n/a | n/a |

Source: DTZ Research

A feature in many of these sales of CRE loans has been the reduction in the number of assets included in the final sale. Not only have the number of assets been reduced in the initial process, but also once a preferred bidder has been selected, these investors are often cherry picking the most appropriate assets and removing those assets considered too problematic.

Further sales are expected during 2012.[26] The focus of these loans is centred on Germany, Italy, Spain and the United Kingdom. Growing activity is expected from the German so called "bad banks"—Erste Abwicklungsan-stalt and FMS Wertmanagement—as they run down the portfolios of WestImmo and Hypo Real Estate Holding A.G.

Of sales completed in 2011 and the first half of 2012, discounts have ranged from 30–80 per cent (see Table 3). A gradual increase is expected, particularly as banks shift to the next phase of the workout of non-prime

---

[26] DTZ are currently monitoring potential loan sales with a face value of over €30 billion.

stock. This will result in the final sale prices of these loans being below face value. In some cases, there have been issues with the agreed pricing or assets to include against an uncertain economic backdrop and further potential falls in values. These pressures were highlighted in Morgan Stanley's decision to pull out of a deal to acquire a portfolio of mostly residential loans from Santander, even after Morgan Stanley had reportedly cherry picked assets and was close to agreeing a deal at €700 million, at a discount of close to 70 per cent.

The end value could also be reduced as the appetite amongst bidders, especially the private equity investors, starts to wane. Demand for the super larger loan portfolio sales that are currently being seen is unlikely to be sustained forever. This would see activity shifting over the next couple of years towards the US model where loan sales are traditionally around $200 to $300 million.

Increased regulation will place further pressure on banks to shrink their balance sheets, with the ECBs LTRO providing some short-term relief, by enabling banks to undertake a more orderly discharge of their loans. This could therefore place equity buyers under greater pressure to deploy capital.

DTZ estimate that funds have, on average, an investment period of three years. Some may have the provision, or agreement to extend this with investors. Those funds raised before 2009 will be, in 2012, under greatest pressure to deploy capital or risk returning equity to investors. DTZ's data suggests that opportunity funds account for 55 per cent of available capital, with value-added funds represent a further 24 per cent (See Figure 23).

Looking at unspent capital, the top 50 funds account for 53 per cent of available capital. The pressure to deploy this capital could see funds investing on less favourable terms. This is more likely to impact fund managers who have a relative smaller range of funds where the risk of returning capital could harm the sustainability of their business and endanger their core fee income. It is interesting to note that, in early 2012, Morgan Stanley agreed an annual extension to its MSREF VII Global fund. It also had to return some equity to investors. (See Figure 24).

Looking to 2013 and beyond, it is interesting to note that the style of funds is changing. Those funds currently seeking to raise capital are, at the time of writing, focussed more towards value-added opportunities, with just 28 per cent seeking more opportunistic purchases. The lower proportion of opportunity funds is welcome, as this is unlikely to saturate the market with too many funds seeking similar investments.[27]

---

[27] See *DTZ Insight, Great Wall of Money, Less capital due to lower gearing*, March 6, 2012.

Figure 23. Available capital by fund style

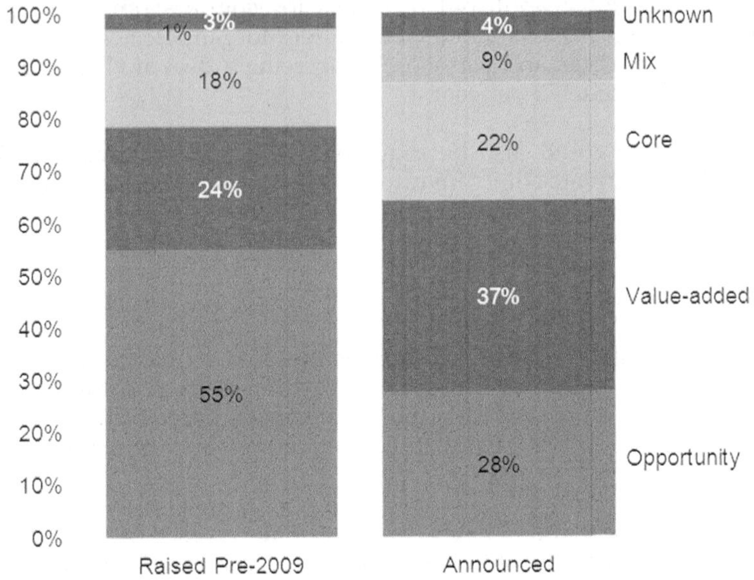

Source: DTZ Research

## 2.6. Conclusion

As this Chapter has highlighted, lending to CRE across Europe has played an important role in the growth and development of Europe's investment market. At its peak, aggregate gearing in Europe's investment market reached 62 per cent. Whilst gearing has reduced, largely reflecting an increase in the value of equity holdings, the amount of debt outstanding to EU CRE has remained elevated and is still above the level registered in 2007. The slow response in the market can largely be put down to the liquidity supports put in place by central banks. These have enabled banks to extend and amend loans, in many cases up to a period of five years. This has provided banks with some breathing space to deals with their troubled loan books without the need for releasing stock to the market at distressed prices. For the banks, this means there is still much work to do.

As Ch.1 highlighted, financing is no longer easy and is getting more expensive; capital is getting tighter; business is becoming less attractive and

**Figure 24. Unspent capital by individual funds raised pre-2009**

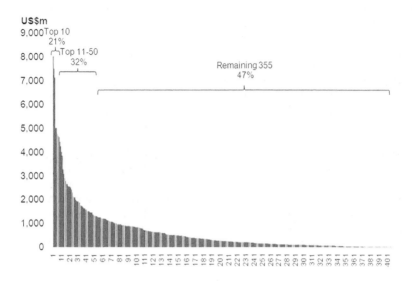

Source: DTZ Research

increasing pressure from regulators is placing greater burdens on the banking sector. These pressures have become increasingly evident in the past couple of years as many banks curtail new lending, retreat back to their home market, or in extreme cases withdraw from CRE lending on a more permanent basis, for example, Commerzbank, as discussed above. The surveys DTZ has undertaken, earlier in 2012, affirm these challenges that face the market, with a clear downward shift in sentiment in 2012, compared to 2011, as sovereign debt and the financial crisis persists in Europe.

Short-term lending, traditionally of five years, combined with recent loan extensions, means that much of the debt originated or refinanced towards the peak of the market is due for refinance in 2012 to 2015. Based on DTZ's debt funding gap analysis, it is estimated that close to €1 trillion of loans are due for refinance between 2012 and 2015. This presents a huge challenge to the industry at a time when lending capacity is being curtailed.

In 2012 and 2013, DTZ estimates the funding gap, the gap between the existing debt balance and the debt available to replace it, to be a gross $182 billion, with the United Kingdom, Spain, Germany and France having the highest exposures.

Europe's reliance on banks as its main source of funding for CRE has also highlighted a weakness in the market when alternative sources to date have been relatively limited. Over 90 per cent of lending to CRE in Europe comes through banks, with only limited participation by other sources, mostly CMBS, but also some through insurance companies. This is in stark contrast to North America, where traditional bank lending represents just 60 per cent of outstanding lending. There, other sources of finance, CMBS and lending from insurance companies and other institutions represent a much higher proportion of activity. This, combined with longer lending terms, up to 10 years, insulates the market from short-term volatility in capital values and reduced lending capacity from particular lending groups.

Evidence of lending from insurance companies, including those based in the United States, is now emerging. Although the trend is slow, it is a welcome shift towards providing a more diverse base of lending that will place Europe's lending markets on a much firmer footing and providing much needed liquidity to the CRE market. DTZ estimates that up to $75 billion of additional lending capacity will be available from insurers and other non-bank lenders in the next two years, providing some relief to the estimated funding gap.

Additionally, there is also sufficient new equity from funds to plug the funding gap. The challenge remains in matching the equity to the debt in the market. With much of the equity currently targeting core assets and much of the remaining troubled assets secondary or tertiary, there remains a gap in matching the debt to the equity. Additionally, where equity is targeted at secondary assets, investors are seeking discounts significantly above the levels banks' are willing to dispose at.[28] As a growing number of loan sales emerge, producing a shift towards more secondary assets, greater clarity in pricing for the market is expected. As loans are transferred to private equity houses, we do expect to see an increase in enforcement and the release of product to the market. Already in the United Kingdom, there have been a number of assets sales emerging from the RBS (Project Isobel) and Lloyds (Project Royal) loan sales coming to the market and providing attractive opportunities for traditional equity buyers. This will take time and will provide a host of opportunities in 2012 and way beyond.

---

[28] This will be discussed in further detail in Ch.3.

# Chapter 3

# Opportunities in Refinancing and Recapitalising Legacy Commercial Mortgage Loans, CMBS Loans and Assets: A Private Equity Perspective

Stefan Jaeger,

Colony Capital LLC

## 3.1. Introduction

The effective closure of the CMBS market since the second-half of 2007 and the struggle of banks to deal with the fall-out from the continuing financial crisis, has resulted in structural changes to the composition of CRE debt markets that are, in 2012 and beyond, opening up appealing investment opportunities for the private equity industry. As discussed in the previous two Chapters, banks, traditionally the major source of European CRE debt, are in a long-term deleveraging process that has already led to a severe contraction in available financing.

At the same time, the other source of capital during the CRE investment boom of 2004–07, the CMBS market, continues to suffer from low demand and issuance volumes. However, despite this contraction in the supply of CRE debt, there is continued investment activity and sustained demand for CRE debt. The first source of demand for CRE debt in Europe is the estimated €100 billion[1] of equity capital, available to be invested into European CRE, leading to potential demand for debt financing of €100–150 billion (assuming a 40–50 per cent equity contribution). The second source of demand for CRE debt in Europe is the need for borrowers to find refinancing solutions for existing financings. Total refinancing requirements in European CRE are estimated to total more than €1 trillion over the next four years[2] creating huge demand for CRE debt and equity injections to refinance and recapitalise borrowers. As a result the debt markets, specifically the senior secured and mezzanine debt market for CRE, are suffering from a sustained imbalance in demand and supply over the foreseeable future. With banks continuing to de-lever, potential uncertainty

---

[1]  "DTZ Insight, Global Debt Funding Gap: New non-bank lending offsets EBA impact", DTZ Research (May 11, 2012) (Nigel Almond) (the DTZ report). See further Ch.2.

[2]  *DTZ report.*

regarding macro-economic conditions and concerns regarding sovereign debt and inflationary pressures expected to continue for an indefinite period, it is likely that cash constrained refinancing situations will provide many attractive investment opportunities for years to come.

For opportunity funds, the threats to and distress in commercial mortgage loans and CMBS markets, raises the prospect of a vast opportunity set to deploy capital in senior, mezzanine and common equity in refinancing and recapitalisation of cash constrained borrowers. In fact, the market disloca-tion that exists, in H2 2012, is viewed by many industry professionals as one of the largest investment opportunities in a generation. Many private equity firms have sought to capitalise on distressed and refinancing opportunities and have launched funds specifically targeting these opportunities. However, a major obstacle to the manifestation of these opportunities has been the intervention of several European governments[3] and the European Central Bank which has slowed the pace of deleveraging. For example, the lending facilities provided to the banking system by the European Central Bank have eased liquidity concerns for many banks. If it were not for these interventions a lot more CRE assets and debt may have been sold outright, post 2008, at deep discounts as banks required liquidity. By intervening, governments may therefore have delayed a normalisation and price adjustment process in CRE and debt markets.

Nevertheless, as stated above, the opportunity that has arisen out of the financial crisis is vast. It is, however, recognised that government intervention may have resulted in such opportunity being not as profitable for distressed asset buyers, as it might have otherwise been. Thus, rather than buying distressed assets outright, as expected by many at the onset of the financial crisis, the opportunity in 2012 and beyond, lies in the debt investment world and revolves around refinancing and recapitalising CRE assets through senior, mezzanine and equity injections. For the private equity investor these transactions are often safer, but offer less absolute returns.

This Chapter will examine the structural changes in the debt markets for CRE, which have led to a significant imbalance of demand and supply. This Chapter will show how this dynamic offers private equity investors opportunities to achieve attractive risk-adjusted returns, when pursuing senior, mezzanine and equity investments, resulting from cash constraint refinancing and recapitalisation situations. Senior and mezzanine debt are, a complementary form of investment to the more traditional common equity investments for the private equity industry, offering a different risk-reward profile. Well-capitalised private equity investors with close

---

[3]  Ireland, Italy, Spain, Greece and Portugal have all participated in bailouts of their banking systems since the financial crisis and a number of banks across Europe, including in Germany and the United Kingdom have been nationalised.

relationships to borrowers and financial institutions will be well positioned to benefit from the market dynamics and opportunities discussed within this Chapter.

## 3.2. The supply and demand imbalance in CRE financing

At the time of writing, the European CMBS market remains, for the most part, closed. Demand for primary CMBS bonds in Europe is at best sluggish.[4] Most of the investor base in the asset class in the secondary market, is, at the time of writing, constituted by hedge funds, whose capital allocation to CMBS is opportunistic rather than long-term. Hence, the major hurdle to the revival of CMBS is to attract a new long-term investor base that can sustain a primary market.[5] As this requires a longer-term effort, a near-term revival of the CMBS market seems unlikely.

At the same time as the CMBS market remains closed, European financial institutions are in the midst of dealing with the aftermath of the financial crisis and continue to be put under stress from lingering concerns regarding sovereign debt. This applies particularly to European banks, where write-downs have lagged behind the United States and sovereign exposure is high and consequently concerns are most acute. Coupled with the need to raise further equity capital and to comply with new regulation, banks are left with few other options than to reduce their exposure to the CRE sector, which is, as described in Ch.1, a capital intensive, risk-based business.

The continued closure of the CMBS market and a severely reduced supply of CRE financing from the banking sector cannot match the huge demand for refinancing of legacy assets and have resulted in a squeeze of the so-called loan to value (LTV) ratios and higher risk-adjusted returns for CRE debt. In CRE finance the LTV ratio, which measures the outstanding notional of a loan divided by the value of the underlying property securing the loan, is an important metric. Following the financial crisis, this ratio decreased in both the numerator and denominator of the equation. CRE market values have fallen for most properties in Europe. While there are certain exemptions in prime/core property markets where prices have returned to, or exceeded their former 2007 peak levels, most properties are valued significantly below their peaks. In, particularly secondary and tertiary property values across Europe are suffering. As a result, properties now often require an equity injection, even if they were refinanced at the same LTV. Additionally, however, leverage levels in property transactions are now generally assumed to be between 40–70 per cent LTV, down from around 75–90 per cent before the financial crisis. As a result, the equity required in a refinancing could be as much as double, compared to what would previously have been required.

---

[4]    For the reasons behind this see Ch.1.
[5]    See further Ch.20.

Furthermore, the scarcity of lending capital has meant that debt pricing has increased sharply from the levels observed prior to the financial crisis. These conditions, of lower leverage at higher pricing levels, are a vast opportunity for non-traditional lenders with CRE expertise to originate and invest into CRE debt and/or recapitalisation equity at very attractive risk-adjusted returns.

### 3.2.1. The supply side

#### 3.2.1.1 The CMBS market

At the height of the CRE boom from 2004–07, CRE investment activity benefited from the strong growth and abundance of cheap debt at very high leverage ratios. In Europe, the CMBS market grew from c.€17 billion in 2004 to a peak of €65 billion in 2007, with an increase (that never materialised) to over €100 billion expected in 2008.[6] Despite this very strong growth trajectory, it is important to keep in mind that even at its peak, issuance levels of CMBS always represented between 10 per cent and 15 per cent of the overall European CRE financing market.

Since the financial crisis, demand for CMBS has significantly reduced. In Europe, the primary CMBS market remains effectively closed as a result of reduced investor demand and more stringent regulation. As discussed in further detail in Ch.1, the period 2008–12 saw no more than a handful of European transactions totalling less than €5 billion.

#### 3.2.1.2 The banking sector

At the same time as funding from the CMBS sector has contracted, banks are deleveraging to meet tighter capital requirements and to comply with increased regulation. Furthermore, European banks are facing severe challenges on the funding side. Morgan Stanley estimates that banks require refinancing for €1.7 trillion of maturing debt between 2012 and 2014.[7] While initiatives by the European Central Bank, such as the Long-Term Refinancing Operation (LTRO) have eased some of the immediate concerns faced by banks in 2011 and 2012, European banks will nevertheless have to refinance these cheap sources of debt at some point in the future. It seems highly plausible that these refinancings will come at a higher cost than in the past.

One of the major reasons for this is that European banks are holding a large amount of sovereign bonds and some of the cheap funding provided by the European Central Bank during 2010–12, has been used by European banks

---

[6]  See further Ch.1.
[7]  "Banks Deleveraging and Real Estate", Morgan Stanley Blue Paper (March 15, 2012), Francesca Tondi, Bart Gysens and others (*The Morgan Stanley Report*).

to further increase these holdings, heightening concerns surrounding European bank solvencies. This has resulted in a higher cost of capital for European banks[8]. In combination with increased regulation facing the banking sector (e.g. tighter capital requirements of a minimum 9 per cent core capital and Basel III) this means that European banks are under pressure to deliver.

Estimates assume that banks, either directly through balance sheet lending or indirectly via covered bond programs, represent more than 90 per cent of the CRE lending market in Europe with total outstanding of €2–2.5 trillion. Morgan Stanley estimates that banks are set to reduce their exposure to CRE by €300–600 billion, or 12–25% of their 2012 CRE balance sheet exposure.[9]

European bank deleveraging, while proceeding more slowly than many expected due to heavy government intervention, has already had a strong impact on CRE lending. For instance, the *De Montfort UK Commercial Property Lending Market* report shows a clear contraction of lending into the UK CRE sector. The report shows a fall of debt held against UK commercial property from c.£228 billion to £212 billion or 6.8 per cent within a year.[10]

The below factors summarise the drivers that have led to a situation of severely reduced appetite amongst banks to lend to the European CRE sector:

### Sovereign debt concerns

Many of the major European CRE lenders also have significant exposure to European sovereign debt. This has significantly constrained the amount of lending European banks are able and willing to provide to the CRE sector. Some major European CRE lenders have temporarily stopped lending to, or, are permanently withdrawing from the market and many banks are generally re-trenching to their domestic markets.[11]

### Expectations for European economic growth are relatively low

---

[8] For further information regarding sovereign debt holdings of European banks see "Europe's Sovereign Debt Crisis and its Impact on U.S. and European Financial Institutions", Navigant Consulting, Inc., Howard Schneider, Vikram Kapoor.

[9] *The Morgan Stanley Report*, p.17.

[10] See the *De Montfort Report*.

[11] For example, in November 2011 Germany's Commerzbank announced a temporary suspension of all new business for its Eurohypo CRE arm, pending a review. In March 2012 Commerzbank, which through Eurohypo previously was one of the largest CRE lenders in Europe, announced a run-down of Eurohypo and an intention of "clearly scaled-down core activities in the CRE business" to be part of a new Commerzbank segment. In June 2012 Commerzbank then announced a fully exit from CRE lending citing the "continuing uncertain situation in financial markets, the heightening sovereign debt crisis and the increasing regulatory burdens." At the time of writing, Eurohypo's entire €56 billion real estate loan book is to be transferred to Commerzbank's non-core asset division to be wound-up. See further Ch.1.

Most economists expect European economic growth to be lethargic for the foreseeable future.[12] For CRE, this implies low rental growth. This means capital values are unlikely to appreciate through strong rental growth, which in turn raises concerns within existing debt providers to CRE, regarding both the provision of new and refinancing debt.

### New regulation for the banking sector

Basel III and other regulatory initiatives across Europe mean that the capital required to be held by banks when lending to CRE is increasing. This has an impact on the profitability and consequently appetite banks are displaying for lending to CRE.[13]

### Changes in funding conditions

The banking industry is contracting and undergoing structural changes in funding conditions, significantly reducing the profitability of CRE lending. Most banks used to profit from the arbitrage of extending long-term loans using cheap short-term funding, so-called maturity transformation. As funding costs for banks increase, the profitability of CRE lending is declining.

### Overexposure of banks to CRE

Morgan Stanley estimates that European banks have CRE lending exposure of c. €2.4 trillion equivalent to c. 10 per cent of their loan books. It is likely that these banks wish to reduce their exposure, to bring it at least in line with historical averages which are significantly lower.[14]

Furthermore, many banks are forced to deliver and reduce their exposure to CRE in order to repay government aid they received during the financial crisis.

### Banks require additional equity capital

In 2011, the European Banking Authority conducted stress tests that resulted in European banks having to plug a €115 billion capital shortfall. European banks are, at the time of writing, required to reach and maintain a 9 per cent core capital ratio. This is considerably more than the amount they are required to hold under Basel III. This short-term need to raise significant amounts of capital, has severely constrained European banks ability to lend to CRE.

Faced with banks less willing to lend to CRE, many borrowers find it increasingly difficult to obtain bank financing. In cases where banks are willing to extend leverage, these loans are targeted at core-type properties with lower leverage and stricter conditions than prior to the financial crisis.

---

[12] For further information refer to the IMF's World Economic Outlook, April 2012, which predicts real GDP contraction in the first half of 2012 with a slow recovery in 2012. Overall European projected growth is 0.2% in 2012 and 1.4% in 2013.

[13] See further Ch. 16.

[14] See the *Morgan Stanley Report*, p.9.

### 3.2.1.3   The German Pfandbrief Market

A further well established supply of financing to the CRE market is via the German *Pfandbrief* market. *Pfandbriefe* are covered bonds issued by German banks under the German *Pfandbrief* Act. The market is the benchmark for European covered bonds and has proven resilient to stress and has performed well throughout the financial crisis. While funding costs are still relatively low in the *Pfandbrief* market, which are passed through to borrowers, the loans underlying the *Pfandbrief* remain on banks' balance sheets. Therefore the same regulatory pressures apply to this funding source as to the banking market as a whole and only limited further capacity can be expected.

### 3.2.2.   The demand side

On the demand side, there is continued investment activity and demand for CRE debt. In 2011, total transaction volumes in commercial property in Europe were approximately €120 billion, which was around half of 2006 and 2007 peak volumes. There is an estimated €100 billion of equity capital[15] available to be invested into European CRE. Assuming an average 50–60 per cent LTV *v* 70–80 per cent LTV pre the financial crisis) this implies demand for debt financing of €100–150 billion. However, future acquisitions are only one demand factor. As stated above, the second driver for strong loan demand in Europe is of course the need for borrowers to find refinancing solutions for their outstanding loans. Total refinancing requirements in European CRE are estimated to total over €1 trillion in the next four years creating huge demand for CRE debt in the near future. Approximately €50–100 million of this so-called "maturity wall" relate to CMBS with the remainder relating primarily to bank financings. Not all of this debt will be refinancable, given amongst other things the squeeze in LTV ratios described above. DTZ estimates that the funding gap (debt that cannot be refinanced through voluntary property sales or straight debt refinancing) in Europe amounts to around €90–100 billion.[16]

## 3.3.   What happens at loan/CMBS maturities?

When a loan or CMBS transaction comes to maturity there are several possible permutations that could materialise. Given the supply/demand imbalance that exists and the scarcity of available debt for CRE in the markets in 2012, most of these outcomes are predicated by cash constraints. Such situations offer great opportunities for the private equity investor to provide capital, in order to facilitate a refinancing and/or recapitalisation of legacy assets in the form of senior, mezzanine and/or equity capital. The

---

[15]   *DTZ report.* See further Ch.2.
[16]   *DTZ report* and Ch.2.

points below summarise the potential outcome that can occur at maturity; there could also be combinations of these outcomes:[17]

### Refinancing without equity injection

This is a likely outcome in low leverage loans backed by high quality assets. Often these financings will also be relatively small. In these cases, principal would be repaid at maturity through a refinancing.

### Refinancing with equity injection

For financings that feature leverage higher than available in the market place, or, where underlying property values have declined, any funding gap between the existing debt and the new debt available at refinancing could be plugged through an equity injection by the borrower and/or new equity provided by a new investor.

### Voluntary property sales

This involves the borrower selling the properties in the open market to repay the loan with the sales proceeds. This way the purchaser effectively provides equity to fill any funding gap. It is mainly an option for smaller portfolios, as large scale portfolios are somewhat constrained by the availability of financing to the buyers, unless the buyer is an unlevered or low-leverage cash investor. Another option is for the borrower to sell the properties individually or in smaller sub-portfolios, before the loan maturity, with the aim to reduce leverage to a level and size that can be refinanced under market conditions. The latter strategy is, however, often restricted through release pricing conditions and lenders being concerned by the borrower selling all good assets and leaving them with the harder to sell properties (so-called "cherry-picking").

### Portfolio break-up

For larger portfolios of assets, where the property quality and / or overall leverage ratios are in line with market expectations, but the portfolio size is too large to refinance given the scarcity of debt that exists, at the time of writing, a possible option would be to split the portfolio into sub-portfolios and refinancing them separately.

### Extension

A very common route post the financial crisis has been to extend loans with the hope of being able to refinance them at a later stage if market conditions improve. Often extensions are then combined with rapid amortisation through cash sweeps and/or voluntary property disposal plans to increase the possibility of a refinancing. Extensions are mainly agreed where the underlying properties generate sufficient

---

[17] The description of these outcomes is loosely based on the descriptions of possible outcomes at maturity in German Multi-Family CMBS transactions. For further information please refer to "German Multi-Family CMBS, Half-time Review and Outlook", *Barclays Capital Securitisation Research* (January 10, 2011) (Christian Aufsatz).

cash flows to service existing debt. Rather than an ultimate solution, an extension is often agreed between lender and borrower to buy some time while attempting to work on another solution. This strategy has often been criticised by market participants and has been dubbed "extend and pretend."[18]

## Restructuring

Loans that mature (or reach the end of extension periods) can be restructured. This can often be a very complex process, particularly in CMBS financings, given the sheer number parties and their potential diverging interests. In a CMBS transaction, for instance, a restructuring needs to be agreed by, inter alia, sponsor, borrower, servicer, various classes of bondholders, hedge counterparties and potentially junior or pari-passu ranking lenders outside the CMBS financing. In a widely distributed bank financing a restructuring can be just as complex. Restructuring often involves write-downs by existing lenders in exchange for equity stakes (debt-for-equity swaps), as well as extended maturity profiles.

## Default and property liquidation

A default is likely in over-levered loans where the underlying portfolio exhibits cash flow problems and often increasing vacancy. Often these situations result in insolvencies, foreclosure or receivership and ultimately result in the liquidation of the underlying properties or shares in the borrower under distressed conditions.

From a private equity investor's perspective, the most attractive investment opportunities arise in cash constraint situations. While investment opportunities can arise in several of the above cases, it is likely that the most attractive returns are available in situations that are facing cash constraints upon refinancing as may be seen in the Uni-Invest deal that matured in February 2012.

*Uni-Invest case study*
The case study of Uni-Invest is good example of the investment opportunity available to private equity firms arising at debt maturity. The case illustrates certain of the outcomes described above. Certain features of the Uni-Invest transaction may also set a template for future European CMBS workouts, albeit most transactions will have bespoke features, making a carbon copy of the transaction unlikely.
Uni-Invest, a Dutch property company that held approximately 200 secondary and tertiary office properties in the Netherlands, defaulted in 2010 on a single loan that was securitised. The originator and special servicer initially extended the loan for one year and adopted an asset

---

[18] See further Ch.5.

disposal strategy to fund principal payments. However, a further collapse of the global CRE market prevented the strategy from making any headway.

The loan returned to default status, and in February of 2012 the CMBS became the first European CMBS transaction to default not only on the underlying loan, but also on note maturity. This enabled the senior Class A noteholders to gain control of the workout process and thus the special servicer formed a steering committee of 20 members, representing 82 per cent of Class A noteholders (the most senior part of the capital structure), to help find a resolution.

The committee adopted a "dual-track strategy" in which two proposals were considered: a loan acquisition bid by a consortium of private equity bidders and a restructuring and asset disposal solution proposed by a third party asset management company. Ultimately, the proposals went to vote and the private equity consortium's bid won more than the required approval of 75 per cent of Class A noteholders.

With a €160–180 million equity investment, the private equity consortium acquired the loan from Uni-Invest, giving them control over the underlying assets. Class A noteholders received 40 per cent of their principal upfront, and the remaining 60 per cent rolled over into new bonds at favourable credit terms, essentially as a form of vendor financing. Those who did not want to rollover into the new bond issuance could elect to take an additional 35 per cent of their principal amount.

Compared to the competing proposal, the private equity bid was seen as more favourable to the senior noteholders, as they received principal back immediately. Additionally, the rollover into new privately held bonds, potentially enabled Class A noteholders to treat this remaining principal as a performing asset for regulatory capital purposes, with the new equity injection serving as a cushion to bondholders

As the first European CMBS transaction to default at final maturity, many in the industry were unclear as to how the workout would resolve itself. Typically in a CMBS, junior noteholders retain control during a workout; however, in this case the note default switched the control to the senior noteholders. This proved to be the pivotal moment in enabling private equity players to acquire the loan in a bid that wiped out junior positions. It is likely that the ultimate proposal, selected by the special servicer, would have been the more complicated, and probably painful, restructuring proposal if junior noteholders had retained control, as it offered them potential to recover a portion of their principal. Rather, the strategy adopted by the special servicer, enabled senior noteholders to play a key role in deciding the resolution of a complicated CMBS structure and this particular approach may serve as a template to further European CMBS deals that default on note maturity.

## 3.4. New sources of capital: Who could plug the gap?

The hangover following the investment boom years in European CRE debt is particularly pronounced. As discussed earlier in this Chapter, the combination of increased regulation, structural changes in the banking market, the need for many market participants to de-lever and the outlook of anaemic economic growth, will mean that lending will remain constrained and lending terms will remain conservative for the foreseeable future compared to those terms offered in the market prior to 2007. Most lending will focus on the safe properties that are highly marketable and generate strong cash flow with long remaining lease terms, so-called core-type CRE assets. Borrowers are generally aware of the issue and are seeking to diversify their funding away from the traditional banking market, wherever possible. This brings strong incentives for new lenders to establish themselves within the market. It is important to note, however, that despite a contraction, commercial banks will likely continue to be the largest providers of financing to CRE in Europe. Any transition to new capital sources supplementing the banking market will take years to materialise, as these new capital providers will first have to raise appropriate funds and build the necessary infrastructure and relationship networks.

### 3.4.1. Capital structure

The figure below illustrates the primary styles of property and the various sources of capital that make up a typical capital structure against these properties. The property types shown range from the safest (so-called core assets, typically characterised by stable cash-flows arising from long-term lease contracts with high-quality tenants, prime locations and low capital expenditure requirements) to the most risky (so-called opportunistic assets often characterised by low, volatile cash flows and high capital expenditure requirements). It also illustrates potential new capital sources that have come to the market aiming to plug the gap that has been left behind by the withdrawal of traditional bank lenders and the CMBS market. What is noticeable is a contraction in available leverage ratios compared to prior to the financial crisis. Furthermore, when going up the risk-scale in terms of property types the scarcity of capital increases severely. Often now the perceived safe haven of core assets has led to very "thin" returns/margins and better risk-adjusted returns being available in secondary and tertiary value-add and opportunistic investments, particularly when investing in senior and mezzanine positions within the capital structure.

### 3.4.2. Insurance companies

One of the potential new sources of debt capital going forward will be large institutional investors (pension funds, insurance companies, sovereign wealth funds, etc.), which look to increase their exposure to CRE either

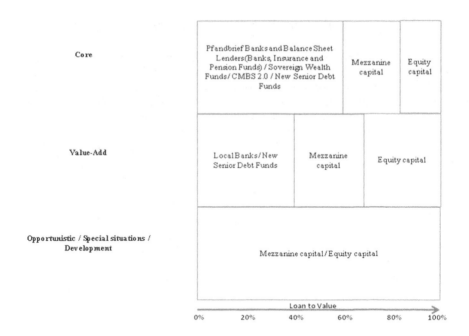

directly or indirectly. In particular, attractiveness of lending to CRE increases for insurance companies compared to directly investing into CRE, as a result of Solvency II regulation.[19] This is because upon implementation of Solvency II regulation (proposed for January 2014) insurance companies will be required to put aside an increased amount of capital for direct CRE investments, thereby making indirect CRE investments such as CRE debt relatively more attractive. Some of these investors have historically low allocations to CRE, in particularly CRE debt. These allocations are likely to increase over time, once the attractive risk/return profiles offered by the CRE debt markets become more widely advertised.

### 3.4.3. *Private equity*

Due to its existing infrastructure to invest in CRE, its wide relationship networks and its flexible investment approach, the private equity industry is another new source of debt capital that can help to address the funding shortfall in Europe. Private equity funds generally have the ability to invest opportunistically across the capital structure. The combination of a sustained supply/demand imbalance in the availability of debt and the consequent increase in the cost of debt described earlier are gradually leading to a closing of the often observed "pricing gap", i.e. the gap between the cost expectations of the borrower and the return expectations

---

[19] See further Ch.16.

of private equity funds. The market environment, at the time of writing, therefore represents a very attractive investment opportunity for the private equity industry and other institutional investors. In essence, the financial crisis has created opportunities for the CRE private equity that allow it to invest in CRE in the alternative form of debt at compelling risk-adjusted returns. Of course, given the cash constraint nature of many refinancing situations, equity capital can also provide attractive returns to private equity investors.

## 3.5. Where are the opportunities from a private equity perspective?

This section describes the opportunity for private equity capital to be deployed which has arisen out of the scarcity of CRE debt capital available in Europe in 2012 and outlines potential investment features and returns. There are a number of different ways to invest capital within the CRE sector, available to the private equity investor, within the context of refinancing these broadly extend to the provision of senior debt, mezzanine debt and equity capital. There are further investment opportunities for the astute private equity industry, arising out of the failure to find sufficient financing, such as the purchase of and/or financing of distressed loans, loan portfolios and CMBS bonds, which are covered elsewhere within this book.[20]

### 3.5.1. Senior debt capital

As senior lenders retrench further and the CMBS markets remain closed,[21] there is a clear attractive investment opportunity at attractive risk-adjusted returns in the senior debt space that results from the refinancing needs of legacy CRE loans and CMBS bonds.

In the European environment of lethargic economic growth that exists at the time of writing, senior secured CRE loans provide income with relatively low risk features:

- Most secure part of the capital structure with asset security implying a low default probability and loss severity.
- Covenants that allow lenders to take control. If covenant breaches occur lenders rights are strong, which contrasts with the covenant-light approach of the 2000s.
- Lower advance rate against re-priced capital values following the financial crisis.
- High degree of subordinated capital (generally in the range of 35–50 per cent).

---

[20] See Ch.13.
[21] Please refer to para 3.2.1 for further information.

- Generally less widely distributed, as most transactions are now with a single lender or small tightly organised group of lenders (club deal). In the past wide distribution and diverging interests have prevented CMBS investors from coordinating effectively in the event of a restructuring.
- More detailed underwriting information allows for higher-quality due diligence to be undertaken and better information flow post transaction closing facilitates monitoring.

While some pension managers and insurance companies have recently started to access the markets directly, it is likely that their lending capacity alone will be insufficient to plug the gap left behind by banks reducing their exposure due to the sheer size of the market and the capacity of such insurance companies. Furthermore, it is likely that many large institutional investors (pension, insurance managers and sovereign wealth funds) may prefer to leverage the credit capabilities and expertise of specialists rather than accessing the market directly. With extensive relationships, strong risk evaluation skills and well established CRE investment platforms, the private equity industry is in a strong position to provide the senior debt investment platforms and fund vehicles sought by these investors.

During the 2000s, CMBS pricing evolved into the pricing benchmark for CRE debt. But the dislocation in the CMBS market and the absence of new issuance means that CMBS prices can no longer serve as the pricing benchmark within CRE finance. Therefore the few bank and insurance originated debt transactions have provided the only pricing points available in 2012. These have been at very attractive margins on a risk-adjusted basis. At the time of writing, newly originated senior secured debt in Europe is pricing at Euribor/Libor + 2.50–6.00 per cent, with LTV ratios that are significantly reduced at 40–65 per cent loan-to-value and stronger covenant packages.[22]

A further attractive investment opportunity for senior debt capital is the European market convention to provide senior loans on a floating rate basis. Such floating rate loans exhibit low price sensitivity to changes in interest rates in secondary loan markets. From an investor's perspective the floating rate element provides inflation protection. While this is mostly not of great concern to most investors, due to low inflation expectations, there is a medium-term probability of this becoming more important should inflation pressures increase due to the sustained period of monetary easing being pursued by most central banks in 2012. Given the floating rate nature of European senior commercial mortgage financing, they offer protection and, on a relative basis, even potential upside. The combination of the above factors (attractive pricing, comparatively low risk, a favourable risk-adjusted return outlook and a secure position in the capital structure)

---

[22] See further Chs 1 and 9.

means that senior CRE debt is an attractive investment opportunity for the private equity industry, which traditionally has been an equity-only investor.

However, in H2 2012, only a handful private-equity sponsored senior debt funds have been launched by private equity platforms[23] and the combined capital these funds are looking to raise will only be a drop in the ocean compared to the overall refinancing challenge facing European CRE assets. As a result of this, it is likely that these funds will be faced with very attractive investment opportunities and somewhat limited competition for the foreseeable future.

### 3.5.2. *Mezzanine debt capital*

As senior debt is now typically only available up to maximum of 65 per cent LTV, a number of new mezzanine funds, often sponsored by private equity investors, have emerged in Europe between 2010 and 2012. These funds have aimed to provide financing up to an additional 20–30 per cent of asset value, aiming to plug (at least part of) the funding gap that has been left behind by retrenching banks and the absence of CMBS funding.

Given its position within the capital structure, mezzanine debt typically requires a lower rate of return than common equity and can therefore be an attractive tool for borrowers in need of refinancing, to plug a potential financing gap. Mezzanine lenders are typically able to provide financing, without requiring direct control over the assets and therefore they allow borrowers to refinance or acquire assets with less of a cash outlay. Mezzanine, in its various forms, tends to be a private investment instrument and unlike CMBS bonds, the asset class is generally illiquid and not traded—this is because mezzanine investments are often highly tailored to the specific requirements of the borrower and mezzanine investor, limiting its transferability to other investors. As a result, there is less price volatility, which makes mezzanine capital highly suitable for the private equity investor. Therefore, most private equity investors take a longer-term stable view, focusing on the credit fundamentals of the underlying property security, when investing in mezzanine.

In CRE mezzanine debt capital mainly takes the following forms.

- B-Note: Subordinated interest in a first ranking mortgage secured by CRE. In the case of B-Notes the relationship with the senior financing is regulated through an intercreditor agreement between the mezzanine lender, the senior lender, sometimes the borrower and hedge counterparties (if any).[24]

---

[23] See fn.19 in Ch.1.
[24] See further Chs 14 and 15.

- Mezzanine loan: Loan secured by a share pledge over the borrower who owns the underlying CRE.
- Preferred equity: Typically in the form of a partnership agreement with the common equity provider.

The negotiation of these contracts is often a complex process, as these tend to be highly tailored and specific to individual transactions. In the market emerging since 2011, learning from the often meagre control rights afforded to subordinated investors during the credit boom, mezzanine lenders place particularly importance on the controls and protections afforded to them through the credit agreement and the intercreditor agreement, as will be seen in ChapterChs 14 and 15. The main areas of focus typically revolve around covenants, control, events of default and enforcement rights. Covenants in particular, are an important instrument to monitor performance. In the case of covenant breaches, certain control and potentially enforcement rights are triggered for the mezzanine lenders. As covenants are of particular importance, the main types are described here, typically falling into three categories:

- Financial covenants: Designed to monitor financial performance. They include LTV ratios, minimum interest coverage, minimum/maximum capital expenditure.
- Negative covenants: Designed to prohibit the borrower from taking certain actions and restricts the ability to leak cash out of the borrowing structure. Typically, they include restrictions on the ability to incur additional debt, restrictions on liens and dividends, asset sales and capital expenditure.
- Affirmative covenants: Designed to facilitate the information flow between the lender and the borrower. These covenants typically include reporting requirements, delivery of other financial information and compliance certificates, as well as an obligation to adequately insure the properties and hedge non-property related risk such as currency and interest rate risks.
- While transaction-specific, expected returns on mezzanine debt instruments range from 10–20%+ depending on the nature of the specific transaction. Depending on the type of asset and mezzanine capital instrument LTV ratios in mezzanine can range up to 85 per cent for B-Notes and mezzanine loans and higher for preferred equity instruments.

### 3.5.3. *Equity capital*

At the time of writing, most equity investors investing in CRE, targets "core" assets. The reason for this is that many investors have lost money as a result of the financial crisis and therefore have returned to the CRE markets with a strategy that is perceived to be the least risky. This has led to capital moving into assets that are perceived to provide less volatile returns.

The consensus view is that core assets are a safe haven for capital during economically uncertain times. The hunger to invest into core assets has led to a recovery in core asset markets in various European cities such as London, Vienna and Frankfurt.[25]

This has masked the real distress that continues to exist in many segments of the CRE market, particularly the secondary and tertiary property markets. As described above, it often remains difficult for property owners with financings coming due, to refinance value-add and opportunistic-type CRE without the injection of equity. As banks have tried to extend and restructure loans they typically require equity injections to amortise principal, adjusting at the same time, for fallen asset prices and/or stricter lending criteria. Part of the gap left by retrenching banks can be plugged through new capital sources providing senior and mezzanine financings as described above. However, there remain a large number of financings that also require the injection of common equity.

Attractive private equity investment opportunities for equity capital exist, to assist borrowers with good assets, but insufficient equity capital. Such situations are cash constraint and here the injection of common equity or the acquisition of the asset with new equity can provide assistance in the deleveraging and refinancing of such assets.

Given the scarcity of capital often available in such situations, risk-adjusted returns can be attractive within the value-added and opportunistic space, particularly when compared on a relative value basis to core investment strategies. Returns on European CRE within the value-added and opportunistic space, at the time of writing, are expected to provide returns from 15 per cent upwards, depending on the nature of the specific transaction and the leverage available/deployed.

## 3.6. Conclusions

The wave of required refinancing in European CRE in 2012 and beyond, in combination with the structural changes that banks, as the traditional debt providers to CRE in Europe are undergoing, make it highly likely that European CRE debt markets will remain dislocated for the foreseeable future. As highlighted in this Chapter, the continued imbalance between the supply and demand for debt and equity, in refinancing legacy CRE loans, CMBS and direct property, will offer private equity investors attractive opportunities in 2012 and beyond, in the European CRE markets.

During the investment boom of 2004–07, capital for opportunistic CRE investments and debt for secondary and tertiary assets was abundant, but since the financial crisis, this situation has reversed. Most investors are

---

[25] Source: CBRE.

looking to CRE as a safe haven investment and most capital is reserved for core/prime assets. In contrast, a disproportionately small amount of capital, compared to the size of the opportunity, is made available for financing and investment in distressed and/or secondary and tertiary CRE that requires recapitalisations and refinancing, even if these assets are fundamentally sound and cash-flow producing.

This is somewhat ironic, as unlike during boom times, risk taking today is being rewarded and consequently the best investment opportunities in CRE today arise as a result of a cash constraint situations in the context of refinancing needs. It seems at the very least doubtful that investing equity into a core asset with a mid single-digit return should be a more attractive risk-return profile than investing in senior and mezzanine debt or common equity instruments secured by cash-flow producing and leased secondary CRE, which often receives more than twice the return on investment.

With banks continuing to de-lever, potential uncertainty regarding macro-economic conditions and concerns regarding sovereign debt and with inflationary pressures expected to continue for the foreseeable future, it is likely that cash constrained refinancing situations will provide many attractive investment opportunities for years to come.

As always, close relationships and strong origination capabilities allow access to these opportunities. Private equity investors with strong networks to originate and capacity to execute will be well positioned to benefit from the market dynamics and opportunities discussed in this Chapter.

# Chapter 4

# Legacy of European CRE Lending, The Lessons Learned During The Downturn and CMBS 2.0

Nassar Hussain,

Managing Partner, Brookland Partners LLP

## 4.1   Introduction

This Chapter will develop on the discussion set out in Ch.1, by providing a brief overview of the legacy of CRE lending in Europe over the past decade with a focus on the size of the CRE debt market and CRE debt maturities, origination levels and performance. During this period, as highlighted in the previous chapters, the European CRE debt markets witnessed unprecedented growth levels, but have since the second half of 2007, along with various other sectors, suffered from significant liquidity and performance issues. These issues have impacted both the bank and capital markets, reducing the availability of debt and with limited alternative lenders entering the market at the time of writing, it has, as highlighted in Ch.2, created a significant funding gap. As discussed, banks were the largest providers of CRE debt in Europe with approximately 75 per cent of market share and it is expected that it will take a number of years before the banking sector recovers and even then there is likely to be significantly reduced appetite to originate CRE debt exposure to the levels seen during the boom years.[1]

As well as alternative lenders, the capital markets are expected to play a larger role in future CRE debt financing, but this will be subject to the various participants having confidence in and a proper understanding of CMBS structures. The financial crisis has exposed some of the weaknesses in historical CMBS transactions. This Chapter also explores some of the key lessons learned since the advent of the financial crisis, in relation to the structuring of CMBS transactions in the context of the issues that many market participants have had to face relating to loan defaults and enforcement, consensual extensions and restructurings, availability of information, voting mechanisms and the role of transaction counterparties. The CREFC, through its CMBS 2.0 Committee, has also issued a

---

[1]   See further Ch.9.

consultation paper on July 24, 2012 on the market principles for issuing European CMBS 2.0. Many participants from the industry contributed valuable time to the discussions and debates of the CMBS 2.0 Committee and it is hoped that the final market principles when issued will improve and increase overall confidence in future CMBS structures. Please note that the author is Chair of the CREFC's CMBS 2.0 Committee[2] and the contents of this chapter are the views of the author and not the CMBS 2.0 Committee or the CREFC.

## 4.2 Legacy of European CRE Lending

### 4.2.1 Size of the European CRE debt markets

As highlighted in Ch.1, the banking market has dominated CRE lending in Europe and banks significantly increased their exposure to CRE in the years 2000 to 2007. European banks are estimated to have, at the time of writing, an estimated exposure to real estate loans of approximately €2.4 trillion (according to Morgan Stanley analysts).[3] The current balance of outstanding European CMBS loans is estimated at approximately €100 billion. Unlike North America, alternatives to the banking market in Europe have been limited and even CMBS in Europe accounts for less than 10 per cent of outstanding debt levels (compared to approximately 22 per cent in North America) with the remainder being provided by banks and the covered bond market. Insurance companies and pension funds have historically provided very little CRE debt in Europe although this is now changing, as they adapt to new opportunities in the market and regulatory capital changes under Solvency II.[4] In contrast, in North America Insurance companies (and others) accounted for approximately 20 per cent of the CRE debt markets. Europe is now also witnessing the emergence of various senior and mezzanine debt funds that are looking to fill part of the gap that has been left by the banks and CMBS, as discussed in more detail in Ch.1.

### 4.2.2 New CRE debt origination

As will be highlighted in this book, European banks are in the process of reducing their overall exposure to CRE debt due primarily to capital and funding constraints. Funding for banks has become much more expensive save for those that are able to issue *Pfandbrief* in Germany[5] and in addition with the implementation of Basel III, more capital will be required resulting in lower returns on capital. A number of banks (including RBS, Lloyds,

---

[2]  See further Appendix 3.
[3]  See the *Morgan Stanley Research Report* (Blue Paper: Banks Deleveraging and Real Estate, March 2012).
[4]  See further Ch.16.
[5]  See Ch.2.

Commerzbank, Soc Gen, various Irish banks) have announced large reductions in their CRE debt exposure and this is likely to continue in 2013 and beyond.

There is little data available in terms of new CRE lending in Europe, however, the *De Montfort Study* provides an insight into volumes of UK commercial property lending through to 2011. It is clear from Figure 1, that the level of new loan originations for the United Kingdom has reduced significantly each year from 2008 onwards whilst the level of extensions has continued to rise.

**Figure 1: Volume of UK Gross Commercial Property Annual Lending**

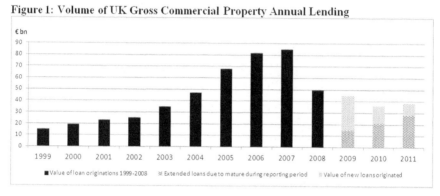

Source: De Montfort Study "The UK Commercial Property Lending Report – 2011 End-Year

In terms of CMBS issuance, there has been very limited new supply for 3rd party placement since 2007 as set out in Figure 2 below. Whilst a number of transactions have been completed many of these have been retained and/or used for repo purposes with the ECB or Bank of England. At the time of writing, Tesco has completed £3 billion of CMBS issuance in the form of five transactions since 2009 but, as referred to in Ch.1, these have been fully amortising and credit linked to Tesco and as such they are bought off the back of Tesco's corporate risk and rating as opposed to the underlying real estate risk. There have been three transactions that would constitute CMBS transactions in the traditional sense and these are from Deutsche Bank's platform comprising the Chiswick Park, Merry Hill loans (where the loans were secured against shares rather than the underlying real estate) and the Vitus German multifamily, Flore 2012-1. It was hoped these transactions would represent a re-opening of the CMBS markets, but due to market conditions, limited new investor appetite and legacy issues with CMBS, this has not yet fully materialised. At the time of writing, whilst there has been increased interest in conduit lending from banks, this has not resulted in loan origination on balance sheet and it is expected that many of the earlier deals will be agented CMBS transactions with a focus on more conservative asset classes such as German multi-family (as per Vitus, Flore 2012-1). (See Figure 2).

*Figure 2: European CMBS Issuance*

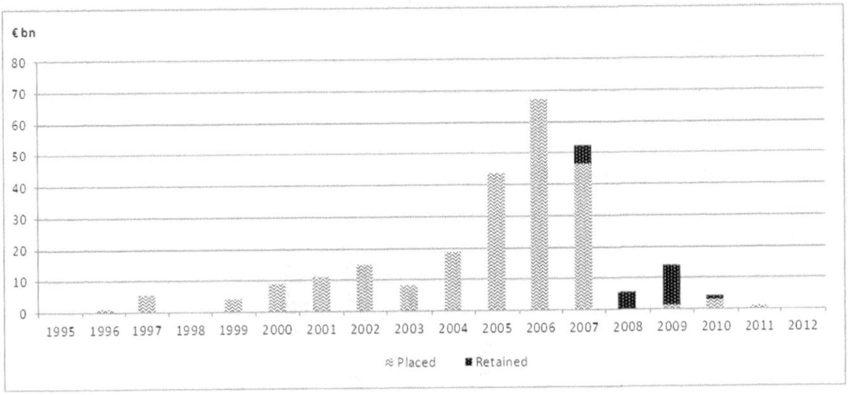

Source: Bloomberg, Bank of America Merrill Lynch Global Research 2012

### 4.2.3 CRE loan maturities

As set out in Figure 3 below, the peak years for maturities for loans originated by banks in Europe is 2012–14 with the largest peaks being in 2012 and 2013 and the largest exposures being in the United Kingdom and Germany. The maturity profile shifts from year to year depending on the level of extensions completed by banks so the peak may be extended to the next year in question until such time as the policies on extensions change. The banks appear to have been reasonably flexible with extensions provided cashflow coverage has been sufficient.

The peak years for maturities for loans originated as part of CMBS issuances is 2013, followed by 2012 and 2014. Generally speaking, CMBS loan servicers have tended not to be as liberal as the bank market with extensions, although in less creditor-friendly jurisdictions extensions and standstills have been more common. Another feature of CMBS transactions is the tail to final maturity of the notes which is required for rating purposes to allow sufficient time for a loan (or from the maturity date of the last loan in a pool of loans) to be refinanced or worked-out from its maturity date. Typically on note maturity, control over loan enforcement passes to the most senior noteholders and this is likely to increase the incidence of asset sales. The peak years for note maturities are not until 2016 and 2017, see Figure 4.

74

*Figure 3: Maturity Profile of Bank European CRE Loans*

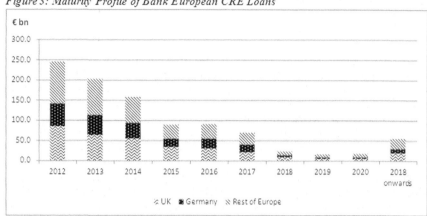

*Source: CBRE, Bank of America Merrill Lynch Global Research 2012*

*Figure 4: Maturity Profile of Note Maturities*

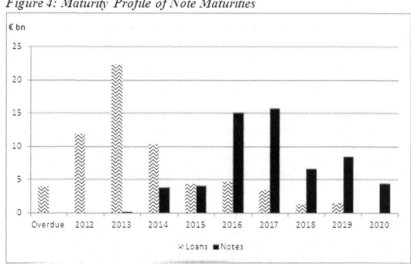

*Source: Bloomberg, Bank of America Merrill Lynch Global Research 2012*

### 4.2.4   CRE loan performance

*4.2.4.1   Comparative default rates*

There have been certain views in the market that CMBS loans have performed particularly badly. This is a misconception and is likely to be due to the negative publicity surrounding all securitisation transactions following the US sub-prime crisis as well as the media coverage on certain high profile CMBS work-outs. To date, CMBS loans have performed well in comparison to CRE loans originated and held on the balance sheets of banks and in comparison to other structured finance asset classes.

Based on research published by BAML in January 2012 in the United Kingdom, as of 2011, 7 per cent of CMBS loans were in default compared to 26 per cent of balance sheet loans. In Europe, as of September 2011, 11 per cent of CMBS loans were in default in comparison 10 per cent of balance sheet loans (see Figure 5 below). Given both the availability of publically available information and the more flexible approach taken by banks to extensions and restructurings, the performance of CMBS loans would be expected to be better than the reported figures.

CMBS loans have typically comprised "cleaner" assets than those contained in balance sheet loans and, on the whole, any debt below investment grade was sold separately as part of a B note or junior debt which were predominantly acquired by commercial banks, building societies and specialist funds including CDO funds.[6] (See Figure 5).

The default rate of CMBS loans was higher than corporate and retail loans in Europe, but the differential drops significantly if balloon defaults are excluded. In addition, the peak years for maturities in the European leveraged loan market are 2014 to 2015 (two years later than the European CMBS market) and there would be an expectation that default rates for corporate loans will increase over time. (See Figure 6).

In relation to other structured finance asset classes, on a global basis, from 1990 to 2011 CMBS performance compares favourably to RMBS and structured credit generally both at investment grade and non-investment grade ratings in Fitch's Global Structured Finance Average Annual Impairment Rates (see Figure 7). During this period, CMBS had an average annual impairment rate of 3.34 per cent compared to 6.73 per cent for structured finance generally. Impairment of European CMBS loans however increased markedly in 2011 and is likely to deteriorate further in 2012 and 2013 as the markets experience the peak in maturities with limited refinancing capacity available.

---

[6]   See further Chs 14 and 15.

*Figure 5: Default Rates in CMBS vs Bank Loans*

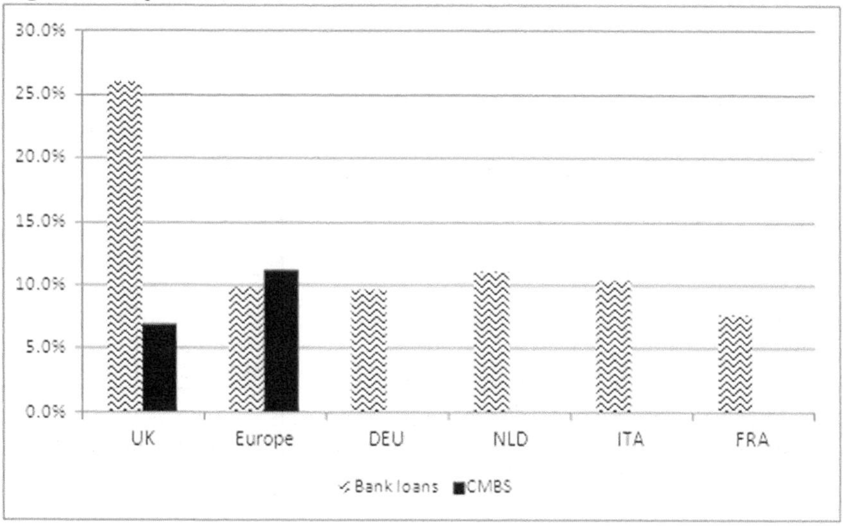

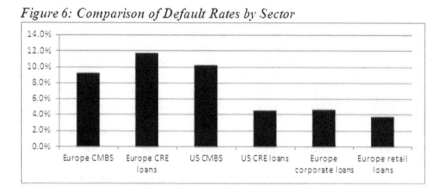

Source: Bank of America Merrill Lynch Global Research 2012

*Figure 6: Comparison of Default Rates by Sector*

Source: Bank of America Merrill Lynch Global Research 2012

**"Figure 7: Fitch global structured finance average annual impairment rates: 1990–2011"**

| Sector | Global SF | ABS | CMBS | RMBS | SC |
|--------|-----------|-----|------|------|-----|
| AAA | 0.53% | 0.01% | 0.02% | 0.79% | 0.91% |

| AA | 1.79% | 0.04% | 0.16% | 2.29% | 2.25% |
|---|---|---|---|---|---|
| A | 3.55% | 0.17% | 0.38% | 5.25% | 6.01% |
| BBB | 6.43% | 0.45% | 1.10% | 9.72% | 6.68% |
| BB | 13.14% | 3.10% | 3.42% | 18.44% | 12.64% |
| B | 21.98% | 14.79% | 12.91% | 26.50% | 25.67% |
| CCC | 57.75% | 39.64% | 37.31% | 66.97% | 53.02% |
| Investment Grade | 2.83% | 0.15% | 0.41% | 4.09% | 3.62% |
| Non-Investment Grade | 22.39% | 10.50% | 10.85% | 28.03% | 25.00% |
| All | 6.73% | 0.90% | 3.34% | 8.91% | 8.13% |
| Source: "Fitch Ratings Global Structured Finance 2011 Transition and Default Study" March 16, 2012 | | | | | |

### 4.2.4.2  Causes of delinquencies

Based on BAML research from 2007 to 2011, approximately 85 per cent of loans in UK and European CMBS transactions failed to repay at their maturity date. Whilst this improved in 2011, it is likely to increase again in 2012 and 2013 as the market approaches the peak in maturities. The level of defaults during the loan term have been relatively low with 3.3 per cent in the United Kingdom and 7.3 per cent in Europe. The most notable defaults on CMBS transactions have revolved around those that are secured on secondary assets (e.g. Opera Uni-Invest, EPIC Industrious, REC6 Alburn, Gemini Eclipse) and most defaults generally relate to the significant drops in property value resulting in higher leverage and the limited refinancing capacity available in the market. (See Figure 8).

The analysis from Moody's in Figure 9 below, sets out the reasons for CMBS loans transferring across to special servicing and confirms the increased incidence of loans defaulting on maturity, especially in 2012. However, it also shows a marked increase in payment defaults during the term of the loan and LTV defaults are also likely to increase as servicers tend to call for valuations closer to the maturity of a loan.

### 4.2.4.3  Default rates

Figures 10 and 11 below, confirms the continued increase in the rate of special servicing transfer events and loan defaults and these are expected to continue to rise into 2012 and 2013 as we reach the peak of maturities.

*Figure 8: Composition of CMBS Delinquencies*

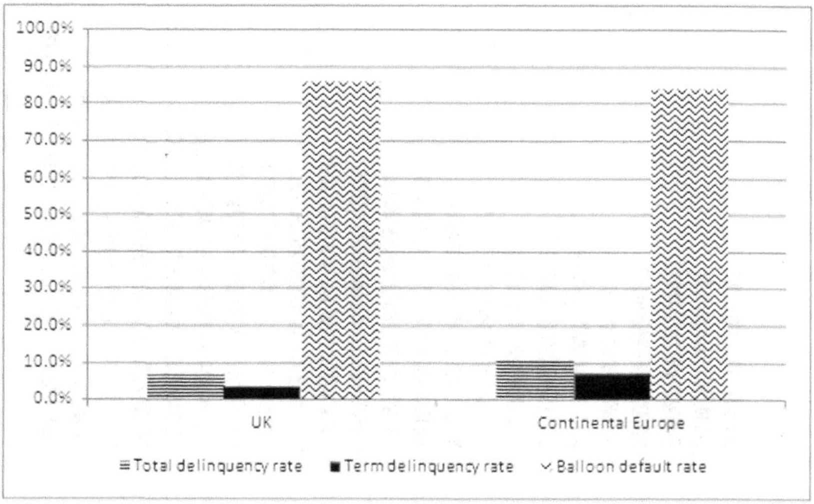

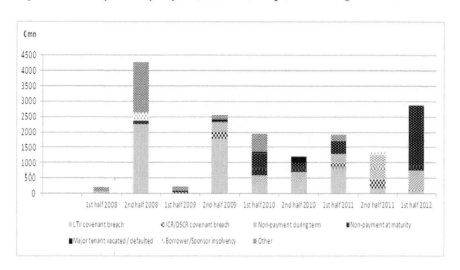

Source: Bank of America Merrill Lynch Global Research 2012

*Figure 9: Reasons for Transfer of CMBS Loans into Special Servicing*

*Figure 10: CMBS Loans in Special Servicing*

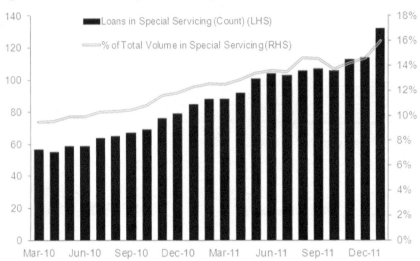

Source: *Moodys Investor Service, Morgan Stanley Research 2012*

*Figure 11: European CMBS Loans Delinquency Rate*

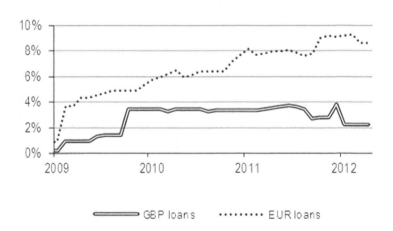

Source: *Bank of America Merrill Lynch Global Research 2012*

### 4.2.4.4 Conduit performance

There are different methodologies for measuring the performance of the CMBS conduits established by various banks in Europe. The three CMBS conduits that have tended to face most criticism from investors have been Titan Europe (Credit Suisse), Talisman (ABN Amro) and Eclipse (Barclays) and this may be due to a variety of reasons including default rates and loan and CMBS structuring.

Figure 12, (Pie chart detailing Conduit Performance—Special Servicing), from Moody's, sets out specially serviced loans per conduit as a percentage of total CMBS loans in special servicing that Moodys rated. Based on the latest statistics from Moodys the conduits with the highest incidence of loans in special servicing were Titan (Credit Suisse), Eclipse (Barclays) and Windermere (Lehmans).

**Figure 12: Conduit Performance—Special Servicing**

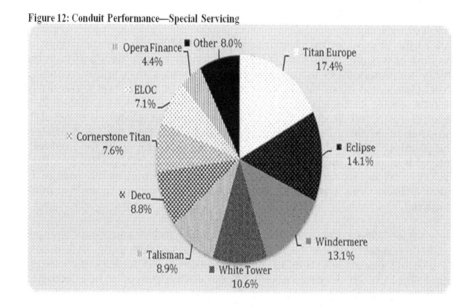

*Note: Although not explicitly stated in the rating agency research reports, where the source refers to a rating agency report, the statistics only include loans rated by that rating agency, i.e. where a particular loan is not rated by that rating agency, it does not form part of those statistics.*

## 4.3 Improving CMBS structures: Lessons learned during the downturn and CMBS 2.0

As mentioned in the introduction to this Chapter above, a number of lessons have been learned in relation to the structuring of CMBS transactions, in the context of the issues that many market participants have had to face since the advent of the financial crisis relating to (i) loan defaults and enforcement, (ii) consensual extensions and restructurings, (iii) availability of information, (iv) voting mechanisms and (v) the role of transaction counterparties. In order to encourage future CMBS issuance, it is important that these lessons are incorporated into future CMBS structures as part of what the industry refers to as CMBS 2.0. The rest of this chapter sets out some of the key issues faced as part of the experiences of restructuring a number of CMBS transactions from a structuring perspective.

### 4.3.1 *Noteholder identification, liaison and voting provisions*

One of the key issues that has arisen during CMBS loan restructurings, at the time of writing, is the time it takes to identify noteholders and then the ability for noteholders to organise themselves in a meaningful manner.[7] Noteholders also do not wish other noteholders or the market generally to become aware of their CMBS holdings and wish to ensure that if they become restricted from trading due to receiving material non-public information as part of private deal discussions that they are appropriately and promptly cleansed. To avoid noteholders becoming restricted inadvertently it is also very important that as part of any informal discussions they do not disclose to each other price sensitive information or engage in actions/discussions which in themselves would result in them becoming restricted.[8]

Noteholders have sometimes also shown apathy to less significant changes to CMBS transactions that have still required a general meeting. In addition, the existing system which relies on the issuance of RIS notices or messages being sent through clearing systems has not always proved to be effective in reaching the beneficial owners of the notes and a number of general meetings fail as a result of not reaching appropriate quorum levels. Whilst the situation has, at the time of writing, improved quite materially it could be further improved by simplifying the voting process for certain limited matters and creating a forum through which noteholders can register their interests in a transaction on a confidential basis.

---

[7] See further Ch.10.
[8] See further Ch.7.

### 4.3.1.1  *Noteholder identification and liaison*

The ability to identify noteholders and organise them in a meaningful manner has increased in recent years through the role played by a number of financial advisory firms specialising in CMBS restructurings and tender offers. However, for future transactions, a CMBS noteholder "forum" could be utilised to facilitate the identification of and communications between noteholders. The participating noteholders should be primarily responsible for the operation of any meetings and subsequent actions undertaken by the forum. A "forum co-ordinator" could also be appointed at the outset with experience of interacting with and/or representing noteholders, or, they could be the party that manages the relevant investor reporting website (e.g. the cash manager). On the issue date of each transaction, the lead manager(s) would provide the forum co-ordinator with a list of the initial investors which would form the basis of the forum. Future noteholders would be invited to identify themselves to the forum co-ordinator who would use this information to contact noteholders for the purposes of the forum.

Any noteholder that is a member of the forum or any transaction party (including the issuer, cash manager, trustee, servicer and special servicer) should have the right to request the forum co-ordinator to send a notice on its behalf to the other members of the forum to arrange meetings. It would be necessary for any such notice that is issued, confirms whether any discussions with other noteholders will comprise any "price sensitive information" and the proposed mechanism and responsibility for "cleansing" the same.

### 4.3.1.2  *Voting rights: Negative consent*

Negative consent processes can be used for certain limited matters to reduce the time taken to pass resolutions, deal with noteholder apathy and save time and costs by avoiding formal general meetings. They have already been incorporated into recent CMBS issuances under the DECO programme. In such a process, a meeting of the noteholders does not actually take place and it only requires noteholders to participate if they wish to object to a particular proposal. A formal notice detailing the resolution would still be distributed, but the notice will contain a statement requiring noteholders to inform the note trustee in writing within a certain number of days if they object to such a resolution. Unless more than a specified percentage makes a written objection to the resolution, it will be deemed to be passed. A negative consent process should preferably only be used for technical or administrative matters by the transaction counterparties and should exclude significant issues, such as basic terms modifications, and waiver or acceleration of a note event of default.

### 4.3.1.3   *Voting rights: Connected parties*

In a number of transactions, borrowers or transaction counterparties or their affiliates have acquired CMBS notes or junior debt and this has created clear conflicts of interest when voting is being undertaken or rights are granted on matters that may impact the holder of such debt. Should a borrower or equity sponsors or any actual/prospective transaction counter-party or their affiliates acquire or otherwise control notes, the relevant holder of the notes should be prohibited from exercising any voting or rights or attending any meeting of the noteholders.[9]

### 4.3.2   *Servicing and controlling party rights*

### 4.3.2.1   *Servicing standard*

There has been much debate on the appropriateness of the servicing standard used by servicers in CMBS transactions. As will be discussed in the following three chapters, the typical language requires the servicer/special servicer to maximise recoveries at the loan level on a present value basis taking into account the interests of the lenders as a collective whole as opposed to any individual tranche (other than taking into account subordination). In addition, it may apply generic standards such as applying the standards of a reasonably prudent lender.

The responsibility of the servicer is therefore to focus at loan level only and to ignore the impact of matters that occur at note level such as liquidity facility drawings, servicer advances and sequential payment triggers. This can sometimes create unusual results where a servicer strategy may maximise recoveries at loan level but may negatively impact the level of recoveries at note level or recoveries as between different noteholders due to the manner in which certain structural features at note level operate. A number of these matters can be addressed by changing the structural features at CMBS level such as the appraisal reduction mechanism on liquidity facilities (e.g. so that liquidity facilities are not drawn on junior tranches when the prospect of recovery on those tranches is very low) or improving the definition of sequential triggers (so for example once has loan continues past its original maturity date regardless of an extension that loan is included in the cumulative percentage of loans required for a sequential trigger to operate).

The role of the servicer can become difficult and unduly complex if it has to start taking into account the interests of individual noteholders, however, whilst the servicer clearly need not take into account note level facilities or mechanisms (other than any swap termination payments that reduce or increase the level of recoveries at loan level) in determining and applying

---

[9]   See further the DPO section of Ch.14.

their strategy under the servicing standard, they should be more open to hearing (with no obligation to act upon) representations from noteholders (on the impact of the servicer's proposed strategy on note level facilities or mechanisms). In addition, servicers should improve their overall communication with noteholders through regular public meetings (and presentations being distributed to the market) which provide information on loan performance and work-out/recovery strategy. By making these meetings/presentations public there is no risk of market abuse or inadvertently restricting noteholders.

The discount rate applied by servicers can have a significant impact on the course of action a servicer decides to take when applying the servicing standard and it is important that servicers have consistent principles for the evaluation of any discount rate to be applied pursuant to a PV calculation under the servicing standard. This is not always the case.

### 4.3.2.2 *Appointment of servicers and special servicers at outset*

Certain agented CMBS transactions have no servicer at all (e.g. Mall Funding, LoRDS1) and certain CMBS conduits (Real Estate Capital in particular REC5 Plantation Place and REC6 Alburn) have not had a special servicer identified and appointed at the outset. This has created various issues and all CMBS transactions, whether conduit or agented, should have an independent third party servicer and special servicer designated as part of the structure at the outset. Where there is no concept of a servicer it results in an increased emphasis on the role of note trustees who by their very nature do not wish to exercise any of the type of discretion that servicers exercise on a daily basis. Consequently costly and time consuming general meetings may be required in order to give note trustees directions on what actions to take, e.g. enter into standstill arrangements.

### 4.3.2.3 *Representations on appointment of replacement special servicer*

There has been much market discussion on whether, on lucrative special servicing appointments, the replacement special servicer has financially incentivised the party with the right to replace the special servicer to influence their appointment. Whilst this issue can be addressed through democratising the power to replace amongst a broader group of noteholders (as referred to below) any replacement special servicer should also be required to represent and warrant prior to its appointment that it has not offered any inducement or other incentives to any controlling party or any transaction counterparty or their advisers involved in the appointment process.

85

### 4.3.2.4 *The role of the servicer in making loan amendments/restructuring discussions*

Many borrowers complain of the uncertainty they face when dealing with servicers in understanding what authority the servicer has to agree certain types of loan amendments and if the servicer does not have the authority then there should be a much clearer noteholder process. This Chapter has already touched upon the latter relating to noteholder identification and liaison. The servicer also needs to know that they have the requisite power to act on a range of clearly defined matters through engaging appropriate professional advisors and organising and liaising with noteholders. In so doing, the servicer's liability concerns for actions it may take are addressed and the servicer may have to face greater liability as a result of not taking the action. The servicing agreement should explicitly state that the servicer, on behalf of the issuer, can and is expected to take such action to agree amendments to loan documentation that the servicer believes are consistent with its obligations under the servicing standard.

### 4.3.2.5 *Restructuring negotiations without the servicer*

In a number of restructurings, borrowers have attempted to negotiate restructurings directly with noteholders through an ad-hoc group and to side-step the role of the servicer. This has created issues where certain noteholders have felt disenfranchised from the process, or, where different terms have been struck with different noteholders. A servicer is typically required to take into account the interests of all noteholders and the servicer's involvement should reduce the likelihood of such instances arising. The transaction documentation should provide that the servicer be informed of any meetings between the borrower and noteholders and have the right to attend such meetings. The borrower should only have the right to meet with the noteholders without the servicer being present, if for whatever reason, the servicer does not wish to participate.

### 4.3.2.6 *Restructuring discussions constituting possible event of default*

Historically, facility agreements have stated that there will be an event of default if the borrower "commences discussions with one or more of its creditors with a view to rescheduling any of its indebtedness". Such language has inhibited discussions between borrowers and servicers as to potential restructuring strategies on certain restructurings. The servicing agreement should clearly permit the servicer to waive such a provision in advance of such discussions or allow for "without prejudice" discussions to take place.

### 4.3.2.7 *Loan sales by servicers*

In many CMBS transactions, the sale of loans by the servicer is not permitted and this reduces the potential options that are available to servicers where it determines that a sale of a loan is likely to maximise recoveries.[10] This was sometimes prohibited due to the accounting requirements faced by conduits established by US investment banks. Where such prohibitions do not apply, the CMBS transaction documents should permit the possibility for a loan sale, provided it is consistent with the applicable servicing standard and a sale of the loan would be the optimal method after considering the estimated proceeds for all other potential methods of realisation along with the risks and costs with respect to such other methods.

### 4.3.2.8 *Ability of servicers to raise capital for essential capex or opex*

On certain CRE and CMBS transactions the borrower has, at the time of writing, on occasions entered into insolvency in less creditor-friendly jurisdictions or assets are sold at potentially lower recovery values due to the inability to raise additional capital to fund costs and expenses necessary to improve or preserve the value of the underlying property (e.g. payment of property protection expenses, buildings insurance, capex to reposition a property) or short term opex to avoid insolvency. Greater flexibility would be available in these instances if the servicer had the ability, subject to certain controls, limitations and caps, to raise additional capital (where it is not already provided for in the liquidity facility or through a servicer advance facility) to fund such costs and expenses.

### 4.3.2.9 *Controlling party, dynamic control valuation event and replacement of the special servicer*

As will be discussed in the following three chapters, CMBS transactions have a concept of a "controlling party" that is appointed with respect to each loan in a CMBS transaction. The controlling party for a particular loan typically has certain rights, most notably the ability to appoint an operating adviser, replace the special servicer and have consultation or consent rights in relation to certain amendments for such loan.

In some CMBS transactions, the controlling party does not change based on a control valuation event, or in many deals, once the control passes to the notes, the most junior tranche of notes is not subject to a control valuation event and the valuable rights associated with it (in particular the replacement of the special servicer) remain with a lender or class of notes that are heavily out of the money and whose interests are not aligned with more senior noteholders. This has, to date, potentially created situations

---

[10]  See further Ch.7.

where controlling parties have undue influence on special servicers and therefore the outcome of a restructuring/work-out process and demand for acquiring debt which has such valuable controlling party rights has increased dramatically notwithstanding that any special servicer will be required to act independently pursuant to the servicing standard.

The calculation of which party is the controlling party or controlling class (in the case of the CMBS notes) should therefore always be dynamic and based on a specified valuation process and the principal amount outstanding of the relevant tranche whether reduced due to amortisation, pre-payment or write-offs.

In addition, it is important that the rights of the controlling class do not unduly empower the holder(s) of a single tranche of debt and that the ability to replace the special servicer. Accordingly, while the controlling class should benefit from consultation rights, the right to replace the special servicer should be assigned more broadly to a wider group or class of noteholders or a broader group of noteholders should have a veto right on the appointment of a replacement special servicer by the controlling party.

### 4.3.2.10 *Replacement of the primary servicer and other transaction parties with a pure service function*

Whilst a special servicer can be replaced, it is usually very difficult to replace other transaction counterparties, which has not, in the past, always encouraged high levels of performance. This could be rectified by providing for the replacement of all transaction counterparties. For example, if requested by more than 10 per cent of noteholders in aggregate, a noteholder vote can take place to replace transaction parties without cause (including the primary servicer, the cash manager, forum coordinator, the note trustee and if appropriate mechanisms are put in place, the security trustee).

### 4.3.3 *Role of note trustees*

The role of the note trustees has also come under much debate as CMBS transactions can sometimes be subject to increased costs or delays due to the requirements placed on note trustees and the unwillingness of certain note trustees to exercise any level of discretion whatsoever.[11] In certain instances, general meetings have been called on matters where the cost and process was arguably unnecessary (e.g. REC 3 Foundation—replacement of asset/property manager) or where a process is delayed due to the note trustee looking for additional indemnities, before proceeding with a course of action. The role of note trustees should therefore be limited to the oversight of mechanical processes and checking compliance with or, if

---

[11] See further Ch.10.

appropriate, passive monitoring of prescribed objective criteria. Note trustees should generally not be required to exercise any discretion, but where note trustees are asked to exercise any discretion then the note trustees should have the ability to obtain appropriate expert advice including legal, accounting, financial or property advice, at a reasonable cost which is charged to the transaction. The note trustee should place primary reliance on the use of the expert advice to make any determination and rely on the standard market liability terms of professional advisers rather than seeking additional indemnities in addition to the standard deal level senior ranking indemnity already provided. The documentation should also establish at the outset, whether any role of the trustee allows the trustee to request additional indemnification (and from whom). A trustee should only be permitted to withhold exercising discretion in the absence of an indemnification where both the reliance on expert professional advice and the standard deal indemnity are clearly insufficient in relation to the level of any potential claim they may face.

### 4.3.4 Valuations

Valuations are an essential tool in assessing the credit risk on a loan, both at the outset and on an ongoing basis. They provide important information in relation to the level of leverage and implied equity in a deal, and the quality, marketability, performance and suitability of the underlying real estate collateral as well as important market data on comparables. Valuations are, however, not always an exact science and there will always be a certain degree of variation between different valuers. Lenders have sometimes historically accepted the practice by borrowers of "valuation shopping" where borrowers select and present their choice of valuer at the outset who they know will give the highest potential valuation. The borrower may also have the ability to select and instruct the valuer of their choice on future valuations. In addition, a number of CMBS transactions have no provision for adequate periodical valuations and even where they do servicers have been reluctant to call for valuations unless the loan maturity is approaching. Consequently, many CMBS transactions report LTVs that are historical in nature and have no bearing to the actual leverage on the underlying properties and therefore the credit risk of the loan.

It is important that underlying loan agreements provide for annual valuations commissioned by the servicer. The servicer should have the discretion to waive the provision of an annual valuation pursuant to the servicing standard, provided it sets out the reasons for the exercise of such waiver in the quarterly reporting. A valuation should always be obtained every twelve months where a loan event of default has occurred and is continuing. Whilst the potential identity of any valuer can be discussed with the borrower and the controlling party, the determination of which valuer should be used, should ultimately only be made by the servicer. If the servicer reasonably believes that there has potentially been a material decline in the value of the underlying property, it should also have the power to request an additional valuation (except if it has only been a few months since the annual valuation), which should (unless an event of default has occurred) be a desktop valuation. Noteholders should also be able to direct the servicer to request either a desktop valuation or a full valuation if a valuation has not been obtained within 12 months.

### 4.3.5  *Transaction structure features*

#### 4.3.5.1  *Class X notes and excess spread*

CMBS transactions are typically structured so that the aggregate interest that accrues on the loans exceeds the aggregate amount of interest that accrues on the CMBS notes and certain CMBS level expenses. This excess amount is commonly referred to as the excess spread. One of the most contentious issues in existing CMBS transactions has been the extraction of excess spread by the arranging bank or the creation of tradeable securities out of the excess spread which are then sold or retained by the arranging bank to third parties.[12] Many CMBS transactions provided revenue for the originating or arranging bank through the extraction or sale of at least a portion of this excess spread and this revenue stream was structured and defined in a number ways including class X notes, deferred consideration, residual interest or retained interest. Whilst part of this revenue stream could be utilised to recover certain upfront transaction costs of the CMBS transaction, it could also yield significant profits for arranging banks and certain class X note structures have permitted ongoing revenue extraction even when the underlying loans are stressed or distressed and there are significant shortfalls to noteholders or liquidity facility drawings.

The main historical issues with such revenue streams and in particular class X notes have been the lack of disclosure of the detailed structure, certain structural features (e.g. how extraneous expenses are met) that potentially result in shortfalls for noteholders which would otherwise be met by excess spread, shortfalls to noteholders or liquidity facility drawings at a time when the beneficiary of the revenue stream continues to receive payments and the potential for default interest, consent fees, increased margins and ongoing excess spread to be paid to such beneficiary after the loan maturity.

In order to mitigate against these issues clear disclosure is required on (i) the existence and nature of any such excess spread revenue streams, (ii) the calculations by which it is determined; (iii) whether it is to be retained by the originating bank, servicer/special servicer or the borrower or their affiliates; (iv) which expenses will or will not be effectively absorbed by the this revenue stream; (v) whether such revenue is paid senior or subordinate

---

[12] See further Ch.5.

to payments due on the other CMBS notes; and (vi) whether the liquidity facility drawings or servicer advances can be used to support the revenue payments.

Furthermore, holders of such excess spread revenue streams should not benefit from default interest, increased loan margins, consent fees on a restructuring and interest after loan maturity and careful consideration should be given to switching off the revenue payments after there have been material loan defaults.

### 4.3.5.2 *Principal payments—definitions and sequential triggers*

Issues have arisen on CMBS transactions on how different types of principal receipts should be allocated in all scenarios such as the application of the allocated loan amounts and release premiums whether due to property sales or property refinancings. It is important that this is clearly defined, together with ensuring that the party responsible for determining the allocation receives all information required in order to determine how to treat the allocation of the relevant principal.

Many CMBS transactions further have a sequential trigger based on the cumulative number of loans as a percentage of the principal amount outstanding of the total portfolio being in default (with no standardisation on the percentage of defaults or the nature of defaults). There has also been some debate, as well as court hearings, on whether loans that are extended as part of a restructuring should form part of the sequential trigger, as they would have otherwise defaulted. To provide clarity, loans which are subject to a material payment default, after any applicable grace or cure period, or that reach their original maturity date (unless an extension is specifically provided for and permitted in the original loan documentation), regardless of whether a standstill or extension is agreed by all of the parties, should be included towards the sequential trigger threshold calculation.

### 4.3.5.3 *Liquidity facilities (and servicer advances)*

In many CMBS transactions, the appraisal reduction mechanism in liquidity facilities has not been structured to fully take into account whether interest paid on certain tranches will be fully recoverable. With the significant decline in real estate values and performance since the advent of the financial crisis, many senior noteholders find themselves in a position where the liquidity facility is being drawn to cover interest shortfalls on junior tranches that have no prospect of recovery. In these instances, the repayment of the liquidity facility will ultimately come from proceeds that would have been paid to more senior noteholders, thus reducing their recoveries.

Appropriate mechanisms should therefore be considered which restrict the amount that can be drawn from the liquidity facility to pay interest on certain notes, if there has been a decline in the collateral performance/value. For instance, the liquidity facility may not be available to pay interest shortfalls on any notes that have been valued out in accordance with the definition of a control valuation event, or, on the basis of a calculation of estimated recovery proceeds from time to time, they will suffer a principal loss of at least 90 per cent of their principal amount outstanding.

To avoid uncertainties on renewals of liquidity facilities, as has sometimes been the case, the procedure for renewing the liquidity facility should also be clearly laid out in the documentation with clear responsibility allocated to a single transaction counterparty (typically the cash manager) to deal with the renewal process.

### 4.3.5.4   Hedging

As will be discussed in Ch.8, hedging structures in some CMBS transactions have come under criticism due to the extended maturity of swaps compared to loans (e.g. Gemini Eclipse, Titan NHP), the lack of disclosure (e.g. LoRDS1) and favourable rights for the swap counterparty (Gemini Eclipse). The use of long dated swaps has typically been due to borrowers looking to achieve the lowest funding costs (where there is a negative yield curve), favourable ratings treatment as a result of locking in part of the refinancing risk on loan maturity and for the bank/swap counterparty potentially increased profits.

Generally, the maturity date of any hedging should be similar to the maturity of the loan and there should be full disclosure of the hedging details and structure. To the extent that the maturity date of any hedging arrangements extends beyond loan maturity, consideration should be given to including the hedging termination costs in the calculation of any LTV or control valuation event calculations.

### 4.3.5.5   Note maturity

To date, the European CMBS markets have only witnessed a single transaction reaching note maturity (Opera Uni-Invest) and this unique event created some uncertainty on who has responsibility on note maturity and the process to be followed.[13] The CMBS transaction documents need to contain adequate provisions to address what will happen if the notes are not repaid at their maturity date. For instance, if a loan remains outstanding twelve months prior to the final maturity date of the CMBS notes, the special servicer could be charged with providing various work-out options for noteholders to consider which should also include an analysis of the

---

[13]   See further Ch.3.

optimum method of enforcement and which type of insolvency procedure to use. If no option proposed by the special servicer receives approval by the requisite number of noteholders, the note trustee for the CMBS should be deemed to be directed by the noteholders to appoint the relevant insolvency practitioner based on the analysis of the special servicer, or, if none, the analysis of its own professional advisers, in order to realise the secured assets of the issuer at such time as the security for the CMBS becomes enforceable in accordance with its terms.

### 4.3.5.6. *Asset and property management*

In legacy CMBS deals, insufficient consideration was given to how asset/property management issues would be addressed where borrowers, or their affiliates, were also the asset managers/property managers and whether such borrowers or their affiliates were fully qualified to undertake such roles. The role of the asset/property manager is an extremely important one especially when there are property performance issues and the ability to replace the asset/property manager is fundamental, especially on a loan event of default. On a number of restructurings, or defaults, it has not been possible to replace the borrower, or its affiliate as an asset/ property manager, unless an insolvency process is followed. In certain jurisdictions, the insolvency process may be unduly costly, time consuming and the special servicer may lose control of the recovery process to a local insolvency administrator appointed by the courts (e.g. Germany).[14]

It is important that any asset manager or property manager should be reputable, with relevant experience in managing properties of a similar nature. The terms of their appointments should be set out in separate agreements and such terms should be in line with market standards, particularly in relation to fees and the duties of the parties. It is recommended that should the asset management and property management be carried out by the borrower or one of its affiliates, the terms of such appointment are on an arm's length basis and can be terminated by lenders (directly or indirectly) through duty of care agreements on a loan event of default occurring.

### 4.3.5.7 *Less creditor-friendly jurisdictions*

Where properties are located in less creditor-friendly jurisdictions, the corporate structure of the borrower group and the related security structure should be designed to provide the lenders with an efficient and effective process for taking enforcement. In many instances, since the advent of the financial crisis, borrowers have been in a position to hold lenders/servicers to ransom, by threatening to push their companies into insolvency unless certain fees are paid or they are given an ongoing role in any restructuring

---

[14] See further Chs 6 and 17.

or sell-down which also attracts certain fees. Also, junior lenders threaten to withhold their consent to a restructuring and thus cause an insolvency event unless certain fees are paid. This is typically in jurisdictions which are less creditor-friendly such as France, Germany and Italy.

Offshore holding companies or trust or fiduciary structures should, if possible, be put in place together with appropriate share pledges to allow enforcement proceedings to take place in creditor-friendly jurisdictions. In addition, measures should be taken to ensure that the COMI of the holding company will remain in the creditor-friendly jurisdiction. Further, all intercreditor agreements with other subordinate creditors should contain release provisions in order to allow the servicer or special servicer to enforce over its security without obstruction as a result of these other subordinate debt positions.

### 4.3.5.8 Synthetic securitisations

In certain synthetic CMBS transactions, it is unclear in whose interests the servicer is required to act, the noteholders or the originating bank who continues to hold the underlying commercial mortgage loans. The originating bank has also usually acquired credit protection through a credit default swap (CDS). This creates conflicts of interest as it is usually the bank which is also the servicer and losses on the commercial mortgage loans will result in the bank receiving payments under the CDS. Restructurings can also constitute credit events under the CDS documentation which requires negotiations with the beneficiary (i.e. the bank) in order that certain payment mechanisms can be agreed. It is therefore rare for loans in synthetic CMBS transactions to be restructured unless the bank also owns a junior loan/equity and is therefore incentivised to consider and take forward a restructuring.

The servicing arrangements for synthetic CMBS securitisations should be structured to adequately protect noteholders. The servicer should be appointed by the issuer and the note trustee rather than by the originator, so that the servicer will act in the best interest of those parties and the servicer should be required to service the loans in accordance with a servicing standard similar to that used on cash CMBS transactions. As far as possible, the servicing arrangements should be designed to closely match the arrangements used on cash CMBS and create adequate incentives for the servicer to act in the best interests of the noteholders (and, where applicable, the junior lender) without creating any conflict between the duties of the servicer and the interests of the lender of record as swap counterparty, even where the lender of record is itself performing servicing functions (whether as master servicer or delegate servicer).

The ability of the credit default swap protection buyer (typically the lending bank) to influence any amendments or modifications to a loan and the definition of credit events in the credit default swap documentation should be fully disclosed in detail. Also careful consideration should be given to the definition of restructuring event so that it also reflects the nature of restructurings that have occurred in recent years, which have primarily involved extensions where the determination of future receipts of principal or interest is not always certain.

### 4.3.5.9  *Warranties*

In the period up to 2007, the loan representations and warranties given by originating banks to the Issuer were diluted with little resistance from noteholders or rating agencies. The representations and warranties covered a range of areas relating to origination, due diligence, the properties and the security. Breach of a representation and warranty typically resulted in the originating bank buying back the relevant loan. There have only been a few cases of loan buy backs for such breaches in European CMBS (e.g. the Tintagel House Loan in the Bellatrix (Eclipse 2005-2) CMBS bought back by Barclays Bank (Servicer: Capita Asset Services)) and this is primarily due to the limited level of representations and warranties that were given and not all servicers fully pursing such claims. The European CMBS industry needs to produce a set of detailed and objective representations and warranties for use in future transactions. Any disclosure or exception to a representation and warranty should be set out immediately below the specific representation and warranty.

### 4.3.6  *Disclosure and transparency*

### 4.3.6.1  *General*

The European CMBS industry requires significant improvement in (i) the overall levels of disclosure and (ii) standardisation of disclosure across transactions. This applies to pre-issuance and post-issuance disclosure of property and loan information, valuation reports, loan level and CMBS level documentation (in particular intercreditors), hedging, property and loan data and cashflow models. It is also important that both primary and secondary investors have access to the same level of information. Improving disclosure is a necessary pre-requisite to rebuilding investor confidence in CMBS and encouraging ongoing liquidity in the sector.

Key disclosure issues that have arisen on transactions include:

- Limited information on junior, pari-passu or super senior debt and any related entrenched rights, purchase and cure options and enforcement rights;
- Entrenched rights of junior lenders or control parties not disclosed in sufficient detail;

- Limited information on hedging, including nature of hedging, structure, maturity or the mark-to-market valuation;
- Limited information on structural features such as class X notes or control party mechanics;
- Lack of access to documentation in most cases limited to CMBS documents and even then access is available only at the Issuer's office in person;
- Very limited or current valuation information is made available;
- Ongoing loan level reporting lacks detail and any meaningful commentary;
- On certain deals basic information such as the LTV of the securitised loan is not provided;
- RIS notices are not always issued when key events occur;
- Lack of provision of transaction data at all or in an appropriate format;
- Provision of cashflow models to enable ongoing modeling, assessment and pricing of CMBS Notes has not been consistent;
- Enhanced information is made available to primary investors compared to secondary investors.

Disclosure matters must be adequately addressed in the full chain of documentation commencing with the loan and through to the servicing agreement and cash management agreements. It must also be addressed at the time of issuance, as otherwise it is too late to remedy. Information and data provided by the borrower in its regular reporting should be in a format that can be used in the loan level reports prepared by the servicer (i.e. in an electronic and downloadable format) and should be provided within a timeframe that enables servicers to prepare reports with adequate time prior to the note interest payment dates.

Access to information should also be made available to all in an electronic downloadable format through the servicer or the cash manager on an investor reporting website maintained by a party to the transaction, a third party website or both.

There should also be greater disclosure in relation to:

- Conflicts of interest, e.g. ownership of debt by the special servicer; the appointment of affiliated entities by transaction counterparties and the related fees;
- The identity of the borrower and the ultimate sponsor(s) holding a certain percentage of the equity;
- Key information in respect of the transaction counterparties including the business, experience, financial standing and ownership of the key transaction parties. In relation to the servicer and special servicer, there should be disclosure on their experience in relation to the loans and collateral (and the country in which the collateral is located) which form part of the CMBS and the ability of the servicer or special

servicer to implement potential work-out strategies with or without consent (e.g. restructuring, enforcement, sale of loan);
- Fees payable to the transaction counterparties and their professional advisers where these are being met out of transaction cashflows should be fully disclosed;
- The recipients of any material ancillary cashflows such as loan prepayment penalties, loan consent fees, loan default interest or gains on hedge terminations.

It is important that the CMBS industry does not create disclosure requirements that result in borrowers deeming CMBS to be far too onerous as a funding source, with commercially sensitive information being made available publicly to all, including competitors and tenants. This would result in a competitive advantage to the balance sheet lending market (where the information would only be seen by the lending banks) and whilst this is not at the time of writing, a real threat, as the banking market hopefully continues to improve, it will become increasingly so. Some will argue that the cost of accessing the capital markets comes with increased disclosure requirements, however, it is important that there is some recognition of trying to achieve an appropriate balance and hence subject to certain restrictions (e.g. not resulting in market abuse) information should not be disclosed would prejudice ongoing commercially sensitive negotiations by the borrower (e.g. sale, lease renewal or rent review negotiations) which in the reasonable opinion of the servicer would be materially prejudicial to noteholders.

### 4.3.6.2    *Transaction documents*

CMBS level transaction documents (including the servicing agreements) should be made publicly available. Loan level documents which deal with cash flows and security, which have a significant impact on the CMBS (e.g. the loan agreement, intercreditor agreement and hedge agreements) should be made available. In the absence of any of the above documents being made publicly available, the summaries in the offering circular should be detailed and should include all material information (and failure to disclose such information should constitute a breach of warranty).

### 4.3.6.3    *Investor reporting*[15]

Key improvements in CMBS investor reporting would include:

(i)    Enhanced loan level reporting, including more commentary on individual loan performance and the properties on which each loan is secured;

---

[15]    See further Ch.12 and Appendix 4.

(ii)   Enhanced portfolio level reporting, including a summary of the aggregated loan portfolio and property characteristics and commentary on any significant changes to overall portfolio performance;

(iii)  Watch listed loans and events, including the reasons for transfer to the list;

(iv)   Specially serviced loans and events, including the reasons for transfer to the list;

(v)    Recoveries and application of proceeds on any property or loan disposals, including the application basis (i.e. pro-rata, sequential or reverse sequential as between loans);

(vi)   Loan covenant breaches and causes as well as any cures or remedies by the borrower or junior lender (to the extent not covered in portfolio level reporting);

(vii)  Any recovery action taken in relation to a loan, including enforcement/foreclosure, loan sale(s) and restructurings/work-outs; rationale for selecting a particular recovery option over another (all to the extent publically disclosable) (this may alternatively be included in the portfolio level commentary above);

(viii) For worked-out loans, a detailed loss determination including cost items and distribution of recoveries. Breakdown of the collateral sale proceeds, e.g. sale price, sale costs, receiver cost, special servicer costs (special/work out/liquidation fees), legal costs, and allocation of the net sales proceeds in the waterfall of payment;

(ix)   Any loan extensions exercised (or exercisable) in the period or historically;

(x)    Any previous restructurings agreed between the finance parties;

(xi)   Details of controlling party (where there is an A/B structure) or controlling class;

(xii)  Details of any control valuation events that may have occurred in the period (and details of the basis on which control passes from the junior loan to the securitised loan;

(xiii) List of all material triggers/events referred to in the offering circular, such as counterparty-related triggers, performance triggers, issuer events of default and available funds caps, and in particular sequential payment triggers;

(xiv)  Details of issuer level fees and costs in the period including transaction counterparties and professional advisers (where fees are paid out of transaction cashflows);

(xv)   List of all key parties and their current ratings (both short-term and long-term) together with any related trigger levels.

(xvi)  Details of any hedging including: counterparty and notional, applicable rates, mark-to-market valuations, payments made/received, any collateral postings;

(xvii) Appropriate issuer level commentary including commentary on:
- Any liquidity facility drawings in the period;
- Any sequential payment mechanism triggers in the period;
- The application of any available funds caps, deferred interest or similar interest shortfall mechanisms; and

- Details of any rating action and a summary of the reasons for action taken in the period.

## 4.4 Conclusion

The European CRE debt markets will continue to face challenging times over the next several years whilst additional refinancing capacity is established, legacy issues are worked through and banks, insurance companies and pension funds become more familiar with the revised regulatory framework. Whilst banks will continue to be the core providers of real estate debt capital, alternative real estate lenders including the insurers and new debt funds will establish themselves with varying degrees of success. The capital markets offer the broadest and deepest potential investor base and should play a much larger role in the new landscape. Europe's experience with CMBS to date has been mixed with a number of concerns over structural and disclosure issues but with strong relative performance to date of (i) CMBS loans to balance sheet loans and (ii) CMBS to other structured finance products. There is of course a continued risk that performance of CMBS loans and therefore CMBS could deteriorate further as we hit the peak of maturities. Many of the structural features of European CMBS were borrowed from the United States, adapted on an ad-hoc basis by certain issuers and then adopted by other issuers without careful consideration. Industry wide initiatives led by organisations such as the CREFC (and its CMBS 2.0 Committee) and publications such as this together with pressure from new investors, will be crucial in ensuring that the structures in CMBS 2.0 are far more robust and more appropriate for the European CMBS markets. What shape the new capital markets based debt products will take in coming years is uncertain but CMBS 2.0 is expected to comprise a core part of any capital markets offering.

# Chapter 5

# Asset Managing Legacy Commercial Mortgage Loans and CMBS Loans

Paul Lloyd,
Head of Loan Servicing, CBRE Loan Servicing

Paul Lewis,
Director, CBRE Loan Servicing

## 5.1.   Introduction

There are many issues surrounding the asset management of commercial mortgage loans and loans held within a CMBS structure. This Chapter will tackle how the role of a facility agent, servicer and special servicer has been transformed since the vintage 2004–07 originations and how they have had to adapt. In highlighting these improvements in service levels, this Chapter will focus on the issues that the servicer and special servicer have had to overcome in a very turbulent market which, at the time of writing, continues to worsen rather than showing signs of improvement. This Chapter will look at the sources of capital and the lack of its availability and then deal with several other key topics such as: the Market Abuse Directive, servicing standards, the ability to contact respective parties held within a transaction and examine the role of the special servicer and the options available to a special servicer in problematic transactions. This Chapter will not attempt to cover every eventuality on a transaction but will highlight the key fundamental issues faced by the facility agent, servicer or special servicer.

## 5.2.   Lack of available finance

As of 2012, the majority of finance available in the CRE finance market seems to only be available for very good quality prime assets in prime locations. The decrease in valuation experienced by these assets is not as significant as those seen for secondary and tertiary assets. The realisation of the actual risks associated with real estate lending has partly been responsible for banks reducing their exposure to the sector. Furthermore, the continued regulations being placed upon banks to ensure that they improve their capital adequacy positions has impacted upon banks' willingness to engage in real estate lending. Whilst some banks that have realised their losses, commentators might argue that many banks have not actually done so sufficiently since the market downturn. Many have had their capital bases diminish continually to levels requiring government intervention through recapitalisation.[1]

The net effect of the shortfall in bank lending to the real estate sector has created a large shortfall in funds available to refinance maturing loans, as well as to originate new transactions. The funding gap, at the time of writing this Chapter, has been estimated to be in the region of €175 billion to €200 billion, as illustrated below by a CBRE/De Montfort University model from 2010.

(See Figure 1: European Commercial Real Estate Debt Maturity Profile).

**Figure 1: European Commercial Real Estate Debt Maturity**

As at end of 2010

€960 billion of debt maturing in the next 10 Years, of which 55% is due to mature in the next three years alone

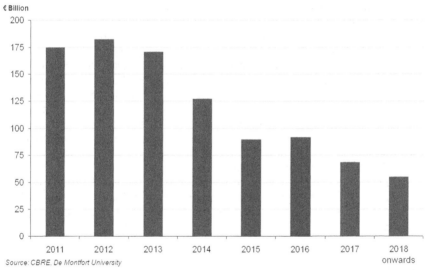

*Source: CBRE, De Montfort University*

It is difficult to calculate the funding gap as of 2012, owing to the lack of correlation between trends in the lending market and direct CRE investment activity. Much of this can be attributed to banks' ongoing "extend and pretend" strategies, which means that short-term loan

---

[1]  In June 2012, Spain became the fourth and largest eurozone economy to seek an international bailout when it requested up to €100 billion for its banking system.

maturities in the 2012–14 period could be inflated above the €200 billion mark. There were initial signs that insurance companies and pension funds would make up the gap in bank lending. However, it has become apparent that although these new entrants can bring fresh capital, they cannot wholly replace the role played by banks in the CMBS market. The lack of trading of the secondary and tertiary assets has made this end of the market very illiquid, especially when the parties able to sell will not discount transactions sufficiently to entice purchasers. Until this gap is bridged, we are some way from these sub-prime assets readily trading, as in previous cycles.

The type of financing is also being restricted by new regulation. Solvency II, for example, has incentivised insurers to allocate more capital towards directly sourced debt products. The reason for this change in allocation is due to the exceptionally high capital charge for holding securitised products, which includes CMBS.[2] The capital charge for holding CMBS AAA rated notes would be 35 per cent compared to a much more palatable 4.5 per cent on a low levered commercial property loan. This would provide a considerable advantage for direct lending over any form of "collective investment products". The downside of this regulation is that it disincentivises market participants from reigniting the CMBS market and entice insurers and pension funds to buy into CMBS transactions as well as the continued origination of new debt. Both can co-exist together in the market and will only assist in plugging the funding gap.

## 5.3. Servicer's response time

There are also significant delays in the time it takes for Servicers to engage with sponsors and noteholders to examine an impending loan maturity. However, the lack of a single decision maker and appointment of advisors at all levels, (i.e. note, servicer and sponsor levels) and conflicting requirements of different creditors have also hindered the timeliness of solutions. If the servicer acts more prudently and interacts a lot earlier in the life cycle of the loan, then the length to resolution could be reduced and consequently the costs would be diluted over time. The example of the CMBS deal, White Tower 2006-3, which is detailed below as a case study, was one whereby the resolution was better than expected and did not involve a plethora of external advisors or conflict between creditors. This initially involved the replacement of the original special servicer on the transaction with a different special servicer. The incoming special servicer was able to utilise its own in-house skills to enable its team to act in accordance with the servicing standard and ensure that recoveries were maximised. This was without the need to appoint a financial adviser or restructuring/workout expert.

---

[2]   See further Ch.16 which will deal with the regulatory pressures faced by the industry in 2012 and beyond.

The key achievements at the outset and throughout the workout process were:

- Innovation in the Channel Islands insolvency procedure resulting in enhanced value recovery through limited enforcement and protection of offshore status;
- Engagement with noteholders to vote through amendments to transaction documentation averting a forced liquidation of the assets and enabling time to develop the workout strategy to be implemented.
- Action taken six weeks after replacing the incumbent special servicer to defend the structure against action from HMRC; and
- Flexible real estate liquidation strategy enabling responsiveness to market conditions.

The points outlined above allowed the special servicer on the transaction, CBRE Loan Servicing, to maximise recoveries to noteholders, as highlighted in the Note Pricing Table below, and deliver the following:

- £1.1 billion recovered over an 18 month time period, a 17 per cent premium to their valuation at the time of the special servicer's appointment; and
- Class A Notes rallied from trading at a c.30 per cent discount to being fully repaid in 12 months and Class D note prices have also rallied from around 5p to being fully repaid since the appointment of the special servicer. (See Figure 2: White Tower 2006-3 PLC Note Pricing Oct '08-May '11).

Figure 2: White Tower 2006–3 PLC Note Pricing Oct '08–May '11

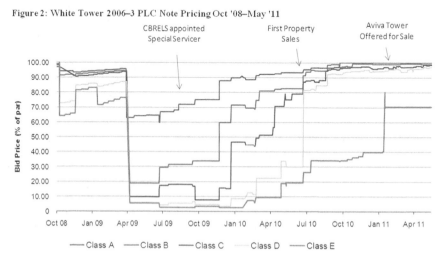

Source: Markit

Certain aspects of deals are currently preventing foreclosure, meaning "standstill" or "forbearance" has been more common. These include hedging that is heavily "out of the money" for the transaction and long dated swaps, which are even further out of the money due to current swap curves. As swap counterparties often rank super senior (i.e. ranking at the top of the payment waterfall), they are less likely to agree to any amendments to finance documents or participate in anything, which would be for the benefit of the sponsor/obligor, even if such an amendment would be in the interests of the whole loan. Swap counterparties generally want their money back and to reduce their internal costs for carrying these out of the money positions.[3] Often there is considerable conflict experienced between other finance parties such as the junior lenders and swap counterparts. This can make resolutions even more challenging due to the lack of consensus and conflicting priorities. For example, if in a particular transaction the special servicer wanted to waive certain requirements under the finance documents, where such actions required the consent of all finance parties, (which included the swap counterparty as well as the junior lender), this creates an issue, because as mentioned above, the current environment encourages the swap counterparty to refuse any type of amendment to the finance documents due to the fact that they simply want to be paid out of their swap positions. In addition, unless the junior lender receives any upside (bearing in mind that it's current position is more than likely to be valueless or "under water" due to the fact that in a sale or enforcement scenario, there will be insufficient funds to fully repay the junior lender) they are not incentivised to allow the special servicer to make any changes, when the junior lender can continue to receive its current interest, so-called "clipping its coupon". Ironically, the result of such conflicts is often simply inertia and further deterioration of the collateral which does not benefit any party.

## 5.4. Noteholders' meetings

Noteholders' meetings in a CMBS deal are convened by the note trustee sending out a notice to the relevant stock exchange requesting a meeting on a certain date. The notice for this is usually three weeks at a minimum. It is sometimes very time-consuming obtaining a quorum at a noteholders' meeting. The original noteholders in a CMBS may have sold their positions many times over and people who used to deal with the bonds in-house within an institution might no longer be employed on these trading desks. As the United Kingdom does not have a bond register for loan trading, akin to those in the United States, it can be difficult to discover the identity of parties. These factors all contribute to the difficulty of obtaining a quorum at a noteholders' meeting. The conclusion, dependant on the clarity of presented information, can then take weeks if not months thereafter if additional information is needed for the final decision.

---

[3]   See Ch. 8, which details the issues surrounding swaps and hedging.

### 5.4.1. *Discovery of the identity of noteholders*

It is often impossible to inject fresh equity into a CMBS structure without subordinate noteholders agreeing to being further subordinated below where the new injection of funding is placed within the structure. A fresh equity provider would clearly want there to be an advantage following its cash injection and as a minimum, they would usually expect to inject their capital which would subordinate the "out of the money" creditor classes. The fresh equity would then take a share, prior to or pari passu with, the creditors/noteholders.

As discussed above, one of the most difficult issues that a servicer faces is trying to track down the holders of each class of noteholder. This is paramount when decisions need to be made on transactions and votes need to be cast by noteholders due to quorums that are set within the securitisation documents. It has been suggested by several commentators that this would be a much easier and timely process if noteholders had to register their positions to a registrar, who would be the contact point when noteholders' meetings were to be convened. This is a practice used in the United States for the loan sale market, whereby a register is kept for all holders of loans, whether traded at issuance or in the secondary market. This would clearly speed up the decision making process and reduce the usual three week notice needed to convene a meeting. However, the downside to this is the ability for a noteholder to remain anonymous if required as a private entity or fund.

### 5.4.2. *Consequences of delayed access to noteholders*

One of the consequences of delayed access to noteholders is the resulting negativity that noteholders have of servicers and note trustees. The belief of noteholders is that both these parties are not performing well and hence need replacing in the CMBS. Such replacement has proven to be difficult as the replacement of a primary servicer is virtually impossible, unless it has been negligent under a transaction. To examine this, the servicer's role firstly needs to be broken down and examined as two separate roles, primary and special servicing and then secondly consider the role of the note trustee.

When deals were originally put together the primary servicer's role was akin to that of a loan facility agent with limited discretions. It was never envisaged that they would be performing tasks that they perform at the time of writing (albeit documented but not expected to undertake) hence their replacement was never in question at the outset. Furthermore, the role of a special servicer was ultimately never expected to be needed in the European CMBS market. This view may be, in hindsight, described as naïve, but as highlighted in Ch.1, the CRE lending market and economy was booming and there was never any concept of a faltering market and property prices reducing instead of increasing. Some issuing banks had chosen third party special servicers instead of setting up their own teams exactly due to the reason that they would never be needed and therefore did not need the expense of setting up a team that may never be needed.

Fast forward to post 2008 and note trustees are, at the time of writing, under pressure from noteholders as it is perceived that they are very reluctant to do anything due to liability and litigation.[4] They are generally not real estate-minded teams and have very limited discretion available to them. As a consequence, they are unlikely to take any action without legal advice and consultation and will probably require an all noteholder vote to take any action that affects noteholders. This, again, increases time to resolution and adds additional costs onto the fees that go through the waterfall, that eventually impacts the junior lenders or controlling class of noteholder.

## 5.5. Concerns of creditors and noteholders

Post 2008, many concerns have materialised when speaking to creditors/ noteholders in relation to their holdings in CMBS. The majority of issues tend to arise as loans move towards maturity. As discussed above, creditors/noteholders often view servicers as not proactive enough in dealing with impending maturities too late in the loan cycle. However, some prudent servicers have changed their watch list criteria, whereby a loan automatically becomes a watch listed item 12 months from maturity instead of six months. This is a new development that has occurred post 2009. Watch listed items are those which require the servicer to become more diligent and in some instances take specific action if the situation deteriorates further. These would include loan maturities, continually reducing ICR/DSCR and other covenants, non-delivery of financials and loss of a major tenant amongst others. There are specific guidelines on these, which have been created by the Commercial Real Estate Finance Council (CREFC); however, a servicer may also introduce their own additional or more stringent watch listed items. There is an argument by both creditors and proactive servicers that a loan should be put on a watch list 18 months from maturity instead of 12 months.

A concern for creditors/noteholders is the different way in which servicers report to the market. This is done through different end user repositories such as Bloomberg, CTS link, the servicer's website or the trustee's own portal. The possible lack of transparency (e.g. information being posted on websites that are password protected) may result in loan or portfolio information being inaccessible to all parties. This potentially makes the notes more illiquid as potential buyers or deal followers are unable to assess an investment opportunity. The form of reporting from individual servicers varies significantly. If required by the issuing bank, some servicers provide

---

4    See further Ch.10. where this will be examined in detail.

CREFC Europe-type reporting, which has been evolving over numerous years into the current version of the European-Investor Reporting Package (E-IRP).[5] Where this is not required by the issuing banks the servicer has made in-roads in to creating their own bespoke investor reports, which in their eyes stand them ahead of their peers due to the details and data that is enclosed therein. However due to the non-standardisation of these reports it is sometimes difficult for an investor to assess the performance of their positions from one deal versus another.

### 5.5.1. "Extend and amend"

The "extend and amend" restructure, or "extend and pretend" as it is also sometimes termed, represents an extension to the loan maturity date usually in exchange for an uplift in margin or a more punitive amortisation profile. It is usually only possible (by way of either documentary restriction or good practice) to extend the loans to a point two years before the maturity of the notes, the so called "tail" of the CMBS. Both of these terms developed in the period 2007 to 2011 whereby the "extend and pretend" term resulted in deals being extended for a period of time, often in the hope that the market would improve based on a perception that the parties who were extending were "pretending" that there was not a problem, and perhaps over time it would resolve itself and the loan would get back on track. After all a "rolling loan gathers no loss". The "extend and amend" mentality briefly improved the position somewhat, as some issues were addressed and hence the underlying deal was amended to encourage improvement and in some circumstances persuaded the equity to inject funds back in to the transaction. This mechanism provided a "hopeful" window of opportunity to "do something with" the underlying collateral.

However, if secondary and tertiary loans are continually extended, and equity providers remain reluctant to inject further capital into a transaction, there will be a further deterioration in asset value, which would be purely as a result of reducing lease length. For example, if you have an asset which is about to mature and there is no ability to fund any capex to enhance the asset as at today you have a possible lease tail of potentially three years. If you then just extend the loan for a further year and again, there is no investment in that year to improve the asset's position in the market, then all that has happened in that one-year extension is the lease tail has diminished from three years to two years with a clear effect on the value of the asset. This raises a question, as to whether a servicer, acting as a "prudent lender", should actually just extend a loan, without a proper action plan in place to improve the asset's saleability at the end of the extension period. The answer is probably no, as if the market remains stagnant and no value enhancing investment is being performed on the asset, this could be viewed as being irresponsible and negligent.

---

[5]  See Appendix 4.

### 5.5.2. *"X Class" coupon and the Chiswick Park case study*

An area of contention has always been the X Class coupon, which is the deals' profit taken by the "issuing bank". It has been mentioned that these issuing banks should themselves be bearing some of the consequences when a default occurs, including loan maturity and general non-payment defaults. If this were built in to transactions at the outset, as the Chiswick Park CMBS that Deutsche Bank AG recently issued at the end of 2011[6] (the X Class would be subordinated in a default scenario), then this would be a way of releasing equity back into a transaction, at the discretion of the servicer, in order to meet capex requirements and general working capital to at least try to stabilise a loan and its collateral.

Additional nuances/details on the Chiswick Park transaction were as follows:

- Improved disclosure of documents: the loan agreement and property valuation are now made available prior to issuance and all securitisation documents, other than opinions, are made available on the trustee website after closing;
- Simpler and more extensive bondholder governance of the issuer: more use of written resolutions and deemed consent; lower quorum and majorities; ability to replace transaction parties;
- Making it clear how a loan that would have defaulted barring an amendment/waiver should be treated. For instance, should such a loan count as a defaulted loan for the purposes of calculating a sequential payment trigger?;
- Excess spread (often called Class X (see above)). This cashflow which has typically been paid to the issuing bank of the CMBS transaction and has been senior in the waterfall has provoked much anger among investors who have seen the sponsor continue to get paid cash even when there have been losses incurred or about to be incurred on investment grade bonds. There was significant pressure, on new transactions, to have this cashflow subordinated upon certain credit events; and
- 5 per cent retention rule as required under CRD2.[7] The retention requirement was viewed as being largely irrelevant by investors. Of greater relevance to investors, with respect to the alignment of interests between the arranging bank and noteholders, was the manner in which excess spread was to be shared between the parties. However, the Chiswick Park transaction was a single borrower, single asset transaction which makes it easy for investors to conduct due diligence in some detail, which they did. By contrast, in the US market, where CMBS transactions contain a large number of loans, investors in new transactions generally have been in favour of such

---

[6]  See Deutsche Banks' Deco 2011—E5.
[7]  See Ch.16.

retention. In the United Kingdom and Europe, the issue has not had to be addressed and so has been of lower priority.

## 5.6. Transparency

Transparency, from an investor's point of view, must include everything associated with a loan transaction that is of value when assessing the pricing of the position held. The Market Abuse Directive (MAD) was introduced into UK legislation in 2005 and has gone some way to improve the dissemination of information flow to the market.[8]

The framework of MAD attempts to ensure that the levels of information disclosure to the market are correct and insider dealing and market manipulation are identified and dealt with appropriately. When MAD came into force, there were a number of institutions that were unsure as to the level of disclosure required to ensure compliance. Many were also unsure of information to be published in the market place and whether such information would be market sensitive or not. This resulted in an inordinate amount of data in the capital markets that did not help an investor assess what was material and what was not, potentially delaying their due diligence prior to selling or investing into a particular issuance. This initial period was followed by a requirement to improve the quality of information disclosure and its distribution. This dissemination process has gradually improved over time with only more pertinent information being published, although, at the time of writing, there is still room for improvement, but the education of servicers and special servicers through specific forums has definitely assisted.

Improvement centres on the way in which this information is distributed to the market. Effective distribution of pertinent information is paramount to the success of MAD. Such distribution should be made available on a cash manager, note trustee or other related third party website enabling full access to market investors. These portals should enable easy access to information which is not password protected so that, as per the requirements of MAD, there is no restriction on accessing this information. However, a servicer that sits on the fence and worries about perception instead of the requirements of MAD has decided that more information, rather than less is best and therefore they are fully covered as they have covered all bases.

An area which was not disclosed was any newly instructed valuation under a particular loan transaction. Servicers were prevented by valuers and issuing banks from releasing full valuations that were supplemental to the original valuation that was undertaken at origination. Some servicers

---

[8]   See Petersen, A.V., *Commercial Mortgage-Backed Securitisation: Developments in the European Market*, 1st edn (London: Sweet & Maxwell, 2006), Ch.13.

would simply disclose the new valuation figure whereby others would release the new figure with details of the assumptions used. The assumptions are key, as sometimes they may change from day one, due to market conditions and hence a rebalance of a creditor's position may be required to include these new assumptions. If the assumptions are not known then the investor is not making a fair comparison, or in other words, using two sets of differing assumptions which inadvertently will give different values and hence cannot be compared. If the market has, however, moved and the initial assumptions are no longer valid, i.e. a long-term hold with a single tenant versus the same asset with varying lease profiles with different covenants, then it is very difficult to use the new valuation as a comparison.

As previously described in this Chapter, the past few years have seen many loan extensions. This could easily be interpreted as some servicers not understanding the effect of an extension of a loan to the future value deterioration. This simply means that merely extending the loan without any regard to the reducing lease term until expiry immediately has a negative effect on the underlying collateral. An extension must be beneficial to creditors/noteholders and show that the servicer is acting like a prudent lender, as if they were the holder of the loan. Extensions may be viewed as beneficial if there is an action plan to put new funding into the collateral to hopefully enhance its value from where it sits today. Moreover, an extension may be needed in order to liaise with tenants to perhaps re-gear their leases, whereby they may accept a few years rent free for an extension of potentially five years on the lease expiry and hence improving the potential to refinance the loan at maturity. As stated above, an element of hope is believed to have been the thought behind some of these extensions, but the market has not improved for the majority of transactions, especially for secondary and tertiary assets. Furthermore, the extension of loans for a period of one to two years has actually pushed them into a time when a plethora of other loans are maturing with a limited amount of market funding to refinance such loans.

One final point to note is the lack of transparency across each deal. Every deal has its own reporting requirements as established by its servicer, which may be either via the European-Investor Reporting Package (E-IRP), described above and set out in further detail in Appendix 1, or bespoke reporting provided directly by the deal servicer. This reporting is clearly an off shoot of the borrower reporting supplied periodically by the sponsor/obligor. The servicer needs to understand exactly what is being reported by the borrower in order to relay this out to the market and the noteholder audience.

## 5.7. Difference in the role performed by a CMBS servicer and loan facility agent

It is useful to differentiate the roles performed by a servicer of a CMBS and a loan facility agent as there are very clear fundamental differences, which should not be confused when discussing types of lending products and asset management. The loan facility agent is an agent on bilateral and syndicated loans and is also an agent on loans prior to them being syndicated. Their role is fairly limited as they take instructions from the majority lenders and cannot use discretion unless this was negotiated into the finance documents at origination. The loan facility agent will be responsible for collecting rental income from borrowers and distributing these funds to the lenders on the transaction. They will also collect period reports, including property reports (if produced) along with borrower/sponsor financial information. These are then distributed directly to the lenders. The loan facility agent is then the "middle man" per se between the borrowers and lenders.

The primary servicer of a CMBS, however, has certain limited discretions over and above that which has just been described for the loan facility agent. These will include decisions surrounding the following areas and will depend on a particular deal:

1.  Exercising all of the respective rights, powers and discretions of each of the lenders, the loan facility agent and the loan security agent in relation to the relevant whole loan and its related security in accordance The services in this regard shall include (without limitation) the following (all in accordance with the provisions of the relevant facility agreement and related documentation):
    (a)  Taking any necessary action to maintain the security in relation to any relevant whole loan and property;
    (b)  Monitoring each whole loan at all times;
    (c)  Procuring and supervising the services of third parties (excluding any sub-contracted third party) which may be necessary or appropriate in connection with the servicing of the whole loans;
    (d)  Collecting all payments due from the borrower in respect of any whole loan and distributing to the cash manager in accordance with the respective waterfall (see (f)));
    (e)  Monitoring any casualty losses and administering any proceeds related thereto;
    (f)  Keeping records with respect to amounts paid under each whole loan and determining amounts representing principal, interest, prepayments, prepayment fees, collections on guarantees or insurance or related security, break costs, administrative charges and payments, insurance proceeds and all other amounts;

(g) Maintaining appropriate ledgers in connection with the amounts referred to in (f) above, and ensuring that correct transfers are made to the appropriate accounts;

(h) Reconciling and validating all accounts and ledgers on a quarterly basis;

(i) Conducting communications and dealings with the borrower in relation to all matters concerning each whole loan and its related security;

(j) If required by the senior lender, taking the actions referred to in the servicing agreement in relation to any amendment, modification or waiver;

(k) Giving instructions to the loan security agent in respect of the whole loan and its related security;

(l) Taking the specified actions upon the occurrence of a servicing transfer event and upon the occurrence of a specially serviced loan becoming a corrected loan;

(m) Notifying the loan security agent, the junior lender representative and the special servicer on the occurrence of a servicing transfer event, and notifying the lenders and the loan security agent upon a whole loan becoming a corrected loan;

(n) In the case of the special servicer, consulting with the junior lender representative prior to taking the specified actions;

(o) Calculating the valuation reduction amount upon the occurrence of an appraisal reduction event, obtaining an updated valuation in the specified circumstances and adjusting the valuation reduction amount to take into account such valuation;

(p) Preventing the forfeiture or irritancy of a head lease or obtaining relief on the court in respect of such forfeiture or irritancy;

(q) Taking all reasonable steps to recover and enforce all sums due to the lenders from the borrower;

(r) In the event a receiver or administrator is appointed, in the case of the special servicer, agreeing with the receiver or administrator a strategy for best preserving the loan security agent's and the lenders' rights and securing any available money from a property and agreeing the terms of and executing a receiver's or administrators' indemnity in connection with the appointment of the receiver or administrator subject to certain conditions;

(s) Establishing and maintaining procedures to monitor compliance with the terms of the finance documents regarding the insurance of the property or properties, procuring the payment of premiums under an insurance policy and, in the event any insurance policy has already lapsed or the property is otherwise not insured, informing the lenders and arranging such insurance;

(t) Negotiating, agreeing and accepting any compromise, abandonment or settlement of any claim for compensation by the loan security agent or the lenders or any claim by the loan security agent or the lenders under any insurance policy and directing amounts paid under an insurance policy to the order of the loan security agent (or in the case of loss of rent cover, paid directly into the account specified for the receipt of rental income under the relevant facility agreement);

(u)   Providing additional reports, documents and information set out in the relevant servicing agreement (generally in the CREFC E-IRP format)

(v)   Providing to the lenders and the loan security agent any information concerning any whole loan and its related security in order to inter alia, enable the lenders to prepare a profit and loss account, balance sheet and directors' report etc. and providing further information and reports which the lender and/or the loan security agent may reasonably require;

(w)   Providing to the lenders, in relation to each whole loan, a monthly activity report detailing any activity or action taken, if any, in relation to the relevant whole loan in the preceding month (including but not limited to lease requests, modifications, lets, etc).

The impact of the discretions determines how the asset management of a loan or portfolio of loans is undertaken on a CMBS or balance sheet loan. When a loan is originated it will generally be executed with a cashflow that has been scrutinised, not only by an internal underwriting section of the financial institution, but also the internal credit department. Certain stresses are placed upon the loan in relation to the underlying real estate to ensure that specific market decisions will not distress the portfolio enough to provide insufficient cash to service the debt.

Many transactions have asset managers that are related to the borrower/sponsor. When some of the first European transactions were documented the requirement in situations of sponsor and asset management relationships was that a quarter of the annual rental income was placed on deposit under the control of the servicer, in case the asset manager had to be replaced or even removed with funds from the transaction. This reserve ensured that the loan could continue to pay its debt service for at least a further quarter, whilst the servicer identified a replacement. This requirement was relaxed over the ensuing years due to borrower pressure and the quantum of transactions an actual borrower would originate with their lending bank. The rating agencies also adapted to it, as this did not affect the ratings of transactions, as the presumption was that in a conduit program how often would this event actually happen and were there sufficient funds from the remaining loans to cover note coupon.

## 5.8. Levels of property data and loan information given to CMBS loan servicers

One thing that was very clear from the outset was the differing level of property data and loan information that was given to a servicer of CMBS loans. This was more of an issue with third party servicers rather than in-house servicers. In-house servicers were fortunate that they had access to all information that their origination team had at hand, which included all cashflows, legal opinions of specific jurisdictions and copies of the credit papers. The detail of a credit paper would be paramount to a servicer or even a loan facility agent so as to see how the underwriting team and credit department have stressed the loan. This would give an insight to the servicer/loan facility agent of potential changes to watch out for as market and property fundamentals change. It must be remembered that the European CMBS market was a volume driven business whereby some investors invested due to high level "credit metrics" rather than the knowledge of the underlying collateral. This applies also to the servicers/loan facility agent whereby the role of a primary servicer was initially believed to be solely that of a payment/collection agent and hence not an employee with an ability to understand property. Over the past few years, primary servicers have sought to address this through recruiting individuals who understand property and providing learning and development packages for existing staff.

One key factor that in-house servicers were able to do, was to work with their origination teams in order to get standard templates for reporting purposes incorporated in the underlying finance documents. This was, and still is, paramount to enable the servicer to reduce the costs in system development to cater for numerous types of reporting to upload into their systems. The more standardised the reports became, the easier it was for the servicer/loan facility agent to compare across loans and portfolios and easily assess errors and market/ property changes. This has not significantly changed since 2005–07 legacy deals but definitely needs to happen, as it saves time and effort on behalf of the servicer/agent when trying to scrutinise the deals and prevent further issues by taking appropriate actions.

### 5.8.1. *Impact of new regulation*

As the real estate financing regulatory landscape continues to change with new regulations, such as Basel III and Solvency II[9] and the reduced lending by banks, it will be important for the servicer/agent to be able to cope with the expected higher demands put on them by the new alternative financing sources. The servicer/agent will have to adapt to the diversification of the requirements of the varying funders including insurance companies, senior

---

[9] See Ch.16.

debt funds, mezzanine lenders, each having their own reporting require-ments to their own investors. Systems for a servicer/loan facility agent are therefore the driver behind any kind of success, as this will provide automation and ability to stress portfolios directly and give comfort to their clients. This provides immediate benefits to servicers, but it is an expensive investment and one which some servicers /loan facility agents have yet to drive forward. A system needs to provide scenario analysis to allow the addition or removal of assets and tenants to assess the effect on covenants and future debt service coverage. It must allow for upload ability of periodic reports and prior to acceptance into the system, the generation of an exceptions report. These are the costly development requirement. Therefore, as a minimum, a system must be able to create investor reports to the creditors along with the simple invoicing to borrowers of their monthly or quarterly loan interest and amortisation along with the automated tracking of borrower obligation such as financials, quarterly monitoring reports, etc.

## 5.9. The role of the special servicer

Special servicer replacements are generally undertaken by either the junior lender on a loan or the controlling class or controlling party in the notes. The controlling class is sometimes the junior tranche of notes in the CMBS structure. The special servicer does not have to have been negligent to be replaced. The controlling parties are able to change the special servicer, a concept which is not universally favoured by some servicers, especially if they have been active in performing their role. However as track records continue to improve for special servicers it is expected that, at the time of writing, more replacements will occur over the coming years in order to maximise recoveries for creditors.

### 5.9.1. Courses of action open to the special servicer

Set out below is a short guide to the various options that are typically open to a special servicer of a distressed CMBS deal. This list is not exhaustive and a typical CMBS workout may encompass a number of different strategies. Each of the options below requires careful consideration and as a minimum will require further legal and restructuring/insolvency advice before implementation. Typically, the route that a special servicer takes will be very dependent on the specific factors relative to the deal and the requirements of the servicing standard. It is also very dependent on jurisdictional risk, for example non-consensual solutions are currently more favoured in lender-friendly jurisdictions.

### 5.9.1.1 *Consensual restructuring solutions*

Consensual workouts typically consist of either a restructure of the creditor structure or terms or the debt. They almost always consist of the continued standstill or forbearance by the special servicer from taking enforcement action whilst the borrower implements an asset management strategy.

#### 5.9.1.1.1. Extensions/Amendments

Loan extensions provide the borrower with further time to either improve the value of the assets or allow for market conditions to improve. For the special servicer they have some key attractions. They are cheap and quick to implement and often require very little approval and can be implemented without any formal consent from bondholders or other finance parties. Often loans are extended before they default thereby avoiding special servicing altogether. They may also be attractive to more junior creditors as they ensure continued payment of interest coupons and may provide enhanced "option value" by allowing sufficient time for asset value recovery and principal enhancement. Typically the servicer or special servicer will seek improved terms as part of the deal, for example, higher margins, partial paydowns or cash sweeps. They may also make certain demands of the borrower such as new asset management resource or disposal targets.

However, loan extensions could also have certain negative implications which need to be considered. These are:

- The potential for further asset value declines either through deterioration of market conditions or increased obsolescence of the property and consequent reduced recovery to lenders;
- They do not necessarily incentivise sponsors to improve recovery prospects;
- They do not generally allow for the introduction of new capital to maintain and improve the assets;
- They may simply be deferring a problem which in itself is not a solution; and
- They may require additional hedging arrangements.

#### 5.9.1.1.2. Re-capitalisations

Recapitalising the equity and debt tranches of a capital stack can have significant advantages. The goal is usually to provide a more stable platform for the continued asset management of the collateral in the interests of all stakeholders. It avoids the need for a potentially damaging insolvency/liquidation process. It can often provide an incentive for the equity holders to enhance value whilst allowing the lenders to participate in any potential future value enhancement. It also allows for new capital to be introduced into the structure, allowing for further investment and value enhancement. They tend to be a particularly useful tool for loans with assets that are not suitable for a liquidation strategy such as large operating businesses. Recapitalisation could typically involve one or more of the following:

1. A write-down of one or more loan tranches possibly in exchange for a new equity (a debt for equity swap) in the vehicle or a new subordinated debt piece;
2. The introduction of new capital either as new equity and debt, potentially at a more senior level to existing debt holders;
3. The amendment of debt terms or interest payable to specific loan classes or bondholders. This could also involve the deferment or "payment in kind" (PIK) or subordination of some interest payable; and
4. Using solvent restructuring techniques such as "schemes of arrangements"[10] to implement restructures, though given the complexity of most legacy CMBS structures, this has proved relatively rare.

Whilst often attractive, recapitalisations are often not straight forward to implement and their cost and complexity may make them difficult to structure effectively. Since the market downturn in 2007, few have been undertaken successfully. The reasons for this are numerous but include:

- There is typically no mechanism for the special servicer to undertake recapitalisations unilaterally. They will often need consents from all finance parties and may be further complicated where there are also multiple tranches of bonds. Typically all classes will have to vote in favour and this may be difficult to achieve where there are conflicting economics (e.g. "in" or "out of the money"). This may be further complicated where there are other creditors with differing priorities, e.g. swap providers. To be successful, recapitalisations need careful structuring. If this is not achieved, the result may be long-term deadlock between the bondholders/finance parties which can result in further value deterioration or stagnation;
- Recapitalisations have proved very difficult to achieve on loans that represent a smaller proportion of a larger "conduit" securitisation. Often these deals do not obtain the same level of attention as the effect of the recapitalisation is diluted by the other deals in the securitisation. The exposure to other loans may also make the various consent requirements more difficult to implement; and
- The costs of these types of restructure can mount very significantly as different lenders and bondholder classes often need their own financial and legal advisers. This can make recapitalisations a

---

[10] See further Ch.17.

relatively expensive option when compared to other more cost-effective solutions such as enforcement and liquidation particularly for liquid saleable assets.

### 5.9.1.1.3.  Discounted pay-off (DPOs)/Tender offers

Typically discounted pay-offs will involve either a sale of the loan to a borrower, related party or the servicer undertaking to release the security on a loan in exchange for a final discounted pay off of the loan. A release of security in this way can be attractive as it can be relatively straightforward for the special servicer to implement unilaterally and cost-effectively. It avoids the negative market perception and costs of enforcement and it may enhance recoveries as the borrower may be considered a "special purchaser" and pay more than the market might. This approach may be complicated where the special servicer has no power to release a junior debt. In such circumstances the junior debt may require some enhanced level of compensation to obtain or "buy" their consent.

A derivation of this approach is the tender offer, though this is generally conducted at bond level rather than loan level. In such circumstances the borrower, sponsor or a third party may offer to buy out all the bonds in each class of a securitisation. If successful, the borrower or third party can then effectively control the senior debt. Tender offers have tended to be successful when the level of distress felt is not too high and all bondholders/lenders can receive a reasonable market price for their bonds. In circumstances where some noteholders are significantly "out of the money" it may be problematic to distribute value across bond classes in a way that all holders fell is appropriate. By their nature, tender offers are generally not handled directly by the special servicer, who only has a role to act at loan level.

### 5.9.1.1.4.  Continued forbearance (or standstill agreements)

This is where the special servicer simply undertakes not to take any enforcement action for a pre-defined (usually short) period of time. Such a "standstill agreement" is usually put in place to buy time to undertake certain asset management initiatives or undertake a consensual sale of the property. Providing the borrower co-operates with the special servicer, this can have the effect of achieving an orderly workout or sale of the property without the negative impacts of an insolvency. It may also allow time for the borrower structure to be sold rather than the asset which has an immediate tax saving benefit. This approach does not, however, enable the special servicer to take full control of the assets and careful consideration needs to be given so as not to be at risk of becoming a "shadow director" or "mortgagee in possession". However the special servicer can usually build in certain requirements that can be imposed upon the borrower as a condition of their continued forbearance. It tends use a short-term solution to achieve a specific goal, but it can also be useful as a tool to prevent the borrower from filing for an unwelcome or premature insolvency process in some jurisdictions.

### 5.9.1.2. Non-consensual solutions

#### 5.9.1.2.1. Enforcement and liquidation

This is perhaps the most widely expected route for a special servicer to follow. Loan documents are typically well structured for such an eventuality and the special servicer can usually take enforcement action without any consent from the various bondholder classes or finance parties.

The type of insolvency procedure depends largely on the jurisdiction of the loan and the property but the special servicer would typically enforce such a way as to retain control of the sales process and not surrender this to a court appointed body for example. It is also essential that the special servicer seeks to undertake the sale in an orderly well-structured fashion. Unlike non-distressed sales, the seller is usually unable to provide any representations or warranties to the buyer. Without careful pre-sale due diligence, this can provide buyers with additional risks that may have a pricing impact. In the United Kingdom, enforcement is usually undertaken by way of a fixed charge receivership process which is usually quick and simple to implement. In some circumstances it may be possible to undertake a sale of the borrower structure, either through appointment of administrators over certain borrower entities or exercising share pledges, assuming this is within the security structure. A sale of the borrower structure may have additional tax advantages, though in reality few examples of this have been executed in practice to date.

#### 5.9.1.2.2. Enforcement and asset management

Depending on the level of security inherent in the loan documentation and the jurisdiction of the borrower/asset it may be possible to enforce and pursue a longer- term workout. This is usually straightforward to implement through a UK fixed charge receivership process but can more be problematic through administration of exercise of the share pledges. Often this approach will be needed where there is limited market demand for the assets or where they need further asset management to make them saleable. It is also useful where a change of asset manager is required, as this can often not be undertaken outside of enforcement. Often a new asset manager cannot be effective without the introduction of additional capital and the special servicer will need to consider whether there is any mechanism for the introduction of capital.

This approach has the advantage of allowing the lender to take control of the assets, without having to sell immediately and crystallise losses. A long-term enforcement process can, however, be costly and negatively impact on workout strategies for example by presenting a negative perception to potential occupiers or buyers. If such an approach is considered, the Special Servicer may also need to consider whether it is appropriate to introduce new interest rate hedging arrangements if the existing arrangements have terminated.

5.9.1.2.3.    Sale of the loan

This approach is undertaken independently of the borrower and can therefore be consensual or non-consensual. During 2011 and 2012 loan sales became an increasingly popular method of realising capital from distressed loans by balance sheet lenders. They have remained relatively difficult to implement in European CMBS structures originated before 2011 as servicing agreements do not typically convey the power of loan sales onto the special servicer. Some more recent deals have sought to rectify this. A sale of the loan is often perceived as a convenient way of realising proceeds without the cost and risk of a lengthy enforcement process. There is often more liquidity in the loan sales market than there is in the asset market which could enhance recovery further.[11] In a CMBS structure, where the special servicer has no power to implement a loan sale, the note trustee will typically require a majority of vote of all classes. As with the previously considered tender offer option, this will involve providing consent payments to more junior bond classes which often makes it uneconomic for the more senior "in the money" classes.

### 5.9.2.    Definition of servicing standard

The definition of servicing standard has been discussed for several years as this has been one of the major issues impacting some servicers/loan facility agents. Some participants prefer a highly prescriptive "tick box" process, which dictates what can and cannot be done when using discretion. However, for a few, the servicing standard is sufficient to be able to take a view on particular issues by utilising common sense and commerciality. The "tick box" process would be very constraining and would clearly reduce the ability and increase timeliness of decision making. The definition below really emphasises that the decision that a servicer has to make should be determined as if it were the owner of the loan and that it has applied the same rationale as it would do on similar commercial mortgage loans for other portfolios.

"Servicing standard" means the requirement that the servicer services, administers, enforces and realises the debt and manages any foreclosed real

---

[11]  See further Chs 3 and 4.

property pursuant to the servicing agreement in the best interests of and for the benefit of the senior lenders (including any holders of notes) and the junior lenders (as determined in the good faith and reasonable judgement of the servicer) as a collective whole but taking into account the subordination (in accordance with the terms of the intercreditor deed) of the junior debt, in accordance with the terms of any and all applicable laws, the finance documents, the servicing agreement, the intercreditor deed and in furtherance thereof, in accordance with the higher of:

(a) the same manner in which, and with the same care, skill and diligence with which it services and administers similar commercial mortgage loans for other third-party portfolios; and

(b) the same care, skill and diligence which it would use if it were the owner of the loans.

In each case, giving due consideration to the timely collection of all scheduled payments of principal and interest under the whole loan or, if the whole loan comes into and continues in default, and if in the good faith and reasonable judgment of the servicer, no satisfactory arrangements can be made for the collection of delinquent payments, the maximisation of recovery on such whole loan to the lenders (as a collective whole, but taking into account the subordination of the junior lenders to the senior lender which may result in a loss being suffered in respect of the junior debt in circumstances where the senior lender suffers no loss or a lesser loss) on a present value basis, but, in either case, without regard to any potential conflicts of interest specified in the following paragraph.

> "The servicer is required to adhere to the above standards without regard to any fees or other compensation to which it is entitled, any relationship it or any other party may have with any party to the transactions contemplated in any securitisation, the ownership of any note, the senior debt or any interest in the junior debt by the servicer or any affiliate thereof, or the ownership, servicing or management by any of the servicer for others or itself of any other mortgage loans or properties. The servicer or any of its affiliates may become the owner or otherwise hold an interest in the notes, the senior debt or the junior debt with the same rights as each would have if it were not the servicer, as the case may be. Any such interest of the servicer in the notes, the senior debt or the junior debt will not be taken into account by any person when evaluating whether actions of the servicer were consistent with the above standards."

The servicer must not be influenced by any party other than undertaking the diligence themselves and passing any proposals through their own internal servicing committee.

## 5.10. Conclusion

As this Chapter has shown, the servicer, facility agent or asset manager has, since the peak of the market in 2007, had to review and improve their service levels to clients, but most of all attain a better understanding of the market and underlying collateral in order to deal with problematic transactions. There are a lot of theoretical approaches to dealing with specific examples of defaulting loans but very few practical examples. However, the number of practical examples increases each month, with maturing and defaulting loans. Even the theory is re-tested especially when many deals are unique in respect of jurisdiction of borrower/obligor, location of assets and finance document legal jurisdiction.

However, as the market continues to falter and loans begin to fail to repay at maturity, due to the lack of financing available to specific assets, the intellect of the servicer, special servicer and asset manager, will undoubtedly change with each new experience of restructuring, workout or enforcement. To this end, the expectation would be that the ensuing defaulting loans will be resolved in a timelier manner, whereby the special servicer has already produced a workout strategy prior to the actual default. This means working more closely with the primary servicer of the performing CMBS, which is something that does need to occur more often. Moving forward, we will see many more differing examples of distress in the CRE world and the way in which the parties deal with them, due to the complexities, will be for another chapter in a future edition.

# Chapter 6

# Servicing Distressed Legacy Commercial Mortgage Loan and CMBS Loans: Workouts, Enforcements

Matt Grefsheim,

Director – Special Servicing, Hatfield Philips

## 6.1 Introduction[1]

With five years since the advent of the financial crisis and the global economy unwinding, the commercial mortgage loans and CMBS markets have learned many lessons that have affected both the CRE industry and those that practice therein.

As set out in Ch.1, not since the dot com bubble burst in 2000 has a fairly niche sector had such an impact on the global financial markets. The irony is that CMBS, together with other structured finance products had, as demonstrated in the first edition of this book, arguably, been such a powerful force for good before the credit crisis morphed into a global financial crisis.

As discussed throughout this book, the CMBS market started in the United States, before bringing many of the lessons learned there, to Europe. These financial structures were invented to help homeowners and businesses access the wholesale capital markets, and it is troubling to see them, at the time of writing, continuing to destroy the very people that they were intended to help.

This Chapter will consider some of the issues and challenges faced, when working out CRE loans in the three key European territories—the United Kingdom, Germany and France—and highlight some of the practices that can be used to ensure the optimum workout for creditors, which is usually also the best outcome for borrowers and their tenants.[2] The Chapter also

---

[1] The author is grateful for the contribution of his specialist colleagues to this Chapter, in particular Benedetto Mischi to para.6.3, Jonathan Agar to para.6.4, Philip Byun to para.6.5 and John Muldoon to para.6.6.

[2] The focus is on these three countries as, whilst the experiences set out throughout this Chapter have been drawn from the working out of CRE loans with properties in almost

includes case studies of CRE loans to illustrate the issues and resolutions faced by loan servicers and those that advise them.

The United Kingdom, German and French markets all have very different legal systems and to some extent financial and economic systems, which leads to varied and unique servicing strategies in each country. It is therefore critical to address each market individually and engage with the formal legislation and the informal modus operandi that each country possesses.

If there is one overarching lesson from the financial crisis, it is that there is no such thing as a single European market or a single way of working out a CRE loan. No two CRE loans are the same and there is no "road map" to show how to work out the CRE loans originated at or prior to the peak of the market in 2007. Each European market needs to be approached with specialist teams, because understanding a country's cultural idiosyncrasies is often as important as the legal wording of a document; "black" may actually be "grey" or even seem "white" in some courts across Europe.

The other key area that this Chapter will touch upon is the expanding role that loan servicers are assuming in order to achieve value for creditors. The most important part of this is the management of CRE from the relatively benign (but often ignored by the borrower) property maintenance, all the way through to assessing change of use, where appropriate. The Chapter will also consider the thorny subject of intercreditor agreements, which are dealt with in detail in Chs 14 and 15 and what may be changed in the future.

## 6.2 The UK: "Predictable, but not without challenges"

From a CRE loan servicer's perspective, the United Kingdom and Germany are relatively straightforward jurisdictions to work out CRE loans, but that does not mean that the CRE loans themselves are not without their problems.

The United Kingdom has a legal system that does not obstruct asset management initiatives and provides and environment that allows a swift and effective conclusion to workouts.

When a loan defaults in the United Kingdom, the lender will identify a solution and negotiate with the borrower to see if they can be part of the

---

every European country, the United Kingdom, France and Germany are the largest markets and, moving forward, they are likely to continue to be the largest markets for CMBS, for a number of years.

solution. If the borrower can be part of the solution, then a role is negotiated, if not then the lender is generally free to act without further borrower involvement.

This means that the skill of the loan servicer in the United Kingdom has been seen more in maximising headline value, rather than looking for solutions to resolve the underlying problems, but it is important to stress that it is not a loan servicer's role to act as a property speculator.

There are a few key lessons learned with regards to understanding enforcement impact and having contingency plans. Firstly, where possible, it is beneficial to negotiate a consensual deal with the borrower and support the valuation of any "consent premium." Secondly, enforcement can provide stability and does not always negatively impact value, as it can enable cash to be redirected/introduced, when the structure may not otherwise allow. Thirdly, enforcement does not necessarily mean sale and the loan can still be restructured.

Figures 1 and 2 provide a summary of the relevant UK enforcement and insolvency proceedings that loan servicers need to be aware of when working out CRE loans in the United Kingdom.

## 6.3 "The Mystery of CMBS loans in France"

France combines the more pragmatic and indeed clinical approach to business generally associated with northern European cultures, with the much more informal approach associated with business in Mediterranean countries. In short, the documentation surrounding CRE loans is usually as good or as bad as that of the United Kingdom or western continental Europe, but the interpretation of such documentation is often much more philosophical, meaning creditors (and the loan servicers acting on their behalf) must be prepared to adopt different and evolving strategies.

As a result, the main concern for loan servicers, special servicers and CRE creditors is the optimum way to navigate the complex French insolvency system, in order to minimise the cost and loss of control for creditors.

It is also true that the French statutory provision is perceived as more debtor- than creditor-friendly, but under certain conditions it can, unexpectedly, turn out to be relatively efficient from an economic perspective.

In France, enforcing on a CRE loan and its underlying security, is theoretically possible without giving rise to insolvency proceedings, but in practice, enforcement against a commercial mortgage borrower will lead to an insolvency proceeding. This means that borrowers facing financial

**Figure 1: UK enforcement and insolvency proceedings, Part 1**

| Criteria | Fixed Charge Receiver | Administrator | Administrative Receivership |
|---|---|---|---|
| Role | Appointed only over assets e.g. property, shares, rents Primary duty to secured creditor | Officer of the Court Duty to all creditors Appointed over whole business and assets | Pre 2003 Security including Floating Charge or Capital Markets Exemption (e.g. Industrious) Appointed over business and assets Primary duty to secured creditor |
| Cost (of appointment) | All depend on role Usually lower cost – narrower role – approved by secured creditor | All depend on role Wider role so usually most costly – approved by creditors | All depend on role Wider role so can be more costly - approved by secured creditor |
| Timing of appointment | Can be appointed shortly after formal demand | Varies – in Court or out of Court Can be quick but longer than receivership | Can be appointed shortly after formal demand |
| Cost (of implementation / impact on recovery of debt) | No empty rates or tax - If Receiver over shares - Can protect tax structure – e.g. SDLT saving | Regulatory exemption from rates: tax payable as expense. Can protect tax structure – e.g. SDLT saving | No empty rates or tax Can protect tax structure – e.g. SDLT |

*Source: CRE Finance Council Europe*

difficulties will usually seek some form of arrangement or protection through a preventative proceeding such as safeguard.

One key aspect of French law is that, regarding CRE debt restructuring, a majority of creditors can approve a debt reduction programme which is binding on all creditors, eliminating the cost in both time and money associated with CRE loans, where the *mezzanine* providers can hold more senior debt to ransom. Debt rescheduling of up to 10 years can be imposed, with a minimum 5 per cent payment after the second year.

### Figure 2: UK enforcement and insolvency proceedings, Part 2

| Criteria | Fixed Charge Receiver | Administrator | Administrative Receivership |
|---|---|---|---|
| Senior debt situations | Gain control of the asset to pursue recovery of principal debt | Duty to act in interest of all creditors, including unsecured – but not to detriment of secured creditors | Gain control of the asset to pursue recovery of principal debt – with a duty to obtain best price reasonably attainable |
| Junior debt situations | As per Senior Debt – duty to obtain best price reasonably attainable | As per Senior Debt | As per Senior Debt |
| Time period | No time restriction | Initial 12 months – can apply for extensions | No time restriction |
| Operating business | Limited powers LPA receiver cannot trade a "business" Receiver of Shares can control as shareholder | Very wide powers and can trade business | Very wide powers and can trade business |
| International recognition | Lacks international recognition | International recognition – may be advantage in cross border situations | Lacks international recognition |
| When other creditors are involved | No moratorium i.e. no protection from other creditors | Moratorium – leave of court required for creditor action – e.g. stop winding up petition | No moratorium - but have control of all business and assets subject to security |

The key requirement for servicing defaulted CRE loans in France is to negotiate and reconcile the problems between the borrower and the lender so as to facilitate the loan as amicably as possible. There are a number of lessons which have been learned by lenders in the recent past,

The lack of insolvency publicity allows less value deterioration. The French insolvency proceedings allow, in certain circumstances, the marketing of the asset as a going concern, driven formally by the borrower, and this process can provide the best value for lenders.

In addition, it has been proved on the market that a court-sanctioned asset sale gives comfort to potential purchaser that there will be no claw-back or third party claims which may have recourse against the sale itself. This is another positive windfall of certain insolvency proceedings. Similarly, real estate borrowers often believe that an administrator can better protect the assets, especially where there is the prospect of problematic sponsors or threatening creditors. This leads to cases where the lenders and the borrower may have the same target, i.e. asset protection and value enhancement, but different timing and views on how to unlock such value.

The general recommendation for lenders is to avoid safeguard when possible. The loss of control over bank accounts reduces the leverage which the lenders may have over the borrower. More importantly, the risk of having a loan restructuring and postponement of payment superimposed by the safeguard administrator can negatively affect the recovery for lenders especially from a timing and control perspective.

At the opposite end of the spectrum of proceedings available to borrowers, the conciliation proceedings allow lenders to still retain control over the negotiations aimed at a loan restructuring and debt recovery, given that the insolvency administrators (*conciliateur*) has only a role of facilitator in such negotiations, and cannot force their own view or plan. Furthermore, conciliation proceedings may allow for repositioning of the asset so the borrower may exit from an insolvency status and return to a going concern status.

The lesson learned in the current cycle of insolvencies relating to French real estate SPVs, is that lenders must be prepared for a negotiated approach with different degrees of control over the recovery process. The hope for the future, is that the French legislature will implement more straightforward insolvency regulations and move towards a system where lenders enjoy a greater degree of control in the enforcement of their security packages within insolvency proceedings. We believe such process will not happen quickly but the hope is that no stigma or prejudice is anymore attached to lenders' behaviour in the French CRE loan business, to prevent such changes.

Figures 3, 4 and 5, provide a summary of the relevant French enforcement and insolvency proceedings that loan servicers need to be aware of when working out CRE loans in France.

### 6.3.1 Case study: Cœur Défense

An example of the perils of trying to pursue a loan aggressively through the courts in France is the CMBS deal, *Cœur Défense*, which was a loan originated and sold in July 2007 by Lehman Brothers, prior to its collapse. The loan subsequently defaulted in early 2008. The CMBS investors have challenged various actions taken in the deal with the result that the loan has been the subject of a number of judicial proceedings and conflicting judgments.

**Figure 3: Enforcement and Insolvency Proceedings in France, Part 1**

| | Mandat ad hoc | Conciliation | Quick Safeguard | Safeguard | Redressement | Liquidation |
|---|---|---|---|---|---|---|
| Timing | Before insolvency | Before, and no more than 45 days after, insolvency | Before insolvency | Before insolvency | After insolvency | After insolvency |
| Duration | No limit, usually 3 to 6 months | Max 4 months + possible 1-month extension | 3 to 6 months | Long (observation period up to max 18 months) | Long (observation period up to max 18 months) | Long (6 months to 2 years to recovery) |
| Cost | Moderate | Moderate | Variable | High | High | Variable |
| Lender Involvement | Voluntary | Voluntary | Voluntary/imposed | Imposed | Imposed | Imposed |
| Outcome | Freely negotiated agreement | Freely negotiated agreement | Pre-packaged safeguard plan | Observation period, followed by safeguard plan, sale of certain assets possible | Observation period, followed by continuation plan or sale plan (all or some assets) | Liquidation sale |

*Source: CRE Finance Council Europe*

Cœur Défense was built in 2001, replacing the former Esso Tower in *La Défense*, the business district west of Paris. It is a €2.11 billion office property, secured with €1.6 billion debt and c.3.77 million square feet.

The whole loan was a typical CMBS transaction structure with a French property-holding SPV (French PropCo and Luxembourg parent (Luxembourg HoldCo). It was, for a CMBS loan, a typical underlying security package, but without a detailed process for managing assigned cash flows after notification of assigned debtors.

The whole loan restructuring plan, initially fell under court-imposed *"procédure de sauvegarde"* (safeguard procedure), under French law. The safeguard procedure introduced by Loi de Sauvegarde des Entreprises on July 26, 2005, allows a solvent company facing insurmountable difficulties to be restructured under the court's supervision.

The whole loan faced three on-going events of default. The loan had been un-hedged since the insolvency of the original hedging provider, Lehman Brothers on September 15, 2008, and the failure to find a replacement hedge provider within 30 days triggered the first event of default. The borrower filed for insolvency in November 2008, as a result of the 80 per cent LTV covenant breach.

131

**Figure 4: Enforcement and Insolvency Proceedings in France, Part 2**

| | Mandat ad hoc | Conciliation | Quick Safeguard | Safeguard | Redressement | Liquidation |
|---|---|---|---|---|---|---|
| Positives | Confidential<br><br>Voluntary participation<br><br>Freely negotiated<br><br>Binding only if agree<br><br>Lender can end, enforce<br><br>Lender still controls cash, accounts, assigned receivables<br><br>Ad hoc agent role akin to mediator, relatively neutral<br><br>Flexible process<br><br>Flexible outcome | Confidential<br><br>Voluntary participation<br><br>Freely negotiated<br><br>Binding only if agree<br><br>Lender can end, enforce<br><br>Lender still controls cash, accounts, assigned receivables<br><br>Conciliator role akin to mediator, relatively neutral<br><br>Fairly flexible process<br><br>Fairly flexible outcome<br><br>Court recognises or approves agreement<br><br>If court-approved, new money lender gets super-senior lien<br><br>If court-approved, no suspect period look-back prior to approval | Faster (no observation period)<br><br>Willing majority creditors can ensure the plan is imposed on minority creditors | Blocks enforcement by other creditors for their prior claims<br><br>Rescheduling plan can be imposed despite reluctant creditors with divergent interests<br><br>Borrower's directors stay in power<br><br>Lender can challenge court decision ordering commencement of proceeding | Blocks enforcement by other creditors for their prior claims<br><br>Rescheduling plan can be imposed despite reluctant creditors with divergent interests<br><br>Varying degree of reduction in management power of borrower's directors<br><br>Other creditors of prior debts can take no action | No debt rescheduling<br><br>Borrowers directors stripped of power |

Figure 5: Enforcement and Insolvency Proceedings in France, Part 3

| | Mandat ad hoc | Conciliation | Quick Safeguard | Safeguard | Redressement | Liquidation |
|---|---|---|---|---|---|---|
| Negatives | Launched without lender involvement | Launched without lender involvement | Requires the prior launch of conciliation proceeding | Can launch without lender involvement | Can launch without lender involvement | Can launch without lender involvement |
| | Non-participating creditors can enforce | Non-participating creditors can enforce | Unwilling minority creditors can have a plan imposed on them by majority creditors | Public awareness | Public awareness | Public awareness |
| | Negative inference from unreasonable stance | Possible negative inference from unreasonable stance | | Loan acceleration invalid if based on launch of proceeding | Loan acceleration invalid if based on launch of proceeding | Possible activity continuation period of 3 months renewable once |
| | Ad-hoc agent neutrality only relative | Conciliator neutrality only relative | Limited to financial creditors | No payment of prior debts or enforcement in observation period | No payment of prior debts or enforcement in observation period | Individual creditor enforcement blocked |
| | if no agreement, other proceeding will usually ensue (lost time, value) | If no agreement, other proceeding will usually ensue (lost time, value) | Limited to borrowers with turnover of €20m or more (or 150 or more employees) | Administrator can terminate or continue on-going contracts | Administrator can terminate or continue on-going contracts | No lender control on proceeding |
| | | If no agreement and notice to pay is given, easier for borrower to get an extension | Requires court approval of plan | Lender commitment maintained | Lender commitment maintained | No lender control on sale process |
| | | | Recently introduced, no practical experience yet | Risk of up to 10 yrs debt rescheduling imposed | Risk of up to 10 yrs debt rescheduling imposed | No lender control on cash, accounts |
| | | | | Risk of claim reduction if approved by majority creditors in committees | Risk of claim reduction if approved by majority creditors in committees | Value deterioration |
| | | | | Borrower's directors stay in power | Borrower's directors stay in power (subject to limitations) | |
| | | | | No lender control on cash, accounts | No lender control on cash, accounts | |
| | | | | No lender control on proceeding | No lender control on proceeding | |
| | | | | Senior rank of post-commencement debts | Senior rank of post-commencement debts | |

The safeguard procedure was re-opened in November 2008 in relation to the French PropCo borrower and its Luxembourg HoldCo. These proceedings lasted until February 25, 2010, when the judgments which had opened the safeguard proceedings, in respect of both companies, were annulled by the Paris Court of Appeal, essentially reinstating the transaction to where it had been previously, that is, in default since October 2008. The rental assignments were also confirmed.

On March 8, 2011, the *Cour de Cassation* (the French Supreme Court) reversed a decision of the Paris Court of Appeal which had held that safeguard proceedings could not be commenced in relation to *Heart of La Défense SAS* (Hold) and its sole shareholder *Sarl Dame Luxembourg* (Dame).

However, in January 2012, the loan took on a new twist when the Versailles Court of Appeal confirmed the opening of safeguard procedures for the holding company Dame and its subsidiary Hold – the holding company formed for Coeur Défense.

It is important to understand initially why the safeguard (moratorium) proceedings, which would have meant the loan was immune from enforcement action, were established. Firstly, the borrower intended to prevent loan acceleration, security enforcement, and the lender from capturing its rental income. Secondly, the borrower intended to open safeguard proceedings in respect of the Luxembourg parent as well, so as to prevent enforcement of the share pledge. It is clear that the commercial view of the borrower was that by restructuring and postponing repayments associated with the loan, the equity position would have still retained some hope value, as long as the borrower could have been able to control the operations and investments associated with the property, so to benefit from a potential value added asset management strategy or simply by a lucky upturn in the real estate cycle.

*Cœur Défense*—Lessons learned:

- The French legal system can be ambiguous;
- Creditors profoundly dislike safeguard;
- The effects of safeguard are very similar to insolvent reorganisation;
- Safeguard results from debtor's choice to seek protection rather than negotiate with creditors;
- Creditors perceive safeguard as giving borrowers an unfair advantage in negotiating a restructuring arrangement;
- Using safeguard to protect one's investment may now affect a borrower's future ability to raise debt;
- Where a borrower may has no viable option, a safeguard is strategically useful;
- Market withdrawal/strategic blocking/resolution of lender negotiation: a borrower may use it to by-pass negotiation with creditors and to buy time in refinancing (debt postponement);
- Borrowers perceive securitised loans as much more complex and costly to restructure;

- The French system encourages and nearly demands consensual arrangements to be reached, whether the borrower is exercising hold out rights or negotiating a real need—the court will not distinguish the difference.

The *Cœur Défense* case is emblematic in showing how a borrower's unwillingness to negotiate with its own creditors has brought far reaching consequences for the creditors involved. There is no way to avoid the risk of safeguard for the lenders, aside from engaging proactively at the borrower's table in an open and effective way, so that the debtor will perceive the outcome of a consensual agreement as potentially beneficial over the safeguard outcome.

## 6.4   German restructuring of large loans requires creativity

With a boom in securitised commercial mortgage lending in Germany between 2005 and 2007, many loans have been falling due since 2011, whether through scheduled maturity, or because they are approaching the limits to which they may be extended. Most CMBS transactions limit loan extensions to two years before note maturity (the tail), unless noteholders vote otherwise.

While there are standard tools for restructuring and enforcing on property SPVs in the United Kingdom, there is less of a standard approach in Germany, and the standard tools are not necessarily best suited to maximise recoveries to creditors.[3]

German properties are subject to German security law. However, the relevant loan agreement may be under English law and the SPVs (and their bank accounts) are as often as not, domiciled in other jurisdictions, such as Luxembourg or the Netherlands, with loan covenants to maintain the COMI (Centre of Main Interests) in such countries for insolvency purposes. This means that a special servicer in Germany needs expertise in other jurisdictions as well.

Common reasons for CRE loans to be transferred to special servicing are the after-effects of overleverage in a boom market, or occurrences specific to the property, such as major tenants moving out, or, being liquidated. Borrowers, who are "out of the money", can prove themselves to be co-operative, or obstructive, in the hope of ensuring compensation for their assistance. Furthermore, borrowers may also be interested in entering into new agreements, e.g. loan restructuring or new asset management terms for an asset management affiliate of the borrower.

---

[3]   See further Ch.17.

Loan sales, while attractive in principle, may be difficult to carry out in practice. As discussed in further detail in Ch.7, some servicing agreements and powers of attorney do not envisage loan sales as recovery strategies and do not give the special servicer adequate powers. Some loans include a B lender whose co-operation cannot be procured by the special servicer. So, in practice, the special servicer may need to determine a specific recovery strategy and decide how best to implement it. The special servicer may find some loans have asset management strategies best served by avoiding insolvency, others by enforcement of some type.

In Germany, enforcement often causes insolvency and as will be set out in Ch.17, a new insolvency law has come into force in 2012 has changed the regime. Advantages which are relevant to special servicers, include the ability to nominate an insolvency administrator, and creditor committee meetings happening earlier in the enforcement process. It remains to be seen whether easier debtor-in-possession insolvency plans, coupled with more rights for creditors to challenge the plan, will result in better outcomes for secured creditors of SPVs. In any event, creditors have taken to lodging preventative declarations (*Schützschreiben*) at courts where they suspect an application for debtor-in-possession self-administration will be applied for.

Enforcement also typically diminishes an asset's value. The well-trodden secured lender enforcement routes against German real estate assets are standard tools, available in almost all circumstances. These are forced administration (*Zwangsverwaltung*), by which a local court appoints a receiver to take over management of a property from its owner, and forced auction (*Zwangsversteigerung*), by which a court forces an auction process over a property.

Forced administration is straightforward to obtain (as long as the enforceable title is correctly set out) and efficient, but is comparatively expensive (10 per cent of rent or 5 per cent of imputed rent if unrented). Properties under forced administration (and their income) are outside the reach of an insolvency administrator of the owning SPV.

Forced auction is less straightforward to obtain, and can take time. It is relatively inexpensive and has the advantage over consensual sales of extinguishing any forced mortgages registered on the property, affording clean title to a purchaser. Conversely, such forced mortgages remain in force with a consensual sale, therefore reducing the value—even if the underlying claim would otherwise be classed as an insolvency claim—and ranking behind secured financial debt.

Forced auctions are widely considered to be less effective for sales of more complex assets and portfolios, but a first secured lender can decline to release security, if its claim is not fully met through the hammer price. To facilitate a transaction, a secured lender can give a bidder a guarantee to release its security if a reserve price is met (*Ausbietungsgarantie*), with a break-up fee if the bidder is outbid on the day. As with forced administration, an insolvency administrator of the owning SPV receives no income from this process.

Forced auctions and forced administrations are often detrimental to both the borrower and the lender because the full value of the asset is never realised. For this reason, as far as the interests of insolvency administrators and secured creditors are concerned, there is an incentive for the two to agree so-called "cold forced administration" (*kalte Zwangsverwaltung*) and enter into a realisation agreement. This ensures that the insolvency administrator takes formal responsibility for administering the property, while setting out duties and undertakings from property managers, real estate asset managers and secured creditors as appropriate. The realisation agreement sets out a mutually agreed process for disposals as consensual sales.

This model has become commonplace in German insolvencies, but is not always so easy to negotiate in other jurisdictions, where German property is involved, even where the incentives are similar to those in Germany. However, there are other enforcement routes if borrowers are being un-cooperative.

Enforcing on share pledges over the equity in borrower SPVs is possible, in principle, in most situations. This might usefully serve the purpose of removing obstructive sponsor influence and unhelpful borrower directors. In practice, there are several obstacles. Enforcement is generally over a pledged shareholding of 100 per cent of the borrower. If the enforcement is not co-ordinated with an ultimate buyer, the exercise of a pledge on an equity shareholding above 95 per cent triggers German real estate transfer tax. And, if a share pledge enforcement is being contemplated by a secured lender, it would normally follow that the borrower is not facilitating the due diligence that would enable the secured lender to secure an ultimate buyer. Some jurisdictions require the exercise of a share pledge to be implemented by way of an open auction process. This is unwieldy and moreover allows a borrower with nothing to lose to declare insolvency beforehand, thus defeating the purpose of exercising the share pledge in the first place.

In some jurisdictions (e.g. Luxemburg), the share pledge agreement typically includes a pledge over voting rights. This allows a secured lender to ensure immediate control of the borrower and avoid any nuisance insolvency filing.[4] It remains unclear whether the prolonged control of borrowers through exercise of voting rights can go unchallenged, should the nominal shareholder wish to contest the pledge and insist on monetisation of the pledged shareholding.

---

[4]   Please see para.7.3.2 for further discussion on this particular workout strategy.

Where insolvency is to be avoided, some innovative structures have emerged (see the case study set out in para.6.4.1). If an asset management plan is best carried out by solvent borrowers, or if the sponsor wishes to "hand back the keys" and co-operate to avoid insolvency, this can normally be achieved with creative structuring. To avoid penalties under Germany's strict insolvency laws, restructuring opinions are often sought, which can entail substantial loan restructuring to achieve the desired outcome. Creditors may only wish to undertake such actions, which benefit the borrowers, if the creditors capture the economic benefits thus obtained by the borrowers.

Figures 6 and 7 below provide a summary of the relevant German enforcement and insolvency proceedings that loan servicers need to be aware of when working out CRE loans in Germany.

### 6.4.1  Case study: Talisman-7 Finance Ltd, Mozart Whole Loan

**Figure 6: Enforcement and Insolvency Proceedings in Germany, Part 1**

| Scenario | In court | | | Out of court |
|---|---|---|---|---|
| Criteria | Land charges | Share Pledges | Insolvency | Third Way |
| Options | Forced auction  Held by court | Forced auction or private sale | Statutory proceeding  Reform:  Pre-insolvency proceedings with pre-packed plans as alternative | Mutually agreed  Implementation of independent trustees  Replacement of managing directors by experienced individuals for workouts |
| Control | Lenders | Lenders | Insolvency administrator, chosen by court  New Reform | As agreed |

*Source: CRE Finance Council Europe*

#### 6.4.1.1  History

The €940 million Mozart CMBS loan, originated in 2007, was secured on around 100 German commercial offices and retail premises. The Mozart loan defaulted in January 2010. Post-default, it had a valuation deficit of around €200 million and its restructuring is one of the most complex CMBS loan transactions ever undertaken in the European market.

138

### Figure 7: Enforcement and Insolvency Proceedings in Germany, Part 2

| Scenario | In court | | | Out of court |
|---|---|---|---|---|
| Criteria | Land charges | Share Pledges | Insolvency | Third Way |
| Duration | Approx. 1 year | 4 to 6 weeks | Potentially several years | As agreed |
| Costs | Percentage of the proceeds | Not relevant | Can be high, approx.: Assets €500k: Fees K€ 250-450 Assets €5m: Fees €500k-€1m Assets €25m: Fees €2-4m All fees are per legal entity in a portfolio. | Mutually agreed Often a combination of a retainer and a contingency fee |
| Benefits | Common proceeding Widely accepted | Common proceeding Widely accepted | Administrator gains control of asset management Servicing agreements end | Tailor-made structures are possible |
| Downsides | Can cause insolvency Long proceeding Negative effect on value Asset-based benefits of the portfolio are lost | Can cause insolvency Who shall buy? Lenders need to create means to take the shares Risk of subordination to be avoided Balance sheet issues may need resolving simultaneously Real estate transfer tax | Administrator enforces to liquidate Lenders have no control over the proceedings Asset based, all benefits of the portfolio are lost | Requires to certain extent the consent of all parties. Borrower's consent may be replaced via share pledge Obstructing lender's consent may be replaced under ICA provisions |

*Source: CRE Finance Council Europe*

By the time the loan defaulted, the portfolio of properties was already deteriorating in terms of both dilapidation and value, due to a lack of investment by the sponsor. There was no incentive for the sponsor to invest further in the portfolio, as it had been losing equity value steadily since

2007. From early 2010, the sponsor was no longer obliged to inject further funds. The sponsor was nevertheless prepared to co-operate with the special servicer to avoid insolvency.

### 6.4.1.2   *The problem*

The expiry of a guaranteed interest covenant in January 2010, meant imminent illiquidity. Due to large deficits in scheduled interest payments at the borrower level during the restructuring negotiations, significant liquidity facility drawings had to be made at the CMBS issuer level.

The restructuring had to take into account the rights of numerous stakeholders and complex documentation. It necessitated stabilising the corporate structure to provide for a new asset management strategy which would have been difficult to implement under insolvency proceedings. Intercreditor agreement drafting issues and certain lender issues made resolution very complex to achieve due to the lenders in the structure having divergent economic interests and the special servicer sought to avoid requiring consents from out-of-the-money lenders.

### 6.4.1.3   The restructuring

The borrowers obtained a *Sanierungsgutachten* (German restructuring opinion). Under a share purchase agreement, a newly founded Luxembourg entity, Sanchez S.à r.l. (whose shares were pledged to the creditors) acquired 94.9 per cent of the shares in the borrowers' parent. Sanchez S.à r.l. itself is owned by a charitable foundation (the whole structure being known as an "orphan trust". This structure allowed the creditors to exercise a degree of influence, without actually owning equity, which was not permitted by the CMBS documentation. Further, the share purchase agreement provided for a call option to acquire the remaining minority interest, at a later point in time in the restructuring.

In order to avoid triggering German real estate transfer tax, the borrower entities needed to be converted to a different legal form. To convert them, sufficient equity had to be created in them. The restructuring used the different over indebtedness treatments in Luxembourg and Germany to create a stable debt structure.

On signing, a loan extension of 3.25 years to April 15, 2015 was agreed, to allow a new asset manager to co-ordinate investment and conduct an orderly sale of the properties thus resulting in an orderly amortisation of the debt. The amended loan also allowed the borrowers to defer interest if capital expenditure and tenant incentives proved to be more value-enhancing, or if funds were not available.

Following the closing of the share purchase agreement, Sanchez S.àr.l. became a borrower in its own right. A portion of the debt was assumed on closing by Sanchez S.àr.l., and the borrowers owe a corresponding contingent consideration to Sanchez S.àr.l. Thus sufficient equity was created in the German borrowers to allow their conversion to a different legal form. This contingent consideration can only be paid from borrower profits, and is repaid only after the debt portion still owed by the borrowers has been paid. As this tranching of the Mozart facility took place only at the borrower level, it did not alter the rights of the creditors under the Mozart intercreditor agreement.

Various binding tax rulings were sought from the German and Luxembourg tax authorities to bless this structure. While it is more complex than would be necessary for most loans, it demonstrates that radical CMBS loan restructurings are possible, despite various contractual restrictions and imprecisions, and despite a lack of unanimity among all stakeholders.

The Mozart restructuring used several techniques which can each be used in isolation (e.g. orphan trust). This restructuring used the full panoply because of imprecise documentation and the need to limit consents from entities other than the operating advisor.

## 6.5   Location, location, location

As was set out in the beginning of this book, historically, one of the most compelling reasons for the existence of CMBS was that it allowed a huge diversity of property types and locations to secure finance. The premise was that you could have a bundled portfolio of broadly similar assets, whose risk profile and returns were amortised.

Latterly, and in the frenetic early 2000s, many structures just bundled whatever they could, such that loan servicers now service loans which included within a single securitisation property ranging from orange groves in Spain to multi-million pound office blocks in the major cities of Europe.

The result is that a loan servicer must maximise returns on both good and not so good properties in some very desirable, and many equally far from desirable locations. While geography will play an important part, it is possible to limit the categorisation of a 'good location' to the tight remit of either the financial or retail areas of the major cities. For a 'good property' it really is limited to grade 'A' offices and the equivalent retail.

### 6.5.1   Mixed properties in a good location

#### 6.5.1.1   AMG Portfolio Loan (Windermere VIII)

The AMG Portfolio Loan (Windermere VIII) is a good illustration of where loan servicers have serviced loans secured on both good and bad (mixed) properties in a good location. Through a judicious management of opposing creditors' interest and thorough underwriting of the sponsor's refinancing proposals, the special servicer took the action to enforce the sale resulting in a successful outcome for all creditors.

The AMG portfolio loan consisted of a portfolio of five office properties with 458,424 sq ft net lettable area, in the heart of the insurance district of the City of London. The whole loan at origination in 2006 consisted of £330 million of debt, including a B-note[5] consisting of three sequentially subordinated junior lenders.

Following the sale of two properties in 2007, the structure, as at April 15, 2010, when the loan matured and transferred to special servicing due to non-repayment at maturity, consisted of a £153 million A-Note and a £20 million B-note.

The sponsor's historical efforts to refinance the loan, by positioning the properties as a development site (banking scheme or courtyard scheme) proved unsuccessful.

A 60-day standstill was executed during which property-related due diligence was completed, development plans assessed, cash flow models constructed to assess sustainable net operating income, updated valuation of £139.7 million, was obtained and finalised and refinancing proposals were prepared both by the sponsor and the special servicer.

The sponsor's three year refinancing proposal migrated from initially being, in July 2010, a new £20 million working capital facility, to a £20 million day one amortisation from new equity injection, at the point of enforcement in October 2010.

An administrator and a new asset manager were appointed in November 2010, as the sponsor's final proposal did not sufficiently address refinancing risk and lacked a credible business plan.

The property was marketed in Spring 2011 and sold to a purchaser in June 2011 paying off the loan in full.

---

[5]   See further Chs 14 and 15.

Post completion of the property sale, the special servicer engaged with the controlling party, administrator, sponsor and a leading counsel (QC), and obtained the advice of the QC on February 16, 2012, that a liquidation fee was payable by the borrower.

This case demonstrates that in most cases the borrower's first proposal is not its best proposal. However, at the same time, thorough underwriting analysis and prudent due diligence, it needs to support any counterproposals and negotiations to be undertaken with a borrower in order to extract the most attractive proposal.

### 6.5.2 Good and mixed properties in a poor location

At the other end of the spectrum, many loans have what in the pre-crash market would have been considered prime property but in the post crash market are considered secondary, but not necessarily tertiary locations. Many were of a very high quality being recently built or refurbished to a high standard.

The strategy for these properties needs to take account of the prevailing local economies which are often uncorrelated to what is happening nationally.

Many of the options relating to the bricks and mortar are discussed in the next section on asset management. However, in conjunction with a possible asset management strategy the special servicer would also look at several other options including a detailed assessment of the borrower's current business plan with a view to assessing the conditions of the loan terms.

For example, given an acceptable cash flow, the servicer would determine whether there was an achievable level of amortization during a loan's extension period allowing the conversion of the loan rate to floating from fixed. The special servicer will also look at other ways to restructure the loans including the possibility of merging two loans resulting in a lower combined LTV or increasing the diversification within the loans; and finally the implementation of an asset management initiative during an extension period.

While properties situated in a good location attract stronger market interest, this still demands a thorough and critical analysis of the real estate fundamentals and legal workout options and strategic management of the various ranking creditors. For properties situated in a poor location, the ability to achieve a full recovery is further strained by lack of available financing and the limited scope of investors. In some cases, the workout strategy for assets in mixed locations will entail a segregation of assets into immediate disposal, mid-term asset management and exit, and long-term hold, asset manage and exit.

## 6.6 Asset management—Refocusing on the real estate

One of the characteristics of the post 2007 boom decline in CRE values across Europe was the realisation that many property owners, whose assets sat within CMBS structures, lacked a fundamental understanding of how to manage complex, multi-tenanted, mixed use assets and portfolios.

An abundance of cheap money and the seemingly endless increase in capital values in the run up to 2007/08 created a wave of CRE investors whose primary focus was in leveraging assets as highly as creditors would allow, extracting cash and then looking to exit as quickly as possible. In a rising market with low interest rates and aggressive lending, it's an irresistible model and the importance of understanding the assets and their true performance took a back seat to the financial engineering considerations.

When the financial crisis took hold and CRE values started to fall, asset trading slowed, and it rapidly became apparent that many CRE owners lacked the knowledge, personnel and financial resources necessary to react to the changing climate for CRE. Couple this with the fact that their motivation evaporated as quickly as did their equity, and the loans and their servicing and asset management were left in a perilous situation.

The post 2008 Lehman's world, where tenants want lower rents, shorter leases, longer rent-frees and more frequent breaks has left many of the newer and heavily geared landlords reeling. They have quickly found themselves out of their depth and just as quickly, it has become apparent that they often lack any detailed knowledge of their assets, have no meaningful relationship with their tenants and have little idea of how to manage active portfolios.

These factors mean that when loans default, the special servicer often finds themselves faced with a plethora of problems, ranging from higher vacancy rates, than were previously reported by borrowers, through to gaping holes in capex budgets and the rapid decline in values, resulting from the general assumption that every tenant intended to break their lease, or, vacate at the first available opportunity.

Throughout the early 2000s, the strategy to amass large portfolios spread over wide geographical areas, differing asset classes and even different countries, now looks totally flawed. Today, the special servicer finds itself in a position of having to untangle administrative and legal headaches, whilst trying to design appropriate strategies to exit the troubled assets within the portfolios in a manner which extracts greater recoveries for the lenders.

In many cases, the best recovery is likely to be achieved by an immediate sale of the underlying asset, especially where the lease and income profiles are stronger today than they would be if the asset were held in the medium term. However, as the market for secondary assets has, at the time of writing, remained challenging, the period post 2010, has led to more importance being placed on developing robust asset management strategies for assets that need repositioning prior to sale.[6]

Whilst it is important to stress that the special servicer is not a long-term asset manager, and indeed is often constrained by the lack of time brought about by the rigidity of CMBS structures, note maturities and tail periods, it is equally important to make clear that the special servicer does not want to conduct 'fire sales' in circumstances where value recovery can be enhanced by applying better asset management strategies.

Many of the strategies for gaining control of assets have been covered elsewhere in this and previous chapters but, in this section, it is worth focusing on how asset management can deliver enhanced recoveries for creditors.

Asset management is not a new concept. Experienced, long-term real estate investors, property companies and CRE professionals have long understood the importance of sweating assets to improve their performance. As has been said above, many investors, new to the sector in the mid-2000s, did not have these skill sets to fall back on.

Developing an asset management strategy for any asset involves the creation and implementation of a sound business plan at a real estate level. To do this requires an owner, or by default, the special servicer to develop a sound understanding of the underlying bricks and mortar. An appreciation of the property's micro location, the occupier market it serves, and the wider economic factors affecting its performance and exit value, is vital.

The majority of assets that find their way into special servicing, tend to be more difficult to sell in the market that exists at the time of writing, as they typically suffer from short lease profiles, non-investment grade covenants and a lack of investment in terms of capex and tenant improvements by the borrower.

As a result, one of the first steps of a loan servicer is to analyse whether the borrower is part of the problem or the solution. If the borrower does not understand how to maximise the value of their assets and is either unwilling or unable to invest new equity or capex, they often have little of any value to contribute. The option to enforce, remove the borrower and start afresh with a new approach, delivering focused asset management is often a better way forward. In instances where borrowers do know what they are doing and have a sensible strategy, it is more likely that the special servicer will look to work with the borrower.

---

[6]  See further Ch.5.

Developing a business plan for the asset(s) requires thorough research, building knowledge and creating a strong team of multi-disciplinary professionals that can look at delivering enhanced performance.

As stated above, the starting point is to understand the real estate and what can be done with it. In order to do this, a loan servicer would typically commission a new independent valuation, often known as a 'Red Book' valuation. In addition, a "Broker's Opinion of Values" (BOV) would also be sought, which is a more market-facing assessment of what an asset will trade for in the market. In parallel with this process, the servicer should consider the wider- and longer-term potential to reposition the assets before disposal.

This typically involves developing a strategy that might involve a combination of the following:

- Re-gearing or prolonging tenant leases, by trading potentially over-rented income for longer lease commitments;
- The appointment of new agents to freshen up the marketing of vacant space;
- Enhancing marketability by means of targeted capex programmes to enhance marketability;
- Assessing the potential for changes of use, or re-profiling uses within buildings;
- Reviewing local planning policies to assess redevelopment angles;
- Pursuing dilapidations claims, either to maximise revenue to reinstate space when tenants vacate or strategically to encourage tenants to renew their leases;
- Reducing a tenant's cost via better management of service charge expenditure; and
- Engaging with existing tenants to see what can be done to improve the building's performance, by better tailoring the way the property operates, to suit the tenant's occupational requirements.

The potential value that can be added, via the implementation of any given asset management strategy, then needs to be considered on a net present value (NPV) basis, to help decide whether a better recovery can be obtained by selling immediately versus implementing the medium-term business plan to optimise value.

Even if the decision from the NPV analysis is to sell the assets immediately, asset management can still add short-term value, through the appointment of the most appropriate interim asset manager and/or sale agents. This enables the marketing effort to be maximised, so that the maximum number of potential purchasers are approached and then, when sales are agreed, data rooms and contracts are drafted and ready for issue as soon as heads of terms are agreed. Delays in the conveyancing and due diligence process have unwound many a good deal, so it is important that what is actually being marketed reflects the reality of what is happening on the ground. Whilst this may sound like common sense, it is easy to lose value by choosing the wrong agent or allowing a disengaged borrower to run an uncoordinated sales process.

### 6.6.1 Asset management in practice

#### 6.6.1.1 Case study: Rowland Hill Shopping Centre, Kidderminster, UK

The Rowland Hill Shopping Centre, consists of c.42,500 sq ft of accommodation in Kidderminster, UK, with tenants such as Santander Bank, First Choice Holidays and Bon Marche. It forms part of a portfolio of commercial premises which were securitised in 2007 as part of a £90.75 million portfolio securing a loan within the Windermere XI CMBS plc securitisation.

Rowland Hill Centre was identified as one of several properties that would benefit from strategic asset management prior to launching the sale. Under the special servicer's guidance, Cordatus Partners (Cordatus) were appointed to asset manage the improvements recommended by LPA receivers RS Morgan and RJ Goode (of GVA) and Hatfield Philips International, the fixed charged receiver and special servicer to the Westville Portfolio respectively.

Cordatus' appointment mandated them to asset manage the centre to provide optimisation of recovery for the creditors. Active management intensive initiatives included engaging with all tenants on a one-to-one basis, pursuing rent arrears and identifying strategies for securing tenants and improving the asset's WAULT (Weighted Average Unexpired Lease Term). Due to previous under investment, there had been a prolonged decline in income and occupancy. To arrest this decline, it was agreed that Cordatus would implement a comprehensive refurbishment of the asset to provide an improved retail environment to attract both retailers and shoppers.

Specific improvements included for example, relocating the public toilets to increase footfall through the centre, installing automatic doors to the centre's rear entrance to reduce the 'wind tunnel' effect that was being created and to maximise short term income until such time as the refurbishment scheme allowed the re-launch of the centre.

At the time of writing, this refurbishment continues. Once the refurbishment is completed, the marketing of vacant space and re-signing of existing occupiers to longer leases will commence in earnest, along with initiatives to enhance mall trading income, tidying up title issues and generally preparing the investment for sale.

Selling the asset prior to the implementation of the asset management programme would have given purchasers the ability to discount heavily their bid prices due to uncertainties regarding tenant intentions, short-lease profiles and the cost of turning the centre around. Instead, much of this uncertainty has been removed and a purchaser can look to continue the good work started by Cordatus.

## 6.7 Intercreditor agreements—a time for change?

An intercreditor agreement (ICA) is where two creditors agree in advance as to how they will deal with their competing interests in their common borrower. In this section, the role of the junior lender, senior lender and special servicer and their rights and responsibilities in relation to the servicing of the loan are discussed.

### 6.7.1 *Junior lenders' "Consent and Consultation"*

One of the often overlooked areas of working out CMBS loans, is the role that junior lenders play and the rights they have in a securitised AB loan.[7]

It is imperative for junior lenders to understand their consent and consultation rights, especially when a default has occurred on a loan because, contrary to popular belief, the junior lender can still exert a significant amount of influence on the direction of any default resolution strategy.

### 6.7.2 *Who services the AB loan?*

Typically, as will be dealt with in detail in Chs 14 and 15, an intercreditor agreement (ICA) is entered into by the senior and junior lender, where the ICA empowers the senior lender (or servicers selected by the senior lender) to service the AB loan on behalf of both the senior and the junior lenders. When the loan is securitised, the servicer under a servicing agreement assumes the responsibility for servicing the AB loan. The servicer will act as the 'master servicer' on all performing loans within this securitised pool.

As set out in Ch.7, if an event of default (or if the servicer deems an event of default to be imminent) which adversely affects the interests of either lender occurs, the servicing of the AB loan will be transferred to a "special servicer", whose responsibility it is to resolve defaulted loans. However, the junior lender can, in certain instances, replace the special servicer with respect to an AB loan with a special servicer of their choice.

---

[7] Such rights will be set out in detail in Chs 14 and 15.

### 6.7.3 Are there limitations to the servicer's ability to take action with respect to an AB loan?

Loan servicers hold exclusive authority to administer loans and manage all decisions on behalf of the creditors. Loan servicers are required to service the loan in accordance with the applicable loan documents, laws and a standard of best practice known as the "servicing standard".[8] A servicer's authority to manage a loan is balanced by various consultation or consent rights held, for the most part, by the junior lender.

Set out below, is a general comparison of such consultation and consent rights.

(a) **Consultation rights**
  - "Consultation rights", require a servicer to update the junior lender with regards to a certain action and consider their suggestions prior to taking this action;
  - Consenting to material alterations; approving the borrower's business plan; granting consent with respect to general leasing matters or changes in property managers; releasing escrows held in connection with the loan.

(b) **Consent rights**
  - "Consent rights", require the servicer to obtain specific approval of the junior lender prior to taking certain actions;
  - Extending the loan maturity; modifying the monetary terms of the loan; changing the loan structure from debt to equity; releasing or substituting any collateral in the loan; permitting the borrower to take on additional subordinated debt; accelerating after a default has occurred and commencing foreclosures against the property.

Borrower requests may vary from a requirement for consultation to consent as they are dependent on what has been negotiated by the original junior lenders at the time of purchase of the original loan. There is a clear distinction between the types of junior lender rights. Thus it is essential that junior lenders understand whether a particular borrower request received by a servicer, triggers a consultation right or a consent right, when considering their response. After all, an opinion offered as part of a consultation is not binding, whereas the need for a consent is.

### 6.7.4 What path does a servicer assume when requesting junior lenders' consultation or consent?

If the servicer receives a request from a borrower they will normally perform the following:

---

[8] Dealt with in detail in the previous chapter and the next Chapter.

- Review whether the request can be carried out—is it permitted by the documents, evaluate the performance of the loan; e.g. is there a default outstanding?
- Due diligence work and assessing any possible impact as a result of approving the request;
- Ensuring there would be no material deterioration of the loan as a result of approving the request;
- Review relevant documentation to establish if the junior lender needs to be consulted or if consent needs to be abstained;
- Go to credit committee with the request to seek approval before sending the request to lenders;
- Send the request to relevant lenders with sufficient supporting documents to allow them to understand and comment as appropriate.

In the event that the servicer does not receive a timely response, or in cases of urgent need, the servicer may take immediate action, if necessary, to protect the interests of the lenders, the so called servicing standard override.[9] In the event that the junior lender rejects the servicer's request, the servicer is commonly prohibited from taking the requested action. If the junior lenders reject the request, the servicer is typically required to propose an alternative course of action for the junior lenders to approve. This, too, can be rejected. However, loan agreements will typically stipulate that the junior lender must agree a course of action within a time frame (often 60–90 days) or permit the servicer to proceed without obtaining further consent from the junior lender.

## 6.8 Conclusion

The main lesson learned since the start of the CMBS shutdown is that Europe is far from having a single set of rules and regulations applicable in loan workouts and restructurings. Not only has this impacted on how restructuring could take place, it will also have a significant impact on how the CMBS market will evolve moving forward.

The United Kingdom and German markets have proven to be more straightforward for implementing and effecting loan workouts and when the market returns, its is anticipated that most, if not all, major loans, will be originated from these territories.

While the legal systems do differ in the United Kingdom and Germany the basis on which they operate share the key criteria of clarity and interpretation which favours neither borrower nor lender and therefore allows resolution based on the contract terms. Unfortunately, the rest of

---

[9]  See further Chs 5 and 7.

Europe does not always share this transparency in terms of how to interpret what a contract means or, even post interpretation, how to apply the law as specified.

In France, experience shows that the law, or more precisely its interpretation, is often ambiguous and the insolvency system "appears" more debtor-friendly. From a special servicer's perspective the key in France is not to let the legal environment deter one from pursuing the desired outcome, but it may require more negotiation and reconciliation than in Germany and the United Kingdom.

Experience also shows that lenders across Europe will need to change their practices for managing loans. As discussed in this chapter, defaulted loan enforcement, modifications and extensions can be costly and time consuming requiring expertise some lenders wouldn't historically been expected to have. Outsourcing to a servicer to engage their depth of experience in effective solution analysis and loan workout implementation is valuable in saving in time and cost when dealing with a defaulted loan and it is expected that this will continue to occur more frequently in 2013 and beyond.

# Chapter 7

# Servicing Commercial Mortgage Loans and CMBS 2.0: the Legal Issues

James A. Spencer,

Senior Associate, K&L Gates LLP

## 7.1.  Introduction

Loan servicers have been front and centre of European commercial real estate (CRE) loan workouts and restructurings in the post financial crisis era. Their role has been challenging and is set to become increasingly so as a significant proportion of existing European CRE debt is expected to go into default (if it has not already) as borrowers face the consequences of being over leveraged. Moreover, an alarming funding gap has emerged which will hinder the ability of borrowers to refinance. In the United Kingdom alone, there is an estimated £299 billion of outstanding debt secured on commercial real estate, an estimated £73 billion of which may not be able to be refinanced in the market that exists at the time of writing.[1]

As the previous two Chapters have described, loan servicers are, at the time of writing, faced with the difficult role of maximising realisations on CRE loans in a challenging economic landscape within often rigid and limited documentary parameters, which has restricted servicers being able to utilise all the tools that should otherwise be available to them. In the case of CMBS loans, a sizeable proportion of the underlying real estate collateral is less than prime quality and the underlying finance documentation has often been too borrower friendly. This has presented servicers with additional challenges beyond those of simply having to be as effective and creative as possible, within an economic landscape that neither the securitisation parties nor finance documentation contemplated.[2]

---

[1]  Figures based on De Montfort University's 2012 annual survey into bank lending to property, and includes both securitised and balance sheet loans, as well as loans held in NAMA. The survey also sets out the amount of CRE debt (CMBS and other senior secured) maturing over the coming years—£54 billion in 2012; £35 billion in 2013;, £33 billion in 2014 and £22 billion in 2015. The funding gap is due to many factors – as set out in Ch.1, there is little sign of conduit CMBS returning and balance sheet lenders across Europe are either pulling out of CRE lending, retaining capital to meet the latest capital requirements, or restricting the deployment of capital to relatively low leverage lending on prime assets, or in different asset classes altogether. See further Ch.2.

[2]  See further Ch.10 where this theme will be further explored.

This Chapter will explore the role of loan servicers, their duties, obligations and rights and the key provisions of their appointment, before taking a closer look at how servicers have conducted themselves in the realisation and work out of CRE loans since 2008, and the challenges they have faced and continue to face as more and more loans and CMBS deal reach maturity. This Chapter will then shift focus, to consider how the role of loans servicers, their interaction with other stakeholders, and the documentation could be modified in order to provide a more efficient and workable loan servicing solution.

## 7.2. Loan servicing and the role of loan servicers

### 7.2.1. What is loan servicing?

As described in the previous two Chapters, loan servicing is the process of administering, managing, collecting on and realising CRE loans and is divided into two functions: primary servicing and special servicing. Primary servicing refers to the process of collecting payments from the underlying borrower and applying those payments to the relevant creditors; put simply cash collection and cash payment. In addition, primary servicers are responsible for the general administration of the loan, dealing with communications received from the borrower, monitoring compliance and reporting on loan performance to the finance parties and (in the securitised deals) certain of the securitisation parties.

Special servicing refers to the more "intensive care" aspects of loan servicing. Once a loan as transferred from primary servicing to special servicing, the special servicer will be responsible for dealing with non-payment and other material breaches of the underlying finance documents and for determining, and then implementing, the chosen strategy to work out or enforce the loan and its related security. Whilst a loan is being specially serviced, the primary servicer continues to carry out its role of cash management, but its duties to communicate with the borrower will pass to the special servicer, whilst the loan is in special servicing.

### 7.2.2 Appointment of CMBS servicers

Servicers are appointed at the time a CMBS transaction is closed to service all the CRE loan securitised within that transaction on behalf of the CMBS issuer (as owner of, and lender under, those CRE loans) and the CMBS issuer security trustee (as holder of all security granted by the issuer over the loans and its other assets for the benefit of the CMBS noteholders). To carry out this role, the issuer will appoint the servicer as its agent and lawful attorney to exercise all the rights and remedies the issuer has as lender under the finance documents and, in the case of A/B loans, as senior lender under the intercreditor arrangements.

CRE loans are typically structured as syndicated loan facilities, with a facility agent being the link between the borrower and syndicate of lenders and with a security trustee holding the security granted by the borrower on trust for the syndicate. As such, servicers will also be appointed by the facility agent and security trustee as their agent and lawful attorney to carry out and perform their duties and exercise all rights available to them under the finance documents and any relevant intercreditor arrangements.

Whilst the issuer, facility agent and security trustee delegates absolutely all their respective rights and duties to the servicer, it does not follow that the servicer is entitled to exercise such rights and duties within its absolute discretion, or, without boundaries or limitations. The issuer, loan level facility agent, security trustee, issuer security trustee and servicer enter into a servicing agreement that sets out in detail what the servicer can and cannot do on behalf of the various parties in respect of the loans. The next few sections of this Chapter will discuss this in greater detail.

Servicers are granted with powers of attorney from the issuer, facility agent and security trustee and these powers of attorney are an integral part of the servicing documentation. The power of attorney typically appoints the servicer to act as the appointers' attorney in connection with all loans owned within the particular CMBS, but these powers of attorney typically do not list or otherwise identify on its face which specific loans the power of attorney applies to. Whilst this approach avoids the powers of attorney being cumbersome, it can also have the unwanted outcome of borrowers and other third parties querying or being reluctant to accept that a particularly power of attorney gives the servicer authority in respect of a specific loan. Moreover, these powers of attorney will not be sufficient or effective to enable servicers to execute all acts they may need to carry out in the discharge of their duties. This is particularly relevant for special servicers where, for example, executing land charge enforcement documentation in Germany will require the special servicer to be armed with a German language and German law vollmacht (power of attorney) which clearly relates to a specific loan.[3]

### 7.2.3.  *Servicing standard*

As set out in the previous two Chapters, a standard feature in all servicing agreements is the obligation on the servicer at all times to act in accordance with the servicing standard. The servicing standard is one of the key principles of loan servicing, providing a benchmark against which a servicer's performance can be judged. Whilst the definition of servicing standard differs from deal to deal, it generally places an obligation on the

---

[3]  For the approach of servicers in Germany see Ch.17.

servicer to service the CRE loans in the best interests of the creditors, acting to a standard of skill and care which is the higher of that which it would service its own portfolio of CRE loans and that which it applies to third party CRE loans, but taking in account the standard of skill and care of a reasonably prudent lender of CRE loans, with a view to the timely receipt of payments due in respect of the loans and maximising recoveries to the creditors on a net present value basis.

Where a loan is tranched, the servicer will be required to maximise recoveries to the issuer and the junior lender as a collective whole, but taking into account the subordination of the junior lender. The servicing standard will also set out what obligations (at law or by contract) the servicer should comply with and, in the case of conflict, in which order of priority. It must first and foremost act in accordance with any law applicable to it or any entity which it acts on behalf of. It follows therefore, that it can't be obliged by the servicing agreement, or by any instruction or direction it may receive thereunder, which would cause a breach of law. Thereafter, priority is usually given to the loan document, then any intercreditor agreement (where relevant), before the servicing agreement. Whilst the servicing standard will typically rank the intercreditor agreement in priority to the servicing agreement, it is sometimes the case that the intercreditor agreement will state that, in the case of conflict with the servicing agreement, the servicing agreement will prevail (effectively overriding the conflict priority set out in the servicing standard).

A second important feature of the servicing standard is that it lays down the parameters for how the servicer must act in connection with any conflicts that may arise between its own interests and those of the issuer and other parties it represents. The servicing standard makes it clear that in the discharge of its duties, the servicer cannot have regard to the fees or other compensation it receives, any relationship it or any related entity has with any other party to the CMBS or underlying loan, nor any ownership interest it or any related entity has in any underlying loan or otherwise in the CMBS. In essence, the servicer should, at all times, place the interests of the creditors above its own interests or the interests of related entities. Whilst in practice it is often difficult for servicers to totally separate and disregard their own interests when making decisions, what should never be allowed to happen is servicers acting solely in their own best interests. By way of illustration, servicers have often (more so in the period 2004–10) had related entities holding either junior classes of notes in the CMBS or holding junior tranches of the underlying loans and so this element of the servicing standard is of paramount importance to protect the CMBS noteholders as a collective whole.

### 7.2.4. *Cash collection and reporting obligations*

As discussed above in this Chapter, the primary servicer will typically remain responsible throughout the life of a loan for collecting payments from the underlying borrower and then distributing those payments to the finance parties. Where the loan is tranched, this will typically involve paying the collections into a tranching account and then applying those collections in accordance with the priority of payments agreed between the senior lenders and junior lenders. In the case of a securitised loan, the servicer will pay amounts due to the CMBS issuer into its collection account. At this point, the responsibility for dealing with cash passes to the CMBS cash manager, who will distribute all amounts paid to the issuer to the noteholders and other securitisation parties in accordance with the securitisation priority of payments. As such, it should not be the responsibility of the servicer to concern itself with how loan level collections will be distributed at the CMBS level. This is discussed in further detail below.

The primary servicer's other main function, particularly where the loan is securitised, is reporting. In CMBS transactions, the servicer is obliged to periodically report to the note trustee, issuer and other key parties, in a standardised form, how the loan is performing (which in Europe typically follows the Commercial Real Estate Finance Council's European-Investor Reporting Package (E-IRP)[4]). When a loan transfers to special servicing, the special servicer is required, in addition to the primary servicer's periodic reporting obligations, to provide a periodic progress reports on the workout of the specially serviced loans. Together these reports are of fundamental importance to the noteholders as their primary source of information on the underlying portfolio's performance. In the context of CMBS deals and in recognition of the requirements of the Market Abuse Directive (MAD),[5] the primary servicer is also responsible for preparing, on the CMBS issuer's behalf, notices to be issued to the market which disclose non-public information which is likely to have a material impact on the value of the underlying loans.

### 7.2.5. *Modifications, waivers and consent under the finance documents*

Whilst servicers are empowered to agree to modifications, waivers and consents in connection with the underlying finance documents on behalf of the lenders, they may do so only in accordance with the parameters laid down in the servicing agreement and, where applicable, the intercreditor arrangement.

---

4   See Appendix 4.
5   Directive 2006/3/EC. See further Petersen, A.V., *Commercial Mortgage-Backed Securitisation: Developments in the European Market*, 1st edn (London: Sweet & Maxwell, 2006), Chapter 13.

Subject to controlling party consent and consultation rights (discussed in greater detail below), servicers are empowered to agree to consents or waivers contemplated by the terms of the underlying finance documents provided that the conditions laid down in the finance documents which need to be satisfied prior to a consent or waiver being given have, in the opinion of the servicer, been satisfied. Servicers may also agree to consents, waivers, amendments or modifications which are not contemplated by the finance documents, but the servicer must be satisfied that agreeing to such matters is in accordance with the servicing standard and either not material or will produce aggregate greater recoveries to the lender on a net present value basis than liquidation of the underlying CRE. Some legacy CMBS servicing agreements allow the servicer to consent to matters which wouldn't satisfy the two above mentioned conditions, if they obtain confirmation from the rating agencies that the proposed agreement would not result in the rating of the CMBS notes being downgraded. However, in practice this option is very rarely utilised as rating agencies have to date proved reluctant to, in effect, underwrite servicers' proposals in fear of noteholder actions; the role of the rating agencies should be limited to providing an opinion as to the likeliness of the notes being repaid and receiving interest.[6]

Furthermore, if the lender is dealing with a request to extend the loan maturity, then such matters are subject to further requirements, particularly for CMBS loans. In CMBS servicing agreements, a servicer is permitted to consent to a loan extension provided that the loan is, as explained in Ch.6, not extended into the "tail period" of the CMBS, the two or three year period immediately prior to the final maturity of the CMBS notes, and provided that there is no other material default apart from the maturity breach. The reason for limiting an extension to the commencement of the CMBS tail period is that the tail period allows the issuer a period of time in which to realise the loan portfolio and conclude any loan level enforcement action (based on the projected typical timeframe for enforcement processes in any particular jurisdiction) before the notes fall due for repayment, so that the issuer can avoid defaulting on its payment obligations which would create a note event of default. If a servicer wanted to extend a loan into the tail period it is typically required to obtain the consent of each class of notes in the CMBS structure. Since obtaining noteholder consent is a time consuming and difficult process, this is not something a servicer is likely to wish to do, unless it sees this as being the only viable option to maximise recoveries on the loan.[7]

The work involved in deciding whether or not to agree to consents, waivers and modifications is often time consuming and will often involve the preparation of internal credit papers, credit committee approval, detailed analysis of cashflows and projections. Such matters are often dealt with in

---

[6]  See further Ch.11 for the role of the Rating Agencies.
[7]  See further Ch.10 where this topic will be discussed further.

primary servicing with a view to restructuring a loan before it goes into default. Given the relatively low basis point fee which primary servicers are entitled, servicers will often charge the borrower a fee for agreeing to the borrower's request. The servicing agreement contemplates servicers charging such a fee, provided the fee is reasonable and the servicer has notified the securitisation parties that they have charged a fee to the borrower.

### 7.2.6. Enforcement

Special servicers are responsible for dealing with the enforcement and workout of specially serviced loans.[8] Whilst a consensual workout with the borrower is preferable this frequently is not possible and so special servicers must determine how best to utilise the various rights and remedies available to the finance parties in the loan documentation, particularly the security, in order to maximise recoveries to the creditors/noteholders. It is within the special servicer's discretion to determine the best strategy to achieve this, but often the special servicer is required to notify the various parties it represents before commencing with any enforcement action and provide such parties with periodic progress updates. Despite special servicers being granted powers of attorney to enable them to carry out enforcement action in the name of the security holders, local law requirements and practices may not recognise such powers of attorney and so special servicers may need to obtain local law compliant powers of attorney, or, in some cases require the security holder itself to execute documentation in order to facilitate an enforcement procedure.

One particular concern arising from enforcement is addressed in all servicing agreements: mortgagee-in-possession or its equivalent outside the United Kingdom. As a general rule, special servicers are prohibited from taking any action which would cause the finance parties to be considered in possession of the underlying real estate. The risk from being in possession of the real estate is that the finance parties could be responsible for any liabilities attaching to the real estate as if they were the legal owners—this could include environmental liabilities and business rates. The approach differs from deal to deal, but the servicing agreement will usually allow a special servicer to take actions which would cause the finance parties to become in possession of the real estate if they set up an SPV to take possession, which would ring fence any liabilities that could arise from being in possession, or, in some cases, if the special servicer has first carried out an environmental assessment of the underling real estate or obtained the consent of the note trustee. In the case of real estate located in England and Wales, the risk of possession can readily be avoided by appointing a receiver (who can sell the real estate as well as strategically asset manage the real estate prior to sale), however, in much of continental Europe such course of action is not possible.

---

[8] Please see Ch.6 for further discussion and commentary on loan workouts in England, France and Germany.

As a general rule, special servicers will want to avoid enforcing the mortgage over the real estate to exercise the power of sale contained therein. In some jurisdictions, such as Germany, this is by far the most expensive, time consuming route available and can often take control of the process away from the special servicer. Thus, taking enforcement action of this kind is often the last resort where all other options are not viable.[9]

It is worth noting, that some enforcement procedures require the loan debt to have been demanded before the procedure can commence. The obvious risk of demanding payment from the borrower is that the directors or managers of the borrower may then be duty bound to file the borrower for insolvency. This is, almost without exception, considered unhelpful for secured creditors—not only does it add an additional level of complexity, but it will inevitably increase costs, reduce recoveries and cause significant delays, as well as risking the loss of the finance parties control over the general workout strategy of the borrower.

### 7.2.7. *Controlling party consent and consultation rights*

Despite the broad discretion of servicers to exercise the lender's rights in order to maximise recoveries, key amendments to the terms of the underlying loans and key actions in respect of such loans, such as accelerating the debt or enforcing the security, are often subject to consent rights in favour of the controlling party.

Where the whole loan is held in a CMBS, the controlling party will be the controlling class, which is usually defined as the most junior class of notes which, based on the aggregate outstanding principal amount of the issuer's loan portfolio, would see more than 25 per cent of the principal balance of that class of notes repaid. If the loan is tranched, then the controlling party will be the most junior lender in respect of which a CVE is not continuing (typically defined by reference to expected recoveries, based on the most recent valuation of the underlying real estate, being low enough that the junior lender would expect to recover less than 25 per cent of its principal loan commitment), before passing to the next most junior lender, or, if there is no other junior lender, then the senior lender. Where the senior lender is a CMBS issuer, then the controlling party will be the controlling class.

The documentation surrounding consent and consultation rights is often complicated and requires servicers to fully analyse the terms of the servicing agreement and, where the loan is tranched, the intercreditor agreement, to understand what matters require the servicer to seek controlling party involvement, and whether that involvement is consent or consultation.[10]

---

[9]  See Ch.17.
[10]  See further Chs 14 and 15.

At the securitisation level, the controlling class will need to appoint a controlling class representative or operating adviser for its consent and consultation rights to apply. Since the controlling class representative (CCR) or operating adviser (OA) is a single entity, it enables the servicer to communicate and discharge its consent/consultation duties more efficiently than if it had to deal with numerous noteholders within a class. Whilst all deals differ to varying degrees, the consent of the controlling class (via the CCR/OA) will often be required prior to consenting to a loan extension, varying the timing or amount of payments of interest or principal, varying other material provisions of the finance documents, taking enforcement action, releasing a borrower from its obligations and releasing security where it is not contemplated by the finance documents (e.g. where the loan is not repaid in full or where an asset sale doesn't meet the specified allocated loan amount (ALA) requirements)). In addition, the controlling class (through the CCR/OA) will often have the right to be consulted with respect to any change in the property manager (where the lenders have a discretion on whether or not to approve a change in property manager) and any release of security (regardless of whether contemplated in the loan documents or not).

Servicing agreements set out in detail the process for obtaining controlling class consent and often require the servicer to give five to 10 business days prior notification of its intended course of action and the controlling class (through the CCR/OA) is entitled to raise objection and propose an alternative course of action within that timeframe. If the CCR/OA does not respond within the specified timeframe then it is deemed to have given its consent and the servicer may proceed with its intended plan. If the CCR/OA does respond within such period, then there is typically a limitation on dialogue continuing for a period usually 30 to 45 days, after which, if no agreement is reached between the servicer and the CCR/OA, the servicer can proceed based on its own proposal. In addition, the servicer will also benefit from what is known as the servicing override – this entitles the servicer to take immediate action or to liaise with the CCR/OA for a shorter period of time that the servicing agreement otherwise requires, if to do otherwise would be contrary to the servicing standard. The servicer override can be an important tool for servicers since the CCR/OA acts on behalf of junior stakeholders and thus may base its objections/decisions on what would only benefit the interests of those junior stakeholders.

In the case of A/B loans, the junior lender's consent rights whilst it is the controlling party are typically the same as those of the controlling class, although in some deals they can be more encompassing and, in some instances, the junior lender will also have certain entrenched rights which it retains even after a CVE. In addition, the junior lender will often have consultation rights with respect to any matter which the servicer considers to be a "significant action" with respect to a loan or its security.[11]

---

[11] Junior lender consent and consultation rights are discussed in more detail in Chs 14 and 15.

Some CMBS deals provide that in the absence of an OA or CCR identifying themselves in writing to the servicer, the servicer should proceed on the basis that there is no OA or CCR appointed. Other deals are silent on the position where an OA/CCR has not come forward. In those instances, a prudent servicer may wish o contact the market, requesting any OA/CCR to identify themselves. A peculiarity arises, where a party or class are in control (and thus has the right to appoint an OA or CCR) but they do not exercise such a right in order to get a "seat at the table", to agree, approve or just be consulted on key restructuring/workout strategies. Some noteholders view appointing an OA or CCR as a poisoned chalice, opening oneself up for challenge from other noteholders within the controlling class for which that OA or CCR represents. As such, an OA/CRR is more likely to be appointed where one particular organisation owns the entire controlling class. Furthermore, if a noteholder appoints itself as OA, then this can limit the noteholder from trading its notes. This is because the OA, when exercising its consent and consultation rights, will become privy to price-sensitive information which may affect the price of its notes. The MAD (and the rules of the various European jurisdictions implemented MAD into national legislature) create an offense for those trading securities based on price-sensitive information, known as insider dealing.[12] Accordingly, noteholders may not wish to appoint themselves as an OA because they will not want to have their general ability to trade their notes fettered, even at the cost of losing a degree of control over the proposed actions of the servicer.

### 7.2.8. *Special serviced loans and corrected loans*

CRE loans will be serviced by the primary servicer unless and until any one of a number of events occurs with respect to the loan (known as servicing transfer events). Once a servicing transfer event occurs, the special servicer will take over responsibility for servicing that loan and addressing the particular matter which caused the loan to switch to special servicing.

The list of servicing transfer events varies from deal to deal, but typically, include the following events: (i) failure to repay the loan on its maturity; (ii) any other payment default which is more than 60 days past due; (iii) the borrower is unable to pay its debts as they fall due or is subject to insolvency or any analogous proceedings; (iv) the servicer has received notice of enforcement action, or proposed enforcement action, being commenced with respect to the underlying mortgage property; (v) the borrower is in default of any of its other material obligations beyond any applicable grace period; and (vi) in the reasonable opinion of the servicer, there is imminent risk of a default arising which is likely to remain un-remedied for a specified period.

---

[12]  See Ch.13 of the 1st edn.

In the case of tranched loans, the intercreditor agreement will often state that a servicing transfer event will not occur for so long as the junior lender is exercising (or is within the period to exercise) its cure rights in respect of the default which has caused a servicing transfer event. However, it will not be possible to stop a servicing transfer event arising following a maturity breach or insolvency of the borrower.

Despite the transfer to special servicing, as stated above, the primary servicer will remain responsible for collecting debt service and processing payments to the finance parties, as well as administrating hedging arrangements and CMBS reporting obligations and will continue to receive fees for these duties. However, primary servicers often find themselves in a position where the loan has not switched to special servicing (because a servicing transfer event has not yet arisen) but they are nonetheless carrying out quasi-special servicing services. As discussed below in this Chapter and in Ch.5, CMBS 2.0 should provide a mechanism for loans transferring to special servicing in these types of scenarios.

Whilst not often seen in practice, it is possible under the servicing agreement for a loan in special servicing to "flip" back to primary servicing if it has become a corrected loan. Typically, a loan will become a corrected loan if, in the case of payment default, the default has been remedied and no further payment default occurs, for a specified number of consecutive payment periods, or for other defaults, the event which caused the transfer to special servicing event has ceased to exist.

### 7.2.9. Fees

Servicer fees are split into four components—the primary servicing fee; the special servicing fee; the work out fee; and the liquidation fee. In addition, servicers are entitled to recover out-of-pockets cost and expenses reasonably incurred in the performance of their duties.

Primary servicers have historically been entitled only to receive the primary servicing fee, typically in the region of five basis points per annum of the outstanding balance of all loans and payable on each note payment date. The fee rate is designed to reflect the fairly straightforward cash management and administrative nature of their role. However, as indicated above and in the previous two Chapters, in practice primary servicers have often found themselves in circumstances where loans are in, or heading towards, a distressed position but have not yet been transferred to special servicing, and are carrying out special servicing functions without being appropriate remunerated for such services. This Chapter will discuss below how the primary servicer remuneration structure could be amended in CMBS 2.0 to address this anomaly.

Special servicers are entitled to a special servicing fee, typically in the region of twenty five basis points per annum of the outstanding balance of all specially serviced loans and payable on each note payment date. This higher fee is designed to reflect the additional work and expertise required to properly service loans in special servicing.

Special servicers are also entitled to two performance based fees: the workout fee and the liquidation fee. The work out fee arises where a specially serviced loan becomes a corrected loan and for so long as it remains a corrected loan. The quantum of the workout fee is frequently one per cent of all principal and interest received on a corrected loan and is intended to reward the special servicer for converting a non-performing loan into a performing loan.

The liquidation which incentivises the special servicer to maximise recoveries arises in the event of liquidation of a specially serviced loan or its underlying property. The quantum of the liquidation fees is frequently one per cent of the net liquidation proceeds received and is typically paid to the special servicer on the note payment date following receipt of such proceeds. The securitisation level documentation architecture is usually structured such that the payment of the liquidation fee to the special servicer reduces principal recoveries to the creditors/noteholders due to the fee being paid out of funds that would otherwise be available for distribution to the creditors/noteholders. Notwithstanding how the securitisation documentation contemplates the liquidation fee being paid, there are numerous examples of the special servicer, on behalf of the issuer, charging the liquidation fee to the borrower under the fees/costs indemnity and expenses provisions in the underlying finance documents. This can avoid a shortfall being incurred by the creditors/noteholders, but only when the net liquidation proceeds are sufficient to discharge in full all loan liabilities and cover the liquidation fee. If such proceeds are not sufficient then charging the liquidation fee to the borrower may, so far as the creditors/noteholders are concerned, have the same net effect as paying the liquidation fee at the securitisation level. Further complexity can arise if the underlying loan is tranched—in such circumstances careful consideration should be given to the terms of the intercreditor documentation as to how servicer fees are expected to be recovered from the issuer and/or the junior lender, and if charging the liquidation fee to the borrower would contradict such terms.

The special servicing fee and liquidation fee rates are applied equally to all loans within a CMBS, irrespective of the loan size and irrespective of how much involvement and activity has been taken by the special servicer. Consequently, for large loans or where very little work has been carried out by the special servicer in connection with the realisation of the liquidation proceeds, the liquidation fee can represent something of a windfall payment. Conversely, for small loans or where a great deal of work has been carried out by the special servicer in realising the liquidation proceeds, the liquidation fee may not adequately reward the special servicer. Changes to the special servicing fee and liquidation fee structure aimed at making sure special servicers are remunerated appropriately, regardless of the loan size, are discussed below.

### 7.2.10. Liability, termination and replacement of servicers

The liability that loan servicers owe to their appointers is typically limited to losses and liabilities incurred as a result of the servicer's breach or its wilful misconduct or fraudulent activity. Of fundamental importance to servicers, the servicing agreement should also state that servicers are not responsible or liable for the loan portfolios performance or any shortfall in ultimate recoveries. Moreover, servicers are also indemnified for any losses or claims they may incur in the discharge of their duties.

Servicers who diligently discharge their obligations should remain appointed as servicer for the life of the loans, with their appointment automatically terminating when the last of the recoveries on the last loan in the CMBS portfolio has been received. However, a fundamental control right for the issuer security trustee is the right to terminate the servicer if certain material events occur with respect to the servicer. Whilst varying from deal to deal, the right to terminate the servicer will usually arise where: (i) the servicer has caused a payment not to be paid on its due date; (ii) the servicer has breached any of its other obligations and such breach is materially prejudicial to the interests of the creditors/noteholders; (iii) the servicer is insolvent or any insolvency or similar proceedings have been taken or commenced; (iv) the servicer ceases to carry on its business or is unable to discharge its duties; and (v) the servicer's continued appointment would result in the notes being downgraded or put on negative watch. Whilst a matter of negotiation, the servicer will usually benefit from grace periods for certain of these events allowing it time to remedy the breach and avoid the issuer security trustee being able to terminate its appointment.

As seen in the previous two Chapters, whilst neither the issuer nor the issuer security trustee have a right to terminate the servicer without cause, the controlling class typically has the discretionary right to terminate the special servicer at any time and appoint a replacement of servicer of its choosing, provided that the replacement servicer satisfies certain condition contained within the servicing agreement. The use of this right in practice has been hotly discussed in the market post the 2008 financial crisis. Initially included to provide the controlling class with a degree of control in the event that the special servicer was underperforming, there have been a number of instances where the controlling class has terminated existing special servicers and replaced them with special servicers affiliated or otherwise associated with the controlling class. This has raised concerns in the market, particularly from the more senior classes of noteholders, that the newly appointed special servicer will work out specially serviced loans or otherwise carry out its duties in a manner favourable to the interests of the controlling class, giving disregard to the servicing standard which they should comply with at all times. The debate continues at the time of writing.

## 7.3. Legacy loan workout

Since 2010, many of the loans securitised before the origination bubble burst in late 2007 have been defaulting and servicers have had to determine the best strategy for working out such loans in a manner which maximises recoveries to the creditors/noteholders on a net present value basis. The nature of defaults that have been the trigger for workouts range from maturity and other non-payment breaches, financial covenant breaches (such as loan to value and interest cover ratios) as well as borrower insolvency. Regardless of the nature of the default, the typical starting position for all special servicers is that enforcement of the security is, more often than not, the least attractive option to maximise recoveries; not least because enforcement of real estate level security is, particularly in mainland Europe, a lengthy, costly and court led process.[13]

The workout strategy adopted by servicers varies from loan to loan, but typically falls under two headings: consensual loan workout or restructuring and security enforcement.[14] Consensual workouts can consist of a combination of standstill, loan extension or other amendments to the loan terms which typically set out an agreed asset disposal and de-leveraging programme, with the intention that the process will be carried out by the borrower in a consensual and orderly manner, but under the close supervision of the servicer. As would be expected, security enforcement involves exercising the power of sale contained in the mortgage or, where the security package enables, the equity in the borrower. As mentioned, this route is often avoided where the borrower is prepared to work with its creditors, but where it is not, then servicers may be left with little option but to enforce the security in order to take control over the real estate.

In addition, security over the borrower equity can, in some jurisdictions, be used in a different way, by replacing the management control of the borrower, in order to try and execute an orderly sale of the portfolio outside of formal enforcement proceedings. This option, which this Chapter will label as quasi-enforcement, has proved a valuable alternative to enforcement and enables the servicer to achieve a consensual and orderly wind down of the borrower portfolio without the sponsor's involvement.

---

[13] See Ch.17.
[14] Please see Ch.5 for further discussion on active asset management as a workout strategy.

### 7.3.1.  Consensual workout

For any consensual workout to be successful, it requires the borrower and its sponsor to work with the servicer until all its assets are realised and have been distributed in discharge of the debt. Where the borrower has indicated its willingness to work with the servicer in a post default scenario, the servicer's first step may be to issue a standstill or forbearance agreement pursuant to which it agrees not to take any action in respect of the default for a specified period of time and subject to certain conditions. The standstill or forbearance agreement is a useful tool for servicers as it can, first and foremost, reduce the risk of the borrower filing for insolvency, particularly in the case of a maturity payment breach. Secondly, since a standstill doesn't waive the existing defaults, it will focus the borrower's mind to come up with a repayment strategy that will be acceptable to the servicer, in the knowledge that if it fails to do so, the servicer can terminate the standstill and proceed with enforcement action.

There have been many loans which servicers have also agreed to extend the maturity in order to allow the borrower further time to repay the debt. As seen in Ch.5, whilst many market participants refer to this as "extend and pretend", indicating that simply pushing out the maturity achieves nothing more than delaying the inevitable, many loan extensions which servicers have granted, are more involved than just changing the maturity date. The extended loan will often require the borrower to deliver a business plan for the period of the extension which will set out how the borrower will conduct an orderly sale programme of the properties and repay the loan. The programme may commence with an initial period of capital expenditure at the property to improve market value. Where possible, the servicer will look to the sponsor to inject fresh equity to fund such capex, but where this can't be agreed, and assuming there is little or no surplus cashflow to fund such capex, servicers may be willing to permit a certain amount of cashflow to fund capex ahead of debt service charges. Whereas many loan agreements require the borrower to achieve a sale price of a specified percentage above the allocated loan amount for each property, this is frequently unachievable and unrealistic in the market, at the time of writing, and so extended loans frequently amend this provisions to say any disposal must be approved by the servicer and the entire proceeds of such sale (less costs of sale) are applied in full in repayment of the debt. In deals which haven't yet hit maturity and have a fairly small amortisation profile, servicers may also take this opportunity to put in place cash sweep provisions which look to amortise the loan down beyond its scheduled repayment profile out of surplus cashflow instead of allowing those funds to go out of the deal to the borrower.

Consensual restructurings can be the most appropriate method to maximise recoveries to the creditors/noteholders, however, a servicer can't be certain that the borrower will remain willing to work with the servicer once the loan has been restructured and, if that happens, then the servicer will need a default to arise, before it will be in a position to proceed with any other work out strategy.

### 7.3.2. *Enforcement and quasi-enforcement*

Formal enforcement of security, as discussed above in this Chapter, is typically carried out where there are no other viable workout options available. Enforcement of security over English real estate represents somewhat of an exception to this rule, as servicers can appoint an LPA receiver to execute an orderly sale of the real estate in a manner and on terms acceptable to the servicer, unlike for example a court led sale process in Germany where the servicer has very little involvement or control.[15]

The servicer may have the option of enforcing real estate level security or share level security. Depending on the jurisdiction of the borrower and the real estate, enforcement of the share level security may be the more attractive option if it can be carried out and completed in a quicker period of time than real estate level enforcement; share level enforcement will most certainly be a less costly process than real estate level enforcement. Moreover, share level enforcement may present an opportunity for the purchaser to acquire the real estate (indirectly) in a manner which would avoid relatively high land taxes. Where a tax saving is possible, purchasers may be willing to share that saving with the servicer, which can thus increase recoveries.

As mentioned above in this Chapter, CMBS deals, in particular, prohibit or restrict the servicer's ability to enforce the security in a way which could cause the finance parties to be mortgagees-in-possession (or the equivalent outside of England and Wales). However in some cases, it may be that, in order to maximise recoveries when operating in fairly limited local law parameters, it is necessary for the servicer to take possession of the real estate so that it can, for example, engage in a period of active asset management prior to exercising the power of sale. If taking possession is required, servicers may wish to, or be required to, set up an orphan SPV entity to take possession in order to ring fence potential liabilities.

Quasi-enforcement is the process of exercising rights contained in the security documents, in a manner which achieves a greater recovery on a loan than would be achieved by formal enforcement. One form of quasi-enforcement which has been used on numerous occasions has been to exercise the voting rights attached to the shares in the borrower in order to replace the incumbent board of directors with independent third parties directors. Prior to exercising these voting rights, the servicers will have canvassed corporate service providers and discussed, on a confidential basis, the status of the borrower, its indebtedness and the servicers general

---

[15] See Ch.17 and also Chs 5 and 6.

strategy to work out the portfolio. In return for taking the appointment, the new directors will receive an annual fee and, in some cases, a success fee upon conclusion of the workout strategy. Once the directors are appointed then the discussion above in this Chapter regarding consensual workout applies equally. The new directors are ultimately duty bound to the act in the best interests of the company and so servicers should not consider this strategy as taking control of the borrower—the new directors may at any time decide not to continue with an agreed workout strategy. By the same token, servicers should take all necessary steps to ensure that they do not become shadow directors of the borrower and thus it is fundamentally important that the new directors act autonomously from the servicer and consider the servicers proposals and requests accordingly—they should not simply do whatever the servicer requests.

### 7.3.3. *Junior lenders*

As a final note to this section of this Chapter, and as mentioned earlier in this Chapter, in the case of A/B loans, the junior lender will enjoy a degree of consent and consultation rights which are typically conditional upon whether or not a CVE has occurred. As a consequence, over recent years services have frequently been faced with junior lenders using the mechanisms available to them in the documentation to challenge the valuations used to determine the occurrence of a CVE, either by challenging how the calculation of the CVE was initially made or by exercising their right to request another valuation (often referred to as a challenging valuation) to be used to calculate the CVE.

In addition, junior lender cure rights[16] have, perhaps unintentionally, resulted in an unnecessary delay where immediate action is needed to enforce and protect the interests of the finance parties as a whole. This is because intercreditor agreements typically prohibit the servicer from taking action to accelerate the loan or enforce the security whilst the junior lender is able to exercise its cure rights, irrespective of whether or not it actually exercises such rights in the applicable period. Whilst the logic to this is clearly understandable, going forward, servicers would undoubtedly benefit from some form of override to take action during a junior lender cure period where such action is necessary to protect the interests of the finance parties as a collective whole.

## 7.4.   CMBS 2.0 and the future of loan servicing

The exact role of loan servicers for the next round of originations, particularly those ear-marked for CMBS (assuming market appetite for such product returns), is one which may be debated at length. At the time of

---

[16]   Junior lender cure rights are discussed in further detail in Chs 14 and 15.

writing this Chapter, the Commercial Real Estate Finance Council Europe has just issued its discussion paper on *Market Principles for Issuing European CMBS 2.0* (the *CMBS 2.0 Discussion Paper*),[17] which includes a section on the role of loan servicers for future transactions. The principles contained in the *CMBS 2.0 Discussion Paper* are, as stated therein, only suggestions of best practice for a new CMBS market and ultimately it is down the market participants to decide which principles should be endorsed or not. This section of the Chapter will seek to identify some of key areas which are likely to change in future deals[18] and consider some of the suggestions contained in the *CMBS 2.0 Discussion Paper* relating to loan servicing.

### 7.4.1. Servicing standard under CMBS 2.0

As discussed in para.7.2.3 above, the servicing standard in some legacy CMBS deals states that the servicer should act in the best interests of the creditors/noteholders and maximise recoveries for the creditors/noteholders. Furthermore, the *CMBS 2.0 Discussion Paper* suggests that the servicing standard should require servicers to take into account the interests of the noteholders and that servicer should be open to hearing representations made from noteholders on how a servicer's workout strategy may impact the noteholders. However, loan servicers generally do not have, and should not be expected to have, the capital markets expertise and resources to evaluate how decisions made at the loan level will impact the creditors/noteholders, particularly given both the complexity of securitisation waterfalls and the conflicting interests of the various classes of creditors/noteholders. To do this would detract them from their primary obligation of servicing the underlying loan portfolio. Moreover, the servicer is appointed by the issuer, not the noteholders, and so in the absence of any direct contractual nexus between servicer and noteholders it is difficult to rationalise why the servicer should owe a duty to the noteholders. Accordingly, there is a view that CMBS 2.0 deals should, contrary to the *CMBS 2.0 Discussion Paper*, limit the duties of the servicers to consideration of the creditors' interests only and expressly state that servicers are not obliged to consider the interests of the noteholders.

### 7.4.2. Loan sale

CMBS deals, unlike many other types of ABS securitisations, tend to be structured as static collateral pools which should not be changed during the life of the deal. As a result, many deals expressly prevent loan servicers from selling loans in the course of their duties because servicers are not

---

[17] See further the discussion on CMBS 2.0 in Ch.4.
[18] The early CMBS 2.0 deals in the market, such as DECO 2011 – CSPK, are all secured by Deutsche Bank originated loans, provide a useful indication of the changes that market participants have made to loan servicing, but such deals should not be considered entirely representative of a new CMBS 2.0 market.

appointed to seek arbitrage opportunities on the issuer's portfolio.[19] However, in a workout context, loan sales can often produce greater recoveries for the creditors/noteholders than can be achieved through a consensual or enforced sale of the underlying portfolio. Loan sales can be concluded in a matter of days compared to asset sales which take weeks, if not months, to complete. During recent years, servicers have received offers from the borrowers on a number of deals to purchase the debt at a discount (commonly referred to as a discounted pay off or DPO[20]) but, due to documentation restraints, servicers have not been able to proceed with DPOs, even where a DPO would have had the best outcome for the creditors / noteholders. Accordingly, a key tool for the servicer's toolbox in CMBS 2.0 should be the ability to sell defaulted loans as part of a workout strategy, and this view is supported in the *CMBS 2.0 Discussion Paper*.

### 7.4.3. Remuneration

As indicated above in this Chapter, the fee structure of legacy CMBS can result in servicers being remunerated too much or too little compared against the amount of work involved.

Firstly, with regard to primary servicers legacy deals were structured on the basic assumption that loans would either be performing (and so in primary servicing) or in default (and in special servicing). No-one envisaged the primary servicer would be carrying out services akin to those carried out by the special servicer, but without being remunerated for this additional workload. To address this issue, CMBS 2.0 deals should not only provide the primary servicer with discretion to transfer the loan to special servicing in these types of scenarios but also entitle it to charge additional fees to compensate it for the additional work it carries out.

Secondly, with regard to special servicers, the special servicing fee and liquidation fee rates in legacy CMBS deals apply equally to all loans within a CMBS, irrespective of the loan size and irrespective of how much involvement and activity has been taken by the special servicer. Consequently, for large loans or where very little work has been carried out by the special servicer in connection with a loan workout, the special servicing fee and liquidation fee can, as stated above, represent something of a windfall payment. Conversely, for small loans or where a great deal of work has been carried out by the special servicer in realising a loan, the special servicing fee and liquidation fee may not adequately reward the special

---

[19] Whilst generally prohibited, servicers are empowered to sell loans when (i) its re-sale back to the originating bank due to a breach of representation or similar in the underlying loan sale agreement and (ii) when directed to do so by the issuer security trustee when it is trying to liquidate the issuer's assets following acceleration of the CMBS notes. This can be compared to say a portfolio manager's duties on a cash CDO or other arbitrage securitisations where assets can be traded frequently during the life of the deal to take advantage of price variation opportunities.

[20] See Ch.14.

servicer. To create a level fee structure, CMBS 2.0 deals should include different basis point fee rates, with smaller loans receiving higher basis point special servicing fees and liquidation fees, whilst larger loans receive smaller basis point fees.

### 7.4.4.   *Note legal final and loan workout*

As the notes on early legacy CMBS deals approach legal maturity, creditors/noteholders are trying to open dialogue with servicers to find out the servicers' plans to realise the loan portfolio before the notes mature. As already discussed, servicers generally are not obliged to consider the interests of the noteholders and that extends to considerations over whether a realisation strategy will result in recoveries being obtained before the notes mature. However, despite the tail period acting as a buffer to allow loans to be worked out before maturity, it was envisaged that, if a loan didn't repay by the start of the tail period, servicers would enforce the security and sell the real estate. In practice, this is not necessarily the case because enforcement, as discussed above, is not ordinarily the best strategy to maximise recoveries and the servicer may proceed with a longer period of workout in order to improve the issuer's recoveries. This could result in the issuer not receiving the proceeds of recovery in time to meet its payment obligations on the notes.

Accordingly, there is a disconnect in legacy CMBS between servicers obligations to maximise recoveries and the obligation of the issuer to repay the notes at legal final. In addition, if the notes are not repaid at maturity, then the general assumption has been that the issuer security trustee will enforce its security package over the issuer and effectively direct the servicer to liquidate the issuer's asset, however, this approach raises concerns over whether this would be in the best interests of the noteholders as a whole and if the issuer security trustee is best placed to direct such a process.

CMBS 2.0 deals are likely to address these concerns by introducing a procedure for loan servicers and noteholders to discuss how the loan portfolio will be worked out in the run up to legal final. It is envisaged that if the servicer does not expect the portfolio to be repaid, or workouts to be completed, on or before the legal final maturity, the servicer will prepare a workout plan at least six months prior to legal final. The senior class of notes would have the right to approve or reject the plan (which represents a change from the standard approach in CMBS that control rests with the most junior class of noteholders) and if the plan is not approved then the default position would be for the issuer security trustee to take steps to commence a liquidation of the issuer's assets.

The *CMBS 2.0 Discussion Paper* suggests that borrowers and noteholders should be permitted to meet with each other without the servicer's attendance (if the servicer has not indicated it will attend such meeting) to discuss loan amendments and restructurings. However, there is a view that advocates that CMBS 2.0 transaction documents and the loan agreements for loans destined for CMBS 2.0 should expressly prohibit noteholders and borrowers from engaging in direct communication with each other without the express consent of the servicer. To allow otherwise would run contrary to the basic principles of loan servicing and would cut across the privity of contract that exists between borrowers and the issuer (on the one hand) and the issuer and the noteholders, via the note trustee (on the other). It is not necessarily the case that the noteholders interests are aligned with the interests of the issuer (as the actual lender) or indeed the interests of any junior lender and so therefore what is in the interests of certain noteholders may not necessarily be what a servicer would determine to be the best course of action in accordance with the servicing standard.

### 7.4.5. *Rating agency consent*

Some legacy CMBS deals oblige the servicer to obtain the prior consent of the rating agencies in order for the servicer to take certain types of action at the loan or intercreditor level. In practice, rating agencies have adopted the approach that they will not respond to requests for consent as they do not consider it correctly so, to be their role in the industry to act as a check or balance on loan/intercreditor structuring or workout, but only to appraise the ratings of the CMBS notes as a result of any changes at the loan level. As a result, where deals have required rating agency consent, servicers have been required to seek note trustee consent to waive these provisions. Note trustees generally speaking, are not prepared to give consents without first obtaining the consent of the noteholders. To avoid this issue in the future, CMBS 2.0 deals should not place any rating agency consent requirements before actions can be taken at the loan level. The only exception to this should be in the case of loan extensions where the servicer wishes to extend the maturity into the CMBS tail period.

## 7.5.  Conclusion

Loan servicing is an integral function within CRE financings and, as this Chapter and the previous two Chapters have outlined, whilst servicers are generally given broad powers and discretion in the performance of their roles, the documentation can, at times, place unnecessary restrictions on what they can do. This Chapter advocates greater servicer discretion and arming servicers with additional tools to help facilitate loan workouts and restructurings. However, the future landscape of servicing, particularly in CMBS, is yet to be mapped out as servicers wait, with baited breath, for CMBS 2.0 issuance to commence in earnest and the loan servicing requirements of investors to be fully outlined.

173

As liquidity in both the commercial mortgage loan and CMBS markets remains stagnant at the time of writing, servicers face challenges to their own businesses as legacy deals begin to run off and with it their fee income. Servicers of the future will need to be more than just servicers reliant on CMBS portfolio instructions; those with real estate experience, experienced asset management platforms and investment teams will be best placed to profit from the next boom, or indeed the continuing bear.

# Chapter 8

# Derivatives in Legacy Cre Financings and their Role in Future Transactions: How Derivatives Continue to Impact Restructurings and Finance Strategy

Mark Battistoni,

Director, Chatham Financial

Jonathan Lye,

Senior Hedging Adviser, Chatham Financial

## 8.1. Introduction

Derivatives such as interest rate swaps have provided, and continue to provide, at least one important function within most CRE financings in Europe: ensuring that a borrower's ability to satisfy interest cover and debt service covenants is unaffected solely by movements in interest rate markets.[1] This function is so relevant to CRE lenders' underwriting processes that it manifests as a hedging requirement in most variable-rate loans and is by definition the basis for fixed-rate financing structures. Derivatives have performed this important function very well, except in the obvious case of the bankruptcy of Lehman Brothers, which necessitated the unanticipated replacement of any Lehman entity providing hedges to borrowers. Perhaps counter-intuitively, this includes long-dated interest rate swaps, certain aspects of which will be featured in this Chapter. Notwithstanding this view, there is no denying that the overwhelming perception of derivatives within the CRE community is negative. This Chapter will consider what can often appear to be a shadowy and arcane corner of CRE finance. As the title suggests, it will comprise a mix of backward- and forward-looking analysis in pursuit of the threads connecting derivatives to any given financing strategy.

---

[1] Although some CRE transactions involve currency and inflation risks requiring foreign currency and inflation derivatives, these are relatively rare. This Chapter focuses on interest rate hedging, although many of the concepts will be relevant to other types of hedging. Property derivatives are not covered in this Chapter.

In a truly global sense, the historically poor reputation of over-the-counter (OTC) derivatives, at the time of writing, has plumbed to new depths amongst some CRE market participants since the advent of the financial crisis. Specific to Europe, the CRE community has had its share of transactions in which derivatives were more than just innocent bystanders. This stems from the fact that derivatives, used as hedges, were undeniably the vehicles through which movements in interest rate markets delivered acute financial distress to a large number of CRE investments. This Chapter will start by demonstrating how and why derivatives—interest rate swaps in particular, but not exclusively—exacerbated the property sector and credit market problems, as interest rates fell, alongside property values and liquidity in the credit markets. The legal and structural quirks of derivatives (which have tended to make bad situations worse, especially in CMBS transactions) will also be considered.

For a sector as large and diverse as European CRE finance, it is perhaps not surprising that market resilience has, at the time of writing, prevailed. Despite some fairly high profile debt debacles made worse by derivatives such as swaps—with still many to be resolved—there has not been a knee-jerk reaction away from structures involving variable-rate loans hedged with derivatives in favour of financing structures which avoid their use (e.g. those involving fixed-rate loans). The second section of this Chapter focuses on what lessons market participants and stakeholders at all levels—lenders, CMBS arrangers, ratings agencies, borrowers, legal advisers, and servicers to name a few—have gleaned while managing legacy transactions and dealing with the derivatives and the challenges raised by them since the financial crisis. New deals and restructured loans are changing shape. Inherent to this change, capital markets for both debt and equity are evolving, almost as fast as the regulatory environment.[2] This is not confined to Europe or to its CRE markets. Examining the intersection of lessons learnt and top-down changes under way, this Chapter highlights a few paradigms which are most likely to affect derivatives' usage within CRE financings in 2013 and the coming years.

Above all, this Chapter aims to be less subtle than its corresponding chapter in the 1st edn (published before the financial crisis).[3] The second sentence of the authors' Chapter in the 1st edn of this book was in hindsight, a gross understatement, *"However, the extent to which derivatives can shape costs over the life of a CMBS financing is not always fully appreciated."* It is fundamental to the content of this chapter to distinguish between the appreciation and appropriateness of derivatives within a financing structure (which can protect against uncertainty) and the appreciation and appropriateness of hedging decisions taken on any given financing (which can have a different

---

[2] See Ch.16.
[3] See A.V. Petersen, *Commercial Mortgage-Backed Securitisation: Developments in the European Market*, 1st edn (London: Sweet & Maxwell, 2006), Ch.6, which contains a detailed description of the main interest rate derivatives used in CRE financings: swaps, caps, collars, step-swaps, swaptions and flexi-swaps.

or greater financial impact on transactions than anticipated). To this point, the massive downward shift in interest rates in the wake of the financial crisis was not at all predictable, but the behaviour of the derivative instruments (i.e. their costs and valuations over time) with respect to changes in interest rates, was entirely predictable. As the example cases in this Chapter will demonstrate, the economic impact certain hedging strategies levied on CRE transactions have had on transactions, at the time of writing, has been staggering.

As a final note within this introduction, consideration should be given to why hedging requirements exist in the first place. In most cases the income from a property asset is a relatively fixed quantity. This income is not at all linked to the interest rate environment applicable to variable rate loans, meaning that if interest rates were to rise, the borrower may be in a position where its income is not sufficient to cover the interest payments under a variable rate loan.[4] The ratio of net operating income (NOI) to interest expense in a given period (the Interest Cover Ratio, or ICR) is one of the fundamental tests in CRE finance. By how much would variable rates on any given CRE loan have to rise, such that the ICR falls from fairly healthy levels (well above 1.50) to the point at which income fails to meet interest payments (below 1.0)? Absent a hedge, for many loans this result could occur if variable rates were to rise by as little as 100 to 150 basis points. Given that variable rates can shift by these sums in a matter of months (upward as well as downward) the interest rate risk to a variable-rate loan is real. For perspective, since 1999 three-month variable interest rates in euros and sterling have shifted by at least 100 basis points during a calendar year six and five times, respectively. See the Annex to this Chapter, Figures 5 and 6, for charts of the recent history of three-month inter-bank rates and selected swap rates.

For readers with a desire for more tangible examples applied to example financing scenarios using actual European data from the past decade, please see Figure 1. To illustrate the basic principles for why derivatives are a valuable tool in a CRE financing, this tables track the effects of variable rate movements and swap rate movements on ICR, at two-year intervals over the seven-year terms of two hypothetical European financings, one in GBP and one in euros. The financings are assumed to be originated in September 2003, with NOI of 6 per cent of the initial property value in each scenario. Case 1 is for the quarterly GBP LIBOR index, whereas case 2 is for quarterly EURIBOR. To give further colour on the applicability of hedging on different types of loans, each case contrasts debt with a reasonably low loan-to-value (60 per cent) and 100 basis points margin with that of a more aggressive LTV (80 per cent) with a commensurately higher margin of 150 basis points. (See Figure 1).

---

[4]   This is measured through the Interest Cover Ratio (ICR) and managed by making hedging, in some form, a condition of such loans.

Figure 1: Why Hedge? Hedged and Unhedged ICR tests for CRE financings drawn September 2003

| Case 1: GBP 7-Year Debt based on 3-month GBP LIBOR<br><br>Type of Loan / Test Date: | 3-Month LIBOR | ICR at Prevailing LIBOR | Swap Rate to Maturity | ICR at Prevailing Swap Rate |
|---|---|---|---|---|
| 60% LTV, 100bps Margin / Sept 2003 | 3.69% | 2.13 | 4.75% | 1.74 |
| 60% LTV, 100bps Margin / Sept 2005 | 4.60% | 1.79 (-0.35) | 4.48% | 1.82 (+0.08) |
| 60% LTV, 100bps Margin / Sept 2007 | 6.82% | 1.28 (-0.85) | 5.72% | 1.49 (-0.25) |
| | | | | |
| 80% LTV, 150bps Margin / Sept 2003 | 3.69% | 1.45 | 4.75% | 1.20 |
| 80% LTV, 150bps Margin / Sept 2005 | 4.60% | 1.23 (-0.22) | 4.48% | 1.25 (+0.05) |
| 80% LTV, 150bps Margin / Sept 2007 | 6.82% | 0.90 (-0.54) | 5.72% | 1.04 (-0.16) |

| Case 2: EUR 7-Year Debt based on 3-month EURIBOR<br><br>Type of Loan / Test Date: | 3-Month EURIBOR | ICR at Prevailing EURIBOR | Swap Rate to Maturity | ICR at Prevailing Swap Rate |
|---|---|---|---|---|
| 60% LTV, 100bps Margin / Sept 2003 | 2.15% | 3.17 | 2.80% | 2.63 |
| 60% LTV, 100bps Margin / Sept 2005 | 2.14% | 3.18 (+0.01) | 2.67% | 2.72 (+0.09) |
| 60% LTV, 100bps Margin / Sept 2007 | 4.72% | 1.75 (-1.43) | 4.28% | 1.89 (-0.74) |
| | | | | |
| 80% LTV, 150bps Margin / Sept 2003 | 2.15% | 2.05 | 2.80% | 1.74 |
| 80% LTV, 150bps Margin / Sept 2005 | 2.14% | 2.06 (+0.01) | 2.67% | 1.80 (+0.05) |
| 80% LTV, 150bps Margin / Sept 2007 | 4.72% | 1.21 (-0.85) | 4.28% | 1.30 (-0.45) |

To read the table, start at the top row of each loan for its "test date" of 2003. The ICR test is first calculated using the variable rate as the interest assumption (second column) and then using the prevailing swap rate (fourth column.) The rows below show how the unhedged ICR would develop over time as variable rates changed (second column) and how prevailing swap rates would lead to different ICR results, if an unhedged borrower chose to hedge at the 2005 and 2007 test dates. In short, the degradation in ICR would have been substantial over this time horizon for unhedged borrowers.

The above illustration contains actual market data, not worst-case theoretical possibilities. Clearly, loan underwriting assumptions can vary due to the institution making the investment, but only a very brave investor or lender would underwrite the entire term of a variable-rate loan using the initial variable rate during the underwriting phase.[5] The impetus for hedging variable-rate loans is clearly to decrease uncertainty for a system in which NOI from property rent is not expected to ratchet up and down with interest rate cycles. The obvious uncertainty is whether variable rates will rise detrimentally over time, relative to NOI. For lenders who may be tempted to let borrowers float until rates rise until a certain level, the less

---

[5] Typically, lenders and borrowers will use the market swap rate to the full loan term plus a conservative buffer as a proxy for the ex-margin interest rate assumption, not the short-term variable rate.

obvious uncertainty is whether or not hedging after variable rates have risen will result in ICR results in line with those that influenced the original loan pricing. As Figure 1 shows, it could be that a borrower—by hedging at the end of the fourth year—locks in a materially worse interest cover ratio for the final three-year period of the loan term.

## 8.2. Legacy transactions: How and why derivatives exacerbated *other* property sector problems

This section will now consider the costs associated with derivatives used for hedging in CRE financings. There are a variety of important figures to absorb as set out in Figure 2. Examining these costs in detail, on a backward-looking basis, illustrates the magnitude of the ramifications of any hedging decision made at the loan's inception. The further detail in Figures 3 and 4, also help reveal some of the factors that led to such hedging decisions.

The blessing and the curse of derivatives is that they can do just about anything their users want; they can resemble loans or disaster insurance policies depending on the product and asset class or market. Even within fairly common or "vanilla" interest rate derivatives for CRE debt, there are numerous ways to analyse derivatives, especially since vanilla strategies can be combined fairly easily into limitless permutations, in order to tailor the interest rate profile to the financial characteristics of the underlying property investment. However, the flexibility of an OTC derivative may result in a strong temptation to try to achieve more than just interest rate risk management. Whilst using the business plan to build the hedging strategy and to drive hedging decisions, it is important that the full cost implications of any potential derivative instrument over the full term of the loan are clear to the purchaser.

An important question to consider is which derivatives-related costs feed into any finance strategy framework. There are four separate categories over the term of a property loan: initial costs (payments due at closing), on-going costs (payments made on or about interest payment dates), opportunity costs (unrealised losses, if any, at any point prior to an actual exit),[6] and exit costs (payments due upon early termination or on the maturity date of the loan, whichever comes first).[7] The first and second

---

[6] The terminology is intended to simplify a rather complex construct: the mark-to-market value of a derivative instrument during the loan term. As will be demonstrated later in this chapter, it is possible for a swap or other hedge to be a substantial liability during the loan term; this is not problematic unless the property investor is considering repaying the loan for any reason. These events typically trigger the payment of the hedge liability. This restricts opportunities for repayment such as refinancing or selling the property, and can thus be seen as a cost.

[7] Taking opportunity costs one step further, this terminology relates to crystallising the mark-to-market value of the derivative. It may only be applicable to a few remaining

categories are self-explanatory. The third is not, but it can be seen as another way of describing the mark-to-market valuation of the derivative; if out-of-the-money to the borrower, the borrower would have costs to settle the contract early. The category of opportunity costs—brought into sharp focus in recent years in many CRE financings—reflects the potential for unrealised derivative losses to paralyse workout or restructuring options on an asset. A large opportunity cost can scupper a property refinancing or make the option of an early sale unviable. The exit *costs* in the fourth category will be minimal or zero if the exit date is the loan maturity date and the derivative is coterminous with the loan; but they can be substantial otherwise.

These costs and the impact thereof are demonstrated in Figure 2.

### 8.2.1. *Overview*

Figure 2 shows three cases of actual market pricing (which does not include any loan margin) for a range of GBP-denominated derivatives used in various hedging strategies, and the derivatives-related costs in hindsight. The hypothetical variable-rate loans and derivatives in cases 3, 4 and 5 are assumed to commence on September 15 in three separate years—2003, 2005, and 2007, respectively.[8] This illustrates the scale of potential differences in the derivatives-related costs of loans and to give basic insights of how and why derivatives exacerbated other problems within CRE financings. It is not intended to suggest that these strategies were the most popular hedge strategies employed at any particular point in time, or that seven-year loans were the most popular variety on offer within the past decade.

The percentages show the ex-margin interest expense—hedged and unhedged—for a few sample hedging decisions. To the extent the seven-year period is not completed at the time of writing, the market forward rates complete the data. It should be clear that no one had a crystal ball at these times, so any decision-maker would have only had the information available at the time. In each case, the interest rate environment at inception was such that the swap rate was quite different than the prevailing floating rate LIBOR. In case 3, the swap rate was actually higher than LIBOR at inception but it would have given the most economically favourable seven-year result (3.97 per cent is lower than any other figure in the far right column). Again for case 3, the up-front costs of caps at 5 per cent and 6 per cent and the fact that LIBOR was fairly high at points during

---

interest periods on a hedge, or to several years, and the severity depends on the type of hedge and the difference between the hedge rate and the prevailing market rates. Some hedges have no exit costs (such as a cap with up-front payment) and all hedges which are coterminous with a loan will have no exit costs if the loan goes to term.

[8] The exit cost for the 2007 vintage seven-year swap is assumed to be zero as the mark-to-market valuation amortises to zero at the hedge maturity, which coincides with the maturity of the loan. See the upper right corner of Figure 3 to see the trend (although the data does not yet reach the zero line in the figure).

Figure 2: Derivative cost* comparison tables for hypothetical 7-year variable-rate interest-only loans (GBP)

| Case 3: September 2003<br><br>Derivative Strategy: | Initial<br>Cost | On-going<br>Costs (pa) | Opportunity<br>Costs | Exit Costs at<br>loan maturity | 7-year Hedged<br>Interest Cost<br>(pa) |
|---|---|---|---|---|---|
| Unhedged (LIBOR= 3.69%)** | - | 4.16% | - | - | 4.16% |
| 7-year Interest Rate Swap | - | 3.97% | 3.70% | - | 3.97% |
| 6% 7-year Interest Rate Cap | 1.30% | 4.11% | - | - | 4.30% |
| 5% 7-year Interest Rate Cap | 3.01% | 3.89% | - | - | 4.32% |
| 30-year Interest Rate Swap | - | 4.88% | 18.40% | 18.40% | 7.51% |
| 7-year Interest Rate Swap<br>with 23-year Extension<br>Option at 6% | 2.94% | 3.97% | 3.52% | - | 4.39% |

| Case 4: September 2005<br><br>Derivative Strategy: | Initial<br>Cost | On-going<br>Costs (pa) | Opportunity<br>Costs | Exit Costs at<br>loan maturity | 7-year Hedged<br>Interest Cost<br>(pa)*** |
|---|---|---|---|---|---|
| Unhedged (LIBOR = 4.60%) | - | 3.19% | - | - | 3.19% |
| 7-year Interest Rate Swap | - | 4.49% | 8.10% | - | 4.49% |
| 6% 7-year Interest Rate Cap | 0.46% | 3.14% | - | - | 3.21% |
| 5% 7-year Interest Rate Cap | 1.20% | 2.91% | - | - | 3.08% |
| 30-year Interest Rate Swap | - | 4.40% | 27.40% | 27.40% | 8.31% |
| 7-year Interest Rate Swap<br>with 23-year Extension<br>Option at 6% | 1.60% | 4.49% | 7.74% | - | 4.72% |

| Case 5: September 2007<br><br>Derivative Strategy: | Initial<br>Cost | On-going<br>Costs (pa) | Opportunity<br>Costs | Exit Costs at<br>loan maturity | 7-year Hedged<br>Interest Cost<br>(pa) |
|---|---|---|---|---|---|
| Unhedged (LIBOR = 6.82%) | - | 2.41% | - | - | 2.41% |
| 7-year Interest Rate Swap | - | 5.51% | 9.40% | - | 5.51% |
| 6% 7-year Interest Rate Cap | 1.80% | 2.35% | - | - | 2.60% |
| 5% 7-year Interest Rate Cap | 4.60% | 2.25% | - | - | 2.90% |
| 30-year Interest Rate Swap | - | 4.86% | 28.20% | 28.20% | 8.89% |
| 7-year Interest Rate Swap<br>with 23-year Extension<br>Option at 6% | 1.15% | 5.51% | 8.05% | - | 5.67% |

* Source: Chatham Financial. It should be noted that these indicative costs do not reflect any applicable credit or transaction charges as these are highly negotiable and specific to each transaction.

** Initial rate at the start date of the hedge.

*** For cases 4 and 5 these are estimated using market forward rates when calculated prior to loan maturity date.

the seven-year term meant that on average, the cap strategies were more expensive than a swap or an unhedged strategy. For each of the three cases, the only hedging strategy with exit costs is the 30-year swap; this cost is blended into the seven-year result for easy comparison.

For cases 4 and 5, the up-front costs of the caps would have been well worth paying, given that LIBOR trended lower and lower during the seven-year term. Also note that in cases 4 and 5, the 30-year swap rate at inception is below the seven-year swap rate and well below LIBOR. Case 5 shows us the paralytic effect of the opportunity cost of a 30-year swap, sitting at an eye-watering 28.2 per cent of notional value. The costs at exit are zero for the strategies that are coterminous with the loan. As anyone hearing the term "long-dated swap" post-financial crisis has observed, this is not the case with the swaps with maturities longer than the term of the loan. Finally, the seven-year Hedged Interest Cost (pa) shows us that in case 3, the best hedged outcome would have been to swap, in cases 4 and 5, the best hedged outcome would have been a 5 per cent and 6 per cent cap, respectively.

### 8.2.2. *Notes on derivative strategy column*

For comparison, each case begins with an unhedged strategy, with the initial three-month LIBOR index rate shown for further reference. Next appears the seven-year vanilla swap —a strategy which synthetically fixes the interest rate on a variable-rate loan—and is also considered a "base case" market assumption of the average LIBOR over the term. The next two strategies below the swap are also seven years in term, but they are pure caps on LIBOR paid by up-front cash with no further obligations from the borrower. The lower cap strike rate is dearer in each case, given it would provide greater protection, or higher potential future pay-outs to the borrower over the seven-year term. The 30-year swap is about the longest example of a "long-dated swap" that could appear as a hedging alternative in certain CRE loans, given market practices in the last decade. These were typically justified by lenders if the properties financed contained long-dated leases, but counter-examples do exist. It is worth considering the exit costs for this strategy, which are also shown graphically below, relative to coterminous swaps and other long-dated swaps. The strategy, at the bottom of the list, is that of an otherwise vanilla seven-year swap, but with an option purchased up-front, giving the borrower the right to enter into a swap at 6 per cent for a further 23 years (to a total of 30 years) at the end of the seventh year. The rationale for including this strategy in these tables is considered below.

### 8.2.3. *Notes on initial costs*

Any up-front premium for a hedge strategy is expressed as a percentage of the loan amount. For each of the three cases, this column shows the potentially stark contrast in up-front costs associated with two of the most commonly elected hedging strategies, swaps and caps. In considering the decisions of those making hedging decisions that, may, with hindsight, be seen as preposterous, it should be recalled that any initial costs would be paid out of equity capital, which is very dear to many property investors and therefore the amount expended initially has a large bearing on future return metrics. When the rate achievable by an interest rate swap, at no up-front cost, is well below the strike rate of a cap with a remotely palatable premium, it is natural to put an additional emphasis on the premium. Faced with this decision, it could "feel like" this initial cost amount would be wasted, even though intellectually one can understand that rates could fall and the amount paid on the cap will be more than recuperated via lower on-going interest costs.

### 8.2.4. Notes on on-going costs

Each sum is shown in a per annum rate, and is averaged where appropriate (for unhedged and capped strategies). This is the swap rate for a swap, and the average three-month LIBOR setting at loan reset dates for the cap strategy, after accounting for any cap payments received under that hedge. As a result, a 5 per cent cap contained lower on-going costs than a 6 per cent cap in each of these cases. Had the analysis included cases with 8 per cent and 7 per cent caps, on-going costs for these strategies would have been identical because LIBOR did not rise above 7 per cent during the analysed period. Last, both seven-year swaps have the same *on-going costs* because the swaps are identical; had the hypothetical borrower chosen to embed the option premium into the swap rate, the *on-going costs* would have differed (which is effectively expressed in the right-hand column).

### 8.2.5. Notes on opportunity costs

Each figure shown is the maximum negative mark-to-market valuation of the derivative occurring during the term of the seven-year financing, expressed as a percentage of the loan amount. This is the point at which the derivative was the most "under water," or contained the highest unrealised liability from the borrower's perspective. Again, this is described as an opportunity cost since at whatever moment in time a borrower might wish to make a decision (such as to sell the property and repay the loan, restructure, etc.) the obligation to settle the derivative contract at that point in time could impede such a decision. Note the difference in opportunity costs for a variety of swap tenors hypothetically executed in September 2007 over a seven-year term, as set out in Figure 3 below.

It should be noted that whilst mark-to-market valuations of swaps will (from the perspective of a borrower paying a fixed rate under the hedge) be liabilities to the borrower in times of declining interest rates, it is also possible for a swap to be an asset if the opposite were true. This could arise if a period of relatively high inflation (or inflation expectations) emerged following the extremely low interest rate environment at the time of writing. The potential issues that arise from a swap being an unrealised asset to a borrower are discussed in para 8.3.1 below.

Figure 3: Further Detail on Opportunity Costs

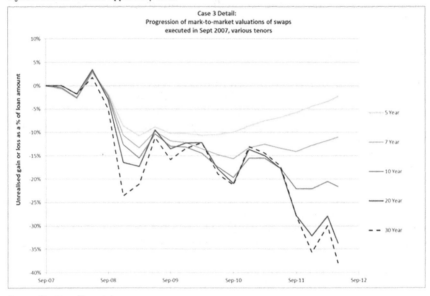

Source: Chatham Financial

### 8.2.6.  Notes on exit costs at loan maturity

Each sum in this column reflects the derivative settlement costs, assuming an exit from the swap on the loan maturity date. That is, only "overhanging" derivatives such as a long-dated swap would result in this category of costs in each case. A possible variation to the cap strategies, one in which the premium is deferred until the loan maturity date, would be an exception. For long-dated swaps, the magnitude of such costs or benefits, depends wholly on market interest rate levels (LIBOR plus expectations of LIBOR in the future, or forward LIBOR rates) at the relevant swap early exit date.

### 8.2.7  Notes on seven-year hedged interest costs

Each sum reflects the actual average per annum costs of LIBOR interest payments plus (or minus) any net hedge payments (or receipts) and other costs over the seven-year term of the loan, undiscounted. This can be seen as a simplistic measure of the effective ex-margin rate of interest delivered by the strategy chosen.

With the benefit of hindsight, taking interest rate risk would *not* have devastated the borrowers in these example financings. Such a strategy would not have given the best overall interest costs across the board, but it was fairly close. For the seven-year hedged interest costs, case 5 gives a particularly stark contrast between interest expense under a "base case" vanilla swap and that of a fairly "loose case" hedging strategy of a 6 per cent cap (5.51 per cent *v* 2.60 per cent), but the rest of the results are inside this spread, with the exception of the long-dated swap. It was somewhat rare for a cap strategy such as this to be chosen prior to the financial crisis, since there was no general expectation LIBOR would actually fall from its prevailing (high) levels in a material manner.[9] By contrast, a swap strategy involved no up-front costs and "locked in a gain" relative to LIBOR at the time. The interest rate curve creating this paradoxical gain was inverted, not due to market expectations that LIBOR would fall substantially over time, but because demand for long-dated gilts tended to outstrip supply. This phenomenon raised prices for those gilts and thus lowered yields on the "long end" of the curve.

### 8.2.8   Conclusions

It is hard to focus on any other figures besides the exit costs of the long-dated swaps, once all the information is arranged in these categories. Even if averaged over the seven-year term of the loan, the simplistic all-in interest cost is above 7 per cent in each case, which was almost twice that of the vanilla swap rate. Recall that these figures do not include any loan margins, as well!

At the risk of belabouring an important point about the state of mind of some borrowers at the time, electing a swap strategy, surely gave a sense of instant gratification to be locking in a better hedged rate than the prevailing LIBOR. For long-dated swaps, the hedged rate could have been materially lower than LIBOR. For those faced with such a possibility, it may not have felt like a risky decision, given that a long-dated swap was, in theory, hedging refinancing risk. That is, if interest rates rose it would protect the owner from a corresponding reduction in asset value, due to higher discounting of the future cash flows on the property. However, the opposite effect is felt if interest rates fall. The consequences of either would be present at the end of the loan, regardless of whether or not the investor continued to be the owner. Ironically, any such decision thus may have brought with it a sense of prudence, since it was addressing several risks at once

Yet each of the assumptions underlying the sense of prudence was flawed, as we now know with the benefit of hindsight.[10] One objective way to

---

[9]   This is in reference to a single hedging strategy applicable to an entire loan term. For borrowers with business plans well shorter than the loan term, it was fairly common for them to select a swap for the "front end" of the loan and a cap on the "back end." The cost of the cap could be blended into the swap rate to avoid the additional equity typically required for the cap premium if paid up-front.

[10]   The first flawed assumption was that property values would tend to rise as interest rates fell. The second flawed assumption was that any "break costs" on a derivative could be

describe the rationale for these decisions (again, in hindsight), is to try to quantify how tempting the long-dated swap strategy actually was over time, as demonstrated in Figure 4.

Figure 4: The "Temptation" Spread

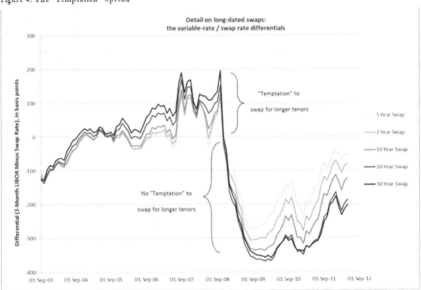

Source: Chatham Financial

Figure 4 depicts a way of looking at how inverted the swap curve has been over the past decade. For any date on which the lines representing various tenors of interest rate swaps are above the "0" differential, the curve was inverted. "Temptation" was present because long-dated swaps had lower rates than LIBOR, and in most cases much lower rates than other tenors of swaps as well. The magnitude peaked at just below 200 basis points in late 2007, but it averaged nearly 100 basis points for 30-year swaps from late 2006 to late 2008.

One last point on refinancing risk is that if this had really been a major concern, one would have probably observed numerous instances of borrowers purchasing options to extend their coterminous swaps during the period of maximum temptation. The justification would have been because the depressed "long end" of the yield curve made such options quite far "out of the money" and thus reasonably affordable at strike rates

---

efficiently embedded or "rolled" into a new hedge. The third flawed assumption is that credit markets would permit similar levels of gearing at reasonably similar margin levels at the time of any exit or refinancing.

186

similar to medium-term average LIBOR and swap rates at the time of roughly 6 per cent. Comparing the far right columns in Figure 2, one can see that the additional expense for this refinancing risk was available to borrowers at a premium ranging from only 1.15 per cent to 2.94 per cent if paid up-front or adding 16–42 basis points to net interest expense if averaged over the seven-year term of the loans.[11] Partially because of the high cost of equity capital required to fund such options, but mostly because refinancing risk was not a genuine concern, these transactions did not take place to any large degree.

## 8.3. Lessons learnt and the winds of change: Hedging and derivatives in future CRE transactions

The recipe of mixing over-optimistic property investors with over-aggressive lenders was not a new one when the property bubble burst in the late 2000s in many European CRE markets. The derivatives involved certainly magnified the bad combinations in some cases, so it was conceivable that the CRE finance market would have relegated derivatives out of CRE financings in a hurry. However, as stated above, the market's resilience has kept derivatives strategies front and centre in deals, albeit with a more limited role. As financial institutions' regulatory capital requirements for debt and derivatives become stricter,[12] funding costs have also risen such that some choices formerly available to CRE borrowers and lenders are no longer practical. But the market has not changed structurally, at least for the moment. For example, one can still borrow from a bank on a floating basis and hedge with a swap. Or, one can still borrow from an insurer with similar fixed-rate terms and make-whole provisions as in the past, should that be preferable. At the extreme, it is still possible for a borrower to secure a five-year 85 per cent LTV bank loan and hedge it with a 30-year swap. There is no viable market for this activity at present, because the costs have risen substantially. But if a borrower were willing to pay the premium it would take to make such a deal happen, it could probably do so. There is a trickle of CMBS transactions flowing,[13] to the delight of many observers hoping for a renaissance in capital markets transactions, although these few instances are quite different flavours than the CMBS of the past.

A version of self-regulation has thus unfolded at the time of writing. Just as 90 per cent LTV rates for commercial property loans are no longer available, some practices that led to the worst examples of how not to manage interest rate risk with derivatives have been summarily dismissed by stakeholders

---

[11] Figure 2 assumes the option premium is paid up-front and thus does not contribute to on-going costs, but the premium is divided by seven when calculating the seven-year hedged interest cost (pa) in the far right column.

[12] See further Ch.16.

[13] See Chs 1, 2, 4 and 20.

most directly involved. A few of these are detailed below to give readers a sense of the impact of derivatives on the future of CRE finance. More national and supranational forms of regulation are underway as well. Where derivatives markets meet debt markets, the two most salient regulatory thrusts are the increased regulatory capital requirements for financial institutions (Basel II/III, Solvency II) and the mandatory use of clearing houses for OTC derivatives by Alternative Investment Fund Managers (AIFM).[14]

Higher regulatory capital requirements are already being phased in on debt as well as derivatives transactions by most financial institutions[15] operating in Europe, and it is fairly intuitive that this extra capital buffer directly increases the cost of holding loan assets on balance sheet, versus 2007. Any higher funding cost a bank or other lender might have relative to its funding regime in the past is evident in the loan margins one witnesses today. Likewise, any financial institution entering into a derivative contract with a client such as a borrower (whether or not it is the affiliate of the lender) will need to set aside higher capital buffers. These costs are specific to the derivatives; they would not have the same risk weightings as their underlying loans, except if by coincidence. The risk weightings vary by derivative as well, meaning that a certain hedging strategies that are more credit intensive than others (such as swaps relative to caps) should bring relatively higher regulatory capital charges, all things being equal.

In this regard, only one meaningful trend has appeared. For major lending banks with derivatives desks—including arrangers of CMBS[16]—the regulatory capital regime change is a mixed blessing: it presents higher costs but an opportunity to package higher costs in a way that could suit their interests. True, borrowers who delve into the details of derivatives pricing could be disappointed to find higher charges than may have existed in the past. Yet many borrowers may not notice this detail until it is effectively too late to change funding sources, and only a minority would compare such costs in detail prior to making their debt type and lender decisions (although this would be advisable). Further, since regulatory capital charges are specific to each bank's internal controls and in any case do not need to be formally disclosed to the counterparty, the line between conservative regulatory capital assumptions and increased profit from the transaction

---

[14] See further Chs 12 and 16.

[15] There is a lively debate, at the time of writing, between competing financial institutions as to which group of banks are failing to adopt the Basel III requirements in order to meet short-term targets, at the expense of those who are following the guidance diligently. American, Swiss, French and German institutions have each taken turns of criticising each other.

[16] Although the vast majority of the lending risk may be offloaded to the capital markets via the securitisation process, the derivatives desk cannot easily replicate this feat. Therefore, unless they replace themselves in whole or in part with a suitable institution, the CMBS arranger's derivatives desk or third party hedge provider, as the case may be, can be expected to pass along to the borrower the full regulatory capital charge to which it is subjected at closing.

can be blurred. For other lenders such as insurers and debt funds, the pricing methodology is generally not as refined as that of bank lending or CMBS; as such, there are no noteworthy trends to report at the time of writing.

Rarely, if ever, are new financial regulations greeted with open arms by all market participants, but the prospect that CRE investors could be required to cash collateralise an interest rate swap on a variable-rate loan has been greeted with near-universal disbelief since the autumn of 2010 when the notion first appeared. This is the scenario potentially resulting from EMIR, if CRE borrowers (typically SPVs of entities that would otherwise be classified as "financial counterparties" under definitions within the AIFMD) are captured by the new regulations. The source of the consternation is that CRE finance hinges on the principle that a property or mortgage secures the debt capital providers, not cash or other liquid securities. Posting of initial cash margin plus daily cash margin, if needed, to a third party (a central clearing counterparty under the EMIR rules, not the lenders) against any unrealised losses on a hedge would compel the borrower or its sponsor to contribute additional cash to the deal to the extent the mark-to-market value of any derivatives changed for the worse. This poses a serious liquidity risk to the investor, which ironically would only arise due to a contract designed to reduce a real risk on the investment (interest rate risk).

The system for clearing would likely be quite strict, so any failure to uphold the margin obligations with the clearing house would lead to an automatic termination of the derivative contract by the relevant central clearing counterparty in the interest of counterparty protection. This would almost certainly violate the covenants of the financing and lead to a borrower default. At the time of writing, the EU regulatory process, still underway, may yet yield sufficiently vague language such that there is a tacit —but for political reasons, not an explicit—exemption for SPVs controlled by AIFMs. This would effectively permit the CRE sector continue to provide the status quo of variable-rate loans hedged with derivatives for SPV borrowers, should they elect to do so, for the foreseeable future.

Apart from those affected by regulatory changes, it is now worth considering what other practices within CRE finance have tended to be modified or discontinued with respect to derivatives. The paragraphs below continue with listing some of the lessons learnt and some of the questions faced by those who have been directly and indirectly involved in these examples post the financial crisis.

### 8.3.1. Ratings agencies[17]

Overall, a minority of balance sheet debt transactions in European CRE transactions involve issuer ratings. For CMBS transactions in Europe and elsewhere, however, ratings are a necessary ingredient. As well as performing other important functions in the securitisation process, ratings agencies necessarily concern themselves with some of the details of how any derivatives effectively insure against covenant breaches in their stress tests, as well as ensuring hedge counterparty viability of the term of the notes. At the time of writing, there are no substantive changes to ratings evaluation processes related to a further divergence between levels of market interest rates and CRE capitalisation rates, although this may feed into the ratings assigned by indirect means in transactions in 2013 and beyond. The primary lesson concerning derivatives and interest rate risk management, as evidenced by changes to ratings standards of the major ratings agencies, involves counterparty risk. This is the risk that the hedge provider (often, but not always, an affiliate of the arranger to a CMBS) is unable to perform its obligations throughout the life of the hedge contract for whatever reason (insolvency or otherwise).

As referred to above, if interest rates rose dramatically, the hedge providers would be the party with large (and uncontained) unrealised liabilities, and the borrower would be dependent on the hedge provider's ability to maintain the hedge in all circumstances. To protect against this potential non-performance risk, in light of the destabilising events related to the near-failures of Bear Stearns and Merrill Lynch and the failure of Lehman Brothers as hedge providers in rated deals, ratings agencies have adopted much more rigorous standards. These feed their way into finance documents as downgrade provisions or "ratings events" applicable to the borrower's or issuer's hedge counterparty.

The changes set out above are welcome in principle. If interest rates were to rise dramatically post-closing, any interest rate derivatives taken out by the borrower would contain substantial value. This value contained in the hedge instrument (regardless of hedge strategy chosen) could evaporate if the hedge provider to CMBS transactions were to fail. Yet some questions remain, primarily involving the costs of protecting the issuer (and ultimately the bond investors) against such an evaporation of value. Since there is no market for this type of insurance, arrangers will struggle to provide the level of transparency and consistency, demanded by would-be borrowers, who bear the costs of the insurance directly via higher spreads on their swaps or higher premiums on caps.

On that point, should the cost of iron-clad derivatives counterparty insurance be borne by the borrower? How iron-clad is it, too, given that banks may be forced to ignore the collateralisation or counterparty

---

[17]  See further Ch.11 for a discussion of rating agencies and their role in the market.

replacement terms if the banking sector goes into full panic mode? If bearing the (potentially substantial, i.e. double-digit number of basis points) cost, should the borrower expect a competitive process to ensure he is not limited to the arranging bank as hedge provider, when other counterparties could meet the strict ratings requirements more easily and at lower cost? What calculations will the arranging bank use to arrive at charges related to downgrade provisions? How likely is it that an arranger's cost indication may change between signing a term sheet and closing, and what is the recourse if these costs are excessive in the eventual opinion of the prospective borrower? Will CMBS arrangers, without the highest of ratings, effectively be compelled to introduce highly-rated third party hedge providers to the CMBS arrangement and underwriting process in order to ensure the issuance can have an AAA-rated tranche? If so, what ranking will a hedge provider require in order to underwrite the risk of a swap?

### 8.3.2. Lenders

For brevity, this broad category is limited to commercial and/or investment banks with balance sheet or syndicated CRE lending platforms, both of which have played a major role in European CRE debt finance over the last two decades. For new CRE lending operations, not much has changed, apart from what has been mentioned above, concerning regulatory capital charges. Relatively routine adjustments to generally accepted terms within the standardised derivatives documentation (i.e. transaction confirmations and Schedules to the ISDA Master Agreement, not intercreditor agreements) have arisen in response to events like the bankruptcy of Lehman Brothers.

The material changes in recent years have been largely confined to the realm of pricing: of credit risk; of the increased cost of meeting regulatory capital requirements; and of determining the settlement amounts payable on early termination of the derivative, in each case as applicable. There is no "right answer" for what a credit charge should be, but there has been rather broad acknowledgment that when interest rate levels were higher, most CRE lenders priced counterparty credit risk fairly aggressively, for the magnitude of risk they were actually taking. It is likely that their credit models did not give a material probability to interest rate levels and asset values falling in tandem. With respect to determining the proper mark-to-market settlement amounts, another factor is responsible: the bank funding market has migrated away from LIBOR/EURIBOR. These inter-bank lending rates are no longer used as much since most banks' short-term wholesale funding models proved deeply flawed in the first phases of the financial crisis and interbank lending at such rates has not always been available.[18] Today, banks fund themselves using either longer-term funding

---

[18] The manipulation of LIBOR and other inter-bank published lending rates erupted as a scandal in 2012, but the inter-bank lending that serves as the foundation for LIBOR submissions all but ceased in the aftermath of Lehman Brothers' 2008 bankruptcy (as did other short-term funding sources for banks). The inter-bank lending exception is overnight

or using extremely short-term inter-bank loans, typically overnight (with rates such as SONIA and EONIA, which are well lower than LIBOR and EURIBOR levels).

Since LIBOR and EURIBOR are thus artificially high due to inter-bank mistrust, borrowers with fixed-rate swaps on their books should, in theory, benefit from these short-term rates' impact on the replacement rate used to calculate the mark-to-market valuation of the swap. Perversely, they do not. Any benefit of a slightly higher LIBOR/EURIBOR curve is eroded by lower discounting due to the lower rates of the SONIA or EONIA curves.

For restructuring situations, two main themes have emerged. The first is that lenders in some cases have found it necessary to forgive certain portions of borrower liabilities as part of the restructuring, but any write-downs are confined to the debt. This necessitates a partial termination of the associated derivatives so that the notional amount on the hedges matches the new, lower debt quantum. The seemingly simpler solution would be to write down both the debt and the derivatives, but this is not the case for reasons explained below. Also, if a CMBS arranger holds none of the notes, its derivatives desk will be isolated in any potential restructuring scenario. The second is that lenders' derivative desks have progressively applied hefty funding charges wherever possible. These cannot be levied retroactively without some event (termination or amendment) involving the derivatives transactions. The result has been implied credit margins on the restructured derivatives well in excess of those of the restructured debt.

There is some logic to this, since most restructuring operations tend to defer payments that would otherwise be due to hedge counterparties and so by extending existing loans this should justifiably include some compensation to the hedge counterparty due to the time value of money concept alone. In practice, it is difficult to convince a borrower that extending a loan would require the full termination of the existing hedge(s), with any liability arising from the settlement costs, giving rise to funding charges plus new credit charges on the full term of the new hedge covering the longer maturity date. In such cases, the dynamics of the lender-borrower relationship tend to dictate the extent to which funding charges are applied. Borrowers with little negotiating leverage will typically pay higher funding charges than those with more favourable circumstances. The trend of sole legacy lenders bringing in multiple syndicate banks to participate in the restructured loan has not been helpful to borrowers' negotiating leverage, since it is generally considered "cleaner" if all new lenders are on equal footing with respect to loan amounts and hedge amounts. A legacy swap which could have been left mostly "as is" would require termination and reinstatement in order to put all new hedge providers on equal footing,

---

deposits, which carry less risk but do not serve as a very helpful benchmark variable rate. Note the Wheatley Report in teh Uk has recommended a complete overhaul of the way LIBOR is calculated.

despite the consequentially higher funding charges applicable to the derivative restructuring. The predictable result is a tendency for the economic terms of the "lowest common denominator" amongst the new bank group to prevail.

### 8.3.3. CMBS investors

This stakeholder group in CRE finance has experienced substantial economic degradation at the hands of derivatives, given that their assets ranked below the hedges in most creditor waterfalls within European CMBS structures. Other major failings detailed elsewhere in this book led bond investors to effectively vacate the European CMBS markets in droves,[19] but complaints related to derivatives have been rife. Near the top of the list is inadequate disclosure of the potential liabilities resulting from derivatives employed by borrowers (i.e. "hedge debt" ranking in priority to amounts due to the bond investors). Although not knowing the specific details of the derivatives in place when buying the notes was frustrating enough, it proved difficult for many bond investors to obtain adequate information later on, about what derivatives were in the structure, or what their valuation might be at any given point in time. If and when the granular details emerged, it was not the only bad news presented, given that the situation may have already spiralled out of control. For example, the *opportunity cost* of 28 per cent in Figure 2 in para.8.2 above, which, if realised as an *exit cost*, would rank directly ahead of a bond investor, would hardly have been welcome news.

With the benefit of hindsight, it is likely that a portion of CMBS investors would have stress-tested some of the hedging strategies employed within originations and applied a haircut to deals containing objectionable or questionable derivatives. It is worth repeating that although no structure would have been perfectly suitable for all stakeholders at the time of most of the CMBS activity in the mid-2000s, the concept of "hedge debt" as another way of describing the *opportunity cost* described earlier from the borrower's perspective, is, at the time of writing, etched firmly in bond investors' minds for the foreseeable future. Consequently, this group is unlikely to permit hedge liabilities to rank senior to the AAA notes in any future securitised transaction, without full disclosure of the terms of the hedge arrangements and these being appropriately reflected in the bond pricing. If hedge liabilities are to continue to rank senior (for reasons involving other topics like ratings agencies or regulatory changes), many market participants suggest that such liabilities are capped to a known amount. Simply put, "hedge debt" may have lost its diplomatic immunity for ever. Although the tangible ripple effect is that the credit charges for swaps are higher for the borrower if the hedge provider is pari passu

---

[19] See further Ch.1.

relative to super-senior, the cost difference should not itself be material enough to dissuade a borrower from choosing a swap if that is the preferred strategy.[20]

Looking to the future, would-be CMBS investors will have to continue to prioritise their needs so that the general formula for lending to CRE investors by the capital markets meets the needs of all parties and is sufficiently standardised to develop economies of scale. A consensus on avoiding opportunity costs of derivatives over a full seven-year term should be one of the top priorities of market participants. This may be appealing to a wide enough investor base so as to eventually achieve a certain level of liquidity in the primary and secondary markets, given it would increase certainty of yields and it could lead to simpler structures than those prevalent in floating-rate deals. Rather than tinkering with the old formula, this hypothetical scenario involves CMBS investors pushing to adopt a new one—albeit a formula that could closely resemble the fixed-rate portion of the US CMBS market.[21] The US fixed-rate CMBS market is very robust by any measure, and part of this robustness stems from its extremely investor-friendly prepayment terms. Ostensibly the loans are not pre-payable, but the documentation typically allows the borrower to exit as long as the bond investors are made whole using replacement collateral in the form of highly creditworthy fixed-income instruments such as US treasury bonds or agency securities. This process is called defeasance.

Migration to fixed-rate loans (whether CMBS or otherwise) would certainly obviate the need for derivatives, since pricing a fixed-rate loan over a chosen benchmark rate would bypass the swaps market, even if the benchmark happened to be a quoted swap rate for any reason. This hypothetical market development is not a prediction, but just one example supporting the idea that if, in 2013 and beyond, there is indeed sufficiently deep and consistent investor demand for trade-able CRE bonds in Europe, there is a way for the market to adapt.

### 8.3.4. CMBS arrangers

This category comprises banks which eventually (whether immediately or in a post-funding event) sell on to capital markets the debt used to fund CRE investments. In some respects this category blurred unhelpfully with other sources of CRE debt finance, as competition for debt capital in a

---

[20] The difference between a swap credit charge depends on more than just the ranking of the hedge provider in the waterfall of payments, but if moving from *senior* to the senior debt to pari passu, the increased cost is not likely to be a deal-breaker for most borrowers. Conversely, the costs associated with moving a hedge provider to a *junior* ranking might have that effect.

[21] Replicating the defeasance-based system used in the US fixed-rate CMBS market would not remove opportunity cost from the European CRE finance realm, but it would change its form and make certain aspects more complicated in the process. The costs and administrative burdens of defeasance can be materially higher than those of swaps.

frothy market intensified. The consequence is that their original roles as initial lender, CMBS arranger-originator, hedge provider and potentially servicer as well could dwindle down to only that of hedge provider in some cases. When a balance-sheet lender makes a poor loan and suffers a loss as a result of its underwriting, it can only point the finger at itself. Things are clearly different in the CMBS arranger space and although there are a lot of nuances and possible caveats, the lack of "skin in the game" by arrangers is often cited as one of the main reasons why the CMBS market has yet to fully reopen in Europe.[22]

If the parties to which the arranger sold the notes rank well behind its derivatives desk in underwater positions, the derivatives desk is in a conspicuous position of advantage and it is fairly easy to picture the awkwardness of the situation. Borrowers and CMBS investors alike—alongside the many other parties working on restructurings—would welcome any economic relief that derivatives providers could offer to a restructuring scenario.[23] One means for this to come about relates to the same regulatory changes causing loans and hedges to be more expensive. Banks need to hold a large capital buffer against assets and, since banks focus on return on capital, it is costly to face swap counterparties with a large mark-to-market valuation (a liability for the borrower) regardless of its ranking in the security waterfall. The "regulatory capital relief" the bank would achieve if the swap were terminated could be substantial. The valuation, as described in the first section (see Figure 2), can be quite large indeed, so even a modest percentage of the amount of regulatory capital held against the swap asset could be material to a bank. Irrespective of the continuing credit risk, in a potential restructuring scenario this factor makes the derivatives desk's most favourable economic outcome a termination of the derivative.

The larger question is about full or partial forgiveness. Alas, no derivatives amnesty has thus far hit the press, and the rationale surrounding forgiveness merits both a technical and common sense discussion. The short technical explanation is that derivatives are not treated like debt within financial institutions; their profit is effectively accrued at inception (not over time) and the risk is, almost always, fully hedged by an actively managed trading book. The end result is that the mark-to-market valuation of the derivative instrument is not able to be "written down" similar to an impaired loan, so from an accounting standpoint any "haircut" it offered to take on a derivative would be a new loss, not the recognition of a previous write-down. To put in much more practical terms, if the derivatives desk of a CMBS arranger set a precedent by taking a "haircut" on the derivatives for whatever reason, it would be difficult to contain the news and to prevent the proverbial long queue forming outside its doors.

---

[22] See further the detailed discussion in Ch.4.
[23] See Ch.20.

### 8.3.5.  Servicers and special servicers[24]

Clearly, borrowers and lenders of all varieties have had to manage the economic impact of derivatives within CRE transactions on their bottom lines. The impact of derivatives on the loan servicing community has been less direct, but in many respects just as substantial. As scrutiny of terms and covenants within CRE loans arose amid general market turmoil when the credit crisis changed into a full-blown financial crisis, the demand for information increased dramatically, especially when a deal passed into special servicing. These firms had to quickly move from having a basic knowledge of how a hedge works within a loan, to a much more detailed understanding of the theory. Servicers needed to be armed with granular information on the actual loans in their charge and any derivatives linked to those loans.

Starting with pure economics, this included knowing the current and past market valuations of the derivative(s) associated with a loan and what the valuation could be in various interest rate scenarios in the future. The information available on the loans made this process easier, in some cases, than in others. Moreover, they needed to learn the practical trading mechanics and documentation-driven rules governing potential full or partial derivative termination processes. As if this "baptism by fire" were not enough, servicers further needed to become well versed in the legal ramifications of acting, or failing to act, on the derivatives within the capital structure of a deal, which would typically entail complex linkages to the debt and in some cases, no clarity as to what the "correct" procedure should be, due to conflicting information within the documentation available. Although servicing groups affiliated with lenders had information advantages, such as easier access to derivative valuations and internal expertise on which to draw as needed, independent providers have closed the gap in subsequent years by relying on third-party valuation providers, hedging advisers and of course legal advisers, to augment their resource base.

### 8.3.6.  Borrowers

The most prevalent theme emerging from this stakeholder group is risk aversion, and the risk most intently averted has depended on the situation. In restructuring scenarios, aversion to liquidity risk largely trumped cost sensitivity and interest rate risk. Because of the high cost of equity capital or an aversion to contributing further equity at all, a "cashless" hedge restructuring was a double-edged sword. By and large, borrowers have taken the necessary steps to get the restructuring done, sometimes being resigned to their fate, as price-takers on the new hedge, alongside the new debt package on offer. To date, it has been relatively rare for borrowers to push hard for a particular strategy, rather than the one that was simplest or facilitated the deal most favourable for the lender or lenders.

---

[24]  See Chs 5, 6 and 7 for a detailed discussion of loan servicing.

In extension scenarios, there has been a greater emphasis on cash flow risks. Such risks typically entailed re-shaping interest costs over the new term, via the derivatives, to take advantage of lower interest rates such that the borrower would meet its financial covenants more securely from the date of the extension. Since many extensions took place well in advance of the original loan maturity date, borrowers could leave the existing hedge in place to its original term and add a follow-on hedge to the extended term, or they could "extend and blend" by terminating the existing hedge and rolling its termination costs into a single new (but off-market) hedge, covering the full term. The former was typically more efficient economically, whereas the latter could make more sense from a covenant standpoint, even if some double-charging occurred on the amended derivatives.

For new lending scenarios, the main theme among borrowers has been interest rate risk aversion. There is a bit of a schizophrenic aspect to this, however, which merits some explanation. It is not so much that borrowers are keen to capture upside benefit or "win" on their interest rate hedging decision. It is more defensive in nature: if interest rate movements can be seen to limit their options on the underlying business plan for the investment, borrowers are willing to pay a bit extra to remove this future interest rate risk. It is not as simple as stating that all borrowers are averse to swaps, willing to pay whatever it takes to purchase a full-flexible hedge such as a cap to meet their hedging requirements. This decision takes several extra steps and compromises, and is more thoughtful than a one-dimensional approach in the end.

The following is a more complete version of this decision-making process, which the authors have experienced in the wake of the financial crisis. A borrower has survived the gauntlet of challenges of the European CRE markets, some of which were due to plummeting interest rates. Naturally, the borrower will take that into account when making future decisions that concern interest rates, such as on a new loan for a new investment opportunity. Many of the borrower's CRE investment colleagues will have heard stories of transactions failing, as a result of particular hedging strategy choices, even if such colleagues did not directly experience such an event. The borrower will have heard that swap strategies caused many regrets in the market at large because they created unknown liabilities over the term of the loan, potentially limiting refinancing opportunities. The borrower is thus tempted to elect to pay the additional up-front cost for a cap. The deal would still meet the borrower's investment hurdles, even allowing for the additional equity required for a cap at a rate that would effectively guarantee the interest covenants would be satisfied.

However, the borrower knows that all markets ebb and flow, so could equally envision a scenario of regretting choosing a cap, when interest rates are historically low. Should interest rates happen to rise, this would lead to potentially much higher interest costs than with a swap, as a result of floating up with the rising rate in addition to the cap premium. After all, with interest rates being historically low it stands to reason that they could rise, perhaps substantially. At an impasse, the borrower will consider what tolerance the deal has for some additional costs, during certain phases of the investment. After about 42 months, the need for flexibility is highest. The borrower is therefore fine to swap the first 42 months, but thereafter would need a cap. The borrower learns that a cap for months 43–60 would be easily affordable, especially if the borrower were to pay for it, by increasing the front-end swap rate accordingly. The borrower did not invite complexity from the start, but it came after interrogating its sensitivity to potential costs over the investment term. This story encapsulates the main lesson learnt by borrowers at the time of writing. In short, borrowers have learned to analyse the hedging/derivative strategy decision considering the impact of their unrealised gains or losses on the hedge over the term of the loan.

## 8.4. Conclusion

Interest expense is a big line item in CRE investments, and managing it effectively over the life of an investment is in the interest (so to speak) of all parties. Market participants rightly focus a great deal of attention on the margin component of interest, but the other component (the base rate or LIBOR, depending on the type of loan) is also important, albeit for different reasons. Derivatives used to shape the non-margin component of interest expense have played an increasingly visible role in the past decade. Much recent attention to derivatives—namely, specific derivatives such as long-dated swaps—has been negative, of course. Although the role is changing for a variety of reasons highlighted in this Chapter, it is likely that derivatives will continue to play an important role within CRE financing packages in 2013 and beyond.

Due to the tension between risk management and cost management, designing and implementing the best means to mitigate interest rate risk in European CRE financings has been a balancing act for lenders and borrowers alike. Witness the restructuring challenges for many distressed situations involving derivatives (not just interest rate derivatives, but these are most prevalent), and it is clear that the balancing act continues well beyond the initial deal structuring and closing processes. Advisers, law firms and special servicers have played enormously important roles in rectifying certain inconsistencies concerning derivatives' structural aspects and documentation, as they have addressed harsh realities where derivative liabilities compounded other serious financial challenges at the property level. It has been a learning process for many parties around the proverbial table, and in some cases it has been a painful experience for all concerned. Increased awareness of the sensitivity of a loan to its accompanying derivatives transactions is a welcome side-effect of these tribulations.

This awareness will be useful as the CRE lending paradigm changes. The continuing distress witnessed in H2 2012, within the banking sector—European and global—is spawning new participants in the European CRE lending markets, and they will benefit from past experience. Whereas bank funding has been traditionally a mainstay in Europe, debt capital in the near- to medium-term is likely to increasingly come from private or sovereign debt funds, insurance companies, newer incarnations of CMBS such as CMBS 2.0,[25] private placements arranged by smaller specialist intermediaries, or other entities with the means to plug the "funding gap"[26] so readily cited in the media. The role of derivatives within these other types of CRE financings is not as well established, but it cannot be assumed away.

It is clear that a focus on managing interest expense will evolve and continue to play an importance part in this market. It is not clear which of the many changes underway will be lasting and which will be fleeting. One certainty is that emerging regulations will make this balancing act more complicated for new lenders and the old guard in the medium term with respect to the ways derivatives are selected and managed over the life of a CRE financing. Encouragingly, many stakeholders within CRE finance have launched a variety of efforts to avert previous mistakes and to embrace certain subtle changes to debt capital markets for the European CRE sector. Some of these involve derivatives: more lenders are restricting swap maturities to the loan maturity date; lenders and borrowers are increasing the specificity of acceptable hedge strategies at the term sheet stage; bond investors are pushing for the hedge provider to rank pari passu instead of super-senior; and all parties are paying much closer attention to the maximum liability that is possible under the hedging strategy. These are positive signs. Changes, a mix of both bold and subtle, are welcome. (See Figures 5 and 6).

---

[25] See Ch.4.
[26] See Ch.2.

Figure 5: LIBOR and Swap Rate History since 1999 (UK)

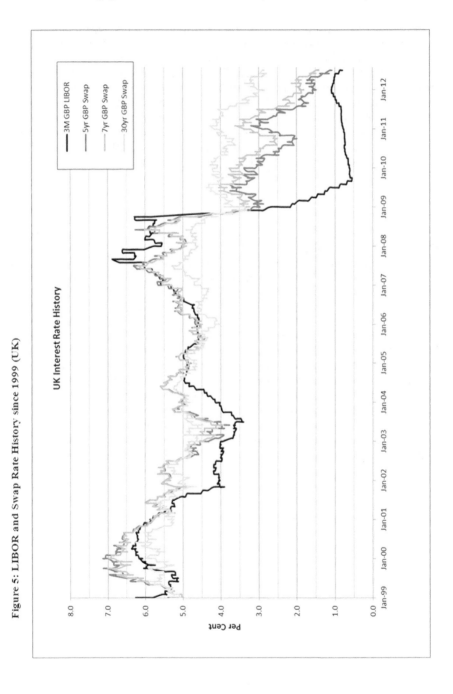

Figure 6: EURIBOR and Swap Rate History since 1999 (Euro)

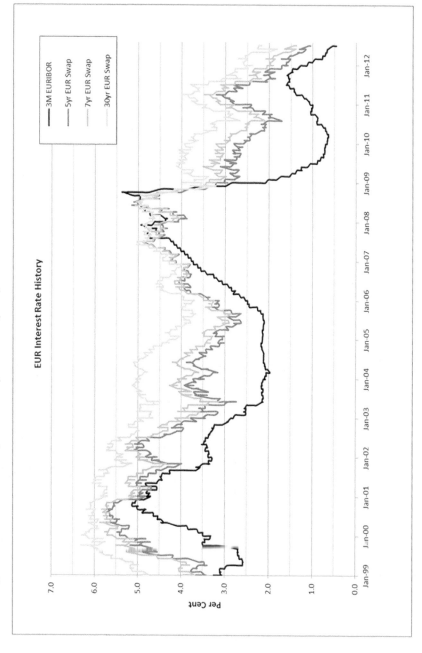

# Chapter 9

# The Economics of Commercial Lending and CMBS Origination

Christian Janssen,

Portfolio Manager, Real Estate Finance Fund, Renshaw Bay

## 9.1. Introduction

This Chapter sets out to analyse the economics of commercial real estate (CRE) lending and CMBS origination. Given the dramatic changes that have taken place since 2007, the Chapter will, similar to Ch.1, look at two periods of time, the decade from 1998 to 2007 and the period from 2007 to date in an attempt to discern what might await the CRE finance industry in the period 2013 and beyond. The aim will be to understand the drivers and the economic conditions of the relatively successful golden era of 1998 to 2007, the structural and secular changes that have surfaced since the financial crisis and how those changes have affected the CRE finance industry. With these fundamental data points and in order to avoid any significant repetition and overlap of topics in other Chapters of this book, this Chapter will explore how different lenders, portfolio lenders as well as debt capital markets oriented lenders, operated their businesses. It will also consider the economics of commercial lending and CMBS origination, how the competitive CRE lending landscape has changed during these periods and might continue evolving, and what types of lenders will be active in 2013 and beyond.

## 9.2. 1998–2007

The decade of 1998 to 2007 proved to be a successful time for direct and indirect CRE investments. The fundamental conditions in this period of time, the non-inflationary consistent expansion (nice) period, provided for an attractive environment for CRE lenders. Calm and steady economic growth (see Figure 1), relative interest rate stability (see Figures 2 and 3) and increasing CRE values were ideal conditions for CRE lenders.

Figure 1. UK GDP Growth – Year-on-Year

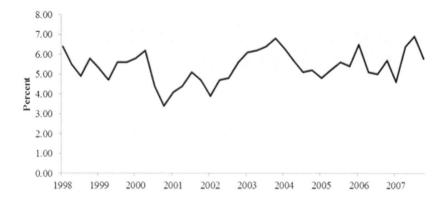

Source: Office of National Statistics

Figure 2. 5 Year GBP Swap Rates

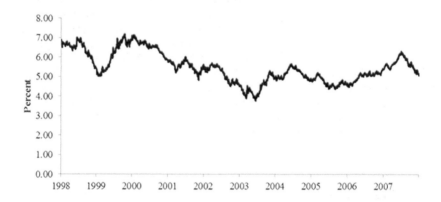

Source: Bloomberg

### 9.2.1. *Portfolio lenders*

As highlighted in Ch.1, in the early 1990s, the CRE finance market was comprised mostly of commercial and specialist mortgage banks, and insurance companies. But over the years, banks started increasing their market share, until in the late 1990s, they had a virtual monopoly in the CRE financing market. This transition was driven by their increasing

Figure 3. IPD Total Return Index and IPD Capital Growth Index

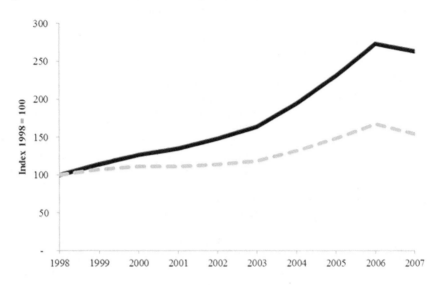

Source: IPD (Investment Property Databank)

appetite for CRE debt and, for the traditional commercial lenders, the increasing focus in financing their CRE portfolios with cheap and abundant debt. For the purpose of this analysis, this Chapter will focus on the two dominant funding strategies for portfolio lenders. The specialist mortgage lenders, the main group of them being the German mortgage banks, relied heavily on the issuance of covered bonds. This provided a stable, cheap and long-term funding strategy that matched their assets and liabilities and was well suited for the purpose.[1] Given the leverage restrictions and overcollat-eralisation requirements for *Pfandbrief* issuance, only 65 to 80 per cent, depending on the quality and leverage of the loans, of their mortgage loan book balance was financed this way. That meant that a significant amount of unsecured corporate debt, in addition to some degree of equity capital, was required to finance the remaining part of their balance sheet. However, corporate debt, in the form of unsecured recourse bonds and loans, was also available at attractive levels. The tight pricing of this debt was influenced, especially for German Landesbanken until the mid-2000s, by the explicit government guarantees and the consequent high corporate ratings and, overall, by what has been identified as the implicit backing of banks by their respective national governments. The other group of portfolio lenders

---

[1]    See further Ch.2.

were the traditional commercial banks. Their financing structure relied less on dedicated long-term secured debt, but rather on customer deposits and cheap unsecured short term debt. While it has always been the role of the banking sector to be the system to intermediate short term liabilities to medium and long-term assets, the increasing reliance on ever shorter financing was leading, in the mid 2000's, to some significant imbalances.

After the Russian debt crisis and the bursting of the dot-com bubble, from the early 2000s until 2007 the world was awash with liquidity. The over-reliance on cheap and plentiful debt, combined with the pervasive view that CRE was a safe and steady asset that rarely fell in value, led to the proliferation of business models that were very highly levered.[2] Commercial and specialist mortgage banks were operating with leverage ratios that often exceeded 20 and 30 times their equity base. Specialist mortgage banks were financing themselves with a term structure that more closely matched the maturity profile of their assets, whilst commercial banks were increasingly financing themselves on short commercial paper.

The business model of CRE lending is simple and straightforward. Lenders make loans that earn interest and fees that exceed the lender's cost of capital. Of course, this capital is comprised of equity and different types of debt and an easy way to increase the ROE is increasing the corporate balance sheet leverage. There were three factors that facilitated and encouraged and made it almost inevitable that banks would actively engage in such behaviour. First, the cost of debt was cheap: short-term debt for many banks, be it overnight borrowing or short-term corporate paper, was close to LIBOR/EURIBOR flat, covered bonds were priced at swaps plus a few basis points (bps), and even medium-term unsecured corporate debt was being priced only slightly wider. Secondly, the supply of debt was readily available in a seemingly indiscriminate manner. Thirdly, the regulatory framework either allowed such high degree of leverage, or, very often the banks manipulated, arbitraged or structured their way around higher regulatory requirements. There might be a fourth factor that should not be forgotten. While bankers might have been over-enthusiastic in their approach to the CRE finance business, the fault cannot be placed just on their shoulders. Rating agencies and regulators failed to identify or act on the fragility of the business model. However, banks were only able to increase their cheap leverage because investors were willing to provide them with abundant capital, with little or no restraints or controls. And, of course, these practices were, at least for a period of time, successful as equity returns increased and so did compensation packages.

Equally relevant was the fact that, in large commercial banks, the process of measuring risk and allocating the appropriate cost of capital to different activities within the banks was a highly unscientific and arbitrary process. As has been seen in the aftermath of the credit crisis, many banks'

---

[2]  See Ch.1.

information systems were so flawed and lacking that they did not know what loans, and therefore risk, they had on their balance sheet. In addition, the risk model of many banks was not suited for appropriate measurements of risk, let alone stress testing their portfolios. Poor models, lack of detailed and updated data, weak risk controls and an overoptimistic assessment of their underwriting and credit capabilities led to poor and flawed credit and risk decisions. In many instances this led to an under-allocation of capital to their CRE financing business, with the unintended consequence that CRE finance, along with certain other businesses within banks, benefitted from internal subsidies and misallocation of capital costs.

This meant that the economic capital being used for CRE lending was attracting very high returns. When a bank's debt is priced cheaply (See Figure 4 below, particularly the period from 2001 until 2007) and its financing costs are allocated evenly across business lines, without regard to the level of risk of business, there are few limitations to the leverage ratio that can and will be used. Not unsurprisingly, this encouraged banks to increase their origination and holdings of CRE debt, which in turn increased the availability of debt for CRE investors, who pushed up CRE values and in turn increased the level of transactions in the market. If a bank can finance itself at LIBOR +10 bps and has a leverage ratio of 25x, then a loan priced at LIBOR +70 bps still produces an ROE of 15+%.

Figure 4. Sample of European Banks' Five Year CDS Spreads

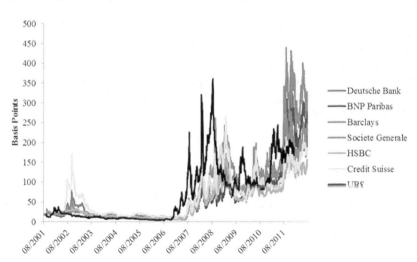

Source: Bloomberg.

When the CRE and debt fundamentals did not support CRE values or debt quantum being secured on the properties, some of the more aggressive lenders started to underwrite future value and rental growth based on exceedingly optimistic forecasts and business plans. Some lenders also engaged in a number of financial engineering strategies and also used longer dated swaps to capitalise on the inverted yield curve present at that time. These activities often went side-by-side with a lowering of underwriting, due diligence and credit standards.

While CRE borrowers are generally considered experienced professional investors, some of the risks they accepted—and sometimes demanded—by agreeing to higher leverage and complex hedging strategies, they did with the tacit encouragement of the banks.[3] Only a few banks were not caught up in the "irrational exuberance", a term coined a decade earlier but certainly applicable in the circumstances of the mid 2000s. Given the attractiveness of the CRE finance it was only natural that banks would try to increase their origination and holding volumes. With large transaction sizes that could be executed with a relatively small number of staff, the CRE finance market was well suited to be a volume-based business.

The mispricing, and probably also the misunderstanding of risk in CRE debt market, reached its peak in the first half of 2007. While there were some initial signs that leverage, structuring, liquidity and pricing had been pushed to the limit, firms continued and increased the frantic pace of origination in 2007.

But while this seemed a veritable virtuous circle, the fundamentals of the CRE market were not keeping pace with the debt and liquidity fuelled CRE prices. In 2008, when the liquidity in the debt market started being reduced, the upward trend in property prices started reversing, and the end of the highly pro-cyclical pattern of high liquidity/cheap and abundant debt/ever increasing price/ever higher returns ended. The "nice" economy had officially run its course.

### 9.2.2. CMBS originators

The parallels between the portfolio lenders and the CMBS originators, and the CMBS market, are not unsurprisingly, numerous. The CMBS of European CRE debt in the form of CMBS conduits started, slowly, in 1998 and relatively quickly gathered pace, culminating in the dramatic and abrupt termination in late 2007 or early 2008. See further Chs 2 and 4 for the volume of CMBS deals.

Investment banks, mostly US ones, that had successfully entered and capitalised on the US CMBS market, saw the European bank led, portfolio lending market as an attractive opportunity to replicate their US business

---

[3]  See furtherCh.8.

plans. As a result, the 1998–2007 decade was particularly attractive for CMBS originators. A large and somewhat complacent and unsophisticated European market that had experienced no capital markets competition, proved to be a fertile ground for a small group of investment banks to take market share and profit.

The liquidity spill-over, driven by the commercial banks, was indirectly benefiting the CMBS market. The same dynamics that portfolio lenders were experiencing with cheap short term funding were trickling down to structured investment vehicles (SIVs). These SIVs were able to borrow large amounts of money from banks with a very small amount of equity. The leverage ratios in some cases were even higher than the ones the banks had. These SIVs would buy up large quantities of CMBS, as well as other structured finance products, pushing down margins.[4]

For practical purposes, what had started as a way to diversify the sources of finance for CRE debt, ended up being a mostly bank liquidity, and eventually also a bank retained risk, driven market. The CMBS market ended up with a similar pattern of quick growth in the origination of loans and issuance of CMBS, that made similar mistakes to the banks: reduction in underwriting, credit and due diligence standards, introduction of complex derivatives, and a fair amount of financial engineering that sometimes only benefitted the CMBS originators, to the disadvantage of the CMBS investors or borrowers.

This book has highlighted that the initial CMBS model in Europe remains dislocated and frozen. The industry has gone through a significant re-trenchment—issuance of conduit-style, true sale CMBS transactions in Europe has been virtually non-existent since 2008, and staffing level at CMBS originators and at ancillary support service companies, with the exception of special servicers,[5] has been reduced dramatically. Some of the biggest CRE lenders, such as Eurohypo, Société Générale, HRE, not to mention virtually all investment banks focused on CMBS, have exited the market and stopped originating loans or have gone out of business. Equally important, as highlighted in Ch.1, the investor base and investor demand for CMBS has vanished. This lack of demand and market liquidity, combined with the deterioration in the credit performance of CMBS bonds, have pushed the CMBS product into a vicious circle of widening spreads, fewer investors and lower liquidity. Clearly, these are not conditions attractive or conducive to new CMBS issuance.

*9.2.2.1. Economics of CMBS origination*

As discussed in Ch.1, the economics of the business of a CMBS originator can be broken down into several component parts and are conceptually

---

[4]  See further Ch.1.
[5]  See Chs 5, 6 and 7.

very straight-forward and simple: an originator makes loans at a certain level of pricing, packages them into securities and sells them to investors at tighter pricing levels. The pricing difference is the retained profit for the originator. The basic economics for portfolio and originate-to-distribute lenders are fundamentally similar. The main difference to portfolio lenders is that CMBS originators remove the credit risk from the balance sheet upon closing of the CMBS, and that they endeavour to monetise the excess spread by selling it to third party investors.

However, it is useful and important for the purposes of this Chapter to analyse the details of the CMBS origination-to-distribute model to understand how the economics of CMBS origination were derived and how CMBS originators might be able to do it in the future. The economics of a loan are relatively simple. The borrower will pay the lender origination fees, interest, principal and under certain circumstances prepayment fees. In a few instances and in more speculative loans there might be PIK interest components, exit fees and profit share arrangements, but it would be generally accepted that these are not likely in CMBS loans. The costs associated with the origination of a loan, i.e. documentation, due diligence, valuations, etc. would generally be paid for by the borrower and therefore would not affect the economic dynamics. While traditional CMBS issuance could be comprise of fixed or floating rate bonds, the vast majority of "conduit" issuance was in floating rate format, which will be the focus of this Chapter as it considers the typical life cycle of a loan.

CRE has traditionally been viewed as a fixed income asset class, due to the relatively fixed nature of the rental income generated by the CRE assets. While there is some empirical evidence that over longer periods of time CRE asset values and rental income do provide a moderately effective hedge against inflation, it is however, poorly correlated with short-term interest rate movements. Therefore, given that CMBS issuers need to originate actual or effective floating rate assets, the originator will also generally enter into hedging arrangement to hedge the interest rate risk. This was traditionally done, as discussed in the previous chapter, mostly with swaps or sometimes caps. If the loan was a floating rate loan, the swap would be entered directly with the borrower, and if the loan was a fixed rate loan the lender would enter into a swap with its derivatives desk and novate it to the CMBS vehicle. Whichever option was used, hedging activities comprised a significant portion of the economics for a CMBS loan originator.[6] Meanwhile, whilst the loan is on the originators balance sheet, it would earn interest in excess of the short-term funding costs of the bank or the CMBS desk. This was defined as "positive carry".

Once a pool of sufficient size and with the right degree of diversity and compatibility was assembled, the structuring, rating and documentation

---

[6] See further Ch.8.

process would take place. The costs associated with these activities would generally be borne by the originator of the CMBS.

While some loan originators would try to optimise their economics by syndicating parts of loans, generally the higher leverage portions of loans, i.e. junior loans or B-pieces,[7] the fundamental mathematics of the exit strategy are the same as if the whole loan was securitised. The basic reasons for syndicating the junior portion of the loan ranged from simple—rating agencies might assign a low rating to a highly levered loan, there might not be strong demand for such a tranche—to structurally more nuanced—the required coupon for a lowly rated tranche might cause the tranche to be either priced at a discount or be susceptible to available funds caps. Lenders followed a simple decision making process: if B pieces or junior loans could be sold at higher prices/lower margins to loan investors than to bond investors, then loan originators acted rationally and sold the loans to loan investors instead of re-packaging them as CMBS securities.

Once a CMBS was marketed and sold and bonds had settled, the final economic tally could be assessed. An originator would aim to sell all the bonds in a CMBS, but if it failed to do so, it would generally be required to hold any unsold bonds on its trading book at the appropriate mark-to-market. For the purpose of this analysis, it is assumed that originators sold all of the bonds. Generally, the margins on the bonds would be set at a level so that the bonds would be sold at par. In some circumstances, particularly for the most junior classes, either because the net interest margin of the loans was not sufficient to pay the full margin on all the bonds (either from day one or under certain prepayment scenarios), then the margin of certain bonds would be set at a level lower than the market clearing discount margin, leading to below par pricing.

In order to illustrate the economics of CMBS origination a hypothetical, but not a-typical, CMBS conduit transaction is analysed below. Figure 5 portrays a £500 million securitisation structure of eight loans with the characteristics of Figure 6 below. The securitisation is comprised of five tranches, and utilises a simplified sequential pay structure with an X-class[8] (or deferred consideration) and running transaction costs of 15bps per annum.

A range of economics (low and high) has been chosen as different types of transactions had different levels of costs and profit. As demonstrated in the above example, the transaction generates a profit for the originator of approximately 1 per cent to 3 per cent, i.e. £5 million to £15 million (see Figure 7). As shown below, the significant part of the economics and the vast majority of profits of the CMBS originator are determined by the value

---

[7] See Chs 14 and 15.
[8] See Ch.5.

Figure 5. Sample CMBS Structure

| | | | Securitisation Structure | | | |
|---|---|---|---|---|---|---|
| | Bond Size | Bond Balance (£) | Price (%) | Price (£) | Margin | Discount Margin |
| AAA | 75% | 375,000,000 | 100.00% | 375,000,000 | 0.25% | 0.25% |
| AA | 10% | 50,000,000 | 100.00% | 50,000,000 | 0.40% | 0.40% |
| A | 7% | 35,000,000 | 100.00% | 35,000,000 | 0.70% | 0.70% |
| BBB | 5% | 25,000,000 | 100.00% | 25,000,000 | 1.00% | 1.00% |
| BB | 3% | 15,000,000 | 95.912% | 14,386,729 | 2.00% | 2.75% |
| Total/W.A. | 100% | 500,000,000 | 99.88% | 499,386,729 | 0.39% | 0.41% |

Figure 6. Sample Loan Collateral Pool

| | | Loan Collateral Pool | | |
|---|---|---|---|---|
| Loan | Balance | Amortisation | Margin | Term (Years) |
| 1 | 140,000,000 | 1% Per year | 1.12% | 6.00 |
| 2 | 106,000,000 | Interest Only | 1.05% | 5.50 |
| 3 | 78,000,000 | 1 Year IO, 1% per year | 0.90% | 7.00 |
| 4 | 55,000,000 | 1.75% per Year | 1.40% | 6.00 |
| 5 | 39,000,000 | Interest Only | 0.70% | 5.00 |
| 6 | 27,000,000 | 1.5% per year | 0.78% | 6.50 |
| 7 | 16,000,000 | 2 Year IO, 1% per year | 0.95% | 7.00 |
| 8 | 39,000,000 | 2% per year | 1.25% | 5.00 |
| Total/W.A. | 500,000,000 | | 1.06% | 5.95 |

of the excess spread and its ability to be extracted in an efficient and timely manner by way of an X-class or deferred consideration.

The key feature of these interest-only X-Class payment streams is that they can cease if loans prepay or default. In a CMBS transaction backed by a pool of loans with an expected average life of six years, if no prepayments occurred and all loans performed to maturity, the X-Class would expect to receive excess spread cashflows for six years. (See Figures 7 and 8).

If loans prepay before maturity this would directly lead to reduced excess spread payments, and therefore a reduction in the potential profits an originator would make.

In Figure 9, certain loans prepay during the transaction with the reduction of the cashflows seen in the reduction in the height of the bars representing the quarterly payments to the X-Class.

Figure 7. Summary of Sample Economics for a £500 million CMBS

|  | Low | High | Footnotes |
|---|---|---|---|
| **Loan Origination** | -100.00% | -100.00% | |
| Origination Fees | 0.35% | 0.65% | |
| Carry | 0.25% | 0.60% | 1) |
| Derivatives P&L | 0.15% | 0.40% | 2) |
| Securitisation Origination Expenses | -0.35% | -0.55% | 3) |
| Sale of Bonds | 99.88% | 99.88% | 4) |
| **Sub-Total (%)** | **0.28%** | **0.98%** | |
| **Sub-Total (£)** | **1,386,666** | **4,886,666** | |
| X-Class/Deferred Consideration (%) | 0.80% | 2.19% | 5), 6) |
| X-Class/Deferred Consideration (£) | 4,005,708 | 10,950,000 | |
| **Total (%)** | **1.08%** | **3.17%** | |
| **Total (£)** | **5,392,374** | **15,836,666** | |

Assumptions/Footnotes

| | |
|---|---|
| 1) | Assumes 6 months hold, Loan Interest at L+80/120 (Low/High), Funding at L+0/50 |
| 2) | Assumes 3-8bps profit PV-ed |
| 3) | Legal, Accounting, Rating |
| 4) | Junior Bonds might be sold at |
| 5) | High End Value assumes PV of zero prepayment |
| 6) | Low End Value assumes PV of worst prepayment scenario in 10,000 Monte- |

Figure 8. Sample Excess Spread Cashflows - Base Case

Hence, the importance in a CMBS transaction of loan level call protection (protecting against reduced excess spread due to loan defaults is more challenging task). In Europe, call protection was achieved by the inclusion of prepayment fees in the loans. While some longer-dated CMBS transactions may have had prepayment lockouts, or defeasance structures,

**Figure 9. Sample Excess Spread Cashflows - Prepayment Case, No Prepayment Fees**

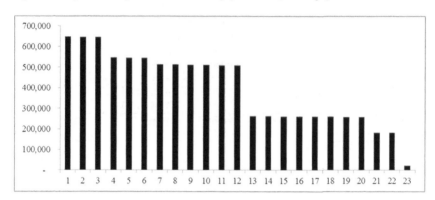

some had more sophisticated yield maintenance or make-whole provisions. For typical CMBS conduit transactions, loan level prepayment fees were the dominant mechanism used.

Figure 10 shows the same prepayment profile as Figure 9, with the significant difference that, particularly in the early years of a loan, prepayment fees were paid when loans prepaid, increasing the cashflows at the time of the prepayment and compensating the X-Class investor for the future reduction of excess spread.

**Figure 10. Sample Excess Spread Cashflows - Prepayment Case, With Prepayment Fees**

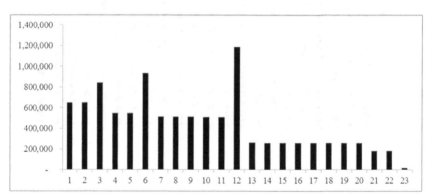

The design of prepayment fees and structuring to optimise the stability of the excess spread is an interesting, complex and controversial topic, but is beyond the remit of this Chapter.

### 9.2.3. Fundamental operating parameters and differences between CMBS originators and portfolio lenders

A key requirement for a CMBS originator is to have a high degree of visibility and stability in the execution of a CMBS in order to have a high degree certainty in the level of profitability of a transaction. Unlike portfolio lenders that try to match assets and liabilities and where liabilities are known at the point of origination, CMBS originators originate loans and face several factors that introduce uncertainty and risk into their business.

Portfolio lenders generally have a well-defined financing structure to match the assets they are originating. Insurance companies and pension funds have real and actuarially defined liabilities, investors, including CRE debt funds, have target returns, hurdle rates and carried interest targets to reach, etc. Most of these liabilities are defined, or will be defined, at or shortly after the origination of a loan. CMBS originators on the other hand are intermediators with relatively short-term hold parameters.

## 9.3. Economic risks of CMBS origination

A CMBS originator has several challenges. These are:

- Extended execution period

There is generally a three to 12 months delay between the time of origination and the time at which CMBS bonds are actually sold. A CMBS originator might require three to six months to accumulate enough reasonably compatible or homogenous collateral to put together a pool of loans. At the height of the CMBS market, some platforms issued over one €/£ billion of CMBS per year (some significantly more). Most conduit platforms issued less than that and therefore the accumulation period was reasonably long. In addition, the fact that European CMBS issuers did not combine or pool their loans, contributed to the extended periods of time to achieve reasonably sized pools of loans. Once the pool is assembled, originators required approximately three months to get the deals rated by the rating agencies, document the transaction and market the bonds.

- Uncertain rating outcome

The outcome of the rating process is uncertain. While a number of the CMBS issuers claimed, during this period, they had the rating agency "models", such statements are difficult to reconcile with the reality, that the rating agencies never released detailed parameters to replicate their models. While rating agencies may have had internal models to analyse loans, a significant component of their analysis and eventual capital structure allocation was based on subjective "non-model" overrides.[9]

The high degree of variability in rating outcomes was due to the radically different analytical approaches used by each rating agency, which led to rating agency "shopping" and arbitrage.

• Lack of homogeneity

Additional variability was partially due to the fact that loan documentation, loan structuring, leases, etc. vary from jurisdiction to jurisdiction, from loan to loan and from originator to originator. The lack of a homogenous European market and therefore the ability to make the analysis more predictable and formulaic made the rating outcome more volatile and unpredictable.

• Lack of credit hedging

The lack of instruments to hedge credit spreads exposes CMBS originators to economic risks. As noted above and in Ch.8, the vast majority of the CMBS market in Europe was a floating rate market. While loans could be originated as floating rate loans as well as fixed rate loans, all "conduit style" fixed loans where hedged with interest rate swaps or caps that effectively hedged the interest rate risk between the date origination of the loan and the issuance of the (mostly) floating rate bonds. However, originators had few, if any, cost effective choices to hedge credit spread variations over such extended period making it very difficult to ensure that the economics expected at loan origination were actually realised when the CMBS priced.

• Commercial real estate value volatility

CMBS originators were exposed to CRE values changing between the time of origination and CMBS sales which could affect the credit quality of the loans. This could have a positive outcome of values improved during the hold period, or be negative if values deteriorated. For example, a 75 per cent LTV priced at LIBOR plus 100bps could become an 80 per cent LTV and be mispriced by the time it was securitised, or become a 70 per cent LTV and have a successful CMBS execution.

• Negative convexity and adverse selection

Another somewhat uncontrollable factor was the tendency of borrowers prepaying loans, sometimes while they were still on the lender's balance

---

[9]  For a detailed discussion of rating agencies and their role in the market see Ch.11

sheet. Generally, the loans being prepaid were the ones which had improving credit characteristics, such as increasing CRE values, and were therefore able to get higher leverage and tighter pricing from other lenders. The ones with deteriorating credit attributes did not prepay as readily.

### 9.3.1. Potential impact on economics

Given the factors outlined above, it is surprising that the CMBS market enjoyed the success it had for the period of time it did. It is also somewhat surprising that CMBS originators where willing to assume the level or risk that they did. Given the economics of a CMBS transaction highlighted above, relatively small spread widening could change the economics of a CMBS transaction from profitable to loss making.

Using the same hypothetical transaction shown in Figure 5, if CMBS bonds spreads widen by 10bps on average (see Figure 11 below), the value of the zero-prepayment excess spread declines by 15 per cent. However, the actual total economics drop by 19 per cent, because the junior bonds will need to be sold at an increased discount in order to avoid an available funds cap issue (i.e. the loan margins are not high enough to pay the bond interest in full).

**Figure 11. Potential Impact On CMBS Economics Due To Spread Movements.**

|  | Discount Margin | Stressed Discount Margin | Delta |
|---|---|---|---|
| AAA | 0.25% | 0.31% | 0.06% |
| AA | 0.40% | 0.50% | 0.10% |
| A | 0.70% | 0.87% | 0.17% |
| BBB | 1.00% | 1.24% | 0.24% |
| BB | 2.75% | 3.42% | 0.67% |
| Total/W.A. | 0.41% | 0.51% | 0.10% |
| Excess Spread (%) | 2.19% | 1.84% | 0.35% |
| Excess Spread (£) | 10,950,000 | 9,207,974 | 1,742,026 |

Similar variability could arise if the capital structure varied due to loans having leverage at closing as compared to at origination due to CRE value declines.

### 9.3.2. *Perfect storm and a lost decade*

A particularly dramatic example of the convergence and synchronisation of most of the risks discussed above occurred in 2007. With balance sheets full of loans earmarked for securitisation, many of the CMBS originators suddenly found themselves with loans that had been financed on a short-term basis that could not be sold in the securitisation market. As property valuations deteriorated, so did the allocated capital structures. As market spreads for bonds widened, so did the cost of CMBS issuance.

Originators found themselves in the unattractive position of either having to securitise the loans at a loss (if they had been able to place the bonds at all), or holding the loans on balance sheet, finance them at ever increasing spreads (as treasury departments passed along the increased costs of funding that banks faced), allocating ever increasing amounts of equity capital to the rapidly deteriorating asset quality and increasing LTVs and, in most cases, suffering mark-to-market (MTM) losses on their positions. Many CMBS originators suffered losses in 2008, 2009 and 2010 that matched or exceeded the cumulative profits they had earned in the prior decade. Not unlike the performance of global stock indices like the FTSE 100 or S&P 500, 2000–10 was a lost decade.

### 9.3.3. *Golden era or fata morgana*

The success of the CMBS market was based on the relatively benign CRE value evolution between 1998 and 2007 that accompanied the "nice" economy, with a relatively consistent upward trend in property values that masked the risk of CRE value volatility. (See Figures 1 to 3).

The period between 1998 and 2007 also provided a very benign spread environment. It is not the goal of this Chapter to explore the underlying drivers of the spread compression, but the proliferation of easy credit, a huge amount of liquidity and a false sense of security, are certainly contributors to the development of an investment requirement in which risk was significantly mispriced.

Figure 12 below shows original bond margins of CMBS transactions over time. It is only in 2007 that the tide started turning.

## 9.4. The future

Other parts of this book discuss at length the current state of the CRE finance market, and in particular, the funding gap.[10] This section of the chapter will now explore and try to answer the question of who will be the

---

[10] See in particular Ch.2.

Figure 12. AAA and BBB CMBS Origination Margins from 1998 to 2007

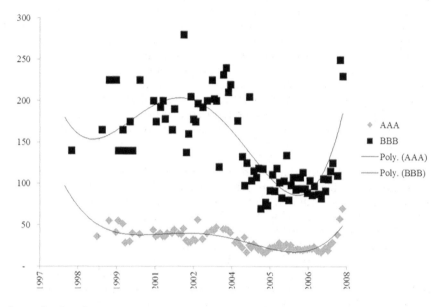

Source: Renshaw Bay

lenders in the future and in addition why and what are the economics of the different participants? While some jurisdictions require banking licences to be able to lend[11], the critical question to address has as much to do with the legal or regulatory framework for the lending entity as the liability/funding structure of the lender. That in turn should be driven by the business plans and risk tolerance of the entity.

This Chapter will not explore the regulatory intricacies of the capital, regulatory and liquidity requirements imbedded in Basel III, Solvency II, CRD IV and the other regulatory and central bank initiatives, as these are discussed in detail in Ch.16. However, it is worth noting here that the relevant and practical outcome of those requirements has seen, at the time of writing, significantly higher regulatory capital and liquidity buffers for regulated entity. These items, combined with significantly higher financing costs have been translated into much higher CRE debt pricing and lower LTV loans by banks.[12]

While banks will probably continue to be the dominant providers of CRE debt in Europe for the foreseeable future, partially because it will take some

---

[11]  See further Ch.17.
[12]  See Chs 2, 13 and 20.

time for alternative providers to emerge and acquire market share (but also because banks are only very slowly and deliberately reducing their CRE portfolios to avoid a CRE market crash driven by an even larger reduction of the available financing) the future composition of market share of CRE debt providers will certainly change. A more mature and functioning model is the United States one, where banks' share of the CRE finance market is approximately 50 per cent. The other 50 per cent is split between portfolio lenders such as insurance companies, pension funds and capital markets investors, particularly CMBS. While it is unlikely that Europe will, potentially ever, see such a diversified source of CRE finance, the current 90+ per cent bank dominance will need to be reduced and this is being actively pushed by regulators.[13]

Banks have started to adapt to the regulatory environment, liquidity and to some degree match funding requirements affecting the CRE assets on their balance sheets. In order to reduce the costs associated with the business, optimise their returns and make up for the economic drag imposed by their large, under-priced and often underperforming legacy portfolios have started changing the characteristics of their new lending. To date, the loan origination of the banks have tended to be of lower leverage and shorter duration than in the past, with many limiting their exposures to 55 to 60 per cent LTV and three- to four year term. Pricing has shot up to LIBOR +275 to 400bps (and higher) for loans that five years ago would have been priced at LIBOR +75bps or lower.

That has left some significant gaps in the CRE debt spectrum that will be filled by CRE debt funds, insurance companies, pension funds and other real money investors. These entities will focus on either higher leverage or longer term loans that banks are no longer providing, or they will compete directly with banks in their core products, as highlighted in Figures 13, 14 and 15 below. The vertical axis indicates LTV ratios and the horizontal axis the tenor of the loans. The darker shades correspond to the highest focus, while the lighter shades are of lower interest.

## 9.5. Who are the likely future issuers of CMBS in Europe?

Given the current challenges described above for the originate-and-distribute as CMBS model, it is a relevant question to ask who the potential future issuers of CMBS in Europe could be and why these entities would be attracted to this business model.

It might be easier to start by listing who is less likely to be adopting such a strategy. Insurance companies, pension funds and other real money, asset-liability matching portfolio lenders are not structurally incentivised to adopt what is in essence a short-term hold strategy. Their business is

---

[13] See Chs 16 and 20.

Figures 13, 14 and 15. LTV and Term Origination Parameters for Banks, CRE Debt Funds and Insurance, Pension Funds, respectively

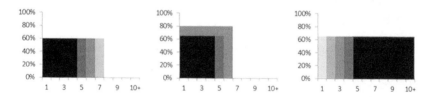

currently focused on originating specific types of loans with specific tenor and leverage criteria to match a well-defined set of liabilities and obligations, and not to deploy capital in a short-term fashion to generate economic returns. It cannot be ruled out that CMBS issuance might be an appropriate and effective method to sell off portfolios of loans in instances when they need to monetise assets or as a portfolio and liquidity management exercise. However, that would require that the loans are underwritten and documented in a manner that would allow these companies to have this option, which is currently not always the case, but clearly is not an insurmountable challenge or irreversible pattern. On the other hand, while CMBS might not be a programmatic tool for these types of companies, CMBS issuance is certainly a strategic and opportunistic avenue open to them.

This leaves a more likely set of potential candidates that could adopt programmatic CMBS issuance as the basis for their business models including banks and specialist financial institutions, including private equity-style, closed ended CRE debt funds. The structure of future CMBS will need to take into account a series of changes. Structures will probably be more conservative and overall leverage will be lower. In addition, some of the expenses of a securitisation will have increased, in some cases, for example liquidity facility costs, dramatically with far lower supply.

For the purpose of the following analysis, it is assumed that a CMBS originator is able to originate a portfolio of loans similar to the one shown earlier in the Chapter, but with a few significant adjustments to reflect current loan characteristics. The LTVs of the loans range from 60 to 65 per cent, the pricing has increased to an average of LIBOR +325bps with origination fees of 1 per cent, and more limited prepayment optionality and higher prepayment fees. These last two points should dramatically simplify and clarify the profit extraction mechanisms.

By definition the balance sheet utilisation for a CMBS originator will vary dramatically as it accumulates collateral and then securitises it (see Figure

221

16). In order to optimise the capital utilisation, a CMBS originator will require access to short term funding that can be easily drawn and repaid, in addition to a certain level of longer-term capital. This can be easily accomplished by banks.

Figure 16. Indicative Origination and Securitisation Timing and Balance Sheet Usage

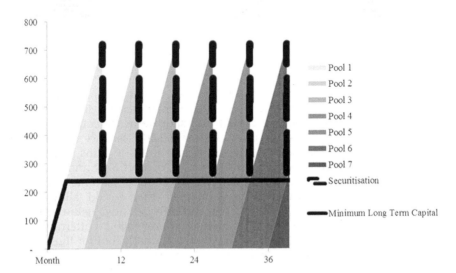

The capital structure below assumes a more conservative leverage position incorporating an amalgamation of data points from recent European transactions and some US standards, like a 30 per cent subordination for the AAA classes. The pricing shown below in Table 1, is also extrapolated from data points and opinions gathered from potential investors in CMBS and actual pricing for other structured credit asset classes. For the avoidance of doubt, this is not intended to be a reflection of what is or will actually be achievable, but a reasonable and justifiable expectation of the current market.

The "current" economics shown in Table 1 combined with the loan pricing that is currently achievable make new origination a non-starter. Originating loans with pricing that matches the pricing of the bond capital structure would be meaningless for a profit seeking CMBS originator. A basic tenet is that CMBS spreads need to be tighter than whole loan margins.

Even assuming that bonds price, on average, 50bps tighter than the table above would only generate a small CMBS profit. The economics for a CMBS originator begin being seriously interesting at the levels shown in Table 2.

222

Table 1. Sample Securitisation Structure for a £500 million CMBS – Current Pricing

| | | | Securitisation Structure | | | |
|---|---|---|---|---|---|---|
| | Bond Size | Bond Balance (£) | Price (%) | Price (£) | Margin | Discount Margin |
| AAA | 70.0% | 350,000,000 | 100.00% | 350,000,000 | 2.75% | 2.75% |
| AA | 15.0% | 75,000,000 | 100.00% | 75,000,000 | 3.75% | 3.75% |
| A | 10.0% | 50,000,000 | 100.00% | 50,000,000 | 4.75% | 4.75% |
| BBB | 5.0% | 25,000,000 | 100.00% | 25,000,000 | 5.75% | 5.75% |
| Total/W.A. | 100% | 500,000,000 | 100.00% | 500,000,000 | 3.25% | 3.25% |

While the differential pricing between the different classes of bonds might be debated, the simplified focus should be on the weighted average bond margin of LIBOR +250bps. This should make intuitive sense. If a portfolio of loans are originated at LIBOR +325bps and the bonds priced at LIBOR +250bps and on-going securitisation expenses add another 35bps to the liability stream that leaves an annualised, nominal profit of 40bps (of course, that differential can also be achieved by widening loan margins).

Table 2. Sample Securitisation Structure for a £500 million CMBS – Target Pricing

| | | | CMBS Structure | | | |
|---|---|---|---|---|---|---|
| | Bond Size | Bond Balance (£) | Price (%) | Price (£) | Margin | Discount Margin |
| AAA | 70.0% | 350,000,000 | 100.00% | 350,000,000 | 2.00% | 2.00% |
| AA | 15.0% | 75,000,000 | 100.00% | 75,000,000 | 3.00% | 3.00% |
| A | 10.0% | 50,000,000 | 100.00% | 50,000,000 | 4.00% | 4.00% |
| BBB | 5.0% | 25,000,000 | 100.00% | 25,000,000 | 5.00% | 5.00% |
| Total/W.A. | 100% | 500,000,000 | 100.00% | 500,000,000 | 2.50% | 2.50% |

The detailed breakdown of the CMBS economics, using the same format as in the prior section of the Chapter to ease comparison, is in Table 3. Several of the assumptions have been adjusted to reflect the economic environment that exists at the time of writing.

The single, stand-alone transaction economics set out in Table 3 are somewhat lower, but not materially different from what we saw in the earlier part of this Chapter. How the single, standalone CMBS transaction

Table 3. Summary of Sample Economics For a £500 million CMBS

**Summary of Sample Economics For A £500m CMBS**

|  | | Footnotes |
| --- | --- | --- |
| **Loan Origination** | -100.00% | |
| Origination Fees | 1.00% | |
| Carry | 0.25% | 1) |
| Derivatives P&L | 0.20% | 2) |
| CMBS Origination Expenses | -0.65% | 3) |
| Sale of Bonds | 100.00% | 4) |
| **Sub-Total (%)** | **0.80%** | |
| **Sub-Total (£)** | 4,000,194 | |
| X-Class/Deferred Consideration (%) | 1.39% | 5) |
| X-Class/Deferred Consideration (£) | 6,969,354 | |
| **Total (%)** | **2.19%** | |
| **Total (£)** | **10,969,548** | |

| Assumptions/Footnotes | |
| --- | --- |
| 1) | 6 months hold, Loan Interest at L+325 bps, Funding at L+275 bps |
| 2) | 5bps profit PV-ed over 5 Years |
| 3) | Legal, Accounting, Rating Agency, etc |
| 4) | Junior Bonds might be sold at a discount to par |
| 5) | High End Value assumes PV of zero prepayment scenario @10% |

economics translate into the economics of a CMBS origination platform is shown in Table 4. The economics are based on the assumption, as stated above, that an originator would finance a portion of its loan origination with short term debt provided by a warehousing facility and that at steady state, and originator could issue four CMBS per year. While this might seem like an ambitious target—even at the height of the CMBS boom few CMBS platforms managed that pace— the shortening of the origination and CMBS process is one of the fundamental changes that the CMBS industry needs to achieve.

The above calculations look enticing; however they ignore the fact that originators will need to retain a 5 per cent stake in their transactions as prescribed by new regulatory standards described in detail in Ch.16. For the purpose of this analysis, it will be assumed that the retention will be comprised of a vertical slice of all the classes of bonds. In a £500 million CMBS that would mean a £25 million retention earning LIBOR +250bps. Not only does this mean that the originator will require an increasing amount of capital to be deployed for this retention, but also that this will be a relatively low yielding set of bonds.

Table 4 CMBS originator economics

| CMBS Originator Economics | | |
| --- | --- | --- |
| Steady State Long Term Capital Deployed (£) | 250,000,000 | 6) |
| Steady State Annualised Profit (£) | 43,878,190 | 7) |
| **Annualised Profit** | **17.6%** | |

| Assumptions/Footnotes | |
| --- | --- |
| 1) | Assumes CMBS originator funds 2/3 of origination with short term debt, 1/3 Own Equity Capital |
| 2) | Assumes 4 originations per year |

The capital allocated to the retained bonds could in theory grow to, in the example set out in Table 4, £500 million over a five year period of time (£2 billion CMBS per year * 5% * 5 years), eclipsing the initial assessment of only requiring £250 million to run the CMBS origination business. While LIBOR +250bps is, in the Table 4 example, the market clearing price of bonds for investors that have a business plan to own and hold bonds, CMBS issuers will generally not have a significant appetite for long term holdings and probably have a higher return threshold.

A CMBS originator could decide that some of the above stated profits may be used to subsidise the part of the business tasked with retaining the bond portfolio. Assuming that the desired bond return threshold for a CMBS originator is 7 per cent and that LIBOR +250bps equates to a fixed rate equivalent to 3.5 per cent (assuming an average LIBOR rate of 1 per cent), the annual return shortfall would amount to £875,000. Over five years that equates to £4.375 million. If this amount is withheld from the initial £11 million of profit shown above, that would leave a profit allocable to the originate-and-distribute part of the business of £6.59 million. Performing the same calculations as before, the annualised return on the £250 million capital allocated to this part of the business is 10.6 per cent (see Table 5). This return is still attractive, but not as overwhelming as before.

The crux of the analysis in Table 5 is that a liquid and competitive CMBS market could be an attractive business proposition for some banks and some dedicated CRE finance specialists, including some CRE funds. The critical question is whether there will be cost-effective mechanisms to mitigate some of the risks present in the current volatile environment, such as credit spread volatility and CRE asset value declines, and whether there will be counterparties willing to provide the products and services required, such as short-term warehousing facilities and derivatives. However, the two most critical questions are, whether the pricing differential between direct lending and CMBS bonds will be achieved and whether CMBS bond investors will materialise in sufficient numbers in 2013 and beyond.

Table 5 CMBS originator economics – adjustment for retention requirements

| CMBS Originator Economics - Adjustment for Retention Requirements | | |
|---|---|---|
| Retention Requirements per transaction (£) | 25,000,000 | 1) |
| Target Return on CMBS holding | 7.0% | 2) |
| Actual Return on CMBS holding | 3.500% | 3) |
| Annual Shortfall (£) | 875,000 | |
| Aggregate Shortfall over life of holding (£) | 4,375,000 | 4) |
| Remaining CMBS Profit (£) | 6,594,548 | |
| Annualised Profit from CMBS Origination Business (£) | 26,378,190 | 5) |
| **Annualised Profit** | **10.6%** | |

| Assumptions/Footnotes | |
|---|---|
| 1) | 5% CMBS size, vertical slice |
| 2) | Assumption, this may vary by CMBS originator |
| 3) | Assumes 5 Year LIBOR average of 1% |
| 4) | Assumes 5 year average life of bonds |
| 5) | Assumes 4 CMBS per year |

The challenges faced by potential new entrants in the market, and particularly capital markets oriented lenders, will either be solved by significantly higher CRE lending pricing or by wider participation at competitive pricing of investors and counterparties. It is likely that the markets may well witness the former first and the latter second.

## 9.6. Conclusion—The case for CMBS

This Chapter has highlighted that there are reasons to be hopeful about the future possibilities of a renaissance and revival of the European CMBS market based on the need for a diversified, balanced and competitive CRE finance industry in Europe. Certain conditions that could be the fundamental drivers to break the vicious circle mentioned above and convert it into a virtuous circle of competitive pricing, wider investor participation and increasing liquidity are, at the time of writing, beginning to surface.

The first of these drivers is the sizable funding gap that is and will be present in Europe for the foreseeable future as detailed in Ch.2. The second driver is the concerted effort by the CMBS industry, through the Commercial Real Estate Finance Council Europe (CREFC) as highlighted in the introduction to the Appendices to this book, to improve the CRE lending and CMBS markets and eliminate some of the correctly identified shortcomings of the CRE lending and CMBS transactions of the boom years. The third driver is that CRE asset values are now more sustainable as are the relative value proposition between CRE debt (and this includes CMBS) and direct CRE investment, and the relative value proposition between CRE debt and other "Credit" fixed income investments as shown in Figure 17.

Figure 17. iTraxx Spreads

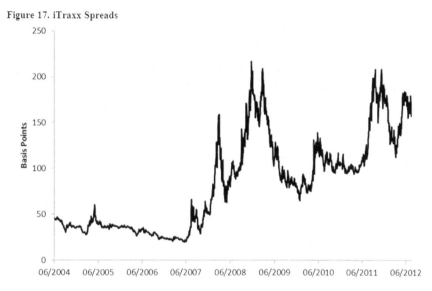

Source: Bloomberg

As highlighted throughout this book, the fundamental purpose of the CMBS market was to provide a mechanism to connect capital sources with users of capital in an efficient, transparent and efficient way. The underlying goal was to provide liquidity, standardisation in documentation and information, to ease the underwriting for investors, to make it comparable and open and to help CRE finance evolve from its traditionally more bilateral, tailor made, in some sense capricious and shrouded in bank credit committee mystery. This aim was to assist not just lenders and investors, but also borrowers. CMBS was supposed to transform illiquid loans into liquid standardised securities, with a number of structural and credit enhancements that appealed to a large swathe of investors, seeking an indirect CRE fixed income investment and allowing these investors to choose the exact level of risk they wanted to take by selecting specific tranches with varying credit subordination, all in an active, broad, liquid market with low bid-ask spreads and transaction costs.

The new issue CMBS activity, at least in what has historically been the early part of the life cycle of a loan—originating loans, warehousing them on a balance sheet while the originator accumulates enough collateral into a pool of loans to an acceptable size, presenting it to the rating agencies, structuring and documenting the CMBS transaction, marketing it and then selling (all of) the bonds—is a resource-intensive and specialised process. The availability of a large and active market was aimed to facilitate the streamlining of the investment process by allowing a certain degree of specialisation and division of labour and to break down the traditional fully integrated business model prevalent in Europe and lead to a more efficient and cost-effective model. The originators could focus on origination, servicers could focus on servicing, and investors could focus on investing. The market is eagerly waiting for these goals to be fulfilled and market participants, through the CREFC and efforts such as this book, are working hard to educate regulators and those that have a guiding hand in how the CRE and CMBS markets emerge from this period, to ensure these goals may be fulfilled.

As of mid 2012, the market is comprised, with a few exceptions, of originate-and-hold lenders. The originate-and-syndicate parts of a lender group have been morphed into the originate-in-a-club, which is really just a subset of the originate-and-hold group, and the originate-and-distribute group, again except for a few institutions, the prime example being Deutsche Bank, are mostly hoping for "something" to happen for the market to revive and the economics of being in the CRE and CMBS business make sense once more.

# Chapter 10

# The evolving role of Issuers And Trustees in CMBS Transactions

Sean Crosky,

Partner, K&L Gates LLP

Emma Hamley,

US Bank Trustee Limited

JP Nowacki,

Structured Finance Management Limited

## 10.1. Introduction[1]

When the previous edition of this book was first published, the European CMBS market was a robust and vibrant part of the securitisation industry, with annual issuance volumes continually increasing, both through banks using conduit programmes to securitise the CRE loans they originated and property companies using CMBS structures to refinance their borrowings.[2] However, the intervening period and in particular the period post 2008 has been a tumultuous period for the global CMBS market and for its participants. The commercial mortgage loan and CMBS markets have witnessed a decrease in value (at times, a very significant decrease in value) of the underlying CRE as well as the inability of borrowers to refinance their securitised facilities at maturity. This has resulted in the restructuring and/or enforcement of many of the loans underlying these structures, although these subjects are not the topic of this Chapter and are discussed elsewhere in this book.

This fundamental deterioration in real estate market conditions placed CMBS deals under stresses which were not anticipated when the transactions were structured and executed. As a result of these stresses, the role of various parties in the CMBS market has evolved from those previously envisaged. At times, this evolution has taken place at a rapid

---

[1] The authors would like to thank Robert Berry and Debra Parsall of Structured FInance Management Limited and Laurence Griffiths of US Bank Trustee Limited for their suggestions on this chapter.

[2] See further Ch.1.

pace (for example, the implications of the *Eurosail* decision discussed further below). Often the parties at the forefront of this evolution are those appointed to have an ongoing role in the transaction. These parties include the trustees and issuers in the securitisations, who have been required to consider, and deal with, issues and situations which for the most part were not envisaged in the structuring or documentation of the securitisation.

This Chapter will consider the position of a trustee and issuer in a pre-financial crisis CMBS transaction as understood at closing. This Chapter will also consider a number of the issues which have arisen since 2007 in the stressed environment of the CMBS market and which have direct implications on the role of trustees and issuers in these transactions. Finally, the Chapter will consider the role of the trustee and issuer going forward including a brief consideration of the implications of CMBS 2.0 in respect of new CMBS transactions as discussed in detail in Ch.4 and whether the market should consider any other issues which these parties have had to face in their existing roles on legacy deals.

The majority of European CMBS transactions were executed at the note level under English law. The discussions in this Chapter will be limited to European CMBS deals, and in particular, those executed under English law (although many of the comments can be transposed to non-English law securitisations in the European market).

## 10.2. The role of the issuer and trustee in a CMBS transaction

Neither the issuer nor the trustee is involved in the arranging or structuring of a CMBS transaction, as their role only comes into effect on the closing of the transaction. Prior to that time, neither party has any formal connection with the underlying loans or the originator. However, following execution of the transaction, along with the servicer[3] and other agents of the issuer, these are the parties whose role continues throughout the life of the transaction and the parties who are required to deal with any issues which arise.

### 10.2.1. The issuer

In CMBS transactions (as with most other securitisations), the arranger or originator will appoint a corporate services provider to establish the issuing vehicle (the Issuer). Often the corporate services provider is not appointed until the terms of the transaction have been structured and negotiated and the drafting of disclosure documents and legal documents has begun. The issuer will not be involved in negotiating the commercial terms of the

---

[3] Discussed in Chs 5, 6 and 7.

transaction (such as representations relating to the assets or the terms of the swaps[4]) nor will it be involved in carrying out due diligence on the portfolio of assets or commissioning reports such as those relating to the valuation of the underlying properties. Rather it will rely upon the arranger and reports and opinions of the advisers to the arranger (such as legal counsel and accountants).

The corporate services provider will provide directors for the issuer and will also provide company administration and accounting services. The corporate services provider is generally an organisation that provides these services to a number of issuing vehicles and specialises in the structured finance market. The issuer will be set up as an orphan company. In many common law jurisdictions this means that the shares of the issuer will be held either directly on trust for charitable purposes or by a holding company whose shares will be held on trust for charitable purposes. In other jurisdictions, the orphan structure may be established through the shares being held by a trust or foundation structure (such as the stichting structure in The Netherlands). By this structure, the issuer is not related to the originator or any other party to the transaction. This structure is driven by rating agency requirements which require the issuer to be independent to the originator and established as an orphan vehicle and be bankruptcy remote.[5]

On closing, the issuer will issue notes into the capital markets and with the proceeds of the issuance the issuer will (i) where the securitisation is refinancing a portfolio of loans originated by a bank, purchase the loans from the originating bank (often the deals are called CMBS conduit deals[6]) or (ii) where the securitisation is refinancing debt of a property company, provide a loan to the property company which will be secured over the underlying assets and may be used by the property company to refinance its existing debt or purchase new assets. A conduit deal may consist of one or a number of loans. As described in Ch.14, in conduit deals, the underlying loan will usually be tranched, with only the senior tranche (often referred to as the A loan) being sold to the issuer and securitised. The junior tranche (or tranches) and issues relating to such junior tranches are not the subject of this Chapter.

CMBS transactions were structured on the assumption that, throughout the life of the deal, the issuer would use the payments it receives on the underlying loans to repay the noteholders (and other creditors) until such time as those parties have been repaid in full. This would either be achieved through the underlying loan repaying principal throughout its life or, more often, being refinanced by the borrower at maturity, with the proceeds of such refinancing being used to repay the loan and redeem the notes

---

[4] See further Ch.8.
[5] The role of the ratings agencies is discussed further in Ch.11.
[6] See Ch.4 where the conduit deals issued prior and post 2007 are discussed.

accordingly. After repayment in full of its secured liabilities, the issuer would be wound up, and the securitisation would come to an end. At least this was the theory behind these structures. Unfortunately, events of the last few years and their effect on the commercial property markets have meant that things have not run in quite the way it was assumed that they would run when originally structured and executed.

Sometimes the issuer is seen as merely a conduit to financing or a "post-box", with no real position in the transaction other than to act as the issuing entity for the financing. However, this ignores the legal reality of the issuer—it is a company with directors, who have duties and obligations, as well as liabilities under the companies law of the entities' jurisdiction of incorporation. Sometimes an issuer may be seen as solely owing duties to the noteholders. However, this does not accord with the position under English law. Under English Companies Law, as a general principle, the directors owe their obligations to their shareholders rather than their creditors, until such time as the entity is nearing insolvency, at which point their obligations become owed to their creditors. The obligations of the directors under companies law can at times place stress on a structure. For example, the directors may have agreed to non-petition language in the documents (which essentially is a provision under which all parties to the transaction agree with the trustee not to petition for the winding up of the issuer). However, under general companies law, there may be a time in the transaction when the directors have a duty to start to wind-up the issuer, irrespective of the position under the documents. It is generally considered that such obligations take precedence to the documents, albeit they are likely to be exercised only on a very limited basis.

### 10.2.2. The trustee

The appointment process of a trustee in a securitisation is similar to the process described for the corporate services provider. The trustee may be the corporate trust entity of a financial institution or it may be a stand-alone corporate trust company. In either case, the trustee will generally be an independent legal entity, separate from other parties to the transaction.

In a CMBS transaction with English law trust documents, as with other securitisations, two trusts are established under the documents. The same corporate trustee will usually act as trustee of both trusts, and the roles may be merged into one trustee position (although in the CMBS world this is generally not the case). However it is important to note that in all cases, the trusts are very separate legal structures.

In a securitisation, the issuer will grant security over all of its assets to secure its obligations to its creditors (who will then be referred to as secured creditors). This security is granted to the security trustee, who is appointed to hold such security on behalf of all secured creditors of the issuer. The beneficiaries of the security trust will include the noteholders, as well as the other creditors of the issuer, such as the swap counterparty, liquidity provider, corporate service provider, third party agents and the trustee itself. This trust is referred to as the security trust.

The security trust will usually be effected through a deed of charge or security trust deed, under which the security trust will be established and the issuer will grant security. This document will also enunciate certain matters relating to the security trustee including powers, indemnities and liabilities, as well as the position regarding conflicts between beneficiaries. The document will also set out matters relating the acceleration of notes on a default and enforcement of security subject to the trust.

The security trustee generally will only have an active role in the event of a default at the note level, in which case it may need to accelerate the debt due under the notes, enforce the security and liquidate the assets of the issuer (which in a CMBS transaction will be the rights of the issuer under the loan agreements underlying the structure). It should be stressed that enforcement of the security at the securitisation level is distinct from enforcement of security at the loan level. Enforcement at the loan level will be pursuant to the security arrangements at the level of the underlying loan—the security trustee is not able to enforce security over the underlying properties in a CMBS transaction, it can only enforce the security granted by the issuer. It should also be noted that an enforcement of security at either the loan level or the note level does not automatically result in an enforcement at the other level, although it may have effects (such as cessation of regular payments under the loan where the loan level security is enforced) which result in enforcement at the other level in the structure.

The second trust established at closing in a securitisation is the note trust. Under this trust, the issuer will grant to the note trustee to hold on behalf of all noteholders the covenant to pay. The only beneficiaries of the note trust will be the noteholders. The note trustee effectively acts as the conduit between the noteholders and the issuer and is the entity through which any decision making powers of the noteholders are affected.

The note trust will generally be established pursuant to a trust deed under which the trust is established, the note trustee appointed and the powers, indemnities and liabilities of the trustee are enunciated. Where more than one class of notes are issued, the trust deed will also contain provisions relating to conflicts between classes and in whose interest the note trustee should act. As a general rule, the note trustee will be required to act in the interests of the most senior class of notes then outstanding.

The role of the note trustee is less limited than the role of the security trustee. The note trustee may be required to act throughout the life of the transaction, with regard to any amendments, modifications or waivers required by the issuer to the securitisation documents. The note trustee may be required to convene meetings of noteholders to discuss such issues, or it may (in conjunction with the security trustee) decide that the requested matter falls within the discretion of the note trustee. Where a default occurs at the securitisation level, the note trustee may also be required by the security trustee to liaise with noteholders regarding potential acceleration and enforcement.

Throughout this Chapter, despite the separate nature of the trusts, we shall refer to the trustee in the singular, without specific reference to the different roles of a security trustee or note trustee. This is partially for ease, but also on the basis that the same entity will usually perform both roles and in the market it is not uncommon to refer to the two trustees in this manner.

### 10.2.3. CMBS structures

A CMBS transaction is structurally slightly different to many other forms of securitisations, whose underlying assets are originated under standard documents and generally (although not always) have a smaller principal balance. These deals often have granular pools of homogenous assets with similar profiles and characteristics. Owing to the nature of the underlying loan or loans, CMBS structures generally are not made up of homogenous loans, but rather of one or more loans originated under slightly different documents with a variety of profiles and underlying structures. It was not uncommon for a CMBS to include a variety of loans with security across a number of sectors, and in many deals, jurisdictions.

This means that the role of the servicer is quite different in a CMBS transaction to other securitisations such as an RMBS or auto loans deal. In the latter types of deal, the servicer has certain discretions regarding the underlying portfolio, and anything beyond this will require the consent of the issuer and the trustee. For example, a certain portion of loans may be restructured, but beyond this threshold, the issuer and the trustee are involved (although the reality is that if these thresholds are breached, the securitisation is probably facing cash flow issues and potential default for breach of certain ratios).

However, a CMBS transaction may only have one or a few loans underlying it, and the servicer appointed has a very wide degree of discretion in servicing the loans (and, where applicable, putting the loan into special servicing). These issues are discussed in Chs 5, 6 and 7, however it does mean that to an extent, matters which in other types of securitisation may require the consideration of the trustee (and, indeed the issuer) are generally managed by the servicer (or special servicer) (which will be referred to throughout this Chapter as the servicing entity).

One final difference in a CMBS is the existence of a controlling party, which will generally be the class who has the most junior collateral interest in the loan. This entity may move up the tranches (from most junior to next most junior, etc. and even potentially to the classes of notes) where the value of the portfolio decreases in value.

The controlling party may have certain rights on the occurrence of events such as a payment default under the loan. This may mean that the most junior creditor with a collateralised interest in the structure effectively may have control in certain events such as payment defaults and restructurings. This is quite different to a securitisation such as an RMBS or an auto loan securitisation where the most senior class of creditors will generally be the party to drive any such discussions and means that the position of the trustee and issuer on the occurrence of certain events in the underlying loans is slightly different to that in other types of securitisations.

## 10.3.   The times, they have changed...

History has shown us the weakness of believing models are infallible. It is not uncommon for events to unfold not as expected, which results in the assumptions of the model ceasing to be valid. This is very much what we have experienced since 2007 in the structured finance market (and in particular, in the CMBS market), and the trustees and corporate service providers have often been the entities adapting their position as best as possible to meet the challenges which have arisen. These parties have rallied to the cry and balanced the need to be proactive and engaged within the limitations of their roles and their need to avoid opening themselves up to inappropriate liabilities given the nature of their mandate.

This has meant that the role of the trustee and issuer has evolved (and continues to evolve at the time of writing) from the roles which were originally envisaged for them. This section of this Chapter will consider the roles these parties have assumed during the financial crisis and other developments which have been part of this evolution. One common theme is that issuers and trustees are having to consider a broad spectrum of issues which it was never envisaged at closing that they would be required to consider. As established in Chs 5, 6 and 7, the structure of a CMBS utilises the expertise of the servicing entity to provide advice and guidance on such issues to the issuer and trustee. However, in conjunction with the servicing entity, the issuers and trustees are being required to consider matters as diverse as swap modelling, valuation procedures, enforcement and insolvency issues across a number of jurisdictions as well as many standard securitisation issues such as contractual interpretation and considering amendments and waivers.

Hindsight is a powerful tool, and many of the issues that are seen in the structured finance markets potentially may have been avoided (or at least minimised) had we the benefit of hindsight at execution. This section of the

Chapter has the benefit of hindsight, and should not be read as a criticism of the parties who arranged, structured and documented CMBS transactions, but merely an enunciation of the issues which have arisen.

### 10.3.1. *Documents, drafted for theory, but being used in practice*

One of the major issues facing trustees and issuers over the last few years has related to documentation. Parties to CMBS transactions have found themselves faced with the need to seek directions from the court on documentation issues as well as being requested to agree to amendments and modifications to the documents. Whilst these aspects of the transaction at the loan level have generally been managed by the servicing entity, there have been regular occurrences where issuers and trustees have also had to consider these issues in detail.

As discussed in Ch.1, CMBS transactions, by their very nature, are highly structured deals, with a number of layers. The underlying layer is the loan facility, which may then have been tranched through an intercreditor agreement, under which certain aspects of the underlying facility may have been modified or amended (such as waterfalls). The senior loan was then securitised, and further amendments and modifications may have been made to the underlying structure (or the cash flows which derive from the senior loan). This complexity, when combined with the speed at which CMBS transactions were executed in the heydays of 2006 and 2007 meant that not every issue was addressed or dealt with in the tomes of documentation produced for each transaction.

One of the main issues arising in documentation is the fact that CMBS transactions were often considered to be "cookie cutter" deals at the securitisation level; like RMBS transactions minimal amendments were required between "repeat" deals. However, this was not necessarily always appropriate. As mentioned earlier, CMBS transactions are generally not homogenous structures with identical loans. Rather, due to the nature of the financing, there will most likely have been active negotiation of the underlying facility. This means that consideration needs to be given to the structure, both legal and economic, for each loan. For example, in a CMBS, there may be a selection of loans, some of which are partially amortising, other which are bullet repayment. There may be other deals which only have one or the other type of loan in them. These differences may have significant impact on aspects of the securitisation.

When a transaction continues to perform, the documents are generally not subject to detailed analysis post-closing. However, when a transaction is under stress, issues often arise which require detailed consideration of the position under the documentation. It is at these times that it becomes evident that either the documents do not entirely work together, or, do not address certain issues.

Documentation issues are arising most frequently when the transaction is nearing default and enforcement of the underlying loans. When drafted, detailed consideration and analysis was generally not given to the position of the transaction at this time. To date, issues are arising which are not specifically dealt with in the documentation. In this situation, the servicing entity and/or the issuer and trustee (depending on what the specific issue relates to) are required to consider the parameters of their powers and any discretion which the documents may permit them. As a general statement, the parties to these deals have been proactive in addressing these issues and ensuring that a transaction is not caught in a stalemate. This has meant that the trustees and issuers have had to be engaged with a variety of highly complex issues and consider the ramifications of various positions and proposals. As such, parties have been required to act within documentation which may not at all times provide a clear process for any such action.

A related issue is the ability for a trustee to agree to certain waivers and amendments when provided with a rating agency confirmation (a RAC). The requirement for a RAC was built into various parts of the documents, such as regarding the transfer of roles from one entity to another, or for other types of amendments and waivers. This mechanism aimed to avoid the cost and time of seeking noteholders consent for matters envisaged in the documents, yet at the same time giving comfort to the trustee that this action was not adverse to the interests of the noteholders.

Over the last few years, trustees have faced issues regarding RACs and when and in what form the rating agencies will give them. This in particular has been the case with the downgrading of financial institutions and the effect such a downgrade has on the transaction. The rating agencies have taken different approaches on RACs, however, as a general rule, RACs are not as easy to obtain as originally envisaged when drafted into the documents. In order to facilitate transfers and relatively straight forward amendments which require a RAC, trustees have had to consider whether they can get comfortable without a written RAC, as required under the documents. Sometimes comfort has been obtained from telephone conversations with the rating agencies or press releases of the rating agencies, where they have stated that a certain event will not in and of itself result in a downgrade of the notes. In other cases, trustees have had to consider alternative ways of getting comfortable with the absence of a RAC without incurring the costs of seeking noteholders consent to what may be transfer of roles entirely within the ambit of the documentation.

Where formal amendments are required (and RACs and other documentation provisions do not benefit the making of the amendment), the consent of the noteholders may be sought. Alternatively, where the trustee has comfort on matters relating to the amendment and the effect of the amendment, the trustee may exercise its discretion to agree to such amendments without the consent of the noteholders. However, owing to the variety of issues which have arisen on documentation, there is no general position regarding the method by which documents are formally amended. Where no formal amendments are required, the servicing entity or the issuer or trustee may agree to interpret provisions in certain ways depending on the level of comfort they are able to get on such matters.

### 10.3.2. *To what extent is servicing entity delegation a full delegation*

When transactions were structured and executed, some people in the market considered the issuers to merely be "brass-plates and letter boxes" with no real capacity to deal with issues in the transaction. However, this is far from the truth. As mentioned above, the issuer is supported by professional directors and a corporate services provider, who often will be a specialist in the structured finance market. Further, such "brass-plate" views ignore the legal reality of the situation—the directors have obligations under the companies law of their place of incorporation which place real responsibilities and liabilities on the directors themselves. This position is supported by case law in a number of jurisdictions which has emphasised the reality of the position of the director (see *Weavering Macro Fixed Income Fund Limited (in Liquidation) v Peterson and Ekstrom*[7] in Cayman Islands).

However, directors on behalf of a company may delegate the authority of the company to specialists as agents or delegates without breaching their fiduciary duties under companies law. As mentioned above, CMBS transactions were structured such that a specialist entity was appointed to service the underlying portfolio of the loans in the name of the lenders (one of which is the issuer as holder of the senior loan). The parameters of the delegation are generally very wide, and are drafted such that the servicing entity is appointed to service, administer and manage the loans. However, there are a number of formulations of the delegation, and it may include specifically (or by implication) ancillary and other rights relating to the loans. The ability of the servicing entity to act in the name of the issuer is effected through a power of attorney. As a general principle, this structure has meant that the servicing entity is able to effectively service the portfolio without seeking instructions from the issuer (which in turn would require instructions from the security trustee) on servicing decisions.

Yet this does not mean that an issuer no longer has any duties with regard to the underlying loans and their collateral. When issues arise outside the ordinary course of the servicing (such as potential litigation) consideration needs to be given to who has the authority to bring the claim in the name of the issuer. This may require analysis of the delegation language and consideration of the ambit of the power of attorney granted to the servicing entity.

---

[7]   Grand Cayman Courts.

Further, although the issuer does not have any duty to actively monitor the servicing entity and its activities, where the issuer becomes aware of matters, a prudent board would discuss these issues with the servicing entity, to ensure that the directors understand what is being done by its agent. To this extent, one of the features of the financial crisis in the CMBS market has been the level of engagement between the issuer and the servicing entity, and where required, the trustee, issuer and the servicing entity.

Under the servicing arrangements, servicing entities deliver regular reports on the assets to the issuer and the trustee. At the time of writing, prudent issuers are considering these reports and minuting such consideration and any questions asked of the servicing entity. This ensures that the issuers are complying with their fiduciary obligations and considering issues as and when they arise, yet at the same time relying on the expertise of their agent.

### 10.3.3.  Limited recourse and the PECO question

One of the general features of securitisation structures (including CMBS) is that the securities issued are limited recourse debt. As a legal concept, limited recourse debt means that the obligation of the issuer to repay any creditors is limited to any proceeds from the underlying assets. To the extent that no assets remain (after repayment of underlying debts or liquidation of the portfolio) the obligation of the issuer to repay such debts is extinguished through the operation of law. This structure means that the issuing vehicle can never be balance sheet insolvent as its liabilities will always be limited by reference to its assets. This ensures that the issuer is unlikely to be susceptible to winding up proceedings, and is often described as meaning that the issuer is an insolvency remote vehicle. This structural feature is required by rating agencies in their analysis of a securitisation's credit strength.

However, prior to the implementation of the Taxation of Securitisation Companies Regulations 2006, in the United Kingdom there was a question as to whether a special purpose vehicle incorporated in England and Wales could issue limited recourse debt without there being an issue as to the deductibility of interest paid on the notes by the issuer. This had a significant impact on the securitisation market involving English real estate assets (both residential and commercial) which were generally securitised through an issuing vehicle incorporated in England and Wales.

In order to create a structure with effects similar to limited recourse, the "post-enforcement call option" structure (the PECO) was developed. Under the PECO structure, an additional special purpose vehicle is established, the PECO holder. The PECO holder will grant an option to the trustee which can be exercised when there are no further remaining assets of the issuer. In these circumstances, the PECO holder will purchase all remaining notes for a de minimis sum. The noteholders agree to this process through the terms and conditions of the notes.

The PECO structure was considered by the market as providing similar comfort to the issuer and the directors as a traditional limited recourse structure (i.e. the structure was considered insolvency remote). In fact, the structure was considered as being commercially equivalent to limited recourse provisions by both the rating agencies and the major accounting firms.

As stated above, limited recourse provisions should mean that the company will never be balance sheet insolvent. Without this, there is the possibility that a company may be balance sheet insolvent. Although a company can be balance sheet insolvent, yet at the same time continue to trade (and indeed be considered a creditworthy entity), there may be times when such balance sheet insolvency has an impact on the securitisation or on the duties of the directors. In the absence of limited recourse provisions, the impact of any balance sheet insolvency needs to be considered.

From a documentation perspective, depending on the parameters of the drafting, an event of default may be triggered by the issuer being deemed unable to pay its debts due to balance sheet insolvency or the legislative equivalent to such wording (in the United Kingdom, s.123(2) of the Insolvency Act 1986). From a companies law perspective, a point may be reached when a company is balance sheet insolvent under which the directors have concerns that they are trading whilst insolvent and as such, have specific obligations under the companies law (although this will also generally need to be combined with cash-flow insolvency).

Whilst there is no uniform position in the CMBS market, a number of transactions did include a balance sheet insolvency event of default (whether expressly or through reference to s.123(2) of the Insolvency Act 1986). The interplay between such an event of default and the PECO structure was considered by the Court of Appeal in *BNY Corporate Trustee Services Limited v Eurosail-UK 2007-3BL Plc*[8] (*Eurosail*).

Whilst the *Eurosail* case concerned an RMBS transaction affected by the insolvency of Lehman Brothers, it has very direct implications for CMBS transactions using English issuing vehicles which predate the Securitisation Taxation Regulations. *Eurosail* considered the circumstances in which an event of default linked to s.123(2) may be triggered and whether the existence of a PECO structure has any effects on the legal analysis of s.123(2) of the Insolvency Act 1986.

---

[8]   [2011] EWCA Civ 227.

The Court of Appeal confirmed that the existence of a PECO in a transaction was not the same as having a limited recourse provision in the document, and whilst it meant that a transaction was bankruptcy remote, it did not mean that the liabilities of the issuing vehicle would always be limited to the assets of the issuing vehicle.

As such, where a transaction includes a balance sheet insolvency test akin to that considered in the *Eurosail* transaction, directors need to consider what s.123(2) of the Insolvency Act 1986 actually means. In a relatively detailed consideration of the meaning of balance sheet insolvency under s.123(2) of the Insolvency Act 1986, the Court of Appeal gave some comfort to directors through its statement that "section 123(2) of the Insolvency Act 1986 applies to a company whose assets and liabilities (including contingent and future liabilities) are such that it has reached the 'point of no return'". The Court drew upon Professor Sir Roy Goode for the "point of no return" test, however, they did not further enunciate the parameters of the test (and suggested that any such enunciation would be "positively dangerous"), suggesting each case needed to be considered individually on the basis of its particular facts.

The decision of the Court of Appeal in *Eurosail* has a number of implications for the directors of issuers in CMBS transactions which include a PECO structure. The first one is that a PECO structure does not have the same legal effect as limited recourse language. The second implication is probably more worrying. The *Eurosail* transaction involved a RMBS deal whose notes had a legal maturity at least 20 years in the future. However, CMBS transactions generally have a shorter period to legal maturity, owing to the shorter maturity profiles of commercial mortgages when compared with residential mortgages. The court noted that the closer the maturity date of a liability, the more likely that the balance sheet test would need to be considered and could possibly be triggered. Where a CMBS deal has a legal maturity in the next few years and its assets have a value considerably below the debt due to be repaid at maturity, directors whose transactions include a balance sheet type event of default will need to consider whether they have reached the "point of no return". This could have very unexpected consequences for a transaction and for the investors in a transaction.

### 10.3.4. PECOs in operation

Another issue which has arisen in the last few years is the actual operation of a PECO.

PECOs are generally structured such that they can only be exercised following enforcement of the security granted by the issuer and following a declaration from the trustee that there are no further assets of the issuer to be liquidated and disbursed to secured creditors. However, two issues arise in the actual operation of this structure.

The trustee is not obliged to make such declaration unless satisfied of its costs (which may include the costs of an adviser required for any determination under the PECO). However, in a Catch 22 position, under the documents, the issuer should have no further assets, so it is difficult to see how this can be done through strict adherence to the documents. Another issuer arises for the issuer and potentially the holding company of the issuer. On the exercise of the PECO, these entities will be wound up. However, where the vehicles are only partially capitalised, there may not be the funds available to pay for the orderly winding up of the vehicles.

Solutions to these issues are available. These can include the issuer and the trustee retaining funds to meet their costs and the costs of liquidation, although this does mean that these parties have to agree to act outside the limited parameters set in the documentation. Alternatively, they could seek the consent of the noteholders to the structure of any exercise of the PECO and the resultant winding up of the issuer.

However, the PECO structure was developed to be automated in process. As this may not be possible for a number of transactions, the actual operation of the PECO is another example of an area where the trustees and issuers are required to consider their position beyond the parameters on the documents. Where the PECO is unable to be exercised, the directors of issuers may seek advice from insolvency specialists and place themselves into a voluntary insolvent liquidation. This was never the assumption for these structures, yet may well be the way CMBS transactions without limited recourse are terminated (and indeed, we have seen examples of this recently).

### 10.3.5.  *Litigation can be an asset*

In a securitisation, as discussed elsewhere in this Chapter (and in this book), at closing, a portfolio of assets is sold to the issuer. Whilst generally the term "assets" refers to the principal assets underlying the structure (such as commercial loans, residential loans or auto loans), strictly speaking, the assets which the issuer owns comprise a number of additional rights. These include any rights transferred by the originator as part of the sale process (both contractual rights and security rights—these together are often referred to as "ancillary rights" or "related collateral") as well as the contractual rights which the issuer has directly against third parties to the transaction. Often these additional assets are difficult to give a quantum to at closing (whereas an underlying loan is easy to value).

Whilst a transaction continues to perform, the assets of the issuer other than those relating to the underlying receivable originating assets and security are less likely to be actively considered (or to have any real value). However, once a transaction is in trouble and the "traditional assets" of the structure (and by this is meant the loans underlying the securitisation and their security) no longer have sufficient value to cover the debt owed to the noteholders, the issuer (or its agents, in particular the servicing entity) will need to consider whether there are any other assets of the structure which could increase the receipts available to the issuer to satisfy its debts as and when they fall due.

This will often involve considering whether the issuer has any contractual claim against any third party (either directly through contractual relationships between the issuer and a third party, or as part of the assigned "ancillary rights" or "related collateral"). These may include considering whether any representations were incorrect at the time they were given (such as representations given as to the assets on the date of transfer) or whether any specialist adviser (such as a lawyer, valuer or auditor) gave advice which was negligent. In the former case, the third party may have an obligation to remedy such breach (with regard to assets, generally by repurchasing the assets in question) and in the latter, the issuer may have a claim either in contract or tort.

Consideration needs to be given as to who is the appropriate person to bring the claim against the third party in question. Although it may be the trustee or the servicing entity (either acting in their own name or in the name of the issuer pursuant to a power of attorney) who is the most appropriate claimant, generally this position will fall to the directors of the issuer acting as the issuer.

When the transactions were structured, however, it was not envisaged that the issuer would need to bring litigation against a third party. As such, funding for litigation by the issuer is generally not contemplated in either the corporate services agreement or in any of the securitisation waterfalls. In fact, some waterfalls appear to limit the ability of an issuer to be reimbursed by reference to "costs incurred in the ordinary course of its business." Where the waterfall is silent (or merely refers to "costs, fees and expenses of the issuer"), it is probably clearer that litigation costs could be covered by the waterfall.

However, consideration should be given to the fact that the issuer has been established to raise financing to purchase a portfolio of assets (and as mentioned above, these assets are not limited to the underlying loans in the structure, but also include rights against other third parties) and the fact that the directors have a duty to promote the success of the company and an obligation to manage the issuer in the best interests of their shareholders, and as such, manage income for the issuer. Moreover, as a claim in litigation is a real asset of the issuer (and in some cases could potentially be a very significant asset of the issuer), it is arguable that any costs in protecting the claim should be covered by "costs incurred in the ordinary course of the business" and as such covered as a senior expense in the waterfall. On this basis (and subject to the issuer having reasonable grounds on which to argue its claim either against the third party or before a court) issuers should be able to accept that whilst not explicitly envisaged in the structure, the ability to protect an asset of the structure such as a claim against a third party should be covered by the waterfall.

The nature of some of these claims, however, can cause issues for both the issuer and the trustee. As the claims will be subject to legal privilege, the issuer (and the trustee, if involved) need to consider how best to notify noteholders without prejudicing the privileged nature of any advice. Further, information regarding the claim unless publicly disclosed may result in those who have notice of the claim being caught by insider trading and other securities regulations. Issuers and trustees need to consider how best to protect their position and the position of the noteholders, without breaching any securities regulations. Noteholders may need to agree to cease trading ("block their bonds") until such time as the claim becomes public nature, which may be problematic for some noteholders.

An additional question arises as to whether the issuer needs noteholder consent to bring a claim against a third party. Whilst the actual position probably varies depending upon a number of factors including quantum of potential claim, applicable limitation periods, strength of advice regarding the claim and nature of the claim, there may well be a situation when the reverse is probably correct, that is, that the issuer has an obligation to bring the claim unless indemnified by noteholders and instructed not to bring the claim. It is possible to consider situations where a failure to bring a claim could potentially expose the issuer (and trustee) to liability.

### 10.3.6.  Liquidity facilities, a drain on a structure?

Another issue which has arisen over the last few years involves liquidity facilities and their cost to a transaction. The structures were rated on the availability of liquidity facilities, and require the issuer to renew the facility on an annual basis.

However, depending on the date of a particular transaction and the regulatory profile of the liquidity facility provider, the annual cost of the liquidity facility provider may be significantly higher than originally modelled.

Prior to the implementation of Basel II, liquidity facilities under 365 days did not require regulatory capital to be retained by the provider. However, with the implementation of Basel II, liquidity facility providers are required to hold regulatory capital on the basis of the rating of the senior tranche of notes (or, in some cases, an independent rating given to the facility itself).

The decline in value of the underlying portfolio of assets in many CMBS deals has resulted in, at times, significant decreases in the rating of the senior classes of notes. This has increased the regulatory cost to the liquidity facility provider in providing the liquidity facility on a given transaction.

Depending on the date of execution of the transaction and on the date of implementation of Basel II by the liquidity facility provider's national regulator, as well as the wording of the facility itself, the liquidity facility provider may be able to claim the costs of any increase in regulatory capital required by the facility to be covered by the transaction. Claims for increased costs are highly technical in nature with limited ability for an issuer or trustee to challenge the increase. Further, the increase needs to be considered by the issuer and trustee on the annual renewal of the facility, where its benefit may be heavily outweighed by the cost to the structure (which is structured to be senior to any payments due on the notes).

Another issue affecting liquidity facilities and their cost to a transaction has been the downgrade by the rating agencies of a large number of banks that provide such facilities in securitisations. Once the liquidity facility provider no longer has the minimum rating required under the documentation, the issuer is required to draw down the entire facility as a standby drawing. The standby drawing may be a cost to the structure as it accrues interest that is senior to other interest costs, and for some transactions, when combined with an increased costs claim, can have an unanticipated impact on the cash flows of the transaction.

### 10.3.7. The approaching wall of legal maturities

Potentially, one of the most significant issues facing participants in the CMBS market is the approaching wall of legal maturities of CMBS transactions. In the coming years, a large number of the CMBS transactions executed prior to 2007 will reach their legal maturity.

Unlike RMBS deals, where the underlying loans amortise over the life of the transaction, in a CMBS transaction, the portfolio will often consist of bullet repayment loans or loans with a limited amortisation profile. This places a refinancing risk on the structure, as a loan will only be repaid at maturity if the underlying borrower is able to refinance the securitised debt.

The combination of a collapse in the value of commercial real estate assets across many jurisdictions and sectors in Europe as well as the lack of appetite amongst banks to refinance commercial real estate loans means that the anticipated refinancing of many of the securitised loans is unlikely to happen.

The rating agencies insisted that the structures include a tail end period (usually two years) which would allow the servicing entity to enforce and liquidate any loan which was unable to be refinanced at maturity. This structure was expected to avoid the issue that loans may still be outstanding at the point of legal maturity of the CMBS notes.

However, as discussed in other chapters in this book, we currently have a CMBS market where a large number of the loans are subject to restructuring, whether it be through the execution of standstill arrangements, entering into formal restructuring process, or at times enforcement of the security and/or liquidation of the assets. The quantum of assets subject to this process and the depressed value of commercial real estate across Europe has meant that we are facing issues where the servicing entity is trying to comply with its obligations under the documents (which generally limit the ability to agree to extensions of loans if such extension would mean that the loan matured within a certain period of the legal maturity date) yet at the same time is trying to maximise recoveries from the assets in accordance with the servicing standards.

This means that there is a very strong possibility that a number of CMBS transactions may hit their legal maturity date without resolution of the issues regarding the underlying loans. One way to avoid this would be to extend the legal maturity of the notes. However, this is not necessarily a straightforward process.

In securitisations, certain amendments are considered modifications so fundamental that they require the consent of all classes of noteholders and generally have a higher quorum for meetings and for resolutions. These amendments are referred to as "basic terms modifications". An extension of the legal maturity of the notes would generally be a basic terms modification and as such would require a "super" majority and "super" quorum in order to be passed by the noteholders.

In order to facilitate such an amendment, it is assumed that the noteholders would require detailed information on the restructuring of the underlying loans as well as any work out plans of the servicing entity. They would then need to consider these plans before being asked to approve them and extend the legal maturity of the notes. This process could take months rather than weeks and needs to be started considerably before the legal maturity date. However, to date there generally has only been limited discussions of such proposals in the CMBS market.

Further, one of the inherent issues of a basic term modification is the fact that it often will be structured to require the consent of all classes of noteholders unless the trustee declares that consent of only the senior class will not materially prejudice the interests of the other junior classes. This declaration is very difficult for the trustee, as this would require getting comfortable with the projected recoveries of the structure under the proposed extension and considering in detail the effect of any proposal on the ability of the junior classes to be repaid. In light of this, it is unlikely that a trustee would be able to get sufficient comfort in order to exercise its discretion to make any such declaration.

As such, it is likely that any extension would require the consent of all noteholders. There have been some distinct differences of opinion over what to do with the structures, with some senior holders wanting to liquidate so they get repaid, whereas junior noteholders may have a greater interest in keeping the structure in existence to maximise recoveries. These types of issue have been played out in both the tranches of the loan as well as the capital stack of the CMBS.

Failure to extend the legal maturity date of the CMBS makes a payment default inevitable unless the servicing entity has liquidated all assets and a liquidation waterfall has been run. One of the problems with hitting this stage is that it effectively limits the ability of the servicing entity to maximise recoveries, unless parties agree to work through legal maturity. Rather, the best that generally can be hoped for, is a minimisation of losses.

Once the notes hit legal maturity, the issuer and trustee are left with limited options. The trustee has the ability to accelerate and enforce. However, even if the trustee enforces, all it has control over is the senior tranche of the loan. The trustee could liquidate this position, otherwise the trustee and the noteholders still have to wait until the underlying loan is enforced and security liquidated. As mentioned above, this effectively limits the ability to maximise recoveries as the market would be aware that any sale of underlying assets is essentially a forced sale.

As such, there is a need in plenty of time prior to legal final for the market to consider how to manage the approaching legal maturities of a large number of CMBS transactions. Without appropriate dialogue between all parties involved, the structures may find themselves in very difficult positions, where any effective ability to manage the process and maximise recoveries is taken out of the hands of the servicing entity and other parties and instead relies upon the marketability of the assets under a perceived forced sale scenario.

## 10.4. Conclusion

In the "Life of Reason", George Santayana gave the world an oft-misquoted piece of advice *"Those who cannot remember the past are condemned to repeat it."*

The issues in CMBS transactions which participants in the CMBS market have had to consider over the last few years, issues which are enunciated and discussed in this Chapter as well as other Chapters of the book, are ones which the CMBS community needs to remember and try and avoid repeating.

The market has taken the lessons learnt and considered whether the next wave of CMBS transactions should be structured in a different manner to the previous wave of European CMBS deals. The result is the development of the highly commendable CMBS 2.0 initiative—a topic which is discussed in detail in Ch.4 of this book. The most recent CMBS deals from the DECO conduit have incorporated CMBS 2.0 technology, with some of the changes effecting the issuer and trustee. In particular, the bane of many parties experience of the last few years, issues with noteholder communication and amendments to documents, has been amended through permitting negative consents in the documentation.

Thus, in principle, the issuers and trustees have taken Santayana's warning to heart. CMBS market participants continue to learn from issues which arise from legacy transactions, issues which are expected to continue to arise on a case-by-case basis in 2013 and beyond.[9] Whilst there has been a limited flow of new CMBS deals, the parties to CMBS transactions are using the knowledge gained for new transactions in other securitisation sectors.

Issuer and trustees are considering the implication of a number of points in the documents, which they previously may have not analysed in quite so much detail. A rigorous analysis of the structure is required going forward, and all parties need to be part of this. The arranger, the originator, their respective counsel and the parties discussed in this Chapter all need to be part of an increased vigilance and analysis of structures, cash flows, mechanics and asset due diligence to ensure that the next flow of securitisation transactions, whether they be CMBS, RMBS, auto loans or more bespoke structures, do not suffer from the limitations and problems of the pre-2007 market. Indeed, the market probably has the best opportunity ever offered to try and rectify these issues and hopefully create a new, vibrant and trusted securitisation market that will once again transform itself through innovation.

---

[9]  This is especially so given the profile of debt maturity discussed in Ch.2.

# Chapter 11

# A Hitchhiker's Guide to the Role of Rating Agencies in the European Commercial Mortgage Loan and CMBS Markets

Cynthia Ma,

Senior Associate, K&L Gates LLP

## 11.1. Introduction

In the wake of the global financial crisis that began in August 2007 and a year later saw the collapse of Lehman Brothers, in a most spectacular manner, and almost unimaginable in the preceding 20 years, the world economy has become an environment which is heavily policed by regulators, where the fundamentals of the economic policies of governments and central banks are repeatedly challenged. Investment bankers have since been condemned and held to be the very culprits who were primarily responsible for the transfer of sub-prime mortgage credit risks to the capital markets through structured financings that triggered the financial crisis.

As the crisis unfolded, the affected world turned its criticisms on the "gate-keepers" of capital markets—the credit rating agencies (CRAs), whom they supposed to have at their disposal, analytical tools to help investors to identify the credit risks inherent in financial instruments, which enable them to make an informed judgment as to whether to invest in the instruments. The criticisms had been directed towards the potential conflicts between the CRAs' involvement, in designing the structural specifics of the securities on the one hand and as producers of unbiased opinions of the creditworthiness of those securities on the other. There were also heavy concerns that CRAs received payments from the issuers of securities for their rating services and such a business relationship would suggest that CRAs could be more willing to accommodate certain issues than in cases where they were not on the payroll of the issuer.

This Chapter examines the role of the CRAs in the EU commercial mortgage loan and commercial mortgage-backed securities (CMBS) markets. The Chapter is divided into four main sections. Paragraph 11.2 sets the scene by explaining the basics of credit ratings and explores the typical procedures in the process followed by CRAs in rating structured finance instruments. The Chapter then proceeds to consider in para.11.3 the elements of rating analysis: the rating models, methodologies and criteria used by CRAs for commercial mortgage loans and CMBS in the EU. Paragraph 11.3.1.1 provides an overview on the fundamental concepts employed—in one form or another—in any credit risk analysis: namely, the concepts of default probability and loss severity. An appreciation of these concepts will aid the understanding of the approaches adopted by CRAs encountered in their numerical analyses.

Paragraph 11.3.1.1 will further consider how these parameters are determined for a single mortgage loan as well as a pool of mortgage loans as in the case for CMBS (para.11.3.1.2). Moody's MoRE Analysis will be offered as a real life quantitative model for analysing CMBS in the appendix to this Chapter for readers who are interested to get a flavour of how the rating concepts and techniques are employed by a CRA in practice.

In addition to the quantitative models, the qualitative methodological considerations, too, are important elements of the rating process. These include detailed legal analyses of the transaction structure, the security package, the payment priorities among creditors of different seniority, other relevant intercreditor arrangements, and the assessments of credit enhancements and the quality of servicing of the mortgage loans. These considerations which provide the major inputs in CRA's rating models will be discussed in para.11.3.2 below.

Finally, in para.11.4 the Chapter will focus on the regulations put in place, post financial crisis, to regulate the businesses of the CRAs, in an attempt to avoid and manage conflicts that arise between the CRA being an independent rater of financial products and at the same time that it being remunerated by the issuer of the products. In particular, the Chapter will trace the history of the regulation in Europe of the CRAs and their activities, dating from the *"Statements of principles regarding the activities of credit rating agencies"* published by the CRA task force of the International Organization of Securities Commissions (IOSCO) in 2003 to the post-crisis to the European Regulation on CRAs (Regulation 1060/2009) (CRA Regulation), as subsequently amended by Regulation 513/2011 (CRA II).

## 11.2. Basics of credit ratings and the rating process[1]

### 11.2.1. What are credit ratings?

Credit ratings are independent opinions issued by CRAs on an entity's ability to make payments of its debts on a timely basis. Credit ratings may be provided on the issuer's general creditworthiness and/or of its particular debt obligations, for instance, a bond issue, euro medium-term note programme or a credit default swap with the issuer as the reference entity. When assigned to an issuer itself (such as a corporate) a credit rating provides an assessment of the likelihood of default by the issuer, given its ability to make payments under its debt obligations in time and in full. Credit ratings may be issued on a long-term or short-term basis. Long-term credit ratings are given on debt securities lasting more than 12 months (which apply to most CMBS) while short-term ratings are for short-term debt securities, with a maturity of less than 12 months as in a commercial paper issuance.

The main CRA players in the EU commercial mortgage loan and CMBS markets are Standard & Poor's Rating Services (S&P), Moody's Investors Services (Moody's) and Fitch Ratings Limited (Fitch). DBRS Ratings Limited has also emerged as a credible alternative to the three major players in the CMBS arena, post the financial crisis.

Given that credit ratings form part of the investors' assessments of the credit risks associated with debt securities, it is important to realise that they are not investment advice per se; for although credit ratings may affect the initial pricing of a debt securities, they are not indicative of its market liquidity. Credits ratings provided for debt securities, when they are first issued, are not guarantees of their credit risks in the future—they do not guarantee that an investment will pay out or it will not default. The ratings reflect the opinions of the CRAs, at a specific time, having evaluated the then available current and historical information[2] and the potential impact of foreseeable future events which can be anticipated at that time. Subsequent to the initial rating, ongoing rating monitoring enables CRAs to review and update their opinions throughout the life of the securities.

---

[1]  See references: (1) "Guide to Credit Ratings – what are credit ratings and how d they work?", Standard & Poor's Financial Services LLC, Vol. 1.4, 2011 (2) "Guide to Credit Ratings Criteria – why criteria are important and how they are applied" Standard & Poor's Financial Services LLC, Vol. 1.0, 2010 (3) Marc Adelson, "Introduction to the Rating Process", Adelson and Jacob COnsulting, LLC, American Securitisation Form 2008.

[2]  This is rather similar to the nature of a balance sheet in the sense that it provides a "snapshot" of the financial affairs of an entity as at a particular date.

## 11.2.2. *Outline of a rating process for structured finance instruments*[3]

In forming its opinion, a CRA applies its own model and methodology in order to assess the credit risks associated with debt securities. Despite the difference in their respective model and methodology, the typical rating process for CRAs is broadly "analyst driven": a process in which an analyst of the CRA takes the lead in evaluating the debt obligation following a request from its issuer and acting as the point of contact between the CRA and the issuer. In conjunction with a team of specialists, the analyst will organise and conduct the appropriate quantitative and qualitative analyses, according to the CRA's own methodology. The analyst then produces an assessment of the instrument-specific documentation and of other relevant information, to be submitted to an internal rating committee for review and voting.[4] Sometimes, the committee's comments may feed back into the rating process through the revision of standard assumptions of the CRA. Once the decision is finalised, all ratings are ultimately mapped into an alphanumeric scale, benchmarked to the historical performance of bonds of similar characteristics. The rating result will be notified to the issuer as a rating opinion letter, that will also be published and disseminated to the public. The CRA may also provide life-long ratings in the form of ratings surveillance to monitor these rated debt issues.

As in the case with corporate bond credit ratings, the issuer pays the CRAs their fees for rating structured finance instruments. However, as highlighted in Ch.1, there is one crucial difference: the process of securitisation pools together individual receivables assets, into portfolios with potentially heterogeneous obligors, each of which corresponds to a tranche of debt of a different seniority that reflects a different position in the transaction's capital structure. The allocation of cash flows to these tranches is determined by subordination covenants that are specific to the transaction. As a consequence, CRAs need to understand the risks that affect the credit positions of the debt tranches arising from the subordination structure, in addition to default risks associated with the collateral pool.

Thus, strictly speaking, a structured finance rating is an opinion expressed by a CRA, on the likelihood that the cash flows generated from the underlying asset pool will be sufficient for the servicing and repayment of the debt claims *associated with a particular tranche*, e.g. one often hears about a "triple-A rating" for the most senior tranche within a CMBS structure.

The key to the reliability of structured finance ratings therefore lies in the accuracy of the CRA, in assessing the credit risk associated with the

---

[3] "The role of ratings in structured finance: issues and complications", Committee on the Global Financial System Working Group Report, Bank for International Settlements, January 2005.

[4] For S&P, the amount of analytical work that has been carried out during the rating process is gathered into the so-called Ratings Analysis Methodology Profile (RAMP). The RAMP is then reviewed and discussed by the rating committee prior to a vote on the assigned rating.

underlying collateral pool and the accurate modelling of the distribution of the cash flows from the asset pool to different groups of noteholders holding notes of different seniority. The rating process for structured finance instruments may be thought of as following a "two-step" approach with:

- a first step in employing analytical models to assess the credit risk of a collateral pool that involves detailed quantitative modelling of the cash flows based on the results of the credit risk analysis; and
- a second step in transaction-specific structural analysis as set out in the securitisation transaction documentation that focuses on legal assessments and evaluations.

See paras 11.3.1 and 11.3.2 below for further details.

During the CMBS rating process, CRAs liaise extensively with arrangers/ originators on their analysis of cash flows, credit enhancement and structural features of the transaction. This results in the arrangers of a CMBS transaction tailoring the debt tranches with reference to certain rating levels and corresponding CRA requirements. Given the influence that CRAs may exert in the early stages of the transaction structure, their involvement may be seen as part of transaction origination by the arrangers to the extent that the CRA models are employed to pre-structure the transactions and that the CRAs are heavily engaged in dialogues with the arrangers, with a view to finalising the structure.

## 11.3. The two-step approach to CMBS ratings

From the standpoint of CMBS, the first step is a portfolio credit risk analysis of the cash flows generated by the assets—a collateral pool of commercial real estate (CRE) mortgage loans and how such cash flows are to be affected by the probability of the underlying borrower's default; while the second step, within the two-step approach, concerns the structural analysis of the risk characteristics on the liabilities side (i.e. the CMBS notes) by assessing and evaluating the specific structure of transaction, primarily the payment waterfall and the subordination of the various noteholders and parties.

The structural analysis step is essentially the detailed modelling of the cash inflows, using the results of the portfolio credit risk analysis as input scenarios to stress test cash outflows as determined by the transaction's payment waterfall and subordination structure, in order to inform on the structure's credit loss tolerance level.

Thus the two-step rating process may be pictorially represented as in the below diagram:

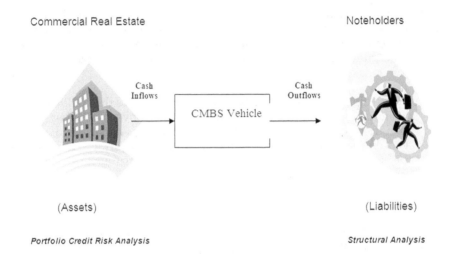

Commercial Real Estate

Noteholders

Cash Inflows

Cash Outflows

CMBS Vehicle

(Assets)

(Liabilities)

*Portfolio Credit Risk Analysis*

*Structural Analysis*

### 11.3.1. Fundamental credit concepts behind the CRAs' rating models and the credit risk analysis of the CMBS collateral

#### 11.3.1.1.  Single CRE loan credit risk analysis

##### 11.3.1.1.1.   Concepts and measures for CRE mortgage loan credit risks[5]

The concepts behind the credit risk analysis is best introduced with respect to a single CRE mortgage loan. These concepts may then be employed in similar analyses of a CMBS secured on a pool of CRE mortgage loans, which are more complex due to the existence of correlations between the loans.

There are three parameters that are important in quantifying the credit risk associated with a single CRE mortgage loan: the "probability of default", the "exposure at default" and the "loss given default". CRAs base their analytical models on all or some of these parameters, though the emphasis and assumptions used in quantifying them differ in their own models.

The "probability of default" (PD) (also known as the "default rate" or "expected default frequency") is strongly associated with the characteristics and creditworthiness of the underlying borrower of a securitised asset and as discussed below, it is dependent on the borrower's likelihood to default under a set of certain economic circumstances.

---

[5]   Christopher Marrison, *The Fundamentals of Risk Measurement* (McGraw-Hill, 2002).

- The "exposure at default" (EAD) is the lender's exposure at the time of default and is equal to the outstanding amount of loan principal and interest accruing at that time.
- The "loss given default" (LGD) (also commonly known as "loss severity") represents the loss as a percentage of the EAD. The loss suffered by the lender is determined as the EAD plus all administrative costs relating to the default, minus the net present value of any amount that is recovered from the obligor as explained in the following formula:

$$LGD = (EAD + Administrative\ Costs - Recoveries) / EAD$$

Inevitably, the credit risk of a CRE mortgage loan depends on the characteristics of the underlying CRE property securing the loan and the loan structure. It transpires that the influence of these two factors may be captured, to a large extent, by the debt service coverage ratio (DSCR) and loan-to-value (LTV) measures associated with the CRE mortgage loan.

The dependence of credit risks on the underlying CRE property are driven primarily by the uncertainty in the income streams produced by the CRE property and the market value of the property at different times. The prime focus of the CRAs is, therefore, whether the underlying property generates sufficient cash inflows from its tenants to cover the scheduled mortgage payments by the borrower; and that the market value of the property will be at a level, at the time of default or maturity of the loan, that allows the repayment of the principal outstanding under the loan. As a consequence, the analyses on the cash inflows and market values of a CRE property form the basis to characterise PD, EAD and LGD in terms of DSCR and LTV.

The cash inflow of a CRE property is measured by the property's underlying net operating income (NOI) (i.e. the revenues less operating expenses or EBITDA) or net cash flow (NCF) (i.e. NOI minus tenant allowance, commissions, capital expenditures not recoverable from tenants other fixed charges and expenses). The level of NOI or NCF is dependent on:

(i)    the property type (e.g. retail, office, hotel or multi-family);
(ii)   the quality of property (e.g. construction quality, neighbourhood, the quality of the property relative to the national market for that property type, local market and competition);
(iii)  the creditworthiness of the underlying tenants (e.g. tenants profile and quality of income);
(iv)   the structure and terms of the underlying leases (e.g. long-term fully repairing insuring leases);
     i.    diversity benefit from cross-collateralisation amongst other properties;

 ii. the historical level of vacancies and rents on the property and other similar CRE properties in the same geographical region; and

 iii. the economic cycle of properties within the local CRE market.

The extent of the NOI coverage for the borrower's loan obligation can be measured by the DSCR, which is often calculated as the current NOI on a property, divided by the actual mortgage debt service obligation.[6] DSCR is a good indicator of PD because it links the likelihood of the borrower defaulting on a loan directly with the amount of cash generated from the CRE property that enables the borrower to service the various payment obligations under the loan and to the eventual repayment of the loan (barring refinancing) at maturity.

In addition to the cash inflows, CRAs also assess whether the market value of the CRE property stands at a level, that in the event of default, the sum to be recovered from enforcement on the property will be sufficient to repay the outstanding amounts under the mortgage loan plus associated enforcement costs and this is expressed by LTV. LTV is an important indicator of the potential LGD since the magnitude of the loss suffered upon the borrower's default will be an amount by which the outstanding debt on the property exceeds the property value at a specific time.

It is worth pointing out that a CRE loan mortgage carries very little credit risk at origination, as the lender typically requires a good buffer for both leverage and debt service cover. For example, underwriting thresholds of an initial LTV of 70 per cent and DSCR of 1.3 at loan origination would mean that the property value would have to drop around 30 per cent before it becomes a concern for the lender. Subsequent to origination, the market value of the property is expected to fluctuate during the term of the loan and the main credit risk driver will be the inherent future uncertainties in the cash inflows and market value of the property, which CRAs aim to quantify and capture in their quantitative models that determine the PD and LGD.

### 11.3.1.1.2. Model for PD

An approach to the modelling of PD for a single CRE mortgage loan will now be outlined.[7]

---

[6] CRAs, however, often use a more conservative form of DSCR measure given by the NCF divided by a stressed refinance constant (a debt constant that is higher than the actual amount of debt outstanding in order to account for potentially unfavourable refinance conditions when the end balloon payment becomes due and payable at the maturity date of the mortgage).

[7] See for example, Jun Chen and Jing Zhang, "Modelling Commercial Real Estate Loan Credit Risk: An Overview" Moody's Analytics, May 3, 2011 and Jun Chen, "Monitoring Real Estate Loan Risk" Moody's Analytics, May 17, 2011.

The process of modelling PD begins by the quantification of the dynamic processes and uncertainties surrounding the CRE asset by considering whether:

(a)   the future NOI streams and the market values of the property are able to cover the amount of debt outstanding at all times; and

(b)   the borrower's likelihood to default under the mortgage loan having accounted for the economic factors affecting the borrower.

In regard to (a), the future streams of NOI of a CRE property will depend on the set of financial conditions specific to the property and the market environment it operates in. Because of the unknown fluctuations and uncertainties that may manifest themselves under those financial conditions; the values of the future NOI stream, theoretically speaking, may be discerned as following an "infinite" number of possible paths or "realisations". One also observes that the evolution of the market values of the property over time—usually correlated with NOI (since a higher NOI will make the property worth more)—is also affected by the general conditions in both the capital and CRE space markets.

In regard to (b), there is evidence that at the time of financial distress and when a shortfall arises due to insufficient NOI to cover scheduled mortgage payments and results, the borrower will either:

•   use its own funds to cover the shortfall if the shortfall is temporary and is one that may be cured;[8]

•   sell (with the lender's permission) the property if the market value stands at a level high enough to allow it to pay back the outstanding amounts of principal and interest owed out of the sale proceeds; or

•   miss the scheduled mortgage payments and wait for the lender's decision to foreclose the property or restructure the debt.

Consider a particular pair, *i* of NOI and market value of the property at a future time *t*, *(NOI, Market Value)*$_i$, the PD at *t*, $PD_{it}$, with respect to *(NOI, Market Value)*$_i$ is mathematically given by:

$$PD_{it} = P(X_{it}) \times P(Default/X_{it})$$

where,

•   $X_{it}$ denotes a particular set of financial variables at the loan, property and market levels that manifest at time *t* that would give rise to *(NOI, MarketValue)*$_i$;

---

[8]   This would usually be the sponsor injecting equity, given that CRE deals are usually structured with SPVs.

- $P(X_{it})$ represents the probability that $X_{it}$ is realised and may determined by statistical data available on the basis of extensive observed historical data of commercial property financials; and
- $P(Default/X_{it})$ measures the conditional probability of default given that $X^{it}$ is realised and captures the exercise by the borrower of any one of its three "default scenarios".

Theoretically, however, with reference to a particular property, there can be other pairs of NOI and market value that may be realised at time $t$ that corresponds to different financial variables at $t$ and so the overall $PD_t$ at $t$ may be obtained by integrating over all possible value pairs of $i$:

$$PD_t = \int PD_{it} = \int P(X_{it}) \times P(Default/X_{it})$$

Determination of $P(X_{it})$

In order to determine $P(X_{it})$ for a particular property $w$ by statistical data available on the basis of extensive historical data of commercial property financials, we may decompose $P(X_{it})$ as the sum of two main probabilities that correspond with two independent sources of risks that may affect the value pair *(NOI, Market Value)*$_i$ for property $w$, namely: $P_{m,w}$ and $\epsilon_{n,w}$

$P_{m,w}$ is dependent on the overall market movement (the "market" or "systematic" risk) and $\epsilon_{n,w}$ relates to risks that are specific to the property $w$ (the "non-systematic" or "idiosyncratic" risk) such that:

$$P_{i,t} = P_{m,w} + \epsilon_{n,w}$$

A Monte Carlo programme[9] will then be used to simulate values for $Z_k$ based on the simultaneous random simulations of $P_{m,w}$ and $\epsilon_{n,w}$

Determination of $P(Default/X_{it})$.

The assumption that a loan would automatically default if the market value of the property at time $t$ falls below the outstanding loan amount owed at that time is a major consideration in the determination of $P(Default/X_{it})$. In additional to the market value, market-wide factors also play a significant part in a borrower's default:

- key asset level financial ratios (DSCR, LTV and loan size) – lower DSCR and higher LTV leads to higher PD;
- market cycle factors—strength of CRE space market and capital markets—weak space market and therefore high vacancy rate and weak capital market and therefore negative price changes will both lead to higher PD;

---

[9]   Laurence Goldman, "Risk Analysis and Monte Carlo Simulation", Decisioneering Inc, 2000.

- market condition at origination—loans originated in stronger CRE market environment will lend to higher PD due to looser underwriting criteria; or
- core versus non-core property type—non-core property types tend to have higher PD due to higher operating business characteristics.

Holding constant the values of DSCR and LTV, there will be more equity accruing to the borrower under good market conditions and it will be more likely to hold onto the property without defaulting. In contrast, there will be less equity incentive for the borrower to retain the property in situations where the prevailing market condition proves to be deteriorating.

Taking all of such factors into consideration, the probability that the borrower will default at time $t$, and in respect of a particular property $w$, is:

$$P(Default/X_{i,t})=f[T_1(DSCR_{i,t,w}),T_2(LTV_{i,t,wt}),...]$$

where $f$ is a logistic function to capture the non-linear relationship between $P$ $(Default/X_{i,t})$ and the explanatory variables and the values of $DSCR_{i,t,w}$ and $LTV_{i,t,w}$ may be calculated by reference to a particular $(NOI, MarketValue)_i$

### 11.3.1.1.3. Model for LGD

An important aspect of credit rating is to identify the severity of the loss once the borrower has defaulted under the loan. Loss severity is measured by LGD. In the event that the lender decides to take enforcement action and sell the property in order to recover the amounts owed to it following the loan default. LGD is a function of the disposal value of the property (which determines the recovery) with respect to the outstanding amounts owed under the loan together with administrative costs. The quantitative model for LGD therefore focuses on the two types of losses:

(i) the amount by which the outstanding amounts owed under the loan exceed the recovery amount and this is the LTV level at time of default $t$; and

(ii) the empirical variables that represent the transaction and administrative costs, $Y$.

For a particular realisation of $(NOI, MarketValue)_i$ at time $t$ in respect of a property $w$:

$$LGD_{i,t,w}=g[T_3(LTV_{i,t,w}),Y]$$

where $g$ is a linear factor and $T_3$ is a linear transformation function.

As a first approximation, in the scenario of negligible transaction and administrative costs, the LGD is reduced to:

$$LGD_t = \frac{Loan_t - Value_t}{Loan_t} = 1 - \frac{1}{LTV_t}$$

Thus, LGD is an inverse function of the LTV for an efficient CRE market, where transaction costs are negligible.

Another useful parameter employed by CRAs is the concept of "expected loss" (EL) that may be determined in terms of PD and LGD as:

$$EL_t = \frac{\sum_{i=1}^{N}\left(PD_{i,t} \times LGD_{i,t}\right)}{N}$$

where $N$ denotes the total number of all realisations of the NOI and market value pairs at time $t$.

### 11.3.1.1.4.  Summary observations

As a numerical method that produce accurate estimates—the use of random sampling is known to generate paths of NOI values at all times $t$ that mimic those actually observed—Monte Carlo techniques are, nonetheless, very computer source-intensive and can require long computation times to produce the results. In the situation of a CMBS transaction, where there may often be a pool of CRE mortgage loans, rather than a single loan, the calculation using Monte Carlo techniques would be further complicated by the introduction of correlations between the loans within the pool.

Moreover, although the use of Monte Carlo methods leads to accurate results, it is nonetheless a numerical technique that relies on the correctness in the assumptions fed into the model by CRAs in the first instance. CRAs place different emphasis on the credit concepts in their respective analysis. While S&P makes PD their main focus, both Moody's and Fitch place expected loss and LGD at the heart of their rating analyses. At the time of writing, S&P has proposed a lifetime default probability concept that is driven by each loan's S&P-specific LTV and DSCR and consultation on the proposal with the industry is underway.[10]

---

[10]  Albert Yoan, "After Business Drought, S&P Proposes Overhaul of CMBS Ratings", Doww Jones Newswire, June 4, 2012 and "Request for Comment: CMBS Global Property Evaluation Methodology", Global Credit Portal, Rating's Direct, Standard & Poor's, June 4, 2012.

### 11.3.1.2. CMBS collateral loan portfolio credit risk analysis

In the context of a CMBS, which are collateralised by a pool of CRE mortgage loans, the quality of the CRE mortgage pool is the most important driver of the credit ratings of the CMBS notes issued. In analysing the loan pool, credit concepts and parameters for a single CRE loan as outlined in the last section—PD, LGD and EL—remain relevant where the collateral pool consists of a pool of CRE mortgages. In theory, one may calculate the probability distribution of the income generated[11] from the underlying CRE loan pool and use this to estimate the probability that the income pool will be sufficient to meet the scheduled payments of principal and interest under the notes at each certified rating, having taken into account of:

- the PD of the individual borrowers within the CRE pool (and how these may vary over the life of the CMBS transaction);
- the LGD for each of the CRE loan; and
- crucially, the default correlations between the CRE loans within the pool.

The effects of correlation cannot be overlooked when one comes to consider a portfolio of credit risks. Correlations describe the extent to which the loans, within the CMBS pool, tend to default at the same time. This could happen due to market factors, for instance, the whole economy is in recession and adverse conditions triggering the default of the tenants of the underlying collateral properties. Such correlation effects produce loss distributions that are skewed—with years of low losses punctuated by a number of years of high losses. The description of this type of correlation and the potential anomaly in the loss distribution profile of a CMBS loan pool is one of the most difficult aspects that dominate the credit analysis of a CMBS loan pool.

The choice of the CRA's modelling approach will depend on the specifics of the CRE loan pool, such as the number and homogeneity of the loan type, borrower classes and historical performances as shall now be illustrated.

#### 11.3.1.2.1. Homogeneity versus heterogeneity

Traditional asset-backed securities (ABS) portfolios consist of large, well diversified and homogeneous pools of assets (e.g. residential mortgages receivables) with no significant exposure of an individual asset relative to the overall pool. Idiosyncratic risks, which are specific to each individual underlying asset, are thus less important, where there is a homogeneous pool. Under these circumstances, the default characteristics of ABS follows the law of large numbers, so that the underlying assets present stable and predictable loss distributions, as a result of which one may adopt the so-called "actuarial approaches" that assume each originator's unique

---

[11] See A2, Appendix for further details.

underwriting policy gives rise to the portfolio's characteristic loss and recovery patterns that are stable over time.

In contrast, CRE mortgages tend to be "heterogeneous" (i.e. lack of uniformity and relevant historical information about them is relatively limited) so that credit risk analysis of a CMBS loan pool would invariably based on individual assessments of the underlying properties securing the mortgages.

### 11.3.1.2.2.   Pool and loan size

The credit risk profile of a CMBS pool changes in accordance to loan and pool size: given a similar loan size, the smaller the pool the greater the effect of default of any loan in the pool will be; and likewise pools with loan or borrower concentrations merit closer scrutiny because they give rise to greater risk of default of the pool. In fact, CRAs often decide whether a property-specific "loan-by-loan" approach or an actuarial analysis should be adopted in accordance with the size diversity of the loan pool. The actuarial approach, involving the evaluation of the credit characteristics of a sample of loans selected from the pool, is likely to be adopted by CRAs in circumstances where the loans have been originated with uniform underwriting standards (i.e. that the distribution of the loan balances is not skewed given a sufficiently large number of loans). If any of these conditions is lacking, CRAs will rely more on a loan-by-loan analysis.

The size of the loans will also impact on the rating analysis of the CMBS notes because as the size of the loans within the pool increases, CRAs will require the credit enhancement to step up so that on the random default of a loan of large size within the pool, any monies through recovery will still be sufficient to pay down the higher-rated classes of CMBS notes, thereby enabling the credit rating of the pool to be maintained and not be affected by the default of that loan.

### 11.3.1.2.3.   Pool DSCR and LTV

On the assumption that the PD and LGD of each loan in the pool is highly dependent on its DSCR and LTV respectively, CRAs will review a large sample (approximately 40–60 per cent) of the individual loans in order to make assessments, by property type, of the pool's NOI and NCF, as well as the market value of the collateral property securing each loan, from which the pool's DSCR and LGD may be determined.

### 11.3.1.2.4.   Correlations

One approach to measuring and quantifying CMBS portfolio correlations is the covariance credit-portfolio model. The model defines the EL (i.e.

expected loss) and unexpected loss (UL) of the portfolio in terms of the EL and UL of the individual loans within the portfolio. While EL in respect of a loan may be interpreted as being the amount that the lender may expect to lose on average over a number of years, UL is the standard deviation of the loss in respect of that loan and is a function of LGD and PD.

Without delving into the mathematical details, suffice it to say that the loss correlation between the loans in a CMBS portfolio may be determined either on the portfolio level or on the loan level.

On the portfolio level, the portfolio UL may be expressed in terms of the UL of each loan together with a term representing the loss correlation between the loans within the portfolio. The "loss correlation term" may be in turn expressed in terms of the average PD for all the loans in the portfolio and the average percentage LGD for the portfolio.

In contrast, in a loan level treatment, the loss correlation is calculated from the joint PD that both loans will default at the same time and the respective PD of each of these loans. The EL of the portfolio may then be determined from the joint PD.

As an alternative, the correlated defaults for a portfolio of CMBS loans may be simulated by the use of Monte Carlo simulation techniques that utilises a Merton-based criterion to the effect that if the random values for the underlying collateral property fall below a certain pre-set level, the loan goes into default.[12]

Under this approach, one begins by creating the random number for the property value in respect of each borrower, then a test is carried out to see if it is less than the pre-set critical value, and if that is the case, the borrower is deemed to have defaulted and the LGD may be calculated. The LGD for all borrowers are then aggregated to give the loss distribution for the portfolio. As for a typical Monte Carlo simulation, the process is repeated thousands of times with different sets of market values until there are sufficient results to generate the loss distribution.

For all the borrowers in the loan portfolio, the changes in the asset values are correlated through common market risk variables (such as interest rates, etc.) that produce the correlated defaults. Under this approach, there is no need to assume a probability distribution for the losses since a loss distribution is produced directly by simulation.[13] The different steps in this simulation model may be summarised as follows:

(a)    determine PD for each borrower;

---

[12]   See A.3.1 of the Appendix.
[13]   See A.3.1 of the Appendix.

(b)     determine the critical threshold for market value of the underlying collateral property;

(c)     determine the correlations between the market values of the underlying properties;

(d)     create un-correlated random numbers, $n$;

(e)     create un-correlated market values of the underlying properties, $z$;

(f)     record a loss if $z$ is below the threshold; and

(g)     create the loss distribution.

Steps (e) and (f) in the procedure above are to be repeated thousands of times to generate an accurate loss distribution. For a specific property $i$, the threshold market value $z_i$ may be expressed in terms of a combination of market risks as well as idiosyncratic risks:

$$Z_i = \beta_i m + \epsilon_i$$

where $m$ denotes a single market index that is associated with a particular market sector which influences the market value of the property in question.

### 11.3.2.   *Qualitative considerations on methodologies and criteria used by the CRAs in rating CMBS transactions*[14]

#### 11.3.2.1.   *Qualitative adjustment factors*

Having elaborated on the quantitative modelling aspects of a CMBS rating process, this Chapter will now turn to the qualitative factors that CRAs may consider when making adjustments in their models.

As the central aim of the rating process for a CMBS transaction is to assess if the cash flows and inherent value of the CRE collateral properties are sufficient to meet the payment obligations under the notes, the issuer's expenses and re-financing on maturity; there is a whole host of factors relating to the property, the cash flow, the nature of the security and insolvency issues that can impact on PD and LGD.

##### 11.3.2.1.1.   Property

The following are the main considerations by the CRAs on the property:

•     Some property types have higher operating expenses and so small revenue changes may result in a notable decrease in the net cash flow and increases the PD as a result;

---

[14] See the references: Benedicte Pfister, "Moody's Approach to Rating European CMBS", CMBS World, CMSA, Winter 2002; "Rating Criteria for Fitch's US CMBS Multiborrower Rating Model", Commercial Mortgage Criteria Report, Structured Finane, Fitch Ratings, January 4, 2008.

- The quality of the properties and their location contribute towards its attractiveness to new tenants and thereby sustaining the cash flow.
- The requisite skill and expertise of the property manager and its experience in managing similar property portfolio will also have an impact on the cash flow.
- The borrowers are expected to maintain adequate insurance cover on the CRE properties in an amount sufficient to protect the continued cash flow during any reinstatement of the property and thereby preserving the lender's security value. The insurance cover will include fire, casualty (including terrorism cover), general liability and rental interruptions, etc. It is also expected that any insurance proceeds will be paid directly to the lender.
- Alterations or developments on the property permitted under the loan documents may affect adversely the value of the property and the borrower's financial position in such a way that its ability to make scheduled payments under the loan becomes impaired.
- Where property substitutions are permitted under the loan documents, tests must be present to ensure that the substitute property will be of equal quality and value to the substituted property in order that the collateral value is not reduced.
- Representations and warranties must be in place in relation to condition of property concerning good repair, structural defects and damages. Borrower covenants in relation to property maintenance and compliance with planning laws are essential to preserve the property value.
- The structure of occupational leases in relation to the CRE properties such as the terms, break options, rent reviews and the ability of the tenant to terminate the lease will have a direct impact on the cash flow.

11.3.2.1.2.   Cash flows

The manner of collection and the legal protections of the cash flows from the collateral CRE properties are both relevant to rating analysis. The optimum collection arrangement for the cash flows is achieved by the immediate payment or transfer of all rental income by the tenants by way of an irrevocable direction from the borrower into an account held with a suitably rated account bank in the issuer's name.

However, in practice, rental income may be received, in the first instance, into an account controlled by the property or asset manager, the borrower or the arranger/ originator and this may present "commingling" issues between the rental income and the cash belonging to those parties. In the insolvency of any of those parties, the rental income (albeit in transit) will fall under the bankrupt entity's estate and the lender/ issuer will only have an unsecured claim over that cash and, from a rating perspective, this is a total credit loss for the issuer. Commingling risks may be reduced by having designated segregated account over which a trust is declared or security is created so that the bankrupt entity effectively only serves as a custodian of that cash.

Another source of risk on the cash flows relates to the account bank, where deposits are treated legally as an unsecured debt on the bank's insolvency and the debtor may be subject to potential insolvency set-off rights. The ways to mitigate such risks include:

- the creation of proper security over the account;
- the stipulation that the account bank should be of a certain credit rating; and
- the requirement that in the event of a downgrade of the account bank, the transaction document has prescribed procedures to transfer the issuer's accounts to a suitably alternative rated bank.

### 11.3.2.1.3. Security

Since the security created over the CRE property is the only recourse to secure monies for the noteholders on a loan default, CRAs' main focus on the rating analysis will be on the effective and timely enforcement of the security and the enforcement costs incurred when the enforcement process is materially affected by the insolvency proceedings and formalities in the jurisdictions of the property and the borrower.

As a starting point, the "basic" security package that the CRAs expect to see on the loan level consists typically of the following:

- first-ranking security over the property;
- assignment of rental income and insurance;
- first-ranking security over all agreements relating to the ownership and management of the property;
- first-ranking security over rental accounts and other accounts (e.g. reserve accounts);
- first-ranking security over the shares, goodwill and uncalled capital;
- first-ranking security over the benefit of any guarantees and subordination agreements, if any, of the borrowers;
- first-ranking security over the other assets of the borrower; and
- any additional third party security in the form of guarantees given in respect of the borrower's obligations under the loan.

### 11.3.2.1.4. Insolvency issues

The enforcement of security under a loan on the borrower's insolvency poses certain challenges to the issuer and of particular concern from the rating perspective is the length of the enforcement process. For instance, the enforcement process may be delayed by a moratorium by the creditors on the proceedings and this will delay the receipt of cash and therefore the recovery of the amounts owed under the CMBS notes.[15] CRAs therefore require a detailed analysis of the legal effects of the applicable insolvency proceedings.

The legal analysis also includes an assessment on the application of the most appropriate governing law—that of the borrower's jurisdiction or that of the location of the property. Within the EU, the EU Insolvency Regulation 2002 establishes a set of rules that would help to determine which law is to be adopted in the face of potential competing insolvency officers being appointed in different EU jurisdictions. For multi-jurisdictional borrowers, CRAs tend to look to the jurisdiction with the least favourable insolvency procedures as a means of stress testing in the credit assessment.

Where there is any anticipated delay in the enforcement process, the CRAs will look for liquidity coverage to be provided for the duration of the delay and in most cases, for the period up until the completion of the liquidation and realisation of the security.

Another source of delay of the enforcement process is the complexity of the commercial arrangements, as a result of which enforcement costs will increase and allowances will be made in the rating consideration.

11.3.2.1.5.   Miscellaneous considerations

Other factors that CRAs take into account in the rating process include the loan structure, cross-collateralisation with other loans and structural enhancement.

*11.3.2.2.   Legal and structural considerations[16]*

Legal considerations and structural analysis by CRAs supplement the quantitative process and are a critical part of the rating process. The cash flows may be interrupted if any obligations of the borrower and/or the issuer to make payments under the transaction documents (on both the loan and notes levels) turn out to be unenforceable.

In practice, the rating analyst will work with issuers and their own legal counsels to ensure that any unanticipated legal issues will not impact adversely on the cash flows in the transaction; and in some cases, to recommend that increased credit enhancement measures to be put in place.

---

[15] See further Ch.6.

[16] See the references: Judith O'Driscoll, "Standard & Poor's Rating of European CMBS, Legal & Structural Considerations"; Andrew Petersen, *Commercial Mortgage-backed Securitisation: Developments in the European Market* (Sweet & Maxwell, 2006); Judith O'Driscoll, "European CMBS, Loan Level Guidelines" Structured Finance Ratings, Standards & Poor's, September 2004; and "CMBS Rating Methodology" DBRS, October 2005.

In terms of the legal analysis of the transaction structure, the key considerations for CRAs are:

- separation of the seller risk from the originator risk through a true sale mechanism;
- servicing issues concerning the originator acting as the master servicer and special servicer;
- the bankruptcy remoteness of a special purpose vehicle to hold the assets;
- servicing practice of defaulted mortgages;
- representations and warranties made by the originator in respect of the mortgage and the property; and
- subordination, priorities of payments and credit enhancements.

### 11.3.2.2.1. True sale structure

In structured finance transactions, because of the need to achieve a legal true sale (i.e. arm's-length sale of the receivables), the preferred choice of CRAs for the "buyer" of receivables is a special purpose vehicle (SPV) set up to bear no corporate relation to the seller/originator. It is normally structured so that the SPV is established in a jurisdiction so that cash flows passing through the structure are not subject to double taxation.

The need for legal true sale stems from the fact that the loans and the related security should no longer remain the assets of the seller following the sale in order that in the event of the seller's insolvency, the assets are isolated from and therefore not subject to claims by the creditors or a liquidator.[17] It is crucial that the seller retains no legal or beneficial interest or equity of redemption over the assets. A true sale structure may be jeopardised if the SPV is not a truly separate legal entity from the seller, which may happen if, under accounting rules for reporting purposes, the SPV is to be consolidated into the seller group of companies and would therefore be included in the seller's insolvency proceedings.

### 11.3.2.2.2. Limited recourse

Structured finance instruments are built on limited recourse financing and CRAs will look for covenants between the transaction parties to the effect that they agree contractually that their recourse to the issuer for any debt owed to them in the transaction is limited to their pro rata share of the proceeds of realisation of the collateral property on enforcement, with the remaining "un-paid" portions of their debts extinguished. Hence, limited recourse provisions make it improbable for the SPV to go into insolvency that allows CRAs to assign high credit ratings to their debt obligations.

---

[17] This is often as "bankruptcy remote".

### 11.3.2.2.3.  Servicing[18]

The skill, knowledge and experience of the loan servicers—be they the master servicer, primary servicer or special servicer—form a key element of CRA rating assessment because of the prominent roles they play in servicing the loans to ensure prompt receipts of cash flows by the issuer.

In the context of CMBS transactions, the role of special servicer is favoured by CRAs as special servicers deal with loan defaults, security enforcement and workouts in a prompt and timely manner to minimise the disruption of cash flows and losses while maximising recovery for the noteholders. To expedite the procedure, CRAs expect to see transaction documentation to provide transfer of the mortgage loans from the master/primary servicer to the special servicer upon an event of default that appears to be imminent. It is also important that the special servicer is knowledgeable in workouts and have resources and connections to real estate and legal specialist to ensure speedy actions.

### 11.3.2.2.4.  Subordination and credit enhancements

An all-important feature of structured financings, is the contractual subordination between the financing parties and any other secured party (e.g. trustee, servicers, cash manager, paying agents, swap provider, liquidity facility provider and the like) of amounts owed to them. This is prescribed by the priorities of payments ("waterfalls") as agreed amongst the parties, both in respect of the pre- and post-enforcement scenarios. The ranking of the secured creditors in the waterfalls directly impacts the likelihood of the noteholders of the different classes of notes getting paid on time and in full if there is insufficient cash flows in the structure for distribution or there is a delay in the receipt of cash, which may in turn impact negatively on the ratings on the junior classes of notes that will be paid further down the waterfall.[19] CRAs will work with arrangers to ensure that there is adequate credit enhancement in the forms of subordination between the different classes of notes, cash reserves, liquidity facilities and swaps to ensure there are always sufficient cash flows in the structure to support the rating of the most senior class of notes.

So far, our analysis has taken a neutral stand with respect to CMBS collateralised by both floating rate ("floaters") and fixed rate loans. However, analysing transactions with floaters requires an additional credit enhancement adjustment (determined by stressing short-term interest rates[20]) on the base-line credit enhancement for fixed rate loans, in order to

---

[18]  See further Chs 5, 6 and 7.
[19]  Please refer to section A.4 "CMBS cash flow analysis" in the Appendix of this chapter for further details.
[20]  This typically involves 1-month LIBOR to assess the credit impact of the floating interest rate exposure on the loan.

compensate for floating rate risks. Such an adjustment incorporates the impacts of the potentially higher interest advancing costs and additional term defaults associated with interest payment volatility.

As an example, Moody's has developed an approach to analyse the impact of the floating rate risk on CMBS based on the concept of expected loss of the underlying loans—by incorporating higher term default frequency and higher loss severity resulting from additional interest advancing costs. The approach incorporates loan specific inputs such as: term to maturity, terms of the borrower extension options, DSCR and LTV ratios, to be spread over LIBOR and the strike rate of the interest rate cap, if any. Such loan specific information and the stressed interest rate assumptions are then used to calculate an adjustment for each rated class of notes within the CMBS structure.

## 11.4. EU Regulation on CRAs[21]

### 11.4.1. Pre-financial crisis EU regulatory environment

Up until the global financial crisis that began in the summer of 2007, the regulatory treatment of CRAs in the EU mainly consisted in the CRAs adopting, on a voluntary basis, certain best practice principles and standards. The CRA task force of the International Organization of Securities Commission (IOSCO) published in September 2003 the *IOSCO Statement of principles regarding the activities of credit rating agencies* that aimed to improve investor protection and fairness and the transparency of the capital markets.

These principles encompassed four main objectives:

- quality and integrity in the rating process;
- independence and conflicts of interest;
- transparency and timeliness of ratings disclosure; and
- confidential information relating to non-public information.

Shortly afterwards in December 2004, the CRA task force produced the *Code of conduct fundamentals for credit rating agencies* (the IOSCO CRA Code) based on the statements of principles. A number of CRAs including S&P, Moody's and Fitch implemented the high-level standards set out in the IOSCO CRA Code in their own practice.

---

[21] Jonathon Katz, Emmanuel Salinas and Constantinos Stephenoce, "Credit Rating Agencies – No Easy Regulatory Solutions", Crisis Response, Public Policy for the Provate Sector, Note Number 8, The World Bank Group, October 2009.

### 11.4.2. Post-financial crisis EU regulatory environment

Following the financial crisis and collapse of the financial markets, CRAs received heavy criticisms for failing to reflect the credit risks in certain structured finance instruments in the first instance and also being incapable to adjust their credit rating assigned to these instruments in response to a set of fast deteriorating market conditions as the crisis deepened.

Amidst the decline in faith for CRAs in respect of the central role they played in the structured finance markets, the EU Commission acknowledged that the IOSCO CRA Code was inadequate and put into force on December 7, 2009 the *Regulation of the European Parliament and of the Council on Credit Rating Agencies (Regulation 1060/2009)* (the CRA Regulation).[22] Furthermore, under the *Regulation of the European Parliament and of the Council amending the CRA Regulation (Regulation 513/2011)* that took effect on June 1, 2011, the responsibility for registration and ongoing supervision of the CRAs was transferred from the national competent authorities to the EU Securities and Markets Authority (ESMA) and granted certain additional powers to ESMA. The transfer of responsibility and powers to ESMA became effective on July 1, 2011.

The legislations take the form of a regulation in order that they may be directly applicable in each Member State within the European Union.

### 11.4.3. Aim and scope of the CRA Regulation

In its legislative proposal for the CRA Regulation published in November 2008, the EU Commission stated that CRAs "contributed significantly to recent market turmoil" through their rating of structured credit products. The CRA Regulation responds by addressing the issues surrounding the rating practice of these products.

It is worth noting that credit ratings produced in relation to private placements and not intended for public disclosure or distribution are exempt from the CRA Regulation. The CRA Regulation defines a "credit rating" as,

"an opinion regarding the creditworthiness of an entity, a debt or financial obligation, debt security, preferred share or other financial instrument, of an issuer of such a debt or financial obligation, debt security, preferred share or other financial instrument, issued using an established and defined ranking system of rating categories." (Art.3(1)(a) of the CRA Regulation).

Research recommendations under the MAD Investment Recommendations Directive (2003/125/EC) and investment research defined in MiFID

---

[22] Regulation (EC) No. 1060/2009 of the European Parliament and of the Council of 16 September 2009 of Credit Rating Agencies [2009] OJ L302/1-31.

Implementing Directive (2006/73/EC) are not regarded as credit ratings for the purposes of the CRA Regulation, and nor are opinions on the value of a financial instrument or a financial obligation (Art.3(2) of the CRA Regulation).

Since December 2010, credit institutions, investment firms, insurance and re-insurance undertakings, collective investment schemes, pension funds and alternative investment funds may only use credit ratings for regulatory purposes if they are issued by CRAs established in the European Union which are registered in accordance with the CRA Regulation. CRAs approved for registration by ESMA are able to issue credit ratings anywhere in the European Union and they will be included on a list in the European Union's Official Journal and appear on the website of the EU Commission.

### 11.4.4. CRA Regulation and structured finance transactions

A number of provisions in the CRA Regulation that are of most impact on the rating practice of CRAs in relation to structured finance instruments deserve particular attention.

#### 11.4.4.1. Independence

The independence of CRAs from the issuers of structured finance instruments are questioned on two grounds:

(i)    Provision of "structuring advice"—CRAs cannot be regarded as completely independent from the issuer as they are heavily involved in providing indications to the issuer during the structuring and documentation stage as to what is, and what is not, acceptable within the parameters of a certain rating for a class of notes. Unlike traditional corporate bond issues, CRAs' presence and inputs in the early structuring phases of structured transactions that lead to the expression of what some may call an "ex-ante opinion" shapes the final structure of the transactions.

(ii)   "Issuer-paid" model—CRAs are paid their fees for the provision of credit ratings by the issuer and therefore are viewed to be incentivised to providing a favourable rating.

The CRA Regulation responds to the concern in (i) by requiring that CRAs should not be allowed to carry out consultancy or advisory services. In particular, CRAs should not make proposals or recommendations regarding the design of a structured finance instruments. However, CRAs should be able to provide ancillary services where this does not create potential conflicts of interest with the issuing of credit ratings (para.22, preamble and paras 4 and 5, section B, annex I of the CRA Regulations). Ancillary services are not part of credit rating activities; they comprise market forecasts, estimates of economic trends, pricing analysis and other general data analysis as well as related distribution services (para.4, section B, annex I of the CRA Regulations).

In response to the concern in (ii), art.7(5) of the CRA Regulation provides that compensation and performance evaluation of rating analysts and persons approving the credit ratings shall not be contingent on the amount of revenue that the credit rating agency derives from the rated entities or related third parties.

### 11.4.4.2. *Management*

The CRA shall have an administrative or supervisory board. Its senior management shall ensure that (para.1, section A, annex I of the CRA Regulation):

(a)   credit rating activities are independent, including from all political and economic influences or constraints;

(b)   conflicts of interest are properly identified, managed and disclosed; and

(c)   the CRA complies with the remaining requirements of the CRA Regulation.

Where the CRA rates structured finance instruments, at least one of the independent members and one other member of the administrative and supervisory board should be an expert in securitisation and structured finance (para.2, section A, annex I of the CRA Regulation).

### 11.4.4.3. *Rating methodologies and models*

CRAs must use rating methodologies that are rigorous, systematic, continuous and subject to validation based on historical experience, including back-testing (art.8(3) of the CRA Regulation).

CRAs must ensure that they monitor credit ratings and review and monitor their credit ratings and methodologies on an ongoing basis at least annually, in particular where material changes occur that could have an impact on a credit rating (art.8(5) of the CRA Regulation).

However, art.23(1) of the CRA Regulation provides that ESMA, the EU Commission or any public authority in a member state should not interfere with the content of credit ratings or methodologies.

*11.4.4.4.   Transparency and disclosures*

When methodologies, models or key rating assumptions used in rating activities are changed, CRAs must (art.8(6) of the CRA Regulation):

- immediately disclose the likely scope of credit ratings to be affected;
- review the affected credit rating as soon as possible and no later than six months after the change; and
- re-rate all credit ratings based on those methodologies, models or key rating assumptions if the overall combined effect of the changes affects those credit ratings.

Of particular relevance to structured finance instruments is that CRAs should ensure that methodologies, models and key rating assumptions such as mathematical or correlation assumptions used for determining credit ratings are properly maintained, up-to-date and subject to a comprehensive review on a periodic basis and that their descriptions are published in a manner permitting comprehensive review (para.34, preamble and para.9, section A , annex I of the CRA Regulations).

In the desire to enhance transparency of the credit rating process, Article 8(1) of the CRA Regulation places an obligation on CRAs to disclose to the public the methodologies, models and key rating assumptions it uses in its rating activities. The CRAs must not charge a fee for the provision of such information (art.13 of the CRA Regulation) but it will be interesting to see how is implemented, given that a large number of publications regarding the details on quantitative models are still beyond reach of the public if they are not subscribers to the CRAs' services.

CRAs are required to disclose any credit rating, as well as any decision to discontinue a credit rating, on a non-selective basis and in a timely manner. In the event of a decision to discontinue a credit rating, the information disclosed shall include full reasons for the decision (art.10(1) of the CRA Regulation).

CRAs must ensure that credit ratings are presented and processed in accordance with the requirements set out in s.D (Rules on the presentation of credit ratings) of annex I of the CRA Regulation). Additional obligations apply for structure finance instruments:

- where a CRA rates a structured finance instrument, it must provide in the credit rating all information about loss and cash-flow analysis it has performed or is relying upon and an indication of any expected change in the credit rating;
- the CRA must state what level of assessment it has performed concerning the due diligence processes carried out at the level of underlying financial instruments or other assets of structured finance

instruments. The credit rating agency shall disclose whether it has undertaken any assessment of such due diligence processes or whether it has relied on a third-party assessment, indicating how the outcome of such assessment impacts on the credit rating; and

- where the CRA issues credit ratings of structured finance instruments, it must accompany the disclosure of methodologies, models and key rating assumptions with guidance which explains assumptions, parameters, limits and uncertainties surrounding the models and rating methodologies used in such credit ratings, including simulations of stress scenarios undertaken by the agencies when establishing the ratings. Such guidance must be clear and easily comprehensible.

## 11.5. Conclusion

This Chapter has highlighted that CRAs serve a vital function in CMBS transactions. Credit ratings help to reduce information asymmetries by providing information on the rated CMBS to the investors and monitor performance of these securities.

An overall awareness of the different phases of analysis and input factors generally employed by the CRAs is therefore useful information to anyone who participates in this type of financing. While quantitative modelling plays a critical to the rating process, so too do qualitative assessments of the underlying CRE mortgage properties and the legal assessment of the transaction structure. Knowledge on the role CRAs play and the tools they employ will help build a mutually beneficial basis to serve the financing needs of all parties associated with the transaction.

Following the global financial crisis, the EU Commission has laid down regulations which it hopes, will improve the transparency and disclosure of the rating process of CMBS as well as the management of conflicts of interest that exists between CRAs being an "independent assessor" of the credit risks associated with CMBS and their involvement in the structuring of the CMBS transaction. Because of the highly structured nature of CMBS, it is indeed a difficult line to draw between when the CRA is an independent assessor and when it may be considered as a "structure" and it remains to be seen how the CRA Regulation can attain an acceptable level of segregation between these conflicting roles.

Finally, on a speculative note, the quantitative models that have been employed by the CRAs have reached a level of mathematical sophistication that is intelligible to a group of specialists that still find themselves in the minority. The CRA Regulations have categorically confirmed that none of ESMA, the EU Commission or any public authority in a member state should interfere with the content of credit ratings or methodologies. On the one hand, it is only correct that a CRA should have the right to follow its own methodologies to form its own view on a CMBS transaction. Standardisation of methodologies will only destroy the benefit to the investors and public since alternative aspects and perspectives on the credit risks associated with a transaction structure keep them better informed overall on the nature of the securities. On the other hand, it had always been the case, the quantitative and to some extent, the qualitative aspects of the rating process in relation the CMBS transactions will move forward with research conducted by the CRAs themselves and the wider circle of the credit research community. In short, they are still left on their own, as they were before, to unfold the mystery surrounding the modelling of correlations and the like.

The increased level of discourse and transparency required of the CRAs will no doubt open up further research opportunities, but at the same time, increase the heat of competition amongst the CRAs.

Finally, the CRA Regulation may serve to address the cosmetic aspects of conflicts management within a CRA's practice. However, the real value of a credit rating rests on the exercise of judgements by CRAs in the selection of correct, relevant assumptions and mathematical tools for their rating process. It is uncertain as to how much of the element of subjectivity has been addressed by the CRA regulations.

*Matching assets with liabilities: CMBS rating analytic framework—a practical example—Moody'sMoody's' MoRE Analysis[23]*
Putting the credit concepts into perspective, this appendix outlines Moody'sMoody's' rating approach to real estate analysis for CMBS in EMEA—the MoRE Analysis—as an illustration of how the conceptual framework of credit risk analysis works in practice. There are four modules to the MoRE Analysis.

## A.1.  Data input

The arranger of the CMBS transaction is typically requested to provide information of the loans on the data template that Moody's has developed, which includes borrower, loan, property and tenant data. The template contains the optimal amount of necessary data for analysing the CMBS portfolio.

---

[23] See update on Christian Aufsatz and Ifigenia Palmeri, "Moody's Real Estate Analysis for CMBS Transactions in EMEA", Moody's Investors Service, June 30, 2005 and Christian Aufsatz, Emmanuel Savoye, Marco Szego and Ifigenia Palimeri, "Moody's Approach to Real Estate Analysis for CMBS in EMEA: Portfolio Analysis", Moody's Investors Services, April 24, 2004.

The data template takes the form of an excel spreadsheet that records the essential characteristics of the collateral loan pool and forms the fundamental link between data provided by the loan originator and the credit analysis of Moody's. Alongside the data template, Moody's also reviews the loan agreements, property valuation reports and other relevant documents to enhance its understanding of the loans and the security the borrowers provide. For information that the arranger or originator is unable to provide on the data template, assumptions on the missing information will be made by Moody's to allow the analysis of the portfolio.

## A.2. CRE asset analysis

Because of the heterogeneous nature of CRE properties and the relatively little historical information available on them, a significant of the CMBS loan portfolio credit analysis is carried out at the level of individual property. The analysis consists in determining the probability-based annual cashflows from the CRE property (in terms of NOI or NCF) and PD of the CRE loan. Moody's adopts a static approach (as opposed to the "dynamic" sampling techniques used in the Monte Carlo approach but does nevertheless produce a good approximation and is more time effective) such as its binomial extension method that involves determining a probability based DSCR and the use of a "diversity score" of the tenant base on a loan-by-loan basis. The analysis also incorporates the specific assumptions for the property as well as any qualitative adjustments agreed by Moody's' rating committee.

The starting point of the CRE analysis is the estimation of cash inflows generated by each property on an annual basis. This information is available through the lease profile provided by the underwriter in respect of the property. The model then applies certain re-letting assumptions at the lease-break date such as:

- the probability of the current tenant staying on;
- the vacancy period;
- the term of a new lease; and
- a new rent.

From such information, the model computes a probability-based cash inflow for each tenant and then summarises these cash inflows on a property and loan basis to assess the amount of cash available for debt service. Consequently, a probability-weighted DSCR for each year is determined.

The analysis also takes into account the quality of the expected income flow on a loan-by-loan basis with reference to the credit rating of the tenants (where available) as well as the number and the diversity of tenants in occupation of the property that secures a particular loan. The credit quality and the diversity of the tenant base is measured by a "diversity score", which is calculated using Moody's binominal extension technique.[24] Having calculated the DSCR and diversity score for each year, it may then be determined how many tenants defaults would lead to a loan default.

In determining the final annual PD, structural elements at the loan level that include reserves, guarantees and non-SPV borrowers will also be taken into consideration.

Another important aspect of the annual PD is that over the life of a loan, its annual PD is influenced by the amortisation schedule. The lower the scheduled amortisation, the lower generally will be the default risk during the term of the loan; but low amortisation also results in an increase of the re-financing amount and therefore increases the default risk at maturity. A good indicator of the PD at the re-financing date is the LTV—i.e. primarily the market value of the property at the re-financing date, which is dependent on factors such as tenant quality, the weighted average remaining lease term and the tenant diversity at the re-financing date.

## A.3.   CRE portfolio analysis

Having determined the expected cash inflows and PD on a loan-by-loan analysis, the next step is to use these results to compute the loss distribution of the loan portfolio and the expected loss.

A loss distribution is essentially a curve that allocates a corresponding probability to each cumulative loss scenario. A dynamic model that utilises Monte Carlo techniques simulates defaults and recoveries of the underlying loans (vis-à-vis LGD) within the portfolio and computes the portfolio's loss distribution and timing characteristics.

### A.3.1.   Modelling defaults

In order to compute LGD, there is an assumption that the loan has defaulted. An event of default is not deterministic, since they depend on the underlying stochastic variables that influence them. Moody's stimulates loan defaults by the use of a multifactor model that equates the default rate of each loan $k, Z_k$, with a location factor, a property type factor, a global factor and an idiosyncratic risk factor; the correlations between these factors are captured by the correlation terms in the model:

---

[24]   Arturo Cifuentes and Gerard O'Connor, "The Binominal Expansion Method Applied to CBO/CLO Analysis", Moody's Investors Service Global Credit Research, Structured Finance Special Report, December 13, 1996.

$$Z_k = w_c C + w_{PT} PT + wZ + \sqrt{\left(1 - w_c^{\ 2} - w_{PT}^{\ 2} - w^2\right)}$$

where, $C$ is the location factor, $PT$ is the property factor, $Z$ is the global factor and $\epsilon_k$ is the idiosyncratic risk factor, which are all independent random variables with a given distribution. $W_c, W_{PT}$ and $w$ measure the correlations between $Z_k$ and $C$, $PT$ and $Z$ and they reflect the interdependence of the loans within the portfolio if they share similar characteristics.

The model generates a random value for each of the variables in the equation at a time $t$ that gives a value $Z_k$ for each loan at $t$. $Z_k$ is then compared with the annual PD of the loan (as provided by the CRE asset analysis stage above), which acts as a boundary value (or trigger level) for defaults, to establish the occurrence and timing of a default. For each set of values generated for the random variables, this procedure is repeated for each loan $k$ within the portfolio. The simulation is then reiterated by the generation of another set of random variables, with which the model will calculate another set of values for $Z_k$ and then, in the same manner, determines if and when each of the loans within the portfolio default at each time. A default distribution will be generated following several millions runs of the simulation process that determines the timing of defaults of the portfolio.

### A.3.2. Modelling LGD

Once the timing of the loan defaults—which is given by the default distribution—are known, the model proceeds to calculate the LGD by comparing the loan amount outstanding with the property value at the time of enforcement (see below) in order to determine any potential loss; taking into account scheduled amortisations, the anticipated accrued interest amounts until the time of recovery realisation and the transaction costs involved with the enforcement actions on the property. Enforcement costs and timing assumptions are generally dependent on the jurisdictions in which the property and the borrower are located, the structure of the loan, the type of assets in the pool and the nature of the security. For instance, some EU jurisdictions are considered more "creditor-friendly" than others due to the difference between their respective enforcement procedures. Moody's ranks the United Kingdom and the Netherlands to be the most "creditor-friendly" jurisdictions while Greece, Portugal and Italy are considered to be "debtor-friendly". In terms of the loan structure, any significant rights of a "B" noteholder to control the enforcement process may also have far-reaching impacts on the enforcement costs and timing.

Additional structural considerations that will also be incorporated into the analysis are:

- the prior ranking claims of the loan;
- the pari-passu ranking of the loan with other loans; and
- any exposure of the borrower to swap termination payments.

Since the property value at the time of enforcement is unknown when the portfolio is first analysed, Moody's utilises a simulation to model this uncertainty based on empirical observations that property values follow cyclical trends where phases of property growth are followed by phases of property decline, but subject to a long-term growth rate. These observations give rise to a mathematical expression that enables us to determine the property value at time *t* in terms of the initial value of the property, known as the initial model value and an exponential function dependent on the growth rate. The model also incorporates correlation assumptions (again generated by a multifactor model similar to the above) in the expression to reflect the degree of diversity of the property pool and its impact on the correlations between defaults and severities. Moody's then models the growth rates of the property values by using a mean reverting process together with historical volatility data from the EU and US real estate markets.

The initial model value for each property in the pool is the appraised values provided by the arrangers/originators with appropriate adjustments to reflect Moody's views of the property value. Such adjustments include the ongoing expenses or capital expenditures for the property, the void period, renewal probabilities for key tenants, sustainability of the valuer's assumptions, the date of the valuation report and discount/capitalisation rates that reflect the tenant quality or rating.

Each run of the simulation process produces the values of the properties with the loan portfolio at the time of default, which are then used to compute the values of LGD.

## A.4.    CMBS cash flow analysis

The final stage of a CMBS rating analysis provides the link between the asset side (the loan pool) analysis and the liability side of a CMBS transaction (the CMBS notes). This translates the loss distribution of the loan portfolio into an expected loss for each class of the CMBS notes.

Once the expected loss distribution for the portfolio is obtained, for each loss scenario on the assets, the corresponding loss for each class of notes is calculated taking into account the structural features of the notes for the CMBS transaction. The liability structure consists broadly of the following:

- sequential-versus-pro rata cash allocation down the priority of payments waterfall;

- any trigger that changes the allocation of cash flows down the waterfall;
- principal to pay interest mechanisms;
- the benefit of expected spread on the notes; and
- reserve fund mechanisms.

Moody's model measures the impact of each loss scenario on the notes, from which an expected loss may be calculated for each class of notes within the CMBS structure. Finally, these results are mapped onto Moody's idealised expected loss tables to determine the rating of each class of notes.

# Chapter 12

# The Future of Commercial Mortgage Loan and CMBS Information management

Damien Georges and Raj Singh,

Hipercept, Inc.

## 12.1.  Introduction

In the commercial mortgage loan and CMBS markets that exists at the time of writing, success in building and maintaining a profitable and thriving CRE investment business requires not only an understanding of CRE market opportunities and risks, but also understanding regulatory requirements and responding to CRE investor demands for increased transparency. Successful CRE investors should be able to demonstrate that they have controlled and repeatable risk and performance management processes, built upon a foundation of accurate and up to date data about their CRE investments.

Given the arrival of CRE as an asset class in its own right, as highlighted throughout this book, in the commercial mortgage loan and CMBS markets that exist post financial crisis, there is a widespread issue at institutions that invest in CRE, related to the ability to consolidate and standardise information about their CRE investments which may be generated and managed across disparate—and often globally dispersed—internal business units and external agents. For example, it is not uncommon for large CRE investment managers to contract with dozens of different third-party property managers, each of whom manage vital tenant and lease information in their own particular systems. For CRE lenders, who do not have direct control over the third parties who may be managing information on behalf of borrowers, the situation is more problematic. Lenders rely on borrowers to provide information, which is limited in scope by the information covenants in the loan documents. For both investors and lenders, regional and jurisdictional differences with respect to CRE law and leasing norms and non-standardised accounting methods, complicate matters further.

All of this complexity presents a challenge when it comes to mortgage loans and CMBS. Understanding the collateral behind each instrument is difficult enough for a direct CRE investor, but for the mortgage loan or CMBS investor, there are the added challenges of complex investment structures and insufficient borrower or asset level servicer reporting.

In this Chapter, the challenges outlined above will be considered in more detail. This Chapter will discuss the ways in which the CRE investor, lenders and industry bodies are currently coping with such challenges and will conclude by making a case for the commoditisation of CRE asset information with the goal being to streamline the sharing of information through acquisition, operation and sale or transfer of CRE assets.

## 12.2.  Risk management

Access to accurate and timely information across many and various categories is required by investors seeking to understand and manage the risk and performance associated with a CRE investment, regardless of whether that investor has invested directly in properties or in property-backed debt via direct mortgage lending or investment in CMBS.

Managing different types of risk requires access to different types of information. The three main categories of risk faced by a CRE investor or lender are: (i) tenant risks, (ii) space market risks and (iii) capital market risks. Tenant risks relate to the possibility that a tenant will be unable to meet its legal obligation to pay rent. Space market risks are the economic risks related to the cyclical nature of the CRE market: rents and asset values rise and fall in cycles, as the supply of space leads or trails the demand for space. Finally, market risks relate to the availability and cost of capital required for the financing of CRE investments. These three categories are closely linked and general economic conditions can impact upon property values in many ways simultaneously. For example, energy price inflation in an economy can lead to a change in the growth outlook for tenants in a particular sector at the same time as it impacts capital markets via a monetary policy response to the inflation. However, these three categories of risk will each be considered separately, to reflect the differences in the types of information that are relevant to understand and manage these risks.

### 12.2.1.  Tenant risk

Understanding exposure to tenant risk is imperative for effective portfolio risk management. Too often, tenant credit risk is ignored or misunderstood, leading to material impact to cash flow and ultimately valuation of the asset. The loss of a single tenant in a portfolio can lead to the breaching of LTV and DSCR loan covenants that put an entire investment at risk of default.

The main indicators of tenant risk are related to a tenant's solvency, or, its ability or propensity to break a lease contract. The credit ratings of some tenants can be obtained from credit rating agencies such as Standard & Poor's, Moody's and Fitch[1] or, via reports produced by Dun and Bradstreet or Experian. For retail tenants, data on tenant sales, if available and accurate, can provide an indication of business sustainability. Where retail sales data is tied to tenant rent levels and is thus regularly supplied to landlords, evaluating trends and stress scenarios can provide significant insights into the health of a tenant's business and thus their propensity to default on rent payments. The best indication that a tenant may be in trouble is recent trends in the company's financial health, or, an increase in rental arrears or delinquency. However, this information provides, at best, a trailing indicator of tenant default probability rather than acting as an early warning of potential future issues.

Many leases contain options for the tenant to end or "break" their lease contract. Predicting which of these options a tenant will exercise is a major part of forecasting the performance of the underlying real estate. Having accurate information about the tenant break options in a portfolio is important, but so is understanding how a tenant is using the leased space. For example, is the space being subleased to another entity, or is the space sitting empty? Tenant use of the leased space is typically the best indicator of whether an option will be exercised or not.

Predicting the impact that specific tenants have on a portfolio is not an exact science. However, in a large portfolio with hundreds or thousands of tenants, statistical distributions of tenant performance are more predictable. The performance of tenants within the same industry sector or the same geographic region will be correlated due to their common exposure to local or regional economic and market factors including the availability of skilled labour, changes in taxation, local economic growth rates, etc. Therefore, it is critical to understand the level of exposure to (or concentration in) specific sectors or regions, particularly if there are known stress factors in those sectors or regions. Information about a tenant's industry sector and business activities is routinely collected at the time of leasing; however the ability to analyse tenant concentration risk requires centralised collection and standardised categorisation of tenant information across the investment portfolio, which is often lacking.

### 12.2.2. Space market risks

At the macroeconomic level, CRE investments exist at the intersection of two markets: the space market and the capital market. The space market is the market for leasable space, where developers, builders and landlords are on the supply side and tenants on the demand side. Space market risks are those associated with the cyclical nature of the relationship between the

---

[1]    See further Ch.11 for the work of the credit rating agencies.

supply and demand of leasable space in a market. These cycles are the result of the time it takes for the prevailing rental rates in a market to adjust to changes in the amount of available space. Since rental rates are one of the key drivers of new development, CRE markets often lurch between conditions of undersupply and oversupply, as developers react to changes in rental prices, by ramping up and then slowing down construction activities.

Changes in the space market affect the income and value of a property through various effects, including changes in downtime and leasing incentives, but the primary variable is the rental rate. As market rental rates fall, tenants with break options are more likely to exercise them and new leases are signed at rates lower than the ones that are expiring. The information required to manage space market risks has to do with the production and consumption of leasable space, for example: total current leasable space; "space absorption" which is the rate at which available space is being leased; development costs, which are driven primarily by the cost of raw land in a market; and, new construction starts. All of these data points, as well as the prevailing market rental rates, are usually available in mature markets from CRE brokerages or specialised CRE servicing companies.

### 12.2.3. Capital market risks

The final category of risks that must be managed by CRE investors and lenders are those related to the financing of properties and the market value of properties as capital investments. Put simply, the value of a property is made up of two components: the income producing potential of the property and the value placed upon that income stream in capital markets, where investors can chose between properties and other income producing assets. The ratio between a property's market value and the income generated by the property is known as the capitalisation rate or "cap" rate. The cap rate is determined by the relative attractiveness of commercial properties, vis-à-vis other investments in a given market at a given time.

The various methodologies that are used to value CRE assets all take into account capitalisation rates. When the cap rates in a market rise, asset values are written down, which can breach LTV covenants in mortgages or make refinancing assets more difficult, even if the underlying performance of the assets remain unchanged.[2] Capitalisation rates are closely related to interest rates, which are determined by open market transactions and can be easily obtained from market information providers like Bloomberg or Reuters.

The risks related to financing properties are primarily interest rate risk, foreign exchange (FX) rate risk, counterparty credit risk and liquidity risk.

---

[2] See further Ch.3.

Interest rate risk, driven by interbank lending rates in the market such as LIBOR or EURIBOR, is market priced daily and easily attainable. FX rates are also highly liquid and easily attainable with market data feeds. However, managing these risk exposures via hedging instruments can result in significant break costs if markets move against a hedged position[3] It is important, particularly for lenders, to factor these liabilities into measures such as LTV calculations.

Counterparty credit risk for investors is the tenant risk discussed above. For lenders, it is borrower creditworthiness or, for non-recourse lending against a specific asset, the asset's performance which is critical. Information availability here is often dictated by information covenants or other terms set out in the loan facility agreement. Loans have historically been underwritten to differing standards and can sometimes have few if any reporting requirements for borrowers.

Liquidity risk is the risk stemming from the lack of marketability (returning an asset to cash) of an investment that cannot be bought or sold quickly enough to prevent or minimise a loss. In the context of CRE, this applies to the relatively illiquid physical asset but also to access to funding or to hedging instruments. Investor costs of funding can vary significantly based on a borrower's ability to provide lenders sufficient transparency into the performance and risk inherent in their business or in the specific asset being funded. This same transparency into the underlying borrower or collateral is equally important to lenders who may wish to sell or securitise CRE loan positions.

## 12.3. Performance management

Managing performance and risk are closely interrelated concepts since one cannot manage performance without also managing risk. However, they each require different data and techniques. Risk management is about measuring and forecasting things that can impact investment performance. Performance management is concerned with measuring and forecasting performance itself.

The key indicators of performance from the point of view of an equity investor in CRE are operational income (i.e. yield), asset value appreciation and return on investment. The information that an equity investor requires to forecast these performance metrics are many and various, but can be grouped into following broad categories:

- Income – i.e. rental and miscellaneous income from existing leases;
- Operating expenses – i.e. taxes, insurance, legal fees and leasing costs, etc.;

---

[3]  See further Ch.8.

- Capital expenditures – i.e. repairs and maintenance, refurbishments and development costs, etc.;
- Space leasing assumptions – i.e. market rents, void periods, tenant concessions, etc.; and
- Capital market assumptions – i.e. cap rates, cost inflation rates, etc.

As discussed above, obtaining accurate and up-to-date information in all of these categories can present a significant challenge to CRE investors with large and diverse portfolios. The challenge for CRE lenders is even greater, as the information covenants in typical commercial property loans do not force borrowers to provide detailed operational information on a frequent basis.

Typically, covenants require borrowers to provide basic financial and lease information on a quarterly or annual basis. In volatile CRE markets, this reporting frequency is insufficient to alert lenders to material changes in the risk and performance of the underlying assets. Furthermore, the format in which information must be provided is often not specified, which makes it difficult for lenders to consolidate information received from different borrowers in order to gain an overall view of the health of the collateral securing their loans.

The performance of a CRE secured loan or CMBS investment is of course closely related to the performance of the underlying properties. However, because debt is always senior to equity in the capital structure, lenders or bond holders get paid before equity holders earn their returns. Thus loan performance is less volatile than asset performance; the return on equity must drop to zero before the return on debt begins to be impacted by a decline in the performance of an asset.

To forecast the performance of their positions, lenders and CMBS investors must monitor interest and debt coverage ratios, covenant compliance and value at risk, which is the difference between the outstanding loan balance and the current asset value less any costs in the transaction that would be incurred in the case of a default and forced sale. Calculating these metrics accurately requires the same detailed property, lease, space market and capital markets data required by equity investors. Investors must integrate their hedging exposure management with their performance management process. Without understanding the impact of a derivative instrument such as an interest rate swap on the overall performance of an investment, the investor is left with incomplete and potentially misleading investment performance information.[4]

---

[4] See further Ch.8 where the impact of derivatives on CRE mortgage loans is discussed.

## 12.4. Investor demands for increased transparency

In addition to expecting a solid return from their investments, many investors, particularly large institutional investors, now demand regular detailed reporting on the operating performance of the underlying assets in their portfolio as well as details on exposure to tenant and space market risks. Historically, investment managers have typically provided quarterly financial reports highlighting income and capital appreciation or depreciation and historical and/or projected returns along with some commentary on asset management strategy, market "outlook" and so on. Some investment managers currently provide supplemental reporting in addition to their basic financial reports, which contain high-level operating statistics (occupancy, leasing activity, debt maturities, etc.). However, at the time of writing, there is a trend towards investors requesting much greater detail from investment managers; for example: complete rent rolls, tenant sales figures, rental arrears by tenant, etc.

In an effort to better manage the risk and performance of their assets, some investors have gone as far as setting up shadow asset management teams and implementing their own real estate information management solutions (utilising one of more of the approaches described in para.12.6.3 below), which they attempt to populate with granular tenant and lease-level information which they request from their investment managers. There are several well-known pension and sovereign wealth funds that have implemented property management systems internally in order to collect and store information about the tenants and leases in properties in which they have invested indirectly through funds or other investment vehicles.

At the time of writing, the authors are not aware of any lenders or CMBS investors attempting to obtain a similar level of transparency. This is probably in recognition of the inherent limitations with respect to control and access to information related to debt investments, which were discussed above. Notwithstanding these current limitations, it is safe to assume that, over the coming years, lenders and CMBS investors will begin to seek the same level of transparency into their real estate investments as equity investors have recently begun to.

## 12.5. Regulatory impacts

Investment managers increasingly face similar burdens in complying with regulatory requirements as banks and insurers. Recent regulatory reforms aimed at investment managers seek to address issues ranging from systemic risk to investor protection, transparency, governance and taxation. Some of these regulatory initiatives, discussed in detail in Ch.16, have arisen from G20 actions following the financial crisis. However, the driving force behind regulatory reform remains financial market regulators and central banks within national and regional jurisdictions globally.

Examples of the many regulatory initiatives facing investors and lenders include, among others, the European Commission's Alternative Investment Fund Management Directive (AIFMD), which comes into effect under the local regulatory regimes of European nations in July 2013, the Dodd-Frank Act, Foreign Account Tax Compliance Act (FATCA), review of the Markets in Financial Instruments Directive (MiFID) and a revision of the Undertakings for Collective Investments in Transferable Securities (UCITS).[5]

Some of the greatest operational implications for CRE investors arise from AIFMD. Under AIFMD, the fund manager will be required to:

- Establish and maintain a permanent risk management function;
- Ensure that the techniques, tools and arrangements are in place to monitor the liquidity risk of the fund;
- Proactively and demonstrably manage third party outsourcing arrangements;
- Establish formal securitisation monitoring procedures including monitoring exposures within the pools underlying securitisation tranches; and
- Improve reporting transparency regarding fund performance and the fund manager's risk exposure.

Alternative Investment Fund Managers (AIFMs) must establish and maintain a permanent risk management function to implement risk management policies and procedures for identifying, measuring and monitoring all risks relevant to each fund's investment strategy. This function should ensure that the fund's risk profile is consistent with the fund manager's risk limits for market, credit, liquidity, counterparty and operational risks. This risk management function must be separated both functionally and hierarchically from the business.

In addition, AIFMD will require AIFMs to conduct periodic back-tests, or reviews of past forecasts, in order to determine how well fund managers understood their risk exposures and how accurately they forecast the performance implications of that risk exposure.

Under the AIFMD, managers investing in tradable securities and other financial instruments based on repackaged loans should ensure that transaction sponsors, originator credit institutions or original lenders:

- Retain a net economic interest in the instruments of greater than 5 per cent;

---

[5]  Some of these are discussed further in Ch.16.

- Base credit granting on sound and well-defined criteria and clearly establish the process for approving, amending, renewing, and re-financing loans;
- Operate effective position administration and monitoring of their credit risk-bearing portfolios and exposures;
- Adequately diversify each portfolio;
- Maintain documentation regarding their policy for credit risk, including its risk appetite and provisioning policy; and Describe how they measure, monitor and control that risk.

Further, the securitisation sponsor, originator or lender should ensure that the fund manager has readily available access to all materially relevant data on the credit quality and performance of the individual underlying exposures, cash flows and collateral supporting a securitisation exposure. The fund manager should have access to information that is necessary to conduct comprehensive and well-informed stress tests on the cash flows and collateral values supporting the underlying exposures.

AIFMD also requires that AIFMs assuming exposure to the credit risk of a securitisation position on behalf of one or more Alternative Investments Funds (AIFs) need to be able to properly identify, measure, monitor, manage, control and report the risks of these products and should pay particular attention to assessing the risks arising from mismatches between the assets and liabilities of the fund.

Fund managers need to have access to relevant asset level and loan level information to be able to perform this analysis. Such information includes the percentage of loan payments more than 30, 60 and 90 days past due, loan default rates, prepayment rates, loans in foreclosure, collateral type and occupancy rates, tenant credit ratings, etc. as well as concentrations of risk exposure to sectors, geographies, and currencies embedded in the securitised products.

Where the underlying exposures are themselves securitisation positions, AIFMs should have such relevant information not only on the underlying securitisation tranches, such as the issuer name and credit quality, but also on the characteristics and performance of the pools underlying those securitisation tranches.

Regulatory bodies are driving the need for more accurate and available data; a focus on transparency is a consistent theme across the AIFMD and other major pieces of market legislation. Investors and lenders who are best able to provide this transparency will be equipped not only to navigate pending regulations but to lower their borrowing or funding costs, more effectively mitigate risk exposure and to improve their investment performance through better decision making.

## 12.6. Current environment

Faced with the imperatives described above, with respect to risk and performance management and regulatory impacts, the CRE investment industry currently suffers from insufficient technology tools and a lack of information standards which result in inefficient and ineffective business processes. Compared to other industries and other asset classes within the investment world, there are no widely adopted standards for exchanging CRE information between organisations. Given the newcomer status of CRE as an investment asset class in its own right, there are also very few tools available on the market for managing CRE information and providing the types of analytics required by CRE investment managers and lenders. Furthermore, the fact that CRE has traditionally been a very illiquid asset resulting in a local industry means that as global investors and lenders have begun to invest in CRE they are forced to interact with a large number of local counterparties: managing agents, brokers, valuers, lawyers, leasing agents, etc. When information is passed between these numerous parties, details are often omitted leading to a breakdown in data integrity.

### 12.6.1. Lack of information standards

Despite numerous attempts over recent decades, there remains no widely accepted standard for describing CRE investments and benchmarking performance. Some of the organisations that have made attempts at establishing standards, with varying degrees of success, include the Open Standards Consortium for Real Estate (OSCRE), the International Property Databank (IPD) and the Commercial Real Estate Financial Council (CREFC), through its European-Investor Reporting Package (E-IRP). The E-IRP covers, from lender and securitisation investor's perspectives, a broad range of data at the property, tenant, loan and securitisation investment levels, which could begin to address the transparency the financing community requires. Importantly, this work has been closely coordinated with related transparency initiatives among Europe's central banks.[6]

Where these organisations have made progress toward commonly accepted information standards, it has generally been within isolated segments of the industry. For example, CREFC has focused on the lending and securitisation investor needs through the E-IRP, whereas IPD has tended to focus on investment and fund managers. OSCRE has been very active among property management firms and software vendors. These organisations tend also to be geographically focused. There are local CRE standard bodies in almost every country within the European Union.

---

[6] See further Appendix 4.

For the market to accept and implement data and reporting standards requires either a significant profit motive or the forceful hand of regulatory bodies. The profitability of utilising standards has proven illusive to date, in part due to a lack of appropriate information management tools. Further, relatively loose loan underwriting standards at the height of the last credit cycle did not create appropriate links between greater borrower reporting transparency and lower funding costs. With transparency at the top of lender and regulator agendas, there is a convergence of commercial and regulatory compliance imperatives for the transparency which comes from information and reporting standards.

In time, some of these organisations may gain the critical mass necessary to credibly claim to be the CRE information standards organisation, but for the time being there is no standard that a firm within the CRE investment industry, particularly a global firm, could adopt to streamline the collection of data from providers such as managing agents and lawyers, for internal asset and investment management and for external reporting to stakeholders such as their lenders, investors or joint venture partners.

### 12.6.2. Lack of tools

The CRE investment industry, at the time of writing, in terms of the types of market players involved and the current business models, is relatively new. Historically CRE has been owned by private landlords with long-term investment horizons or public CRE investment trusts. Financing was provided by traditional lenders in the form of first lien mortgages.[7] In the boom years up to 2007, the CRE investment industry has expanded to include a great number of private equity firms, insurance companies, sovereign wealth funds, endowment managers, and so on. On the lending side, securitisation and loan trading became commonplace and a vibrant trading market appeared. Software vendors have been slow to keep up with these changes. The solutions currently available in the market were designed to address the needs of property managers, valuers, leasing lawyers, and other traditional users. New tools targeting the investment and lending industries and focused on cash flow budgeting and forecasting and on portfolio analytics have recently begun to emerge. However, the adoption of these new tools is still very limited and their utility has yet to be proven

### 12.6.3. Common current approaches

CRE investors and lenders have typically attempted to overcome the challenges described in this Chapter in one of two ways. The most common approach has been to implement property management systems that have been heavily customised to produce reporting that is meaningful and useful

---

[7]    See further Chs 1 and 2.

to investors and lenders. This seems to be an obvious solution given that property management systems are already designed to store and process much of the information that is of interest to owners and lenders (leases, tenants, billing history, account receivables, etc.). Furthermore, in some cases, CRE investors have been able to mandate that all of their service providers use that investor's own property management system so as to avoid the need for "double entry" or consolidation of the information at a later point in time.

The primary drawback of this approach is that property management systems are generally designed to be used to store detailed transactional information and to carry out repetitive processes such as billing tenants and paying invoices, rather than to support the more ad-hoc and high-level process risk and performance analysis that CRE investors and lenders are interested in. These systems are also normally designed around the requirements of local markets and require heavy customisation when used for international CRE portfolios.

The second approach that is commonly attempted is to develop one's own data warehouse, data collection and aggregation framework and to combine these with a generic reporting tool. This approach can be more flexible and can provide more robust analytical capabilities than attempting to customise a property management system; however there are serious challenges here as well. The biggest challenge is designing a data model that is comprehensive enough and flexible enough to capture all of the information that a CRE investor or lender will need to capture from the various disparate sources in different jurisdictions. The task of designing such a data model typically takes anywhere from three months to over a year and the final product often falls far short of expectations in terms of the scope of data it can capture, the quality of what is captured and the flexibility of accessing and manipulating it. This requires subsequent phases of remedial design and re-works. Even after the data model has been designed, the development of the actual data warehouse can take several months. There are several well-known instances of CRE investors having spent several years and several million pounds on data warehouse projects, without receiving anywhere near the value they expected in terms of improved transparency of the risks and performance profile of their portfolios.

For example, a well-known, US-based CRE investment firm recognised they had difficulty with collecting and reporting of CRE information. With a mix of direct ownership and joint venture partnerships they were collecting lease-level information from third party property managers in a property management accounting system and consolidating that data in Excel. Their internal technology group had convinced them they could build a data warehouse that would extract information from their property management system and provide the operational reports they needed to run their business. After a year of development and deployment and an investment of more than two million dollars, the asset and portfolio management groups were unhappy with the results. The data, where available, was of dubious quality. There was also recognition among the users of the solution that more valuable data was available in valuation models and excel workbooks than in the data warehouse. After continuing the project for another year they finally abandoned it, recognising that they could never produce information that the business could trust. With the business constantly second guessing results, the benefit of automation was lost.

## 12.7.   The future

### 12.7.1.   CRE information standardisation

The ability to obtain timely and accurate information in the CRE industry, as in any domain, depends on the existence of an effective data governance framework. Data governance, whether applied in a single business, or across an industry, is focused on the standardisation of definitions and ongoing monitoring for conformity to those definitions through the implementation of policies and procedures and formation of governance bodies responsible for data quality. The core of a data governance framework is a universally accepted data standard, developed from the top down, by deconstructing the information required by the users of the standard including the underlying detailed data elements. It is only by ensuring the integrity of low level data that top level metrics can be made reliable. For example, funds or investments are comprised of underlying deals and/or positions; positions are comprised of assets and/or loans; assets are comprised of properties; loans are comprised of underlying obligors; properties are comprised of leases, or units based on property types. If lease-level data is not standardised, there can be no reliance on investment level risk and performance metrics.

Definitions, and related codes and lookups should be standardised and document in a centralised and managed library that cannot be edited by the general user population. These values should be reviewed and maintained by a data governance body and should only be adjusted based on functional need. All changes, if deemed necessary, must be approved, documented, and disseminated to the user population. This degree of control ensures that information is classified according to a centrally managed taxonomy to which all users of the information can refer.

Through the simplification of the environment brought about by an accepted standard, information management processes becomes inherently streamlined. Having a centralised information repository in addition to data standards would aid in the normalisation of data and simplify the implementation of data governance by providing a single site for the application of data quality policies and procedures. Within this repository, data can be captured at the lowest level in the information stack, and programmatically consolidated to the highest level through automated queries and reports, thus removing the greatest operation risk—the human element—from the consolidation and reporting process. This method also enables the deconstruction of information from the top down, allowing for an auditable chain of methodology and thus increasing confidence in data and reducing operational risk. Business intelligence, or the ability to dynamically create analytics, is a direct product of standardisation and data governance. Effective business intelligence strategies and scenarios, coupled with a reliable method of data capture allows for data to be turned into information.

Working with a global client, the authors have seen the benefit of defining data standards and enforcing their implementation across the enterprise. The client has actively standardised their CRE definitions and forced their disparate globally decentralised business units to confirm to them. Even when data submission must be manual and automated integration is impossible, the result of a uniform business and technical validation process means that executives in the global operating unit are not exposed to information that is not approved. Without ever reviewing potentially incorrect information there is confidence in the data and ultimately the platform. This has lead to continued investment in an information management strategy that provides quality information about the CRE portfolio.

### 12.7.2.  A CRE information exchange

At the time of writing, senior executives within asset management firms that invest in CRE often lament that they cannot get the same level of accurate and timely information about their CRE portfolio as they do from their fixed income and equity portfolios. This is because CRE assets are not treated like other investment instruments that are traded in public markets. CRE assets are passed from owner to owner, each time requiring the new investor to rebuild all the underlying information about the asset. Quite often this is done manually, in the new owner's property management and accounting system. This is costly and time consuming for direct investors. For mortgage or CMBS holders it means that gaining visibility into the collateral securing their investments may require the manual collection of information from dozens of source systems and literally hundreds of hours spent reviewing non-standard reports and documents and creating comparable reports.

In the author's opinion, the clear way forward is the creation of an exchange or clearing house for CRE asset and investment information that enables the seamless transfer of information between buyers and sellers, managers and investors, and borrowers and lenders. With the support of some of the large institutional investors, a critical mass of assets and investments could be reached that would ensure that this exchange becomes the go-to place for collection and dissemination of CRE information. With this type of exchange in place, investors would have far greater access to the information they need to understand the performance value and risk of their holdings.

With advances in technology, the realisation of a global CRE exchange is no longer a pipe dream. The maturity of cloud computing, decreases in the cost of information storage and transmission, improvements in internet security, and the growing acceptance of software-as-a-service models have cleared the way for the creation of a cloud-based information exchange for the CRE industry. With the support of standards and statutory bodies, and investors and managers who understand the importance of transparency, organisations such as Hipercept are currently developing next generation platforms for the ongoing tracking and maintenance of investment grade CRE investments.

## 12.8. Conclusion

In the challenging markets that exist at the time of writing, CRE investors are struggling to effectively manage their CRE portfolios. Whether they are exposed to CRE via direct equity investments, loans or debt instruments, even the most basic details about their portfolio are often elusive. Within the investment community, the focus needs to be on the sharing of information so that value and risk can be more optimally measured and understood. By working towards better principles for defining and managing data, leveraging a coordinated approach; brokers, owners, advisors, managers and investors will be able to significantly streamline their operations and lower the barrier of entry to this investment class.

This Chapter has outlined the current challenges facing the mortgage and CMBS market in understanding the fundamentals behind underlying collateral and the major influences driving change. Without efficient access to accurate information about their investments, investors are unable to effectively manage risk, make effective decisions, and conform to regulatory reform. Only with the establishment of generic open platforms for the ongoing management of CRE collateral and methods for collecting, standardising, maintaining and sharing CMBS and loan investment information will investors be able to access information critical to understanding investment performance and risk. At the same time, with the availability of this information investors and managers will be better positioned to meet regulatory mandates and investor demands for increased transparency, such that CRE can once again become a distinct asset class of choice.

# Chapter 13

# Finding Value in Post-Crisis Commercial Real Estate Debt: an Investor's Perspective

Sa'ad Malik,

Managing Partner, Rhino Investment Management LLP

## 13.1.  Introduction

As set out in Ch.1, the European CRE sector and related debt markets have suffered unprecedented turmoil since late 2007, when they were shut down by the global liquidity crisis that followed the collapse of the US sub-prime market and subsequent recessionary contagion. The combination of this sudden freezing of public and private debt markets, and, at the time of writing, continuing Europe-wide market uncertainty, has resulted in a major re-pricing of credit risk and tumbling CRE values.

### 13.1.1.  Background to the crisis

The expansion of the European financed CRE market through 2007 was tied to surging economic growth, historically cheap cross-border debt and corporate and state-level rationalisation of real estate holdings. Private debt (e.g. local mortgage banks) and equity have, as demonstrated throughout this book, historically dominated CRE lending, but banks increasingly migrated to an "originate-to-distribute" model based on CMBS issuance and syndication to predominantly specialist "fast-money" debt investors.[1] Consequently, record debt volumes were advanced during the peak years of 2005–07, as set out in Ch.2.

The rapid increase in demand for senior debt led lenders to materially relax lending criteria (motivated by low interest rates, poor risk models and lax regulation), and outpaced risk transfer. As a result, CB Richard Ellis[2] estimates that circa €960 billion of largely illiquid commercial CRE debt is

---

[1]  Bank-sponsored SIVs purchased AAA- and AA-rated CMBS, hedge funds found compelling yield pick-up in junior BBB- and BB-rated tranches versus corporate credits and CDOs specialised in the full range of subordinated CMBS, B Note and mezzanine investments. See further Chs 1, 2, 4 and 20.

[2]  CB Richard Ellis, *Real Estate Finance ViewPoint*, Winter 2011. See further Ch.2.

sitting on lenders' balance sheets post-crisis. Hence, banks are under intense pressure to manage deteriorating portfolios, deleverage and improve capitalisation. However, they have generally avoided action which might incur large write-downs, preferring instead to grant loan extensions to stressed borrowers (dubbed the "extend and pretend" strategy by commentators).[3] Widespread government and central bank support, in the form of liberalised regulation and liquidity, has to date also substantially eased the pressure on troubled lenders to sell at the bottom of the market, thereby avoiding the shock of a "fire sale" across the banking system.

Largely, certain under-capitalised banks have exited CRE altogether, or retrenched to core markets, due to a confluence of factors:

- the near-closure of syndication and securitisation markets has removed the sector's most efficient liquidity providers who cannot operate and manage risk profitably in a hold-to-maturity market;[4]
- adverse and evolving risk-weighted regulatory pressures, resulting in large volumes of tied-up capital and depressed returns on equity;[5]
- the need to resolve internal capitalisation issues, manage legacy positions and support existing client refinancings; and
- domestic pressure to extend debt to competing sectors, such as small businesses under the UK's Project Merlin (see Ch.2) initiative.

Therefore, as loans which were originated through 2007 reach maturity, the market is unable to absorb this wave of refinancing, as set out in Figure 1.

Despite substantial fresh equity being raised, the extent of the shortfall between depressed CRE prices and available senior mortgage debt is sobering. For example, DTZ estimates that through 2013 alone, loan maturities will expose a CRE debt-refinancing gap of c.€145 billion.[6] Hence, with c.€480 billion of European CRE debt due to mature during 2012–14, recent outcomes at CMBS loan maturity (See Figure 2) raise material short-term concerns.

The stagnant mortgage market will not pick up until banks, which were formerly the default lenders for the most efficient portion of the CRE debt stack, again become motivated sellers, lenders and investors. Since banks hold the vast majority of outstanding CRE debt,[7] resolution of the overhang on their balance sheets, is key to the present investment opportunity.

---

[3] See further Ch.5.
[4] Such lenders as witnessed in Chs 1 and 2, include major arrangers of CMBS issuance as well as traditional syndicated lending platforms.
[5] Treatment is particularly severe for non-investment grade assets such as subordinated B Notes and mezzanine debt. See further Chs 14 and 15.
[6] DTZ Insight, Global Debt Funding Gap, May 2012. Estimated refinancing gap of $182 billion converted at a $/€ exchange rate of 1/0.795. See further para.2.5.3.
[7] Predominantly bilateral mortgage loans and senior CMBS paper taken over from SIVs.

**Figure 1: European Commercial Real Estate Debt Maturity Profile**

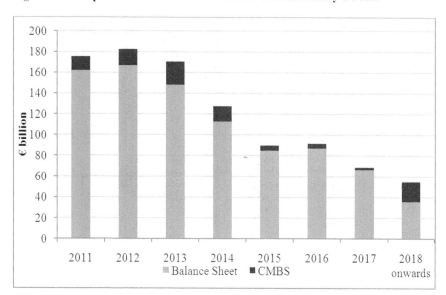

Sources: CB Richard Ellis, De Montfort University, Fitch Ratings

### 13.1.2. The investment landscape

The European CRE debt crisis is firmly rooted in dysfunctional credit markets. Regulation and legacy issues have barred traditional senior debt providers from the market, creating an opportunity for alternative sources of capital to provide liquidity to the bank market and to plug funding gaps left by the retraction of senior balance sheet and CMBS financing.

To date, large UK and German lenders have been the most proactive managers of legacy mortgage and CMBS risk, closely followed by "bad banks" such as Ireland's NAMA. Until the time of writing, the standard has been private off-market disposals with little price transparency (such as discounted pay-offs by sponsors), but as the large scale and urgency of the problem becomes apparent, banks are expected to start conducting large public "auction" processes (e.g. Royal Bank of Scotland).

In comparison with banks, a relatively limited proportion of outstanding CRE debt is held by non-bank institutions including asset managers, life and pension companies. However, since these parties do not have quite the same distressed legacy exposures or regulatory and capital burdens as

Figure 2: Maturity Outcomes of European CMBS Loans

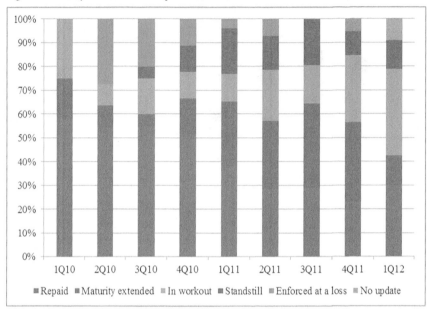

Sources: Fitch Ratings, Morgan Stanley Research

banks[8], they are anticipated to dispose of assets more selectively. For example, insurers are expected to retain high quality, conservatively leveraged debt with strong recovery prospects. Similarly, debt funds typically have the expertise to manage impaired assets through to recovery, though will execute sales to raise capital for investment or to take profits.

Initially, market participants expected that banks would resume post-crisis mortgage lending at reduced advance rates of around 60 per cent,[9] versus a maximum of c.85 per cent at the peak of the market in 2007. Combined with declining CRE values, a significant funding deficit would then be exposed at refinancing. Hence, a raft of high-yield debt funds emerged to provide subordinated "stretch-senior" or "mezzanine" debt from 50–80 per cent LTV.[10] However, many banks have not yet resumed lending, even at these levels. Therefore, the lack of senior debt is, in fact, the main funding constraint at the time of writing. Thus, various senior debt platforms have been launched by alternative lenders including insurance companies and managed debt funds.

---

[8]   However, non-bank institutions may have their own regulatory and capital pressures as highlighted later in this Chapter (e.g. para.14.2). Further see Ch.9.
[9]   In line with advance rates for *pfandbrief*-eligibility (e.g. German covered bonds).
[10]   See Ch.15.

The CMBS primary market has, as witnessed in the opening chapter to this book, also been effectively closed since 2008, due to the cessation of lending activity and loss of the core SIV investor base. Moreover, there is presently insufficient economic and regulatory incentive for all stakeholders to stimulate meaningful volumes of CMBS 2.0 product.[11] Post-crisis, public securitisations have been either bespoke structures to benefit from ECB repurchase schemes, customised corporate credit transactions[12] or else sample structures to gauge investors' preferences. Hence, CMBS is evolving, with a clearer focus on alternative risk transfer for challenging forms of CRE debt.[13]

### 13.1.3. Summary

To date, five years into an extended market dislocation, investors still struggle to establish value or coherent investing strategies, and the combination of limited new debt finance and short available timeframe for resolution of certain positions (e.g. CMBS legal final maturities) presents significant challenges for investors, seeking to accurately estimate exit values and recoveries in legacy CMBS product.

The combined lack of liquidity in the European banking system and inflexibility of available debt is expected to define the current investment opportunity up to 2017. Thus, prospective investors with flexible capital and return expectations are well-positioned to take business from conventional debt providers at historically attractive risk-adjusted returns linked to either seller distress or shortage of available debt rather than straightforward credit risk.

## 13.2. The European CRE debt investor base

Any discussion of the CRE debt investment offering in H2 2012 must start with capital supply and investor preferences. As stated above, the universe of European debt investors has altered materially since the liquidity crunch. Traditional investors have exited or retreated to core markets, whilst new capital sources are emerging to bridge the gap between equity and senior debt. Moreover, the ever-evolving regulatory landscape and shifting impact on certain classes of investors (particularly banks in respect of encouraging deleveraging and/or new lending), continues to constrain liquidity. Each class of current investor has unique investment objectives and restrictions, as outlined in the following sections:

---

[11]   A detailed discussion of CMBS 2.0 is set out in Ch.4.
[12]   See further Chs 4 and 20.
[13]   For example, the non-mortgage debt underlying the DECO 2012 MHILL Ltd transaction.

*Figure 3: Summary of CRE Investor Types*

| Investor Type | Current Status | Potential Trends |
|---|---|---|
| Banks | – €2.4 trillion[14] balance sheet exposure.<br>– Need to deleverage and improve capital positions.<br>– Limited origination and syndication capability. | – €300-600 billion estimated requirement for balance sheet reduction.<br>– Significant decline in senior CRE debt and subject to strict parameters.<br>– Limited potential for CMBS exit. |
| Funds | – Fundraising for portfolio acquisitions plus mezzanine and senior debt. | – €25 billion of capital for private equity CRE strategies.<br>– Increased fundraising expected in order to meet decline in bank market. |
| Insurance Companies | – Early stages of increased CRE lending.<br>– Regulatory clarity could spur expansion of mandates across sector. | – Lending driven by proposed regulation.<br>– €50-100 billion capital availability over up to ten years. |
| Pension Funds | – Allocation predominantly to equity.<br>– Expansion of Solvency II could encourage CRE lending. | – Potential source of senior lending only subject to proposed regulation.<br>– Potential buyers of limited volumes of bespoke credit tenant CMBS. |
| Private Banks & HNWIs[15] | – Largely cash holdings.<br>– HNWIs pursuing defensive, capital protection strategies in CRE equity. | – Flexible capital with conservative return expectations is highly suited to senior debt funding or priority CMBS. |
| Corporates | – Few suitable opportunities for direct investment, and also limited debt available. | – CRE debt may provide off-market exposure to suitable deals.<br>– Complementary business strategy for opportunistic investment. |

*Source: Morgan Stanley Research*

### 13.2.1. Banks

Banks have drastically curtailed their involvement in the CRE loan investment market to prioritise capital and liquidity issues. Hence, at the time of writing, they are drivers of investment opportunity (as sellers) rather than a major source of new investment capital. Many lenders have

---

[14] Morgan Stanley Blue Paper, Banks Deleveraging and Real Estate (March 2012), (the Morgan Stanley Report).
[15] High net worth individuals.

exited this market altogether, with CRE lending undermined also by retrenchment to domestic markets or migration to competing business areas.[16] Moreover, the lack of clarity and continuing evolution of regulation surrounding Basel III and European Banking Authority rules are a key obstacle to investing in new debt (in terms of promoting both deleveraging and new origination).[17] In 2012, banks are only originating CRE loans on a highly selective basis:

- lending against high quality cash flow and collateral in domestic markets, to support key institutional relationships (e.g. refinancing existing facilities);
- minimising funding costs and risk-weighted capital charges on loans and related hedging (e.g. meeting lending targets through *pfandbrief-eligible* business);
- typically five-year loans up to 65 per cent LTV and typically maximum €50 million participations on a bilateral or club basis, with upfront fees of 1.0–2.0 per cent and coupons based on a three-month floating index plus 2.5–4.5 per cent;
- ensuring robustness of primary documentation, including control through covenants; and
- maintaining liquidity for the purpose of risk managing exposures.

Certain institutions are also, opportunistically, acquiring performing loans in home markets as competitors exit non-core portfolios (e.g. Morgan Stanley Research estimates that c.30 per cent of European CRE loans are held cross-border).[18] Furthermore, there may be opportunity for US banks, which are further along in resolving core capitalisation issues, to expand into portfolio acquisitions from divesting European lenders.[19]

Banks have, to date, largely chosen to retain senior CMBS exposures rather than exiting at large discounts. Moreover, their secondary desks have become increasingly active proprietary traders across all tranches and combined with hedge funds, are perceived to represent the majority of European CMBS trading. However, at the time of writing, as Eurozone turbulence worsens, ratings pressure on CMBS increases and non-core balance sheets are trimmed, trading banks are entering a notable risk-off phase.

---

[16] For example, the agreement between the UK government and four major high street banks to promote small business lending (Project Merlin).

[17] See Ch.16 for a further discussion on this area.

[18] See the *Morgan Stanley Report*.

[19] See Ch.19 for a discussion of foreign direct investment into Europe to take advantage of this opportunity.

### 13.2.2. Funds

In H2 2012, funds and asset managers are the most flexible and diverse class of investor encompassing core, opportunity, sovereign wealth and hedge funds, amongst others. Their mandate is broad within defined asset classes due to the lack of bank-style regulation. Hence, risk appetite and return criteria can vary enormously based on investors and market conditions.[20] In the broadest terms, annualised return targets range from 5–6 per cent for senior debt funds, through 20+ per cent for private equity.

Of course, hedge funds and opportunity funds have always participated in primary and secondary CMBS markets, but funds have noticeably increased involvement in more illiquid European debt since 2008.[21] For example, US and continental European funds in particular are seeking cross-border opportunities in order to capture attractive returns from new mezzanine debt investment. More recently, as discussed in Ch.9, a lack of bank lending has also led to the growth of managed senior debt funds targeting newly-originated investments from 0–65 per cent LTV.

Should a large-scale bank sell-off occur in 2013 and beyond, fund activity is set to increase exponentially with pressure to put substantial amounts of investors' capital to work in portfolio acquisitions (e.g. private equity firms have already allocated roughly €25 billion to European CRE).[22] Moreover, the high potential yield and short term to resolution of legacy loans suits fund capital which seeks a relatively prompt return on investment.

### 13.2.3. Insurance companies

Insurers have historically been investors in varied CRE debt in order to match-fund their liabilities and the proposed Solvency II regulations are expected to considerably improve risk-weighted capital treatment (and thus, profitability) for tailored, long-dated senior mortgage lending.[23] Hence, with sizeable capital reserves and limited legacy issues, insurers should be well placed to become a default source of CRE funding, albeit (as set out below) not with the overall capacity to close the funding gap a significant degree.

Some insurance companies have already established senior debt platforms for institutional quality debt product, but short-term expansion is expected to be limited until regulations are finalised in the coming years.[24] However, many firms prefer to participate in third-party arranged syndicated loan facilities which avoid the considerable costs of developing bespoke

---

[20] See further Ch.9.
[21] See Ch.3.
[22] The *Morgan Stanley Report*.
[23] See Ch.16.
[24] Examples include Aviva, Legal & General and M&G Investments.

origination and servicing infrastructure. In the short term, although insurers are unlikely to fill the void created by the downturn in European bank lending, they are anticipated to have as much as €50–100 billion of capacity for CRE lending over the next ten years.[25] However, they are not expected to have interest in purchasing seasoned sub- or non-performing stock.

Given insurers' focus on matching liabilities, short-dated secondary CMBS with significant ratings[26] and price volatility is not a preferred investment option. Thus, investment is typically limited to primary issuance with conservative characteristics (e.g. credit tenant lease transactions).

### 13.2.4. Pension funds

Pension fund allocations to CRE are predominantly to equity. However, if the Solvency II proposals are extended to these institutions, there may be strong incentive to meet liabilities through senior lending, particularly with the added benefit of long-term, secure cash flows and yield pick-up versus corporate bonds.[27] Moreover, long-term credit tenant CMBS is also likely to remain attractive for bespoke exposure to highly-rated cash flow and assets.

### 13.2.5. Private banks and HNWIs

UBS/Campden Research[28] estimates that c.12 per cent of investable private wealth is allocated to CRE. Although private banks and family offices have historically preferred direct CRE assets and traditional fixed income products, market turmoil has diminished investment opportunities across sectors. Hence, some commentators estimate that amongst this investor group, up to two-thirds of assets may be held in cash or cash-equivalents, generating limited returns.

However, global HNWIs are increasingly looking for security and to take advantage of exchange rates by buying western European CRE (especially prime London) with conservative yield requirements, with resultant opportunity for private banks to provide senior debt to core clients. The flexibility and defensiveness of this capital is particularly well suited to all formats of CRE debt, including CMBS, with sophisticated HNWIs attracted to this area as a compelling hybrid of traditional fixed income and real estate investing.

Hence, many HNWIs are, at the time of writing, exploring the potential to migrate from pure equity investment to deploying capital passively in CRE debt, with preferable security and return features. CMBS in particular,

---

[25] See the *Morgan Stanley Report*.
[26] Investment criteria are often reliant on public credit ratings.
[27] Dealt with in Ch.16.
[28] *European Family Office Survey 2011*.

represents an exciting prospect due to the low barriers to entry and ease of investing in and risk managing this asset class. Thus, European private banks are now exploring the potential for collective senior debt and CMBS investment vehicles in order to meet potential demand for low-cost exposure to institutional grade CRE and cash flows.

### 13.2.6. Corporates

The combined lack of suitable supply in the direct investment market and scarcity of debt funding is leading many CRE firms to consider debt investments. Corporates are increasingly viewing this option as an efficient alternative means of gaining exposure to institutional quality assets and potentially acquiring off-market access to the underlying CRE through (negative) control in senior or mezzanine enforcement scenarios.[29]

However, since this strategy deviates materially from corporates' core competencies and long-term business objectives, CRE debt is purely an opportunistic, complementary strategy to their core business model.

### 13.2.7. Summary

As European banks deal with legacy and regulatory concerns in 2013 and beyond, their inflexibility will, as demonstrated in Ch.9, result in alternative lenders without such severe constraints playing a larger role in this dislocated market. The key consideration for investors is to deploy flexible capital, in areas which are underserved by former default lenders, to maximise risk-adjusted returns across the capital structure.

## 13.3. Investment formats

Having established fundamental asset-level investment criteria and return requirements, investors have three distinct routes for CRE debt investment:[30]

- first-ranking commercial mortgage loans (e.g. whole loans or A/B note participations);
- subordinated mezzanine debt secured against a borrower's shares;[31] and
- CMBS notes which are ultimately secured against first-ranking mortgage loans.

---

[29] For example, Delancey's involvement in the REC No.5 CMBS (Plantation Place).
[30] State-guaranteed covered bonds such as German *pfandbriefe* are excluded from this discussion.
[31] See Chs 14 and 15.

The table below provides a simplified overview of these products and frames the discussion:

| *Investment Feature* | *Senior Mortgages* | *Mezzanine Loans* | *CMBS* |
|---|---|---|---|
| Security | – Definable first-ranking mortgage loan(s) plus comprehensive security package. | – Definable non-mortgage junior ranking loan(s) secured by shares of borrower SPV. | – Exchange-listed participation in definable first-ranking mortgage loan(s) plus comprehensive security package. |
| Structural & Credit Enhancement | – Priority ranking ahead of mezzanine lenders. <br> – If bifurcated, A Note is "super-senior" to contractually subordinated B Note. | – No debt subordination. <br> – Structurally subordinated to senior mortgage. | – Priority ranking ahead of mezzanine lenders. <br> – If bifurcated, A Note is "super-senior" to contractually subordinated B Note. <br> – Junior tranches provide enhancement, creating "super-senior" exposure within mortgage debt. <br> – Liquidity or advancing mechanisms minimise cash flow disruption. |
| Credit Ratings | – Private "shadow" ratings can be obtained. | – Private "shadow" ratings can be obtained. | – Publicly rated with regular monitoring. |

| Risk Profile | – First-ranking security (other than hedging). <br>– Tailored to meet investor preferences such as leverage (e.g. A/B Notes), repayment profiles and returns. <br>– Enhancement from junior lenders and equity. <br>– Lack of diversity in single loans can be mitigated by portfolio loans or acquiring bundles of loans. <br>– Most lender control in CRE debt formats. | – First-loss debt behind all priority mortgage and hedging claims. <br>– Maximum exposure upon credit distress. <br>– Negative control rights only, with recourse only to borrower vehicle. | – First-ranking security (other than hedging). <br>– Tailored to meet investor preferences through buying specific tranches reflecting bespoke credit risk, maturity and returns. <br>– Enhancement from junior lenders and equity. <br>– Typically diversified in terms of tenant, property, asset class, jurisdiction and borrower risk plus structural supports. <br>– Least lender control in CRE debt formats. |
|---|---|---|---|
| Control Features | – Passive investment option with no direct property control. <br>– New originations have strict financial and information covenants but legacy debt is typically "covenant-light". <br>– Default gives significant control over management and workout process. <br>– Loans are typically bilateral but club deals have bespoke corporate governance. | – Passive investment option with no direct property control. <br>– Default permits accession to equity position but no control over mortgage enforcement. <br>– Intercreditor provisions may create negative control where mezzanine lender can trigger costs (e.g. stamp duty) upon mortgage enforcement. <br>– Vast majority of loans are bilateral. | – Passive investment option with no direct loan or property control. <br>– Transaction parties appointed at issuance (e.g. servicer) to administer collateral subject to contractual procedures and standards. <br>– Junior tranches are granted certain consultation and approval rights relating to the loans and bonds. <br>– Investors are part of a capital markets syndicate. |

| | | | |
|---|---|---|---|
| *Term* | – Typically 5–7 years with most outstanding debt maturities in 2011–14.<br>– Post-maturity workout in A/B Note structures may be prolonged by intercreditor arrangements. | – Typically 5–7 year maturities with most outstanding debt maturities in 2011–14.<br>– Post-maturity workout in A/B Note structures may be prolonged by intercreditor arrangements. | – Mostly 5-7 year loan maturities (expiring 2011–14) with typical trailing bond maturities of c. three years.<br>– Legal final maturities conclusively restrict investment term but an inflexible timetable can be mitigated by seniority of loan security or by satisfying formal extension procedures. |
| *Return Profile* | – Quarterly coupons (three-month floating index plus margin).<br>– Increased fixed rate origination (e.g. insurers).<br>– Upside limited to nominal value of debt.<br>– Seasoned performing loans are currently priced at annual returns of 15% plus based on expected recoveries (circa 18% plus for non-performing loans).<br>– Returns for new mortgage loans are peaking with all-in gross yields of circa 5% at 60% LTV and circa 8% on 50% LTC portfolio lending. | – Typically payment-in-kind (PIK) interest deferred to maturity but new loans may have some current-pay element.<br>– Upside limited to face-value.<br>– Returns are strong at circa 8-15% but under pressure as mezzanine space becomes crowded. | – Quarterly coupons (three-month floating index plus margin).<br>– Low execution and transaction costs.<br>– "Push-to-par" strategies rely on dislocation arbitrage between bond prices and asset values.<br>– Upside limited to face-value.<br>– Strong risk-adjusted returns, currently comparable with direct investment with yields of 4-8% on first-pay CMBS and 15-20%-plus on mezzanine tranches. |
| *Capital Treatment* | – Dependent on investor. | – Dependent on investor. | – Dependent on investor. |

311

| | | | |
|---|---|---|---|
| *Liquidity* | – Origination and investment require substantial timeframes for diligence due to lack of transparency and large individual lot sizes.<br>– Market conditions are constraining liquidity except for prime assets.<br>– Exit is dependent on health of CRE market and availability of financing. | – Origination and investment require substantial timeframes for diligence due to lack of transparency and large individual lot sizes.<br>– Opportunity is constrained by lack of suitable senior financing and decreasing margins.<br>– Exit is dependent on health of CRE market and availability of financing. | – Traded OTC so there is no official data but the market is active with c.€10 billion of activity estimated in 2011 across more than one hundred individual CMBS issuers.<br>– Greatest liquidity among CRE debt formats due to listing, credit ratings, diversity, tailored risk, small minimum denominations and public information.<br>– Liquidity is greatest in senior AAA- and AA-rated debt versus riskier mezzanine tranches where recoveries are difficult to predict. |
| *Investment Size* | – Individual loans typically range from €10 million – €1 billion, which can prohibit access to larger prime assets except for large institutions or syndicates. | – Individual loans typically range from €10-100 million, prohibiting access to large high-quality collateral for smaller investors. | – Minimum denominations of 50,000 (£ or €) and individual trades usually of €1-10 million face-value, giving small investors access to institutional-grade risk. |

| Barriers to Entry | – No restriction on investors but lot sizes may exclude small investors.<br>– Origination and competitive processes are costly, lengthy and success is not guaranteed.<br>– Asset management requires material investment in infrastructure.<br>– Current lack of bank and capital markets financing for portfolio acquisitions. | – No restriction on investors but lot sizes may exclude small investors.<br>– Origination and competitive processes are costly, lengthy and success is not guaranteed.<br>– Asset management requires material investment in infrastructure.<br>– Significant competition from specialist funds and downward margin pressure. | – Qualified Institutional Buyers (QIBs) only, so non-specialists must invest through qualified intermediaries (e.g. asset managers).<br>– Significant education process for new investors to familiarise themselves with securitised products and structural quirks, particularly in legacy transactions. |
|---|---|---|---|

### 13.3.1. Senior commercial mortgage loans

CRE debt investors are able to participate in either seasoned or newly-originated commercial mortgages, with marked differences between the two investment propositions as described below.

### 13.3.1.1. New origination

There is an acute need for new senior loans in order to refinance the roughly €661 billion wall of European CRE debt maturing through 2016.[32] This presents an attractive risk-adjusted return scenario for active lenders:

- there is limited competition for low leverage but historically high-yielding first-ranking debt, and most borrowers have few efficient alternatives since access to the unsecured corporate bond market is restricted to quoted real estate companies;
- tenders can cherry-pick sponsors and security as well as control lending parameters, covenants and documentation;
- economics are significantly improved versus the lending boom through 2007, as borrowers are more concerned with lack of debt availability rather than costs; and
- new loans are "clean" structures, supported by fresh equity from sponsors.

---

[32] CB Richard Ellis, *Real Estate Finance ViewPoint*, Winter 2011. See further Ch.2.

However, legacy issues and increased funding costs continue to blight the inactive banking sector. Although lenders with access to low-cost covered bond markets (e.g. German *pfandbrief* banks) do have a competitive advantage, especially if base rates spike from current lows, even these banks have restricted mandates in terms of total lending targets, asset quality and lot size (bilateral advances are usually €20–50 million, with scarce large loan capital above €100 million).

Consequently, non-bank lenders are likely to become increasingly valuable sources of senior liquidity, led by large "real-money" accounts.[33] DTZ estimates these alternative lenders will provide approximately $75 billion of liquidity in 2012–13 alone with the result that:[34]

- Numerous insurance companies have established pan-European lending franchises, attracted by the ability to match-fund their liabilities (e.g. fixed rate or inflation-linked returns on loan facilities of 10 years or more), strong relative value versus traditional fixed income investments and potentially advantageous capital treatment and return on capital under the Solvency II regime (first-ranking CRE loans could be considered a favoured asset class).[35] Insurance companies could, therefore, increasingly transfer investment allocations from direct CRE to debt. In fact, Savills estimates that insurers already comprise around one-third of non-bank lenders with capacity to advance loans exceeding €100 million.[36] Observers estimate that this source of debt capital could grow to €50–100 billion over a five- to 10-year term.[37]
- Managed senior debt funds are an emerging class of senior debt investor, with typical gross return targets of 5–6 per cent for leverage up to 65 per cent. These investors have a flexible senior lending mandate in terms of geography, collateral and leverage and in addition, have the potential to migrate beyond traditional 0–65 per cent LTV lending. For instance, providing stretch-senior debt at 50–65 per cent LTV in collaboration with German banks which meet their lending targets mostly through *pfandbrief*-eligible business (50–60 per cent LTV), can present enhanced risk-adjusted returns whilst remaining within strict LTV parameters.
- Whilst pension funds will seek to increase real estate exposure as inflation rises, their allocations are primarily to equity. However, if Solvency II is extended to these institutions and they can resolve internal issues regarding asset/liability ratios, the added benefit of

---

[33] Morgan Stanley Research estimates that up to €100–200 billion of alternative capital could be allocated to replace bank lending over the next five years. See further Ch.9.

[34] DTZ Insight, *Global Debt Funding Gap*, May 2012. See further Ch.2.

[35] Insurers must hold considerable capital against intervals between assets and liabilities, which could be managed well by investing in long-dated senior debt. However, regulations and precise requirements may not be finalised until c.2015.

[36] "Who's in Charge – Borrowers, Lenders or Politicians?" presentation (June 2012).

[37] See the *Morgan Stanley Report*.

secure cash flows and yield pick-up versus corporate bonds may tempt material participation in the senior debt sector.

- Political and market turbulence are driving global HNWIs (e.g. from Middle East, Asian and former Soviet states) to seek safety in prime western European CRE. These clients require passive, institutional-quality investments in typical amounts of €10–30 million, with conservative leverage up to 60 per cent LTV.[38] This represents a clear opportunity for private banks with large cash holdings to provide "one-stop" solutions to select clients and prime assets.

New entrants have previously been impeded by the considerable upfront costs of developing origination and servicing infrastructure, as well as a lack of suitable assets across major markets. However, the risk-adjusted investment case for senior lending is increasingly compelling. This alternative capital can participate in lending sectors where banks are no longer competing such as portfolio lending, non-prime CRE, short-term bridge facilities or higher leverage (e.g. up to 70 per cent LTV). The most exciting prospects are:

- Portfolio acquisition:
  Lending c.50 per cent loan-to-cost (LTC) against single or multiple seasoned loans and/or portfolios of senior CMBS purchased at a discount. This approach has the advantage of both super-senior leverage against re-set asset values and fresh sponsor equity. Anecdotal evidence from recent high-profile transactions suggests gross annual returns of up to 8 per cent are possible, particularly on smaller portfolios of up to €100 million value where other funders may have limited interest.[39] Margins exceed direct CRE lending simply because of non-mortgage security and distance from loan and CRE management. In addition to typically strong sponsorship, senior portfolio lenders may benefit from new relationships with underlying borrowers and from faster principal repayment as positions are worked out; and

- Acquisition bridging:
  Sponsors increasingly require short-term leverage of up to 18 months in order to complete off-market transactions (e.g. discounted pay-offs) within a restricted timeframe, providing a bridge to refinancing. Disregarding reinvestment considerations, the lack of available debt even at conservative leverage of circa 60 per cent, can push gross annual returns up to 10 per cent (far exceeding standard CRE lending).

---

[38] Includes relatively small clients (below c.€20 million of individual liquidity) seeking minority participations in third-party managed investment vehicles with a "club" of sponsors.

[39] For example, Bank of America Merrill Lynch is, in 2012, reported to be providing a 50% LTC acquisition facility to support Lone Star's purchase of a €200 million non-performing portfolio from Société Générale, at three-month Euribor plus 5–6%.

### 13.3.1.2. Seasoned loans

The long-term suspension of European bank and capital markets lending has resulted in a vast overhang of senior mortgage debt that will prove impossible to refinance in full. Despite banks' reluctance to act as at the time of writing, they now encounter considerable pressure to risk-off at meaningful discounts. Therefore, the European banking system is poised for a large-scale discounted transfer of CRE debt risk anticipated to be up to €600 billion in total over three to five years (with circa €300 billion announced to date).[40] Just as the market faces the prospect of a double dip recession, banks are keenly aware that:

- there is no clear route to economic recovery as evidenced by the Eurozone sovereign crisis;
- non-prime CRE values in particular are suffering a pronounced slowdown as loan books continue to deteriorate and capital expenditure needs to escalate;
- most CRE debt is at risk of maturity default due to the effective closure of senior debt markets, and distressed loans have limited prospects of satisfactory resolution;
- government and central bank support for illiquid collateral[41] is gradually being withdrawn (e.g. the NAMA stabilisation scheme has a maximum life, or government rescue packages which are conditional upon strict deleveraging targets);
- harsher regulatory capital treatment,[42] particularly of subordinate or non-performing debt and interest rate hedging, is adversely affecting bank capital ratios; and
- a deep international investor class dedicated to impaired loan portfolios has emerged with the ability to absorb large volumes of product.

In mid-2008, global private equity and opportunity funds foresaw the developing opportunity for large-scale diversified portfolio investing at material discounts to face-value. To this end, approximately €25 billion of private equity capital has been allocated to European CRE, with a large appetite for debt at c.20 per cent plus return targets.[43] Ernst & Young[44] estimates that of the 28 per cent of US distressed investors already active in Europe, most regard this as the larger investment opportunity:

---

[40] *Morgan Stanley Report.* Observers estimate that c. €25 billion may be sold in 2012.
[41] Such as potential loss of state guarantees or the risk of tightening of ECB repurchase criteria (although recent press reports suggest that certain criteria may be broadened in the near term).
[42] In December 2011, Boston Consulting Group estimated that European banks must raise nearly €221 billion or reduce balance sheets by almost one-fifth to meet incoming Basel III rules.
[43] *Morgan Stanley Report.*
[44] Ernst & Young, 2012 NPL Survey (At the Crossroads).

- the distressed European bank market is the greatest source of debt product (DTZ estimates that balance sheet loans represented c.75 per cent of CRE lending at peak, plus c.18 per cent of lending through the covered bond market), allowing investors to ramp up considerable diversified exposures cheaply and efficiently;
- loans are often secured by fundamentally sound but over-leveraged assets, with good underwritten recovery prospects and exit visibility as loans approach maturity; and
- where borrowers are in or approaching distress, lender control is vastly improved and there is upside in recapitalising or partially refinancing borrowers.[45]

Significant discounts to face-value are possible when investing in seasoned loans which are likely to incur principal losses, even where cash flow is strong but underlying collateral values have softened due to external market and funding issues. Here, investment discounts are linked to a combination of seller distress, general re-pricing of risk and the perceived hazard of buying into weak underwriting and documentary standards. Hence, investors are able to purchase nominally "troubled" loans at double-digit yields to maturity with additional upside if recoveries exceed the discounted purchase price (up to a maximum of original face-value). However, purchasers should be prepared to commit material resources to upfront due diligence and continuing asset management.

As the mountain of European CRE debt approaches maturity, investors anticipate material re-pricing across debt formats. Despite banks' willingness to accept realistic haircuts to face-value, most are unable to offer vendor finance, which further constrains asset prices and resolution. Since most loan pools are €500 million plus, all parties have been extremely frustrated by the lack of competitive large-scale acquisition finance which is stalling risk transfer and de-consolidation of the banks' risk-weighted assets. As a result, the marketplace for large loan portfolios is dominated by the most powerful firms which have the human capital and resources to chase marquee transactions. These buyers have either the ability for unlevered investment on favourable terms, or the strongest banking networks.[46] In fact, some commentators predict that re-capitalised US banks may now have the capacity to expand into potential acquisitions of European CRE loans themselves. However, small or new players are deterred from entering the bidding process by the early-stage transaction costs, inability to specify or exclude collateral, lack of supporting debt finance and execution risk.

---

[45] Certain investors seek to acquire defaulted loans in order to refinance or recapitalise borrowers. Likewise, there is growing interest in purchase options relating to defaulted CMBS loans, which may be attached to certain controlling class bonds.

[46] Although most large portfolio transactions have been completed with debt, a sizeable proportion of debt (especially pools of up to €500 million) has initially been funded entirely from equity.

Although there is undoubtedly value in large portfolio transactions emanating from the larger pan-European lenders, smaller investors seeking to invest in smaller loan portfolios of up to €100 million will find more persuasive arguments for engaging instead with small, regional institutions which are offloading their loan books. These banks have smaller exposure to CRE and often less urgency to recapitalise. Hence, they may be willing to transact at lower volumes and also offer outsize discounts on non-core secondary or tertiary stock. At this end of the secondary loan market, bidding competition is significantly reduced along with due diligence and asset management requirements, investment timetables and hence execution risk. Moreover, such small investors may be better placed to either invest without staple finance or to obtain senior funding (e.g. maximum of 50 per cent LTC or €50 million).

This model closely mirrors the United States' highly efficient NPL trading market, in which Ernst & Young estimates around 76 per cent of transactions have a volume below $500 million (and over one-third below $50 million).[47] In addition to creating an entry point for small investors, this level of debt has exciting potential for emerging non-bank portfolio lenders.

### 13.3.2. *Mezzanine loans*

With senior advance rates cut from roughly 85 per cent at peak to c.65 per cent LTV, investors saw a well-defined need for non-mortgage junior debt to plug the lending gap.[48] The argument for mezzanine debt investing is increasingly clear as the need for refinancing becomes more urgent. Consequently, over 100 potential lenders[49] have emerged to invest at 50–80 per cent LTV based on a diverse risk-adjusted return spectrum of 8–15 per cent plus (with both current-pay and PIK elements[50]), which is particularly attractive in comparison with related equity investment.

Committed capital is now available for European mezzanine debt through three main types of active fund:

- core funds targeting high quality assets and cash flow at stretch-senior 50–75 per cent LTVs with an IRR hurdle of 8–10 per cent;
- value-added funds focused on prime or secondary assets requiring repositioning or capital expenditures, at 60–85 per cent LTV and IRR targets of 11–14 per cent; and

---

[47] Ernst & Young, 2012 NPL Survey (At the Crossroads). Transaction volumes are estimated to be circa 36% at less than $50 million, 20% at $50–100 million and 20% at $100–500 million.

[48] Previously, bifurcated senior mortgage debt in the form of contractually subordinated B notes would cover the portion of debt from c.70–85% LTV, with structurally subordinate mezzanine debt providing 70–95% LTV. See further Chs 14 and 15.

[49] Including property investors, non-discretionary funds and specialist mezzanine debt funds.

[50] Some mezzanine providers are also able to negotiate preferred equity-style "promotes" subject to performance tests.

- opportunistic or specialist funds seeking to recapitalise highly leveraged transactions and even development up to 90 per cent LTV with IRR hurdles of 15 per cent plus.

Some highly opportunistic direct CRE players are also seeking to acquire impaired mezzanine debt at option pricing, in order to take over borrower SPVs in restructuring or recapitalisation scenarios. However, outcomes are uncertain and rarely profitable unless for instance, activist lenders seek to frustrate consensual enforcement or to influence restructuring processes through embedded holdout rights.

However, limited capital has been deployed, particularly amongst smaller investment platforms below €250 million of capital, due to the paucity of senior mortgage refinancing (restricted to the highest quality assets) and the following factors:

- intense competition amongst mezzanine funds to deploy large amounts of capital applies downward pressure on economics in transactions with the most attractive collateral and sponsorship;
- either revised return expectations price out many funds raised in 2008–10 with aggressive IRR targets, or funding is too expensive to be accretive to sponsor returns;[51]
- the costs of conducting highly detailed asset level, structural and documentary due diligence and continuing asset management can be prohibitive for smaller transactions (e.g. below €10 million of mezzanine debt) with ironically, the least competition and hence execution risk; and
- the illiquidity of mezzanine debt (due to the loss of the CDO market) means risk is not easily transferred and requires monitoring and management through to maturity.

Thus, in spite of certain strong prospects in mezzanine debt, the segment appears overcrowded at the time of writing. A small number of core funds with large amounts of cheap capital, have priced out smaller or opportunistic competitors. Even so, capital deployment has been weak and will remain so, until senior lending volumes pick up. So, although risk-adjusted returns are still attractive, the investability of mezzanine debt is relatively-speaking less exciting than some other CRE debt formats.

Nevertheless, mezzanine investors can create significant deal pipelines by forming joint venture 0–80 per cent LTV debt platforms with complementary mortgage lenders.[52] This would provide a convenient integrated solution, for borrowers and material operating efficiencies for both lenders (in terms of origination effort and standardised documentation). The

---

[51] Certain funds are also subject to minimum investment multiples, preventing low-coupon investment below a certain tenor.
[52] Such as German *pfandbrief* banks.

scenario is enhanced if an alternative junior CMBS market were to emerge for efficient transfer of such subordinated risk.

### 13.3.3.   CMBS[53]

Securities are considered the most liquid type of European CRE debt. Although there is no official trading data,[54] Royal Bank of Scotland estimates that c.€10 billion of bonds traded in 2011.[55] This is essentially a secondary market for roughly €102 billion of outstanding CMBS issuance[56] with activity led by bank secondary trading desks, credit and hedge funds.

Primary CMBS issuance has been insignificant since the crisis commenced, and for the following reasons there is no clear route to re-establishing meaningful conduit-style issuance:

- arrangers must deleverage before rebuilding origination and distribution platforms;
- there are no large-scale buy-and-hold investors to support new deals since SIVs (which often accounted for two-thirds or more of issuance at peak), exited the market;[57]
- there is no positive arbitrage in securitising newly-originated loans since primary CMBS is still benchmarked against lower-quality secondary paper, and arrangers and investors have no effective hedge against pricing volatility;
- economics are strained by market and regulatory requirements including loss of Class X Notes, the 5 per cent vertical debt holdback under the Capital Requirements Directive and Article 122a monitoring obligations;[58]
- syndicated loans attract more favourable regulatory capital treatment for many originators and investors, and borrowers no longer find CMBS lending competitive; and
- stricter investor and rating agency guidelines have muted diversification and pooling benefits, so that inherent structural features do little besides increasing liquidity.

Hence, recent high-quality issuances are rumoured to have been sold at material discounts. So, CMBS 2.0 presently serves a balance sheet management rather than profit-generating role, providing a convenient exit where traditional syndication or *pfandbrief* routes are unfeasible (e.g. DECO

---

[53]  Refers to both cash and synthetic CMBS transactions, though cash deals are the largest segment of the CMBS market.

[54]  CMBS is traded OTC and so accurate pricing and trading information is unavailable.

[55]  Royal Bank of Scotland, *Trading Opportunities in CRE/CMBS*, February 2011.

[56]  Excludes reference to securities issued for central bank repurchase or government liquidity schemes (e.g. Excalibur Funding No.1 Plc).

[57]  Although insurance and pension accounts may have significant interest in long-dated, fixed rate product, subject to receiving regulatory support.

[58]  See further Ch.16.

2012 MHILL).[59] Alternatively, arrangers may seek to replicate the credit tenant structure employed in the Tesco Property Finance transactions, which provide bespoke long-term, fixed rate corporate exposure to match the liabilities of specific investors such as pension funds. An expansion of the covered bond regime could largely even remove the need for new 0–60 per cent LTV CMBS. Alternatively, CRE investors should explore the viability of a modified CMBS product, collateralised by higher-margin obligations which mitigate capital charges and generate excess spread. For example, in 2013 and beyond, there may be feasible (though smaller-scale) markets for "high-yield" securitisation of stretch-senior or mezzanine debt, NPLs and portfolio acquisition loans.

Although the majority of European CMBS (first to third-pay tranches) is held by banks, pressure to transfer this risk has been muted by the ECB's LTRO initiatives as well as their improved capital positions. Furthermore, banks are reluctant to realise losses on senior paper with strong recovery prospects, so they have only sold down CMBS exposures selectively. The Eurozone sovereign crisis however, is forcing the pace of disposals and at the time of writing, broker-dealers are net sellers. However, prospective secondary CMBS investors have numerous concerns, particularly regarding junior "at-risk" tranches. Thus, the sector has largely been overlooked by peripheral investors such as HNWIs. Specific concerns involve:

- aggressive underwriting standards[60] (particularly in 2006–07 vintages) on largely secondary and tertiary CRE, with growing default histories requiring considerable investor attention;[61]
- the difficulty of analysing multiple loans (and even legal regimes) with variable disclosure, delayed monitoring and little reliable third party cash flow modelling;[62]
- non-standard, complex loan and bond-level documentation, cash flow waterfalls (e.g. Class X Notes) and increasingly detrimental hedging (e.g. senior-ranking swap breakage costs);
- complex and opaque corporate governance structures (e.g. intercreditors) with limited control and influence for individual bondholders;
- uncertain tenor with extension risk in default scenarios even for in-the-money bonds (e.g. Titan Europe 2006-4 (FS) PLC);
- significant ratings migration, opacity and volatility of pricing[63] and no ability to hedge effectively (e.g. no European CMBX), and
- difficulty of ensuring sufficient investment size to justify necessary due diligence (especially in thin junior tranches).

---

[59] See further Ch.4.
[60] Including collateral quality, leverage and "covenant-light" structures.
[61] For instance, noteholder-level restructurings such as in *Opera Finance (Uni-Invest)* following a note event of default.
[62] The cost of subscriptions to Bloomberg, Trepp and Intex services can be prohibitive, not to mention their reliance on the quality of borrower and public reporting.
[63] Sources such as Markit and dealer cover levels are broadly helpful but still require material deal-specific translation.

Nonetheless, secondary CMBS can be an attractive risk-adjusted proposition for investors seeking security and high risk-adjusted returns. The following considerations are critical when assessing the arbitrage between depressed bond pricing and underlying CRE values:

- CMBS is publicly rated[64], representing a liquid and passive investment option with regular public monitoring;
- CMBS is backed by first-ranking mortgages on a diversified pool of definable commercial properties[65] and the ability to tailor risk by investing in specific tranches;
- bonds usually have minimum denominations of 50,000 (£/€) and are traded typically in nominal values of €1–10 million whilst providing access to institutional quality collateral, with low transaction and information costs;
- the discounted pricing of legacy CMBS underpins a "push-to-par" strategy based on CRE fundamentals but retains flexibility for risk management through trading;
- secondary CMBS has a defined investment horizon with the majority of current outstanding CMBS loans estimated to reach their maturity within five years,[66] so there is limited lock-in and relatively clear outcomes in upcoming refinancings and enforcements;
- extension or standstill of defaulted loans post-maturity (and swap expiry) liberates cash flow for sequential hyper-amortisation of senior bonds;
- CMBS underperformance is mostly technically driven but price tightening quickly follows good news in the market; and
- secondary CMBS returns can be commensurate with direct investment (subject to recovery assumptions) but with priority ranking, subordination and structural enhancements (e.g. liquidity).

In H2 2012, the European CMBS market is presently dominated by technical traders seeking short-term relative value versus other forms of structured credit, rather than investing based on CRE fundamentals. Hence, yield compression since 2009 has led traders increasingly to speculate in junior tranches (originally BBB-rated and below), where interest payments and return of principal are precarious.

Also, whilst some sophisticated investors including hedge funds and private equity firms are pursuing value in special situations, this approach is generally unfeasible for the broader investor market. Such specialised investment strategies may include the following:

---

[64] Albeit ratings are far less significant in the secondary market when applying a fundamental, recovery-based approach.

[65] Naturally, diversity benefits will be less apparent in single borrower, single asset and credit tenant transactions. Also, diversity may be regarded as a negative feature in junior CMBS tranches.

[66] Approximately €57 billion of securitised loans fall due through 2016.

- purchasing Class X notes and mezzanine out-of-the-money bonds based on interest-only pricing, assuming continuing interest payments as loans fail to refinance or are restructured;
- exercising controlling class rights to protect impaired bond values (e.g. special servicing transfer);
- acquiring value-impaired CMBS cheaply to negatively control restructuring scenarios, such as blocking stakes in REC No.5 CMBS (Plantation Place), or in anticipation of significant margin uplifts and/or principal recovery upon restructuring or legal outcomes (e.g. valuer negligence claims); or
- acquiring the credit risk of senior-secured and long-dated interest rate swap exposures from hedge providers (at significant discounts to present value) which need regulatory capital relief on volatile positions.[67]

At the time of writing, there is a significant opportunity for investment in carefully selected senior tranches (e.g. first- to third-pay) held by banks, given that outcomes are clearer, before negative selection leaves CMBS pools, with only the weakest collateral. CMBS can satisfy very specific investment objectives:[68]

- **Liquidity:**
  single-borrower transactions secured against prime UK CRE;
- **Upside:**
  credit-intensive pan-European conduit deals secured by multiple loans; and
- **Limited extension risk:**
  synthetic CMBS.

Annual returns of circa 4–20 per cent[69] in bonds reflect a complexity rather than strictly a risk premium to investment in similar corporate debt or direct CRE. Thus, senior notes should be highly attractive to investors taking a risk-adjusted return approach (based on 2012 pricing rather than 2009-pricing) such as HNWIs, private banks and even corporates. Meanwhile, although junior CMBS tranches appear to offer greater total return, they carry disproportionate risk for defensive investors.

Family offices and private banks with large cash holdings could view pan-European senior CMBS paper (e.g. originally AAA- to A-rated) as almost a "cash-equivalent", relatively liquid investment product with a premium to vanilla fixed income products. Discounted senior securities bestow clear advantages for smaller non-institutional investors such as

---

[67] See further Ch.8.
[68] Bank of America Merrill Lynch Global Research.
[69] Yields to expected maturity are deal- and tranche-specific but senior bonds (AAA- to A-rated) typically range from 4–12% with junior notes (BBB-rated and below) achieving 10–20% plus IRR.

HNWIs. Execution is cheap and efficient, investors can participate passively in institutional-grade risk in small denominations, plus coupons and yields to maturity are attractive.[70]

Senior CMBS exhibits exceptional relative value versus comparable direct equity, corporate or sovereign exposure. Moreover, with the great majority of bonds rated AAA at issuance, there is potential to invest vast sums at relatively conservative leverage as banks sell down their risk.

## 13.4. Conclusion

This chapter has demonstrated that value in CRE debt is highly subjective and defined by diverse clusters of private capital. Investors have the ability to set the tone of the CRE financing market going forward in the absence of large pieces of the CRE capital structure. With the anticipated bank deleveraging set to continue in 2013 and beyond, investors must show a flexible approach to collateral, investment formats and return expectations to maximise invested funds and capture compelling risk-adjusted returns. The opportunity lies in meeting the funding gaps in this market from alternative sources of capital, unburdened by the same regulatory and legacy issues as traditional lenders.[71] The key questions for potential investors are:

- Which parts of the CRE debt stack are not functioning or are overlooked by investors?
- Which CRE debt products are investable and at what level of return?
- Which investment format best meets my risk appetite in absolute and relative terms?

In the most exciting environment for private capital since the financial crisis, investors should not seek out only absolute returns at the expense of relatively "easy wins" such as:

- Senior CMBS paper (first- to third-pay) for private banks and asset managers backed by HNWIs;
- Small non-core loan and CMBS portfolios from regional and smaller banks;
- Senior mortgages, and portfolio lending against senior loans and CMBS;
- Stretch-senior lending from 50–80 per cent LTV, with potential exit for banks through a modified securitisation market.

---

[70] IRRs improve as the most senior bonds are increasingly subject to full sequential payment after pool-level credit events (e.g. maturity defaults).
[71] Ch.20 will further develop these and further opportunities.

There is no doubt that the financial crisis will have a lasting legacy on the European debt landscape and many investors may have to reposition or reinvent their platforms to create opportunity. However, it is submitted that inflexibility will lead to a significant loss of opportunity and investors should have this in the forefront of any investment decision in they may be considering in 2013 and beyond.

# Chapter 14

# Leverage and the use of Subordinate Debt

Andrew V. Petersen,
Partner, K&L Gates LLP

Rawle Howard,
Director, BlackRock

## 14.1.  Introduction

As highlighted throughout this book, a unique development in the capital markets over the last two decades, has been the arrival of real estate debt on the global stage as an asset class in its own right. Based on its increasing popularity, the financing and investment of CRE, flourished in the market in the period up to 2007, as a result of a highly competitive CRE lending environment, yield compression and the evolution of attractive capital market exits.[1]

During this period, lenders were forced to be more innovative in structuring CRE loans to keep up with investors' vociferous appetite for CRE assets, and the escalating need for financing leverage and to keep up with their competitors, resulting in CRE turning from a hard asset into a financial one. To win deals, lenders were forced to provide much higher amounts of leverage than they traditionally did, or may have been comfortable with. However, with the capital markets providing an exit, banks were able to package the added leverage related to loans, in a way that appealed to investors across the risk-tolerance spectrum and accommodated a mortgage borrower's desire, to constantly maximise leverage.

Moreover, CRE borrowers' demands for even more flexibility and leverage led to lenders undertaking a constant balancing exercise, between origination volume and their return on their product, without compromising any CMBS exit, or, in the environment that exists at the time of writing, a somewhat dislocated syndication or club deal exit.[2]

---

[1]  See further Ch.1.
[2]  See further Ch.2.

In the United States, where subordinate debt structures first emerged, originating lenders discovered that dividing or splitting a whole loan into multiple tranches enabled them to create a variety of debt instruments which would appeal to a broad array of investors, while meeting the demands of their mortgage borrowers for greater leverage and flexibility. For example, on a highly-leveraged property, the related financing was typically structured so as to produce an investment grade portion of the debt that was included in a CMBS, with the remaining portion of the financing split into one or more subordinated tranches, often tailored to meet the requirements of the anticipated purchaser. Thus, for example, a certain investor's risk and return preference might cause such an investor to prefer a slice of the debt that represented 60–70 per cent of the overall leverage of the financing; with other more opportunistic investors with more aggressive risk and return tolerances preferring more deeply subordinated, higher risk, higher-yielding tranches of the financing, at 70 per cent plus. Methods adopted to achieve this balance or alignment of rights was achieved through the introduction of subordinated debt (junior or mezzanine) and the bifurcating of the commercial mortgage whole loan.

This development was not a new development in "traditional" (i.e. non-securitised or non-capital markets) global CRE finance transactions, with commercial mortgage loans with related birfucated subordinate debt appearing frequently in the market. Gradually, such structures found their way into the CMBS market and 2003 witnessed one of the first European uses of an AB loan structure included in a CMBS deal, where the underlying whole loan was split into a separate participation in the underlying loan, with only the senior tranche being securitised.

Following this, between 2003 and 2007, the CMBS lending market witnessed a proliferation of highly complex modelled subordinate debt structures incorporating a concept of birfurcated or trifurcated real estate loans, comprising of A-1 or A-2, B, C or even D tranches, senior – subordinate tranches and mezzanine or junior debt. As discussed below and in the following Chapter, this practice generated highly flexible structures that built upon the emergence of CMBS as a product of innovation.[3] A product that allowed the subordinate debt to be tailored to comply with the demand in the market, the underlying borrowing group structure and the available lenders (and their legal and regulatory requirements).

As a result, whilst the CRE financing market is operating at a vastly reduced level to the boom years of 2000 to 2007, what is emerging at the time of writing is a dislocated funding market faced with an impending refinancing challenge, where the absence of senior debt is visibly apparent and there are multiple subordinate debt providers faced with a smaller

---

[3]    A.V. Petersen, *Commercial Mortgage-Backed Securitisation: Developments in the European Market*, 1st edn (London: Sweet & Maxwell, 2006), Ch.1.

group of senior lenders chasing the worthy new money and refinancable deals that exist amongst the vast swathes of largely unrefinanceable CRE. This means that, in an increasingly competitive, but still comparatively small market, where in 2012 alone, numerous senior debt funds have been announced as being formed,[4] senior lenders are able to pick and choose the deals and the pricing on such deals, with an increasing amount of senior debt becoming available for good secondary assets with secured income, as well as higher-priced defensive subordinated or stressed/distressed loan-on-loan financing. This is true, even of certain senior lenders that write cheques for substantial senior whole loans that internally will tranche or syndicate the loan to a mezzanine provider or fund set up or controlled by such senior lender. Thus, it has become a rare exception for real estate loans not to be structured with some form of multiple separate subordinate debt. Such structures apply to both single and multi-borrower transactions.

In this Chapter, the debt underlying such structures (mezzanine or tranched junior) will be referred to as subordinate debt, whilst the senior-subordinate structures that will be considered generally take one of the following two forms, with the first being seen as more prevalent in the market at the time of writing:

- a mezzanine loan interest which is documented pursuant to a separate loan and secured by a separate subordinate ranking security package ranking behind the security interests securing the senior or whole loan, or in certain cases a separate security pledge over the equity in the borrower (mezzanine debt);
- a B Loan within an AB loan structure, where the single whole loan is tranched into senior and subordinated tranches which are secured by a single security package (AB debt).

This Chapter will examine:

- the emergence of subordinate structures including the key principles and pricing of such structures;
- the common key principles of intercreditor terms surrounding subordinate structures[5];
- the economics and business case for utilising mezzanine debt and/or AB debt;
- the emergence of recent developments surrounding discounted purchase options (DPO).

---

[4] See *Real Estate Capital*, March 2012, p.14.
[5] Note that the key terms and provisions of an intercreditor agreement will be considered in detail in the following Chapter.

## 14.2. The key principles of subordinate structures

It is important to understand the economics behind subordinate debt structures. Therefore we must examine the key principles that underpin such structures, while noting that there can be variations on all of these principles, as no two deals are the same and that each deal will be faced with unique characteristics based on asset type, obligor or borrower group structure (including any legal and regulatory and other restrictions regarding granting of security or historic tax liabilities).

### 14.2.1. Mezzanine debt

A typical mezzanine secured credit facility (the mezzanine facility) will comprise a term facility that is subordinate to, but coterminous with a senior loan facility. Often the mezzanine facility may increase by any payment in kind (PIK) or other amounts accrued. Typical leverage will be an aggregate of the senior facility and mezzanine facility capped at a certain percentage (say 80.0 per cent) of value of the underlying real estate portfolio. Typically, the aggregate of the senior facility will not exceed the lower of a certain percentage (say 60 per cent) of acquisition costs or a fixed monetary amount.

As discussed further in Chs 4 and 9, pricing is, at the time of writing, increasingly competitive and senior facility pricing will often be provided at a range of rates that will be pegged to LIBOR or EURIBOR plus a certain fixed credit spread, (say 400 to 465 basis points (bps)). There often will be an assumption that for a fixed period of years (say five years) the LIBOR or EURIBOR swap rates will not exceed a certain fixed percentage.

Key terms of a senior loan facility sitting above a mezzanine facility may include: loan to value covenants, with a hard event of default triggered if LTV values raise above a certain percentage (say 70 per cent); a cash sweep triggered if LTV values are above a certain percentage (say 70 per cent) with equity or excess cash, upon such sweep being activated, being swept to repay the senior loan. A cash sweep will often continue until the loan to value reduces below a certain percentage (say 70 per cent) on two consecutive interest payment dates (IPD).

In relation to interest coverage, there will often be an interest coverage ratio included which would trigger an event of default if below a certain fixed level (say 1.30 times). A cash sweep may also be triggered if below a certain falling fixed level (say 1.55 times) and equity or excess cash will be swept to repay the senior loan. Again a cash sweep would continue until interest coverage exceeds such falling fixed level (say 1.55 times) on two consecutive IPDs

An example of further cash sweep/reserve covenants may be seen as follows:

Full cash sweep to the mezzanine facility at following triggers:

- if the LTV is more than a certain percentage (say 85.0 per cent) in year 2;
- if the LTV is more than a certain percentage (say 83.0 per cent) in year 3;
- if the LTV is more than a certain percentage (say 82.0 per cent) in year 4;
- if the LTV is more than a certain percentage (say 81.0 per cent) in year 5;
- if the mezzanine interest cover is less than a certain fixed level (say 1.17 times) to be calculated on a forward and backward looking basis.

### 14.2.2. *Mezzanine debt pricing*

At the time of writing, there is no "typical" pricing of mezzanine debt. Pricing will be dependent on a number of factors, including the size and quality of the deal, the nature of the asset, the number and type of lenders chasing the deal, the economic power of the underlying sponsor and the jurisdiction of the underlying assets. For deals occurring at the time of writing, mezzanine pricing will be in a range from the high single digits to mid-teens percent per annum (all-in coupon) of which an element will often be structured to be payable in cash (cash pay interest) and an element PIKed.

The mezzanine debt may be further structured where the mezzanine lender receives a percentage of excess profits once the sponsor achieves a certain level of internal rate of return (IRR) known as a profit participation. The profit participation will be in addition to any fees and interest payable on the deal.

Typically, a mezzanine lender will want to be compensated for its debt being repaid prior to the maturity date. Although, a voluntary prepayment will be permitted at any time after the first year of the term mezzanine facility, prepayment fees will be payable to the mezzanine lender to protect a certain fixed level of return (say 1.35 times equity multiple) on the mezzanine debt. For example, if the mezzanine facility is prepaid and the mezzanine lender has not received a minimum of 1.35 times on the original principal amount of the mezzanine facility, then the mezzanine borrower will compensate the mezzanine lender for the difference between the amount actually received by the mezzanine lender and an amount equal to 1.35 times of the original principal amount.

331

### 14.2.3. Borrower PIK election period

Typically, on any IPD where there is a cash trap event caused by triggers in the senior facility which has the effect of stopping cash pay interest to the mezzanine facility (The PIK election does not apply to hard events of default), the borrower may make a PIK election where the total coupon is accrued or rolled and forms part of the mezzanine facility balance until the occurred amount is paid down by the borrower. Typically, the borrower will be limited to a maximum of two PIK elections during the term of the mezzanine loan and will not be able to use its PIK election if this would cause a breach of the mezzanine facility hard default covenants. Following any PIK election quarter where the borrower has no remaining PIK elections, a mezzanine facility event of default will be triggered if the mezzanine facility is not cash paid on any remaining IPD (and the cash escrow released to the mezzanine lender).

### 14.2.4. Typical mezzanine security package

Subject to the differences in the overall structures and underlying borrower groups, security for a typical mezzanine facility will consist of a standard security package, which shall include the following:

Shared with the senior facility (on a subordinated basis) or separate second ranking, each to the extent applicable:

- legal charges over the properties;
- fixed and floating security over all the assets of the borrower(s), including without limitation all bank accounts, material contracts (such as managing agent contracts), insurance (including being co-insured), the hedging arrangements related to the mezzanine facility and all shareholder and other intra-group loan balances;
- deed of subordination between the mezzanine lenders and any shareholder loans or equity confirming neither interest nor repayment of any shareholder's loans or equity permitted until mezzanine facility fully repaid;
- a duty of care letter from the managing agents, if any; and
- any other security as required under the senior facility.

In addition, based on potential deal structure and requirements of the mezzanine lender, a first ranking pledge of shares in the mezzanine borrower (or any other appropriate entity depending on the final structure of the transaction) representing control over the entirety of the properties. It is often requested that, in an acknowledgment of the credit support the mezzanine facility is providing and the first loss position it is in, such security is separate and not part of the security package for the senior facility and without any turnover obligation to the senior lenders upon exercise/enforcement or exercise of voting rights attaching to such shares.

### 14.2.5. Valuation

Often, the mezzanine lender shall, at the mezzanine borrower's expense, have the right once per year to call for a valuation in accordance with the RICS "red book" or at any time if it reasonably believes there may be a default or at any time if an event of default is outstanding. Typically, if the mezzanine lender uses this right (in addition to the standard annual valuation provided to the lenders at the borrower(s) expense) that the mezzanine lender will bear the costs of such additional valuation to the extent that this valuation does not result in a cash sweep or an event of default.

### 14.2.6. Documentation

The mezzanine facility will normally be documented by a facility agreement and related security documentation which are normally based on the Loan Market Association (LMA) documentation[6] used for the senior facility (often using the same form of senior facility after it has been negotiated with the senior borrower/sponsor), this agreement will set out (inter alia) the conditions precedent to drawing, representations and warranties, undertakings, events of default triggers, borrowing costs, pro-rata sharing, set-off, and other provisions usual for such transactions.

While the mezzanine facility agreement outlines the relationship between the mezzanine borrower and mezzanine lenders, an intercreditor agreement outlines the relationship among the senior lender(s) and mezzanine lender(s). The intercreditor agreement, includes, amongst other provisions, the right of the mezzanine lender to freely enforce its security without triggering a change of control default or mandatory prepayment obligation under the senior facility. The right of the mezzanine lender to cure a senior event of default and the right to purchase the senior facility if accelerated may also be included. In addition to the foregoing, the senior lender will agree not to change any payment date or maturity, increase or vary any fee or interest payable, increase or vary principal or require amortisation or prepayment, or amend events of default without the prior written consent of the mezzanine lender. Often, it is required that the senior lender consult with the mezzanine lender prior to enforcing its security.

---

[6] On April 16, 2012, in an attempt to aid transparency and liquidity in the market, the Loan Market Association launched its recommended form of single currency term facility agreement for use in real estate multi-property investment transactions. The new document should help, particularly over time, to standardise the approach taken to real estate specific issues and should assist all parties by reducing the time spent negotiating boiler-plate type clauses. Whilst there is not a CRE finance intercreditor in circulation at the time of writing, it is thought that this may in time be produced to assist the market in the same vein as the facility agreement.

The documentation will also contain conditions precedent, undertakings and covenants, representations and warranties, customary for the financings the subject of the deal and in a form and substance satisfactory to the parties and at a minimum mirroring the conditions precedent under the senior facility.

### 14.2.7. The typical features of AB debt structures[7]

There are certain common features existing within AB debt structures. One such feature of AB structures versus commercial mortgage whole loan financings is that, although B lenders lack the right to enforce the mortgage loan security, they do, typically, benefit from certain rights following monetary events of default on mortgage loans, in a recognition that they are (as described above for mezzanine debt structures) in the first loss position.

Such rights are not usually available to junior first loss piece holders in a CMBS, known as the "B piece holders". The B piece holders in a CMBS hold the most junior note interest in a securitised pool of CMBS loans. They hold the "last pay" "first loss" note which do not represent individual loans and have no direct relationship with the mortgage borrower, and should not be confused with the B lenders or B loan holders.

B lenders are not obliged to exercise these rights, which vary from deal to deal and ultimately depend on the sophistication and the needs of the parties. In theory, B lenders would generally only exercise their rights if the expected recoveries from the mortgage loan would thereby be enhanced. The exercise of cure and repurchase rights (which usually include the B lender's right to purchase the A loan as a means of avoiding enforcement proceedings by the A lender following a mortgage loan payment default by making whole a mortgage loan payment) has implications for the A loan and thereby the rated bonds and in such cases, the structure of the intercreditor and servicing agreements are extremely important to AB structures.

### 14.2.8. The attraction of AB structures

AB structures were very popular in a CMBS execution. From the perspective of the most junior investor in a CMBS, as payments to the B loan can be subordinated to the A loan in an AB structure, CMBS transactions with AB loans are preferable to CMBS transactions without.

---

[7] AB Structures were very popular in Europe from 2003 to 2007. See further A.V. Petersen, *Commercial Mortgage-Backed Securitisation: Developments in the European Market*, 1st edn (London: Sweet & Maxwell, 2006), Ch.8. As described herein, their popularity has lessened with the demise of the availability of financiers (and the absence of a fully functioning European CMBS market) that are prepared to arrange or originate a whole loan that will cover the whole of the required debt, although they are still used by certain senior lenders that originate a whole loan and internally tranche such loan into an AB structure.

This is because, depending on the transaction structure, as we have seen above, payments to the B lender may be cut off entirely following an underlying mortgage loan monetary event of default until the A loan has been redeemed in full. In a standard CMBS, by contrast, this will not tend to occur until the most senior class has missed a payment.

Thus, by creating a B loan that is held outside the CMBS, loss severity can be viewed as having been reduced as, following a loan monetary event of default, the A lender benefits from the subordination of payments to the B loan by having the ability to take control over the whole loan and instigate enforcement proceedings before a shortfall has occurred on the A loan, and therefore the rated bonds. This allocates the risks associated with incorporating the additional debt efficiently throughout the market and is preferable to a standard CMBS, in which senior noteholders gain control only after realised losses have eroded the value of the junior CMBS notes. Furthermore, this results in an improvement of the subordination levels of the rated securities versus the subordination levels if the entire loan were included in the CMBS.

Moreover, for multi-borrower transactions, which may pool together various B loans, the additional credit support provided by the subordinated B loans is specific to the separate individual mortgage loans and is therefore not provided to the entire transaction, usually resulting in higher credit enhancement being expected for the lowest-rated level of securitised notes. If losses incurred on any one loan exceed the amount of the B loan, the excess will be allocated to the lowest-rated class of notes. Where B loans provide the only credit support to an A loan in a multi-borrower transaction, there is no pooling benefit for the lowest-rated class of the A loan.

It is important to note, however, that although a higher percentage of the rated securities are considered investment grade in a pool that is made up of A loans, the investment-grade debt as a percentage of the first-mortgage debt (the first-mortgage debt equalling the combined total of all A and B loans) is not higher. In fact, in most cases the investment-grade debt as a percentage of the first-mortgage debt would be lower than if the entire loan were deposited into the CMBS. This is due to the weaker form of credit support provided by the B loans that are not cross collateralised, compared to subordinate bonds, which are cross collateralised. For instance, in a pool made up of A loans, if a loan incurs losses, upon the erosion of the B loans, losses would continue upward into the rated securities and not to the other B loans held outside of the CMBS.

From a prospective investor's perspective there are several benefits to an AB structure. First, the B loan is secured by a preferred form of security, a first mortgage. Also, for many of the institutional B loan purchasers such as insurance companies and banks, risk-based capital reserve requirements are less onerous for B loans than that of subordinate bonds. Having to reserve less capital against B loans effectively increases their overall net yield. When contrasted with investing in subordinate bonds, the primary benefit of the B loan is the ability to isolate risk to one asset. Unlike a subordinate bond where losses can be incurred from any one asset in a pool, the loss potential of a B loan is limited to the asset(s) serving as security to the B loan. This makes it easier than in a whole loan CMBS, where the originator, when placing a pooled bottom class of risk, has to try and sell this risk to an investor willing to take the first loss risk on all of the loans in the pool. As a result, risk is effectively dealt with much more discretely and the risk assessment of potential subordinate debt investors is also much more efficient since the due diligence process of evaluating one asset (the B loan) is considerably easier than evaluation of a pool of subordinate bonds. This is especially so in the European market where there is multitude of loans and variety of asset classes within pools. Another benefit, as we have seen above, is the ability to either purchase or cure upon an event of default. While this feature may not always be a viable option, it may be a potential exit strategy.

## 14.3. Key principles of a senior/mezzanine intercreditor agreement[8]

As discussed above, in a subordinate structure, the legal relationship between the lenders is delineated in an intercreditor agreement (intercreditor), which both grants and limits certain important rights (which may have an impact on the senior lender), to the subordinate lender. Whilst the next Chapter will examine the key terms and provisions of an Intercreditor in detail, this Chapter will briefly set out certain key structural features.

The list below is not intended to be exhaustive and there can be variations on all of these principles as, no two deals are the same and each deal will be faced with unique characteristics based on asset type, obligor or borrower group structure (including any legal and regulatory and other restrictions regarding granting of security or historic tax liabilities). The principles below represent the key terms and principles for an intercreditor governing the relationship between a senior loan (senior loan) made by a senior lender (the senior creditor) and a mezzanine loan (the mezzanine loan) made by a mezzanine lender (the mezzanine creditor). In such a hypothetical case, the principal terms that may be included in the intercreditor are as follows:

---

[8] As recognised in this Chapter, at the time of writing, there is no standard Intercreditor Agreement in the market place. In order to aid transparency, standardisation and liquidity in the CRE market, in February 2012, the CREFC-E established an Intercreditor Working Group to examine industry practices in order to establish a CRE loan intercreditor agreement template for the European market. The working group includes various stakeholders who utilise intercreditor agreements for CRE Loans and a CRE loan intercreditor agreement template and model principles are expected to be published by December 2012. This Chapter will anticipate certain of these issues and set out certain principles which will be considered in further detail in the following Chapter.

### 14.3.1. Acceleration/enforcement

The mezzanine creditor may require the mezzanine loan facility agent/ security trustee to exercise voting rights under the first-ranking share pledge over the mezzanine loan borrower (or if the mezzanine loan borrower is the same as the senior loan borrower, over the borrower's parent company) if an event of default (other than a material default (as defined below)) is outstanding.

The mezzanine creditor may require the mezzanine loan facility agent/ security trustee to take any enforcement action under the share pledge over the mezzanine loan borrower (or if the mezzanine loan borrower is the same as the senior loan borrower, over the borrower's parent company) if a material default (as defined below) is outstanding.

The senior creditor shall not require nor instruct the senior loan facility agent/security trustee to take any enforcement action under any security unless it has first consulted with the mezzanine creditor. In addition, to the extent the senior creditor does not take enforcement action within a certain period (say ninety days) following the occurrence of a senior event of default and the value of the properties is not less than a certain fixed value (say 1.25 times the principal then owing under the senior loan), the mezzanine creditor may instruct the senior loan facility agent/security trustee to take enforcement action.

### 14.3.2. Permitted payments

The intercreditor will contain waterfalls setting out the priority of payments prior to and following the occurrence of a material default.

Prior to a material default (as defined below), interest and principal payments (including any prepayment fees) made by the borrower are to be applied in accordance with the loan agreement.

Upon the occurrence and continuance of a material default, cash will be distributed sequentially according to a post-default waterfall resulting in a cessation of cash to the mezzanine creditor and diversion of cashflow to the senior creditor, provided however, that payments shall not be paid down the post-default waterfall and shall instead be held on a grace period ledger during the continuance of any applicable cure period until such time as the senior loan is accelerated and if the material default is cured within the applicable cure period such amounts shall be paid down the pre-default waterfall.

Material default typically means in respect of the senior loan:

- an insolvency event of default (relating to actual, rather than potential, insolvency events); or
- a payment default, which includes non payment and insufficient payment except as a result of a technical or administrative error that is remedied within any applicable grace period.

Sometimes a breach of any financial covenant under the senior loan shall also be considered a material default although this is often negotiated on a case-by-case basis.

### 14.3.3. Limit on senior loan

There is often no senior loan headroom concept in an intercreditor. This means that any increase in the amount of senior loan will rank behind the mezzanine loan (excluding any increase in amount of mezzanine loan).

### 14.3.4. Cure rights

Upon the occurrence of an event of default (other than certain insolvency related events of default) which is remediable, the mezzanine creditor may remedy that default within grace periods between certain fixed periods (say 15 business days in relation to a payment default and twenty business days in relation to other defaults)—each period will be negotiated depending on the circumstances of the deal.

It will often be requested that cure periods for defaults other than payment defaults should be unlimited for so long as the mezzanine creditor is diligently pursuing a cure, again to be negotiated on a case by case basis. Further, the mezzanine creditor may request that it may take such action to remedy as it considers desirable in the circumstances. For remedy of a payment default or financial covenant default, certain actions may be expressly permitted including:

- prepaying the senior loan (excluding default interest and prepayment fees);
- paying the amount of the shortfall;
- placing a deposit on behalf of the senior loan facility agent/security trustee into a cure loan deposit account in an amount equal to the additional amount of net rental income which would have been required to have been received by the obligor to have complied with the relevant financial covenant; or
- obtaining and delivering to the senior loan facility agent/security trustee an unconditional and irrevocable standby letter of credit payable on demand and in an amount equal to the additional amount of net rental income which would have been required to have been received by the obligor to have complied with the relevant financial covenant.

Typically, an intercreditor will provide a limit on the number of times that a payment default can be cured, so that the cure right may not be exercised more than a fixed number of times, say twice consecutively in any one 12-month period and no more than six times during the term of the facility. It will further be requested that there shall be no limit on the number of times a payment default may be cured where such default is continuing for a 90-day period or more and that there will be no limit on curing other defaults (to the extent the borrower's cure rights are unlimited).

Often it will be provided that any repayment of cure payments made by the mezzanine creditor in respect of cure rights will rank behind the senior loan but ahead of the mezzanine loan. Further, during the exercise of cure rights (and the applicable grace periods for making cures), the senior creditor shall be prohibited from taking enforcement action in respect of any relevant event of default.

### 14.3.5. Purchase/buy-out rights

In recognition that it is best to have an incentivised mezzanine lender in the deal compared to a dis-incentivised mezzanine lender and/or sponsor or borrower, the intercreditor will typically provide that at any time after the occurrence of any event of default under the senior loan or any enforcement action, the mezzanine creditor may elect to acquire the senior loan at par plus accrued interest, any swap breakage costs and funding break costs incurred by the senior creditor as a result of the transfer but excluding prepayment fees and default interest or at a price as otherwise agreed between the lenders. The difficulty in exercising such a right, at the time of writing, is that given the catastrophic fall in values, as discussed in further detail in Ch.2, it is very hard to exercise such a right when the value of the debt will often exceed the value of the underlying collateral.

### 14.3.6. Amendment rights

In further recognition of the interconnection between the senior loan and the mezzanine loan and how they are intended to exist side by side in the same deal, an intercreditor will often provide that certain material provisions of the senior loan finance documents must not be amended or waived without the prior consent of the mezzanine creditor. The material provisions include:

- any change of the date of payment of any amount;
- a change in the amount of any payment or the basis for calculating payments;
- an increase of commitments;
- any change in the term of the facility;
- a release of an obligor;
- a release of security or taking additional security;

- a change to the terms of any financial covenants;
- a change to the definition of events of default;
- a change to the terms of any hedging; and
- rights to assign or transfer.

An intercreditor will typically provide that a mezzanine creditor may amend the mezzanine loan finance documents without the prior written consent of the senior creditor where the changes are:

- a minor, technical or administrative change; or
- following the acceleration of the senior loan or the occurrence of certain material events of default in respect of the mezzanine loan (including payment default, insolvency and material adverse effect), provided in each case no such amendments would increase the amount of the mezzanine loan, increase any other monetary obligation of the mezzanine borrower (apart from equity participation) or amend the maturity date.

### 14.3.7. Consultation

An intercreditor may provide that a senior creditor and a senior loan facility agent/security trustee will notify and consult with the mezzanine creditor (without the need for their approval save for enforcement action) before taking any formal step to exercise any remedy against the borrower or taking any enforcement action (which shall require the approval of the mezzanine creditor), save where the senior creditor reasonably determines that immediate enforcement action is necessary in order to prevent the material diminution to the value, use or operation of the security or a material adverse effect to the interests of the senior creditor under the senior loan finance documents—the so-called senior creditor override—a provision that acknowledges the position of the senior loan and its security and the position of the senior creditor in maintaining control of its security and its recovery on the senior loan.

## 14.4. Why utilise subordinated structures?

Given the additional complexity of subordinate structures, the natural question to ask is why incorporate this type of instrument into real estate debt transaction? It would be much simpler to just have one lender and one loan. But from a business standpoint, the use of subordinate debt is important to a number of stakeholders in a real estate transaction.

From the sponsor's point of view, mezzanine debt typically carries a return that is lower than the return required by the common equity and allows the sponsor to invest less cash in a transaction, whether it is for an acquisition, or, refinance. This additional leverage can be accretive to the deal and usually helps to enhance the deal's internal rate of return (IRR).

From the senior lender's point of view, since mezzanine debt is structurally subordinate to the first mortgage, it provides credit enhancement and a significant capital buffer against collateral value deterioration. Moreover, by incorporating subordinate, the senior lender is able to reduce the amount of risk they would otherwise have to hold on their balance sheet.

From the mezzanine lender's perspective, subordinate debt produces a higher yield than senior debt, because there is more risk involved on a relative basis, but is still collateralised.

### 14.4.1. Recent developments involving discounted purchase options

A major effect of the withdrawal of credit, following the global credit crisis that emerged post 2007, was the ever-decreasing pool of investors buying CMBS. With the origination/distribution model that CMBS shops had relied on effectively closing down,[9] many originators and holders of debt, faced with the prospect of having to sell the logjam or overhang of assets remaining on their books that were destined for a CMBS execution, turned to borrower or sponsor affiliates to buy some of their own debt. Faced with the lack of liquidity in the market driving pricing and values down, borrowers and sponsors saw sense for them to use available cash to purchase perfectly good debt (in their eyes) at a discount to par, either to hold it for yield or retire it.

Thus the DPO market was born and with the market evolving very rapidly and investors in short supply and senior bankers (and their new state shareholders) demanding the mortgage-laden balance sheets of the banks be cleared out before the prospect of any true market in CRE lending commencing once again (and at the time of writing still not fully functioning), a number of originators sought approval from the rating agencies for intended transfers of loans to borrower or sponsor (indirect or direct) affiliates.

A DPO purchase is not without its challenges. In most cases, CMBS documents do not provide for such a transfer without the involvement and agreement of the CMBS parties, being the issuer, noteholders and the B lender. Often CMBS servicing agreements[10] will state that except as contemplated by the issuer deed of charge and the intercreditor agreement, a servicer will not be permitted to dispose of any loan or any B piece. In addition, the usual forms of power of attorney granted under a CMBS deal normally expressly prohibit a servicer from selling the debt to the borrower. Further, typically an intercreditor will not provide for the sale of the debt or

---

[9] See further Ch.1.
[10] See further Ch.7.

B piece and the issuer deed of charge often states that a sale of any of the issuer's loans is not permitted unless the note trustee is enforcing its security. Moreover, as far as an issuer is concerned, it is usually restricted from disposing of its assets unless it has the consent of the note trustee. The note trustee would usually not give its consent unless it gets the consent of the controlling class (which would require them to pass an extraordinary resolution).[11] Moreover, the intercreditor will often contain an absolute restriction on the B lender selling its loan to the borrower or an affiliate of a borrower. Therefore, the B lender would need the consent of the issuer and the facility agent to undertake such a sale.

Notwithstanding these challenges and any prohibitions in the intercreditor, the DPO market still, at the time of writing, remains popular and consent to a transfer of the B loan to a borrower/sponsor affiliate may be sought on the basis that the rights of any B lender (that is also a sponsor or borrower affiliate) should be turned off and should not be exercisable whilst the B lender remains a borrower or sponsor affiliate. This has the effect that, immediately following any such transfer, the B lender will not be able to exercise, have exercised on its behalf (other than by a servicer or a special servicer in accordance with the terms of the servicing agreement) or have accruing to it any cure, enforcement, consultation, approval, appointment and/or control rights (together the "rights") otherwise available to it under the terms of the underlying credit agreement, the intercreditor and/or the servicing agreement.

Typically, following a DPO to a borrower or its affiliate, the Rights should be reinstated (a) for so long as the B lender (A) does not control or manage (in each case directly or indirectly) the management or voting rights in the mortgage borrower or an affiliate of the mortgage borrower; (B) is not controlled or managed (in each case directly or indirectly) by a mortgage borrower or an affiliate of the mortgage borrower; (C) is not party to any arrangements (the "arrangements") with any other entity pursuant to which the mortgage borrower or any of its affiliates would have any indirect control of whatsoever nature in relation to any of the rights; and, for the avoidance of doubt, (D) is not a mortgage borrower or an affiliate of the mortgage borrower, in each case being confirmed to the reasonable satisfaction of the security agent; or (b) with respect to the whole or any part of the transferred B loans, following a subsequent transfer or assignment of such participation by the B lender, as discussed below.

Moreover, the transfer should further provide that each of the servicer and the special servicer will be required to notify the B lender (or any of its designees) with respect to material actions (as determined by the servicer and/or special servicer acting reasonably) to be taken with respect to the whole loan provided that: (A) neither the servicer or, as the case may be, the special servicer will be required to disclose any information to the B lender

---

[11] See further Ch.10 where the role of the trustee is further discussed.

that, in the discretion of the servicer or the special servicer (acting reasonably), as applicable, will compromise the position of the other lenders in the deal or reveal any strategy of the other lenders that could compromise the position of the other lenders with respect to the whole loan; (B) no such notification will be required where immediate action is required to be taken in accordance with the Servicing Standard;[12] and, for the avoidance of doubt, (C) no such rights shall oblige the servicer and/or special servicer to take into account any advice, direction or representation made by the B lender in connection with such notification.

Furthermore, the B lender should agree that, prior to any subsequent assignment or transfer of whole or any part of any transferred B loan being effective (along with the ability to exercise all or any corresponding rights), (i) the B lender either confirms or procures confirmation to a security agent that the subsequent assignee/B lender is a "qualifying lender"; and (ii) the conditions set out in each of the underlying credit agreement and the Intercreditor agreement must be otherwise complied with.

## 14.5. Conclusion

This Chapter has highlighted the purposes, general key features, risks, and benefits provided by typical subordinate structures. Prior to 2007, many regarded the introduction of mezzanine debt and/or AB debt as a positive development, since certain features of the structures behind such debt provided additional benefits that were unavailable to lenders in standard bilateral commercial mortgage loan financings.

However, as has been seen in the market that has evolved since 2007 as discussed in further detail in Ch.4, these benefits may not necessarily translate into improved credit enhancement levels for loans structured as AB loans. That being said, it is generally recognised that the structural features of a subordinate structure ensure that a default of the whole mortgage loan does not necessarily result in a shortfall of funds to, and therefore a default of, the senior loan. In particular, it may be seen that the cure rights of the subordinate lender, the priority of all payments to the senior loan and the enforcement rights of the senior lender reduce the probability of default of the whole loan, leading to the conclusion that subordinate structures provide benefits to rated classes of bonds in single-loan transactions.

Moreover, as is apparent in the restructuring market that has emerged since 2007, whole loan slicing and dicing ultimately creates a variety of interested parties, (whose interests are often at odds) having a variety of consent and approval rights over both "routine" mortgage borrower actions such as

---

[12] For further detailed discussions of the servicing standard and the rights and obligations of the servicer and the special servicer, see Chs 5, 6 and 7.

alterations and lease approvals as well as more complex issues such as material financial modifications. In a whole mortgage loan with multiple pari passu senior tranches, subordinate tranches and possibly mezzanine loans, it is easy to see how a once relatively easy process quickly becomes extremely complicated and convoluted, and will require more time and effort to process, which inevitably leads to increased costs and possibly delays in restructuring the debt.

While certain deemed consent rights are much more commonplace in an effort to streamline this process, as we shall see in the following Chapter, any insolvency proceedings are bound to be infinitely more complex, with the potential for large-scale conflict among the various stakeholders. No more is this apparent than in the market conditions witnessed since 2008. In the more challenging lending environment that exists at the time of writing, workouts and stressed properties are more apparent than in the last decade and the role of the intercreditor in such workouts are usually not viewed as a productive outcome to the innovative structuring that has developed over the last few years, as the parties to the intercreditor attempt to agree what rights they thought they had. In past real estate cycles,[13] e.g. a mortgage borrower may have only had to negotiate with one secured creditor, a mortgage bank or at its worse a small syndicate of such banks. Now, the economic tightrope will be walked by many interested parties—hedge funds, distressed debt funds or opportunistic "vulture" funds, even borrower or sponsor affiliates together with numerous lawyers representing each of the parties. It is, as Standard & Poor's proclaim "difficult to imagine the loss experience improving in that environment."".[14] In the end, only time will tell of the overall impact slicing and dicing and the effect of the "car-crash" intercreditors has had on mortgage borrowers, originating lenders, the restructuring of commercial mortgage and CMBS loans and commercial mortgage loan servicing in general. For now we can merely sit tight, wait for the dust to settle and hope we do not need an ambulance.

---

[13] See Ch.1.
[14] See *European CMBS Outlook—Getting Interesting Again*, July 31, 2007, p4.

# Chapter 15

# The Modern Intercreditor Agreement: Terms and Issues

Diego Shin,

Senior Associate, K&L Gates LLP

Philip Moore,

Principal, DRC Capital

## 15.1.   Introduction

At the time of the writing of this Chapter, only two European non-credit tenant-linked or ECB liquidity-driven CMBS transactions have been publicly placed, since the closing of the CMBS market in 2007.[1] Despite this, the wider commercial real estate (CRE) financing market is still active, albeit at reduced levels to the ones seen at the height of the boom in 2007. During this interval, the commercial mortgage loan and CMBS markets have witnessed a very significant public outcry, directed against the financial industry generally and bankers in particular, some of whom had been responsible for devising highly complex structured finance transactions that have been blamed, no doubt with some justification, for being one of the major contributors to the financial crisis and the general erosion of investor confidence. In reaction to the same, governments and regulators in both the United States and Europe have been busy introducing new laws and regulations.[2] Such laws and regulations are principally aimed at aligning the interests of the parties responsible for bringing these transactions to the market with investors, ensuring that financial institutions that invest in these transactions meet certain standards of due diligence and risk assessment, prior to acquisition of any interests in these deals and increasing transparency and information flow.

Accordingly, the state of the securitisation market, of which CMBS is an integral part,[3] remains in flux. Potential "securitizers" (to use the broad term used in US legislation[4] which broadly encompasses issuers, sponsors

---

[1]   See further Ch.4.
[2]   See Ch.16.
[3]   As demonstrated in Ch.1.
[4]   s.941(a) of the Dodd-Frank Wall Street Reform and Consumer Protection Act, United States Code 15 Ch.78o-11(a) (2010).

and arrangers) face the uncertainty caused by not having a fully developed and consistent legislative framework in place, in addition to a multi-jurisdictional legal regime in Europe. Furthermore, the volatility of pricing demands from investors remains a significant obstacle to ensuring that assets can be originated and priced and exited through securitisation, at a profit. Investors, on the other hand, will need to comply with new regulatory requirements, imposed by legislation which will vary depending on the type of investor, including meeting potential added compliance costs resulting from the inconsistency between the laws and regulations, adopted in both the United States and Europe.

Against this background, it is easy to understand that there has not been significant development to the terms of intercreditor agreements, used in the context of CMBS transactions since 2007. However in the broader CRE loan market, things have changed significantly. Due to this, the scope of this Chapter will be broader than its counterpart in the first edition of this book and will look at intercreditor agreements in their wider context in the commercial mortgage loan and CMBS markets, as they govern the relationship between senior and junior loans.

Using the same concept as set out in the previous Chapter, references to "senior loan" will be used to refer to the senior or "A" interest in a whole loan or the actual whole loan itself, whilst references to a "junior loan" may refer to either a "B loan" or "B tranche" of a whole loan or a subordinated interest to such whole loan, be it a mezzanine or other interest. The use of the term "junior loan" may also be deemed to include references to more subordinated tranches in a whole loan in the context where there are more than two tranches of debt. What this Chapter is not intended to discuss are intercreditor agreements in the context of subordinated loans, debt or equity provided by companies related to the underlying borrowers and which would otherwise be expected to be fully subordinated to the interests of third party lenders financing the transaction.

As was set out in the previous Chapter, the AB loan structure was introduced into European CMBS in 2003. By the time it was being adopted in Europe, the US CMBS market already had a track record of using fairly standardised intercreditor agreements (referred to in the United States, as "co-lender agreements"). The European intercreditor, on the other hand, has been and remains to date "much more heterogeneous"[5], reflecting, among other things, lender preferences and choice of legal advisers engaged by such lenders to draft the relevant documentation, which will have their own drafting styles. These European variants can broadly be categorised as falling within the "European style" or "US style", the latter modelled on the

---

[5]  T. Cascino, S. Haase and E. Gatfield, *From A to B and back again—an update on intercreditor arrangements in European CMBS*, Fitch Ratings, June 5, 2007, p.1.

US CMBS co-lender agreement. Where relevant in this Chapter, differences between the "European style" and "US style" intercreditor agreement will be highlighted.

## 15.2. Priority of Payments

### 15.2.1. Introduction

One of the primary purposes of an intercreditor agreement is to set out the respective lender's right to cash flow generated from the underlying loan. The relevant loan agreement will set out a payment waterfall, that should ensure that costs associated with the running of the income producing property securing the loan and the operational costs of the borrower (usually a special purpose vehicle (SPV)) are met and, if applicable, any hedging costs relating to any borrower-level swaps, are paid in priority to the distribution of any amounts to the loan finance parties. Following payment of such expenses and any fees, costs and expenses due to the relevant agents of the loan, together with amounts available to pay principal and interest due under the loan, will be paid to the lenders, although the loan agreement will usually not set out how those amounts are to be distributed amongst the lenders. It is therefore not necessary for the borrower to be privy to the arrangements between the lenders, and the actual rates to be paid to each of the lenders, can be set out in separate fee letters agreed between such lenders.

The allocation of amounts due to be distributed under an intercreditor agreement will, in common practice, hinge on whether certain triggering events have occurred. First and foremost, there will likely be separate waterfalls that would apply depending on whether certain material events of default are in occurrence in respect of the related loan. Usually, these material events of default will encapsulate, at a minimum: (a) a default in the payment of interest, principal and other amounts due on the loan; (b) a default under certain covenants linked to the cashflow coverage or the loan to value ratio; and (c) certain insolvency events relating to the borrower and related obligors under the loan. Other than the preceding, additional events can be and are commonly included as well, though this will be subject to negotiation between the lenders due to the effect that such events have on the distribution of amounts and ultimately, on the scenarios in which the junior lenders will be absorbing a loss, since the junior loans in such arrangements provide credit enhancement for the more senior positions in the related loan. A junior lender will also seek to ensure that it has the right to cure, where possible, as many of the events may trigger a waterfall switch as further discussed below.

### 15.2.2. Waterfalls

An intercreditor agreement will usually set out a pre-default waterfall and a post-default waterfall. The pre-default waterfall will determine the allocation of payments before certain events of default have occurred. The post default waterfall will set out the allocation of payments after such events have occurred.

There may be some variation to a typical pre-default waterfall from deal to deal (e.g. junior loans which have some element of amortisation may rank in priority to amortisation on senior loans) but a typical pre-material default waterfall is set out below:

"For so long as no Material Event of Default is continuing, on the later of the date that amounts are distributed in accordance with the Credit Agreement or the date that payments are due with respect to any Hedging Arrangement that relates to such amounts, such amounts shall be distributed as between the Finance Parties (in replacement to the order set out in the Credit Agreement) as follows:

- *first*, in or towards any payment due under any Hedging Arrangements (whether or not periodic payments or payment as a result of termination, provided that such termination is not due to a default of or termination resulting from the related swap counterparty);
- *secondly*, in or towards payment of all fees, costs and expenses due and payable to the Security Trustee and its agents under the Finance Documents, (including all fees and expenses of the Servicer and Special Servicer as agents of the Finance Parties pursuant to the terms of the Servicing Agreement) and all amounts expended in connection with the preservation of the rights of the Finance Parties under the Finance Documents, including the preservation of the Property as security for the Whole Loan;
- *thirdly*, in or towards payment of interest due and payable (after taking into account any Cure Payment made in respect of a Non Payment of such interest) to the Senior Lender under the Credit Agreement (including the portion of Break Costs (and income earned thereon) up to the amount necessary to make a complete payment of interest on the Senior Loan at the Senior Loan Rate for the related Interest Period);
- *fourthly*, in or towards payment of interest due and payable to the Junior Lender under the Credit Agreement (including the portion of Break Costs (and income earned thereon) up to the amount necessary to make a complete payment of interest on the Junior Loan at the Junior Loan Rate for the related Interest Period);
- *fifthly*, in or towards payment to the Senior Lender and the Junior Lender, pro rata, according to the amounts due to each of them, of principal due and payable in respect of the Senior Loan (after taking into account any Cure Payment made in respect of a Non Payment of such principal) and the Junior Loan respectively;
- *sixthly*, in or towards payment of Default Interest received on the Whole Loan to the Senior Lender and the Junior Lender, pro rata, according to

348

the outstanding principal on the Senior Debt and the Junior Debt as of the beginning of the related Interest Period;

- *seventhly*, in or towards reimbursement on account of any Cure Payments made by the Junior Lenders pursuant to this Deed;

- *eighthly*, in or towards payment to the Senior Lender and Junior Lender, pro rata, other than to the extent such amounts are paid above, of all other costs, fees and expenses due and payable under the Finance Documents; and

- *ninthly*, in or towards payment to the swap counterparty with respect to any Hedging Arrangement entered into with respect to the Whole Loan in relation to termination payments when the swap counterparty is the defaulting party or reason for termination.

- *Notwithstanding the above*, if there are insufficient collections to pay all amounts of principal and interest due and payable to the Senior Lender and the Junior Lender (or any of them) in accordance with this Clause, the full amount of such shortfall shall be allocated to the Junior Loan."

In contrast to the above, upon the occurrence of a relevant triggering event, a post-default waterfall typically provides that payments due to the lenders are to be distributed sequentially, in order to ensure that higher ranking lenders receive their payment in full, prior to any amounts leaking out, to pay amounts due to the more subordinated classes of lenders. The intercreditor agreement position here may be different than under the underlying loan agreement, as the occurrence of the material event of default, for these purposes, may or may not involve an acceleration of the whole loan. Therefore, the post-default waterfall trigger may cause available proceeds to be applied to pay off lenders in full, whilst such amounts may not necessarily be presently due and payable under the whole loan itself.

Alternatively, it is not uncommon to see waterfalls that provide a staggered approach whilst a material default is continuing (e.g. a payment default) but, prior to acceleration of the whole loan, amounts received from the borrower would be applied firstly to pay amounts due and payable to the A loan whilst amounts that would subsequently be due to the B loan or more subordinated classes of lenders would be placed into an escrow account. The period during which such amounts may be retained in such an escrow account will usually be limited, pending either the acceleration of the loan, or the cure of such default by the junior lenders. If the loan is accelerated, or the default is not cured, amounts in the escrow account would be applied towards payment of amounts due in respect of the A loan, with any excess flowing to the more subordinated positions. If, however, the whole loan is not accelerated within a certain period (a period which is subject to negotiation but, as an example, it may be 90 days to match an interest period), then such escrowed amounts together with any accrued interest in the escrow account would be released to be applied against the B loan, or more subordinated positions in the debt stack. Such retention periods are usually structured to motivate the A lender to assess the impact of the relevant default and to determine whether it should seek to accelerate the whole loan and enforce the related security. However, from a junior lender perspective, such may be seen as an attempt by the A lender to build up a reserve to the detriment of the junior lenders.

An example of a sequential post-default waterfall is set out below:

"For as long as a Material Event of Default is continuing, on the later of the date that amounts are distributed in accordance with the Credit Agreement or the date that payments are due with respect to any Hedging Arrangement that relates to such amounts, such amounts shall be distributed (in replacement to the order set out in the Credit Agreement) as follows:

- *firstly*, in or towards payment of any amounts due under any Hedging Arrangements entered into with respect to the Whole Loan (whether or not periodic payments or payments as a result of termination, provided that such termination is not due to a default of or termination resulting from the related swap counterparty);
- *secondly*, in or towards payment of all costs, fees and expenses due and payable to the Security Trustee under the Finance Documents (including all fees and expenses of the Servicer and Special Servicer as agents of the Finance Parties pursuant to the terms of the Servicing Agreement) and all amounts expended in connection with the preservation of the rights of the Finance Parties, including the preservation of the Property as security for the Whole Loan;
- *thirdly*, in or towards payment of interest due and payable to the Senior Lender under the Credit Agreement (including the portion of Break Costs (and income earned thereon) up to the amount necessary to make a complete payment of interest on the Senior Loan at the Senior Loan Rate for the related Interest Period);
- *fourthly*, in or towards repayment of all principal outstanding on the Senior Loan (whether such amount is due or not);
- *fifthly*, in or towards payment to the Senior Lender of the Senior Lender's pro rata portion of all other costs, fees and expenses due and payable under the Finance Documents;
- *sixthly*, in or towards payment of the Senior Lender's pro rata portion of Default Interest received on the Whole Loan based on the outstanding principal on the Senior Debt as compared to the Whole Loan as of the beginning of the related Interest Period;
- *seventhly*, in or towards reimbursement on account of any Cure Payments made by the Junior Lender pursuant to this Deed;
- *eighthly*, in or towards payment of interest due and payable to the Junior Lender under the Credit Agreement (including the portion of Break Costs (and income earned thereon) up to the amount necessary to make a complete payment of interest on the Junior Loan at the Junior Loan Rate for the related Interest Period);
- *ninthly*, in or towards repayment of all principal outstanding on the Junior Loan (whether such amount is due or not);
- *tenthly*, in or towards payment of the Junior Lender's pro rata portion of Default Interest received on the Whole Loan based on the outstanding principal on the Junior Debt as compared to the Whole Loan as of the beginning of the related Interest Period; and

- *eleventhly*, in or towards payment to the Junior Lender of the Junior Lender's pro rata portion of all other costs, fees and expenses due and payable under the Finance Documents; and
- *twelfthly*, in or towards payment of any amounts due under any Hedging Arrangements entered into with respect to the Whole Loan in relation to termination payments, when the swap counterparty is the defaulting part or reason for termination."

## 15.2.3. Hedging[6]

The above waterfalls contemplate that lender-level hedging, benefiting all, is in place in respect of the loan. If hedging is exclusively in place at the borrower level, then the loan agreement waterfall will usually deal with its payment in priority to payment of amounts due to the lenders under the loan. If, in contrast, no lender level hedging is to be entered into for the benefit of the junior loan, then the CMBS waterfalls would have to deal with the allocation of amounts payable to the related hedge counterparty. Typically in CMBS, there will at least be a basis swap to address the mismatch between the dates on which interest and principal are due on a loan and the date on which proceeds are to be distributed to CMBS bondholders under the CMBS and the floating interest rate mismatch that may arise as a result. Accordingly, if a lender-level swap pays on any date, after which amounts are due on the underlying loan, the actual date of distribution of such amounts, for the purposes of the intercreditor agreement, should reflect that latter date as the date of distribution of amounts under the intercreditor agreement.

A hedge counterparty will expect that the main hedge payments due to it rank at the top of the waterfall. In the context of CMBS, this is important, as the CMBS bonds will require having adequate hedging arrangements in place, as a default in the payment of such amounts will not only result in the probable termination of the underlying hedging arrangement and break costs due to such hedge counterparty, with the corresponding reduction in proceeds available to be distributed to bondholders, but also in the impossibility of bringing in a replacement hedge counterparty if required. However, not all payments due to a hedge counterparty will rank in priority. If break costs are due to a hedge counterparty, for reasons which are imputable to such hedge counterparty (e.g. termination event under the related hedging arrangement in respect of a hedge provider or the failure by the hedge provider to meet its obligations under the related hedging agreement following a ratings downgrade), such amounts will be expected[7] to be subordinated to amounts due to the lenders.

---

[6]  See further Ch.8.

[7]  For instance, see *Swap Criteria for European Structured Finance Transactions*, DBRS, June 2011, pp.17–18.

### 15.2.3.1. Case law in the United States and England

Three cases, two in the US Bankruptcy Court in the Southern District of New York and one in the UK's Supreme Court, in each case relating to the bankruptcy of Lehman Brothers and its affiliated companies, in and around September 2008, have evidenced that US and English law disagree on the validity of such subordination clauses or 'flip clauses' when triggered by the filing of insolvency proceedings of the related hedge counterparty.

The first, *Lehman Bros. Special Financing v BNY Corporate Trustee Services Ltd (In re Lehman Bros Holdings, Inc)*[8] related to two series of credit-linked synthetic portfolio notes issued by an Irish SPV (Saphir) created by Lehman Brothers under the so-called Dante Program. At issue was whether Lehman Brothers Special Financing (LBSF), as credit default swap provider to the transaction, had been validly subordinated under the provisions of the transaction documents, which were expressed to be governed by English law, in respect of its entitlement to distributions in the collateral (being certain triple-A rated bonds) securing the transaction upon the filing of its voluntary case under US bankruptcy law, specifically Ch.11, in October 2008.[9] Prior to an event of default under the related hedging arrangement imputable to LBSF, LBSF would have been entitled to payment of proceeds produced by the collateral in priority to certain bondholders (in this case *Perpetual Trustee Company Ltd*), who would otherwise have been due such amounts as payment due under the related bonds. Upon the occurrence of such an event of default, the priority of payments would be "flipped" and the calculation of the amount due to LBSF as a result of the termination of the hedging arrangement would vary, each favouring *Perpetual* to the detriment of LBSF. As there was no issue of triable fact, Judge Peck heard the matter as a motion of summary judgment and concluded, among other things, that the "flip" to the priority of payments as a result of the insolvency of LBSF breached US bankruptcy law[10] and any attempt to

---

[8]   422 B.R. 407 (Bankr. S.D.N.Y. 2010).

[9]   Lehman Brothers Holdings, Inc. (LBHI) bankruptcy filing in September 2008 was also an event which was capable of triggering an event of default under the credit default swap, as LBHI was the credit support provider and its bankruptcy filing was an express event of default. However, this distinction is immaterial for purposes of the above as each of LBHI's and LBSF's bankruptcy filings predate the date on which the hedging arrangements were notified to have been terminated on behalf of Saphir.

[10]  Specifically under each of: (1) s.355(e)(1) of the US Bankruptcy Code, which reads: "Notwithstanding a provision in an executory contract or unexpired lease, or in applicable law, an executory contract or unexpired lease of the debtor may not be terminated or modified, and any right or obligation under such contract or lease may not be terminated or modified, at any time after the commencement of the case solely because of a provision in such contract or lease that is conditioned on- (A) the insolvency or financial condition of the debtor at any time before the closing of the case; (B) the commencement of a case under this title; or (C) the appointment of or taking possession by a trustee in a case under this title or a custodian before such commencement." (11 USC (2011) s.365(e)(1)); and (2) s.541(c)(1)(B) of the US Bankruptcy Code which reads in part "...an interest of the debtor in property becomes the property of the estate... notwithstanding any provision in an agreement, transfer instrument, or applicable non-bankruptcy law-... that is conditioned on the

enforce such provisions would violate the automatic stay provided for under the US bankruptcy law. Interestingly, this motion for summary judgment was being heard contemporaneously with proceedings brought by *Perpetual* in the English courts and Judge Peck noted that "[i]n applying the Bankruptcy Code to these facts, this Court recognises that it is interpreting applicable law in a manner that will yield an outcome directly at odds with the judgment of the English Courts." For purposes of the US litigation, the case was subsequently settled before appeal to the US District Court and accordingly, the decision is ultimately only persuasive for the purposes of whether it is a binding precedent for future litigation.

Similarly, *Lehman Brothers Special Financing v Ballyrock*[11] related to a hedging arrangement entered into between LBSF and the issuer in a CDO transaction, Ballyrock. Under the related master agreement and indenture, LBSF would have been entitled to a priority ranking in the related waterfall if amounts were due to it as a result of the termination of the hedging arrangements, except that if such termination was due to LBSF or Lehman Brothers Holdings Inc. (LBHI), as credit support provider under the hedging arrangement, among other reasons, due to either having instituted or having instituted against either of them bankruptcy proceedings. The termination payment would be subordinated to the payment of bondholders and capped in the amount of $30,000. Accordingly, upon LBHI's bankruptcy filing in September 2008, Ballyrock exercised its right under the hedging arrangement to call for an early termination date, under all transactions entered into in respect of the hedging arrangement and a termination payment due to LBSF of approximately $404 million was determined. Ballyrock subsequently liquidated its assets and after distribution of amounts due to the bondholders proposed to further distribute a remaining amount of $137 million to bondholders on the next scheduled payment date. Upon the announcement of the proposed distribution of such amounts, LBSF filed a complaint against Ballyrock for a declaratory judgment to obtain, among other measures, a judgment that such proposed distribution would be in violation of applicable bankruptcy law. On a motion to dismiss such complaint, Judge Peck again found that, also citing *Lehman Bros Special Financing v BNY*, the flip clause was susceptible to being interpreted[12] as an ipso facto provision that could not be enforced to deprive LBSF of its rights on account of its bankruptcy filing. Furthermore, there was a detailed discussion of the safe harbour provisions in US bankruptcy law then set out in *Lehman Brothers Special Financing v BNY*.

---

insolvency or financial condition of the debtor, on the commencement of a case under this title, or on the appointment of or taking possession by a trustee in a case under this title or a custodian before such commencement, and that effects or gives an option to effect a forfeiture, modification, or termination of the debtor's interest in property." (11 USC (2011) s.541(c)(1)(B)).

[11] *Lehman Bros Special Financing Inc v Ballyrock ABS CDO 2007-1 Ltd and Wells Fargo Bank, N.A., Trustee (In re Lehman Brothers Holdings, Inc)*, 452 B.R. 31 (Bankr. S.D.N.Y. 2010).

[12] Given that the matter heard was in the context of a motion to dismiss filed by Ballyrock, a full hearing a trial on the matter would subsequently determine whether such the enforcement of such clauses would violate US bankruptcy law.

Such provision allowed, notwithstanding a bankruptcy filing, a swap participant to exercise any contractual right it may be entitled to under the terms of the related hedging arrangement to liquidate, terminate or accelerate a hedging arrangement upon a bankruptcy filing of the other party[13] Judge Peck, in his judgment, made it clear that such safe harbour was to be construed to permit termination and not, as in this case, to subordinate a right to payment but for the bankruptcy filing.

In *Belmont Park*,[14] the UK Supreme Court heard the final Chapter in the *Perpetual* case saga. Rather than being based on carefully worded legislation, applicable English law relevant in this case hinged primarily on English common law and the "anti-deprivation rule" under English insolvency law. The Belmont group were a series of bondholders, other than *Perpetual*, who owned bonds in other series of bonds issued by Saphir. Following decisions by the High Court and Court of Appeals favouring the bondholder view that the "flip" clause was valid and worked to subordinate LBSF's expectation of payment from proceeds realised on the related collateral, Lord Collins, in his leading judgment, found that it is "desirable that, so far as possible, the courts give effect to contractual terms which parties have agreed",[15] that "there is a particularly strong case for autonomy in cases of complex financial instruments such as those involved in this appeal"[16] and specifically, the transaction (and the "flip" clause) had been entered into in good faith and there never had "been any suggestion that those provisions were deliberately intended to evade insolvency law".[17] Furthermore, Lord Collins considered that it was "possible to give a policy [the anti-deprivation rule] a common sense application which prevents its application to bona fide transactions which do not have as their predominant purpose, or one of their main purposes, the deprivation of the property of one of the parties on bankruptcy."[18]

Consequently, the practical lesson to be learnt as a result of the above cases is that, whilst the "flip" in a waterfall triggered as a result of an insolvency filing of the party otherwise entitled to payment is valid under English law, care should be taken to verify whether the jurisdiction in which main bankruptcy proceedings may be brought against that party will also

---

[13] Specifically, s.560 of the US Bankruptcy Code, which reads in part: "[t]he exercise of any contractual right of any swap participant or financial participant to cause the liquidation, termination, or acceleration of one or more swap agreements because of a condition of the kind specified in section 365(e)(1) of this title or to offset or net out any termination values or payment amounts arising under or in connection with the termination, liquidation, or acceleration of one or more swap agreements shall not be stayed, avoided, or otherwise limited by operation of any provision of this title or by order of a court or administrative agency in any proceeding under this title..." (11 USC (2011) s.560).

[14] *Belmont Part Investments PTY Ltd v BNY Corporate Trustee Services Ltd and Lehman Bros Special Financing Inc* [2011] UKSC 38.

[15] Citing Lord Neuberger in *Perpetual Trustee Co Ltd v BNY Corporate Trustee Services Ltd* [2009] EWCA Civ 1160, [2010] Ch 347 (CA) at [58].

[16] [2010] Ch 347 (CA) at [103].

[17] [2010] Ch 347 (CA) at [109].

[18] [2010] Ch 347 (CA) at [104].

recognise such clause. Given that US courts may steer towards finding such clauses in breach of US bankruptcy laws, parties may wish to minimise any adverse impact by, where possible, entering into such arrangements with counterparties subject to, for example, English law where possible.

### 15.2.4. Servicing fees

Whether both lenders will be responsible for payment of the servicing fee and related costs and expenses incurred by the servicer or special servicer is subject to negotiation between the parties. However, from a practical standpoint, it is in the interests of the securitisation that any potential disputes in relation to the administration of the loan are minimised and, accordingly, the servicing of the whole loan is preferable and as noted by the rating agencies, there is an expectation "that the servicer and/or special servicer will have sufficient authority to act in the best interest of both lenders",[19] which would be particularly relevant in the context of an enforcement or workout of the whole loan. It is also possible that the loan will include an indemnity from the borrower, making it responsible for some or part of any servicing fees incurred, particularly following the occurrence of an event of default. If so, such fees may be caught by that indemnity and would not necessarily result in a reduction in amounts available to pay the A loan and B loan.

If servicing fees are usually payable by the transaction as a whole, such fees may be taken from the top of the waterfalls. If, however, the A lender (or issuer) is solely responsible, payment may be achieved by either deducting such amounts from the amounts due to the A lender (by, for instance, reducing the amount of interest payable to the A lender) under the intercreditor agreement, or, by accounting for those amounts in the relevant securitisation waterfalls (if within the context of a CMBS deal) from proceeds already distributed to the issuer under the intercreditor agreement.

As seen in Chs 6 and 7, servicing fees are broken down into firstly the primary servicing fees payable to a servicer prior to the loan(s) transferring upon the occurrence of certain events to special servicing.[20] Such tasks have traditionally been more of an administrative, payment monitoring and borrower interface nature. As a result of the financial crisis and the increased levels of defaults occurring in CRE financing transactions, due to the reduced availability of capital and the general deterioration of the CRE industry,[21] it has become increasingly apparent that servicers have been required to take a more active role which may include undertaking a more frequent monitoring and reporting commitment and/or some of the roles

---

[19]   T. Cascino, S. Haase and E. Gatfield, *From A to B and back again—an update on intercreditor arrangements in European CMBS*, Fitch Ratings, June 5, 2007, p.7.

[20]   See further Chs 5, 6 and 7.

[21]   See further Ch.1.

that are usually performed by special servicers. From a primary servicer's standpoint, such additional or extended obligations will usually result in an increase in the overall primary servicer's costs which were not always contemplated at the outset of the transaction when the fees were agreed. This can be addressed structurally in new transactions,[22] for instance, some transactions in 2011 and 2012 have incorporated the possibility for the primary servicer to charge a modification fee payable by the borrower a condition to a work-out of the loan, which is intended to prevent a premature transfer of the loan to special servicing.

Special servicing fees are the second component that may be stripped at the top of an intercreditor waterfall. These can include basic special servicing fees, liquidation fees and work-out fees. Such fees are payable on top of the primary servicing fee. The two CMBS transactions that have been closed, since the financial crisis began, have modified these arrangements to account for the complexity and size of the loans which are aimed to ensure that special servicers are appropriately compensated but, in respect of larger loans, are not generating excessive profits.[23]

### 15.2.5. Losses due to shortfalls

The primary goal of intercreditor agreements, is to ensure subordination between the different tranches of the loan. One area where this is important, is in the allocation of losses. In the pre-material default waterfall sample included at para.15.2.2, the last paragraph of that clause ensures that the intended credit enhancement that the B loan represents, in favour of the A loan, is preserved in the circumstance where there is a shortfall in available proceeds, even when the pre-material default waterfall applies. This may occur, for instance, following a work-out or restructuring of the loan where the loan, after having been paying under the post-material event of default waterfall, reverts to the pre-material default position but, for instance, the amount payable by the borrower under the loan has been reduced. This paragraph ensures that when a payment is to be made in respect of each of the A loan and B loan where the B loan would, save for the shortfall, have been entitled to any payment in priority to the A loan (as in the case of the sample pre-material default waterfall above), available proceeds are first allocated to meet amounts owing in respect of the A loan, with the B loan absorbing the loss.

---

[22] See the discussion on CMBS 2.0 in Chs 4 and 7.

[23] In these cases, DECO 2011-CSPK and DECO 2012-MHILL, which are both single loan securitisations, the basic special servicing was set at 0.125% per annum, the liquidation fee at 0.50% of the proceeds of sale net of costs and expenses arising from a disposal and the work-out fee at 0.50% of each collection of interest and principal received for so long as the loan remained a corrected loan (i.e. a discontinuance of a monetary payment default for, usually, two consecutive interest periods and the loan not being subject to any other event that would give rise to the loan becoming a specially serviced loan).

### 15.2.6.   Interest rate creep

A diminution of the amount of principal outstanding on a senior loan may have a negative impact on the availability of proceeds, to meet amounts due under more subordinate tranches. As noted above, lenders in the debt stack will agree to an interest rate on their participations that will be calculated based upon the overall rate payable by a borrower under the whole loan. Senior lenders, given their ranking in the waterfall and their priority in respect of recoveries from proceeds generated by the underlying collateral, will agree to a rate of interest that matches the level of risk they are agreeing to in the transaction. Correspondingly, subordinated lenders will invest and accept subordination only if they are paid a rate commensurate to their own position's level of risk.

An example of what is called "rate creep" can be explained by assuming a whole loan in the amount of £100 million is entered into at a rate of 9 per cent per annum. The whole loan is subsequently tranched into an A loan in the amount of £70 million at a rate agreed between the lenders of 6 per cent per annum and a B loan in the amount of £30 million at a rate of 16 per cent. If the A loan is hyperamortised in priority to the B loan in, for example, £5 million that results in a weighted average on the combined A loan and B loan of approximately 9.07 per cent, which means that the whole loan interest rate payable by the borrower under the loan agreement would no longer be able to sustain the B loan rate. This scenario may occur if the post-default waterfall triggers occur, which results in hyperamortisation of the A loan, in priority to the B loan and then the waterfall shifting back, as a result of a cure of the event, to the pre-default waterfall. Another example may be if part of the A loan is wiped out or forgiven. One way to address this issue is to ensure that the A loan rate is expressed to be net of the B loan rate. In the second example, the consent rights typically afforded to the B lender will require that prior to any change to the amount of any payment due under the loan, the prior written approval of the B lender be obtained.

## 15.3.   Amendments, waivers and consents

### 15.3.1.   Entrenched rights vcontrol valuation

In Europe, there are two general approaches to resolving the issue relating to the amount of control given to subordinated lenders. The first, requiring that either any amendments, waivers or consents, or those relating to an enumerated list of specified actions in respect of the whole loan, cannot be taken without the consent of the subordinated lenders, which are commonly denominated "entrenched rights". Any actions outside that list would be taken by the servicer, special servicer or senior lender as relevant. Rating agencies have traditionally not favoured the existence of entrenched rights in a CMBS context.[24] The second, subjecting any subordinated lender approval rights in respect of any amendments, waivers or consents relating to an enumerated list of actions to a 'value out' provision (a "control valuation event"). Under such a provision, if the underlying properties securing the whole loan have depreciated in value to cover both the senior debt and a specified portion of the related subordinated debt, then such approval rights would be disapplied. An example of a control valuation provision is provided below:

> "A 'Control Valuation Event' will occur if at any time, the Market Value of the Property is less than the aggregate of: (i) the A Debt then outstanding to the A Lender; and (ii) twenty-five per cent of the B Debt outstanding to the B Lenders at the date of this Deed"

Hence, if the value of the property, as determined by a valuation obtained pursuant to the terms of the intercreditor agreement, securing the whole loan falls below the full amount of the A loan plus 25 per cent of the B loan, at the time the intercreditor agreement is entered into, the B lender will cease to be able to exercise the relevant control rights. Such calculations will be based on valuations obtained at the times or upon the occurrence of certain events, as set out in the intercreditor agreement. This may or may not coincide with the timings for obtaining valuations under the underlying loan agreement. In fact, such valuations at times cannot be used for the purposes of determining whether a control valuation event is in existence. If a control valuation event is determined to exist, the affected lender will usually have the right to obtain, or instruct the servicer or special servicer to obtain, another valuation at the cost of such lender. The servicer or special servicer may then have the discretion, to be exercised in accordance with the servicing standard, as to which valuation to use for determining the existence of a control valuation event.

### 15.3.2.  Common actions requiring consent

An intercreditor agreement may provide for a combination of both methods described above, i.e. a set of entrenched rights or rights subject to a control valuation event and a list of items in respect of which the facility agent or, if applicable, the servicer or special servicer would be required to consult the relevant subordinated lender on in any event.

Whilst the list of actions that will require the consent of the junior lenders will naturally be subject to intense negotiation and vary from deal to deal,

---

[24] "It is common for the junior lender to have consent rights with respect to issues that will affect the characteristics and/or credit quality of the loan. However, Fitch expects that these consent rights to be structured such that they do not interfere with the day-to-day management of the property, servicing of the loan and, in particular, the timing of the enforcement process. Where amendments can be undertaken only in case all (senior and junior) creditors agree, the question is whether these consent rights grant too much power to the junior creditor." *Fitch Ratings*; pp.4–5.

there are a few that form a very basic list from which negotiations usually start. A sample list is provided below:

> "The [Agent, Servicer or Special Servicer] may not amend or waive any term of any Finance Document or exercise or refrain from exercising any consent, approval, discretion or determination, contained in any Finance Document having the same commercial effect in a manner or to an extent which would or could result in:
>
> (a) any change to the date of payment of any amount to a Lender under the Finance Documents;
> (b) a reduction in the Margin or a reduction in the amount of any payment of principal, interest, fee or other amount payable to a Lender under the Finance Documents;
> (c) a change to the currency of any amount payable under the Finance Documents;
> (d) an increase in, or an extension of, a Commitment;
> (e) any change to the basis upon which a payment is calculated in accordance with the original provisions of that Finance Document;
> (f) any amendment, waiver or supplement to an Event of Default under the Credit Agreement;
> (g) a release of an Obligor;
> (h) a release of any Security other than in accordance with the terms of the Finance Documents; or
> (i) any change to the right of a Lender to assign or transfer its rights or obligations under the Finance Documents..."

The first four items listed above will impact the junior lender's economics in the transaction and will naturally be an area that the junior lender will wish to ensure is not amended without its consent. For the reasons provided in para.15.3.1, the junior lender will also wish to limit any amendments to the economics relating to the senior piece, or any amendment under paras (e) and (f) which can result in a change to the applicable waterfall or lead to the acceleration or enforcement of the loan, that may have an impact on the junior lender's rights to payment (including cash flow). Paragraphs (g) and (h) address the credit quality of the asset and (i) ensures that the lender may exit the transaction on the originally agreed terms, if so desired. Other items are commonly negotiated and added on to the list on a case-by-case basis (i.e. relating to the administration and quality of the underlying property or further events that may result in a change to the applicable waterfall which may result in proceeds being cut off from the junior lender). These will vary depending on the transaction and the bargaining power of the related parties. However, care should be taken to ensure that such actions that may be required for the day-to-day management of the property are not unduly restricted or subject to the delay that a formal approval or consultation process will entail, particularly in a post-default scenario where the servicer or special servicer will be required to take a more active role.

## 15.4.   Cure rights and Purchase option

### *15.4.1.   Cure rights*

As noted in the previous Chapter, cure rights are an important feature for junior lenders, in order to avoid a switch of the pre-material default waterfall to the sequential post-default waterfall and to halt the taking of enforcement action by the senior lender. In addition, such a feature will normally prevent the transfer of the whole loan to special servicing, as will be further discussed below. These rights will usually allow the junior lenders to remedy a payment default and certain other defaults that are by their nature capable of being remedied. The precise list of defaults that the senior lender will agree that the junior lenders may cure will be negotiated on a case-by-case basis, but in addition to a payment or monetary default, it is not uncommon for the junior lenders to be also permitted to cure financial covenants (i.e., loan to value or debt service covenants set out in the loan agreement). Defaults which cannot be remedied by a payment may, at times, be included, though they would in practice be very difficult to cure if at all. Regardless, insolvency defaults would be excluded and to the extent that defaults other than those that can be cured by payment are included, they will usually be events that may be corrected by the borrower, after the fact, such as a breach of representation or undertaking to perform certain actions.

The amount of the cure payment to be made on the occurrence of a payment default will include not only the amount of the shortfall but to the extent, in the context of a CMBS, the issuer, as A lender, has obtained an advance or has made a drawing under the securitisation liquidity facility. The cure payment will also be made to include any related interest and other amounts, including any break costs, that will be payable by the A lender on such advanced or drawn amounts on the following interest payment date. It is possible that the intercreditor agreement provide for the payment of certain additional amounts, though a junior lender will naturally wish to minimise the number of costs that may be chargeable as part of the cure payment.

### *15.4.2.   Exercise of cure rights*

The procedure followed in respect of the exercise of cure rights will usually commence upon the agent, servicer or special servicer becoming aware of the curable default and the giving of a notification to the junior lender, entitled to make such cure, within a predefined period of time. If such event is a payment default, the junior lender will generally be permitted to make a payment, in an amount equal to the payment shortfall due to the senior or more senior lenders, or, if such payment default results in amounts available to pay the senior loan, but results in a shortfall to that junior lender, or those other junior lenders which are subordinated to it, waive on its own behalf and on behalf of any other lenders which are subordinated to it, such shortfall as between the lenders. In the latter case, such waiver would not waive amounts due by the borrower and those amounts would continue to be due by the borrower but would, for the purposes of the intercreditor, be considered waived in order to prevent such event from constituting a material event of default leading to the consequences discussed above. If, on the other hand, such event is a financial covenant default, this may be cured by making a prepayment of the loan, in the case of a loan to value covenant breach, in an amount equal to such amount as would be necessary to ensure that the covenant is subsequently observed. Alternatively, if the event is a debt service or interest cover covenant, such default may be cured by depositing an amount that would cure such default in a controlled escrow account or obtaining an irrevocable letter of credit, payable on demand from a bank or other financial institution meeting certain ratings thresholds, which would provide additional security for the whole loan. Ultimately, if a subsequent material event of default occurs which is not, or is incapable of being cured, whether by its very nature or as a result of cure rights having been exhausted, such escrowed amounts would be available, or such letter of credit would be called, to pay down the whole loan in accordance with the post-material default waterfall. If the financial covenant is subsequently rectified, which may require that compliance with the covenant be maintained for a certain number of consecutive interest periods, any escrowed amounts would be released to the paying curing lender.

Cures are typically required to be made within a prescribed period of time. This period will be negotiated between the lenders, but will account for the nature of the default and the impact any delay caused by the cure process would have on the senior lender. In addition, lenders who need to undertake internal processes to source the cash in the amounts required to make such cures will build in enough time to ensure that such rights can be effectively exercised. Further, any payment cures, other than any escrowed amounts as discussed above, will be reimbursed to the paying lender in accordance with the priority of payments of the applicable waterfall. Such reimbursement will be made after all amounts of principal, interest, expenses and other items due to the more senior lenders have been paid.

No enforcement action will be permitted to be taken during the period afforded to the junior lender to cure the related default. The intercreditor agreement would not provide a grace period upon the occurrence of any other event of default which is not subject to junior lender cure right. In order to address any concerns with the length of time afforded to the junior lender to cure the default, the intercreditor agreement may provide that the junior lender would have a reduced period to notify the agent that it will be making a cure and then have an extended period in which to complete the cure. If the junior lender fails to respond or notifies that it will not be making a cure, the period during which no enforcement action would be permitted would be shorter than if such period was intended to provide the junior lender some time to actually effect the payment or other cure. From a ratings perspective, excessively long grace periods would be considered as detrimental to the credit quality of the senior debt.

### 15.4.3. Limits on number of cures

In order to avoid a scenario in which recoveries under the loan would have been greater had the loan and the related security been enforced earlier, rather than waiting whilst the loan was continuously being cured, junior lender cure rights are usually limited both in the number of consecutive cures that can be effected as well as in the total number of cures that would be permitted during the life of the transaction. Usually cures will be permitted no more than twice in consecutive interest periods and between four and six times during the life of the deal, which will vary, among other reasons, according to the length of the term of the transaction.

### 15.4.4. Purchase option

It may be considered that a purchase option granted to the junior lenders to acquire the more senior loans, upon the occurrence of a material event of default, is mutually beneficial to both categories of lenders, in that the senior lenders would be repaid the loan at par and the junior lender is able to preserve control of the loan in circumstances where its right to cash flow may be halted due to a shift to the applicable waterfall or it ceases to be able to exercise consent or consultation rights as a result of the occurrence of a control valuation event. However, it is often not a practical solution for a junior lender, due to the likely problems surrounding the performance of the loan and the amount of the purchase price that would have to be committed to effect the acquisition. For these reasons, it is not an option that is commonly taken up by junior lenders, particularly, at the time of writing, where availability of financing for CRE assets remains scarce.

The option is often triggered on the occurrence of the same trigger events that will cause a shift to the applicable waterfall in intercreditor agreements. There may be circumstances where the junior lender may be able to have included, within the purchase option trigger events, additional items that may result in a decrease in available cash flow to the junior lenders (e.g. increased costs resulting from the transfer of servicing from a primary servicer to a special servicer) or its loss of consent or consultation rights.

The purchase price will usually be determined by the agent, servicer or special servicer and will normally include:

- the outstanding principal amount of the tranche of the loan being acquired;
- all accrued and unpaid interest, fees, costs and expenses and other amounts owed to the selling lender;

- any funding break costs of the selling lender;
- any amount, including fees, costs and expenses and VAT chargeable thereon due to the servicer and/or special servicer in respect of the loan;
- any interest or other finance charges (including, break costs) payable or which would be due on the next interest payment date by the senior lender with respect to any advance or drawing made by a liquidity facility provider or otherwise in connection with the loan; and
- the reasonable costs and expenses incurred by the selling lender as a result of the acquisition.

Whether default interest and prepayment fees are included in the above will be negotiated on a case-by-case basis, but it is fairly common for such items not to be included. Further, if there is lender level hedging arrangements in place, in respect of the senior loan being sold, relevant hedging termination costs would be included in the above list if such hedging arrangements are not being transferred across to the purchasing junior lender.

## 15.5. Enforcement

As noted in the previous Chapter, the rights of a junior lender to instruct enforcement action are set out in the intercreditor agreement. Any enforcement rights also depend on the security the junior lender holds in respect of the loan. For example, if the junior lender is a B lender under the whole loan, it would be expected that the junior lender and the senior lender would share an interest in the security whilst, if the junior lender's position is that of a mezzanine-type lender, it may have its own separate subordinated security package ranking behind the senior security.

Ordinarily, intercreditor agreements as used in European CRE financing transactions, will either provide the junior lender with no right to cause an enforcement, or a limited right of enforcement. In the former case, the rights granted to the junior lender to cure a specified list of defaults, or to acquire the senior loan upon a material event of default (for which see above) would be argued by a senior lender as representing sufficient protection for a junior lender, faced with a probable enforcement scenario. In the latter case, the junior lender could be prevented from taking any such action through a control valuation type of event. Such tests would ensure that the value of the underlying property is sufficient to cover a full recovery of the senior loan plus an addition buffer, normally determined to be 125 per cent of the senior loan. Further, a junior lender would be prohibited from taking any steps to accelerate the relevant junior loan or enforcement action until the expiry of a standstill period provided that the senior creditor has not itself accelerated the senior loan or commenced any enforcement action.

The length of any standstill period, applicable to the junior lender, would vary depending on the nature of the default in question, such as a payment, financial covenant or other default. These periods are typically heavily negotiated between the parties but it is usual, particularly pre-2007, to see periods oscillating between 90 and 150 days from loan default. On expiry of the standstill period, if the relevant default remained outstanding or, the security trustee or special servicer had not taken any enforcement action and provided always that a control valuation event had not occurred in respect of the relevant junior loan, the junior lender would be entitled to take or instruct the relevant agent or special servicer to take enforcement action.

Absent any right of the junior lender to instruct enforcement action, the senior lender would commonly be able to direct enforcement action. Any such instructions from the senior lender would remain subject to any cure or purchase option rights and timetables, in respect thereof, to which the junior lender would be entitled. During such periods, the senior lender would not be entitled to take enforcement action as discussed above. Usually, when exercising such rights, the senior lender would not be obliged to take into account the interests of the junior lenders, when instructing the relevant party to take enforcement action. In some transactions, the junior lender may be able to have an indirect influence on the enforcement process, by being able to terminate and propose the appointment of its preferred special servicer. Certain conditions will be attached on the identity of any such proposed special servicer which will be discussed below and in Chs 5, 6 and 7, though this right ensures, that for so long as the junior lender has enough equity in the deal, it will be able to have some degree of influence on the management of a specially serviced loan. This power to terminate and appoint a special servicer, will typically be provided in situations where the whole loan is being serviced on behalf of both the senior and junior lenders. However, the inclusion of such a right and additional consent and consultation, as discussed above, may be afforded to the junior lenders in circumstances where the junior loans are not being serviced.

Although the above scope of junior lender enforcement rights is commonly seen in Europe, there may be some variations to the above depending on the transaction in question. For example, certain transactions may provide the junior lender with the power to require the disposal of properties at any time, once enforcement of the whole loan has commenced, if any such disposal proceeds would be sufficient to repay the senior loans. The principle behind these types of variants is to afford the junior lender with a greater voice in the process, where there is enough value in the transaction to repay the senior loans and any additional costs in full.

## 15.6. Transfer restrictions

During the financial crisis it became increasingly common that borrowers or affiliates of borrowers, in an attempt to maximise opportunities raised by financial institutions' needed to address relevant regulatory capital requirements, raise liquidity and dispose of loan assets.[25] Such parties sought to purchase positions in related loans at a discount (so-called DPO)[26], in order to reduce leverage and influence loan administration processes, including prospects of enforcement. Such a trend has also been seen in secondary market trading of whole loan CMBS, where positions have been acquired to exert control over the appointment of special servicers and the consequent influence such would have over the administration and enforcement process of a non-performing loan.

Historically, limitations on the parties whom a junior lender or senior lender have been able to transfer part or the entirety of the position in a loan to, have been typical and would be included as a restriction on transfer in an intercreditor agreement. These have typically followed Loan Market Association (LMA) standards, where the transferee is expressed to be a financial institution, or by way of the inclusion of either a general but narrower description of the type of entities to which such interests could be transferred and/or the inclusion of a "black list" of lenders to which transfers would be prohibited. Such restrictions have been aimed at addressing the potential disalignment of objectives between lenders, whose motivations are influenced by other interests, than ordinary lenders ultimately concerned in achieving a full recovery of proceeds due to it under the loan.

In order to address concerns of undue influence of sponsors, borrowers and their affiliates in the day-to-day administration of a loan, post-financial crisis transactions have sought to restrict the rights which such parties may be entitled to exercise upon an acquisition of the loan. This is dealt with at para.14.4.1, resulting in documentation providing for the:

- disapplication of voting rights in approving any consent, waiver, amendment or any other matter;
- removal of any right to attend any meetings between the other lenders when dealing with matters pertaining to the loan;
- removal of any right to receive any communications or notices prepared for the benefit of the other lenders;
- exclusion of any benefit in the security package securing such loan;
- cessation of any entitlement to receive certain payments (e.g. tax gross-up payments or increased costs); and

---

[25] See further Chs 3, 4, 16 and 20.
[26] See para.14.5.

- excluding the amount held by such lender from any computations used to determine the identity of the requisite proportion of lenders constituting a majority position,

upon such party acquiring an interest in the loan. Furthermore, upon the securitisation of the loan any such acquisition by a related party would be prohibited. Similarly, post-financial crisis whole loan CMBS deals have also gone a step further by treating any bonds held by the sponsor, borrower and their affiliates as if they were not outstanding and, accordingly, carrying no rights for the purposes of any quorum required to pass a resolution of bondholders, computing the necessary majorities required to approve a written resolution and giving instructions to the relevant note trustee.

## 15.7. Servicing

### 15.7.1. Whole loan versus senior loan servicing

As discussed above and in Chs 6 and 7, servicing of a loan consists of two work streams which will depend on the status of the loan as performing or non-performing. The first denominated primary servicing, is mostly administrative in nature relating to the collection of payments due under the loan and their subsequent distribution, monitoring compliance with the loan terms and acting as liaison of the lenders with the borrower, for the purposes of any notices and requests received in connection with the loan and the collateral securing the loan. The servicer may also be appointed by the facility agent and security trustee to exercise their rights under the related loan documentation and intercreditor agreement.[27] Upon the occurrence of a special servicing transfer event upon a default or it becoming apparent that the loan is imminently in danger of defaulting, the role of actively managing the loan and security can be undertaken by a special servicer who will represent the senior or all of the lenders, the facility agent and the security trustee in connection with negotiations with the borrower in order to ensure that the loan performs or reverts to a performing status as soon as possible or, alternatively, seeking to work-out or liquidate the loan in order to maximise recoveries for the lenders.

With the advent of the financial crisis, servicers have found that the distinction between primary servicing and special servicing has become blurred and primary servicers have been called upon to perform certain functions that in the past were carried out by special servicers, as set out in Chs 5 and 6. However, a loan that is past the stage of a foreseeably immediate correction, will require transfer to special servicing, as the costs associated with the administration of such loan and the expertise required

---

[27] See further Ch.6.

in seeking a satisfactory resolution of the loan, will typically be beyond the scope of services rendered by a primary servicer.

The documentation providing for the servicing of the loan will depend on whether the whole loan will be serviced by the same servicer. If so, there are variations as to how this arrangement will be set out. In European-style intercreditor agreements, it is fairly usual for there to be an acknowledgment by the lenders that the whole loan will be serviced by one servicer for the benefit of all the lenders. It is not uncommon for the junior lenders to then become a party to the actual servicing agreement with the senior lender, servicer and special servicer. In CMBS, this process can be quite cumbersome as the documentation is usually agreed simultaneously, with the negotiation and finalisation of the remaining securitisation transaction documents and the involvement of additional third party lenders to the securitisation may prolong and difficult the process. Alternatively, US-style intercreditor agreements will provide a basic framework of key terms of the servicing agreement which would include, among other items, the servicing standard, the method of calculation as to when a lender becomes a controlling party for the purposes of consent, amendment and waiver rights, the criteria for transfer of the loan from primary to special servicing, the fees payable to the servicer and special servicer and the right of the controlling party to terminate and propose the appointment of a special servicer.[28] These basic terms form the backbone of the servicing agreement and the subordinated lenders' agreement to its principal terms. Subsequently, the senior lender (being the issuer in the case of a CMBS) would, in turn, enter into the actual servicing agreement without involvement from the subordinated lenders.

When the whole loan is serviced by the same servicer, the junior lenders typically have the right to terminate and propose the appointment of a special servicer who would, in accordance with the servicing standard and the requirements of the loan documentation and intercreditor agreement (for instance, the consent and consultation of rights of the junior lenders as discussed above), be entitled to direct the enforcement strategy and make all decisions regarding the senior and subordinated loans. Similarly to junior lender consent and consultation rights, the right of the junior lender to terminate and have the right to propose the appointment of a special servicer of its choice, would be dependent on the related junior lender remaining in a "control" position in the loan, meaning that it is not affected by a control valuation event.

If the junior loans are not to be serviced by the same servicer, the intercreditor will provide a general acknowledgement that the senior lender may cause the senior loan to be separately serviced. As discussed above, servicing fees would, in such circumstances, usually be payable by the senior lender alone. The subordinated lenders would have no further

---

[28] See Chs 5, 6 and 7 for these provisions in relation to servicing agreements.

involvement in the negotiation and finalisation of the relevant documentation and would either service the related junior loan themselves, or, delegate the same to a third party. In those circumstances, given that the senior loan will be serviced and the cash management aspects of such servicing would be under the control of the senior lender's servicer, the role of any third party junior lender servicer would be limited to monitoring and receiving distributions paid to the junior lender and interfacing with the senior loan servicer, as to any consultation or consent rights that the junior lender has under the intercreditor agreement.

However, from a securitisation and rating agency standpoint, it is preferable that the whole loan be serviced by the same servicer, particularly following a default in order to minimise any disruption caused by potential conflicts between lenders and delays which may arise as a result when implementing key management actions that are required in a post-default scenario. In addition, from a practical perspective, having one servicer with the power to conduct the whole process independently will facilitate the management of the loan, again particularly in a post-default scenario.

### 15.7.2.   Servicing standard

As set out in Ch.7, the servicing standard will provide the framework in which the servicer and special servicer will service the related loan. It will prioritise the factors that must be taken into account by the servicer and special servicer and will rank those factors in an order of priority which must be followed to the extent that there are any conflicts between them. Firstly, the servicer must act in accordance with applicable law. This factor serves to ensure that no liability is incurred by the servicer in conducting its administration of the loan, particularly to the extent it receives instructions from any of the lenders to take any actions that would constitute a breach of applicable law. Secondly, the servicer will have to account for the provisions of the loan agreement and other finance documents which will be the framework on which the intercreditor agreement is to operate. This is particularly relevant where the borrower is not a party to the intercreditor agreement, as any right, or, other course of action permitted under the intercreditor agreement will need to fit within the rights of the lenders and agents under the loan agreement, as the latter will represent the deal that has been struck with the borrower. The terms of the intercreditor agreement will rank after the finance documents on the above basis. Similarly, the terms of the servicing agreement will need to conform to the rights agreed between the lenders under the intercreditor agreement, again particularly if the other lenders are not a party to the servicing agreement. The standard will subsequently set out the degree of care and standard of skill to be exercised by the servicer and special servicer. Finally, the objective of the servicer and special servicer will be to service the loan with a view towards, pre-default, the "timely collection of scheduled payments" and, post-default, the "maximisation of recoveries" for the lenders taking into account the relevant subordination agreed to between the lenders. An example of a servicing standard is provided in Ch.5.

The servicing standard will frequently need to be considered by servicers and special servicer when considering strategies in order to deal with, particularly, non-performing loans. When assessing compliance with the servicing standard and, consequently, the servicer or special servicer's own liability to the lenders, servicers or special servicers will need to bear in mind that the objective is ultimately to ensure that recovery on the loan is enhanced "on a present value basis". Therefore, for example, strategies that seek to enhance value prior to a disposal will need to pass the test of whether the ultimate recovery will in fact be increased by taking into account, among other things, the investment involved, the period that will need to lapse before the property is disposed and the quantum of projected disposal proceeds which will be received.[29] It is common that in such making such determinations, the special servicer will wish to hedge their exposure to the lenders by engaging third party professional advisors to provide their written advice supporting the ultimate course of action adopted.

### 15.7.3. *Special servicing transfer events*

Whether specified in the intercreditor agreement or in the servicing agreement, the servicing transfer events will provide a list of events that, upon their occurrence, will result in a transfer of the loan or whole loan (as the case may be as discussed above) from primary to special servicing. From a lender's perspective, the administration of the loan will become more active upon such transfer, as the special servicer considers and implements strategies, in accordance with the servicing standard, to recoup and maximise recoveries for the benefit of the lenders taking into account the relevant subordination between senior and junior lenders. Given that such transfer will result in the lenders, if the whole loan is being serviced, or the senior lender, if only the senior loan is being serviced and the junior lenders are not responsible for payment of servicing fees, incurring additional expense as a result of the fees chargeable by the special servicer, lenders will not wish for the servicing transfer to occur too quickly. As previously discussed in this Chapter and Ch.5, this has resulted in primary servicers having been asked to take on a more active role that originally contemplated. However, if performance of the loan is seriously jeopardised or hindered, the lenders may have few alternatives than to accept its transfer to special servicing.

As set out in Ch.7, typically, the list of events that will result in a transfer of the loan to special servicing will, at the minimum, include a payment default either at maturity or, during the term of the loan, which is continuing for a specified period of time. Furthermore, any insolvency

---

[29] See Ch.5.

events affecting the borrower or an obligor under the loan will also result in a transfer. The list may go on to include certain additional events which are deemed by the lenders to be material defaults, which may include a financial covenant default and/or other items as may be agreed by the relevant lenders and servicers. Given the considerations noted above, with respect to lender reluctance to incur additional fees that would be stripped from funds available to be distributed to them and possibly accelerating losses upon the commencement of a disposal process, lenders will wish to avoid including hairline triggers that may cause a transfer of servicing or will prefer to have a say in deciding whether such event should result in a transfer. Regardless, any servicing transfer will not occur during the duration of any junior lender cure period. A sample servicing transfer event definition is provided in para.7.2.8.

### 15.7.4. *Immediate action and servicing override*

As noted in the above discussion of amendments and enforcement, the servicer and special servicer will typically be authorised to take immediate action, if it considers that such action is necessary and consistent with the servicing standard. The authority to take such immediate action will mean that the servicer and special servicer will either be able to proceed with a course of action, without having to wait for the relevant lender to provide a required consent, or, will be able to reduce any periods in which such lender is to respond. Should the servicer or special servicer take such immediate action, the servicer or special will, following the taking of the required action, be required to notify the relevant lender of the action, and provide it with all reasonably requested information and must take due account of any advice or representations made by such lender.

In addition, in transactions where the whole loan is being serviced by a sole servicer and special servicer, the relevant servicer will be instructed to disregard any instructions received from a lender that conflicts with the servicing standard, irrespective of whether such lender is a controlling party under the loan. There is a lesser likelihood that such a provision is included in transactions, where the subordinated loans are not being serviced by the same servicer. However, from a CMBS rating agency perspective, there is an expectation that even in situations where the relevant junior lender is a controlling party, the relevant servicer will have sufficient authority to act in the best interests of both creditors.

## 15.8. 2012 Developments

### 15.8.1. *US Foreign Account Tax Compliance Act (FATCA)*

The US Foreign Account Tax Compliance Act (FATCA) enacted as part of the Hiring Incentives to Restore Employment Act (HIRE) of 2010,[30] amends certain provisions of the Internal Revenue Code of 1986. Most relevant to this discussion is the imposition of a 30 per cent withholding on certain US source payments if such payments, are made to non-participating or non compliant foreign financial institutions (FFIs) that have not entered into a voluntary agreement, to provide information on its US account holders to US Internal Revenue Service.

Whilst the Treasury Regulations implementing FATCA have yet to be issued in final form, if adopted in their proposed form, at the time of writing, US source payments made to non-compliant FFIs would be subject to a 30 per cent withholding. This also applies to FFIs that are affiliated with entities that have US assets. Therefore, if a borrower with US assets or affiliated with an entity that holds US assets, makes a payment to an FFI loan agent with, or affiliated with an entity that holds, US assets, such FFI loan agent will need to procure compliance with the voluntary FATCA regime and disclose the requested information on the ultimate beneficiaries of the loan payments. If such FFI loan agent is not compliant, the borrower would be required to deduct the 30 per cent withholding. Further, if such ultimate beneficiaries (i.e. lenders) are non-compliant FFIs, the FFI loan agent may be required to withhold on distributions made to the lenders. Such withholding obligations would apply to loans entered into (or significantly modified) from January 1, 2013 and the withholding obligations would commence (in respect of interest and fee payments) from January 1, 2014 and (in respect of principal payments) January 1, 2015.

It should be noted that FATCA has been drafted in such a way that it will apply even in circumstances where the US connection is very remote. As an illustration, this may also affect payments made by hedge counterparties where such hedge counterparty is an FFI, with or affiliated with, an entity that holds US assets. If such hedging payments are to be made to a non-compliant FFI, such hedging payments would be subject to the 30 per cent withholding.

### 15.8.2. *CRD*

The implications of art.122a of Directive 2006/48/EC has been discussed elsewhere in this book in the context of its impact on CMBS.[31] However, its impact on AB intercreditor agreements should also be considered, as it may

---

[30] Pub.L. 111–147.
[31] See Ch.16.

fall within the definition of "securitisation" as set out in the directive. For these purposes, the term "securitisation" is defined as:

> "a transaction or scheme, whereby the credit risk associated with an exposure or pool of exposures is tranched, having the following characteristics:
>
> (a)   payments in the transaction or scheme are dependent upon the performance of the exposure or pool of exposures; and
> (b)   the subordination of tranches determines the distribution of losses during the ongoing life of the transaction or scheme."

Whilst market participants and organisations, such as the CRE Finance Council Europe (CREFC) have, in 2012, sought clarifications that the above definition would not capture typical AB loan intercreditor agreements, regulators have not committed to excluding the same from the application of art.122a and have taken the view that the economic substance of the transaction should be analysed to determine whether it is a securitisation.

Accordingly, there is, at the time of writing, concern in the CRE industry that the art.122a "skin the game" and risk-weighting requirements would apply to the tranching of loans under traditional AB intercreditor agreements. In addition, if an AB intercreditor arrangement is a securitisation, the securitisation of the A loan would result in a re-securitisation with the corresponding punitive capital treatment set out in Directive 2010/76/EU.

## 15.9.   Negotiating Intercreditors

Having discussed the technical aspects of intercreditor agreements above and how, in particular, junior lenders might approach the negotiation of these documents and what such parties try to achieve through these discussions, will now be discussed. What follows is not meant to give an exhaustive view on how to negotiate the finer details of the above, but more to give a framework to the practitioner.

Typically, the vast majority of what is documented in an intercreditor agreement will only come into play when a transaction starts going wrong and there are issues relating to the borrower's performance of its obligations. When the deal is performing, a lender will usually only be concerned about when and in what amount it will get paid and accordingly there is no great need to look beyond what is expressed in the payment waterfall. However, the vast majority of what is contained in a typical intercreditor agreement will deal with theoretical outcomes, once things start to go wrong. It is therefore paramount to have a clear idea of what parties are trying to achieve in terms of rights at the outset of the negotiation. This will depend on the asset type, the leverage and also on the other parties involved in the negotiation and the way parties anticipate they might react in a default situation.

Taking the sections above in order, the following is a non-exhaustive list of commercial issues worth consideration for each category.

### 15.9.1. Waterfall

In an intercreditor, the key thing to consider, aside from the ordering of payment, are the events that can cause this ordering to change. Typically these are linked to events of default, but the precise parameters are often up for discussion. For instance, as a mezzanine lender, one should always push to restrict the events that can cut off such lender's cashflow to certain limited events of default. On the other hand, if a senior lender, the converse applies. Other points to note are where the hedging payments rank. This will depend on the relative negotiating power of the hedge provider. The particular payments to consider are hedging breakage costs, as these are the most volatile as exemplified by the period 2008 to 2012.

### 15.9.2. Hedging

The main argument is typically whether the swap should rank senior or *pari-passu* with the senior lender. It is widely accepted that the swap would rank senior, but one would expect this might change given the issues caused by long dated super senior swaps in the structures being worked out at the time of writing.[32] The other points of discussion, are usually where termination payments rank, when the swap counterparty itself defaults. From a junior lender perspective, there is usually no real position to take here, unless it is to use it as a giveaway point for something else.

### 15.9.3. Servicing

This is very much transaction specific and the main discussions are typically around the level of fees. If the CMBS market is ever properly resurrected to pre-2007 levels, one would anticipate a lot of discussion around the powers of servicers, as discussed in Chs 4 and 7. There has been a lot of difficulty caused by the lack of clear guidelines for servicers, in particular, at how servicers look after the interests of different lenders with different priority rankings. At the time of writing, the agency role contemplated in most modern intercreditors provide for as little discretion as possible, as this usually completely controlled by the majority (senior) lenders.

---

[32] See further Ch.8.

### 15.9.4. Entrenched rights

The basic principle is that all classes of lender are going into a transaction on a set of pre-agreed terms and these terms should not be varied on an ongoing basis, given that this changes the credit profile for the other parties to the transaction. Senior lenders have attempted to modify these clauses, in order to have the discretion to vary the term of their senior loan. From a junior lender perspective, the only power a typical junior lender can accept to give to a senior lender, in these situations, is limited to extensions and or certain waivers, e.g. senior lenders may be permitted to be more lenient if they so decide without junior lender consent. A junior lender should not accept any rights for a senior lender to make their loan more onerous for the borrower, without junior lender consent as that takes the parties closer to a senior default with the usual anticipated consequences.

### 15.9.5. Cure rights/purchase options

These are key rights in the context of a default as they allow the junior lender to keep the loan alive and avoid being "cut off/out" by the senior lender if they believe that there is value left in the asset for the junior loan. The key is to ensure that there are sufficient cure rights available and to distinguish between junior lender cure rights from those afforded to the borrower under the underlying loan documents, if at all possible. This will allow junior lenders more time to fix a problem. If these cure rights are deficient, it may become necessary for junior lenders to buy out the senior loan. This is usually done by auctioning a purchase option. This option is usually linked to a default. In this regard, from a junior lender perspective, the key point is to make sure any prepayment or exit fees are waived in the case of the purchase option being exercised.

### 15.9.6. Security package and enforcement

This is the most important part of the intercreditor agreement, as this will govern how recoveries are made and who can control that process. In the senior-centric market that exists at the time of writing, it appears to be widely accepted, that the senior lender has unfettered rights to enforce on their security package, which principally in senior/mezzanine loan structures, will usually include a first ranking mortgage and first ranking share pledge on the asset holding company.[33] The key from a junior lender perspective is therefore to seek, at the time of the structuring of the transaction, a senior share pledge at a company higher up in the structure, with the ability to enforce on that share pledge, without needing the consent of the senior lender and without triggering a change of control event for the senior loan. The ability to enforce can be achieved by setting covenants on the junior loan to be more sensitive than the senior loan

---

[33] See Ch.14.

covenants, such that a junior loan default is triggered before a senior loan default. It is also key to make sure that the senior loan does not cross default with the junior loan for this mechanic to work properly. The last thing to avoid are senior lender attempts to tie obligations to cure senior events of default to the enforcement of this separate share pledge.

If all the above points are achieved, junior lender should have structured a position where they can step into the equity with minimal disturbance to the senior financing in place, which is a precious commodity in today's senior debt-constrained marketplace.

## 15.10. Conclusion

As seen from the above and the previous Chapter, there are numerous issues that parties to an intercreditor agreement will need to consider when negotiating their intercreditor. As a result of legislative and regulatory initiatives post 2009, introduced in the wake of the financial crisis, these issues have multiplied to such a point, that some industry commentators have remarked that the AB intercreditor is at the time of writing effectively "dead". Whilst there remains significant uncertainty as to how some of these reforms will be interpreted in practice (namely, whether an AB intercreditor will be commonly considered to be a "securitisation", as discussed above), many market participants continue to utilise the technology of an AB intercreditor to document the interaction between senior and junior lenders in respect of whole loans. Furthermore, intercreditors structured on the well established principles described above, continue to be one of the most heavily negotiated documents between CRE senior and mezzanine lenders, lending to the same borrower or borrower group. The reports of its death appear "greatly exaggerated".

# Chapter 16

# European CMBS and Regulatory Reform

Stephen H. Moller,

Partner, K&L Gates LLP

## 16.1.   Introduction

Our financial markets are currently in the most extensive period of financial regulatory reform in living memory. The two central and interrelated objectives of the global reform agenda are the strengthening of the world's financial institutions and the extension of regulatory oversight. Very little of the reform is directed solely at CMBS or the wider commercial real estate (CRE) finance markets. However, the consequences of the changes for such markets are profound.

This Chapter will examine the development of the existing framework for bank capital adequacy and its reform in the immediate aftermath of the financial crisis and the implementation of Basel III. This Chapter will then consider the effects of Solvency II on insurance companies (where proposals are, as at the time of writing, still under development, but show every sign of being even tougher in their treatment of CMBS than Basel III). Other proposals which will impact the market will also be examined, these include: "slotting" in relation to CRE loans under the Financial Services Authority (FSA)'s Prudential Sourcebook for Banks, Building Societies and Investment Firms (BIPRU), the reform of the structure of the UK banking industry following the *Vickers* Report and the recent *White Paper on Banking Reform*, the mandatory clearing of certain types of OTC derivatives under the European Markets and Infrastructure Regulation and the potential regulation of the shadow banking sector. The other main aspect of financial regulatory reform of relevance to the European CRE and CMBS markets, the regulation of rating agencies, is dealt with in Ch.11.

The main theme which emerges is that capital adequacy reform is likely to severely restrict the ability of banks and insurance companies to provide credit to the CRE market. In the case of banks, this comes as a result of the need to increase their overall level of capital and the imposition of heavier risk-weights in relation to many types of asset and off-balance sheet exposures. The relative cost of CMBS as against other CRE finance investments will also increase for banks and insurance companies.

## 16.2. Introduction to bank regulatory capital and the Basel Accord

The global framework for bank capital adequacy is overseen by The Basel Committee on Banking Supervision (the Basel Committee). The Basel Committee was set up in 1974 in the wake of the secondary banking crisis and is composed of representatives of the central banks and banking supervisory authorities of the world's largest economies.[1]

In 1988, the Basel Committee published the first version of the Basel Accord (Basel I) which was universally adopted by the world's leading economies. In the European Union, the implementing measure for the Basel Accord is now the Capital Requirements Directive (CRD)[2] supplemented by rules (such as BIPRU in the United Kingdom) made by national regulators.

Basel I established a quantitative test of capital adequacy: the capital ratio which is the ratio of a bank's capital divided by the aggregate of its risk-weighed assets and off-balance sheet exposures. The minimum capital ratio required under the international rules was (and remains) 8 per cent, although national regulators are free to set a higher ratio either generally or for particular institutions.

Under Basel I, capital consisted of core (Tier 1) capital (comprising common equity and disclosed reserves), supplementary (Tier 2) capital (comprising undisclosed reserves and revaluation reserves), general provisions and loss reserves, hybrid capital instruments (for example perpetual preference shares and perpetual debt) and subordinated debt with a minimum maturity of five years. Banks were also required to make certain deductions in arriving at their capital base, for example, for goodwill and also for any investment which the bank had in a subsidiary which carried on a banking business, but which was not consolidated for regulatory purposes by its national regulator.

On the asset side of the equation, Basel I distinguished between financial instruments held for trading purposes (trading book assets) and those intended to be held to maturity (banking book assets). Trading book assets were to be valued on the basis of current market prices. Banking book assets were risk-weighted according to the nature of the obligor. For example, a loan to a central government or central bank and denominated in its own currency (or, in the case of an OECD country, any currency) would carry a risk weight of 0 per cent. Under Basel I, a loan to a private sector corporate

---

[1]  Basel Committee on Banking Supervision: History of the Basel Committee and its Membership (August 2009).

[2]  The Capital Requirements Directive ("CRD") which was adopted in June 2006 and took effect from January 2007 was introduced to implement Basel II. The CRD replaced two directives: Directive 93/6/EEC on the capital adequacy of investments firms and credit institutions which was recast as Directive 2006/48/EC and Directive 2000/12/EC known as the Banking Consolidation Directive which was recast as Directive 2006/49/EC.

entity would attract a risk weighting of 100 per cent. In other words, the minimum capital requirement for a loan of £100 to an OECD government would be zero, whereas the capital requirement for a loan of the same size to a private sector corporate entity would be £8.

Residential mortgage loans attracted a risk-weighting of 50 per cent. In contrast, loans secured on CRE were treated in the same way as other private sector corporate debt and risk-weighed at 100 per cent. In other words, the additional security value of CRE did not result in a reduced capital charge.

Off-balance sheet exposures were first weighted by a credit conversion factor according to the perceived prospect of the commitment being called upon. A direct credit substitute for a loan such as a general guarantee of indebtedness would carry a credit conversion factor of 100 per cent, whereas contingent items such as performance bonds and liquidity facilities would carry a lower credit conversion factor.

## 16.3. Basel II

*Shortcoming of Basel I*

Basel I had unprecedented success in introducing a global standard for bank capital adequacy. Nevertheless, as time went on the shortcomings of its relatively simple methodology became apparent. Basel I differentiated between different types of obligors in the risk weights that it imposed, but it did not differentiate between obligors of differing credit qualities within those categories. This created a perverse incentive for banks to make riskier loans, because the capital cost of making a high margin loan to a corporate borrower of poor credit quality was the same as the capital cost of making a low margin loan to a corporate borrower of high credit quality. Basel II, which was initially published in June 2004, aimed to address this by introducing two alternative ways of risk-weighting exposures to borrowers according to their perceived credit quality.

*Basel I* *Reliance on ratings agencies*

The first method, the "standardised approach", relied upon credit ratings issued by external credit ratings agencies. For example, a claim on a AAA rated corporate would be risk weighted at 20 per cent (rather than 100 per cent as had been the case under Basel I); on the other hand, a claim on a corporate rated below BB- would be rated at 150 per cent. The standardised approach also risk-weighted securitisation exposures (which would include CMBS) on the basis of an external credit rating assessment, although with more onerous capital requirements at the lower end of the credit spectrum than applied for corporate debt. A securitisation exposure which was rated AAA attracted a 20 per cent risk weighting (the same as an equivalently rated corporate obligation), but at BB- level, the risk weighting for a securitisation exposure was 350 per cent (rather than the 150 per cent figure which applied to corporate debt). Securitisation exposures which were rated at B+ or below (or which were unrated) were deducted from capital.

*Internal Ratings*

The second method introduced by Basel II, the internal ratings based (IRB) approach, was designed to be used by the larger and more internationally active banks. Subject to obtaining their regulators permission, those banks would be able to use their own credit risk models to determine rating equivalents for borrowers which they could then use to determine regulatory capital risk-weights. The advantage of the IRB approach was that it allowed further granularity in assigning risk-weights and also allowed banks to take into account not only the probability of borrower default, but also the potential loss given default in assigning a regulatory risk-weighting.

Basel II also introduced a number of refinements in relation to securitisations which had been adopted by certain national supervisors, for example, dealing with the terms on which a call option could be included without attracting a further capital requirement, explicitly recognising synthetic securitisation and providing for liquidity facilities to have a credit conversion factor of 20 per cent (or 50 per cent if they had a duration of more than one year).

Real estate lending benefited from reduced risk weights under Basel II. Under the standardised approach, subject to certain conditions, the risk-weight attached to residential mortgages was reduced to 35 per cent and, while the standardised approach retained a 100 per cent risk weighting for CRE loans,[3] it was possible to achieve a significantly lower risk-weighting under the IRB approach for both residential and commercial mortgages.[4]

Although the Basel II framework rested on the so-called "three pillars" (in addition to the minimum capital requirements determined by the capital ratio, the other two pillars being the supervisory review process and market discipline), the capital ratio remained the sole quantitative test under Basel II.

---

[3] The Basel Committee noted in the Basel II framework document, with a certain degree of prescience, that it would not be appropriate to risk weight commercial mortgages under the standardised approach at less than 100 per cent "in view of the experience in numerous countries that commercial property lending has been a recurring cause of troubled assets in the banking industry over the past few decades". However, this of course did not prevent particular commercial real estate lending transactions from being risk weighted at less than 100 per cent by banks using the IRB approach.

[4] *The Current Financial Crisis: Causes and Policy Issues* published by the OECD in 2008 (at p.6) reports that banks using the internal ratings approach expected the capital weight on residential mortgages to fall from 50% under Basel I to between 15 and 20% under Basel II. Direct comparisons of this type are more difficult for commercial mortgage transactions owing to a greater variance in transaction type.

## 16.4.  The financial crisis

The financial crisis which started in 2007 and intensified in 2008 exposed a number of shortcomings in global financial regulation and also led to specific criticism of the role which securitisation and structured finance had played in the run up to the crisis.

First and foremost, the level of intervention from central banks, regulators and governments which proved necessary seemed in itself to show that the extent and quality of capital held by banks had been inadequate. According to one estimate, at the height of the financial crisis, the US Federal Government provided $6 trillion of assistance to major financial institutions and EU governments provided a further $4 trillion of assistance.[5] A number of special programs had to be introduced to provide emergency credit and liquidity to financial institutions (for example, the Troubled Asset Relief Programme (TARP) and the Term Asset-Backed Securities Loan Facility (TALF) in the United States and the Credit Guarantee Scheme, Asset Protection Scheme and Special Liquidity Scheme in the United Kingdom). The Federal Reserve, Bank of England and European Central Bank were forced to relax rules on eligible collateral requirements for central bank funding and liquidity. In addition, of course, a number of well known financial institutions became insolvent or required government recapitalisation.

However, strengthening the capital ratios of banks was not in itself enough. Lehman's capital ratio had been relatively healthy and had not provided advance warning of the bank's vulnerabilities caused by insufficient liquidity and too much leverage. Northern Rock had also been given the opportunity to leverage up by the low risk-weights attributed to its assets under Basel II: the £113 billion of assets on its balance sheet were risk-weighted at a mere £19 billion.

Indeed, it is arguable that the increased sophistication (and opacity) of Basel II's metrics encouraged over reliance on the capital ratio as a measure of financial robustness and therefore in itself proved dangerous. The CEO of Northern Rock, in response to a question in a UK Treasury Committee hearing, justified the decision to increase the dividend paid to shareholders immediately after the bank made its first profit warning by citing the fact that the bank had just completed its Basel II transition and had surplus capital as a result.[6]

In response to the global financial crisis, the leaders of the G20 commissioned a report by the Financial Stability Forum[7] which was

---

[5]  A.E. Wilmarth, "Reforming Financial Regulation to Address the Too-Big-To-Fail Problem".
[6]  "The current financial crisis: causes and policy issues" (OECD, 2008), p.9.
[7]  "Report of the financial stability forum on enhancing market and institutional resilience", April 7, 2008.

discussed at the G20 summit in Washington in November 2008. At the subsequent G20 summit in London in April 2009, the leaders of the G20 agreed to "establish the much greater consistency and systematic coopera- tion between countries, and the framework of internationally agreed high standards, that a global financial system requires". In particular, the G20 agreed to establish a new Financial Stability Board (FSB) with an enhanced role, to take over the functions of the Financial Stability Forum. They agreed to extend regulation and oversight to all systemically important financial institutions, instruments and markets, including hedge funds and also to credit rating agencies. They also called for new regulatory rules to prevent excessive leverage in the financial system and to build up capital buffers in periods of economic prosperity which would be available to cushion financial institutions in times of recession.

The *Turner Review* in the United Kingdom[8] reflected these concerns and made a number of other recommendations in relation to the calculation of the capital ratio itself, including that the capital requirement for assets held in the trading book be significantly increased. Turner also levelled a number of criticisms at securitisation and structured finance. The "initial proposi- tion" that the securitisation market would lead to diversification of risk and the export of risk outside the banking sector had not actually been achieved. Instead much securitised credit had been sold to other banks or repackaged in the form of CDOs and other forms of structured product and had often been used as collateral for liquidity purposes. There had been too much reliance on "sophisticated maths" and structural complexity. The high levels of leverage used by SIVs and ABCP conduits had not been included in standard measures of their sponsoring banks' leverage and yet during the crisis, as noted in Ch.1, the banks had been forced to take these vehicles and/or their assets back on to their balance sheets as a result of reputational issues and/or liquidity commitments. The use of these vehicles to achieve "maturity transformation" (i.e. the funding of long-term assets with short-term liabilities) also gave rise to risk. Turner saw certain securitisation and structured finance techniques as being pro-cyclical, for example, rating downgrade triggers and collateral haircut requirements, both of which can expose banks to the risk that they have to post more collateral in times of crisis. Securitisation transactions were also viewed as inherently more complex than other investments and often subject to greater price volatility.

Finally, there was a concern that securitisation could result in a "misalign- ment of incentives" in that an originator of an asset might not be as concerned in the credit quality or ongoing servicing of the asset, if it did not retain any ongoing economic interest in the asset. These concerns about securitisation and structured finance (including CMBS) were widely shared by regulators and policy makers and in many ways are reflected in changes made to capital adequacy rules immediately following the crisis and discussions to date about the further changes to be made in Basel III.

---

[8] "The Turner Review: a regulatory response to the global banking crisis" (FSA, March 2009).

## 16.5. "Basel 2.5", CRD 2 and CRD 3: the reaction to the financial crisis

In the aftermath of the global financial crisis, the EU introduced two amendments to the CRD known as CRD 2 and CRD 3. CRD 3 was to a large extent the implementing measure for the series of changes to the Basel II regime announced by the Basel Committee in April 2008 which became known as "Basel 2.5".

### 16.5.1. CRD 2

*skin in the game requirement* [handwritten annotation]

CRD 2[9] introduced the so-called "skin in the game requirement" by introducing art.122a of the Capital Requirements Directive (art.122a). Article 122a provides that European banks cannot invest in a securitisation unless the originator, sponsor or original lender agrees to retain a net economic interest of at least 5 per cent. The 5 per cent net economic interest test can be satisfied by the retention of at least 5 per cent of the nominal value of each tranche of securities sold to investors, or, by the retention of the first loss tranche (and, if necessary, other subordinated tranches) equal to no less than 5 per cent of the aggregate nominal value of the securitised exposures. It can also be satisfied by the retention of an originator interest of 5 per cent in a securitisation of revolving exposures or by the retention of randomly selected exposures equivalent to no less than 5 per cent of the securitisation exposures (although these two further methods are more relevant to the securitisation of residential mortgages and other consumer assets than they are to CMBS transactions).

Article 122a also requires European banks which invest in securitisations to demonstrate to their regulators that they have a "thorough understanding" of the risk characteristics of their securitisation positions and the underlying exposures and also of the relevant originator's reputation and loss experience in previous transactions. Banks are required to implement formal procedures to assess third party securitisation exposures on an ongoing basis. Material failure in this regard can result in the imposition of significant further capital charges.

Unlike Regulation RR of Dodd Frank (the legal provision in the United States which is broadly equivalent to art.122a), the requirements of art.122a fall on banks which are investors in securitisation transactions, rather than originating institutions. This, and the emphasis given to due diligence and monitoring, reflect the fact that a number of European banks had a "heavy

---

[9]    Directive 2009/11/EC.

383

exposure"[10] in US sub-prime RMBS and other third party securitisation transactions which were downgraded during the financial crisis.

Article 122a applies to all new transactions issued after January 1, 2011 (and will be extended to cover all transactions whenever issued with effect from December 31, 2014). Although issuance in the European CMBS market since January 1, 2011 has been limited, at least one recent transaction has included a retention undertaking under which the originator will agree to hold 5 per cent of the securitisation notes.[11]

*← originator holding % of securities*

CRD 2 also made a number of other changes to the CRD including provisions designed to promote cross-border co-operation between banking supervisors, clarification of rules in relation to credit risk mitigation, additional eligibility criteria for hybrid instruments to count as Tier 1 Capital and also specific requirements in relation to the policies and procedures of European banks in relation to liquidity risk management.

### 16.5.2. CRD 3

CRD 3 was published in its final form on December 14, 2010.[12] It increased the capital requirement rules for "re-securitisations" (in other words securitisations in relation to which at least one of the underlying exposures is itself a securitisation as defined under CRD). The definition of a "securitisation" for the purposes of CRD can potentially catch financing transactions which the market would not categorise as securitisations, if the transactions involve an element of subordination between senior and junior debt and involve exposure to a pool of assets.[13] Nevertheless, in most circumstances, conventional CRE financings will not fall into the definition of "securitisation" even if they involve a senior/junior financing structure. It follows that a CMBS transaction which repackages CRE loans will not, in normal circumstances, constitute a re-securitisation.

The rules introduced by CRD 3 in relation to re-securitisations will, however, be relevant to other CRE based capital markets transactions such

---

[10] "Economic crisis in Europe: causes, consequences and responses", the European Commission's Economic and Financial Affairs Directorate's analysis of the financial crisis, cites investment by European banks in subprime mortgages as an initial cause of the financial crisis.

[11] Deco 2011-CSPK £302,342,500 Commercial Mortgage-Backed Floating Rate Notes due 2021 (as disclosed in the Prospectus).

[12] Directive 2010/76/EU.

[13] For the purposes of CRD, a "securitisation" is a "transaction or scheme, whereby the credit risk associated with an exposure or pool of exposures is tranched, having the following characteristics: (a) payments in the transaction or scheme are dependent upon the performance of the exposure or pool of exposures and (b) the subordination of tranches determines the distribution of losses during the ongoing life of the transaction or scheme". See further Ch.15.

as CRE CDOs.[14] They are also relevant to the extent that they impact other capital markets refinancings of CMBS transactions (CMBS transactions clearly are "securitisations" even if they are not themselves "re-securitisations") or credit derivative transactions which reference CMBS transactions. The incremental capital requirements for re-securitisations are onerous, for example, at the AAA level, a securitisation exposure under the standardised approach would carry a risk weighting of 20 per cent whereas a re-securitisation position with the same rating would attract a 40 per cent charge.

In relation to the trading book, CRD 3 equalised the (previously lower) capital charges for securitisations in the trading book with those in the banking book. A third change of specific relevance to the CMBS and other securitisation transactions was the extension of the disclosure requirements for securitisation risks, to cover assets held in the trading book as well as those held in the banking book. The nature of the disclosure was widened to include the bank's objectives in relation to the securitisation activity, the nature of the risks associated with its securitisation positions (including liquidity risks) and the process by which the bank intended to monitor changes in credit and market risk associated with its securitisation exposures.

## 16.6. Basel III ⟷ proposals; not yet passed

*What's the most recent status?*

The Basel Committee published its paper "Basel III: A global regulatory framework for more resilient banks and banking systems" (Basel III) in December 2010 (revised in June 2011). This document and the Basel Committee's related paper on liquidity,[15] contain a series of proposals for the further strengthening of the bank regulatory system following on from Basel 2.5.

Basel III contains various measures designed to increase the quality of capital held by banks. The definition of "common equity" which forms the core of Tier I capital will be tightened up and generally the ability of credit institutions to include capital which is not common equity within their Tier 1 capital will be restricted. Tier 2 capital will no longer be split between Upper Tier 2 and Lower Tier 2 capital. For any instrument issued on or after January 2013 to be included within either Tier 1 or Tier 2 capital, it must be capable of being converted into common shares (or written off) if the issuing credit institution finds itself in financial difficulties.

---

[14] CRE CDOs did not become an established asset class in Europe in the way in which they did in the United States. However, for an example of a European CRE CDO, see Anthracite Euro CRE CDO 2006 Plc.

[15] "Basel III: International framework for liquidity risk measurement, standards and monitoring" (December 2010).

The amount of capital which banks are required to hold will increase dramatically. While the minimum capital ratio will stay at 8 per cent, the minimum requirement for common equity will rise from 2 per cent to 4.5 per cent and the minimum requirement for Tier 1 capital as a whole will rise from 4 per cent to 6 per cent. A new "capital conservation buffer" will be introduced, which will limit the ability of banks to pay dividends and make other distributions if their common equity falls below a certain percentage of their risk weighted assets. For example, a bank which only just meets the common equity required ratio of 4.5 per cent will not be able to make any distributions at all, a bank which has a common equity ratio of 6 per cent will be required to retain 60 per cent of its earnings and only banks which have a common equity ratio of 7 per cent or better will be entitled to make distributions without any restriction.

Basel III also proposes a new "contracyclical capital buffer" which is designed to ensure that banks build up their capital reserves in good times, to cover potential losses in a downturn. National authorities would have the right to require banks to build up an additional buffer of up to 2.5 per cent of risk weighted assets (in the form of common equity) in times of excessive credit growth. In practice, the contracyclical capital buffer would be an add-on to the capital conservation buffer. For example, a credit institution subject to the maximum contracyclical capital buffer would have to have a common equity ratio of 9.5 per cent (i.e. 7 per cent plus an additional 2.5 per cent) before it was able to pay dividends and make other distributions without restriction.

Following recommendations made by FSB, Basel III also provides that Globally Systemically Important Financial Institutions (G-SIFIs) would be required to maintain additional amounts of common equity on top of the amounts required by the capital conservation buffer and the contracyclical conservation buffer of between 1 per cent and 3.5 per cent.[16] The methodology for determining whether banks fall in to the G-SIFI category and the additional capital conservation buffer which should apply to them have been developed further in subsequent rules published by the Basel Committee.[17] The factors to be taken into account in deciding whether banks are systemically important will include their level of cross-border activity, their interconnectedness with other credit institutions, the complexity of their business, the lack or otherwise of readily available substitute institutions or infrastructure to take over the services they provide and their size.

A new leverage ratio will be introduced which will test the size of a bank's Tier 1 capital against the aggregate of its non-risk weighted assets and its off-balance sheet exposures. Unlike the capital ratio, the new leverage ratio

---

[16] "Global systemically important banks: assessment methodology and the additional loss absorbency requirement rules text" (BCBS207, November 2011).

[17] "Global systemically important banks: assessment methodology and the additional loss absorbency requirement rules text" (BCBS207, November 2011).

will focus only on Tier 1 capital and will not take into account risk-weighting or credit mitigation techniques (which can be used to reduce or eliminate the capital charge associated with an asset for the purposes of the capital ratio). The leverage ratio is intended to restrain banks from borrowing excessively to build up large portfolios of assets. The leverage ratio will initially be set at 3 per cent during an observation period.

Moreover, two new liquidity tests will be introduced. The liquidity coverage ratio will require banks to hold sufficient liquid assets which are unencumbered and have a high credit quality to meet net cash outgoings during a 30-day stress scenario. The net stable funding ratio measures the amount of stable funding which is deemed to be available to a credit institution (i.e. sources of debt and equity funding which are sufficiently reliable to be available to a bank during a one year stress scenario) against a stable funding requirement which takes into account, amongst other things, the liquidity risk associated with the bank's assets and off- balance sheet exposures.

Basel III will require banks to make further disclosure in relation to their capital structure, including a full explanation of the calculation of their various regulatory capital ratios and a full reconciliation of all regulatory capital items referred to in their audited financial statements.

Capital requirements for derivatives, repos and security finance transactions will also be increased. The "credit valuation adjustment" will require banks to hold capital to cover the risk of mark to market losses (in other words, risk arising from deterioration in a counterparty's credit-worthiness as opposed to the risk associated with a potential default of the counterparty). An additional 25 per cent capital charge will be applied to all exposures to very large financial institutions and also to unregulated financial firms. Exposures to derivatives counterparties will be made on the basis of stressed inputs. Generally, the capital cost of uncleared OTC derivative transactions relative to transactions which are cleared with a central clearing counterparty will be increased. This appears to be a negative development for the CRE finance sector as interest rate transactions entered into in connection with CRE finance transaction are often bespoke and therefore will not necessarily be capable of being cleared through a central clearing counterparty.

Another theme is a proposed reduction in the importance of rating agencies in assessing regulatory capital. Basel II introduced the use of external ratings for risk-weighting assets under the standardised approach. Under Basel III, banks will have to carry out their own independent assessment rather than simply relying on external ratings. Basel III also tightens the criteria for assessing whether the ratings of a particular credit rating agency are eligible to be relied upon for capital adequacy purposes.

As might be expected for such a wide ranging and fundamental programme of change, the timetable for implementing Basel III extends over of a significant period of time. The changes in relation to the quality of capital will begin to be phased in from the start of 2013 in a 10-year timetable. The leverage ratio will be required to be disclosed by banks from 2015 and is intended to be fully implemented in 2018. The capital conservation buffer and the contracyclical capital buffer will be phased in between 2016 and 2018.

## 16.7.　CRD 4

CRD 4's main function will be to implement the changes to the capital adequacy regime proposed by Basel III including in relation to the quality of capital, the capital conservation buffer and the contracyclical capital buffer, increased requirements for common equity and Tier 1 capital, the leverage ratio, the liquidity coverage ratio and the net stable funding ratio, counterparty credit risk and credit valuation adjustment risk.

In broad terms, CRD 4 follows Basel III closely in relation to each of these aspects, although in relation to the credit valuation adjustment risk, the current proposals contained in CRD 4 are less onerous than those contained in Basel III. CRD 4 does not deal with G-SIFIs, although further discussions with the Basel Committee and FSB are expected in this regard.

However, CRD 4 also deals with certain other proposed changes to the CRD, reducing further the ability of credit institutions to rely upon credit rating agencies and requiring the implementation of a single European rulebook (in other words dispensing with national options and interpretation in connection with capital requirements and, in particular, preventing national regulators from imposing additional requirements or higher standards than those required under general European rules – so called "gold-plating"). CRD 4 proposes European-wide rules in relation to sanctions for breaches of the capital requirements rules (both in relation to institutions and individuals). In general, the proposed sanctions are more punitive then the measures which have been typically applied to date by individual Member States of the European Union.

While the supervision of credit institutions will remain primarily a national responsibility, the European Banking Authority will have responsibility for producing guidelines and technical standards in connection with the new rules.

CRD 4 will consist of a new Directive and also a new Regulation. Under EU law, the distinction between a Directive and a Regulation is that a Directive is implemented in individual Member States through national legislation whereas a Regulation takes direct effect under national law without the need for implementing legislation. Generally, the provisions of CRD 4 which implement Basel III will be contained in the new Capital Requirements Regulation (and therefore will take direct effect).

CRD 4's final text was published in July 2012. It is expected to come into force on or before January 1, 2013 (although the implementation of its requirements will be phased in over a longer timescale as noted above in relation to Basel III).

## 16.8. Slotting

In the United Kingdom, the bank regulatory capital rules introduced by the CRD are implemented by the FSA under BIPRU. BIPRU 4.5 provides for what is known as "slotting" in relation to the specialised lending exposures of banks using the IRB approach. Many CRE lending transactions will constitute "specialised lending" for this purpose. Slotting requires the bank to assign each of its specialised lending exposures to one of five "slots" depending on the perceived credit quality of the exposure. This classification of exposures has to be carried out in accordance with specified criteria which include market conditions, financial ratios, stress analysis, cashflow predictability, asset characteristics, the strength of the sponsor or developer and the nature of the security package.[18]

The combination of the slotting category (which range from "strong" to "weak" and "default") and the remaining maturity of the exposure, dictate the risk weight to be applied to the exposure. For example, a loan falling in category 2 (good) will be assigned a risk weight of 70 per cent if it has a remaining maturity of less than 2.5 years and otherwise will be assigned a risk weight of 90 per cent. A loan in category 4 (weak) will be assigned a risk weight of 250 per cent. In June 2011, the FSA entered into a consultation process on draft proposals to amend the slotting procedure, but encountered opposition from the industry, particularly due to concerns that an exposure which was rated as "weak" in relation to one of the criteria would have be assigned to the overall "weak" category as a result. Given that one of the criteria relates to "market conditions", this gave rise to the possibility that a loan with excellent collateral and other risk characteristics could end up being categorised as weak simply due to current economic conditions.[19]

According to recent reports, the FSA is concerned that many banks which use the IRB approach but which have not adopted the slotting procedure are underestimating their eventual losses in relation to loans which have

---

[18] *FSA Handbook* (London: Sweet & Maxwell) "BIPRU 4 Annex 1 supervisory slotting criteria for specialised lending: Table 2—Supervisory rating grades for income—producing real estate exposures".

[19] "FSA pressures UK banks to reweight property loan risk" (Real Estate Capital 12/2011).

been restructured or are in standstill/forbearance. It is therefore bringing pressure on the banks to move to the slotting regime.[20]

The British Bankers' Association has expressed the view that slotting entails an unnecessarily prescriptive approach to the risk weighting of CRE exposures.[21] There is a concern that, particularly in an economically weak environment, slotting may increase the overall capital requirement in relation to CRE exposures, beyond what would otherwise be necessary and that it will reduce the amount of new CRE lending.

## 16.9. The *Vickers Report* and the White Paper on Banking Reform

The Final Report of the Independent Commission on Banking (commonly known as the *Vickers Report*) was published in September 2011. The *Vickers Report* sets out the Commission's recommendations on reforms to improve stability and competition in the UK's banking industry in the wake of the financial crisis. The principal recommendation is to structurally separate domestic retail banking from global wholesale and investment banking by moving retail operations into ring-fenced subsidiaries which would be legally, economically and operationally independent of their parent banks and other non-retail members of the group. Activities such as taking deposits and providing overdrafts to ordinary individuals and small- and medium-sized enterprises would take place within the ring-fence.

The *Vickers Report* also recommends that large UK retail banks should have equity capital of at least 10 per cent of risk-weighted assets (which would be in excess of the Basel III minimum, even for G-SIFIs). The report recommends that the primary loss-absorbing capacity of the retail and other activities of large UK banking groups should be at least 17 per cent to 20 per cent. It also advocated increased competition in the UK retail banking sector,

In June 2012, the UK Government published a White Paper on banking reform,[22] which endorsed the finding of the *Vickers Report* in relation to the retail ring-fence, increased loss absorbency capacity and enhancing competition in the retail banking sector. It undertook to introduce the necessary legislation by May 2015 and to require banks to comply with the new measures no later than 2019.

---

[20] *Financial Times*, December 11, 2011, "FSA crackdown on understated property risks".
[21] British Bankers Association, October 29, 2010. Response to consultation exercise in relation to "Internal ratings-based probability of default models for income-producing real estate portfolios".
[22] HM Treasury Banking Reform White Paper: Delivering stability and supporting a sustainable economy.

It appears that banking groups making CRE loans will be able to choose whether to do so within the ring-fence or within the non-ring-fenced group. However, the structuring and execution of CMBS transactions on an agency basis would be prohibited within the ring-fence (ring-fenced banks would, however, be able to originate securitisations of their own assets). Ring-fenced banks will also be prohibited from entering into derivative transactions. This raises the prospect of ring-fenced banks entering into CRE loans, but being unable to provide hedging—a potentially complicating factor. Of further significance to the CRE market would be an implementation of the *Vickers Report's* recommendations in relation to increased capital requirements for UK banks, both within and outside the ring-fence, which would further restrict the lending capacity of banks.

## 16.10. ECB and Bank of England collateral requirements and loan level reporting

Following the onset of the global financial crisis, the importance of asset backed securities as eligible Eurosystem collateral for the ECB's monetary policy operations and the Bank of England's lending operations has increased significantly. According to the ECB, asset-backed securities rose from 11 per cent of all eligible collateral used in the Eurosystem in 2006 to 28 per cent in 2008,[23] making it the largest single asset class used as collateral. Asset-backed securities, including CMBS, remain widely used as Eurosystem collateral. In June 2012, the ECB reduced the rating eligibility requirement for CMBS transactions (and also for RMBS and SME securitisations) to BBB. CMBS with a second best credit rating of at least "A" will be subject to a valuation haircut of 16 per cent, those with a second best credit rating of at least "BBB" will be subject to a valuation haircut of 32 per cent. The valuation haircuts applied to other types of securitisation, such as RMBS and auto loan deals, will be the same at the "A" level and will be less onerous at the "BBB" level at 26 per cent.

In December 2010, the ECB decided to introduce loan-by-loan reporting requirements for asset-backed securities with the intention of increasing transparency in the securitisation market and facilitating Eurosystem operations. The reporting template for CMBS transaction was published in April 2011 and is available on the ECB's website.[24] It requires information on the individual underlying properties (including size, use and valuation) and detailed information about the terms and performance of the loan, including in relation to LTV and DSCR covenants, reserve amounts, hedging, delinquency, servicing and originator retention.

---

[23] European Central Bank "Recent developments in securitisation" February 2011.
[24] ECB loan level data template for CMBS transactions: *http://www.ecb.int/mopo/assets/loanlevel/transmission/html/index.en.html* [Accessed August 13, 2012].

In order to be eligible as collateral for the Bank of England's lending operations, CMBS transactions must be diversified and the assets must come from the United Kingdom, other states within the EEA or the United States. Transactions with include construction loans are not permitted. CMBS is only accepted as collateral for certain facilities offered by the Bank of England (such as the Discount Window Facility) and must be rated AAA on issue (and must have maintained a rating of at least A3/A-). In December 2011, the Bank of England announced changes to its eligibility requirements for CMBS including a requirement for loan level information, that transaction documentation and cashflow models should be available to investors, that the issuer provides an overview of the structure using the Bank's standard form and that investor reports are provided in a standard form.

## 16.11.   Insurance and Solvency II

Under European law, insurers and reinsurers (referred to collectively below as "insurance firms") must establish technical provisions to cover future claims from policyholders. The regime which currently governs the assessment of these technical provisions is commonly known as "Solvency I".[25] In April 2009, the European Parliament adopted the Solvency II Directive to lay the foundations for an overhaul of the current rules.[26] Under the latest EU Commission proposals, Solvency II must be implemented by insurance firms by January 1, 2014, although following recent comments from Commissioner Barnier, it appears likely that this will be pushed back to 2015.

Solvency II provides that insurance firms must meet both a Minimum Capital Requirement (MCR) and a Solvency Capital Requirement (SCR). The SCR is based on a value at risk test designed to give a 99.5 per cent confidence level that an insurance firm will be able to meet its obligations over a one year time horizon. The overriding aim of Solvency II is to ensure that an insurance firm has sufficient assets relative to anticipated claims for another insurance firm to be able to take over its assets and liabilities should that be necessary. Solvency II therefore aims to make the valuation of assets by insurance firms for regulatory purposes a more accurate reflection of their market price. This contrasts with a "buy and hold" approach to valuation which assesses the value of the return on the asset if held to maturity taking into account the possibility of default.

In assessing the value of assets for solvency purposes, insurance firms may either adopt the "standard formula" under which a regulatory charge is set

---

[25]   The current European regime for insurers and reinsurers was originally introduced by the Solvency I Directive: Directive 73/239/EEC. The current directives governing Solvency I are 2002/12/EC and 2002/13/EC.

[26]   Solvency II Directive: 2009/138/EC.

by the European Insurance and Occupational Pensions Authority (EIPOA) in relation to each asset class or an "internal model" approved by the insurance firm's national regulator under which the regulatory charge for an asset is calculated on the basis of a model which uses the insurance firm's own assumptions as to projected losses.

Valuing assets on the basis of market prices rather than the likely return if the assets are held to maturity introduces market volatility as an important component of valuation. The period in which the regulatory charges have been assessed for the purpose of the standard formula has been the most volatile in the history of the ABS market. Perhaps as a consequence, the capital charges for securitisations (which will include CMBS transactions) under the standard formula are expected to be far greater than was the case under Solvency I. The current proposals are still under discussion between the European Commission, the European Parliament and various industry bodies and there is some uncertainty about what will emerge. However, it is understood that the calculation of the charge for securitisations and for re-securitisations under the standard formula will be a function of the credit rating of the relevant asset and its duration. For example, under what are understood to be the current proposals, a AAA rated securitisation with a duration of one year would attract a 7 per cent capital charge under the standard formula, whereas a AAA securitisation with a duration of five years would attract a capital charge of 35 per cent. At an AA level, the capital charge for asset backed securities with durations of one and five years would be 16 per cent and 80 per cent respectively. In contrast, the capital charge for a covered bond with a five year duration which is rated AA would be only 5.5 per cent.

According to a recent rating agency study,[27] the capital charges for an insurance company investing at all levels in a securitisation transaction will be a multiple of the capital cost under the Basel rules which would be incurred by a bank investing in the same assets. The charges under Solvency II for a typical CMBS transaction would also be higher than those for a typical RMBS transaction due to an assumed longer maturity of the CMBS relative to the weighted average life of the RMBS transaction and also the non-granular nature of the CMBS pool. There is also a very pronounced difference between the treatment of a CMBS transaction and the capital cost of direct lending by insurance companies: we understand that the capital charge applied to a direct investment in a CRE loan of up to five years duration would be 3 per cent multiplied by the duration of the loan.[28] A further contrast is between the treatment of CMBS transactions and claims on EEA sovereign bonds which are considered to be risk free under Solvency II, notwithstanding recent experience in relation to the volatility of yields (and hence market prices) in relation to certain European sovereigns.

---

[27] "Solvency II and securitisation: significant negative impact on European market" (Fitch Ratings, April 30, 2012).
[28] "Solvency II and real estate", PWC.

Of course, the rules applying to insurance companies using an internal model will be less prescriptive. However, it seems unlikely that regulators will be convinced by proposed internal models which generate capital charges which are very different from those indicated by the standard formula. This is particularly true given that one of the criticisms levelled at Basel II in the context of bank capital adequacy was that the ability of sophisticated banks to use the IRB approach presented an opportunity for many of them to reduce the overall amount of capital which they held.

Solvency II does not currently apply to occupational pension funds, although the European Commission is currently examining the development of new solvency requirements for pension funds[29] and it would be natural to take a similar approach to asset valuation for both pension funds and insurance firms. It is also likely that Solvency II will influence the reform of the capital frameworks for insurance firms and pension funds in jurisdictions outside the European Union and so the ramifications for Solvency II are likely to extend far beyond European insurance firms.

## 16.12. The European Markets and Infrastructure Regulation

The European Markets and Infrastructure Regulation (EMIR) was adopted by the European Parliament on March 29, 2012. The Regulation provides for compulsory clearing of standardised derivatives through central clearing counterparties (CCPs). The clearing obligation only applies where both counterparties are either "financial counterparties" or parties which not financial institutions, but whose activity in the OTC derivatives market exceeds a certain threshold. While all banks and most funds will fall within the definition of "financial counterparty", SPVs established for the purpose of making CRE loans or as issuers of CMBS normally will not. To date, indications from the European Securities and Markets Authority (ESMA) are that the threshold for non-financial counterparties will be set at a relatively high level (and derivatives which can be demonstrated to have been entered into for hedging purposes are excluded from the calculation of the threshold amount anyway). It therefore looks unlikely that CRE lending special purpose vehicles and CMBS issuers will be subject to the clearing obligation. In any event, the clearing obligation only applies to standardised swap transactions (even for parties which are financial counterparties or are non-financial counterparties which exceed the threshold limit). While the technical standards for EMIR have, as at the time of writing, not yet been finalised, it seems that many derivatives which are entered into in connection with CRE financing deals will be too bespoke to be subject to the clearing requirement.

---

[29] "Solvency II: Frequently asked questions (FAQs)" European Commission, question 5.

However, EMIR still has the potential to affect the CRE and CMBS markets as it signals an increase in capital requirements for non-cleared derivatives and therefore will make hedging on a bespoke basis more expensive for end users (including borrowers of CRE loans). To the extent that CRE derivatives do have to be cleared (either because they are subject to the clearing obligation, or because the swap counterparty requires it), the parties will need to consider how to meet the collateral requirements of the clearing house through which the derivative is cleared (or of the broker through whom the clearing is carried out). Almost invariably, the collateral requirement will be in the form of cash or alternatively highly liquid and rated debt securities. Collateral requirements vary according to the mark-to-market value of the derivative for the time being and, therefore, clearing a derivative may present a problem in the context of a limited recourse CRE financing or a CMBS transactions due to a lack of access to cash or other forms of liquidity.

## 16.13. Regulation of the shadow banking sector

In October 2011, FSB published its recommendations in relation to the shadow banking sector.[30] The "shadow banking system", as the term is used in FSB's report, refers to "credit intermediation involving entities and activities outside the regular banking system", it therefore potentially extends to a very wide range of counterparties both regulated and currently unregulated including bank sponsored vehicles such as ABCPs and SIVs and other structured finance vehicles, insurance companies and pension funds, hedge funds and other funds involved in credit strategies (for example long/short credit, distressed credit, fixed income and some multi-strategy funds) and money market funds. CMBS transactions and other forms of securitisation would also fall within this definition of the shadow banking system.

The report highlighted a number of concerns in relation to the shadow banking system. First and foremost, the shadow banking system had grown significantly (one estimate cited by FSB put it at $27 trillion in 2002 and $60 trillion in 2007, a figure which it maintained in 2010). This means that a significant proportion of credit intermediation (traditionally an activity performed by banks) is now conducted outside the regulated banking framework. In aggregate, FSB estimated that the shadow banking system now constitutes between 25 to 30 per cent of the total financial system.

In FSB's view, the growth of the shadow banking system gives rise to a number of systemic risk to the effectiveness of bank regulation. These include maturity transformation, liquidity transformation (the transformation of liquid assets such as cash into less liquid assets), credit risk transfer

---

[30] Financial Stability Board Recommendations, "Shadow banking: strengthening oversight and regulation"October 27, 2012.

(in this context the transfer of credit risk back to banks from the shadow banking system through off-balance sheet exposures) and the build up of excessive leverage. FSB was particularly concerned to make sure that vehicles such as ABCPs and SIVs which are sponsored by banks (and to which banks might have either a commitment to provide liquidity or alternatively a reputational connection) are consolidated on banks' balance sheets. There was also a general concern that the shadow banking system could be used for regulatory arbitrage purposes.

As far as securitisation is concerned, FSB reiterated the need for a retention requirement (as per the revised art.122a of the CRD) and for a move towards the standardisation of securitisation products and greater transparency. FSB mandated the International Organisation of Securities Commissions to carry out further work in relation to the regulation of securitisation transactions.

More generally, FSB committed itself to enhancing the monitoring framework for the shadow banking sector and set up workstreams to examine specific issues the case for further regulatory action in five specific issues: (i) banks' interactions with the shadow banking sector, (ii) the regulatory reform of money market funds, (iii) the regulation of other shadow banking entities, (iv) securitisation and (v) the regulation of securities lending and repos. In a progress report to the G20 leaders in April 2012,[31] FSB stated that the five workstreams would report during Q2 2012.

In March 2012, the European Commission published a Green Paper on Shadow Banking which was supportive of FSB's initiative and which signalled a willingness to consider further legislative and regulatory measures in response.

Hedge funds, private equity funds, CRE funds and other forms of alternative investment funds are, of course, already subject to regulation in Europe, under the Alternative Investment Fund Managers Directive (AIFMD).[32] The AIFMD contains a carve-out for securitisation vehicles which means that special purpose issuers of CMBS transactions should not generally find themselves directly regulated by the AIFMD. However, the AIFMD will affect securitisation (including CMBS transactions) in a number of ways. Article 17 empowers the European Commission to make rules regarding the criteria for securitisations to be eligible for investment by alternative investment funds. In the first instance, these criteria are likely to similar to those adopted for banks under the revised art.122a of the CRD. The AIFMD also requires alternative investment fund managers to perform certain levels of due diligence in relation to investments made by their funds and to ensure that the liquidity profile of their investments is

---

[31] Financial Stability Board,"Strengthening the oversight and regulation of shadow banking" April 16, 2012.
[32] Directive 2011/61/EU.

consistent with their underlying obligations. It is possible that these requirements may inhibit investment by alternative investment funds in relatively complex and illiquid assets such as CMBS transactions.

## 16.14. Conclusion

The regulatory response to the financial crisis has been far reaching (and includes not only the areas referred to above in relation to CMBS, but also other important issues such as remuneration and the regulation of retail investments). It is continuing and is being conducted at great pace. It will take some time for financial institutions to adapt to the new environment. That fact, and continuing uncertainty about the final content of much of the detail of the new rules, will be an inhibiting factor in relation to financial activity for some time.

However, the broad framework is now clear. Banks will be required to maintain more capital and securitisation (including CMBS) will become relatively more expensive for both banks and insurance companies when compared to other forms of debt investment. In particular, it will be much harder for insurance firms using the Solvency II standard formula to invest in CMBS and other types of securitisation if the proposals go through in their form at the time of writing. Other changes, such as the art.122a "skin in the game" requirement, additional disclosure and due diligence requirements for securitisations, the new leverage and liquidity ratios and additional capital charges for re-securitisations, may limit the ability of banks to enter into or refinance CMBS deals. The CRE finance market will also have to deal with increased capital requirements in relation to derivatives (and, in some cases, compulsory clearing) and, in the United Kingdom, the extension of the "slotting" regime.

The extension of regulatory oversight to other market participants, such as alternative investment funds, and the likelihood of further regulation in relation to shadow banking, may also make it harder for new entrants to the market to replace funding lost from the banking and insurance sectors.[33]

On a more positive note for the CRE market, it is hoped that current efforts to standardise documentation and reporting requirements will in time lead regulators to a more nuanced view of the structured finance market which will be supportive of transactions which are relatively simple and undertaken to finance "real assets" (such as commercial and residential real estate and consumer assets). Simplification, standardisation and an alignment between the contractual terms of transactions and commercial expectations will all be important. The challenge for the CRE industry will be to convince the regulators that the financing needs of the CRE market can be met in a way that does not increase systemic risk. Far from ending

---

[33] See Ch. 2.

the innovation which has characterised the CRE and CMBS markets over the years, this will require further new thinking.

# Chapter 17

# Continental European Commercial Mortgage Loans and CMBS

Dr. Stefan Luthringshauser,

Director, Capita Asset Services GmbH

Volker Gattringer and Dr. Christian Büche,

Partners K&L Gates LLP

## 17.1. Introduction (Part I—Market, Development and Outlook)[1]

As more fully described in Ch.1, the global economic and financial market experienced severe distress and uncertainty from mid-2007 onwards. The turmoil of the financial systems, which was initially referred to as a credit crunch, soon turned into a full financial crisis. The collapse of Bear Stearns and Lehman Brothers, in March and September 2008 respectively, were just the starting point of a formerly unknown dimension of failure of the global banking system. Against this global backdrop, many European property lenders including Germany's Hypo Real Estate and the UK's Royal Bank of Scotland were rescued by their national governments. In Ireland, the Irish Government created the NAMA to buy all the Irish banks' major property loans. Iceland's two principal banks, Kaupthing and Landesbanki, were also affected and faltered.

Furthermore, as highlighted throughout this book, at the time of writing, the European economic landscape, despite some occasional signs of improvement, continues to be confronted with major challenges. The fiscal stability of certain eurozone economics is continues to be questioned over its member states' indebtedness. Many economies, for example, Portugal, Italy, Ireland, Greece and Spain (PIIGS), have been facing huge government budget deficits and political uncertainty, resulting in deteriorating credit profiles and widespread downgrades by several rating agencies. European-wide austerity measures, implemented to overcome the escalating eurozone sovereign debt crisis, continues to date to limit liquidity in the market, which in turn impacts the global financial markets in general and the

---

[1]   The views and opinions contained in this article are those of the author and do not reflect in any way the views of Capita Asset Services or K&L Gates LLP.

banking sector as well as CRE in particular. This Chapter will, in Part I, consider these issues when considering the continental European commercial mortgage loan and CMBS markets and their outlook, before offering some concluding remarks. This Chapter will then, in Part II, consider certain specific legal, regulatory environment and developments for commercial mortgage loan and CMBS in Germany.

## 17.2. Changes in European capital requirements and relating regulation

As highlighted throughout this book, CRE mortgage loans became one of the fastest growing lending classes for banks across Europe following the 1990s. European CRE lending activity peaked between 2004 and 2007, which was partly a result of the emergence and quick acceleration of CMBS. According to Morgan Stanley, in 2011, the loan books of European banks hold up to c.€2.4 trillion of CRE debt.[2] In Europe, traditional balance sheet lenders have historically been the main source of CRE financing. However, to date, European banks are increasingly struggling to access sufficient capital at adequate financing terms due to structural changes in funding conditions. Established funding sources are increasingly expensive due to rising costs for short-term unsecured funding, which are being typically raised from the bond markets.

In an attempt to improve liquidity and funding conditions, in December 2011, the ECB provided unlimited three-year loans to European banks in the form of the LTRO. In February 2012, the ECB made available further loans in the form of the LTRO II. However, at the time of writing, lending activity continues to be weak, since banks prefer to hold on to cash or are depositing it with the ECB, in order to improve their capitalisation and equity capital position as requested by impending regulations (e.g. European Banking Authority (EBA) Capital Adequacy Regulation, Basel III, Solvency II). Basel III, with a gradual phasing-in scheduled from 2013 onwards, requires banks to increase their ratio of equity capital to risk-weighted assets from 4 per cent to 7 per cent, which may increase up to 8 per cent to 10 per cent if allowing for an additional required capital cushion. Solvency II, on the other hand, obliges insurers to hold a buffer of significant equity to bridge duration gaps between assets and liabilities. Negotiations regarding the exact capital requirement for insurers are ongoing and not expected to be agreed upon before 2014/2015.[3]

---

[2] See the *Morgan Stanley Report*.
[3] Further examination of the new regulatory framework will be covered in Ch.16.

## 17.3. Loan origination activity by European banks → *substantially tightened*

While some European banks have stopped their lending activity altogether in 2012, many have started to suspend their CRE lending activity and/or ceased all non-domestic CRE financing. Examples include German Euro-hypo and French Société Générale, which started to drastically reduce their CRE activities, especially in international markets, whilst Commerzbank announced in June 2012 that it is to wind up its CRE lending business. The withdrawal from this business contributes to the ongoing decline in the availability of CRE lending in Europe from big ticket lenders. Commerz-bank's CRE portfolio will remain in the legal entity Eurohypo, one of the largest European CRE lenders. IEurohypo was renamed "Hypothekenbank Frankfurt AG" as of August 31, 2012. At the time of writing, Commerzbank indicated that those decisions are attributed to "high capital and the rising liquidity requirements under Basel III" bank regulations. Some other senior debt lenders have reduced their origination activity and tightened their terms on CRE credit facilities by only being prepared to lend up to an LTV of 55–65 per cent against core-stabilised assets let to highly rated tenants. In 2011 and 2012, large transactions by single European banks have become scarce; loan amounts are often limited to a maximum of €50 million. While the European syndication market also continues to be slow, club deals, in which lenders jointly underwrite prior to any deal closing, as opposed to syndication or participation post closing, have been undertaken instead.

## 17.4. Deleveraging activity by European banks

*↳ to raises their capital ratios.*

With limited time until the above mentioned regulations become effective, the lack of funds available to fulfil these capital requirements together with little investor appetite for fresh bank equity capital, forces European banks to raise their capital ratios through deleveraging. There are three main means available: (a) loan repayments; (b) sale of single loans or portfolios; and (c) write-downs.

### 17.4.1. Loan repayments

To date, repayments of maturing loans across Europe have been very limited due to the lack of alternative financing available. If borrowers fail to secure alternative sources of funding at economic feasible terms, repayment is not possible, unless the underlying collateral is being disposed of. While European property market fundamentals are slowly en route to recovery in terms of property rents, values and transaction volumes, market values are in many cases still significantly below the levels they were at on loan origination. On the one hand, this leaves borrowers unable to sell and repay in full, and on the other hand, poses a considerable risk for European banks to create negative equity. These together contribute to a considerable funding gap, which, as discussed in Ch.2, is referred to as the difference between the maturing outstanding debt amount and lending capital available to replace it. To some extent, this funding gap is also a value gap, in which the collateral value is significantly below the current loan amount. The considerable discrepancy between supply and demand for lending is particularly affecting secondary, tertiary and specialised assets. According to DTZ,[4] the EU funding gap figure is estimated to be in the order of €83 billion while the value gap is currently calculated at approximately €42 billion. DTZ estimates that countries with the largest overall funding gaps across all European CRE lending are the United Kingdom (€30 billion), Spain (€20 billion) and Ireland (€9 billion).[5] Unsurprisingly, an increasing share of maturing loans are defaulting as a result.

### 17.4.2.  Sale of single loans or portfolios

European banks have started to offer a significant amount of individual CRE loans or portfolios for sale, especially those with high-risk asset weights or market prices close to the outstanding loan amount. European banks tend to parcel their loans into portfolios to more effectively reduce their loan book rather than selling them individually. While some transactions were executed successfully, others failed due to too low price offerings, which as a result would have prevented the banks from realising any positive develeveraging effect. Examples for market deals include NAMA's sale of the Barclay Brothers' loans in September 2011 relating to three hotels in London (loan amount: €800 million). In addition, underlying swap contracts hedging the loan facility may also discourage the disposal of loans or assets as they may force the banks to take considerable losses on the swaps as typically these have been put in place at times of a high interest rate environment.[6]

### 17.4.3.  Write-downs

While many loans are being extended and restructured, others are being enforced and worked out resulting in the liquidation of the assets. This often requires the bank to write down considerable losses due to the currently subdued market conditions. This option, however, remains the last resort, since European banks are still reluctant to liquidate their assets below holding value. In addition, this process is often time-consuming and lenders are often faced with legal challenges due to cross-border jurisdictions.

---

[4]   See CRE Finance World Summer 2011 "Update on the European CRE Finance and CMBS Status". See further Ch.2.

[5]   See Standard & Poor's Global Credit Portal Ratings Direct, "European CMBS: The Next 100 Days", (September 28, 2011).

[6]   See further Ch.8.

## 17.5. Development of the European CMBS market

As described in Ch.1, securitisation has traditionally supplied banks with a key source of long-term funding. This refinancing instrument enables banks to increase the availability of credit, while decreasing its cost, and to improve the bank's capital position and streamline its balance sheet. Noteholders also benefit from CMBS since they gain direct risk exposure to a well-diversified portfolio of CRE loans.

With loan terms during the origination peak (2006/2007) typically ranging between five to seven years, loan maturities are also, at the time of writing, on the rise, with many borrowers struggling to refinance their facilities. Loan repayments are only very limited and according to Fitch Ratings[7], the default rate of all loans scheduled to mature by the end of 2011 increased to 22.8 per cent. The rating agency expects that more than half of all loans securitised in 2006 and 2007 in European CMBS will default when reaching maturity.

According to the rating agency Standard & Poor's,[8] the unpaid balance of European CMBS loans resulting from loans scheduled to mature between 2009 and 2011 stood at €4.7 billion. The amount of maturing unpaid debt could reach €10 billion by the end of 2012. A further concern in this regard is the upcoming large number of CMBS bond maturities from 2013 onwards, peaking in 2017. A first example for a bond maturity payment default became public in February 2012, when Opera Finance failed to repay €603 million of bonds to its investors backed by a portfolio of offices located in the Netherlands.[9]

European CMBS performances in 2012 show that loans scheduled to mature increasingly remain unpaid. On a per months basis, while February, March and May were quiet months in terms of loan maturity, January and April 2012 recorded large volumes. According to Standard & Poor's Rating Services,[10] 38 of the 51 maturing loans failed to pay on time in January, which equates to €3 billion of €3.7 billion of debt outstanding. In April 2012, a further 29 loans with a total balance of €2.6 billion were due to mature. Fitch Ratings[11] adds that for half of the loans due in April 2012, the maturity dates were extended, increasing the proportion of extended loans from 37 per cent to 40 per cent in total. This equates to some €9.5 billion in European CMBS loans outstanding due to loan extensions since the start of the financial crisis.

---

[7]   See *Property Investor Europe News*, February 13, 2012 "EMEA CMBS 4Q Maturity Default Rise to Continue" – Fitch.

[8]   See *Financial Times*, March 1, 2012 "S&P Warns on European Mortgage-backed Loans".

[9]   See Ch.3.

[10]   See Ch.3, fn 8.

[11]   See *Fitch Ratings Newsletter*, May 2012 "European CMBS Loan Maturity Bulletin".

Despite the European CMBS market being confronted with an increasing number of loans being in breach of their financial covenants, in default or in special servicing, there have been few enforcement actions to date. Fitch,[12] for example, highlighted that in H1 2012, the proportion of loans being actively worked-out decreased from 20 per cent to 18 per cent. Fitch concludes, that to date, the European CMBS market has proven to be resilient with only limited losses being realised.

Whereas a bounce back of the European CMBS market was considered possible in the short term, the ongoing economic and financial crisis, with weak property fundamentals as well as prevailing investor scepticism, are not conducive to any revival in European CMBS market activity as at the time of writing. Following regulatory changes, originating lenders are, for example, required to maintain more risk of the underlying portfolio in their own balance sheet. Furthermore, originating banks are faced with investors demanding more attractive yields to compensate for the limited liquidity available in the secondary markets.

Structural shortcomings have made CMBS increasingly unappealing for investors and lenders alike. Deficiencies of the European CMBS market have been discussed in Ch.1 and there is a general consensus that in order for the market to reopen a number of issues needs to be addressed to realign incentives for all transaction parties involved. There is a call for stricter credit terms including more conservative underwriting, lower loan leverage and lower collateral risk. Deal structures need to become less complicated and loan documentation more standardised to improve transparency. Reporting and data disclosure is another area of improvement necessary including more and better analytics, more standardised and publicly available information. Further, control and governance by the CMBS note holders is another area which requires substantial improvement. For example, the restructuring of a large CMBS securitisation with underlying CRE in continental Europe has been impeded because the English law CMBS documentation failed to specify the note holder majority required for allowing a restructuring of the CMBS notes.

In an effort to revive the European CMBS market, the CREFC has initiated the creation of a taskforce to formulate CMBS 2.0 for Europe. The efforts of the committee are more fully described in Ch.4. Moreover, as noted in the introduction to the Schedules to this book, the CREFC is actively discussing and lobbying EU-wide as well as country-specific regulations, in order to create a level playing field for all transaction parties involved.

---

[12] See *Fitch Ratings Newsletter*, May 2012 "European CMBS Loan Maturity Bulletin".

## 17.6. Alternative sources of lending

According to DTZ research during the boom years, traditional banks made up for around 75 per cent of commercial mortgage lending in Europe, while Morgan Stanley believes this proportion to be as high as 95 per cent when covered bonds issued by banks are also considered.[13] Alternative sources of financing incorporate a great diversity of lenders such as non-bank financial institutions (e.g. pension funds, insurance companies) and specialised managed debt funds. As attractive investment opportunities increasingly emerge for CRE in Europe, alternative lenders have started to enter the European financing market, however, with varying investment strategies and requirements.[14]

Non-bank financial institutions, which adopt a more conservative lending approach, for example, have started to show an interest in European CRE financing since it offers an attractive risk-return and as it enhances their diversification strategy as well as provide access to new asset classes. Unlisted funds have become the main vehicle for non-bank lenders such as insurance companies and pension funds to finance European CRE.

Insurance companies have started to show an interest in the CRE debt finance sector, which is a result of the currently favourable purchasing conditions and the potentially advantageous capital treatment under Solvency II. Insurance companies are prepared to originate loans themselves or make use of purchasing debt from the secondary markets. According to DTZ,[15] some life insurance companies have already become active in the mature European markets including, for example, AIG, Allianz, AXA, Aviva, Legal & General, MetLife, M&G and Canada Life. More players are expected to enter the field in the short to medium term.[16] The exposure to CRE, however, remains limited (less than 2 per cent of their assets). According to Cushman & Wakefield,[17] much like insurance companies, pension funds have increased their appetite for the European CRE financing market, since it offers higher relative returns than traditional fixed income products. In addition, pension funds tend to move into asset classes like CRE, when inflation rates are on the rise and bond yields low.

Managed debt funds are higher return-driven than non bank financial institutions. They are focusing on providing mezzanine or senior/stretched senior debt. By definition, mezzanine finance aims to bridge the capital gap between senior debt and equity. The associated higher risk exposure involved allows mezzanine lenders to demand higher returns on their

---

[13] See the *Morgan Stanley Report*.
[14] See further Chs 4 and 20.
[15] See DTZ Research, November 8, 2011 "DTZ Insight: Global Debt Funding Gap Europe Struggles Despite Positive Trends."
[16] See further Chs 1, 2 and 20.
[17] See "European Real Estate Lending Survey" (Cushman & Wakefield, March 2012).

lending than senior providers. According to CB Richard Ellis,[18] this type of financing is, for example, attractive to CRE investors, HNWIs (e.g. family offices represented by asset managers), institutional investors and specialised debt investment funds, which otherwise would not be able to gain access to this type of property class. CRE investments currently may offer attractive returns and investors often benefit from regulations that favour debt in contrast to direct CRE investments. Diminishing competition from traditional lenders provide an appealing route to diversify the investment exposure of mezzanine lenders.[19] Considering the currently tight lending environment, mezzanine finance often provides a feasible but expensive solution for European borrowers to hold on to their properties which otherwise could end up in workout.

## 17.7. Outlook

Many of the challenges of the financial crisis and failure to tackle them in a constructive manner are highly likely to depress the banking sector in general and the CRE market in particular even more in the short to medium term. The ongoing EU sovereign debt crisis, political and economic uncertainty and its disrupting effect on financial markets have pushed some members of the eurozone into recession. The uncertainty over the future of the euro and the solvency of Europe's banking sector are certainly also restraining market participants' confidence in the CRE market. Liquidity is expected to remain tight due to the ongoing and proposed austerity measures in the eurozone countries, since most of the fiscal and monetary options have already been used to stimulate growth. In addition, it is expected, as set out in Ch.16, that regulators will continue to increase their pressure on banks to streamline their balance sheet (providing adequate equity buffers) and to improve their internal risk models.

### 17.7.1. Loan origination activity by European banks

Most market participants expect credit facilities to become even more restrictive with financing only available for highest quality properties. Lending terms and conditions will continue to become tighter. According to Cushman & Wakefield,[20] maximum LTVs for senior debt in Western Europe have declined from 65 per cent in 2011 to 60 per cent in Spring 2012. Exceptions are prime well-located assets let to a highly rated tenant stock on long leases, which might still be financed at LTV of 65 per cent, whereas peripheral markets (Central and Eastern Europe) are faced with lower LTVs ranging between 50–55 per cent. Investors anticipate less net investment

---

[18] See "The Funding Gap: Is Mezzanine Lending the Solution?" (CB Richard Ellis, Real Estate Finance View Point, Winter 2011).
[19] See further Chs 14 and 15.
[20] See "European Real Estate Lending Survey" (Cushman & Wakefield, March 2012).

activity. However, as some top-quality assets are expected to come to the market, buyers are likely to take the opportunity to realise purchases at low interest rates.

### 17.7.2. *Deleveraging activity by European banks (loan repayments; sale of single loans or portfolios and write-downs)*

Overall, while deleveraging activity has so far been moderate, it is expected to increase considerably from 2012 onwards, since newly imposed EU banking regulation forces banks to meet equity capital requirements.

Lenders anticipate loan performance to deteriorate further in 2012 and 2013 and rating agency Moody's[21] expects the recovery not to start before 2014 and to take longer than previously assumed. With the peak of loan maturities expected throughout 2012–14, refinancing needs will be high. According to Fitch, the value of loans, which are scheduled to mature, is expected to increase from €3.8 billion in 2011 to over €10 billion in 2012 and more than €20 billion in 2013. The rating agency anticipates that the majority of existing loan facilities will be extended and restructured with the banks' joint aim of improving loan profitability while keeping the realisation of losses to a minimum.

While market participants have already been predicting an upturn in restructuring activity over the past two years, which for various reasons failed to materialise, it is expected to pick up from 2012 onwards. Despite the protracted workout process of loan portfolios, the disposal of non-core sub-performing and non-performing loans is likely to pick up in speed in the short to medium term as banks endeavour to free up capital, recover funding, improve profitability and refocus their business model. Therefore there may be more single loans, loan portfolios and CRE assets being offered for sale to the market. Some of the mortgages will need to be embarked upon more forcefully, which will increase the pressure on property values, particularly for low quality non-prime assets outside of top markets. Consequently, yield widening can be expected. With regard to prime quality properties, Fitch Ratings[22] expects that this asset class will also not be able to maintain its low yield levels due to the limited rental growth perspective. Prices achieved, which are likely to remain below previous peaks but higher than 2010 prices, will result in the painful recognition of losses. It remains to be seen if this loss will be accounted for by the lenders via write-downs, or by the current owners, via reduced asset values.

---

[21] See "European Real Estate Lending Survey" (Cushman & Wakefield, March 2012).
[22] Fitch Ratings 2012 "EMEA Structured Finance Snapshot–2012".

### 17.7.3. European CMBS Market

Due to ongoing regulatory changes, economic and political uncertainties, weak property fundamentals as well as excessive investors hurdle rates, rating agencies expect European CMBS only to be a marginal provider of CRE funding in the short to medium term. The exceptions are prime assets; there will continue to be demand for this asset type if properly structured and well underwritten, as proven.[23]

The anticipated surge in loan maturities will dominate the European CMBS market for some time. Due to the borrowers' limited refinancing options for maturing mortgages, many loans, if not restructured successfully, are bound to default and end up in special servicing.[24] Servicers will consider further extending loan facilities to avoid losses, however, according to Moody's, if the underlying cash flows from the property become insufficient for loan payments, the work-out process is highly likely to start with a forced property sale or loan foreclosures. The rating agency therefore expects that enforcement actions may accelerate from 2012 onwards. This may result in more losses being realised, particularly by junior and mezzanine bonds of CMBS transactions.

Although some investors express their interest in CMBS transactions, uncompetitive pricing in Europe apparent since 2010 makes the product unattractive, considering the risks involved. Structural issues, such as rules that require loan originators to retain a portion of their CMBS dealt with in Ch.16, refrain banks from pooling loans into new CMBS. Some of the market participants believe that a revival of the European CMBS market is only expected when banks are showing their own confidence in the transaction by investing their capital into some of the note classes at risk. According to a survey conducted by Ernst & Young,[25] EU investors have mixed views about the revival of the European CMBS market in 2012. Overall, while 43 per cent of the survey participants have a positive outlook for this type of funding, an equal number has a negative view on its return. However, looking into this analysis at country level, it becomes apparent that historically active CMBS countries, such as Germany, have a more pessimistic outlook, while less mature markets such as Poland and Russia have a more positive view on the European CMBS market coming back in 2012 and beyond.

---

[23] For further information please refer to source such as: Standard & Poor's Global Credit Portal Ratings Direct September 28, 2011, "European CMBS: The Next 100 Days; CRE Finance World Summer 2011, 'Update on the European CRE Finance and CMBS Status'".

[24] See further Chs 5, 6 and 7.

[25] See Ernst & Young 2012 "European Real Estate Assets Investment Indicator 2012, As one Door Shuts, Another Opens".

### 17.7.4. *Alternative sources of lending*

Morgan Stanley[26] estimates that the banks' deleveraging activity results in a capital shortfall of €300–600 billion out of which €200 billion could be covered by alternative sources of lending. Cushman & Wakefield adds that this funding gap is not going to be sufficiently bridged by alternative lenders in 2012.

With regard to alternative sources of lending there are a few main players expected to become active over the coming years. According to DTZ[27] and Cushman & Wakefield,[28] institutional lenders, pension funds and insurance companies are expected to increase their lending capacity in Europe, taking advantage of the prevailing funding gap due to the lack of active traditional lenders. Equity capital markets are also anticipated to increase their CRE involvement. Investors surveyed by Ernst & Young[29] envisage overall an upturn in equity finance for 2012 (42 per cent of surveyed investors), which may however only be attributable to the great volatility in that market in 2011, merely suggesting some hope for a more positive picture in the future.

Mezzanine finance providers are expected to reduce their investment exposure in European CRE lending, which is, however, mainly a result of low availability of senior and senior-stretched debt for assets with higher risk exposure.

## 17.8. Conclusion

In conclusion, there can be no doubt, as highlighted throughout this book, that there is a substantial shortfall of funding available for CRE in the EU market. The outlook for the short to medium term, particularly with an increasing number of loan maturities due in 2012 to 2014, is challenging for all market participants and will, without doubt, result in losses realised by all market participants. Some of the losses might be postponed as many primary servicers have taken the approach to extend loan facilities through restructurings rather than defaulting them at loan maturity and transferring them into special servicing for asset liquidation through workouts.[30] Overall, as summarised by Moody's in their central scenario assumptions: "refinancing prospects will remain tiered; lending will remain subdued; fire sales will be avoided, investment will focus on prime properties; prime

---

[26] See Moody's Investor Service Announcement February 9, 2012 "European CMBS: 2012 Central Scenarios".

[27] See DTZ Research, "Money Into Property Europe 2012 Forced Deleveraging Next" (April 25, 2012).

[28] See Cushman & Wakefield, "European Real Estate Lending Survey"(March 2012).

[29] See Ernst & Young 2012 "European Real Estate Assets Investment Indicator 2012, As one Door Shuts, Another Opens.

[30] See further Chs 5 and 6.

property values will remain stable while non-prime property values will fall; and CRE fundamentals will weaken."[31]

While a revival of the European CMBS market is not expected in the short term, the ongoing debate and commitment of participants of all transaction parties provides some encouragement that a more streamlined product with more standardised underwriting and documentation, lower loan leverage as well as lower collateral risk is well able to survive the current economic and financial crisis in the medium term. Efforts of legislators and regulators in 2013 and beyond, will help to find and maintain the confidence of a new investor base for the product.

Alternative sources of funding are increasingly entering the market, however, they are not expected to fully bridge the widening funding gap created by the ongoing deleveraging activity of traditional lenders. Institutional lenders, pension funds and insurance companies are expected to become an increasing supplement provider of CRE finance in 2013 and beyond.

## Part II—Legal and regulatory developments in Germany

Similar to many other jurisdictions, to some extent the focus in Germany as the largest market for CRE financings in continental Europe (hence the focus on CRE finance in Germany in this book) has shifted away from the issues arising in the course of new CRE financings or CMBS to, as noted above, the potential impact of the "wave of loan maturities" of the existing CRE financings and CMBS predicted in the years 2013 through 2017. In the absence of abundant sources for financings or refinancings, both lenders and borrowers find themselves confronted with situations where loans are about to mature, but repayment appears remote. There is no universal remedy as to which steps should be taken in order to best safeguard the respective interests. Possible options include standstill agreements, extensions, restructurings or even enforcement of security or an insolvency of the borrower.

However, there are certain developments worth noting, particularly since a number of developments have occurred in Germany, to facilitate the trading of debt and CMBS in Germany, since the advent of the financial crisis. This part of the Chapter will focus on some of these.

---

[31] See Moody's Investor Service Announcement February 9, 2012 "European CMBS: 2012 Central Scenarios".

## 17.9.  Regulatory Environment and Developments for Securitisations in Germany

Since 2007, many of the issues imposing legal risks to the transfer loans and securities have been resolved by the German courts. For instance, in 2007 the Federal Court of Justice (*Bundesgerichtshof*) ruled that the transfer of loans in a true sale transaction is not prohibited by German banking secrecy rules.[32] More recently, in 2011, the *Bundesgerichtshof* has facilitated the transfer of enforceable titles for mortgages in the event of a transfer of the mortgage.[33] Also in 2011, the ECJ held that the purchase of defaulted debt for a purchase price, below its face value, is not subject to value added taxes if the purchase price actually reflects the economic value of the defaulted debt.[34]

With the continuing financial crisis, though, it has been observed that the legislator in Germany is inclined to tighten the legal framework again. To this end, not only more stringent retention requirements for CMBS as provided for under the CRD have been introduced in Germany, but also further legislation, such as the so-called Risk Limitation Act (Risikobegren- zungsgesetz) of 2008 (Risk Limitation Act) has come into effect, that aims essentially at limiting the transfer of loans and the enforcement of security. Although most of these requirements are specifically aimed to protect consumers, commercial loans are affected nevertheless.

## 17.10.  Transfer restrictions for loans under the Risk Limitation Act (*Risikobegrenzungsgesetz*)

The Risk Limitation Act was originally aimed at protecting consumers against the sale of their loans to third parties. However, it also introduced measures affecting commercial loans in Germany, which took effect as of August 19, 2008.

The transferability of loans has been restricted by the Risk Limitation Act. While it is now possible to agree that the rights under a loan shall not be transferrable or, only to a pre-defined group of persons, borrowers pushing to restrict the transferability of their loans usually have difficulty in making their point. In fact, lenders are reluctant to agree as loans would then not be considered eligible security by the ECB. More importantly, it is no longer permitted for a lender to transfer a loan by way of assumption of contract (*Vertragsübernahme*) to another lender without first obtaining the consent of the borrower and any agreements containing a general consent of the

---

[32] FCJ (*Bundesgerichtshof*), February 27, 2007 (XI ZR 195/05, BGHZ 171), pp.180 et seq.

[33] FCJ (*Bundesgerichtshof*), June 29, 2011 (VII ZB 89/10, NJW 2011), pp.2803 et seq.

[34] ECJ, October 27, 2011 *GFKL Financial Services AG* (C-93/10, OJ C370) December 17, 2011, p.12.

borrower are considered void. This restriction will, however, not apply to a transfer of the facility agent or the security agent.

## 17.11. Increased retention requirements

In Germany, politicians felt that the retention requirements for CMBS set out in art122a of the Capital Requirements Directive 2009/111/EC were not sufficient to adequately protect financial institutions from the risks arising from CMBS. Therefore, in a single-handed attempt to increase the standard of protection, politicians pushed for and eventually succeeded in resulting in the legislator in Germany passing in December 2010, more stringent retention requirements that go beyond those applicable in most other jurisdictions of the EEA. As a result, investments into CMBS by financial institutions regulated in Germany require a minimum retention requirement of 10 per cent to be made by the originator, the sponsor or the original lender applying from January 1, 2015 rather than only 5 per cent as is common in other EU countries. It is thus not unlikely that institutions which are subject to the capital requirements applicable in Germany will face severe competitive disadvantages and critics advocate even a ban on such investments, as they would factually not be allowed to invest into CMBS originated in other countries of the EEA or the US. This becomes most obvious in respect of high quality mortgages which are fully exempt from any retention requirements under the Dodd Frank Wall Street Reform and Consumer Protection Act.[35]

In fact, the retention requirements in effect at the time of writing are a result of ongoing controversial discussions. While originally the German government wished to implement art.122a of the Capital Requirements Directive by requiring institutions to retain 5 per cent with a step-up to 10 per cent coming into effect in 2013, the majority of the parliamentary parties, particularly the left-wing opposition, favoured even more stringent retention requirements rocketing from up to 15 per cent to 20 per cent. Despite expert opinions to the contrary, the politicians felt a need to protect financial institutions from the potential risks resulting from CMBS, particularly from those which were encountered in the US, and to force originators, sponsors and lenders to conduct CMBS in a responsible manner. In light of the tighter requirements and much lower default rates in Germany compared to CMBS in the US and with a view not to drain access to the capital market for small and medium-sized businesses, a transition period until December 31, 2014 was agreed, during which the retention requirement will remain at 5 per cent. The 10 per cent retention requirement will apply for CMBS effected after that date. Although the Government promised to support an increase of the retention requirement with the EC with a view to amend art.122a of the CRD to 10 per cent, a view is forming,

---

[35]  See further Ch.19.

at the time of writing, in Germany that it may make sense to reduce the retention requirement before the step-up will come into force on January 1, 2015.

## 17.12. More clarity on European banking licence requirements

With a view to the approaching "wave of loan maturities" predicted in the years 2013 through 2017, lenders will have to have a tighter focus on the banking licensing requirements in Germany when granting loans or other forms of credits. This will not only be true for new market participants, such as insurance companies, pension funds, debt funds or shadow banks, but all the same for existing lenders in assessing their options, for example when extending maturity dates for loans.

Unlike in most jurisdictions within the EEA, in Germany not only credit institutions within the meaning of the Directive 2006/48/EC, i.e. undertakings whose business is to receive deposits or other repayable funds from the public and to grant credits for their own account, are required to obtain a banking license from the FSA. In fact, the license requirement applies even to undertakings merely granting credits for their own account. Failure to grant credits in Germany without the requisite banking license may result in harsh sanctions, including criminal liability. At any rate, amendment agreements, extensions of maturity dates or refinancing agreements will not be considered void in absence of a banking licence, as was confirmed by the German Federal Court of Justice in 2011.[36]

For CMBS in general, although not yet finally decided by the courts in Germany, it is the majority view in the legal literature that a licence on the part of the issuer will not be required to acquire the underlying loans and security. This view is shared by the FSA in Germany.[37] In contrast, in the case of a refinancing where a credit is granted to a borrower in Germany, the lender may, under certain circumstances, be required to obtain a banking licence in Germany.

Existing lenders will have to assess their options carefully with a view to the banking licence requirements. As such, it is permissible for lenders to enter into standstill agreements with the borrowers without a licence, however, if the terms and conditions of the loan are amended, a lender may require a banking licence in Germany. As currently, the term of most notes still exceeds the maturity date, in order to avoid the insolvency of the

---

[36] FCJ (*Bundesgerichtshof*), April 19, 2011 (XI ZR 256/10, WM 2011), pp.1168–1170 making reference to previous rulings stating that credit agreements are not considered void if the lender has not obtained the requisite licenses from the Financial Supervisory Authority.

[37] Financial Supervisory Authority, guidance notice as of January 8, 2009 on lending business (Kreditgeschäft), available on *http://www.bafin.de* [Accessed August 12, 2012].

borrower, lenders are inclined to extend the maturity date of the loans. Although, there is no new or further funds paid to the borrower, the FSA considers already that the decision to extend the maturity date may amount to the granting of credit, potentially requiring a banking licence in Germany.

In that respect, foreign lenders are in a more favourable position than lenders domiciled in Germany. The FSA allows for some limited exemptions to the licence requirement for foreign lenders, in cases where there is an existing client relationship, or if the initiative for granting the credit comes from the borrower.

## 17.13. When the borrower fails to meet its payment obligations—extensions and standstills

As a result of the wave of loan maturities, standstills and extensions of these loans are, at the time of writing, coming more and more into focus. In the vast majority of CRE financings lenders are, at first glance, sufficiently secured by the assets of the borrowers: mortgages, rent receivables and pledges over almost all of the borrower's other assets. Still, at the maturity date where there are loans that cannot be refinanced in full, for example due to high LTV ratios, or security has substantially decreased in value, to take immediate enforcement action may not be the most promising way to proceed for lenders to recover their outstanding loans.

At the time of maturity the borrowers will find themselves confronted with the obligation to repay the loans in full, together with accrued interest. For borrowers with their COMI in Germany, this usually means that they are required, pursuant to statutory law, to file for insolvency within three weeks following the maturity date at the latest. Failure to do so is a criminal offence. In most instances, this short period of time, however, does not allow the borrower to arrange for refinancing, if at all available, or to negotiate an extension of the maturity date for their loans.

As an insolvency of the borrower is likely to impair the enforcement of their security interests, lenders are expected to seek out-of-court solutions with the borrowers without pushing them into insolvency. Thus, where refinancing is not available at the maturity date, there is likely to be an increasing number of standstill agreements entered into. The purpose of the standstill agreement is, for a certain period of time, to dispense the borrower from its obligation to file for insolvency. But at the same time it allows the lenders to work with the borrowers on the most efficient way to enforce security, without the burden to undergo insolvency proceedings, at additional costs for the insolvency administrator.

Pursuant to s.17 of the German Insolvency Act (*Insolvenzordnung*) a debtor is deemed illiquid if it is unable to pay its debts when "due". As simple as it looks, the Federal Court of Justice has ruled that "due" for the purposes of the German Insolvency Act is not equivalent with "due" for the purposes of the civil law and thus for the purposes of the credit agreement.[38] Rather, for the purposes of the German Insolvency Act, payment obligations that are due under the credit agreement will not be considered as due when determining whether the debtor is illiquid, if the lender does not seriously demand satisfaction of those payment obligations. The requirements for payment obligations to be seriously demanded are fairly low. Accordingly, debtors often prefer a deferral of the payment obligations, i.e. the lender agrees to the payment obligation being no longer due for purpose of the credit agreement. In its ruling, the German Federal Court of Justice, however, explicitly confirmed that a mere standstill with the lender agreeing to be paid at a later time or subordinating its loan, is sufficient to avoid illiquidity. When agreeing to a deferral, it needs to be taken into consideration that default interest may not accrue during the time of deferral and third party security may not be enforceable, whilst this might still be possible under a standstill agreement. In order to avoid any legal uncertainties as to whether the satisfaction of payment obligations has been seriously demanded, written form of the standstill agreement is market practice. This is because if the borrower does not comply with its statutory obligations to file for insolvency it would not only be subject to civil but also to criminal liability.

## 17.14.  The next frontier? – Using English law Scheme of Arrangements when restructuring continental European borrowers

At the time of writing, the use of English law scheme of arrangements to restructure the borrower's obligations is growing in popularity and it is expected that this concept will also be considered for CRE borrowers with a multitude of loan tranches. Principally, such scheme of arrangement can also be used for continental EU borrowers provided they have sufficient connection with the United Kingdom for an English court to have jurisdiction over it. For example, English courts consider English law governed loan agreements to be sufficient to demonstrate such connection.

A scheme of arrangement is a procedure pursuant to Pt 26 of the Companies Act 2006, whereby a company makes a compromise or arrangement with its members or creditors (or any class of them). The terms and subject matter of a scheme are flexible. A scheme may compromise or re-arrange almost any matter which the borrower and its creditors (or shareholders) agree, so long as some form of compensation is provided to those parties who agree to

---

[38]  FCJ, rJuly19, 2007 ( IX ZB 36/07, BGHZ 173) pp.286 et seq.

give up or vary their rights. Principally, a scheme can be used for solvent or insolvent borrowers to effect almost any kind of internal reorganisation, so long as the necessary approvals have been obtained. To become effective and binding on all creditors, regardless of whether they had notice, a scheme of arrangement has to be approved at a meeting of the creditors, or in separate meetings of different classes of creditors, by at least 75 per cent in value and a majority in number of those registering a vote on the scheme and then be sanctioned by the English court.

So far it is not clear whether a UK scheme of arrangement will be recognised by continental European courts. In a 2012 decision, the German Federal Court of Justice ruled that a UK scheme of arrangement will not be binding on German creditors.[39] However, the decision was in relation to the restructuring of a UK insurance company and the recognition has been denied on grounds of regulations which specifically exclude jurisdiction of UK courts over insurance claims.[40] So it still remains to be seen whether it possible or not to restructure a, for example German based, real property SPV by means of a UK scheme of arrangement.

## 17.15.  Recent trends and experiences with the enforcement of CRE- backed loans

The keystone of any financial debt product is its ability to recover from the borrower any unpaid amounts by means of an enforcement of the security. In recent years, the security package which borrowers granted to the lender became quite comprehensive comprising virtually every asset the borrower can dispose of.

There are two principal scenarios under which such security packages can be enforced: outside of insolvency proceedings or in the course of insolvency proceedings. For larger real property portfolio financings recent experience in connection with security enforcements under both scenarios is a bit sobering. The below provides an overview of some typical issues of security enforcements in Germany as the most important continental EU CRE financing market.

---

[39]  FCJ, February 15, 2012 (IV ZR 194/09, BGH Betriebsberater 2012), pp.1561 et seq.
[40]  See arts 8, 12 and 35 of the Bruxelles I-Directive (EC) No 44/2001.

## 17.16.   Out of court enforcement of the security package

### 17.16.1.   *Formal enforcement of the mortgages*

#### 17.16.1.1.   *New enforcement requirements under the Risk Limitation Act*

With the implementation of the Risk Limitation Act, the German legislator intended to ease the pressure borrowers typically experience in the event of an imminent enforcement of mortgages created over their properties. This has been implemented by introducing a mandatory cancellation require-ment before the lender, as mortgage beneficiary, can commence the enforcement. In order to prevent bypassing the law, any agreements to the contrary are considered void and thus unenforceable. Therefore, a lender planning to enforce its mortgage over properties in Germany has to take into consideration that it will require a termination notice period of at least six months prior to taking any enforcement action. Borrowers are therefore in a stronger position when it comes to negotiating standstills or a consensual sale of their real properties. The new law, however, only applies for mortgages created on or after August 19, 2008. As a result, the enforcement of mortgages created prior to the emergence of the 2008 financial crisis; and thus most loans that are scheduled to mature between 2012 and 2014, will generally not be affected.

The effects of the termination requirement are already ascertainable at the time of writing, when it comes to new financings or refinancings of existing loans. Lenders can no longer request from the borrower the granting of mortgages which are immediately due and payable, or which can be terminated at any time without any notice period. Notaries are no longer allowed to issue immediately enforceable copies of the mortgage deed, which is required to initiate a forced sale or a forced administration over the real property. Instead, the lender must provide evidence that the mortgage was terminated and that the notice period of six months has expired. To this end, the lender must present to the notary, publicly certified documents which prove formal service of the enforceable mortgage deed on the owner of the real property. Even though in some cases it has been observed that borrowers waive this requirement, it is currently legally uncertain whether this is actually permissible in light of the purpose of the law. With a view to property owners domiciled outside of Germany, it is recommended to have a German process agent appointed by the property owner in order to expedite the service of the mortgage deed. In the event of a refinancing, the new lender may prefer to have existing mortgages assigned to it rather than requesting newly created ones.

### 17.16.2. Forced sale of the real property

When enforcing the security package, the primary option is always a formal enforcement of the mortgages. There are two principal options: a forced sale, or a forced administration of the underlying real property.

A forced sale process takes at least 12 to 18 months provided the borrower does not further obstruct the forced sale process by initiating court proceedings against the forced sale. Most lenders are therefore looking for other options allowing a faster realisation.

Further, a forced sale typically attracts bargain hunters who often pay less than the fair market value for the underlying properties. The problem is further aggravated when the lenders wish to enforce the sale of a larger portfolio of real properties having a value over €300 million. In the wake of the financial crisis, it is currently very difficult for a potential bidder to receive bank financing for the acquisition of a large portfolio, thus further reducing the price which can be obtained from an auction of the real properties. As a result, a forced sale of the real properties has become more and more unpopular among lenders of larger real property portfolio companies and lenders are therefore looking for other realisation options.

### 17.16.3. Forced administration of the real property

Besides a forced sale, lenders can also apply for a forced administration of the underlying properties. In fact, forced administration and forced sale are often filed simultaneously. The rationale for filing a forced administration is that it allows the lender to enforce its security over the real property's net cash flows during the forced sale process. This is because an insolvency administrator appointed over the assets of a borrower can invalidate any rent assignments and can set aside and claw back any rental income collected by the lender, if the rental income relates to rent periods after the insolvency filing. Such set aside or claw back is, however, not possible if net rental income is distributed to the lenders in the course of a forced administration. Needless to say, that a forced administration is just a supplement allowing to capture the real property's net cash flow during the forced sale proceedings.

### 17.16.4. Consensual sale of the real property by means of a realisation agreement

Because a forced sale proceeding is costly, timely and—for larger real property portfolios—not a viable option and because an acceleration of the loan could increase the likelihood of the borrower filing for insolvency causing additional delays and costs, many lenders try to enter into a realisation agreement with the borrower to effect a consensual sale of the real properties securing the loan.

Obviously, this option would only be worth considering if the borrower is willing to work together with the lender on a realisation of the real properties. It further requires that the borrower is not likely to change its mind and to obstruct such a consensual realisation of the real properties later in the process.

As part of such realisation agreement, the borrower agrees with the lender to apply any realisation sale proceeds towards the repayment of the loan. In addition, the borrower grants a power of attorney to a third party (for example a CRE broker) allowing it to market the real property. A power of attorney in favour of the lender or a security agent would only be valid if the loan and the mortgage are due and payable. However, to avoid an insolvency of the borrower, the lender typically avoids an acceleration of the loan and, instead, prefers the power of attorney to be granted to a third party. As a next step, the attorney-in-fact and the purchaser of the real properties agree on the terms of the purchase agreement which will have to be executed by the borrower and the purchaser. At completion of the real property purchase agreement, the purchaser transfers the sale proceeds either directly to the lender or the security agent, or to a borrower account which is pledged in favour of the lender or security agent. Upon repayment of the loan, the lender and/or security agent releases the mortgages and other related security over the relevant property to allow the purchaser the acquisition of clean title over the relevant real property. The last step would be a waiver of any outstanding amounts allowing a solvent winding up of the borrower. If the borrower is a German partnership, all partners of the borrower need to pass a unanimous resolution approving the disposal of the real property.

### 17.16.5. *Enforcing the pledge over shares in the borrower*

If the lenders do not wish to pursue a forced sale, nor succeed in securing the borrower's co-operation on a consensual sale of the real properties, the lenders' remaining option is an enforcement of the pledges over the borrower shares or partnership interests.

Such share or interest pledge enforcement obviously depends on the borrower's jurisdiction. Many borrowers are companies under Luxembourg law which offers a broad range of enforcement options to the lenders:

The pledgees of a Luxembourg law share pledge can choose between a sale of the borrower to a third party, an appropriation of the borrower shares, or an exercise of the voting rights over the shares in the borrower. This gives lenders a variety of options to exercise control over the borrower, allowing it to replace the asset or property manager or to sell the real properties to a third party. Clearly, each such enforcement option has its own different requirements, shortcomings and benefits. Since 2010, the enforcement of a Luxembourg law share pledge has generally proved to be a viable option for the lender.

In contrast, the enforcement of a share or interest pledge over the shares of a German law borrower has proved to be difficult and is as at the time of writing, rarely seen. This is because, unlike Luxembourg law, German corporate law does not allow the lender or security trustee to exercise voting rights over the borrower shares. An appropriation of the borrower shares by the lender and/or the security trustee is only possible if the borrower shares are listed or traded on a stock exchange. Given that most borrowers are unlisted SPVs, whose shares cannot be publicly traded, the only enforcement option for a share pledge over a German borrower is a public auction and sale of its shares to a third party.

As far as a public auction of the borrower shares is concerned, there are so many obstacles that lenders have typically discarded this as enforcement option. Among other reasons, lenders have shied away from taking control over the borrower, by acquiring its shares, because their loans would then become subordinated in a borrower insolvency if they are lenders and shareholders at the same time. Further, an acquisition of 95 per cent or more of the shares or partnership interests of a German borrower triggers real estate transfer tax of at least 3.5 per cent of the value of the borrower's real properties. Finally, the typical standard form for a German share or partnership interest pledge agreement, which was used pre the 2008 financial crisis, was drafted with a view to a borrower pledging the shares of its subsidiaries. Such standard form did not take into account that it was the borrower's shareholder who was pledging its shares to secure the obligations of the borrower; hence why most of the share or partnership interest pledge agreements proved to have shortcomings which could not be eliminated when the lender contemplates an enforcement of the share pledge. For example, only very few share pledge agreements allow an enforcement when the lender has granted a standstill agreement to the borrower to avoid a borrower insolvency. It would obviously be impossible to find a third purchaser for an insolvent borrower SPV. Further, many share pledge agreements provide for a subordination, instead of a full waiver of the pledgee's statutory subrogation right for the purchase price amount paid by the third party. Thus, a third party purchaser could never acquire the borrower shares on a debt free basis because the pledgee and former shareholder of the borrower would—by operation of law—end up as the borrower's new lender in an amount equal to the purchase price.

## 17.17. Enforcement of the lenders security in insolvency proceedings

In the wake of the 2008 financial crisis, many borrowers were either forced to file for bankruptcy under local applicable insolvency law, or lenders put borrowers into insolvency as part of their realisation strategy, because an out-of-court enforcement of the security package was not available or not the preferred option.

Realisation agreements with insolvency administrators are principally governed by the laws of the jurisdiction in which insolvency proceedings were opened over the assets of the borrower. So, if the borrower is a Luxembourg SPV with real estate located in Germany and the insolvency proceedings over the borrower's assets were opened in Luxembourg, it would be mainly Luxembourg law which governs a realisation agreement between the Luxembourg insolvency administrator and the lenders and/or the security trustee (acting on behalf of the lenders).

Generally, there are two objectives which can be achieved by such realisation agreements: a sale of the real properties by the insolvency administrator and an administration and management of the real properties allowing lenders to capture the net cash flow generated by the real properties until their disposal. The terms and conditions for realisation agreements vary from jurisdiction to jurisdiction. For example in Luxembourg, the insolvency administrator's fee for a disposal of the real properties is regulated by law, while in Germany the fee can be freely negotiated between the insolvency administrator and the lenders and/or the security trustee (acting on behalf of the lenders). Depending on the value of the real property, the fee which a German insolvency administrator may claim varies from 1 per cent to 3 per cent for a disposal and from 5 per cent to 8 per cent of the gross rental income for an administration of the real properties.

### 17.17.1. To file or not to file – lenders' dilemma in a borrower insolvency

While the opening of insolvency proceedings over the assets of CRE borrowers allows a realisation of the real properties for the benefit of the lenders, the appointment of an insolvency administrator can also give rise to additional risks for lenders.

In the first place, insolvency administrators will seek to make avoidance or preference claims invalidating part of the lenders' security package. Since 2010, the assignment of borrower's rental income has often been the subject matter of a preference claim by German insolvency administrators. This is because German courts have ruled that a rent assignment's hardening period only starts when the borrowers' rental claim against the respective tenant has become due and payable. In contrast, such assignment of rental income has principally been upheld under Luxembourg insolvency proceedings.

Similarly, while in German insolvency proceedings, lenders will need to demonstrate compliance with German rules on equitable subordination of shareholder loans. There is no such risk if the insolvency proceedings under Luxembourg law. Lenders are therefore more cautious about filing insolvency proceedings when such proceedings will be under German law as opposed to other more liberal jurisdictions such as Luxembourg.

### 17.17.2.   In search of the COMI – cross border insolvencies in Europe

Because the applicable jurisdiction for insolvency proceedings makes a fundamental difference to their risk position, lenders of CRE typically try to get more clarity on the applicable jurisdiction.

Since May 2002 it is now European law (EU Insolvency Regulation No 1346/2000) which determines the jurisdiction over insolvency proceedings. In theory, the EU Insolvency Regulation provides an answer by stating that the applicable jurisdiction for insolvency proceedings is the court of the EU Member State where the debtor's COMI is located. It further states that the COMI corresponds to the place where the debtor conducts the administration of his interests on a regular basis and is therefore ascertainable by third parties. In the case of a company or legal person, the place of the registered office shall be presumed to be the COMI in the absence of any proof to the contrary.

The EU Insolvency Regulation, however, does not provide a clear definition of COMI. In particular, there has been no guidance on the COMI of a typical CRE borrower which quite often has its registered office in countries like Luxembourg or the Netherlands for tax reasons, while its real estate assets and almost all other assets are located elsewhere in Europe. To date, it has largely been left to the local national courts to decide how the regulation should be interpreted on this point. Not surprisingly, the approach taken by local national courts in the various EU jurisdictions has not been consistent.

In October 2011 the ECJ in *re Interedil*[41] had to decide on the COMI of a real estate SPV which was registered in London while its real estate and almost all of its other assets were located in Italy. The ECJ ruled that the borrower's COMI must be determined by attaching greater importance to the place of the company's central administration, as may be established by objective factors which are ascertainable by third parties. Where the bodies responsible for the management and supervision of a company are in the same place as its registered office and the management decisions of the company are taken, in a manner that is ascertainable by third parties, in that

---

[41]   ECJ, October 20, 2011(C-396/09 (*Interedil Srl in Liquidation/Fallimento Interedil Srl*)).

place, the presumption in that provision cannot be rebutted. Where a company's central administration is not in the same place as its registered office, the presence of company assets such as real estate and the existence of contracts for the financial exploitation of those assets in a EU Member State, other than that in which the registered office is situated, cannot be regarded as sufficient factors to rebut the presumption unless a comprehensive assessment of all the relevant factors makes it possible to establish, in a manner that is ascertainable by third parties, that the company's actual centre of management and supervision and of the management of its interests is located in that other EU Member State.

As a consequence, it is the place of a borrower's central administration which counts in the first place, while the place of a borrower's assets is typically not the decisive factor. Admittedly, *Interedil* has not put an end to the COMI discussion, but it has provided at least some guidance to borrowers and lenders when it comes to determining the COMI of a CRE SPV.

### 17.17.3. Secondary territorial insolvency proceedings—the wildcard in the game

Secondary territorial insolvency proceedings are local insolvency proceedings, alongside the main proceeding, in the country in which the borrower has an establishment. If, for example, the borrower is a Luxembourg legal entity with its COMI in Luxembourg and the borrower's real properties are all located in Germany, a creditor who has his domicile or registered office in Germany, or whose claim arises from the borrower's operation in Germany, could request the opening of territorial insolvency proceedings in Germany. The effects of secondary territorial proceedings are limited to the assets located in the state of its jurisdiction. For lenders of CRE backed loans, such secondary proceedings provide another layer of risk, because the secondary insolvency administrator could, to almost the same extent, raise preference, avoidance or equitable subordination claims, as the main insolvency administrator. Hence, this is why the lenders wish to avoid any such secondary territorial insolvency proceedings.

As mentioned above, the request for secondary territorial insolvency proceedings requires an establishment of the borrower in another EU Member State. The EU Insolvency Regulation defines an "establishment" as any place of operations where the debtor carries out a non-transitory economic activity with human means and goods. While there is almost no doubt that the borrower carries out a non-transitory economic activity with goods (i.e. the real property), the key question is whether such economic activity also uses "human means". In re *Interedil*, the ECJ clarified that an establishment requires a structure consisting of a minimum level of organisation and a degree of stability necessary for the purpose of pursuing an economic activity. The presence alone of goods in isolation, or of bank accounts, does not, in principle, meet that definition.

Similar to the determination of the COMI, the approach taken by local national courts in various EU jurisdictions has not been consistent when deciding whether or not there is an establishment of the borrower. Some German courts have taken the position that for the presence of human means, it would be sufficient for the borrower entity to have engaged local facility or property managers for their real property.[42] Thus even if the real estate SPV has no employees at all, it could still be considered to have "human means" by virtue of their service providers. It remains to be seen whether the legal position of these German courts is considered to be in line with the guidance given by the ECJ in re *Interedil*. In the absence of such clarification by the ECJ, lenders will have to face the risk of secondary insolvency proceedings, such as in Germany which could give raise to additional insolvency-related risks.

# 17.18. Conclusion

The 2008 financial crisis brought about many regulatory challenges and developments in legislation which were aimed at protecting CRE borrowers and regulated financial institutions, in particular banks. One particular example is Germany's increased originator retention requirements for CMBS which will make it in future difficult for German banks to hold CMBS notes. Another example is the enhanced protection of CRE borrowers from an enforcement of the mortgages. Moreover, a further development since 2010, is the emergence of larger non-performing CRE portfolios providing challenges for lenders to realise their security over the real properties. These challenges caused lenders to take a closer look at alternative enforcement routes such as consensual sales of the real estate, realisations by an insolvency administrator, or enforcements of the share pledges over the CRE SPVs. Also, borrowers increasingly used CRE SPVs which had their COMI, not in the same jurisdiction where the real estate was located. This development gave rise to all sorts of issues such as locating the COMI, or, the emergence of secondary insolvency proceedings.

The EU regulatory and legal environment has and will continue to have a large degree of influence on CRE financings in 2013 and beyond. To date, the European CRE financing market has managed to cope with all the new developments and challenges. With the upcoming wave of loan maturities which is predicted for the years 2013 through 2017 the acid test for the EU regulatory and legal environment is still to come.

---

[42] Lower Court (*Amtsgericht*) of Stralsund, ruling (*Beschluß*), May 31, 2012 (12 IN 98/12, not published).

# Chapter 18

# Islamic Compliant Financing of Commercial Real Estate

Jonathan Lawrence,

Partner, K&L Gates LLP

## 18.1. Introduction

CRE has been an increasingly important asset class for Islamic compliant transactions and banks since the publication of the first edition of this book in 2006. During this period, Islamic compliant finance has proved to be an alternative source of funds for investors entering the European CRE market, as highlighted by such high profile London CRE deals, such as the Chelsea Barracks and the Shard of Glass, the tallest building in Europe.

In 2012, Islamic compliant financing is on a growth trajectory, based on demographic trends, rising investible income levels and progress towards harmonisation with global regulation. Whilst the economies of developed economies are, at the time of writing, under strain, CRE market participants are looking to funding alternatives, such as Islamic debt. Islamic banks originating in the countries of the Gulf Cooperation Council (GCC) could emerge as forces to be reckoned with in the new global order of finance in 2013 and beyond.

On 2012 estimates, 26.4 per cent of the global population will likely be Muslim by 2030, against 23 per cent in 2012. The proportion of Muslims in Europe is around 5 per cent of the population. This creates a large market and investor base to consider. The level of harmonisation is increasing between conventional and Islamic banking regulation, thus eroding barriers to entry. Islamic banking services are available in 39 countries on four continents. There are also significant growth opportunities, given that the global penetration of Islamic banking is currently below 2 per cent in CRE finance and the Islamic debt market or *sukuk* accounts for only approximately 1 per cent of global debt issuance.

The United Kingdom has enjoyed an in-built advantage in its attempt to become the hub of Islamic finance in Europe, due to English law often being the governing law of international Islamic finance transactions. An Islamic finance transaction might involve a Swiss bank and a Middle Eastern counterparty, but may well choose English law, to structure their documentation, in order to give flexibility and certainty to both sides.

Nonetheless, other EU jurisdictions (in recognition of this) have sought to attract Islamic finance transactions. For example, in 2010, Ireland introduced a tax neutrality regime for Islamic finance. Ireland has signed over 60 double tax treaties ensuring there is no double taxation for such structures (for example, treaties with Malaysia, Saudi Arabia and the United Arab Emirates). The Irish government has called an Irish government *sukuk* "an option" and Dublin is already well developed as a financial centre, with the Irish Stock Exchange having listed its first corporate *sukuk* in 2005. However, Ireland only has a Muslim population of approximately 30,000 and this may hamper the development of the industry. Nonetheless in 2008, the Irish Financial Regulator introduced a dedicated team to help Islamic compliant funds set up in Ireland.

Luxembourg ruled out a government *sukuk* in 2011. However, the country has attracted over 40 Islamic funds. If Luxembourg could be the first EU country to issue a government *sukuk*, then it would certainly put it on the map.

France has a Muslim population of over 3.5 million. However, the political climate has not been conducive to the development of the industry over the past few years. The United Kingdom has had a first-mover advantage over France and the UK property market attraction for Middle Eastern investors has also put the United Kingdom ahead.

Turkey is a country to watch. Straddling Europe and Asia, its 70 million plus population is 99 per cent Muslim. Companies are allowed to issue Islamic compliant debt and the first corporate *sukuk* has been undertaken by a leading Turkish bank.

## 18.2   CRE as an asset class

To date, Islamic finance has viewed CRE as an investible, tangible asset class on which to base its financial structures. The focus has tended to be on prime or trophy assets: for example, hotels or large office headquarter buildings. However, since 2010, Islamic funds and Islamic banks providing mezzanine finance, have multiplied. In such structures, a conventional senior bank lends the majority of the debt on an interest payment basis, the investors inject their equity and the mezzanine finance tranche is put into the structure in an Islamic compliant way. This is a feasible way of ensuring that deals get done. The senior conventional bank and the Islamic compliant mezzanine lender enter into an intercreditor agreement which governs the way each loan is treated and takes account of the Islamic sensibilities of the mezzanine lender.

Student accommodation has been a major target for Islamic funds given the existence of rental guarantees, steady demand and upward only rental payments. Further developments may be seen in this sector due to a broadening view of social infrastructure to include healthcare, education and social housing sectors. Prime residential properties are still a focus, with an Islamic compliant fund launching in the United Kingdom in September 2011 to offer Islamic investors exposure to this market.

Real estate has been a primary focus of the Islamic finance industry since the 1990s. Islamic property investments began in the residential housing sector, but quickly moved to CRE, which now plays a large role in this sector throughout the world. Initial investments were, and continue to be, effected through investment fund structures. However, the emergence of the *sukuk* in 2003 saw significant changes in Islamic compliant CRE finance.

It is worth considering what qualifies as Islamic complaint finance, as Islamic or *Shari'ah* compliant finance is a different animal than conventional finance. For example, the payment and receipt of interest are prohibited by the *Shari'ah*, making it impossible to lend against CRE in a conventional manner.

## 18.3. What is Islamic compliant finance?

In summary, Islamic finance is the conduct of commercial and financial activities in accordance with the *Shari'ah*. The *Shari'ah* is Islamic religious law, as applied to commercial and financial activities. It is a combination of theology, religion and law. The *Shari'ah* is a guide to how a Muslim leads his or her life (it means, literally, "the way" or "the right path") and is the divine law to Muslims as revealed in the *Qur'an* and the *Sunna*.

*Fiqh*, literally, is the human understanding of that divine law; the practical rules of *Shari'ah* as determined by the *Shari'ah* scholars. The primary methodology used in this interpretation is *ijtihad* (literally, "effort"), or legal reasoning, using the "roots of the law" (*usul al-fiqh*). The roots (*usul*) upon which Islamic jurisprudence are based, are the:

- *Qur'an*, being the holy book of Islam and the word of Allah (a word for God used in the context of Islam);
- *Sunna* of the Prophet Mohammed, which are the binding authority of his sayings and decisions;
- *Ijma*, or "consensus" of the community of scholars; and
- *Qiyas*, or deductions and reasoning by analogy.

The *Shari'ah* is comprised of principles and rules and, historically, its explanation and application has been largely oral. There are also a number of schools of Islamic jurisprudence (the four main schools of the largest branch of Islam (*Sunni*) are Hanafi, Hanbali, Maliki and Shafi). Historically, the different schools are frequently in conflict with respect to the application of the *Shari'ah* to different factual or structural situations. Even within a school there are variable interpretations and there is considerable divergence between South East Asia (particularly Malaysia, Indonesia and Brunei) and the Middle East and Western Asia (particularly Pakistan).

As expounded by *Shari'ah* scholars over the last 1,400 years, and as applied to Islamic finance, the *Shari'ah* is a full body of law. It covers virtually every aspect of commerce and finance that is addressed by a mature body of secular law. Thus, for example, it addresses contracts, concepts of consideration, legal capacity, mutuality, sales, leasing, construction activities, partnerships and joint ventures of various types, guarantees, estates, equity and trust, litigation and many other activities and legal structures. As such, it will influence all aspects of an Islamic compliant CRE finance transaction or the formation of an Islamic investment fund as well as every aspect of the operation and conduct of a CRE business. However, Islamic finance transactions involving non-Muslim parties are governed by secular law, such as English law or New York law.

## 18.4. *Shari'ah* supervisory boards and Islamic finance regulators

In many CRE finance transactions, only one party may care if the deal is Islamic compliant. In that case, it is important that each party represents to the other that it is satisfied with the Islamic compliance from its viewpoint and will not seek to use a later finding of non-compliance as a reason to renege on the transaction.

However, the question remains as to how an investor that wants to make *Shari'ah* compliant investments ensures that its investment is in fact in compliance. Most individuals do not have the expertise to make that determination for themselves. Over the last few decades, the mechanism that has evolved to provide comfort with respect to *Shari'ah* compliance is the *Shari'ah* supervisory board (a "*Shari'ah* board" or a "*board*").

Most Islamic banks, financial institutions and CRE companies and many of the higher net worth families and individuals in the Islamic world have retained one or more *Shari'ah* scholars that comprise a *Shari'ah* board. Each board oversees the complete range of investment practices, and the principles, methodology and activities of operation of all aspects of the business, of the entity or individual that has retained that particular board. Each board is comprised of a different group of individual scholars. Each board renders determinations with respect to structures and undertakings that are confidential to the entity that retains that board, with the result that explanation of the *Shari'ah*, as applied in competitive financial markets, has occurred in isolated pockets rather than a manner that is coordinated across markets or even schools of Islamic jurisprudence.

*Shari'ah* boards may be comprised of one scholar or a group of scholars. Frequently, a board is comprised of one or more of the leading "internationalist" scholars, some regional scholars, and some local scholars. Frequently, the internationalist scholars (who most often populate the boards of the major banks and investment funds) have expertise and experience in sophisticated financial transactions in a wide range of jurisdictions throughout the world, including various secular tax and finance laws and other legal and regulatory regimes and the interplay between those regimes and the *Shari'ah* as applied and considered by specific investors.

The Bahrain-based Accounting and Auditing Organisation of Islamic Financial Institutions (AAOIFI) and the Kuala Lumpur-based Islamic Financial Services board (IFSB) are strong forces in promoting greater uniformity across the schools and across the divide between Southeast Asian jurisdictions and Middle Eastern and Western Asian jurisdictions. AAOIFI standards prescribe additional international financial reporting standards to reflect the specifics of Islamic finance. The IFSB advises domestic regulators on how Islamic financial institutions should be managed and has published standards on stress testing, liquidity, management, capital adequacy and corporate governance.

In April 2012, AAOIFI introduced seven new standards for Islamic financial institutions addressing issues including financial rights, bankruptcy, capital protection and contract termination. As a greater number and variety of multi-national conventional banks and investment banks enter, and expand their range within, the Islamic finance field, there will be increased pressure toward uniformity, if only to facilitate the implementation of internal policies and procedures of these institutions.

The board will perform a number of different roles, including, typically, the following:

- participation in product development activities;
- review and approval of the fund or entity structure and its objectives, criteria and guidelines and issuance of a *fatwa* in respect thereof;
- review and approval of disclosure and offering documents and issuance of a *fatwa* in respect thereof;
- review, approval and oversight of investment and business operational structures and methodology, and issuance of a *fatwa* in respect thereof;
- ongoing review, oversight and approval of transactional or operational variances or applications to unique or changing circumstances; and

- annual audit of the operations of the fund or entity and issuance of an annual certification of *Shari'ah* compliance.

A *fatwa* (singular; *fatawa* is the plural) is a written certification of a *Shari'ah* scholar or board. It has no binding legal effect under secular law in Europe. Over recent years *fatawa* have been structured more like Anglo-American legal opinions, with discussion of the underlying *Shari'ah* precepts. It is common to see a copy of a more general *fatwa* reproduced in the offering circular of a *sukuk* issue.


## 18.5. *Shari'ah* principles

The outlook of the *Shari'ah* on finance is as a type of "ethical investing". It prohibits investment in, or the conduct of, businesses whose core activities:

- include the manufacture or distribution of alcoholic or pork products or, in the case of certain *Shari'ah* boards, firearms;
- have a significant involvement in gaming (gambling, including casinos), brokerage, interest-based banking or impermissible insurance;
- include certain types of entertainment elements (particularly pornography); or
- have impermissible amounts of interest-based indebtedness or interest income.

The activities referred to above are categorised as prohibited business activities. Some *Shari'ah* boards also include the growing, manufacture and distribution of tobacco within prohibited business activities. Some boards interpret the entertainment exclusion more broadly and include cinema and music generally because of the pornography elements of these industries. Hotels are often included because of the presence of alcohol in bars and mini-bars or in-room entertainment. Entities that have prohibited business activities may not be tenants in properties owned and leased by a *Shari'ah*-compliant investor. These prohibitions fundamentally influence the nature and operations of funds and businesses.

Many large office buildings and complexes have tenants that engage in prohibited business activities, such as retail branches of conventional banks, restaurants that serve alcohol, or supermarkets or convenience stores that sell pork, wine and beer. In the purest case, the entire building or complex would be an impermissible investment. However, the *Shari'ah* scholars have taken a pragmatic view. Rules have been developed that allow investment in these properties for certain impermissible uses, such as those just mentioned. For example, if the branch bank serves a retail market, there are insufficient other banking opportunities in the defined area, and the branch bank occupies a small percentage of the property (say, 1 per cent or less), some *Shari'ah* boards will permit the property acquisition and allow renewal of the lease to that branch bank. The development of these rules, as to de minimis impermissible tenancies greatly expanded the universe of properties available for investment.

A fundamental *Shari'ah* principle is the prohibition of *riba*, best known by its prohibition on the payment or receipt of interest. This rule affects every aspect of the manner in which a *Shari'ah* compliant transaction is structured and implemented. In the securitisation field, it (and other principles) precludes pooling of conventional mortgages, credit card receivables, and all interest-bearing debt instruments.

In the area of joint ventures (including partnerships), numerous principles address allocation of work, profit and loss allocations and distributions and virtually all other operational matters. For example, as a general statement, all distributions of profits and losses must be pro rata. Preferred shares are not permissible. In certain types of partnerships (*mudaraba*), one person contributes services and another person contributes capital. If the arrangement suffers a loss, only the capital provider may be penalised in cash. In other types of partnerships (*Sharikat* and *musharaka*), work and capital contribution may be allocated over all partners with corresponding loss sharing. These rules affect CRE business and fund structures and many operational activities and, directly, *sukuk*.

*Shari'ah* principles in relation to leasing are of particular importance because leasing is the primary tool used in the implementation of *Shari'ah* compliant transactions. Examples include the requirement that a property lessor must maintain the leased property. The lessor may not pass structural maintenance obligations, or corresponding obligations such as the maintenance of buildings insurance, to a lessee. In short, the pervasive fully repairing and insuring lease is prohibited. The end-user tenant may not have prohibited business activities and the lease to the end-user tenant must itself be *Shari'ah* compliant. These principles have a critical impact on Islamic securitisations.

As one would expect in light of the development of the *Shari'ah* in Middle Eastern societies that were so heavily focused on trading activities, the *Shari'ah* precepts applicable to sales are especially well refined. Leasing, in fact, is treated as a type of sale—sale of the temporary possession (or usufruct) of property. With only limited exceptions, one can sell only tangible assets. Debt cannot be sold, nor can other financial instruments that do not represent an ownership interest in tangible assets. Further, one cannot sell property that one does not own and possess. These principles have a major influence on the structure of Islamic bonds and securitisations. In addition, there are very particular rules addressing delivery, receipt, ownership, allocation of risk, down-payments and virtually all other aspects of sales transactions. These rules affect both the ability to create secondary markets and the tradability of securitisation instruments.

431

*Shari'ah* precepts that prohibit gambling and uncertainty also preclude most types of conventional insurance and investments in conventional insurance companies, although the unavailability of *takaful* (*Shari'ah* compliant insurance) has led to some practical accommodations to the prohibition on the use of insurance.

## 18.6. Islamic CRE finance structures

To help understand Islamic CRE financing, this Chapter will outline certain of the component structures of Islamic compliant finance. These are primarily the lease (*ijara*) and sale (particularly *murabaha*) structures. Two structures, the *mudaraba* and *musharaka*, are joint venture structures. Each structure is briefly summarised in this section, and each of these structures is also the basis or a component of Islamic bond and securitisation structures.

### 18.6.1. Ijara (lease) structures

The predominant acquisition and operating financing structure in Islamic CRE finance in Europe is the *ijara* (lease). Figure 1 below, shows a basic leasing structure. This example assumes 60 per cent conventional interest-based financing and 40 per cent contribution by the *Shari'ah* compliant investors; these percentages will vary with each transaction.

The investors make their investment into the "project company". For tax reasons, this investment is usually made through a fund and at least one entity is usually inserted in the structure between that fund and the project company. A SPV, the "funding company", is established to acquire and hold title to the property in which the *Shari'ah* compliant investment is to be made (the "property"). The project company contributes its investment (40 per cent of the acquisition price) to the funding company. A conventional interest-bearing loan is made by the "bank" to the funding company (equal to 60 per cent of the acquisition price). The funding company then acquires the property from the seller.

Then, the funding company enters into an *ijara* (*lease*) with the project company, as lessee. The rent payable under the *ijara* is identical to the debt service on the conventional loan from the bank and provides the funds to pay that debt service.

The lease must be *Shari'ah* compliant including:

- the lessor must have ownership of the CRE prior to leasing it;
- the lease period must be specified;
- the CRE asset must continue to exist throughout the lease term;

## Figure 1 – *Ijara* Structure

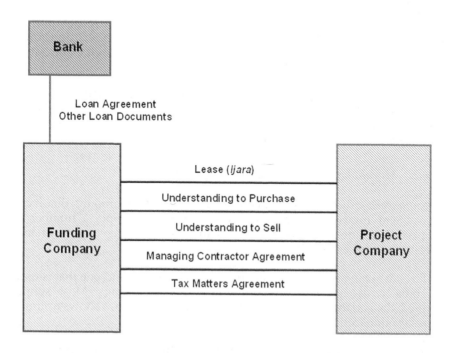

- the lessor must be responsible for maintaining and insuring the property.

Future rents cannot be accelerated under a *Shari'ah* compliant lease. Given that the outstanding principal is paid through the *ijara*, an acceleration mechanism is necessary outside the *ijara* itself. The understanding to purchase performs that function (it also mirrors all mandatory prepayment provisions of the bank loan). The bank, through the funding company, "puts" the property to the project company at a strike price equal to the outstanding principal (and other outstanding amounts).

The project company may also want to sell the property during the period that the loan is outstanding. The understanding to sell provides the mechanism (and also mirrors the voluntary prepayment provisions of the bank loan).

Under the *Shari'ah* rules noted above, and others, a lessor cannot pass structural maintenance and insurance obligations to a lessee. However, a lessor can hire another entity to perform those functions. In this case, the funding company hires the project company to perform those activities pursuant to the managing contractor agreement.

Finally, the tax matters agreement provides that the project company is the tax owner of the property and for income tax (and other) purposes, this is a loan from the bank to the project company. The tax matters agreement outlines the components as between the conventional loan documentation and the *Shari'ah* compliant leasing documentation.

This structure is used in essentially all *Shari'ah* compliant CRE transactions in Europe (with some relatively minor country variations, as appropriate, under relevant tax and CRE laws) and, as noted below, it is easily modified to effect a *Shari'ah* compliant securitisation.

### 18.6.2.  Murabaha (sale at a mark-up) structures

The *murabaha* structure results in OpCo obtaining a cash amount, that it can then spend towards purchasing a CRE asset. In Europe, a number of property investors have used this structure as a banking tool, to finance investor purchases of CRE.

As a result, a *murabaha*, is a widely used sales structure, and one that is used in some *sukuk* and in many working capital financings. Most simply defined, the *murabaha* is a sale at a mark-up. Figure 2 below, shows a simple *murabaha* transaction.

In the simple *murabaha*, "OpCo", a client of "MBank", wants to purchase a commodity, piece of equipment, or other asset. OpCo negotiates the terms of the purchase, including payment terms and precise specifications, with the commodity seller. OpCo then asks MBank to finance the purchase of that asset.

OpCo and MBank enter into a *murabaha* agreement pursuant to which MBank agrees to supply to OpCo a commodity or asset meeting the precise specifications that were negotiated with the commodity seller. The *murabaha*agreement will require OpCo to make payment to MBank for that commodity on a deferred purchase basis.

MBank, in turn, will enter into a commodity purchase agreement with the commodity seller and will purchase the commodity from the commodity seller for immediate payment in full.

Upon accepting delivery of the commodity, MBank will fulfil its obligations under the *murabaha* agreement by re-selling the commodity to OpCo. While there are numerous other applicable rules, two are of particular note:

- MBank must have ownership risk with respect to the asset; and

Figure 2 - Basic *Murabaha* Structure

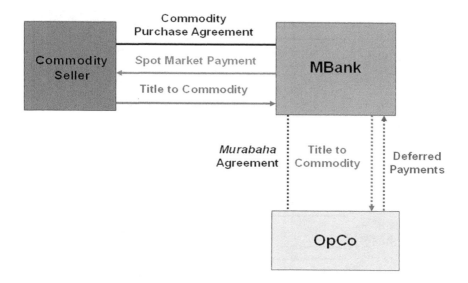

- OpCo can, under most schools of Islamic jurisprudence at the present time, act as the agent for MBank in completing the arrangements between MBank and the commodity seller.

A working capital *murabaha* is shown in Figure 3. This structure is used, in variant forms, in *sukuk* structures.

The transaction, shown in Figure 3, is substantially identical to the *murabaha* transaction shown in Figure 2. The additional element is that OpCo, upon taking title to the commodity (here a permissible metal), immediately sells that metal to the metal purchaser for a cash payment at the same spot market price as obtained in MBank's purchase of that metal from the metal seller (fees ignored). The metal purchaser and metal seller are frequently affiliates. The net result is that OpCo ends up with cash equal to the spot market price of the metal and a deferred *murabaha* payment obligation to MBank in respect of that amount plus a profit factor.

In the CRE context, UK and Irish banks have offered *murabaha*, by taking notional possession of a property's title at closing and then selling the property to the investor at a higher price.

If the bank does not want to or cannot acquire title for regulatory reasons, then the bank appoints a transacting party to act as its acquiring agent. The agent then executes the sale in favour of the ultimate investor.

**Figure 3 - Working Capital *Murabaha***

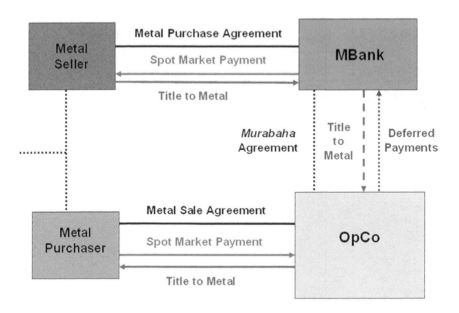

### 18.6.3. *Mudaraba (service provider—capital provider) structures*

A *mudaraba* is a type of joint venture and is a key method for organising and acquiring CRE investments. It is most frequently formulated as a limited partnership, a limited liability company or a fund. The base structure, involves one partner providing services and management (the *mudarib*). One can equate a *mudarib* to a fund manager. In that case, the *mudarib* may sub-contract its duties to an experienced CRE management professional. Usually, the *mudarib* does not provide cash or other in-kind capital. Some *Shari'ah* boards prohibit *mudarib* capital; all prohibit it without the consent of the other partner(s). The other partner(s) (the *rabb ul-maal*) provides capital, in cash or in kind, and generally may not interfere in the management or service component. A simple *mudaraba* arrangement with multiple capital providers is shown in Figure 4.

As a general matter, and with a few modifications, a conventional limited partnership agreement works well to structure a *mudaraba*. For example, while a capital provider may not interfere in the management function, most *Shari'ah* boards permit "minority rights" protections such as are afforded to limited partners, and other rights are permissible in *mudarib* default, breach and infringement scenarios.

**Figure 4 - *Mudaraba* Structure**

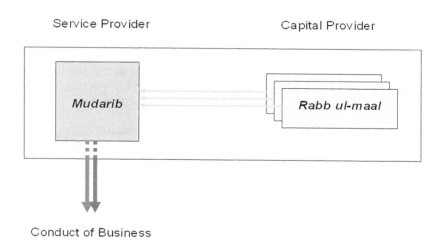

The partnership or fund then acquires CRE assets, most commonly through *ijara* or *murabaha* structures. Profit in a *mudaraba* is that amount that exceeds the capital after deduction of all allowable *mudaraba* expenses. Conversely, loss is the decrease in the *mudaraba* capital. The critical *Shari'ah* rule pertaining to losses, is that all losses are borne by the capital provider (the service provider has lost its services and is not seen as having incurred pecuniary losses). Profit allocations must be specified, and must be pro rata (although formulas specifying different allocations upon satisfaction of hurdles have been accepted). Importantly, there can be no predetermined or conclusive profit allocation to any of the parties and arrangements allocating all profit to a single party are impermissible. More difficult issues arise with respect to scenarios in which a clawback of distributions may be necessary, as with losses subsequent to distributions.

### 18.6.4. *Musharaka (capital provider) structures*

*Al-sharika* is a partnership for profit, *Sharikat ul-amwaal* is a property partnership, and al-*musharaka* is a finance method derived from a partnership contract in which a bank participates with one or more clients. The term *musharaka* refers to a wide range of partnership or joint venture arrangements. In a *musharaka*, each of the partners contributes capital, and there is significantly greater flexibility in allocating management responsibilities among partners; joint rights of management are frequent and usual.

Limited partnership agreements are also useful models for structuring *musharaka* arrangements. Profit and loss definitions are mainly the same as with *mudaraba*, with some fundamental differences. Profits may be allocated in accordance with a points system, and that points system may be structured to take account of the amount of capital contributed and the period of participation. Profit from a specific period or operation may not be allocated to a specified partner, nor may a lump sum be allocated to a specific partner. In the majority view, losses, up to the amount of a partner's capital contribution, must be distributed in accordance with the relative capital contributions of the partners. A partner may not assume liability for the capital of another partner, including by way of guarantee.

*Shari'ah* rules applicable to purchases and sales of interests (*hissas*) from one partner to another (as well as *murabaha* rules) form the basis for securitisation transactions involving *musharaka*.

## 18.7.   The application of CRE finance structures in *sukuk*

Having reviewed some of the typical Islamic finance structures used in CRE acquisition and investment, the next section of this Chapter will consider how such structures have been adapted to develop the market for *sukuk* (*Shari'ah* compliant capital markets instruments) based on CRE assets. Although a number of significant *sukuk* transactions defaulted (or faced near default) with the advent of the global financial crisis, with issuances of new instruments being very limited during this period, one of the most active areas of Islamic CRE finance, both before and after the global financial crisis, has been *sukuk* issuance. In the period 2011–12, the markets have witnessed an increase in the level of issuance of *sukuk* across a number of jurisdictions.

## 18.8.   Asset-based versus asset-backed

Structurally, *sukuk* can be broken into two types of transactions—asset-based or asset-backed. Asset-based issuances are sometimes referred to as Islamic bonds, whilst asset-backed issuances are generally referred to as securitisations. There have only been a limited number of *Shari'ah* compliant securitisations, with the vast majority of *sukuk* issuances being asset-based transactions.

In both types of *sukuk*, the issuing entity (which will usually be an orphan SPV company, as used in CMBS transactions[1]) will issue certificates into the capital markets. The proceeds from the issuance will, depending upon the structure being utilised, either be used to purchase an asset (such as in an

---

[1]   See further Ch.1.

*ijara* structure), be invested (as in a *musharaka* or *wakala* structure) or purchase a portfolio of loans (as in a CMBS). It should be noted that in all these structures, the certificates issued are an indivisible ownership interest in the assets of the issuing vehicle. This can cause some tax issues, which will be discussed later in this Chapter.

The difference between the asset-backed structures and asset-based structures lies in the type of credit risk which the investors are taking under each structure.

A *Shari'ah* compliant securitisation is structurally similar to a conventional securitisation. The issuing vehicle issues certificates and uses the proceeds of the issuance to purchase a portfolio of assets (such as *Shari'ah* compliant mortgages). The issuing vehicle declares security over this portfolio of assets, and in the event of a default, the security trustee enforces this security and may liquidate the assets. As with conventional securitisations, the investors will not have recourse to the seller of the assets on a default; their recourse will be limited to the assets of the issuing vehicle.

As such, the only structural difference between a *Shari'ah* compliant securitisation and a conventional securitisation is the fact that the instruments are certificates evidencing an ownership right in the assets, in relation to the former rather than a debt instrument in relation to the latter. As discussed above, there have been a very limited number of *Shari'ah* compliant securitisations issued (although a larger number have been structured), the most well known of which was the RMBS deal issued by Tamweel in 2008, under which a portfolio of *Shari'ah* compliant mortgages originated by Tamweel was securitised.

Conversely and from a credit perspective, asset-based *sukuk* structures are most similar to a corporate bond. Islamic bonds are based upon the credit of an entity that is participating in the transaction (which may be the seller, guarantor or other credit support provider and will be referred to as the originator). On execution of the transaction, an asset will be sold to the issuing entity by the corporate, or, funds will be invested with the originator. This asset will generate an income for the issuing vehicle. This income will be generated from payments made by the originator under the contractual arrangements with the issuing entity. However, often there will not be any security over the assets of the issuing entity to secure the certificates (and even where transactions do include security over the assets, it may be that the value of this security is difficult to ascertain). Only a minority of *sukuk* are structured to give *sukuk* holders direct recourse to the underlying asset. The majority are structured so that, following a default, the only recourse is to require the originator to repurchase the income-generating asset (either at a fixed price where fixed price undertakings are permitted by AAOIFI or at some other price as set out in the documents).

It should be noted that a large number of *sukuk* issued have essentially been capital raising exercises for the underlying corporate, albeit using CRE assets as a way to access this market. However, there have also been a number of *sukuk* transactions which have been used to raise capital for certain CRE and other projects.

Further, a *sukuk* issuance may be one element of a CRE financing. For example, a CMBS transaction could be executed, which included both conventional bond financing as well as a tranche structured as a *sukuk*. There is increased market interest in the establishment of multi-funding platforms that incorporate tranches of conventional and Islamic finance and there is no reason why these structures cannot be applied to the CRE market in 2013 and beyond.

## 18.9. AAOIFI *sukuk* standard

Under the AAOIFI *sukuk* standard, *sukuk* are defined as certificates of equal value put to use as common shares and rights in tangible assets, usufructs and services or as equity in a project or investment activity. The AAOIFI standard carefully distinguishes *sukuk* from equity, notes and bonds. It emphasises that *sukuk* are not debts of the issuer; they are fractional or proportional interests in underlying assets, usufructs, services, projects or investment activities. *Sukuk* may not be issued on a pool of receivables. Further, the underlying business or activity, and the underlying transactional structures (such as the underlying CRE leases) must be *Shari'ah* compliant (the business or activity cannot engage in prohibited business activities, for example).

AAOIFI has specified 14 categories of permissible *sukuk*. In broad summary, they are securitisations:

- of an existing or to be acquired tangible asset (*ijara*);
- of an existing or to be acquired leasehold estate (*ijara*);
- of presales of services (*ijara*);
- of presales of the production of goods or commodities at a future date (*salam* (forward sale));
- to fund the cost of construction (*istisna'a* (construction contract));
- to fund the acquisition of goods for future sale (*murabaha*);
- to fund capital participation in a business or investment activity (*mudaraba* or *musharaka*); and
- to fund various asset acquisition and agency management (*wakala* (agency)), agricultural land cultivation, land management and orchard management activities.

A factor that had impinged upon the structuring and issuance of *sukuk* and *Shari'ah* compliant CMBS transactions was the lack of *Shari'ah* compliant hedging mechanisms and liquidity structures (which may both be required by rating agencies for a rated transaction). The issue of *Shari'ah* compliant hedging mechanisms was rectified in March 2010, by the publication of the *Ta'Hawwut* Master Agreement by the International Swaps and Derivatives Association and the International Islamic Financial Market. However, this development is still in its infancy compared to the conventional hedging market and will take time to consolidate. With regard to liquidity structures and other forms of credit enhancement (which in conventional transactions will be provided by facilities), various structures have been considered on a transaction by transaction basis.

Prohibitions on *riba* (interest), and on the sale of instruments that do not represent fractional undivided ownership interest in tangible assets, present a seemingly insurmountable problem for Islamic compliant securitisation of conventional receivables, such as conventional mortgages, patent and other royalty payments, credit card receivables, and the full range of other conventional receivables. Many of these receivables will never be made *Shari'ah* compliant in and of themselves, but it seems likely that bifurcated structures will be developed to securitise these assets (just as conventional interest-based financing is used in most international *Shari'ah* compliant CRE and private equity financings).

## 18.10.  Tax and regulatory issues

One issue which needs careful consideration as part of the structuring of any *sukuk* transaction is whether the nature of a *sukuk* can raise any tax or regulatory concerns. These issues by their very nature differ across *sukuk* issuances, depending on the jurisdiction(s) of the issuing entity, of the assets and of the investors.

As discussed above, the certificates issued in a *sukuk* are ownership interests in the assets of the issuing vehicle rather than debt instruments. This can raise a number of unexpected tax issues. In a conventional securitisation, it is fundamental that the issuing vehicle be tax neutral. However, the nature of a *sukuk* may mean that this is not the case. The issuing vehicle may not receive the benefit of tax deductions for interest as no interest is paid on the certificates.

Further, if the instrument is deemed to be an equity-like instrument rather than a debt instrument, transfers of the certificate may incur a transfer tax charge. Additionally, various stamp duty and land taxes may also be triggered in a CRE based *sukuk* structure.

There have also been questions as to whether a *sukuk* is a collective investment scheme, and as such, whether in the EU context, would need to be regulated by certain EU legislation.

In a number of jurisdictions (such as the United Kingdom and Ireland), regulations have been introduced in order to ensure that *sukuk* structures are not taxed in a manner inconsistent with securitisations and other structured debt transactions. These regulations can take the form of deeming the cash flows under a *sukuk* to be equivalent to cash flows under a securitisation (for example, deeming periodic distribution payments to be payments of interest) and deeming the instruments to be debt rather than equity (and as such, removing the risk of transfer taxes being imposed).

Regarding the collective investment scheme issue, this needs to be considered on a case by case basis, as the market has yet to come to a position as to whether or not this is triggered.

## 18.11. Negotiability of instruments

When structuring a *sukuk*, it is important to understand the nature of the asset underlying the structure. Trading in debt above or below par would breach *riba* principles (being interest) and be impermissible. As such, where the assets underlying the *sukuk* are receivables, either the instruments could only be traded at par, or their transfer must be prohibited. These limitations are generally problematic in capital markets transactions, where the ability to trade freely is critical for the creation of liquidity. Many capital markets instruments are held through central clearing systems (such as Euroclear or Clearstream) which require the instruments to be negotiable and tradeable.

The resolution of the apparent *riba* issue lies in the fact that in a number of *sukuk* structures (such as an *ijara sukuk*) the underlying assets are tangible assets rather than debts and through the trust certificate structure (under which the assets are subject to a trust declared by the issuing vehicle in favour of a trustee to be held on trust for the holders of the certificates) the *sukuk* holders have an interest in a tangible asset. This structure means that these *sukuk* can be traded above or below par, and if required by investors, held in central clearing systems.

## 18.12. The *sukuk al-ijara*

The *ijara* structure that is so widely used in Islamic finance (see Figure 1) is readily adaptable to *sukuk* in a number of different ways. The simplest *sukuk* issuance utilising the *ijara* structure is shown in Figure 5. In Figure 5, the structure demonstrates the issuing entity issues *sukuk* into the capital markets and uses the proceeds to purchase an asset from the originator. It then leases the asset back to the originator. Often the *sukuk* holders will not have a security interest in the asset (or, where they do have a security interest in the asset, it may be difficult to enforce). Each *sukuk* holder is entitled to receive the rental income generated under the lease pro rata to its ownership interest in the underlying CRE asset based on the *sukuk* held by it.

**Figure 5 – *Ijara Sukuk***

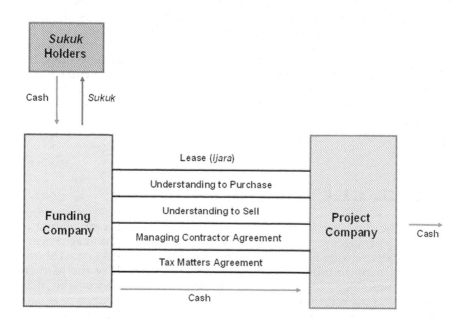

The above *sukuk al-ijara* structure in Figure 5 has been utilised in a large number of *sukuk* issuances across the globe, and is seen by some as the "classic *sukuk*".

In these structures, the rental stream from the *ijara* can be structured to produce a precise cash flow on the *sukuk* akin to conventional debt capital markets instruments. As such, the rate of return can be set as a fixed rate or a floating rate, and the capital return profile can be structured such that it is either through an amortisation schedule, a bullet repayment or a combination of partial amortisation with partial bullet repayment.

Where the structure involves a bullet repayment or partial bullet repayment at maturity, on the maturity of the certificates (or the occurrence of certain other events, such as an event of default), the originator will repurchase the asset at a price fixed at closing. This price will be equal to all amounts owing to the *sukuk* holders. Unlike some other structures, the scholars are comfortable with a fixed price purchase undertaking being used in *ijara* structures. This may be part of the reason why these structures are so popular in the *sukuk* market.

There are some limitations to the use of the *ijara sukuk*. For example, many originators do not own appropriate underlying assets that are subject to *Shari'ah* compliant leases or can be made available for such leases during the *sukuk* term, and, as discussed above, in many jurisdictions, there are significant adverse tax consequences associated with the introduction of the assets into a *sukuk* structure. However, a number of authorities such as those in Ireland, France and the United Kingdom are keen to encourage the growth of Islamic finance within their jurisdictions and have worked with participants in the Islamic finance market to implement regulations to minimise tax issues in *sukuk* and other Islamic finance structures. In fact, London, Dublin and Paris are all keen to try and be the centres of Islamic finance in Europe and have petitioned their relevant tax authorities accordingly.

## 18.13. The *sukuk al-musharaka*

In the *sukuk al-musharaka*, the issuing entity enters into a joint venture or partnership arrangement, pursuant to a *"musharaka management agreement"*, with the party seeking financing (the *"musharaka* partner"). As noted above, each party may contribute capital to the *musharaka*. Each of the partners receives *"units"* or *"hissas"* in the *musharaka* in accordance with their respective capital contributions. The issuer's capital contribution is in cash and equals the proceeds of the *sukuk* issuance. The contribution of the *musharaka* partner is usually an in-kind contribution of a tangible asset (such as a piece of CRE). A *musharaka* structure is depicted in Figure 6.

The issuer and the *musharaka* partner enter into a purchase undertaking pursuant to which the issuer can require the *musharaka* partner to purchase designated units or *hissas* on specified dates either during the term of the *sukuk* or at maturity. Where units are purchased throughout the life of the transaction, the structure is referred to as a diminishing *musharaka*. Economically, this is akin to an amortising bond. However, alternatively, the units may only be repurchased on maturity (or other certain events), in which case the *sukuk* is economically akin to a bond with a bullet repayment.

Under the *musharaka* structure, the issuing entity will receive profit distributions from the *musharaka* and the proceeds from sales of the units or *hissas*, which are then distributed to the *sukuk* holders in accordance with agreed formulae. Although profits and losses are required to be shared between the partners in accordance with their share of total units in the

**Figure 6 –** *Sukuk al-Musharaka*

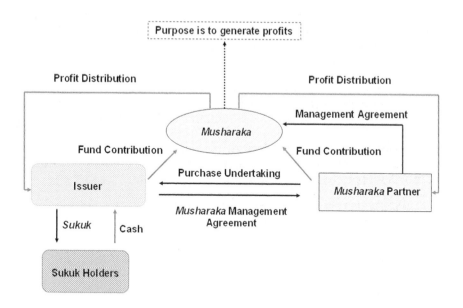

partnership, a number of *sukuk* transactions have been structured such that all profit has been paid to the issuing entity in priority to the *musharaka* partner, until such time as the issuing entities' contribution has been reduced to zero (and the *sukuk* holders have been repaid in full).

In 2008, AAOIFI issued guidelines (the AAOIFI Guidelines) which set out the parameters of how an exercise price under the purchase undertaking could be calculated. Prior to the issuance of the AAOIFI Guidelines, the exercise price would have been stipulated under the purchase undertaking as an amount equal to all amounts owing at the time of exercise to the *sukuk* holders. However, following the issuance of the AAOIFI Guidelines, where the purchaser under the purchase undertaking is the *musharaka* partner, the exercise price cannot be set at closing, but rather is required to be calculated on the basis of the market value of the assets on the date on which the purchase undertaking is exercised. As such, there is the risk that the exercise price may be less than the amounts owing to *sukuk* holders. Although structural mitigates can be built into a *sukuk* transaction utilising a *musharaka* structure (such as reserve funds and *Shari'ah* compliant liquidity features) these may not entirely remove the risk of payment default under the certificates on the exercise of the purchase undertaking.

As such, the use of the *sukuk al musharaka* structure has declined in popularity following the issue of the AAOIFI Guidelines.

## 18.14. The *sukuk al-wakala*

One structure which has been utilised on *sukuk* transactions in the Middle East, at the time of writing, is the *sukuk al-wakala*. This financing structure has been used on a number of funding structures incorporating both conventional and Islamic finance tranches.

In a *sukuk al-wakala*, the issuing entity as investor appoints the *wakeel* as agent to invest the proceeds of the issuance of certificates in accordance with the terms of a *wakala*. The *wakeel* will invest the funds in a portfolio of *Shari'ah* compliant assets, which may be a portfolio of assets or parts of an asset already owned by the *wakeel*. At the outset, the parties to the *wakala* will agree the profit return to the issuing vehicle as investor. This profit return will be paid to the issuing vehicle periodically.

A *sukuk al-wakala* structure is shown in Figure 7.

**Figure 7 – *Sukuk al-Wakala***

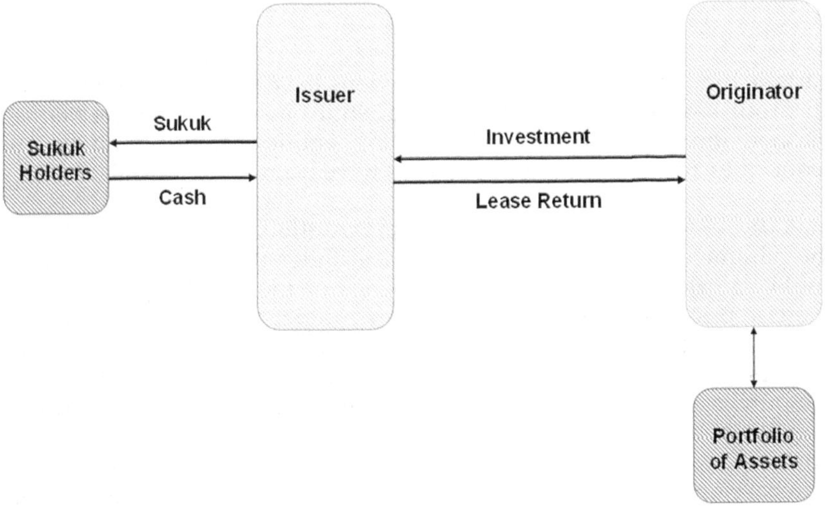

Under a *wakala* structure, any profit is used to pay the profit return to the investor, with the remainder being retained by the *wakeel* as an incentive fee. However, there is a risk that the return generated on the assets may not be sufficient to pay the agreed profit return to the issuing entity, and as such, the *sukuk* holders may suffer a loss. Prior to the AAOIFI Guidelines, a guaranteed profit return structure was utilised in the market. However, following the issue of the AAOIFI Guidelines, the majority of scholars appear to be of the view that a fixed rate of profit return is not acceptable in a *sukuk al-wakala* structure.

*Wakala* structures have been considered in capital raisings by CRE companies, where the companies want to access conventional and *Shari'ah* compliant financing. For example, in the case of a financing of a shopping mall, certain *Shari'ah* compliant parts of the mall could be used as a base for a *wakala*, with the remainder funded by conventional financing.

## 18.15.   The *sukuk al-istisna*

The *sukuk al-istisna* structure has been discussed as an option for project financing, where general bank debt or other forms of Islamic financing are not available. These structures are often referred to as Islamic project bonds. However, the structure also has a number of characteristics which have limited its use by originators.

An *istisna* is essentially an order to a manufacturer to manufacture a specific asset for the purchaser. Under a *sukuk al-istisna*, the originator will agree to manufacture or construct certain assets and deliver those assets to the issuing entity in return for an amount equal to the proceeds of the issuance of certificates.

The issuing entity will then agree to lease the assets back to the originator under a forward lease agreement, under which it agrees to make rental payments to the issuing entity. On the maturity of the certificates or the occurrence of other events, such as an event of default, the originator will be required to purchase the assets from the issuing vehicle for an amount equal to amounts owed to the *sukuk* holders.

A *sukuk al-istisna* structure is shown in Figure 8.

However, as discussed above, there are a number of characteristics relating to these structures. In an *istisna*, there is a construction phase, and then a rental phase. During both phases, the originator will pay periodic rental payments to the issuing entity. There are concerns that during the construction phase, the *sukuk* is only backed by receivables, and as such is not tradable, unless traded at par. Further, some scholars have shown concern about forward leasing, and there is the risk that if the assets are not constructed, any advance rental payments would need to be repaid to the originator.

In light of increased interest in project bonds, it will be interesting to see if these structures become more common, in particular in large multi-funding project finance transactions.

**Figure 8 – *Sukuk al-Istisna***

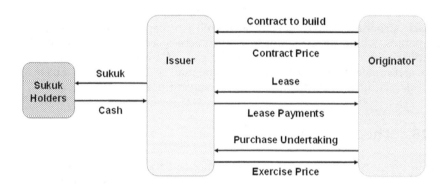

## 18.16. The *sukuk al-mudaraba*

The *mudaraba* structure may also be incorporated into a *sukuk* offering in a number of different variants of the *sukuk al-mudaraba*. A generalised generic form of a *sukuk al-mudaraba* is set forth in Figure 9.

**Figure 9 – *Sukuk al-Mudaraba***

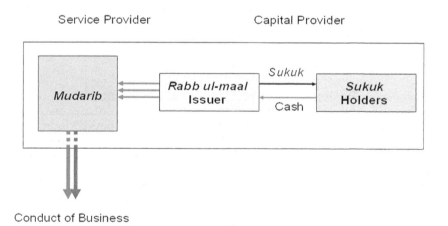

The *sukuk al-mudaraba* is quite similar to the standard *mudaraba* structure presented in Figure 4. The *rabb ul-maal* issuer sells the *sukuk* to the *sukuk* holders and the proceeds of that issuance provide the capital for the *mudaraba*. The *mudarib* will conduct the business of the *mudaraba* as the provider of services. As noted above, this is similar to a limited partnership or limited liability company.

This *mudaraba* may constitute the only entity necessary for the conduct of the relevant business. Or, as is more likely in a complex project or undertaking, this *mudaraba* may enter into joint venture and/or other contractual arrangements with other parties. For example, in a complex project financing this *mudaraba* may enter into a further joint venture with a project sponsor in connection with the financing, construction and operation of the project.

Some of the primary structural considerations will focus, at each level of the transaction, on principles pertaining to allocation and distribution of profits and losses, and the permissibility of capital contributions by the *mudarib*.

A separate set of issues arise in any financing in which capital is needed periodically (these issues also affect other structures, such as the *musharaka*). Consider, for example, the construction of a large-scale project where the construction cycle extends over a period of years and there is no project income during that period. All involved parties will desire that there be certainty of capital availability throughout the construction period. Periodic *sukuk* issuances do not provide that certainty. An initial *sukuk* issuance for the full amount of the construction costs will provide that certainty, but is economically inefficient. The issuance proceeds in excess of immediate needs will be invested in short-term investments (such as *murabaha*) that have low rates of return. Further, the *sukuk* holders will probably expect periodic returns from the inception of the transaction. The project itself will be generating no income (it is in the construction phase) and the reinvestment income will be low. Payments on the *sukuk* during the construction and ramp-up phase are essentially self-funded by the *sukuk* holders.

There have been very few *sukuk al-mudaraba* issuances and following the AAOIFI Guidelines, under which AAOIFI stated that the use of a fixed price purchase undertaking was prohibited in *sukuk* structures, it is expected that these structures will remain rarely used.

## 18.17. The *sukuk al-murabaha*

One *sukuk* structure which probably has limited utility for CRE transactions, yet merits a short discussion, is the *sukuk al-murabaha*. There have been a limited number of *sukuk al-murabaha* when compared to other forms of *sukuk,* however, under certain circumstances, they may be attractive to parties in a capital raising transaction. These forms of *sukuk* generally raise capital for general purposes and are not linked to a specific CRE asset of the originator. However, the capital raised could be used by the originator for CRE purposes.

Figure 10 below shows a bond-type *sukuk.*

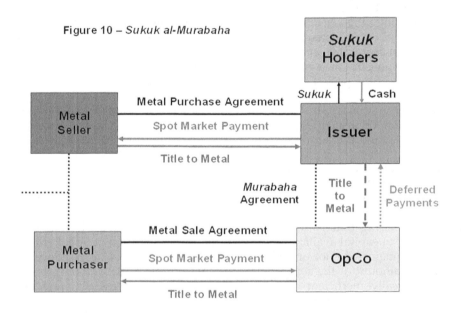

**Figure 10 – *Sukuk al-Murabaha***

The *sukuk al-murabaha* is issued to the *sukuk* holders by the issuer. The *sukuk* represents a "participation interest" in the underlying *murabaha* transaction. The issuance proceeds are used to purchase a metal on the spot market, the metal is then sold to the originator on a deferred payment basis, and the originator sells the metal to the metal purchaser on the spot market. The net result is that the originator holds cash equal to the spot market price of the metal which it can use in its CRE operations and the originator has a deferred payment obligation on the *murabaha agreement* that is used to service the *sukuk.*

Figure 11 below, illustrates a *murabaha sukuk* in which the deferred *murabaha* payment obligations under a pool of *murabaha* transactions are pooled, and the issuer sells a *sukuk* based on that pool.

Under these *murabaha sukuk* structures, the party needing financing (the originator) obtains cash only by selling the tangible asset (the metal or other

450

**Figure 11 – *Sukuk al-Murabaha***

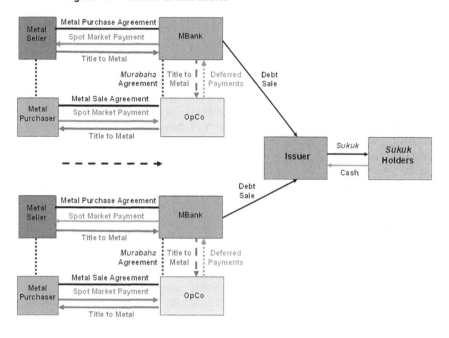

asset). Thus, on an ongoing basis, this *sukuk* does not represent an ownership interest in a tangible asset—it has been sold—and only the deferred debt obligation (a receivable) remains after sale of the asset.

As such, the assets underlying the *sukuk* are debts. One of the general principles of the *Shari'ah* is that debt cannot be traded except at par. As such, the certificates issued in a *sukuk al-musharaka* cannot be negotiable instruments and traded on the secondary market. This limits the possible investor base for these types of instruments. However, there have been a number of recent transactions which have utilised a *sukuk al-musharaka* structure where the investors have agreed to hold the assets for the term of the transaction.

Further, it is possible for a *sukuk* to have a number of underlying structures, including a *murabaha* structure, where the receivables derived from the *murabaha* are a small proportion of the overall structure.

It should be noted that the position of scholars in South East Asia is somewhat different to the position of scholars outside of that region. The South East Asian scholars accept that a *murabaha* may be used as the basis for a tradeable *sukuk*, making this structure a common feature of the capital markets in that region.

## 18.18.  Conclusion

In 2012, the future for the Islamic finance market is difficult to predict, although the hope is that it will continue to grow and develop globally as a true alternative form of funding. If the development in new legislation, to encourage Islamic finance, is an indicator of its future, its future does indeed look bright. In addition to developments in countries such as the United Kingdom, which have been discussed in this Chapter, as at the time of writing, a number of other jurisdictions have tried to encourage the development of Islamic finance. South Africa has announced its intention of executing a sovereign *sukuk* to encourage the South African market, whilst Australia and France have encouraged the development of the Islamic finance markets in their respective countries. Regulators have shown themselves willing to consider Islamic finance structures and equalise the tax position of Islamic finance structures with their equivalent conventional finance structures.

Regarding Islamic CRE finance, based on recent history, it is hoped that the markets continue to see strong growth in this market. Liquidity needs will focus CRE market players on Islamic finance as an alternative financing channel. Progress in product development, coupled with strong demand, should sharply accelerate growth in Islamic finance due to pent-up demand. For example, there is a forecast need for £1.3 trillion of project finance in GCC countries and £60 billion of mortgage finance in Saudi Arabia.

Conventional banks will, as set out in numerous chapters throughout this book, increasingly focus on refinancing, de-risking, improving capital ratios and deleveraging. They will vacate a significant part of the CRE finance field and Islamic finance can help to partly meet the remaining demand, with the result that Islamic finance and investment is poised to enter the mainstream of the global CRE market.

Regarding the *sukuk* market, recent *sukuk* defaults have led to a focus on the position of *sukuk* holders and, in particular, the rights they have to the underlying assets. This has, as discussed above, highlighted the distinction between asset-backed and asset-based structures, comparable to the rights of bondholders under secured and unsecured bonds. In asset-based *sukuk*, the holders can only require the originator to purchase the underlying *sukuk* assets and would have an unsecured debt claim against the originator from the payment of the purchase price after exercising their rights under the relevant purchase undertaking. This credit risk profile may not be what some investors expected. However, there has recently been a surge in *sukuk* issuances in the Middle East and South East Asia, including a number of sovereign issuances. These are very encouraging signs for the continued growth of the Islamic finance capital markets and Islamic finance market as a whole.

# Chapter 19

# Lost (and Found) in Translation: US Cross-border Investments in European Commercial Mortgage Markets

**Anthony R. G. Nolan,**

Partner, K&L Gates LLP

**Diego Shin,**

Senior Associate, K&L Gates LLP

## 19.1. Introduction[1]

In late 2011 and early 2012, the fragile green shoots of recovery began to peek out from the barren blasted heath of the crisis-blown financial markets. Market activity was spurred by a rare confluence of secular trends, which included the strategic imperative of European financial institutions to deleverage and divest assets in order to improve their regulatory capital, leverage and liquidity ratios, a phenomenon that has been described elsewhere in this book.[2] Markets were also impacted by the liquidity provided by pension and investment funds throughout the world, which have been particularly interested in prime commercial real estate (CRE) assets in major European cities.[3] Whilst investment in European CRE has long been regarded as a relative value play for many global investors, North American interest in European CRE has, in particular, proven to be an effective counterweight to the traditional interest of European investors in US CRE opportunities.

As set out in Ch.2, as the European CRE sector and related debt markets have emerged from the massive repricing of credit risk and property fundamentals that occurred during the financial crisis, a significant part of the resurgence in demand for European CRE assets has come from the United States. Indeed, it has been estimated that US investors represented

---

[1]   The authors are grateful for the comments of their tax colleagues, Roger Wise and Tom Lyden to this Chapter.

[2]   See further Chs 9 and 16.

[3]   This Chapter should be read in conjunction with the oportunity for such investors identified in detail in Ch. 3.

almost a quarter of all of investments in European CRE in 2011, up from the year before, with North American investors responsible for fully one third of all such investments in 2010.

There are many reasons why US investors looked to the Old Continent in the wake of the financial crisis in the New World. One reason is that European CRE, which had long been valued as a source of diversification, became more attractive as US mortgage markets were broadly affected by the fall in the residential sector and CRE properties were affected by the steep fall off in tenant demand in US markets. Another is the weakening trend of the US dollar in relation to major European currencies, which affected the demand of US investors for future cash flows denominated in those currencies. Lastly, European CRE capital markets were relatively active at a time that commercial CRE deal volumes in the United States were moribund. While it remains to be seen how the investment story will play out in light of the long-running efforts of the European Union to avert hard devaluations by Eurozone member states, it appears that continuing uncertainty over European fiscal and monetary policy will provide additional attractive occasions for opportunistic private equity investors to obtain interests in fundamentally strong CRE at favourable prices, as discussed in Ch.3.

This Chapter will address some of the trends in global investments in European CRE and touch on some of the strategic and tactical issues that potential investors should be prepared to address when investing in European CRE. These include country-specific features; differences and similarities between investments through interests in mortgages, mezzanine notes and B-pieces; CMBS in Europe and the United States; the CRE debt secondary markets; and problems associated with the economic pressures in the Eurozone.

## 19.2. Post-crisis transactional trends in european CRE

As discussed in Ch.1, structured monetisations of CRE assets since the advent of the financial crisis have included two fully placed non-retained or credit-tenant linked CMBS, the first time such transactions were issued in Europe since the boom markets of 2007. Such issuances have, as discussed in Ch.4, represented an evolution in the structure and disclosure conventions of CMBS from those that prevailed before the crisis CMBS, as they have sought to comply with recent legislative developments and perceived investor concerns.

However, CMBS new issuance volumes have been adversely affected by the pricing volatility of CMBS since 2010, which has often rendered it commercially impracticable for sponsors to proceed with further issuances. Furthermore, legislative and regulatory uncertainty both in the United

States and Europe has made it difficult to issue CMBS in the market, as both arrangers and investors have yet to have a full appreciation of the impact that further legislative developments (and rule-making) may have on the sale and purchase of CMBS by certain categories of institutions. Among areas of concern are art.122a of the Capital Requirements Directive in the EU and corresponding proposals for the Solvency II Directive and proposed US rules that may affect the structures of and disclosures for CMBS transactions, the regulatory capital risk weighting of CMBS tranches of varying levels of seniority and commodity regulation of transactions with more than a de minimis amount of swaps to hedge risks such as those associated with exchange rates or interest rates.[4]

Despite—or perhaps informed by—such opportunities and challenges, there have been several dispositions of performing and non-performing CRE loan portfolios. These have taken several forms, including by way of non-exhaustive examples:

- by joint venture vehicles formed between the vendor and the successful bidder with vendor finance being provided. Illustrative examples of such transactions include Blackstone's acquisition of a c.£1.36 billion UK portfolio sold by The Royal Bank of Scotland in December 2011, Apollo Management's acquisition of a c.€2.1 billion pan-European portfolio from Credit Suisse in late 2010 and Lone Star's acquisition of a €2.3 billion pan-European portfolio from Credit Suisse in mid-2009;
- through a straight acquisition of the portfolio with third party debt being provided. Lone Star's December 2011 acquisition of a c.£900 million UK portfolio from Lloyds with financing, reported to have been provided by Citigroup and Royal Bank of Canada; Kennedy Wilson's acquisition of a circa $1.8 billion UK portfolio from Bank of Ireland, also in December 2011, with Deutsche Bank providing debt and equity financing, and Lone Star's reported acquisition of a €200 million non-performing loan (NPL) portfolio from Société Générale in the first half of 2012; and
- in an auction style atmosphere by distressed lenders or governmentally established bank repositories. The segmented disposals of the Irish National Asset Management Agency (NAMA) and the formerly named Anglo Irish Bank's sale of a $9.5 billion US portfolio to Lone Star, Wells Fargo and J.P. Morgan Chase in late 2011 are typical examples of transactions that are primarily arising as a consequence of the Irish bank bail outs and nationalisations of 2009.

Structures for the acquisition of large CRE portfolios will ultimately depend on the characteristics and factors affecting both buyers and sellers as well as the location of the properties underlying such acquired financial assets. Depending on the size of the portfolios, and subject to considerations

---

[4]   See further Chs 8 and 15.

arising from the specific circumstances of the buyer and the seller, the structure of a transaction is dictated by the eternal question of real estate finance: whether the buyer can make an all-cash bid or whether it will require acquisition financing as a condition to its consummation of the CRE acquisition. A further question is whether the seller can provide such financing to the buyer (whether in the form of straight debt or equity contribution to the purchasing vehicle, or a combination of each of these) or requires payment of the purchase price all in cash.

Correlated with the above decision points are the needs and objectives of the seller, which may be affected by concerns beyond purely economic considerations, such as local law requirements and tax efficiencies. For example, a sole acquisition asset holding vehicle may not comply with applicable local law requirements in certain European jurisdictions (such as France) where only certain limited locally authorised institutions may own or make loans to entities or secured by property located in such jurisdiction. Ever-present tax considerations will also require that the asset owning vehicle be organised in a jurisdiction that is exempt from withholding tax by the jurisdiction with taxing authority on payments it receives in respect of a CRE asset.

As a further example of considerations specific to the buyer or the seller, 2012 witnessed the sale by the German Bundesbank to a Lone Star entity of Excalibur CMBS securities that it had acquired by foreclosing on a Lehman Brothers repurchase facility under the European Central Bank (ECB) liquidity facility programme. This transaction differed from the preceding examples because Lehman Brothers had structured and issued the original CMBS transaction in order to repo such bonds with the ECB as a source of short-term liquidity at a time when markets had become highly illiquid. When the Bundesbank foreclosed on the repurchase facility, it soon became apparent, to at least some observers, that it had neither the expertise nor mandate to manage the resolution of each underlying asset backing the CMBS, particularly in light of the complexity of the assets included within the securitisation, which included a mixture of various direct loan interests and CMBS issued under other programmes. Accordingly, a sale of CMBS under such circumstances would have been premised on immediate recoverability, vis-à-vis, the original exposure: recovery value can affect how the market perceives the structure of a transaction, since resale value can sometimes be enhanced by extricating and repackaging assets (such as the underlying collateral) and selling these in individualised portfolios rather than wholesale.

As the foregoing examples illustrate, context matters in evaluating transactions involving European CMBS. Important considerations include structural and contextual differences among the participants in a trans-action, the types of assets involved in such transactions, how such assets were acquired or originated by the sellers in the first instance and the differential capacity of a wide range of market participants to hold and work out distressed assets. Transactions can be distinguished on the basis of those features, each of which can have a material impact on the structure of a proposed acquisition and valuation metrics. Each of these will be considered in turn.

## 19.3. Asset-level investment considerations

The confection of a winning bid to acquire CRE assets requires a sound strategy coupled with compelling financing and engaged and competent service providers. Moreover, it requires a proper appreciation of the legal technicalities associated with investments in European CRE by international investors. In some respects, this last ingredient can be particularly challenging for investors whose investment experience has been limited to their own jurisdictions, for CRE is uniquely influenced by the law of the place where the property is located. In law, as in commercial life, it truly can be said that the secret of CRE investment is "location, location, location."

Cross-border considerations in Europe are more complex than in the United States not merely because of language and cultural differences, but also because of the fundamentally different evolution of real estate law in Europe and the United States despite converging conceptions of a federal system. In the United States, whilst real estate law and law governing enforcement or foreclosure is specific to each US State, the laws of each US State—particularly with respect to CRE as opposed to residential real estate—can be viewed as relatively homogenous in a very general way, at least if compared to the hotch-potch of various legal systems and concepts evident across national borders in Europe.

As an example, it is fairly typical in the United Kingdom to see borrowing structures with varying degrees of complexity where the borrowers may be located in certain jurisdictions with favourable offshore tax regimes (such as, by way of illustration, Ireland, Luxembourg, Jersey or Gibraltar), or which provide greater tax efficiency, or are required to be used to comply with applicable national law on the basis of the underlying assets collateralising a given loan (the Netherlands or France, among others). Added complexity is introduced to the extent that, the underlying CRE securing such financings may be located in one or more European jurisdictions and to the extent that the documentation governing such loan and associated hedging relationships may be subject to the national laws of another EU Member State. Accordingly, European CRE loans involve an appreciation of various legal regimes (each with its own lending and security requirements) that are distinct from each other. This is a fundamental difference from the US legal framework for equivalent transactions to the extent that standards are essentially sui generis or incompatible with other regimes.

The enforcement of rights in a CRE mortgage depends heavily on the local law governing interests in the subject CRE, the enforceability of subordination and non-disturbance arrangements, and the local power of eminent domain. In addition to the basic impact of cross-border legal systems on the structure and documentation of a CRE loan, the appraisal of value of a CRE project is often a function of planning (zoning in the US) and land use restrictions, which in the experience of investors with a point of reference in the United States, are resolved at the most local level of government. This may depend as much on local conceptions of what is the highest and best use for a loan as on conventional legal doctrine. Therefore, an important consideration for US investors in European CRE is to strategically map the legal concepts and enforcement rights that are relevant to determinations of value to the corresponding concepts to which they are accustomed in their home jurisdictions.

### 19.3.1. Strategy

In order to realise the strategic vision, it is also necessary to have in place a robust platform or service provider network that permits realisation of those expectations, bearing in mind that the ultimate strategy will determine the manner in which a CRE portfolio is managed. In the case of a classic long-term equity management play, it will be particularly important to have a strong servicing and property management capability on an asset-by-asset basis with disposition or favourable refinancing as an ultimate exit strategy.[5] On the other hand, in the case of a distressed lending "loan to own" strategy the most important elements of investment success will be the ability to obtain value by enforcement and ultimate disposition, refinancing or repositioning of the property after enforcement. The application of these considerations to an individual case will depend on the nature of the parties to a transaction and the character of the acquisition of the interest in CRE, as discussed above. However, in order to have a meaningfully realistic exit strategy, the investor should consider having a captive servicer platform (either in-house or appointed via a non-exclusive third party arrangement) to provide the expertise in resolution strategy.

### 19.3.2. Financing

The specific implementation of a portfolio acquisition strategy may be affected by the conditions in which the acquiring party will expect to finance its acquisition. Some basic considerations have been discussed above. Financing terms may be affected by a variety of factors, including whether the CRE acquisition is being conducted on an asset-by-asset basis, or as part of a broader portfolio transaction, whether the financing is structured using securitisation techniques. The objectives and timelines of the bidder that may impact the use of leverage may also affect investment

---

[5] See further Chs 5 and 6.

decisions. In the case of investment funds these generally relate to the fund guidelines and in the case of joint ventures they may require negotiation between the bidders on a common set of parameters.

A key consideration will be the difficulty of obtaining third party debt or equity financing to support the acquisition. As discussed in Ch.2, third-party financing has not normally been available as an option in the difficult environment after 2008, resulting in a relatively prominent need to obtain vendor financing, though financial institutions are now considering with greater interest opportunities to finance portfolio sales on non-performing CRE assets due to the high margins and fees payable and quick repayment. Whilst 2011 and 2012 saw a gradual opening of sources of third party finance, it is uncertain whether the trickle will dry up or will grow into a raging flood. The availability of third-party financing sources provides greater options for an ultimate exit. In this regard, the reopening of the CLO market in the United States may be regarded as a source of optimism, for while it is primarily focused on corporate debt obligations, it may be a harbinger of enhanced liquidity to large loan transactions. If that is taken together with increasing investment opportunities to finance portfolio acquisitions in Europe, a more buoyant level of activity in the short term appears likely. In that sense, there is potential opportunity for investors to take an equity stake in a transaction or provide straight financing (either alone or in syndicate) to third party purchasers to allow such parties to gain exposure to transactions they may have not otherwise been able to access, in so-called "loan on loan" financing. Whether such institutions will prefer an equity or financing role will ultimately depend on the risk/return profile of the transaction that may ultimately cater more to certain types of institutions rather than others.

In assessing the liquidation options for a CRE acquisition, a crucial determinant is the type of bidder involved and how the targeted investor's objectives may impact the structure or financing of a bid. A good example of this may be seen in Blackstone's bid for the Isobel portfolio, as it was reported that the main investor supporting the bid was China Investment Corporation. These types of investors will bring specific needs and requirements to the markets, as outlined in Ch.3.

### 19.3.3    Getting the necessary parties onboard

As discussed above, a crucial element of any strategy that involves a financing option is to determine the optimal source of financing, whether provided by the vendor or by a third party, and the terms of the financing. This will involve very different considerations depending on the nature of the financing party and the way in which the financing is structured. It may be necessary to structure a financing in such a way to satisfy rating agency criteria,[6] if the objective is to create highly rated CMBS securities that satisfy investment guidelines of capital market investors, or alternatively to facilitate the issuance of asset-backed commercial paper by permiting the conduit to satisfy its own rating requirements.

The identity of parties to a financing transaction will be dictated to a great extent by the nature of the transaction. A trustee or security trustee, an administrator, a servicer and a special servicer are all potential parties to a financing transaction. Their roles in the European market are dealt with throughout this book.

### 19.3.4. Certain legal considerations affecting marketing

#### 19.3.4.1. Type of asset or transaction

The amount of due diligence required in respect of a CRE transaction is heavily dependent on the nature of the asset and of the transaction itself. In the case of a whole loan acquisition, the purchaser will have full power to exercise control over the loan and negotiate any work-outs or other resolution strategies with the related borrowers, subject only to restrictions imposed by local law.[7] As described above, a purchaser must appreciate the local laws affecting its proposed exit strategy in relation to each asset it is acquiring. European loan structures can be complex when compared with their US equivalents and can involve a number of very distinct legal regimes. To the extent that a transaction involves non-CRE assets such as synthetic swaps and there may also be exposures to third parties that may introduce counterparty credit risk to a transaction and that counterparty may also have rights to administer or influence the decision-making in respect of the reference obligation.

Apart from the predictable impact that the governing laws of the place of incorporation of each member of a given borrower group may have on a structure, it is also important to consider the various tax considerations that can have an impact on such strategies. These tax considerations may not necessarily be limited to the applicable tax regime affecting the location of where the CRE is situated, but may extend to the relevant entity's place of incorporation and/or where it effectively manages and operates its business, among other considerations.

On the other hand, if the asset is a tranche of a loan, or a CMBS security, the ability of the holder to take actions with respect to it may be materially limited if other parties (whether lenders or bondholders) have contractual rights permitting them to exercise control rights over the asset, such as rights to consult on servicing decisions, special servicing transfers or appraisal reductions, each of which have been discussed in Chs 5, 6 and 7.

---

[6] See further Ch.11.
[7] See further Ch.9.

Furthermore, the extent to which the CRE asset may be out of the money may affect the identity of the party entitled to exercise such control rights, as the controlling party is often defined as a majority of the most subordinate class with at least 25 per cent of its principal amount outstanding. It is worth noting that it is not always easy in Europe to identify such controlling party at any given time because publicly placed European securitisations do not maintain a central register of noteholders and because CMBS securities are often held in book-entry form through Euroclear. This problem of identification is similar to that affecting US CMBS in book-entry form that is held through DTEC.[8] Accordingly, purchasers of non-controlling classes of bonds may wish to take additional steps to identify which institutions are represented within the controlling class where the identity of such institutions can have an impact on how the purchaser's realisation strategy is or can be implemented and whether such strategy is ultimately realistic taking into account such third parties' own interests.

### 19.3.4.2. Control

In the case of CMBS securities, the control determinations can be complicated by many factors, including intercreditor issues between the securitisation and subordinate loans that are secured by the same mortgaged property but are held outside the securitisation structure. These types of intercreditor issues are often apparent in tranched A/B loan structures, where the senior (or A) tranche of the loan is placed in a securitisation and the subordinate (or B) tranche is either held, assigned or is itself securitised in a mezzanine CMBS or CRE CDO.[9] The subordination and intercreditor arrangements are of great importance because the party with control over enforcement rights and other functions such as appraisal reductions will have great influence over determinants of value.

The nature of the asset and the nature and existence of other creditors (such as swap counterparties, junior lenders, senior lenders or mezzanine lenders) may affect the extent to which the purchaser may exercise control rights in respect of the asset. For example, swap counterparties to financing structures often have contractually determined rights to share in cash flow from the charged property, with remedies upon certain events that can include changes to payment entitlements and step-up of rights to direct certain determinations, discussed in Ch.15. To the extent that there are other lenders in the structure, or that rights are held by CMBS bondholders, other parties (such as third party lenders, swap providers or loan servicers) will be involved in the transaction or the administration of the underlying asset in either an ownership, secured party or agency capacity. Any of such

---

[8] See further Chs 4 and 10.
[9] See Chs 14 and 15.

parties may present an obstacle to a purchaser that seeks to implement its own resolution strategy by acquiring a direct interest in the loan CMBS bonds backed by the loan.

A fairly typical example of how such parties to a transaction can directly impact the management of a loan relationship is seen in the rights such parties may have to require the termination and appointment of their nominated special servicer (if any has been appointed). In distressed loans, such special servicers will have primary responsibility in managing the lender/borrower relationship, interfacing with the borrower as to proposed work-out or restructuring plans and ultimately when and whether to take any enforcement action in respect of that loan and its security.[10] It is also possible that such third parties may have certain consent or consultation rights before such prescribed actions are implemented in respect of the related loan or its security. These types of consideration will affect the nature of a CRE investor's interactions with the borrower, as well as the opportunities for realisation of value or liquidity.

### 19.3.4.3.   Facility agent / security agent transfers

In order to maximise the opportunities of realisation on a particular loan asset, the purchaser (or its delegates) normally must be able to interface directly with the borrowers on the underlying loans. Effective channels of communication can be crucial to the ability to engage in modifications of the loan and to understand issues involving the borrower that can affect value. To the extent that any of the existing agents in a loan structure are intending to exit the transaction after the purchaser completes its acquisition of the asset by the purchaser, it is important to ensure that such transfers are permitted and to control the costs and liabilities involved in the same, including, such items as transfers of any related security held in any particular agent's own name. Similarly to what has been described above, local law requirements may have an impact on the selection of any replacements, as certain European jurisdictions regulate the types of entities that may perform certain functions in respect of CRE assets. As discussed in other Chapters, securitisations will usually involve other intermediaries as well, such as a loan agent or servicer or a special servicer who will be a point of contact with the underlying obligors. Following its acquisition of the CRE interest, it will be important for the purchaser to assess the extent of its control over the selection and replacement of this intermediary and to ensure that the preferred intermediary is in the role. The considerations discussed above under "control" will be germane to that assessment.

---

[10]   See further Chs 5 and 6.

### 19.3.4.4.  Restrictions on assignability

The assignability of a CRE loan that has been acquired is an important element to determining the lender's exit, in the case of a direct loan and of the lender's ability to take necessary actions and make needed determinations, in the case of a loan that is financed through a CMBS structure. In cases where a CRE loan or other asset is not capable of being assigned, it is necessary to consider alternative structures such as loan participations or total return swaps. However, these arrangements pose their own challenges, including the continuing interposition of the lender of record as counterparty, facing the party with the actual credit exposure to the underlying borrower. In order to be viable, any transaction must be structured and implemented in such a way that the purchaser or servicer may effectively take lender decisions in respect of a CRE loan.

## 19.4.  Special considerations for US investors

As discussed in Ch.1, CMBS has long represented a source of liquidity for investments in commercial mortgages. The combination of bankruptcy-remote structuring and structured credit enhancement to provide a basis for issuance of highly-rated mortgage-backed securities has long been a potent structuring tool, one that has facilitated capital formation in the CRE markets worldwide.

Although the previous sections of this Chapter have focused on asset-level issues, a crucial set of considerations for transactions sold to US investors relates to the regulatory impact of the structure on US investors, and conversely on the impact that US investors can have on the legal position of a non-US issuer or sponsor.

Commercial mortgage investments that are packaged into securities for sale to investors in the US raise several sets of legal issues. In respect of European issued ABS, these may involve an interplay between US and European legislation, which may impose additional requirements to those which would apply on a purely domestic issuance. [11]From a US perspective, the principal issues involve the registration requirements of and substantive liability under the securities laws, the need to obtain an exemption from registration of the issuer as an investment company, the need to structure the transaction to be eligible for investment by pension plans without causing a prohibited transaction under US pension law and the need to structure the transaction in such a way as to qualify for favourable treatment under US tax law governing real estate mortgage investment conduits.[12]

---

[11]  Recent legislative requirements in respect of European ABS are discussed in Ch.16, whilst this Chapter solely explores US considerations.

[12]  In the interest of space this discussion does not address some areas of law that have not

### 19.4.1. Securities laws

Any offering of securities in the United States or to US persons (including European issuances marketed to US investors) must be registered with the US Securities and Exchange Commission (SEC) unless an exemption from registration is available. The typical exemptions used for CMBS offerings are Regulation D and r.144A under the Securities Act of 1933, as amended (Securities Act). Regulation D applies to private placements of securities to "accredited investors," both on initial sale and on resale, but are not intended for broadly distributed offerings, although the US JOBS Act has relaxed the restrictions on general solicitations of such offerings in certain circumstances. Rule 144A is a resale exemption that applies to offerings to "qualified institutional investors," which are institutional investors that own at least $100 million of securities issued by unaffiliated investors.[13]

Registered offerings of CMBS must comply with the registration and disclosure requirements of the SEC's Regulation AB. This rule sets forth specific requirements for disclosure of information about sponsors, originators, servicers, trustees of a securitisation transaction and also requires significant information about the pool assets, including detailed information about significant obligors as well as static pool information about the current pool and prior securitised pools. In addition, registered offerings must comply with the requirements of SEC Rule 193 to provide disclosure about the underwriting of the securitised assets. Regulation AB requires that service providers certify annually as to compliance with servicing standards. Regulation AB has been in place since 2004 and CMBS offerings

---

affected securitization or private equity transactions in the past but that may have an impact on them depending on how certain rule making activity to implement the Dodd-Frank Wall Street Reform, Consumer Protection and Transparency Act ("Dodd-Frank Act") are carried out. Such areas of potential expansion may include potential regulation of securitisation vehicles as commodity pool operators, impact of swap regulation and restrictions on covered funds imposed by the Volcker Rule. As of the date of writing the potential impact of those issues is too uncertain to assess authoritatively. Therefore the following discussion focuses on areas that have been core regulatory areas and addresses regulatory reform under the Dodd-Frank Act only in the context of how it may impinge on traditional analyses.

13  Registered offerings are subject to liability under ss.11 and 12 of the Securities Act of and s.10(b) and 17 of the Securities Exchange Act of 1934 as amended. Section 11 imposes joint and several strict liability to the issuer, its officers and directors, the underwriters and any experts who have consented to be named as such in the prospectus for losses arising from any material misstatement or omissions in the prospectus, although the underwriters can defend against a claim under s.11 by showing that they had conducted "due diligence." Section 12 imposes strict liability against any person who offers or sells a security by means of a prospectus or oral communication which includes a material misstatement or omission. Section 10(b) and s.17(a) require as a condition to liability, that that the defendant knew or was reckless in not discovering that the disclosure contained a material misstatement or omission. As a practical matter, registered offerings expose the sponsor to greater risk of liability than unregistered offerings because under current law only s.10(b) and s.17(a) provides a basis of securities law liability in those transactions.

in the United States have been structured in reliance on it, with reporting, certification and indemnification provisions that have become quite standard over the years.

In mid-2011 the SEC proposed amendments to Regulation AB that would significantly change the shelf registration eligibility requirements, disclosure requirements and credit risk retention requirements for CMBS offerings.[14] Among other things, the proposed amendments would require that the issuer disclose the payment waterfall in computer programming language to facilitate investor modelling and that in an offering of CMBS that are "taken down" from a shelf registration statement the issuer certify that the structure and assets are sufficient to ensure payment in full of the securities offered under the shelf registration statement. These changes represent a potentially significant expansion of liability for issuers and sponsors of CMBS offerings, although the scope and contours will depend on the terms of the final regulation if and when it is adopted.

Although the disclosure for r.144A CMBS offerings is generally based on the standards of Regulation AB, not all of the requirements of Regulation AB are necessarily followed in all cases depending on practicalities. The proposed amendments to Regulation AB would change this by requiring that the investors in unregistered offerings of CMBS be contractually entitled to require the full suite of Regulation AB disclosure that they would have been entitled to receive in a registered offering. This requirement is expected to erode the distinction between registered and unregistered offerings and to bifurcate the CMBS market into fully SEC-registered deals and truly private deals. Sponsors of CMBS transactions sold into the US would thus be forced to navigate between the Scylla of heightened liability and the Charybdis of reduced liquidity.

While there has been considerable experience with the operation of Regulation AB in US CMBS transactions, many look with trepidation on the potential impact of the proposed amendments to Regulation AB on the wider CRE finance market. In particular, there is a concern that the enhanced disclosure requirements may pose compliance difficulties, particularly where the underlying assets may themselves consist of structured finance securities with respect to which the issuer cannot provide adequate disclosure with respect to underlying assets.

---

[14] The credit risk retention requirements are expected to have less of an impact on CMBS than on some other types of securitisations because of a proposed exemption from the requirement for CMBS transactions in which the first risk of loss is held by a third-party B-piece investor. This proposed exemption reflects the customary way in which the first risk of loss is allocated in CMBS transactions, where a vibrant B-piece market evolved in conjunction with the tendency of special servicers to acquire the B-piece interests for the transactions in which they provide services. See further Chs 1 and 14.

### 19.4.2.  Investment Company Act

Securitisation entities are "investment companies" as defined in the Investment Company Act of 1940, as amended (Investment Company Act), and therefore are required to register as such unless an exclusion from the definition applies. As a practical matter it is imperative for CRE structured finance transactions to operate under an exclusion from registration, because the substantive requirements of the Investment Company Act that apply to registered investment companies are antithetical the requirements of securitisations. These requirements include stringent limitations on leverage that would severely curtail the ability to use financing in a manner that is customary for CRE investments, as well as restrictions on transactions with affiliates and certain other business activities that could hinder the relationships among many parties to the CRE transaction. The consequences of failure to register an investment company for which an exclusion does not apply include administrative sanctions and automatic unenforceability under US law of all contracts that the investment company has entered into.

The most common exclusion for CMBS transactions and other CRE transactions is s.3(c)(5)(C) of the Investment Company Act. That section excludes from the definition of investment company "[a]ny person who is not engaged in the business of issuing redeemable securities, face-amount certificates of the installment type or periodic payment plan certificates, and who is primarily engaged...[in the business of] purchasing or otherwise acquiring mortgages and other liens on and interests in real estate." Many different types of companies in a variety of businesses rely on this exclusion. Such companies include: those that originate and hold CRE interests (such as mortgage participations, mezzanine loans and mortgage-backed securities) and companies that invest in CRE, mortgages and mortgage-related instruments. The SEC staff, in providing guidance on this exclusion, generally has indicated in several No-Action Letters that a company will be considered to be "primarily engaged" in the business of purchasing or otherwise acquiring mortgages and other liens on and interests in CRE if at least 55 per cent of the issuer's assets will consist of mortgages and other liens on and interests in CRE (called "qualifying interests") and the remaining 45 per cent of the issuer's assets will consist primarily of CRE-type interests, such as Tier 1 CRE mezzanine loan.

The SEC is engaged in a review of interpretive issues relating to the status of mortgage-related pools under the Investment Company Act in light of the evolution of mortgage-related pools and the development of new and complex mortgage-related instruments. The review was occasioned by concerns that s.3(c)(5)(C) exclusion has been expanded beyond its originally intended scope by CRE-related investors that have sought to rely on it for exclusions of investments in CRE securities, or other interests that are far afield from classic mortgages and CRE equity interests. This review is unlikely to change the applicability of s. 3(c)(5)(C) to traditional CMBS transactions (unless by changing the interpretation of what it means to be "primarily engaged"), but it may result in a narrow interpretation of its applicability to non-traditional securitisations or to other CRE-related transactions. If s.3(c)(5)(C) were not available, a CMBS transaction with US investors would have to be structured to rely on Investment Company Act r.3a–7 or s.3(c)(7). Rule 3a–7 is an exemption from the registration requirements for securitisations of eligible assets that meet certain requirements relating to ratings, security interests and the like and do not provide for active management of assets for the purpose of realising gains or avoiding losses, while s.3(c)(7) is available for companies that are not contemplating a public offering and whose securities (or in the case of a foreign issuer, whose securities held by US residents) are held only by "qualified purchasers" that have not been formed for the purpose of the transaction in which they are investing and that generally have $5 million or more in investable assets.

### 19.4.3. ERISA

Most privately sponsored US pension arrangements are subject to the fiduciary responsibility requirements of the Employee Retirement Income Security Act of 1974, as amended (ERISA). These requirements apply to investment advisers and similar persons who manage assets of certain US pension plans, regardless of where that manager is located. The require-ments include general fiduciary standards of conduct as well as strict "prohibited transaction" restrictions, which bar ERISA investors from dealing with certain specified parties ("parties in interest") in the absence of a statutory or administrative exemption.[15] ERISA fiduciaries are prohibited from engaging in certain types of transactions involving self-dealing and conflicts of interest with parties in interest. As an example of the breadth of the prohibited transactions prohibitions, an ERISA fiduciary would be prohibited from investing in securities of the plan sponsor or its material suppliers in the absence of an exemption. Actions to recover damages for breach of fiduciary duty may be brought in US courts on behalf of an ERISA investor by another fiduciary for that investor or directly by the US Department of Labor.

The managers of certain private funds in which ERISA plans invest may be considered to be fiduciaries of the ERISA plan, and subject to the standard of care and other restrictions described above. This regulation could result in the servicers of asset pools supporting some CMBS instruments to be considered ERISA fiduciaries, if interests in the pool are offered and sold to

---

[15] ERISA's fiduciary standard is one of the highest standards of care available under US law. A retirement plan fiduciary must act with prudence and undivided loyalty to the participants in that plan. A person providing investment advice for a fee, either direct or indirect, is a fiduciary if (among other requirements) the advice is given on a regular basis pursuant to a mutual understanding that it is the primary basis for the investment decision.

an ERISA plan. For this reason most CMBS issues that are marketed to ERISA plans comply with the requirements of an ERISA exemption, regardless of whether the sponsor or the assets are outside the United States. Also, because of the complexity and severity of the ERISA fiduciary requirements, it is often desirable to structure CRE investment funds to avoid their application. In the case of equity real estate funds, this can be accomplished by structuring the fund as a "real estate operating company" (or REOC).[16]

### 19.4.4. Tax

Tax efficiency is a key consideration for real estate investors, particularly in international transactions. US investors acquiring interests in European CRE would need to consider the effects on a proposed transaction of applicable tax regimes in Europe and the United States.

#### 19.4.4.1. EU Tax considerations

US investors in European CRE must be familiar with the applicable tax laws in relevant European jurisdictions affecting investments in real estate transactions, including such matters as whether the underlying asset is eligible for depreciation and if so the depreciation rate that applies, the treatment of depreciation, whether rental income will be taxed as investment income through withholding or on a net income basis and taxation of capital gains. Relevant considerations for this analysis include whether and under what circumstances rental income from CRE located in the relevant EU Member State and any gain from its sale would be considered source income that is subject to tax in that jurisdiction, whether the US investor's personal tax status has a bearing on the conclusion, and whether that member state has an income treaty with the United States (or other countries through which investments may be routed) and whether the tax treaty has a bearing on the US investor's tax treatment. These questions may be affected by the US tax considerations discussed below.

#### 19.4.4.2. US tax considerations

US investors in foreign real estate must also be concerned about US taxation because US income tax is assessed on net income earned throughout the world, subject to credits for taxes paid in other jurisdictions. The timing of US taxation is subject to complex rules.

---

[16] A REOC is a company that invests in real estate and issues shares that are traded a public exchange. A REOC is in may respects similar to a real estate investment trust, but there are some differences between the two. For example a REOC must reinvest its profits whereas a real estate investment trust is required to distribute profits to its shareholders. REOCs have a greater degree of flexibility than do real estate investment trusts with respect to the types of real estate investments in which they can invest.

**Shareholders in controlled foreign corporations and passive foreign investment companies** Even if a US investor structures its holdings of interests in European CRE or its servicing functions through a local corporation or other entity treated as a corporation for US tax purposes, each US shareholder would need to be concerned about current taxation of its pro rata portion of the entity's "subpart F income" related to the entity's ownership or servicing of CRE interests under the rules governing controlled foreign corporations (CFCs) if the entity is majority owned or controlled by US persons, each of which owns at least 10 per cent of the entity's voting stock.[17] The CFC rules represent an exception from the general rule that US shareholders of a foreign corporation can defer US income tax on the corporation's non-US earnings until the corporation repatriates its earnings to the US shareholders through distribution of a dividend. The taxation of the US shareholders' pro rata share of the income of a CFC is subject to mitigating rules designed to avoid double taxation.

However, if 75 per cent or more of the foreign corporation's gross income is passive income or 50 per cent or more of its assets by value generate or could generate passive income or no income at all, the foreign corporation will be subject to the rules governing "passive foreign investment companies" (PFICs). The PFIC rules encourage US shareholders to pay tax on current income (regardless of whether or not it is Subpart F income and treating capital gains as ordinary income for this purpose) by imposing an interest charge on all distributions in excess of 125 per cent of the average distributions for the prior three years and on gain from the sale of PFIC shares, pro rated for each day of the US shareholder's holding period.

A US shareholder may elect out of the punitive PFIC regime by making an election to treat the PFIC as a qualifying electing fund (QEF). By making a QEF election a US shareholder in a PFIC must include in current taxable income its share of the ordinary income and net capital gains of the PFIC, similarly to shareholders of a registered investment company (i.e. a mutual fund), but regardless of whether the PFIC makes an actual distribution. Such election is effective for the year in which it is made and all subsequent years. To the extent such election applies, the PFIC regime is avoided. However, US shareholders making a QEF election may be subject to tax on

---

[17] Subpart F income generally consists of income that is in principle relatively mobile in the sense of being easily moved between taxing jurisdictions in order to benefit from differences in tax rates between jurisdiction. Subpart F income consists of various types of income, including such things as insurance income and foreign-based company income. This latter is a particularly important income category applicable to most foreign corporations. It includes income from passive investments such as dividends, interest, royalties, capital gains and certain types of rents on real property). It also includes income derived in connection with the performance of technical, managerial, engineering, architectural, scientific, skilled, industrial, commercial or "like services" for or on behalf of any related person outside the country under the laws of which the CFC is created or organized. It also includes services performed by a CFC in a case where substantial assistance contributing to the performance of such services has been furnished by a related person.

phantom income to the extent that the PFIC realizes taxable income or gain that is not distributed to the electing shareholder. The QEF election can only be made if the PFIC provides information on its earnings to its shareholders each year. A mark-to-market election may also be made to avoid the PFIC regime described above—again at the cost of current inclusion even in the absence of distributions—if shares in the PFIC are regularly traded.

**Real estate mortgage investment conduits** US investors financing CRE investments can obtain significant tax efficiencies under the provisions of US tax law relating to entities that properly elect to be taxed as real estate mortgage investment conduits (REMICs). A REMIC is a SPV that pools qualifying mortgage loans and certain other qualifying assets and issues securities that normally represent beneficial ownership of the pooled assets. By electing to be treated as a REMIC a mortgage pool ensures that its "regular interests" will be treated as indebtedness for US tax purposes and avoids taxation as a taxable mortgage pool or "TMP", which is treated as a corporation for US tax purposes.

In order to qualify for inclusion in a REMIC, a CRE interest would have to satisfy certain criteria, including that it consist of a mortgage or other lien on real property, that the holder of the loan have enforcement and foreclosure rights, and that the loan-to-value ratio at the startup of the REMIC be no greater than 80 per cent. The REMIC rules do not distinguish between US and non-US mortgage loans in terms of eligibility for inclusion in a REMIC. However, REMICs have very limited ability to own assets other than qualifying mortgages and assets closely related to them such as mortgage insurance and servicing rights, which may make it difficult for REMICs to use hedging instruments such as swaps.

A REMIC election confers significant advantages, including freedom from corporate taxation at the entity level and treatment of all regular interests in the REMIC (including B-pieces) as debt rather than equity for federal income tax purpose regardless of whether they would qualify as debt under a traditional debt/equity analysis.

However, a REMIC also brings some disadvantages. One of these is that notwithstanding the REMIC's treatment as a flow-through entity that does not pay entity-level taxes, the investors in a REMIC must pay taxes on earnings on their securities issued by the REMIC, and that tax may be assessed at both the state and federal level. Thus investors have little ability to reduce taxes on capital gains. Another disadvantage of a REMIC is that it is required to issue residual interests to entities that are fully taxable in the US as corporations.The REMIC residual interest holders are responsible for paying tax on the income that the REMIC would have paid but for the entity-level exclusion. These residual interests are distinct from B-pieces that represent the economic residual interest but that are treated as regular interests of a REMIC. Because the residual interests in a REMIC are non-economic interests and not entitled to a share of income or gains, they involve the payment of significant amounts of tax on phantom income. In order to sell REMIC residual interests the issuer must pay prospective investors an amount to cover the expected tax liability, with the pricing being based on a prospective residual holder's present valuation of the tax liability over the expected life of the transaction.

Another noteworthy disadvantage of a REMIC is that it is a static pool. Additionally, a REMIC is not permitted to acquire additional assets after the first 90 days from its "start-up date." After that date the mortgage pool is set and the servicer has very little ability to trade or dispose of mortgages. The static pool nature of a REMIC reduces the ability to use pre-funded REMICs to acquire CRE assets opportunistically without a warehouse arrangement. It also makes it difficult to modify or restructure loans, as the REMIC rules generally consider a loan modification to result in a new loan unless the modification is made after default or when default is imminent. A modification that is deemed to be a new loan added to the pool, after the 90-day start up period, will cause the pool to lose its favored status as a REMIC and to be treated as a TMP. Consequently REMIC structures pose challenges for investors that seek to enhance value from CRE loans by aggressive renegotiation. However, these challenges are not insuperable and can often be managed with knowledgeable advice about US taxation of real estate investments.

**Foreign Account Tax Compliance Act** From January 1, 2013 US investors in European CRE will have to be concerned about compliance with the Foreign Account Tax Compliance Act (FATCA), a recently enacted US law that is designed to clamp down on under-reporting of foreign income by US persons. The implementation will be phased in, and the US Treasury Department has proposed rules and guidance that have raised as many questions as they have suggested solutions.[18]

Under FATCA foreign financial institutions (FFIs) must agree to provide information to the US Internal Revenue Service (IRS) or to their withholding agents for transmission to the IRS about US account holders or substantial United States owners. Some countries, where it would be a violation of data protection law to provide such information to the IRS directly, are attempting to negotiate intergovernmental agreements with the US Treasury, pursuant to which FFIs in those countries would provide such information to their own governments, which would provide information in appropriate format to the IRS.

An FFI is broadly defined to include any foreign bank, custodian, broker-dealer, or pooled investment vehicle. The term can also include certain insurance companies. Although direct holdings in real estate would

---

[18] The discussion below of the Foreign Account Tax Compliance Act is general and preliminary because the detailed rules implementing this legislation are only in proposed form and are subject to change.

not cause a foreign investment entity to be treated as an FFI, any real estate-related holding that is structured as a security or derivative would cause such an entity to be an FFI.

In the absence of an agreement with the IRS, a FFI would be subject to withholding at a rate of 30 per cent on certain US-source payments that it receives. These include US-source payments of passive income, such as dividends, interest and rents, received on or after January 1, 2014, and gross proceeds from the sale or other disposition of US stocks or bonds received on or after January 1, 2015. Under rules that have not yet been issued and that will not apply any earlier than January 1, 2017, a compliant FFI would itself need to withhold on certain distributions—referred to as "pass thru payments"—that it makes to any payee or beneficial owner who does not provide the FFI with a certification that the foreign entity does not have a substantial US owner, or does not provide the name, address and taxpayer identification number (TIN) of each substantial US owner.

The proposed regulations under FATCA would create two broad categories of FFIs consisting of certain qualified investment vehicles and restricted funds that would be "deemed-compliant" with FATCA and therefore would have a more streamlined means of complying with FATCA in order to avoid the 30 per cent withholding tax. However, the scope of such entities is limited and they would still be subject to due diligence requirements and registration with the IRS, either directly or through a withholding agent. A potentially important issue for a US investor participating in an investment in European CRE interests may be whether the investment vehicle would be deemed compliant under FATCA.

Under the proposed FATCA regulations a qualified collective investment vehicle (QIV) may qualify as deemed-compliant entities if it is an FFI solely because it is an investment vehicle (and not a bank, custodian, or broker-dealer). Under the proposed rules the QIV would have to be regulated in its country of incorporation or organization as an investment fund and each record holder of debt interests in excess of $50,000 or equity interests in any amount would have to be a participating FFI, a registered deemed-compliant FFI, an exempt beneficial owner, or certain categories of US person (such as a publicly traded company, a regulated investment company, a real estate investment trust). All FFIs in the expanded affiliated group must be participating FFIs or registered deemed-compliant FFIs.

## 19.5. Conclusion

In recent years global economic forces affecting world financial markets have been drawing capital inexorably towards European CRE. The commercial issues and strategic dynamics posed by the movement of money are similar in many respects to those in any relation of buyers and sellers, although, the particular strategic positions of particular players may be influenced by geography. However, a unique confluence of legal issues affects structures for European CRE that are offered for sale to US investors. Cross-border investments also raise unique needs for cross-cultural perception and the ability to translate common concepts of real estate finance into the vernacular, not only of different languages but of different legal systems, in order that US investors can usefully compare their rights in European CRE investments with corresponding rights in US CRE investments with which they are most familiar. The comparison does not stop there, because US investors also need to assess how emerging and inchoate bodies of regulation in the United States and Europe affect their position and affect the relative merits of an investment in any particular jurisdiction. The uncertain nature of developments in the law, in the economy and in commercial practice makes cross-border CRE investments complex undertakings and requires great care in their implementation. However, European CRE investments can represent extraordinary opportunities to achieve high yields for those investors who understand the intricacies and can accurately price risk and reward.

# Chapter 20

# Challenges and Opportunities For Commercial Mortgage Loan and CMBS Markets

Craig B Prosser,

Landesbank Baden-Württemberg

## 20.1. Introduction

As highlighted throughout this book, the dynamics, participants and economics of the European commercial mortgage markets have changed radically since the end of 2006. As noted in Ch.1, CRE activity, by its nature, is a very capital intensive business and has always relied upon significant debt funding. Up until 2007, aided by a plentiful supply of debt and equity capital, real estate in Europe was often traded or revalued within a matter of a few quarters, each time backed by significant amounts of commercial mortgage debt and frequently sold on in a market heavily reliant on the commercial mortgage loan and CMBS markets to maintain this flow of capital from buyer to seller. Favourable regulation, transparency of valuation information at the transaction level[1] and competitively priced commercial mortgage loans, often up to 95 per cent of purchase price, aided the flow of capital within the CRE market. In 2006, the ABS/CMBS markets in Europe were also reaching a peak, in terms of increases in issuance volumes and provided one of many flexible distribution channels for CRE debt. As such, there were few, if any, impediments to the flow of capital between the commercial mortgage debt markets and the real estate equity investor. As well as traditional commercial mortgage lending, the prevailing commercial mortgage loan model, at the time, was the "originate to distribute" model. Under this model, the main actors were the investment banks who were able to originate a loan and within three to six months of closing the whole loan would be distributed either into the balance sheet banking market via syndication or into the capital markets via CMBS issuance and unless the deal was priced incorrectly, the investment banks rarely retained any of the transaction.[2] Meanwhile, commercial banks who

---

[1] When transaction volumes are high, the process of valuation is relatively easy because there are often several examples of comparable transactions available. Reduced transaction volumes, at the time of writing, make comparable transactions scarcer and, therefore, reduce transparency of valuation information.

[2] See further Ch.1.

did not operate a pure originate to distribute model, were pushed to originate riskier commercial mortgage assets such as development loans, lending against operating assets and CRE, in jurisdictions where the legal framework was generally less creditor friendly. This led to an abundance of modestly priced debt being quickly allocated to CRE and the result was yield compression driven not necessarily by fundamentals, but rather by more and more competitively priced CRE debt.

Following a decade of plentiful supply of debt finance, the pendulum has now swung the other way. In 2007 came the global financial crisis. As noted at the beginning of this book, the main buyers of the CMBS senior bonds, at the peak of the CMBS market, had been Structured Investment Vehicles (SIVs). SIVs engaged in the process of buying long dated ABS assets funded by shorter term, lower interest rate, one-year funding. The SIVs, mainly owned by the banks, were highly leveraged and as funding dried up, so did their business and they were either liquidated or wound up. Thus banks began the painful process of deleveraging and as a consequence the flow of debt capital between the real estate investor and the commercial mortgage loan markets dried up. In broad terms, the underlying challenge faced by commercial mortgage loan and CMBS markets in 2012, is to once again play a role in ensuring smooth capital flow between investor and financier.

Since the onset of the credit crunch, the activity in the CRE loan and CMBS markets have contracted for a variety of reasons. These reasons span both "supply side" factors such as the scarcity of bank capital globally, and "demand side" factors including the lack of CRE marketed for sale, due to banks and legacy investors who are, understandably, reluctant to exit unprofitable positions in both the debt and equity space respectively. Underlying these trends is, uncertainty in global financial markets that has been a feature of the markets throughout 2011 and 2012. The shadow over the financial health of many European economies combined with proposed regulatory changes in the form of Basel III, IFRS 9 and Solvency II,[3] has increased the challenges for commercial mortgage debt markets and contributed to the contraction in the supply of new capital to the real estate debt markets across Europe. Such uncertainty also diminishes both bankers' and investors' appetite to allocate capital.

The CRE market may in 2012 be only just emerging from the 2007 global financial crisis and, contrary to the numerous negative headlines and doom and gloom predictions from many market commentators, following the advent of the crisis, the financial apocalypse did not arrive. It came close, and there can be little doubt that the events which culminated in the advent of the financial crisis will take decades to pay for; however, the main tenets of the capitalist model remained intact—investors, financiers and interme-diaries will continue to seek out returns that offer rewards, according to their individual risk tolerances. Accordingly, inextricably linked to the

---

[3] Dealt with in Ch.16.

challenges facing the commercial mortgage loan markets, lie opportunities in the development of creative mechanisms, to assist adaptability of the loan and capital markets, to respond to the changing pockets of capital and evolving regulatory landscape.

The aim of this Chapter is not to offer a prediction on prices of debt, or yields on CRE property, as these will surely fluctuate over time but rather to look at where it is believed the main opportunities and challenges lie in 2013 and the years ahead. Without doubt, the greatest challenge to these markets, remains the resolution of the legacy real estate debt burdening banks' balance sheets across Europe. Only when this process is nearing completion will we see the re-emergence of a properly functioning and transparent debt market for CRE. Furthermore, the more structured the debt market and the amount of sovereign support the financial institutions in any given jurisdiction receive, the longer the resolution is likely take. Unfortunately, as long as legacy debt remains mispriced on the balance sheets of European banks, transaction transparency will be lacking in the CRE market. Lack of transparency increases uncertainty and undermines confidence on the part of investors and financiers. Transactions, often in the form of recapitalisations and loan extensions, are taking place between the bank/servicer and the borrower without coming to the market, based on the individual and unique set of circumstances between the bank and that particular borrower. Transparency of the transactions and the valuation discovery this brings, is critical to the confidence of the commercial mortgage markets in Europe.

This Chapter will first examine the European primary and secondary CMBS markets, looking at their historical role and the challenges and opportunities for the investor and financier in this space. The Chapter will then examine the context of where European commercial mortgage loan markets are as we move into 2013 and will highlight opportunities and challenges these markets present. In particular, the Chapter will consider opportunities for senior and mezzanine debt funds, the potential in the non-performing/distressed debt space, in each case with consideration to the market structure. Finally the Chapter will discuss the challenges and opportunities presented by the evolving regulatory backdrop to European commercial mortgage markets.

## 20.2. Challenges and Opportunities in primary and Secondary CMBS markets

### 20.2.1. *The secondary CMBS market*

Before entering into a discussion on the primary CMBS market, it is worthwhile to examine the progress of the secondary CMBS market, which, whilst thinly traded in Europe with most investors being "buy and hold", is, in 2012, the main source of CMBS product in Europe. Market estimates for the total CMBS outstanding in GBP and Euro are, at the time of writing, at £53 billion and €49 billion respectively.

Figures 1 and 2 serve as a useful guide for discussing the state of the secondary CMBS market and the opportunities which it presents.

**Figure 1: AAA CMBS Bond Spreads 2005-Q1 2012**

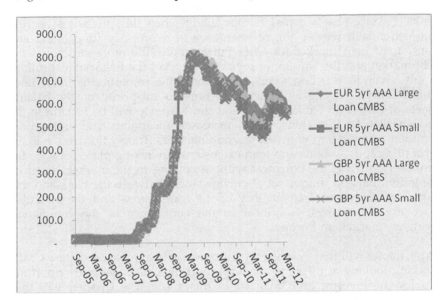

Prior to the onset of the financial crisis, CMBS bond spreads had remained relatively stable; however, post 2007, as the charts show above, the spreads available to CMBS investors widened substantially to a maximum of circa 800bps (AAA), see Figure 1, c.2960bps (BBB), see Figure 2, in mid-2009 and have since undergone a 30 per cent retracement in Q1 2012 to c. 570bps (AAA), see Figure 1, and c.2000bps (BBB), see Figure 2.

Between 2008 and 2010, in the period of extreme stress in the global financial system, investors who took the opportunity to go against the crowd of liquidation and deleveraging were able to purchase CMBS bonds, and for a holding period of one to two years, make a significant multiple on their initial investment. The peak of CMBS spread levels in 2008 and 2009 arose due to fire sale prices from SIVs, banks and flight to liquidity. At the time of writing, the secondary CMBS spreads, whilst not offering the same type of returns that were on offer, at that peak, still offer opportunity for

**Figure 2: BBB CMBS Bond Spreads 2005-Q1 2012**

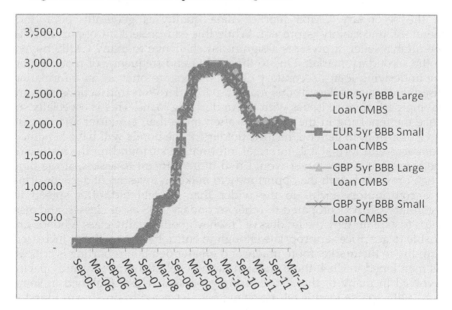

finding good value, relative to other investments in the ABS and CRE debt capital markets. Indeed, relative to the primary CMBS market which is discussed below at para.21.2.2, the secondary spreads are on average, at the time of writing, some 200+bps wider for Class A bonds.

There are several main challenges surrounding investing in the secondary market:

### 20.2.1.1. *Negative selection*

CRE loans in the secondary CMBS market, in broad terms, were originated prior to 2007/8. Original loan terms, on average, were between five to seven years, and occasionally 10 years. Since 2007, in general, in multi-loan transactions, the better quality collateral, has either been repaid or refinanced, and the loans which remain in CMBS issues, are those which struggle to achieve refinancing or have been extended or are in default. Therefore as time passes, the secondary market in aggregate will become one of diminishing quality, which presents a challenge for investors and therefore favours early entrance and careful transaction selection in this market.

*20.2.1.2. Transparency and information asymmetry*

In the secondary CMBS market, data quality is generally poor and, therefore, uncertainty is present. While this can present an opportunity to the nimble seller, it presents a significant challenge to many CMBS buyers in the secondary market. Due to the quality and frequency of reporting on the underlying loans, secondary CMBS buyers are often at an information disadvantage to sellers in this market, particularly on transactions that are having performance issues with the underlying loans. This is especially so, since the reporting in the market is often more than a quarter after events have occurred. In general, historic holders of the bonds will have benefited from access to formal and informal information surrounding the history of the loans that a new buyer would find more difficult to assess, at the time when presented, with the opportunity to make an investment decision. This is a contributory factor to the wider than normal bid/offer spread in secondary CMBS, compared to other secondary ABS asset classes, and also helps to explain why the holders of "money good" quality class A bonds are unable to get prices appropriate enough to entice them to sell. For increased liquidity in the market more timely and greater detail in reporting is critical. As mentioned in Ch.4, there is a significant level of complexity and opacity involved in many of the restructuring processes. This, combined in some cases with sparse loan level reporting, has detracted main stream investor interest in this area. Furthermore, many of the transactions are spread across multiple jurisdictions with different legislative regimes and enforce-ment processes, and the result is that, more often than not, investors' capital allocation decisions, involve the risk of certain legal outcomes, rather than strict commercial fundamentals. Such issues ipso facto add an element of speculation to the secondary market, especially in CMBS tranches lower in the capital structure.

*20.2.1.3. Size/liquidity*

As mentioned above, the secondary CMBS market is generally very illiquid. In the main, holders are characterised as patient (so far) end accounts who will often wait for loan/deal maturity, unless forced by strategic or external events to sell at a discount in the secondary market. With thorough risk and portfolio management techniques, experienced investors are able to make these decisions and trade-offs. The net result to the market is that often it is difficult to acquire bonds in any material size in the chosen class and chosen deal.

*20.2.1.4. Risk of extension/restructuring*

Following the advent of the financial crisis, there was a predilection for banks and their delegated servicers to offer extensions to loans, thereby increasing the weighted average life of CMBS transactions, and decreasing the return to the investor, who purchased at a discount, should no coupon adjustment be passed through.[4] However, towards the end of 2010 and 2011, there appeared to be a shift in attitude towards default and enforcement over extension. Probably this was driven by a combination of the approaching legal final maturities and deteriorating collateral performance.

With these issues in mind, investments in the Class A senior pay bonds present investors with perhaps the best opportunity in the secondary CMBS sector in terms of risk / reward trade off. There is a significant attraction of investing in Class A CMBS bonds, where sequential paydown mechanisms have been triggered, in that there is increased potential for an early return of capital, on a bond that has been purchased at a significant discount to par. However, this investment thesis in the secondary CMBS market has become less attractive, at the time of writing, given the pricing for bonds, more junior in the capital structure and the lack of transparency in certain deals, combined with uncertainty over the underlying valuation moving forward. Deals that have undergone restructurings, with increases in note margins, have been generally successfully received by the market as they offer investors the opportunity to receive net margin income, at levels of c.300bps, rather than purchasing at a discount and receiving current income of c.20bps (being the pre-2007 AAA average CMBS spread). Where such restructuring is possible, therefore, there is an opportunity to widen the investor base and increase liquidity in the transaction.

The challenges mentioned above, are not exhaustive by any means; control rights, voting percentages and valuation risk also present difficulties in the universe of secondary CMBS. A further challenge to consider is how to deal with longer-term hedging where loans are in default. As competition among debt lenders intensified in the run up to the financial crisis, ever more highly-structured and innovative transactions took place. Such structures included the incorporation of interest rate hedges into the loan financing which were often longer than the loan term and now present a significant challenge to both the secondary CMBS and commercial mortgage loan markets. These hedging structures rank senior to the loan amount advanced and were originally put in place in order to fix at a lower rate than, say, the prevailing five year swap rate for a five year loan. This allowed a greater amount to be advanced to the borrower, though added a speculative element on the direction of future interest rates into the financing—a speculation which has turned out badly. Because of the economic crisis and subsequent decline of interest rates to historic lows many of these hedges are now substantially underwater and present a significant challenge, combined with the declines in real estate values, to investors and financiers when contemplating refinancing and default decisions.[5] In many cases, when defaults are called, the swaps are broken and a substantial breakage loss will crystallise, which must be repaid ahead

---

[4]   See further Ch.5.
[5]   See further Ch.8.

of the senior loan, thereby reducing potential recovery values to investor and financier. In other cases, the prospect of multi-million-pound penalties, which fluctuate daily with the Libor curve, also is stalling property sales, by making it more difficult for buyers and sellers to determine the value of a deal, when a swap is involved. Finding solutions to deal with such problems will no doubt assist with the resolution of the legacy loans on banks' balance sheets, as more transactions would be released to the market, bringing greater transparency of valuation information. One pragmatic solution to break the "stalemate" would be to postpone breaking the swap, whilst enforcement and collateral liquidation takes place. This would offer solace, both in terms of reducing the duration for which the swap breakage is payable and, if rates rise during the postponement, would reduce the rate used to calculate the swap breakage. Furthermore, as sales of assets seem to be taking up to one to two years in the market, agreements may be made, where the swap remains in place until sales are finalised. Such an opportunity may be appropriate, for Gemini Eclipse 2006-3 Plc, which has a swap breakage of in excess of £250 million.

### 20.2.2. The primary CMBS market

Aside from ECB repo transactions, there has been relatively little primary CMBS issuance since the onset of the financial crisis in 2006. There are two drivers for this—fundamental and regulatory. The fundamental rationale for investing in CMBS, has been less than favourable over the past few years, as the CMBS product has unfortunately been somewhat tarnished with several high profile defaults, documentation and structures that did not work as anticipated. Furthermore, given the pricing on senior loans and the prices bond investors are willing to pay, the arbitrage between senior debt funding and CMBS bonds is, at the time of writing, questionable. An even greater challenge to the re-emergence of the primary CMBS market, lies in the evolving regulatory environment, which is proving to be challenging for CMBS investments. The main challenge for issuance in primary CMBS, is the evolution of the Basel III regulatory framework. Although Basel III is not due to take effect until the end of 2018, banks are already well underway in terms of planning and preparing for its implementation. Under the Basel III capital rules, it is uncertain as to whether CMBS will be permitted to count towards a bank's liquidity ratio. Such uncertainty is anathema to a well functioning primary CMBS issuance market. Compounding the problem is art.122a of the CRD which came into effect in January 2011, coined the "5% skin in the game" provision. Effectively this directive requires banks originating CMBS transactions to keep 5 per cent of a deal on their balance sheets. Either the advent of a more favourable regulatory environment or the successful adaptation to this evolving regulatory landscape will be critical for the CMBS markets going forward.[6]

---

[6]  See further Ch.16, where the regulatory landscape is dealt with in detail.

As set out in Ch.1, since the onset of the financial crisis, there have been eight CMBS transactions issued. At the time of writing, the most recent transactions, are from Deutsche Bank's platform, true sale securitisations of the Chiswick Park (2011), Merry Hill (2012) and Vitus/Florence loans. The other securitisations were more akin to credit tenant lease securitisations and corporate bonds, rather than the traditional CMBS transactions which have more exposure to real estate risk. When considering the opportunities for CMBS, it is important to remember that even prior to the financial crisis, the CMBS market, whilst very important, was only a small part of the overall commercial mortgage market in Europe. Since 2007, the market volatility across all asset classes, has added to the challenge of arranging CMBS transactions. The risk-on, risk-off rallies which have characterised debt and equity markets' attitude to risk over the past few years, has meant that significant swings in value of the CMBS bonds to be issued will occur between origination and execution, as investors swing between bearish and bullish in their economic outlooks. In a market with imperfect hedging for CMBS, this can eat into profits and in some cases cause deals to be delayed for six months or more (as market conditions switch from risk-off to risk-on), and has contributed to the challenge of issuing primary CMBS paper. Therefore, from 2007 onwards, European mortgage markets have been largely reliant upon funding from the balance sheet banks, especially those able to access refinancing via the German Covered Bond *"Pfandbrief"* market.

The near-term opportunity for primary CMBS will be to provide capital where the balance sheet banks are unable to for a variety of reasons. For instance, at the time of writing, if a sponsor requires debt financing in excess of £100 million it is potentially likely that there will have to be multiple banks at the table in order for the lead arranger to syndicate the risk early on in the transaction. CMBS via a capital market process is largely able to obviate this process and has the potential to offer a rapid execution to the borrower. For the near term, it is likely that the significant opportunity for CMBS lies in large ticket financings for strong sponsors. CMBS will also continue to serve an opportunity to finance, where balance sheet banks and Pfandbrief bank restrictions do not permit or find challenging, such as where counterparty limits have been reached, financing for very large trophy real estate and potentially also for operating assets. For instance, commentators cite one of the reasons that Deutsche Bank chose to finance the Merry Hill Shopping Centre transaction via CMBS, was that the security package was not Pfandbrief compliant. Another area where CMBS is likely to play a role, in the near to medium term, is likely to be in the German multi-family sector. Conservatively underwritten loans to experienced sponsors in the multi-family area are likely to be seen as a good proxy to RMBS and offer yield pick-up, over typical RMBS spreads. Considering 2013 and beyond, and the expected volume and size of the upcoming maturities of German multi-family CMBS transactions, it is likely that the commercial mortgage markets will witness increased securitisations in this area, should markets stabilise as evidenced by the Vitus/Florence deal. Furthermore, German multi-family housing also benefits from strong macro-economic fundamentals; Germany is one of the few western economies not to have experienced a credit or real estate boom over the past decade. It is also likely that CMBS will take advantage of the demand for fixed rate paper in the market and, going forward, if CMBS is able to lengthen its maturity, it would broaden both its investor base and borrower base and attract pension funds who are seeking long-term debt to match their liabilities.

As markets move away from a period of liquidity stabilisation, to that of increasing financing for CRE in the primary markets, and from current analysis this process is already at a nascent stage, it is believed that the primary CMBS market will once again, on a selective basis, offer banks, investors and borrowers an important channel for capital and liquidity transfer.

## 20.3. Dynamics and pricing in the bank debt market

The situation in the commercial mortgage loan markets across Europe is still very much one of deleveraging. For the United Kingdom, this is highlighted in the 2012 De Montfort Survey, which states that the aggregate value of UK CRE debt on banks' balance sheets at the year end of 2011 stood at £212.3 billion, down some 6.8 per cent from the year before.[7] The challenge, therefore, for the European CRE market, is in clearing the legacy loans off the banks' balance sheets to enable the return of a functioning lending market. The current tightness in the supply of debt finance for CRE debt has been steadily increasing since 2007 and manifests itself in the pricing. On average, the margin over Libor for a 60 per cent LTV five year investment loan on CRE in 2007 was about 50–60bps. At the time of writing, this has increased to somewhere between circa 300–circa 400bps. This is approximately a six-fold increase in five years, however the good news is that this is likely to be the peak for margin pricing. In the context of what the financial system has been through, the pricing increase should come as no surprise. Basic axioms of economics underpin the fact that, as the availability of debt decreased but the same number of people needed it, debt became more expensive. The same principles also dictate that, as real estate debt prices increase, so should supply of debt capital, which should in turn subdue demand. This is what European markets are witnessing with the emergence of senior debt and mezzanine debt funds.

---

[7]    See the *De Montfort Report* and Ch.1.

## 20.4.   The senior debt fund opportunity

As supply has diminished from the traditional providers of CRE debt (see para.20.3), and in many cases permanently left the system, due to the nationalisation and closures of banks, new sources of capital have entered into the market to supply real estate debt. Understanding these new sources of capital and their targets provides a welcome opportunity for European real estate debt markets in the second half of 2012 and beyond. There are, at the time of writing, up to eighteen or more institutions that have either entered or increased their presence in the market, with either a mandate to raise a fund for senior CRE debt or are already lending directly into the market on real estate debt. In the main, these institutions are insurance companies or asset managers, seeking to benefit from the relatively high margins mentioned above, which are available on CRE debt. Estimates for the firepower that these funds have or will have are said to be in excess of some €20–30 billion.

However, the not insignificant challenge for these funds will be to deploy their capital economically and in accordance with their criteria, without getting into competitive bidding amongst themselves and also potentially against the banking and CMBS sector. In the short term, the principal challenge for the senior debt funds is to ensure an effective alliance with a number of European lending institutions and leverage these relationships in a mutually productive manner.[8] Success in this area, sound underwriting, combined with the ability to be both flexible on assets, competitive on pricing and management fees relative to the other institutions, will be key determinants to the success of these funds. Financings on prime assets across Europe are an obvious opportunity for the senior debt funds. However, two less obvious, but nonetheless significant, opportunities for the senior debt funds lie in the, at the time of writing, unfashionable sectors of secondary property and CMBS.

### 20.4.1.   *Secondary property versus prime property*

In Q3 2012, prime Office yields in the City of London are around the 5–6 per cent yield range and generally speaking, not too far off where they were in 2007. Secondary properties around the United Kingdom are thinly traded, though can be seen to range between 9–12+ per cent. It is worth noting that at the height of the markets in 2007, secondary asset pricing and prime pricing had very small yield differentials. Price discrimination in the commercial mortgage loan and CMBS markets, between primary and secondary properties, was also largely absent. At the time of writing, the

---

[8]   In July 2012, US investor Kennedy Wilson announced plans to invest up to €2 billion in European CRE loans. A statement from the firm announced a "new framework" with an unnamed "global financial institution". It said the firms would "target the acquisition of circa €2bn of performing, sub-performing and non-performing loans secured by commercial and residential real estate in Europe, with a focus on the United Kingdom and Ireland".

divergence in yield between the two asset classes is very significant and increasing. Between the end of 2012 and the middle of 2014, it is submitted that the CRE markets, will probably come close to the bottom in the pricing for secondary real estate assets. The attraction of achieving a double digit un-levered IRR on secondary assets, in a low interest rate environment, will prove to be too attractive for real estate investors to pass up. Through backing the right property and importantly the right sponsor, capital allocation in the form of senior debt to this sector, at this stage in the cycle, is likely to prove a golden opportunity for the senior debt funds. Similarly, senior debt fund managers, focussing on light infrastructure and operating assets, may be rewarded with above average returns.

### 20.4.2. CMBS

Should the market for senior debt funds flourish in Europe, this could also provide an opportunity for more primary CMBS issuance. Relative to a senior debt fund, the CMBS investor, prior to capital allocation, has full disclosure of the real estate and debt structure, benefits of a rating and low management fees. Furthermore, whilst the market for trading CMBS is relatively illiquid, it is still nonetheless possible to sell this product, rather than hold for five to seven years in a senior debt fund. The ability of the senior debt funds to purchase CMBS assets or to collaborate on an issuance would perhaps serve to enhance relationships between the senior debt fund and their banking sector partner.

## 20.5. The mezzanine debt market opportunity

Prior to the financial crisis, the LTV ratios that banks and CMBS markets were willing to offer were often up to the 80–95 per cent range at an all in margin of c.1–1.5 per cent. Now the LTV ratio most lenders are willing to offer is rarely higher than 65 per cent and is much more sensitive to asset type than before. Many German lenders often cut off their LTV's towards the lower end of a 55–65 per cent range known as a percentage of the *"Beleihungswert"*–an independently assessed value that means a loan is able to be refinanced through the Pfandbrief markets to those institutions that have programmes in place.

The current LTV gap has presented non-traditional lenders with an opportunity to enter into the CRE mortgage markets. Some were already present and buyers of B notes from banks, though there have been many new entrants seeking to achieve private equity type returns of 12–20 per cent IRR from commercial mortgage debt. Market assessments suggest that junior debt and mezzanine funds which are active in the market have been writing tickets with margins of between 750–1350bps for subordinated debt, with generally a cut-off LTV ratio of between 60–80 per cent.[9] Occasionally, and in order to achieve desired IRR returns, it has been necessary for such funds to increase the LTV ratios at which they will lend. Historically very expensive, this debt is not always appealing to property investors. The challenge for the mezzanine and junior debt funds to deploy their capital, relies upon senior lenders (whether traditional providers or debt funds as referred to in para.21.4 above) being active in financing, to facilitate the offering of their product. Given the continued resilience of the Pfandbrief market and the lower range LTV cut off described above, it will be only a matter of time before the emergence of a "Stretch Senior debt fund", which is, at the time of writing, missing from the market and presents an opportunity to allocate capital to what was always termed senior debt. Such funds would allow borrowers to raise c.70 per cent LTV, with the first c.55 per cent LTV advanced by the senior lender and the next 15 per cent LTV coming from such funds and being subordinated to the senior lender (sometimes through separate lenders or even by the same lender that can internally tranche these advances through separate funds with differing returns and risk appetites). If such funds accepted margins of c.500–800bps, it would enable an all-in margin of financing to the borrower of c.400bps, assuming senior debt margins remain in the current 275–375bps range.

In future, the emergence of such a "Stretch Senior debt fund" with banks retaining the 55 per cent LTV level on their balance sheets and joint venture partners in the form of insurance companies, pension funds, asset managers and real estate investors pooling capital to offer total financing in the 65–70% LTV level, will be a much welcome capital source for the CRE market. The challenges will be to devise a structure for the inter-creditor that satisfies the Pfandbrief trustee and the equity investor(s) into the debt fund. Senior debt funds with the ability to invest in the junior part of the capital structure will be able to bring more to the table as a bank's joint venture partner. Aside from seeking out capital satisfied with a 7–9% IRR return in this space, the issue facing structures of such funds will be the creation of broad enough selection criteria for the banks to offer flexibility, to provide the financing seamlessly to the borrower, yet have narrow enough criteria to satisfy the provider(s) of the equity capital into the "Stretch Senior debt fund". In summary, as in the senior debt fund space, partners in this space will need to choose each other carefully, since the funds' equity investor(s) will need to see a strong volume of potential debt for the fund and be satisfied on quality underwriting criteria from the bank(s). Size of such a fund, target returns, ease of operation and costs involved, are all critical factors to ensure a successful product provision.

---

[9] See further Ch.15.

## 20.6. Opportunities in the non-performing/distressed debt space

As we have emerged or are emerging from the financial crisis, there has, in 2012, been a marked increase in the activity surrounding non-performing or sub-performing loan portfolio sales. At the outset, banks were unable to take the hit to capital on the loss that they would have incurred on such portfolios; however, along with the replenishment of capital reserves in some banks, there has been an increase in the volume of portfolio sales at sufficient discounts, to attract keen buyer interest. This is a very competitive market, with the current number of buyers active so far outnumbering the number of sellers. The potential for the sovereign crisis to escalate in Europe towards the end of 2012 and beyond may result in increased sellers in this area, particularly with banks with large exposure to the periphery countries in Europe. Furthermore, as banks shift focus back to their core markets, their non-core and non-relationship assets are likely to find new ownership.

The discounts offered by the seller on a loan portfolio, combined with the potential for more proactive asset management of these non-performing loan portfolios, has attracted the interest of senior debt funders in the market. Financing the acquisition of a non-performing loan portfolio offers much higher margins and more attractive repayment mechanisms, than a straightforward commercial mortgage loan. Additionally, the debt financing of such a portfolio brings with it a diverse book of business and client relationships for banks keen to build their activities in the CRE debt space. Such activities have been helpful in reducing the bank real estate loan book exposures and in bringing transparency to the market in terms of transactions post work out/enforcement of the loans. Sovereign wealth funds have been active in this area as witnessed by China Investment Corporation's involvement in the financing of Blackstone's Project Isobel acquisition from the Royal Bank of Scotland Plc. As credit markets in Europe re-open and confidence returns, the securitisation of such non-performing loans could present an opportunity for much needed capital flow within the sector.[10] Such non-performing loan securitisation will offer efficient matched term financing and even modest leverage, which in theory will enhance returns and lower the haircuts, vendors will take on the assets.

---

[10] At the end of June 2012, it was made known that Royal Bank of Scotland (RBS) aimed to securitise the £550 million Project Isobel senior debt and will likely retain the rated bonds on its balance sheet, to benefit from increased capital efficiency under the incoming Basel III regime, in the first-ever European loan-on-loan securitisation. It was announced that while RBS will attempt to sell the bonds–which have already been rated–potential distribution is a secondary motive behind the principal attraction of securing a lower capital requirement against the rated bonds, relative to a straight balance sheet hold. See CoStar UK June 21, 2012. For an update to this deal see CoStar UK September 28, 2012.

## 20.7.  Challenges of evolving regulation

As discussed above, the evolving regulatory backdrop is creating head-winds in the banking sector through the implementation of Basel III. Similarly, in the insurance sector, a new risk based capital adequacy regime is being ushered in called Solvency II. The uncertainty surrounding the treatment of real estate debt and equity investments under both Solvency II and Basel III represents a major challenge for the CRE sector, as it is seen as delaying much needed capital allocation.[11]

Although the insurance sector has historically allocated a relatively small percentage of its assets to CRE, the capital allocation decisions are generally long-term and provide much needed stability in the market. Indeed, commentators argue that the outcome of the Solvency II regime, may make it more favourable for insurers to become commercial mortgage lenders. Early drafts of the legislative framework were interpreted by market participants, as being very beneficial for insurance companies to invest in CRE loans, as opposed to direct CRE. Furthermore, as drafted, at the time of writing, Solvency II makes it more expensive from a capital perspective for insurers to hold CMBS assets. Drafts of the legislation have offered further clues on the treatment for real estate and, although it is far from certain, commentators believe that it is likely that the capital charge faced by a European insurer investing in real estate debt is likely to be similar to that of an unrated corporate bond.

Regardless of the outcome of Solvency II, further involvement of the insurance sector is key for the European CRE mortgage market and the market is certainly seeing increased activity from the insurers. This is probably driven by the macro-economic backdrop as well as anticipation of favourable treatment under Solvency II when it is implemented in 2014. It is easy to see why real estate debt is appealing to the insurance sector in the macro-economic environment that exists in 2012, when UK and German government debt is yielding all-time record lows, and the insurance sector is looking to other investment opportunities for inflation-linked returns and long-dated credit instruments. Transaction volume during the last quarter of 2011 and first quarter of 2012 has shown, amongst others, Aviva, Allianz and Legal & General to be active lenders in the senior debt market. In terms of assets under management, insurance companies' investment in CRE loans is modest, and their investment in CRE more modest still. Recently, in Q1 2012, AXA reported that it plans to double CRE loans to 2 per cent of its €140 billion of assets from one percent.

The challenge for the commercial mortgage market will be to access this capital in an efficient way and to create structures that are both transparent and flexible enough to replace the capital from the banking sector.

---

[11]  See further Ch.17.

## 20.8. Conclusion

This Chapter has presented a panoramic view of the main opportunities and challenges facing the European commercial mortgage loan and CMBS markets. It has considered the challenge that the evolving regulatory backdrop creates, for both commercial mortgage loan and CMBS markets, with the danger that planned regulation in 2013 and the years to come may impede growth and innovation in the CRE sector and beyond. The secondary CMBS markets remain a place where investors can seek out respectable returns on their capital, relative to other ABS asset classes, though as illustrated in this Chapter, it is not a sector without challenges. The Chapter has also summarised the challenges facing the CRE loan markets, where capital is scarce, and on a more positive note, highlights the opportunities this presents for senior debt and mezzanine funds. The most striking and greatest challenge discussed in the Chapter remains that of reducing the legacy loan books, which is now a process that has, been on-going for five years. This means that the market is probably more than half-way through this process and the increased participants in the non-performing loans space, combined with funding innovations on non-performing loan portfolios, provide a much needed reservoir of activity in this space.

One challenge, perhaps better described as a threat to the market, is that of a shift in focus from the central banks, so that the market becomes faced with the prospect of rising rates, or worse still–suddenly rising rates. Currently banks enjoy the benefits of cheap funding via central bank programmes, such as the three year LTRO. There is a danger that, sometime in the near future, central banks will shift their focus from one of easing and crisis management, to tackling inflation and, therefore, increase interest rates. The challenges of maintaining current financing spreads and LTV levels, when interest rates regress towards their long-run average, is something to which all market participants should give some thought. The unwinding of the unprecedented financial stimulus the banking sector has benefited from, also has the potential to create dislocations in the sector, at a time when it is undergoing a fragile recovery.

Throughout this Chapter the discussion on costs of financing has focussed on the margin over Libor that debt providers charge. From the property investor's perspective it is the total cost of financing (i.e. Libor + margin) relative to the property's yield that is important. Even though margins have increased substantially, the five year Libor rate in 2007 stood more than 400bps higher than 2012 rates, as depicted in the Figure 3 below.

Thus the total cost of debt financing to the borrower is still favourable relative to 2007, for modest LTV loans. If rates revert towards their mean and margins remain at levels witnessed in 2012, then debt financing will become very expensive indeed for the property investor. The hope here is

Chart Showing 5 Year Swap Libor Rates in GBP and Euro 1999-2012

Source: Thomson Reuters

that for rates to rise, rents and values will have increased proportionately. However, the fact that many market participants do not expect or anticipate market rates to move sharply higher any time soon, could in itself exacerbate the eventual effect of a modest and sustained rise in Libor.[12]

As mentioned herein, the key challenge to commercial mortgage loan and CMBS markets remains the resolution of the legacy loans which remain on many banks' balance sheets across Europe. Over time, selective portfolio sales will bring about the clearance of the legacy loans. A comparison may be drawn with the Savings and Loans crisis of the 1980s and 1990s in the United States, which was only really resolved via policy action and the creation of the Resolution Trust Corporation which embraced asset sales and equity partnerships with the private sector on asset disposals.[13] Perhaps the creation of a European version of the Resolution Trust Corporation, which has the ability to recapitalise, manage, merge and close down problematic financial institutions will provide an opportunity to resolve the legacy CRE loans in a more timely manner.

In light of the challenges and opportunities discussed herein, there is a further challenge facing the market which is worth mentioning, although

---

[12] See the *De Montfort Report*. Note that the *Wheatley Report* has recommended a complete overhaul of the way Libor is calculated.

[13] See Ch.1 of the 1st edn..

491

there is not the scope to discuss its implications in full in this Chapter. In the face of such an unprecedented downturn and change within the sector perhaps the greatest issue of all faced by the market will be the ability to attract and retain the human capital necessary to face the current and future challenges of restructuring, origination and servicing of commercial mortgage loans discussed throughout this book. Without doubt, the upheaval that has taken place in CRE markets over the last few years has affected both assets and talent in the sector. As the banks have withdrawn from CRE lending, the expertise and transactional knowledge has become more dispersed. For platforms with the appropriate expertise and creativity, the CRE lending market, despite all its challenges, presents one of the best opportunities in a generation.

Finally, as discussed at the start and throughout this book, CRE is a capital intensive business and as the balance of economic power shifts from west to east, to overcome the challenges in the commercial mortgage markets, participants will need to adapt to seek out the changing pockets of capital. Innovation in adapting to the challenges faced by the sector will continue, as is already seen in the arrival of specialist debt funds and fixed rate products on offer. In addition to traditional sources of capital, debt market participants in Europe will need a more global perspective, in seeking out capital to allocate to real estate debt. South-East Asia, the Americas, the Middle East, Russia, Japan and importantly China will all have an increased role to play in the European commercial mortgage debt markets of the next decade and beyond. After all, as witnessed with the advent of the financial crisis, the effect of globalisation cannot be ignored.

# APPENDICES

# Introduction

## An Introduction to the Commercial Real Estate Finance Council Europe

The Commercial Real Estate Finance Council (CREFC Europe) is a member-led trade association dedicated to promoting liquidity and transparency in commercial real estate (CRE) finance throughout Europe.

CREFC Europe's membership consists of, at the time of writing, more than 67 European companies from the CRE finance industry. Member firms include commercial and investment banks, insurance companies, private equity funds, investment grade and B-piece bond investors, servicers and rating agencies.

In the dislocated CRE and CMBS markets that exist at the time of writing, CREFC Europe provides CRE finance professionals a meeting point to discuss and propose working solutions for market issues at a local, regional, country, pan-European and global level.

In 2011 and 2012, as a result of the fallout from the financial crisis, CREFC Europe formed a number of committees and working groups to focus on creating market principles and guidance publications to help bring confidence back to the European CRE finance and CMBS markets and stimulate the wider CRE economy.

Active committees and working groups include:

- **Lender Committee**
  Loan Due Diligence Working Group
  Loan Hedging Working Group
  Loan Intercreditor Working Group
  Loan Tax Working Group
- **European CMBS 2.0 Committee**
  Pre issuance Disclosure Working Group
  Excess Spread Structure Working Group
  Servicing & Transaction Party Working Group
  Investor Identification Working Group
  Improved Investor Reporting Working Group
  Transaction Structure Features Working Group
- **Regulatory Committee**
- **European Investor Reporting Package (E-IRP) Committee**

Each of these important industry initiatives will be addressed below.

## 1. LENDER COMMITTEE

The Lender Committee offers an opportunity for European CRE lenders to discuss and propose solutions for issues negatively impacting CRE lending.

As highlighted throughout this book, within the European countries there are a variety of lenders ranging from balance sheet lenders, investment banking debt origination lenders, private equity debt funds, insurance firms and *Pfandbrief* lenders. Each of these lenders is currently facing their own funding challenges and each has defined lending practices. The Lender Committee is a uniform voice that unites these differences with common goals of increasing investor confidence, encouraging new entrants, creating liquidity and promoting transparency.

The Lender Committee focuses on improving market standards through the following key points:

- **Human capital:**
  o Market suffers from lack of experienced property bankers due mainly to the negative employment impact of the property cycle
- **Implementing recent lessons learned:**
  o Bring together knowledge recently gained from managing the fallout of the credit crisis
- **Market harmonisation fostering liquidity:**
  o Promote CREFC Europe support for delivery of high quality lending across differing capital sources

The Lender Committee is initially focused on transaction structuring, documentation and intercreditor arrangements as key areas for encouraging better market standards.

In March 2012, the Lender Committee released the *European Commercial Real Estate Lending Principles Guide* (see Appendix 1). This guide offers an initial layout of key principles to be considered when advancing secured investment loans. The recommendations detailed in this guide assume a professional degree of existing knowledge and experience of CRE lending. The guide is intended for senior balance sheet, corporate, capital markets focused and subordinated debt lenders, as well as alternative lenders such as insurance and fund based capital providers.

### 1.1 Loan Due Diligence Working Group

In conjunction with the Lender Committee, a Loan Due Diligence Working Group has been established to focus on "micro best practice" across Europe.

Initially the Loan Due Diligence Working Group and its "micro best practice" discussions will focus on the United Kingdom. Subsequent versions of this document will expand to cover other European jurisdictions.

The Loan Due Diligence Working Group is currently producing an extensive guide for market release in early 2013 that will provide guidance on Transaction and Asset level due diligence and instruction and reliance letters which all will help create market efficiency.

The main areas of transaction due diligence include:

### Transaction due diligence
- Statutory requirements ("Know Your Client"/Money Laundering)
- Inspection of asset
- Borrower entity:
  - (a) Structure/ownership
  - (b) Legal powers and capacity (legal opinions)
  - (c) Tax position
  - (d) Financial resources/solvency
- Project/development appraisals
- Funding of transaction (debt service/repayment)
- Asset management arrangements
- Financial modelling
- Tenant credit analysis

The main areas of asset due diligence include:

### Asset due diligence
- Principal reports
  - (a) Valuation
  - (b) Legal report/certificate of title
  - (c) Building, site and measurement surveys
  - (d) Environmental/ground surveys/reports
  - (e) Asset insurance reports/policies (specialist and general)

### Additional reports
- Planning (zoning)
- Mechanical and engineering (including fixed plant and machinery, e.g. lifts, heating, air-conditioning)
- Utilities (gas, electricity, water/drainage and telecommunications)
- Building services (gas/electricity/telecommunications)
- Deleterious Materials (e.g. asbestos, high alumina cement)
- Mining (e.g. coal, tin, lead, limestone, salt/brine, china clay) survey reports
- Flooding
- Occupational (health & safety, fire precautions)
- Rights of light
- Railway, highway and waterway liabilities
- Specific projects (e.g. Crossrail, High Speed 2)
- Capital allowances
- Energy efficiency/performance.

### 1.2 Loan Hedging Working Group

The purpose of the Loan Hedging Working Group is to examine past and future market practices in loan hedging for CRE finance transactions, in order to create awareness of issues and provide guidance to market participants.

Initial areas of focus include the following:

- Rating requirements
- Compare "old" versus "new" standards and downgrade triggers
- Verification on what can be expected from the regulators
- European Market Infrastructure Regulation/Over-the- Counter Derivatives
- Structural aspects
- Hedge providers rank, rights and voting options?
- Verification of fixed rate swaps or caps for CRE loans going forward

This working group aims to publish a guidance document by year-end 2012. This guidance document will serve as an educational tool for lenders, borrowers and investors.

### 1.3 Loan Intercreditor Working Group

The purpose of the Loan Intercreditor Working Group is to examine industry practices in order to establish a CRE loan intercreditor guidelines and a model template for the European CRE market. The working group includes various stakeholders who utilise intercreditor agreements for CRE Loans.

### 1.4 Loan Tax Working Group

The Loan Tax Working Group's objective is to assist on matters that relate to CRE tax and accounting matters.

In early 2012, the Loan Tax Working Group produced the *European Commercial Real Estate Lending Tax Guide* (See Appendix 2). This guide is designed to assist market participants develop an understanding of the multiple issues a lender should consider, when undertaking a transaction and to provide a template letter of instruction for lenders to allow them to seek appropriate professional advice on tax implications.

The *European Commercial Real Estate Lending Tax Guide* sets out, in general terms, common tax issues that prospective lenders should consider in their decision-making for lending to CRE investment structures. This document takes a high level approach to the situations that may arise and should be considered when examining a debtor's tax position. The document is intended for lenders, loan servicers, investors, restructuring advisors and participants in the European CRE finance market.

## 2. EUROPEAN CMBS 2.0 COMMITTEE

CREFC Europe established the European CMBS 2.0 Committee to issue a set of industry best practice principles for new European CMBS issuances.[1] The background for the committee is as follows:

### Funding gap

As highlighted in Ch.2, the CRE funding gap and debt refinancing block means that there is a need for an alternative source of debt funding, which can potentially be filled by the CMBS new issue market.

### Weaknesses in historical structures

In order for CMBS to again become attractive to investors, amendments to the way deals are structured will need to be made in order to avoid the weaknesses that were exposed during the recent crisis and also to simplify (and where possible, to standardise) structures.

### Single source of guidance

This Committee, comprisly investors, issuers, servicers, borrowers and other market participants, has been established to consider a set of industry principles for new issuance of European CMBS.

Individual working groups within the European CMBS 2.0 Committee are the following:

### 2.1 Pre- issuance Disclosure Working Group

To form principles for pre-issuance disclosure in offering memoranda including conflicts of interest, rights of junior lenders and access to underlying documentation (both pre and post issuance) and, related to this, standardised and updated version of representations and warranties (principal/agented deals).

### 2.2 Excess Spread Structure Working Group

Excess Spread/Profit Extraction Structure for Originating/Arranging Bank (e.g. Class X, retained interest, deferred interest, skim both at bond and loan level, etc.[2])—ranking, impact of restructurings, triggers to switch off based on expected rather than crystallised losses, appraisal reduction type structure on default.

### 2.3 Servicing and Transaction Counterparty Roles Working Group

The role and fees of the primary servicer/special servicer, standardisation of the Servicing Standard (NPV, loan level/note level, who else is covered?, synthetic

---

[1]   See further Chs 4 and 7.
[1]   See further Ch.5.

deals, etc.), standardisation of the level of servicer discretion (increased discretion, improved indemnities, accountability) (verification of service improvements/ enhancements).

### 2.4 Investor Identification Working Group

The working group is to verify an investor identification/register of investors process which will be available to official transaction counterparties. In addition, the group will verify if there is a need for a new potential role of a noteholder representative.

### 2.5 Improved Investor Reporting Working Group

The working group will verify ways to improve and standardise investor reporting and enhanced loan and property surveillance ensuring both lenders and borrowers are incentivised to build this into the underlying loan documentation (regulatory and other requirements). This group will liaise with the CREFC Europe E-IRP and Lender Committee on respective guidelines and standards.

### 2.6 Transaction Structures Features Working Group

The Working Group will focus on the following areas:

- Standardisation of control party (and operating adviser) and junior lender rights with effective appraisal reduction;
- Standardisation of noteholder voting rights;
- Preferred hedging structures (risk of long dated structures, issuer/loan level);
- Optimising transactions structures for less creditor friendly jurisdictions (off-shore companies with share pledge, off-shore reserve accounts);
- Liquidity facilities—Availability, improved and standardised appraisal reduction mechanism, alternative forms of liquidity;
- Asset and property management—Improved ability to terminate; performance assessment; independence from sponsors;
- Synthetic securitisations;
- Servicing; restructuring credit events;
- Valuation standards, standardised instruction letters and reliance/addressee issues; and
- Loan documentation in conjunction with CREFC Lender Committee.

The European CMBS 2.0 Committee has finalised, *Market Principles for Issuing European CMBS 2.0,* which aims to help bring confidence back to the European CRE capital markets and stimulate the further development of European CMBS in order to address the immediate need for senior debt in European CRE transactions. These are further discussed in Chs 4 and 7.

The focus of the principles are on transaction structures, transaction counterparties and disclosure of appropriate levels of information. Key areas addressed include:

- Disclosure requirements for both pre- and post-issuance information as well as investor reporting, investor notices, valuations and cashflow models;
- CMBS structural features, such as controlling party rights and voting provisions;
- Revenue extraction, e.g. excess spread monetisation (including Class X Note structuring); and
- Role of the servicer and other counterparties such as trustees and cash managers.

### 3. REGULATORY COMMITTEE

The purpose of the Committee is to address specific regulatory and legislative issues that impact the European CRE finance industry. In addition, the Committee works with a consortium of trade groups and has an ongoing dialogue with the European regulators as to possible ways to improve transparency in the marketplace and to identify ways to create liquidity. The committee focuses on UK, European and US legislation and regulation such as:

- Bank of England Liquidity Scheme
- Basel II and III
- Credit rating agency reform measures
- Capital Requirement Directives (CRD II, III and IV)
- Shadow Banking
- Solvency II
- US Dodd Frank Legislation and Impact on UK/Europe
- US SEC Rule 17g-5

See further Ch.16 and a discussion of the regulatory environment impacting the CRE and CMBS markets at the time of writing.

### 4. EUROPEAN INVESTOR REPORTING PACKAGE (E-IRP) COMMITTEE

The E-IRP Committee is in the process of updating the reporting package to version 2.0 (E-IRP v 2.0) (see Appendix 4) and is set to introduce further standards in Loan and CMBS reporting. The group is working towards making the package adaptable to various transaction types and considering ways to encourage broader use of the package amongst originators, issuers and servicers.

The E-IRP v2.0 has formed the basis of the European Central Bank and the Bank of England loan level data templates for CMBS transactions used to transfer data amongst market participants. Use of the CMBS template is a requirement for any CMBS loan placed on deposit with the European Central Bank and the Bank of England.

The package continues to evolve to include new developments and requirements of the industry on a periodic basis.

### 4.1 Brief history of the Commercial Real Estate Finance Council Europe E-IRP

In 2004, CREFC Europe started a process of gathering market participants to verify the best way to create a European reporting package. The E-IRP Committee decided that it would utilise the general format of the US IRP and customise the package for the UK/European CMBS markets. Version 1 of the E-IRP was not as advanced as the US Version 4.0 at the time and initially began with the loan Set-Up File, Loan Periodic File, Property File and the Bond File. This was completed in 2005. Subsequently, the Servicer Watch List and Watch List Guidelines were introduced in 2006.

The E-IRP is a "living document" as loans and CMBS structures evolve the information that needs to be captured changes and grows. To accommodate this, CREFC Europe has a permanent E-IRP Committee (industry professionals that include service providers, investors and originators) that meets to address questions and concerns. These comments are reviewed for additions, revisions and/or clarification to the E-IRP.

In late 2007, the E-IRP Committee began the process of updating the reporting package to E-IRP v 2.0 and set out to introduce further standards in CMBS reporting; how to make the package adaptable to the various transaction types and specific to the loan event calculations and ways to encourage broader use of the package amongst issuers and servicers.

The E-IRP package has been designed to provide core assets and loan data that can be utilised as the basis for reporting for many types of capital market transactions secured by European CRE (e.g. covered bonds, syndications, subordinated debt structures and CMBS).

A key point of the E-IRP is that the reporting package can be used across CRE as a sector by balance sheet lenders, by structured finance teams and by bond investors. Reporting packages that can be universal within sectors should create a greater level of transparency than reporting packages catering for individual segments within a sector. By making sure the E-IRP can cover the loans and the bonds it should be a package that is used by the CRE finance sector as a whole and not just by CMBS market participants. CREFC Europe believes this universality of reporting standards is a key benefit to the market as a whole.[3]

### 4.2 Highlights of the CREFC E-IRP Version 2

The key benefits of the E-IRP v 2.0 are:

- Data fields can be used for various loan structures such as whole loan, securitisation, syndication and AB Structures[4];
- Re-defined field definitions, which clarify key concepts;
- Introduction of minimum required fields—with over 600 data fields, the E-IRP v

---

[1] See further Ch.12.
[1] See further Chs 14 and 15.

2.0 highlights key fields that should be populated for basic transaction information flow;

- Introduction of standards for calculating key financial indicators such as interest coverage ratios, debt service coverage ratios and loan to value ratios;
- Financial calculations can be based on the loan agreements and loan structure participation levels; and
- Introduction of methodology for analysing and reporting property income statements. Details on how to report net operating income for various European jurisdictions. This will allow investors to compare property cash flow in a more transparent fashion.

### 4.3 Key issues with implementation of data standardisation

The E-IRP has been successfully adopted by multiple users within the European CMBS markets with the third party service providers being the most immediate beneficiary of the data transfer standards. As of 2012, the European Central Bank and the Bank of England have adopted the E-IRP format for CMBS transactions provided as collateral. However the E-IRP remains a reporting standard with voluntary compliance; there is no regulatory requirement for any market participant to provide the data in such a format. Further, the data contained in E-IRP will only reflect that provided to the lender/servicer from the borrowers.

### 4.4 Ways to incentive borrower reporting compliance

The CRE market is still lacking comprehensive property information from borrowers. Loan borrower reporting incentives are an important driving point for the industry in order to accurately understand the credit risk of the underling loan portfolios in an efficient manner.

How borrowers can be incentivised by banks/lenders is a matter to be determined but crucial to the successful implementation of any reporting standards. Firstly, as any increase in borrower reporting requirement is not encompassed within existing loan documentation, an effective and efficient method must be determined to incentivise borrowers to comply with new requirements. Secondly, in certain instances, such as Germany, privacy laws may prevent the reporting of individual details in a form consistent with any implemented reporting standard. Therefore, any such reporting standard must provide the necessary provisions to accommodate any such restrictions. Lastly in a preponderance of existing loan documentation, the only recourse available to the lender in the event of borrower non-compliance with reporting requirements is to call an event of default. With no incentive, such as the imposition of an increased interest rate, the borrower presumably realises that the lender is not likely to trigger an event of default solely for the non-provision of information, especially if the information is not contained in the original facility agreement.

The E-IRP Committee is, at the time of writing, formulating standard borrower reporting requirements to lenders. In time this reporting format can be a boilerplate within loan documents and submitted in a standard electronics transfer method.

*Intended audience and wider audience*

As CMBS is a key tool in creating liquidity in the structured finance CRE market, CREFC Europe feels that the transparency reporting requirements should be widened to the broader CRE finance markets such as balance sheet lenders and covered bonds. By creating a wider reporting requirement on CRE loans, information arbitrage will not take place within the primary and secondary trading markets for CRE loans.

To date, banks/balance sheet lenders are not required to report in any great detail the performance of balance sheet CRE loans. The extent of bad loans/losses and write-downs in recent times has created a real need for balance sheet lenders to be required to report CRE finance transactions to regulators and central banks in more detail. Further, any inconsistency in reporting requirements may provide a disincentive for market participants to issue CMBS transactions at the cost of compliance—for systems, relationship and information collection—may be viewed as excessive. The unintended result of an acceptable reporting requirement for CMBS without similar application to other lending products could be counterproductive for a re-emergence of CMBS as a viable alternative funding tool.

The above initiatives and the Appendices that follow, are crucial in strengthening, creating transparency and liquidity in the European CRE finance market.

In 2012/2013, many of the initial market principles and guidance papers will be published for market access. Currently the *European Commercial Real Estate Lending Principles Guide;* European *Commercial Real Estate Lending Tax Guide,* E-IRP v 2.0 data files and market principles for issuing *European CMBS 2.0* are published on the CREFC Europe website (http://www.crefc.org/eu). The first three of these are also reproduced in this book, In addition, CREFC Europe encourages all market participants to become active members in the process to effect change within the CRE finance industry. As the market continues to re-develop, CREFC Europe will create additional committees, working groups and initiatives to reflect the ongoing change.

Furthermore, as a benefit of membership, CREFC Europe provides members with the following dedicated services:

- Weekly newsletter informing members of CRE finance news and regulatory updates
- Member discussion groups facilitated through organised committees and working groups
- Bi-annual conferences for members and wider market participants
- Educational "hot topic" events held in London and Germany
- Networking opportunities offered at conferences and educational events
- Members views obtained and collated for legislative consultations by key bodies such as the FSA, Bank of England and European Central Bank
- Key initiatives such as transparency promoted through formulating market reporting standards

Further information in relation to committee papers, conferences, seminars, news, regulatory matters impacting the CRE finance market and membership can be found at *http://www.crefc.org/eu*.

# Appendix 1

## European Commercial Real Estate Lending Principles

Commercial Real Estate Finance Council®
EUROPE

## Contents

## 2 Introduction

### 2.1 Lender Committee

The Commercial Real Estate Finance Council Europe ("CREFC Europe") formed a Lender Committee ("Committee") to further underpin the strategic broadening of its remit. The Committee seeks to offer an opportunity for the providers of finance active in the European Commercial Real Estate market to interact and address issues particular to their business. This Committee is composed of commercial banks, pension funds, insurance companies, finance companies, funds and other private investors. It will examine best practices, effects of regulatory reform and, where possible, standardisation to the sector amongst other initiatives. The Committee's focus is broad in scope but incorporates considerations of:

- The senior balance sheet lending arena;
- The corporate and capital markets arena (such as unsecured debt, convertible bonds, derivatives, debentures and Eurobonds, CMBS, covered bonds / Pfandbrief);
- Subordinated debt (stretched senior, junior, mezzanine and preferred equity); and
- Growing involvement of alternative lender types (institutional, insurance, fund based capital providers).

### 2.2 Best Practices

The crisis of the last few years has meant that lending practices have been rigorously tested and significant insight as to their robustness gained. Meanwhile, there has been a profound reduction in the number of property lending personnel and the supply of debt remains constrained. Europe is seeing a fragmentation of lender type - not just balance sheet using banks and capital market issuers but the appearance of a more mature subordinated debt market and growing interest from new entrants such as the insurance sector. The Committee therefore recognises that there are good reasons to focus on Best Practices:

- *Human Capital*: Banking market consistently suffers from lack of experienced property bankers mainly due to the negative impact of the property cycle in recruitment / training.
- *Implementing Recent Lessons Learned*: Perfect opportunity to bring together knowledge recently gained from managing the fall out of the credit crisis.
- *Market Harmonisation Fostering Liquidity*: Seek to ensure that CREFC Europe supports the aim to deliver a high quality approach to lending that is harmonised across differing capital sources.

The Committee has identified six overarching lending "pillars":

- Transaction Structuring;
- Documentation;
- Due Diligence;
- Intercreditor arrangements;
- Tax
- Hedging

The Committee had already determined to create a set of European principles holistically valid for lending. This paper covers Structuring / Documentation. A tax bulletin entitled "European Commercial Real Estate Lending Tax Guide" was issued in March 2012. Related papers on Due Diligence and Intercreditor arrangements will follow. Specific French and German variations will also be produced to demonstrate CREFC Europe's commitment to representing the wider European market. This work will finally dovetail into the "Market Principles for Issuing European CMBS 2.0" process also being undertaken by CREFC Europe. In effect, CREFC Europe is focusing on ensuring loans are well structured, executed and managed and that those loans that are then ultimately (partially) securitised/syndicated are also subject to well structured, executed and managed securitisations/syndications.

CREFC Europe is part of the working group assisting the Loan Market Association ("LMA") in developing an "LMA Standard" real estate finance facility agreement which should be completed in early 2012. The Bank of England has further sought best practice views from CREFC Europe.

### 2.3 Approach

The following recommendations assume a *professional* degree of existing knowledge and experience. They do not seek to incorporate the obvious basics of property lending but rather focus on areas of importance and controversy and where specific lessons have been learnt. A single advance term secured investment loan with multiple properties has been considered as the base transaction. It is intended that this paper will be updated on an annual basis by the Committee.

## 3 Best Practice Recommendations

*3.1 General*

| Issue: | Recommendations: |
|---|---|
| Ensure related due diligence process is focused not just on property but also corporate aspects. | CREFC Europe is currently undertaking a comprehensive Due Diligence Best Practices exercise with draft papers envisaged in H2 2012. This paper simply highlights certain matters.<br><br>Due Diligence typically includes:<br><br>• Valuation;<br>• Certificate of Title work covering title, planning and lease structure; and<br>• Review of corporate documentation (e.g. Certificate of Incorporation, Memorandum and Articles of Association, recent financial accounts).<br><br>In addition Lenders should consider ensuring appropriate conditions precedent due diligence has been undertaken with regards to:<br><br>PROPERTY LEVEL<br>• Full lease review and tick back to source documentation;<br>• Mechanical and Engineering soundness;<br>• Tenant improvements ("TIs") / capital expenditure assessment;<br>• Environmental contamination;<br>• Energy efficiency; and<br>• Insurance<br><br>CORPORATE LEVEL<br>• Accounting/legal due diligence of Borrower where it is "old" or where historical (contingent) liabilities are suspected of having existed. |

|  |  |
|---|---|
|  | • Tax report that specifically covers the tax implications of purchasing, owning and selling property and the likely cash outflows resulting (please see the Ernst & Young/CREFC Europe "European Commercial Real Estate Lending Tax Guide" on this matter). The desirability of a formal tax report is clear but its absolute need will depend on the transaction complexity and leverage.<br><br>Results of due diligence ultimately should feed into cash waterfalls.<br><br>Ideally such due diligence should be undertaken by independent third parties or, if necessary, Borrower advisers under strong duty of care language and appropriate liability exposure. All due diligence must be addressed to enable reliance with appropriate disclosure language in all relevant circumstances. |
| Cross Border transactions create unforeseen enforcement issues. | The wide range of tax efficient structures often means that UK property may well be owned or managed by vehicles outside of the UK. The Channel Islands is a favoured location, for example. Recent experience has clearly indicated that the normal UK enforcement processes can be adversely impacted by other jurisdictions being involved.<br>For example:<br>• It may be impossible to appoint, or there may be additional costs in appointing, an administrator.<br>• The local law may provide for a sale on enforcement but no ability to take control with a view to holding until better conditions prevail.<br>• Local laws may be new and untested – a lack of clarity as to what they mean.<br><br>The Lender's lawyers should provide clear written advice on the potential enforcement impact of any cross border structure with suggested mitigation strategies. |

## 3.2 *(Condition of) Utilisation*

| Issue: | Recommendations: |
|---|---|
| There may be material payments that need to be undertaken to protect the value of the underlying collateral (e.g. insurance premium or head leasehold payments). | Incorporation of the concept of "Property Protection Loans" as such advances are pre-agreed by the Borrower and allow the Lenders to unilaterally advance sums to cover these items if required to protect their position. |
| Risk that transaction fundamentals change between commitment and drawdown – biggest risk being interest rate movement. Interest Coverage Ratio ("ICR") analysis often considers stressed property cash flows using a static interest rate. | In many situations general best practices suggest incorporating draw stop conditions based on ICR, Loan to Value ("LTV") and Loan to Cost ("LTC") set at the initial underwriting position, not default levels. LTC is also often included to avoid the risk that valuation results lead to a materially higher LTC than LTV. Potentially consider stating a maximum acceptable interest strike rate. |

## 3.3 *Repayment / Prepayment / Cancellation*

| Issue: | Recommendations: |
|---|---|
| Intra Interest payment Date ("IPD") repayment. | Either (i) repayment on an Interest Payment Date or (ii) the margin is made whole to the next IPD. Minimum of 10 business days' notice for repayment. |
| Repayment priority. | Recommend pro-forma documents include requirements for senior debt to be fully repaid in priority to any subordinate debt. Often the precise deal mechanics will adjust this presumption. |
| Clarity on events that require mandatory prepayment. | Recommended to include disposals, lease premiums on surrender, insurance proceeds, compulsory purchase and illegality proceeds. |

513

3.4 *Hedging*

| Issue: | Recommendations: |
|---|---|
| Hedge Counterparty – Following the Lehman Brothers Chapter 11 experience there is greater awareness of counterparty credit positions and changes to that counterparty. | • Compromise of a counterparty being either an original Lender, an approved acceding Lender or a rated counterparty.<br>• Clear implications on failure to perform should be set out.<br>• Rating language may well be at least needed for any capital markets issuance.<br>• No changes permitted to counterparty without Lender and counterparty consent.<br>• Lenders to have ability to require closing out of hedging on insolvency of counterparty. |
| Ensure up front and ongoing agreement of hedging strategy. | Written strategy pre-agreed by all Lenders probably including parameter ceilings e.g. maximum strike rate. No changes without all Lenders consent. |
| Appropriate ranking and security. | Pari passu beneficiary of security; carve outs for any margin call agreements (that are to be used first). |
| Termination rights – no market standard. | The only market consensus is that there is no market consensus regarding counterparty termination rights. Bank hedge desks have increasingly had greater input in the loan negotiation process with a strong focus on when they have the unilateral right to close out hedging positions as opposed to explicit acceleration rights. Historically such termination rights might have occurred on loan acceleration. Now this varies from institution to institution with termination due to insolvency, default, tax event, tax event on merger and force majeure being hotly discussed. Furthermore, counterparty voting rights are also being raised, usually in the post termination period. It must be emphasised that these issues are being repeatedly discussed on a deal by deal basis and CREFC Europe intends to focus on this issue in 2012 within the Loan Hedging Working Group. |
| Hedging levels – automatic mechanisms to cater for over/under hedging. | No more than 105% and presumption of 90% of loan amount hedged at any time but greater permitted if occurs through a non-credit related product e.g. a cap. |

*3.5 Fees, Costs & Expenses*

| Issue: | Recommendations: |
|---|---|
| Up Front Fee – ensure actually paid irrespective of whether loan drawn. | "Payable" at signing and "paid" no later than earlier of first drawdown or expiry of commitment period. Ensure consideration as to who is responsible for paying when the Borrower is a Special Purpose Vehicle ("SPV") – often the main client entity will guarantee such obligations. Current accounting practices require clarity on the reason for the payment. As a general rule 'structuring' or 'arrangement' fees can be recognised at loan commencement. "Participation" fees often are required to be amortised over the loan life. |
| Agency costs tend to increase post default. | Agency Fee needs to flex to take account of work involved post default. |
| Prepayment Fees sometimes unfair when either the Borrower addresses a loan deterioration or where issues occur beyond its control. | Prepayment Fees not payable on cure of (potential) default, increased costs occurring due to illegality or on receipt of insurance proceeds. Prepayment fees should however be distinguished with break costs. |
| Prepayment Fees structured to reflect capital at work. | The current market standard is typically fixed basis point penalties for the first few years. A number of Lenders (especially the non-bank lenders) are starting to advocate margin make whole provisions for a certain number of years. Such a choice is at the discretion of Lenders. |

| | |
|---|---|
| Default margins apply purely on a payment default. In a low interest rate environment many problematic situations can arise without actual payment default occurring. | Historically default margins have only applied on payment default. The introduction of Basel II and inevitably Basel III has demonstrated banks' capital costs rise significantly post any default. Arguably should a default margin apply on any default it could be represented as a genuine pre-estimate of the additional costs of the default which should generally mitigate the risk that it is identified as a penalty and therefore unenforceable. Whilst this approach is being adopted by a growing number of Lenders it is by no means a market standard. An alternative structure which only captures declining deal performance is an LTV/ICR margin grid where a default triggers the highest margin. Finally some law firms are now recommending charging default interest for failure to satisfy a condition subsequent or failure to provide information on time. |

### 3.6  *Accounts*

| Issue: | Recommendations: |
|---|---|
| Rent Account: Practical balance on flow of everyday funds. | • Agent sole signing rights to Rent Account, complete lockbox account.<br>• However it should be queried whether tenants pay directly into that account or not.<br>• The credit crisis is a recent reminder that property costs usually have to be paid irrespective of whether Lenders assumed they did not.<br>• It is generally more practical to get a managing agent to owe a duty of care, collect monies, retain appropriate (and capped) irrecoverable/agreed property costs and then transfer net amount to the Rent Account. Hedging counterparty transfers any payments direct to Rent Account.<br>• Agent then deals with head lease payments, debt service requirements, capex / TI and tax retentions and any surplus goes into General Account where Borrower has signing rights.<br>• Consider whether corporate SPV costs (pre-agreed and capped) come out before or after Rent Account.<br>• Typical to leave Borrower to deal with VAT flows. |

| | |
|---|---|
| Capital Expenditure ("Capex") / Tenant Improvements ("TI") Account | • Given increased focus on Capex a separate identified account is usually justified.<br>• Based on initial and annually updated professional advice (see Business Plan point above).<br>• Funded day one with pre-determined "Catch Up" Capex. Periodic transfers occur in an agreed way to cover identified future Capex obligations and TIs likely to arise.<br>• Only Agent has signing rights and releases as and when required.<br>• Ensure Borrower cannot commit to Capex / TIs above an agreed amount without Lender consent. |
| Tax Account | • Based on initial and annually updated tax advice.<br>• If interest on shareholder debt used as a tax shield then robust accountant opinion on tax deductibility should be obtained.<br>• Pre funded with identified Stamp Duty Land Tax / VAT liabilities.<br>• Periodic transfers from Rent Account on pre-agreed accruals basis to cover corporation tax liabilities.<br>• Only Agent has signing rights and releases as and when required. |
| General Account | • Lenders can lockbox the account on default. |
| Rating | • Whilst arguably not market standard CREFC Europe believes recent history recommends a minimum rating requirement for account providers certainly for accounts where large capital sums flow through. |

### 3.7  Tax / Increased Costs / Other Indemnities

| Issue: | Recommendations: |
|---|---|
| Lenders' own tax position – new entrant funds, insurers, etc that are not classically banks could create risk they are subject to withholding tax from day one. | Initial Lenders to confirm that they are not subject to withholding tax then Borrower takes subsequent change of law risk for such Lenders; subsequent Lenders treated in a similar way. |

### 3.8  Guarantees & Guarantors

| Issue: | Recommendations: |
| --- | --- |
| Use of Guarantees prevalent and shown to have inherent weakness, especially Fund Guarantees. | Acceptances of guarantees are always a subjective decision by Lenders. Common mistakes in their use include failing to take account of Guarantor jurisdiction and consequent enforceability rights, requirement to prove loss, contingent commitments, other guarantees, differentiating between net assets and actual liquidity, whether capital is invested or merely committed and by whom and ensuring guarantees are called long before either liquidity is utilised or unused commitments are drawn or expire unused. Serious consideration of the wording and nature of guarantee tests/covenants is advisable. |
| First demand guarantee or not? | First demand is strongly encouraged. |

### 3.9  Representations

| Issue: | Recommendations: | Notes: |
| --- | --- | --- |
| A lack of market standard approach exists and a number of "bear traps" for the Lender exist. | The LMA process intends to produce a pro forma clause. CREFC Europe feels such a list should at least focus on for each obligor:<br>• Status – status of the obligor and its power to own its assets and carry on its business;<br>• Binding obligations – obligations expressed to be assumed by the obligor are legal, valid, binding and enforceable;<br>• Non conflict with other obligations – the entry into and performance by the | All such representations should be deemed repeated on each utilisation request, the first day of each interest period and when a new entity becomes an obligor.<br><br>"To the best of knowledge" caveat should be resisted. Accuracy of representations is ultimately a risk, not fault, allocation exercise. For example, it may not be the fault of the Borrower that information provided by or on behalf of itself and upon which the Lender has based its |

decision to lend is inaccurate, but the Borrower, not the Lender, should bear the risk.

The fact that a representation is incorrect or misleading is typically only an event of default insofar as it is incorrect or misleading in a "material" respect. Adding materiality language to the representation may amount to "doubling up" on materiality.

obligor of the transactions contemplated by the documents will not conflict with laws or regulations, constitutional documents or other agreements binding upon it;

- Power and authority – the obligor has the power to enter into and perform the relevant transactions and no limit on its powers will be exceeded by the transactions;
- Validity and admissibility in evidence – all necessary authorisations required to enable the obligor to enter into and perform its obligations and to make the relevant documents to which it is party admissible, and all authorisations necessary for the conduct of its business, have been obtained or effected and are in full force and effect;
- Registration requirements – except for specified registration requirements, it is not necessary to register any of the relevant documents in any public place or elsewhere;
- Governing law and enforcement – the choice of [English] law as the governing law and any judgment obtained in England in relation to the

documents will be recognised and enforced;

- Deduction of tax – no day one requirement to deduct for on account of tax from any payment under the relevant documents and there is no requirement to deduct tax from rental income;

- No filing or stamp taxes – it is not necessary under the relevant laws to file, record or enroll or pay any stamp, registration or similar tax in relation to any of the relevant documents and any required disclosures in relation to stamp duty land tax have been made;

- VAT – the obligor is not a member of a value added tax group [other than a group made up solely of obligors];

- No default – no default is continuing or might reasonably be expected to result from the transactions and no other event or circumstance which constitutes a default or termination event under an agreement is reasonably likely to have a material adverse effect;

- Information – all information (including general information, information in relation to the property due diligence reports and information in relation to the valuation) is true and accurate and does not omit relevant information;

- Financial statements – its financial statements have been prepared in accordance with GAAP including, if applicable, IFRS and there has been no material adverse change since the day one financial statements;

- Pari passu ranking – the obligor's payment obligations under the relevant documents rank at least pari passu with unsecured and unsubordinated creditors;

- No proceedings pending or threatened – no litigation, arbitration or administrative proceedings have been started or threatened against the obligor;

- Title to property – the relevant obligor holds legal and beneficial, and good and marketable, title to the relevant property free from security interests and except as disclosed in the property due diligence reports there are no issues in relation to the properties; no other business – no obligor has traded or carried on any other business, it has no subsidiaries and it has no employees or obligations in respect of a pension scheme;

- Centre of main interests and establishment – the obligor's centre of main interests and establishment is in [England and Wales]/[its jurisdiction of incorporation];
- Ranking of security – the security conferred by the security documents is first priority security of the type described;
- Ownership – the obligor is owned by the person or persons identified as part of the credit process.

### 3.10 Information Undertakings

| Issue: | Recommendations: |
| --- | --- |
| Financial Statements | Whilst filing dates and requirements to produce consolidated accounts may influence deal specifics. Timely production of statutory and interim management accounts under recognised accounting standards is vital. |
| Compliance Certificate regularly provided and undertaken on an appropriate basis. | Provided in advance of IPD assessing position at that IPD and signed by 2 directors. |
| Lack of consistent property reporting. | Property monitoring reports provided on each IPD should seek to cover information on:<br>• Existing occupational tenants showing rent, service charges, VAT, key lease terms (annual rent, lease term/breaks, rent review provisions, unusual lease provisions); |

| | |
|---|---|
| | • Management accounts / cash-flows;<br>• Arrears information;<br>• Rent reviews, lease expiries, surrenders and (prospective) new lettings;<br>• Material correspondence regarding insurance; and<br>• Up-to-date capital expenditures and repair/maintenance plans. |
| Business Plans | Provision of annual business plan for approval; especially to cover irrecoverable operational expenses which is a general waterfall deduction. |

*3.11 Warning Milestones – Financial Covenants*

| Issue: | Recommendations: |
|---|---|
| Hard as it is to believe – some deals have no consequence to covenant breach. | Ensure purpose to covenant structure. |
| Too often deals have a simple covenant breach point that moves the transaction from "performing" immediately to "default". | • Cash sweep triggers that occur on ICR/LTV ratios designed to reflect that the deal has moved beyond only a moderate deterioration point<br>• Sweeps create cash liquidity that can be used on appropriate asset management strategies and amortisation<br>• On some deals consider other ratio triggers that allow Lender greater rights e.g. right to have greater sign off on asset management strategies or requirement to replace property/asset manager |
| Ensure Interest Cover acts as an early warning trigger rather than reflecting disaster has already struck. Also recognition than SPV financing means one should be looking at corporate level NOI not pure Net Rent. | Comparison of Finance Costs against Net Operating Income ("NOI")<br><br>**NET OPERATING INCOME**<br>• Not Net Rent.<br>• Unless property has extremely short leases then one should undertake an annual projected income calculation; if short leases do exist where assuming all leases that can break do is often unrealistic, then a 3-month look back annualised figure |

- is perhaps more appropriate (unless also a seasonal cash flow (e.g. hotels) when a one year look back may be considered).
- Net Rent is effectively calculated by taking a forward 12-month projection of Gross Rent and then:

  - Break clauses assumed to occur;
  - Only considering contracted rent;
  - Recognising only contracted rent reviews increases;
  - Ignoring all rental flows where tenant already one+ months in arrears or where insolvent

- And then deducting irrecoverable property costs (including related VAT) such as:

  - Ground rents;
  - (Empty) rates ignoring any short term empty business rates mitigation scheme;
  - Service charges;
  - Insurance premium;
  - Repair and value maintaining Capex; and
  - Agreed and capped property and asset management fees.

- NOI = Net Rent less any approved and capped SPV running costs.
- Interest on cash balances and ancillary income to be ignored unless very compelling rationale.
- Tenant incentives and Capex are arguably items of a capital nature and "below the line".

## FINANCE COSTS

- Interest and fees.
- Finance costs always forward looking projection.
- Take account of hedging; for swaps use the swap rate; for caps use the cap itself or the LIBOR rate for the remaining loan period (especially relevant in an upward sloping LIBOR curve environment) or, at a minimum the 12 month LIBOR rate.

| | |
|---|---|
| Loan to Value – consistent and independent basis. | **LOAN**<br>• Use the standing loan amount unless there is a reason to use the facility amount (e.g. when structure allows for provision of guarantees under facility terms).<br>• Measures of mark to market are not at all market standard. Some situations (e.g. significant loan/hedge term imbalance) may warrant some considerations.<br><br>**VALUE**<br>• RICS Red Book Market Value.<br>• No artificial constructs (e.g. internal leases) to be considered.<br>• Adoption of strict German Mortgage Bank rules in Valuer independence<br>• Lender right to call valuation at least annually and when believes default outstanding or where a default might arise as a consequence of such a further valuation.<br>• Copies of all valuations received by Borrower to be provided to Lenders although to be ignored for covenant testing purposes. |
| Covenants should apply at all times not just on discrete dates. | Only formally tested quarterly but ongoing duty of directors to ensure complied with at all times. |
| Who undertakes the covenant calculations? | The Borrower should prepare the calculations and provide them to the Agent with supporting documentation. The Agent's calculation should prevail on any disagreement. |
| Curing of covenant breaches should be permanent. Where temporary curing this should be severely restricted in terms of time or extent to avoid prolonged artificial maintenance of a transaction. | Make a clear distinction between "permanent" cures and "subsidy" cures. Permanent cures such as capital repayment or cash collateral (when finance costs related to that cash sum are ignored) should be unlimited. Subsidy cures such as cash injection for interest test shortfall should be limited to no more than a maximum of two consecutive IPDs and/or not more than two in any twelve month period and/or four to six times in total. |

3.12  *General Undertakings*

| Issue: | Recommendations: | Notes: |
|---|---|---|
| Negative Pledge carve outs can create issues. | Lenders should adopt an approach that there should be no other liabilities incurred apart from pre-identified specific exemptions. | "Basket" exceptions and wide exceptions language (e.g. "ordinary course of business") should be avoided. |
| Merger / Acquisitions | Not allowed without Lender consent. | |
| VAT | Bar on VAT group unless solely with other obligors as membership of a VAT group gives rise to liabilities for VAT obligations of other group members. | |

3.13  *Property Covenants*

| Issue: | Recommendations: |
|---|---|
| Insurance – more care needed in clause formulation. | • Legal advisers have already tightened insurance provisions. The German Pfandbrief led banks remain extremely focused here recommending a number of aspects be considered as almost mandatory. The Lenders should ideally be co-insured with appropriate non-vitiation, subrogation waiver and loss payee clauses. At the very least the Lenders interest should be noted. A Borrower may seek a carve out that permits proceeds below a certain de minimis threshold to be paid to the Borrower for minor insured events/claims.<br>• In addition an inconsistent approach exists in relation to the use of rating level requirements for insurance counterparties, notwithstanding its use is arguably sensible.<br>• Pfandbrief rules also require insurance to be asset specific (i.e. not a block policy) and the borrower/owner must insure (i.e. insurance via a superior interest holder does not work). |

| | |
|---|---|
| Lenders still require input on leasing matters without this being too intrusive. | Each transaction is far too specific to provide generalised comments. The trust placed in the asset manager, the scale of assets, lease diversity and asset quality are all deciding factors. That said, some consent control over material new leases and cumulative surrenders is still advisable (by % GOI or ICR for example). |

### 3.14 Disposals / Substitution

| Issue: | Recommendations: |
|---|---|
| Portfolio transactions invariably contain property of mixed quality. Applying a dogmatic standard allocated release amount ("ALA") release pricing that applies at all times leads to cherry picking risk especially at a time when poorer properties are illiquid. | <ul><li>If using ALAs then ensure based on qualitative assessments as much as value.</li><li>Consider ALA flexing on basis of updated values and quality review (probably on annual basis).</li><li>Any sweep covenants should also apply to disposal proceeds.</li></ul> |
| Ensure that no transaction manipulation permissible through use of disposals clause. | <ul><li>Sales only on arms' length basis to third party.</li><li>Lender consent specifically required if the net disposal value is below the initial value.</li></ul> |
| Value destruction risk exists on sale of part of an asset (e.g. individual residential sales can lead to remaining "Swiss Cheese" residential block). | Majority or all Lender consent specifically required for part sales. |
| Danger of collateral deterioration and fundamental shift of deal type through poorly controlled substitution rights. | No pro forma substitution clause. To be considered on a deal by deal basis with caution and with Lender consent required – perhaps without having to act reasonably (i.e. absolute discretion). |

3.15  *Security*

| Issue: | Recommendations: |
|---|---|
| Recent history has shown that many creditors have been frustrated in their attempts to enforce and sell the Borrower SPV as opposed to the underlying asset. SPV sale might be desired for reasons of speed, efficiency, SDLT mitigation. A principal stumbling block is the existence of non-consenting other creditors. | Obtain appropriate security over other material liabilities (e.g. subordinate third party debt, shareholder loans) that allow the cancellation or movement of such liabilities to facilitate SPV level (as opposed to direct asset level) sale. |
| Only comprehensive belts and braces security package ensure creditors can maximise their enforcement options. | A strong security package will typically include, but will not be limited to:<br>(i)  A first legal mortgage over the underlying properties;<br>(ii)  First fixed and floating security over all assets of the obligors including:<br>  a.  First ranking charge over rental income and all receipts;<br>  b.  First charge over the bank accounts;<br>  c.  First ranking assignment of insurances with the Lender as co-insured;<br>  d.  First ranking assignment of hedging instruments;<br>  e.  Assignment of the benefit of all relevant (and material) contracts in which the obligors have an interest;<br>(iii)  Charge over the shares in the obligors;<br>(iv)  First charge over all subordinated indebtedness.<br>(v)  Subordination deed and intercreditor agreement (as appropriate);<br>(vi)  Duty of care with each property manager and asset manager; and<br>(vii)  Cross-guarantees or such other structure or instrument to achieve full cross collateralisation of the obligors. |
| Looking beyond the SPV is sometimes desirable to strengthen security position. | Consider whether Holdco security or convertible rights on default might further enhance a specific transaction. |

| Recovery claims from Report Providers rarely considered upfront. | CREFC Europe believes that it may be appropriate to incorporate provisions for prepayments out of the proceeds of claims made against report providers (e.g. claims against solicitors who prepared the certificate of title). |

### 3.16 Changes to the Lenders / Obligors / Other Parties

| Issue: | Recommendations: |
|---|---|
| Allow easy asset management transfer on enforcement. | Lender right to terminate asset management agreements with no more than 3 months' notice on default / acceleration. |
| Change of Control ("CoC") is often structured to trigger mandatory prepayment which is an "after the fact" trigger. | Better to structure CoC as an event of default which is therefore requiring dialogue "before the fact". |
| CoC prevention. | CoC may be declined by banks for deal specific or KYC reasons. In addition another explicit valid reason is consequential increase to cluster risk (i.e. overall group exposure to a lender). |
| Due to KYC / money laundering great focus is given to the legal owning entities. Surprisingly often a lack of focus occurs regarding the entities actually managing the investment (e.g. a GP of a fund) or the asset manager undertaking the core property work. | Lender consent required for CoC of the Borrower, Ultimate Shareholder, Asset Manager and, if relevant, Fund Manager. |
| The mechanisms for the replacement of Lenders has been found wanting. Examples of this are "Tranche warfare", dissenting syndicates, "Loan to Own" strategies, non-bank Lenders with | Overarching proposals:<br>• No Borrower consent rights over Lender assignment of its position. Consultation rights may be a compromise so long as "consultation" is properly defined to ensure no more than non-binding dialogue.<br>• Comprehensive drafting permitting syndication, securitisation and loan |

| | |
|---|---|
| varying requirements, Borrowers restricting assignment to an extent that damages liquidity. | • tranching to facilitate optimised balance sheet management and foster market liquidity.<br>• Due consideration as to whether other Lenders get consent rights in certain circumstances e.g. sales to non-banks or vulture funds pre default or the sale of any subordinated debt by that creditor.<br>• "Yank the Bank" and non performing Lender clauses are contentious but the LMA does have language to include if chosen.<br>• Agent to keep a record of all ultimate Lenders available to all others and Lender disclosure mandatory. The LMA are not in agreement with this point although CREFC Europe continues to see this proposal as sensible.<br>• General prohibition on Borrower or partners related to Ultimate Shareholder taking position in debt. |

*3.17 Agent / Arranger*

| Issue: | Recommendations: |
|---|---|
| Clarification of Agent role required. In most sectors, Agents are actively seeking to reduce their unilateral decision-making powers. Conversely, in Real Estate Finance, Agent roles are often either structured with strong decision-making powers or Agents interpret their role that way. Clarity should be sought. | • Start from presumption that the Agent has no discretionary decision making powers and is a pure processer. Decisions should be made on the instructions of the lending group. While most decisions should be able to be made by Majority Lenders, some particularly important decisions should be reserved to all Lenders (such as amendments to pricing, release of security/guarantees, etc).<br>• If the Lenders determine to empower Agent with some decision making power there should be a specific agency document that clearly sets out what these are.<br>• This does not detract from the need to allow Agents to act unilaterally when to not quickly act is damaging. |
| Agent/Arranger role in club deals. | • Generally one or more of the Lenders will carry out the co-ordination role and will receive an arrangement fee for doing so.<br>• One of the Lenders (often through a related entity) will carry out the role of facility agent (and security trustee, if the two roles are separate) and will receive an agency fee for doing so. |

| | |
|---|---|
| | • The agency / security trustee roles are independent from lending roles and the agent may have separate requirements in respect of the loan and security documentation. |
| Substantial conflicts of interest have been seen to arise e.g. when Senior Agent is also in the subordinated debt or equity. | Agent should have explicit requirement to give due consideration to conflicts of interest. |

### 3.18 *Confidential Information*

| Issue: | Recommendations: |
|---|---|
| Onerous confidentiality restrictions impair liquidity of loan positions. | Recognition that certain parties e.g. in securitisations will not or cannot enter into confidentiality undertakings. In particular numerous lenders have found it challenging to share information with insolvency practitioners/receivers in the run up to an anticipated bankruptcy/enforcement or when potential buyers/asset managers are involved in strategies such as pre-pack administration. Lenders should however give due regard to any information process or recognise certain information is proprietary or price sensitive. |
| Avoid needing Borrower's consent to appointing third party advisers post default. | Ensure pre-agreed mechanism incorporated into documentation. |

**About CRE Finance Council Europe:**

Commercial Real Estate Finance Council Europe (CREFC Europe), part of CRE Finance Council (CREFC) headquartered in the U.S., is the premier trade organisation for the global commercial real estate finance industry and has been active in Europe since August 2004. We are dedicated to promoting the strength, transparency and liquidity of commercial real estate finance worldwide. We have become an effective channel for the industry to influence the regulatory framework and play a vital role in setting industry standards and promote best practices. We also provide educational sessions led by leading industry experts and networking opportunities for all market participants within this key sector of the global economy.

CREFC Europe's focus has expanded far beyond its roots in CMBS to encourage participation and drive involvement from the wider CRE markets. Our Members come from areas across the commercial real estate finance spectrum and include participants from the lending, investing, servicing and professional services communities across Europe.

*www.CREFC.org/eu*

# Appendix 2

## European Commercial Real Estate Lending Tax Guide

Commercial Real Estate Finance Council®
EUROPE

*Quality In Everything We Do*

## Contents

Disclaimer:

This document contains general information only and none of CRE Finance Council Europe or Ernst & Young are, by means of this document, rendering legal, tax, or other professional advice or services. This document is not a substitute for such professional advice or services, nor should it be used as a basis for any decision or action that may affect your finances or your business. Before making any decision or taking any action that may affect your finances or your business, you should consult a qualified professional adviser. None of CRE Finance Council or Ernst & Young shall be responsible for any loss whatsoever sustained by any person who relies on this document.

# Preface

It is a historical reality that Lenders have often neglected to consider the full impact of tax in transactions they undertake. It is indeed not uncommon for the tax aspect to be entirely ignored in a Lender's structuring and due diligence process. Sadly the last few years have visibly demonstrated that tax can and does have material impacts on a Lender's position with this lesson learnt at the worst possible time, namely a loan workout. Lenders have relied on their Borrowers to structure their investments in a tax efficient manner and later realised that tax remains part of the equation, that laws do change and that their Borrowers do not apply an equity view to tax as much as property investment. In a low interest rate environment with property yields in excess of overall medium term borrowing rates, the tax impact is an ongoing issue; indeed with European government deficits as they are we should expect tax take to increase. Managing tax liabilities requires consistent diligence and an adherence to a set of clear rules.

Classic examples abound, a pan European flavour includes:

- The requirement in the UK to file for withholding tax exemptions on rent paid offshore
- The limitation of interest cost deductions in Germany based on EBITDA metrics
- The threat of legal change a few years ago in the Netherlands to disallow depreciation on buildings as a tax deduction, often the main tax shield for leveraged deals
- The continued existence in Italy of withholding tax on interest paid to EU banks notwithstanding general EU free market principles
- The priority ranking nature of capital gains tax in Ireland to a traditional mortgage
- The payment and future recovery of VAT on certain property acquisitions in Spain necessitating a bridge finance structure

Whilst it is generally the case that in most European jurisdictions a first ranking mortgage grants a Lender a first claim on the property, this does nothing to ensure the underlying structure is as bankruptcy remote as possible and that the cash flows the Lender expects to see can actually be delivered.

It is for all these reasons that CRE Finance Council Europe in association with Ernst & Young has developed a document that seeks to achieve only two things. Firstly, it seeks merely to illustrate the myriad of issues that a Lender actually does need to consider. Secondly, it seeks to provide a template letter of instruction to Lenders to allow them to seek appropriate professional advice and ensure that, as best as possible, their business appropriately caters for the reality that tax does matter.

Peter Denton

Chairman, CREFC Europe Lender Committee

## 1. Introduction

This document sets out, in general terms, common tax issues that prospective lenders should consider in their lending decisions to real estate investment structures.

Managing the tax exposure of a structure involves striking a balance between two extremes:

- A simple structure that is easy to operate, and minimises compliance costs, but that is not tax efficient; or
- A complex structure that, while theoretically effective, requires adherence by non-tax experts to strict and inflexible procedures that, from a commercial perspective, may appear arbitrary and highly impracticable. Such structures may be difficult to manage in practice and are likely to be subject to challenge by the tax authorities..

Managing the tax profile of a structure is a lifetime process, where compliance with tax rules and regulations is as pertinent as the quality of the advice received on its establishment.

This document takes a high level approach to the situations that may arise, and should be considered when examining a debtor's tax position. For example, Germany and several other countries have recently introduced very detailed and prescriptive rules that restrict how much interest may be deducted (generally to a maximum of EBITDA or EBIT), whether or not that interest is sourced from unconnected parties. In the course of this report, we will not discuss the detail of such rules, but will flag them up as an issue that you should be aware of.

The purpose of this document is to frame the considerations and questions you should be asking when presented with a property investor's operations and structures, i.e. it is intended to act as a starting point outlining principles and concerns, and should not be treated as a comprehensive check list that addresses all tax risks that could arise.

## 2. Executive Summary

- Managing the tax position of an investment structure is a complex issue that requires informed and careful management.
- A key first step is to assess the operational risk that a property investment structure may present. A non-exclusive list of risk factors and considerations could include:-
  - What is the general quality of investment management?
  - How is tax advice obtained?
  - Is there evidence of a large number of open and unresolved tax issues?
  - Has all tax planning been implemented in accordance with relevant legislation?
  - Is someone taking a global oversight of tax strategy?

- Do operations take place in jurisdictions in which the tax authorities are known to take an a strong line with perceived non-compliance?
- This initial assessment should inform the level of detail and review required to assess for any specific tax risks. Real estate investment structures typically encounter the following tax issues as common risks:-
  - The tax strategy has been implemented incorrectly owing to lack of due care and attention, and is therefore rendered ineffective.
  - The tax deductibility of interest (both internal and external) is restricted.
  - The write-off of underperforming loans triggers unexpected tax charges.
  - Changes in the profile of investors can trigger tax charges at investment level.
- Actions carried out by investors on their own account can trigger tax charges/investigations at investment level.
- 'Offshore structures' (i.e. where real estate is held in a company tax-resident in another, more tax favourable, country) can be incorrectly operated in practice, with often significant negative tax consequences.
- Adopting an inappropriate tax profile for VAT/GST purposes on property rentals can significantly reduce the attractiveness to certain tenant classes.
- Real estate transfer taxes could have been triggered by restructuring of the investment structure.
- Structuring and tax planning to manage withholding tax liabilities and tax leakage on repatriation of cash to the investors proves ineffective.

## 3. Deductibility of Interest and Other Costs

Virtually all jurisdictions will seek to tax the rental profits from properties situated within them. Most property investors will therefore seek to minimise profits at the property SPV level, which in turn minimises the tax paid on these profits.

A generally accepted principle is that interest paid on financing a real estate business can be deducted against the rents received. To prevent abuse of this principle (i.e. by over gearing the business to extinguish net rental income), most jurisdictions have anti-avoidance provisions in place that can restrict the deductibility of debt interest.

Obviously, a reduced deduction for interest increases the amount of tax payable, and hence erodes post-tax returns to investors.

The worst-case commercial risk is that a property SPV in a cash flow neutral or negative situation, owing to a heavy debt burden, finds itself faced with a tax liability it does not have the cash to pay, having paid all its cash out in interest.

We discuss below some common situations in which the tax treatment of interest/loan amounts may become commercially relevant, and why tax due diligence by a prospective lender is advisable.

### *Transfer Pricing/Thin capitalisation*

These rules are now almost ubiquitous. How they are implemented varies significantly from place to place, but the key principle is that a taxpayer should not be able to acquire a tax benefit by entering into a loan agreement with a connected party that is underwritten on non-commercial terms.

In practice, this is most commonly achieved by comparing the loan terms to that which a hypothetical third-party lender would be prepared to lend on (i.e. an 'arm's length basis'), and allowing deductions only to that extent.

Several jurisdictions have 'safe harbour' provisions which simplify this test by setting out in legislation parameters in which they will consider loans to be 'arms length', e.g. a certain debt:equity ratio, interest rates in a certain range, de minimis limits for the rules to apply.

### *'Interest stripping' rules*

Over the past decade, several countries (notably including Germany and Italy) have moved away from targeting perceived abuses involving connected party debt, and are seeking to restrict what they see as erosion of their local tax base by use of excessive debt (be it from an unconnected third party or otherwise.)

How the rules work varies from country to country, but the common theme emerging to restrict the maximum tax deduction for interest to a certain percentage of EBIT/EBITDA or some similar metric. Germany, for example, restricts (in most cases) interest deductions to 30% of EBITDA.

### *Loan write-offs*

The tax treatment of loan write offs/rescheduling is typically a complex one, and tax advice specific to the jurisdiction should be taken in advance of any significant loan restructurings. Generally speaking, the release of a loan will produce an accounting credit to the profit and loss account of the debtor, and advice should be taken on whether this release is taxable or not.

## 4. Investor-Level Risks

Very often, a key tax risk lies not in the actions or inactions of the property investor, but in the actions and behaviours of its owners. The consequences of these can cascade down the chain of ownership and produce undesired and unexpected consequences at the level of the property investment that its managers have no ability to prevent.

Knowing the details and tax circumstances of the investors into an investment can therefore be just as important as knowing details of the investment itself.

There is a broad variety of circumstances in which the actions of the investors might cause issues for the property structure. However, we set out below some common issues that can arise.

## Change of Control

When companies are sold from one owner to another, anti-avoidance rules in many jurisdictions seek to catch two broad classes of transactions:-

a. Where an attempt is made to avoid transfer taxes etc. by selling a corporate wrapper rather than an underlying asset, or
b. The sale of surplus tax attributes (e.g. losses, tax depreciation pools) from one party to another. For example, a bankrupt group of companies will generally leave its administrators/receivers in possession of significant tax losses (trading losses, asset writedowns, etc.) that the group is, obviously, no longer in a position to use.

It should be noted that despite the intent of these rules, commercial transactions at the level of the investors can be caught that trigger unexpected tax consequences. For example, moving the parent company of a group into a trust could trigger German real estate transfer tax in respect of its German properties; or a consortium of investors acquiring control of a UK group could potentially jeopardise the availability of the brought forward losses therein.

It is difficult to set out a general principle here, but if you become aware of a proposed significant change in the ownership of an investment structure, it may be worth investigating further to ensure this does not jeopardise its tax attributes, or trigger an unexpected tax charge.

## Disclosure to Tax Authorities

In the current economic environment, tax authorities worldwide are taking a more stringent approach to auditing taxpayers. In addition, in response to the ever-increasing globalisation of business and political pressures surrounding 'tax havens', there has been a significant move to extend both the theoretical scope and the practical use of information exchange agreements, which allow the sharing of information between tax authorities.

It may well be the case, therefore, that disclosures made by an investor in the course of an enquiry into their affairs could lead to attention being focussed by the tax authorities onto the investments they have made.

In a well-run investment structure, this should not present a significant risk, bar the management time and costs associated with handling the tax authority's queries, but it should be apparent that where you may have concerns about a structure's tax risks, the probability is that others may do as well.

### Majority Investors

Most property investment structures (for example, a limited partnership) are set up such that operational control remains with the fund manager, even though the majority of the economic returns from the structure flow through to the investors.

To combat tax avoidance, most tax systems have special rules that cover companies under 'common control'. However, how a particular tax system may define 'control' has typically evolved away from a simple definition into a complex mechanistic test.

The practical effect of this is that we recommend investigating a structure where one investor owns a majority of the economic interest (even if they are otherwise a passive investor) to ensure that this does not present a tax issue in either the countries of the investment or of the specific investor.

### French '3% tax' and Analogues

As discussed in Section 5 of this report, there can be substantial legitimate tax efficiencies to operating a property structure from an offshore company. Several jurisdictions have, in an attempt to combat the benefits of offshore status, introduced taxes whose purpose is not so much to raise revenue, but to penalise non-disclosure of the ultimate owners of the structure to the relevant fiscal authority.

In France, for example, holders of French real estate are obliged to pay 3% of the value of the market value of their property holdings at 1 January each year. In practice, provided that disclosure is made of the ultimate beneficial owners, and that these owners are resident in a country that has a tax treaty with France, the 3% tax is mitigated. Otherwise, the 3% is levied on the investment structure, not the investors. There is therefore a strong motivation for the investment manager to disclose ownership.

Since the introduction of this tax, most fund agreements now incorporate a clause allowing the cost of any 3% tax charges (e.g. where an investor is from a country without a tax treaty with France, such as many Middle Eastern countries) to be allocated against the returns that the specific investor receives. In the absence of such a clause, an investor in one jurisdiction can erode the returns made by the investment structure. (In France, an investor subject to such a charge causes a 3% tax charge only in proportion to their economic holding of the structure, which mitigates this risk. In other countries, including Greece, there is no such pro-rating.)

## 5.   Offshore Structures

Virtually all jurisdictions seek to tax, in some way, real estate physically located within their borders. However, it is often the case that significant tax efficiencies can be accrued by holding a property in an offshore structure, i.e. that the company or other entity holding the property is located in another jurisdiction that does not tax (or taxes lightly) assets located outside its borders.

For example:-

- If a UK real estate investment is held by a UK company, rental profits and any capital gain on selling the property is subject to UK corporation tax (at a current rate of 26%). If, however, the same property is held by a Jersey company, then only rental profits are subject to UK income tax at 20%, while capital gains are exempted entirely (this treatment does require application to HMRC to obtain – failure can lead to the tenant withholding 20% from gross rental payments). Jersey would not tax either source of profits.
- In Germany, rental profits and capital gains on German property are generally always subject to federal-level corporate income tax at a rate of c. 15.8%. However, German Länder also typically levy an additional Trade Tax on profits arising from a 'permanent establishment' (very broadly, a fixed place of business) within their borders. This can almost double the effective tax rate paid on a German property investment. With care, however, a permanent establishment in Germany can be avoided (and so any trade tax liability as a consequence), and this is best achieved by use of a non-German company.

The key point is that securing these tax efficiencies requires a company to be non-resident in a particular jurisdiction. This is not just a matter of incorporating a company in an appropriate country.

The precise test to be satisfied, and the nature of the requirements to be satisfied, varies from country to country. However, the broad outline common to all of them is no control or management over the company's affairs should be exercised from within the physical boundaries of the jurisdiction within which the property is located.

We recommend careful attention is paid to this issue should you become aware of any of the following. None of these are, in themselves, 'red flags' but they are situations in which the management of the investment structure needs to take greater care to minimise the risk

- The ultimate investors are themselves resident in the country of the underlying asset;
- The investment managers themselves have substantial operations in the country in which the asset is located;
- Key individuals involved in the investment management process are nationals of or resident in the relevant country; or
- There is a general weakness in the investment manager's processes and procedures that might lead to inadvertent breaches.

## 6.   VAT, Sales Taxes and Real Estate Transfer Taxes

The indirect taxation of real estate is typically complex, as it involves at least three stakeholders; the owner of the property, the fiscal authorities and the counterparty in the taxable transaction. One of the key practical risks, therefore, is not so much that tax is unexpectedly payable, but that tax is unexpectedly payable by a third-party

We set out below some broad circumstances in which the risk is elevated:-

### Unexpected Sales Tax/GST/VAT on Rents

In a typical jurisdiction, particularly those with a VAT/GST, the treatment of the supply of property-related items (e.g. rentals, construction work, etc.) is complicated. Typically, particularly in respect of commercial property, the landlord is able to substantially affect whether VAT/GST is charged or not.

### VAT/GST Recovery Issues

One of the key principles applicable to VAT/GST is that the tax is levied at every step in a supply chain, but that a recipient of a supply who uses that supply to generate further taxable supplies is able to recover the VAT/GST they have suffered in making that supply.

If we consider how these principles apply to property, the two key risks should become apparent:-

a. The property owner is unable to recover all of its VAT/GST (if there are substantial construction costs involved, e.g. in a development-type project, this can substantially impact on the economics of the deal.)
b. Certain classes of commercial tenants (principally banks, insurance companies and other financial institutions) are generally unable to recover the majority of their VAT. If confronted with the choice between tenanting two equivalent properties; one of which will be subject to VAT on its rent, the other not, then this tax consideration will undoubtedly factor into their commercial decision-making process. (Conversely, however, a typical commercial tenant will be able to recover all of its VAT, and bar the cash flow issue on having to pay and then recover VAT, will typically not be so concerned about this issue.)

In summary, we recommend that any due diligence/modelling work on an investment structure should seek to establish the VAT/GST basis of how it operates/is intended to operate, as this is one of the key areas in which there is scope for an inappropriate operating model, or failings in compliance, to significantly impact on the expected economic returns an investment is able to generate.

### Sale of Shares Triggers Unexpected Transfer Tax Liability

A sub-set of the above relates to real estate transfer tax. Historically, this has usually been levied on the direct sale of real estate. However, as transfer taxes on the sale of shares have historically been either non-existent or much lower, an increasingly common approach is to sell the shares in an SPV holding the property rather than the property directly.

Many jurisdictions have introduced statutory overrides where, if the underlying substance of a transaction is the sale of land or buildings, the sale of the SPV is subject to real estate transfer taxes.

It should generally be apparent when these rules are likely to come into direct effect. However, there can be cases in which transactions higher up the chain of ownership in a property structure can trigger transfer tax liabilities in respect of properties held further down the chain.

### Tax Planning to Minimise Transfer Tax Liability is Ineffective

Governments have sought to take advantage of rising property prices by increasing the various duties and taxes payable on the sale of real estate. In the United Kingdom, for example, the rate on commercial properties worth more than £500,000 has gone from 0.5% in 1996 to 4% at the current date.

Should you become aware that an investment structure is implementing tax planning in respect of transfer taxes, we recommend that this is one of the areas on which any due diligence/investigation is focused, both around the technical aspects of the planning, and whether the requirements of this planning have been successfully implemented.

## 7. Cash Repatriation and Withholding Taxes

When implementing an investment structure, consideration should be given to the tax impact of repatriating profits to investors. This is particularly important where investors are tax exempt bodies.

### Withholding Taxes

Many jurisdictions levy withholding taxes on the payment of interest, dividends & royalties. Typically, most careful investment structures will ensure that withholding taxes are minimised. Below, we set out some common approaches taken, and also note where failure points commonly occur.

### Tax Treaties

To minimise double taxation (i.e. where two countries would otherwise tax the same item of income), a substantial network of double tax treaties has evolved. Typically, these treaties allow a resident of one country that receives income from another to be subject to tax only in their home country (or, failing that, applies a maximum rate to that which can be levied by the other country). The growth in this network has been facilitated by the OECD, which has developed a model treaty and guidance thereon to assist in this process.

However, a pronounced trend in recent years is that many countries are starting to limit the availability of treaty benefits in response to perceived abuse of the treaty network.

Therefore, many jurisdictions require that a company claiming treaty benefits is able to show:-

- that the company has substance (i.e. that it is not just a name on a piece of paper and has genuine commercial activity), and/or
- that it is actually the beneficial owner of the income it receives. This can catch back-to-back financing arrangements – if a company receives interest income, only to lend it on immediately to another company, arguably it is never beneficial owner of this interest income.

In practice, with care and attention by the managers of an investment structure these requirements can be met, but they do need to take care that the tax structure is supported by commercial reality..

A well-managed and advised investment structure should have this as one of their key tax risk management strategies. If there are concerns about the general approach to corporate governance of the investment structure, then this should be one of the areas in to which any investigation should take place.

## Hybrid Instruments

A hybrid instrument is, broadly, an instrument that is considered equity in the jurisdiction of holder, but as debt in the jurisdiction of the issuer (or, of course, vice versa). This is possible because many jurisdictions draw the line between debt and equity in a different place.

It is generally beneficial for such hybrid instruments to be considered debt in the country making the payments (as interest is generally deductible for tax purposes), but as equity in the receiving country (both for tax purposes, and also for the commercial goals of the investors).

Furthermore, where a country levies withholding tax on dividends, but not on interest (as, for example, Luxembourg does) such hybrid instruments form an essential part of an investment structure's cash repatriation strategy.

Hybrid instruments, however, do present certain risks:-

- Administrative complexity – hybrid instruments can be awkward to operate in practice.
- Anti-avoidance legislation – Several jurisdictions have introduced anti-avoidance legislation to combat use of hybrid instruments. This should have been taken into account when establishing an investment structure.

## 8. Change in Law or Practice

Owing to the current global economic situation, many governments find themselves running significant deficits, and as such, are keen to maintain their tax revenues to the maximum extent possible. However, in many cases it would be politically problematic to raise headline tax rates.

Therefore there has been a trend by some governments to:

- Introduce new anti-avoidance legislation to combat perceived abuses;
- Remove or severely restrict the availability and practical usefulness of long-standing tax reliefs; and
- Revisit the interpretation and approach to legislation to ensure greater certainty of treatment and a more robust compliance framework.

The above all, of course, form part of the normal evolution of a tax system, but the pace has been noticeably accelerated in recent years.

Therefore, although this is not a direct risk in itself, the current commercial and economic environment does significantly raise the risk that an investment structure has been unable to successfully cope with the consequently rapidly changing tax environment, triggering one of the specific risks outlined elsewhere in this document.

## 9. Fiscal Authority Actions for Non-Compliance

A well-run and tax compliant investment structure should generally not have cause to fear an investigation by tax authorities. Although the risk of a tax exposure should never be ruled out (either because tax planning has been put in place but is later held to be ineffective by the courts, or because there is a genuine disagreement on an ambiguous area such as an appropriate arm's length value on an intra-group transaction), provided care has been taken in establishing and operating a structure, these risks can be controlled (and in most cases, quantified).

However, the random audit or inspection remains a well used tool for jurisdictions seeking to defend their tax base.

Any investment manager should therefore operate on the assumption that pre-vention is better than cure, and should ensure that, on an ongoing basis, the controls and procedures it may put in place are documented and maintained in a con-temporaneous fashion to ensure that defending against tax authority investigation can start from the best possible starting point.

An investment structure should carefully consider the approach of the jurisdictions in which it operates, and not necessarily assume that 'one size fits all' in managing its tax risk – its approach will need to be flexed on a jurisdiction by jurisdiction basis.

## 10. Inadequate Procedures and Controls

Managing tax risk should be a continuous process, not a set of one-off actions.

There are numerous situations in which either not seeking tax advice, or not taking the effort to implement it correctly, can present significant tax risks to a property investor.

Therefore, one of the key starting points for any investigation of a property investment structure's tax risk is to assess the quality of its procedures and controls. By its very nature, what an appropriate level of quality needs to be viewed in the round, but we set out below some issues that, if observed, may suggest further investigation is needed. We stress that none of the below are an infallible sign of inadequate controls and procedures (and vice versa, their absence should not be read as a clean bill of health), but more that poorly managed investments tend to have at least one of these issues arising:-

- **What is the quality of the investment management generally**? If financial/ tenant management controls and procedures are inadequate, are their tax-related equivalents any better?
- **How is professional tax advice obtained?** For example, is a very large and complex structure taking advice from a suitably experienced firm of professional advisors?
- **Is there a large number of open and unresolved tax issues?** Particularly where there is little progress being made in reaching agreement with the tax authorities.
- **Are tax planning strategies taking priority over commercial realities?** A failure to structure tax planning around commercial realities is likely to trigger a challenge by the tax authorities in many jurisdictions.
- **Is there someone reviewing and coordinating tax from a global perspective?** It is often the case that something that is tax beneficial in one jurisdiction might cause problems in another jurisdiction on implementation (as a simple example, a high interest rate on a shareholder loan can reduce the tax in the company paying the interest, but could increase the tax bill of the company receiving it). If there is evidence of a 'silo' approach in the provision of tax advice, it may be worth investigating how tax advice is coordinated between countries.

## Appendix A  Template Letter

Dear [X]

## TAX RISK ASSESSMENT

As previously discussed, we ask you to perform an assessment of the [Investment Structure] and whether its nature and operations present a material risk to the safety of the funding that we are considering providing.

Although the specific details of the areas we would like you to cover in your assessment are dependent on your best professional judgement and also on the circumstances of the jurisdictions involved, we would like to concentrate on the following key areas in your review:-

- An assessment of the quality of the tax advice that the [Investment Structure] has taken to date.
- Whether there have been, an announcement has been made in respect of, any material changes in tax law and/or practice that could invalidate this advice.
- Whether there are sufficiently strong procedures and controls to implement this tax advice successfully.
- Whether the tax assumptions made in models of income, costs and exit values are reasonable and prudent. [We intend to provide you with our assumptions and would seek you to confirm the resulting tax impacts are in line with our expectations.]
- A summary and brief description of any currently open tax issues, and an assessment of the potential exposure to which [Investment structure] is exposed in light of these.
- An assessment of the [Investment Structure's] financing structure, and whether this presents obstacles to the tax deductibility of interest and any practical obstacles that may be encountered in cash repatriation
- If any actions carried out at investor level are likely to trigger tax issues charges at the [Investment Structure] level.
- What are the tax consequences of the envisaged exit strategy(ies), and how is the [Investment Structure] managing these consequences?
- If the [Investment Structure] is appropriately treating its real estate portfolio for indirect tax purposes (e.g. has it opted to charge VAT/GST on its commercial rentals, has it put in place real estate transfer tax planning to minimise transaction costs on sale?)
- Please provide a list of initial and ongoing requirements that should be inserted in the financing documentation to ensure the rigorousness and validity of the [Investment Structure] is maintained
- Additional information sufficient to provide reasonable comfort that no material tax exposures not already identified from the above might exist.
- We would expect that your professional indemnity insurance meets the minimum required by your regulator. Furthermore, we would also expect that your professional indemnity insurance coverage applicable to the advice you will be

providing us with is commensurate to value of this transaction. In order to assess whether such coverage is adequate for this transaction, please provide us with details as to your professional indemnity insurance coverage.

- The following wording must be included in the report:
The [Lender], its employees, agents, successors and assigns may rely upon this report in evaluating a request for an extension of credit (the "Loan") to be secured by the [property/properties]. This information may also be used by any actual or prospective purchaser, transferee, assignee, or servicer of the Loan, any actual or prospective investor (including any agent or advisor thereof) in any securities backed by the Loan, any rating agency actually or prospectively rating any such securities, any trustee appointed in the context of the issuance of such securities, and any institutional provider(s) from time to time of any liquidity facility, hedging or credit support for such financing. In addition, this report or a reference to this report may be included or quoted in any offering circular, private placement memorandum or prospectus and [name of advisor] agrees to cooperate in answering questions by any of the above parties in connection with a sale, securitisation or other transaction involving the Loan and/or such securities. Accordingly, this report may be relied upon by any person falling within the abovementioned classes of person as if this report were addressed to that person specifically. This report has no other purpose and should not be relied upon by any other person or entity.

I trust the above performs a reasonable basis for you to report to us, but please do not hesitate to suggest alterations/expansions to our suggested scope of work above.


Yours [faithfully/sincerely]

# Appendix 3

Commercial Real Estate Finance Council®
EUROPE

# Market Principles for Issuing European CMBS 2.0

## *Promoting Fairness, Transparency and Liquidity*

The focus of the Principles is confined to transaction structures, transaction counterparties and disclosure of appropriate levels of information. Key areas addressed include:

- CMBS structural features, such as controlling party rights and voting provisions;
- Disclosure requirements for both pre and post issuance information as well as investor reporting and investor notices;
- Revenue Extraction e.g. excess spread monetisation (including Class X Note structuring); and
- Role of the servicer and other counterparties such as trustees and cash managers.

## CMBS 2.0 Market Principles can be found at: www.crefc.org/eucmbs20

# Appendix 4

# European Investor Reporting Package®

# (E-IRP®)

**Version 2.0**
**Data Files:**
Data File Legends
Loan Setup
Loan Periodic
Property File
Bond File

Commercial Real Estate Finance Council®
EUROPE

| Additional Financing Indicator Code Legend | |
|---|---|
| 0 | Whole loan no additional financing |
| 1 | Whole loan with additional financing |
| 2 | Participated loan structure, no mezzanine financing |
| 3 | Participated loan structure with additional mezzanine financing |

| Amortisation Type Code Legend | |
|---|---|
| 1 | Fully Amortising |
| 2 | Amortising / Balloon |
| 3 | Interest Only / Balloon |
| 4 | Interest Only / Amortising (Hard/Soft) |
| 5 | Interest Only / Amortising (Hard/Soft) / Balloon |
| 6 | Principal Only |
| 7 | Annuity |
| 8 | Linear |
| 9 | Cash Sweep |
| 10 | Trigger |
| 11 | Hyper-Amortisation |
| 12 | Other |

| Accrual Method Legend | |
|---|---|
| 1 | 30 / 360 |
| 2 | Actual / 365 |
| 3 | Actual / 360 |
| 4 | Actual / Actual |
| 5 | Actual / 366 |

| Controlling Party Rights - Material Decisions Legend | |
|---|---|
| SD | Sole discretion (usually if ownership is two thirds or more) |
| V | Veto (usually if ownership is greater than one third but less than two thirds) |
| S | Silent (usually if ownership is one third or less) |
| O | Other |

| Covenant Breach / Trigger Legend | |
|---|---|
| 1 | Interest Coverage Ratio (ICR) |
| 2 | Debt Service Coverage Ratio (DSCR) |
| 3 | Loan to Value (LTV) |
| 4 | Other |
| 5 | ICR / DSCR |
| 6 | ICR / DSCR / LTV |
| 7 | Property Level Breach |
| 8 | Borrower Level Breach |
| 9 | Tenant / Vacancy Level Breach |

| Currency Legend | |
|---|---|
| GBP | Great British Pound (Sterling) |
| EUR | EU Euro |
| CHF | Swiss Franc |
| SEK | Swedish Krona |
| USD | U.S. Dollar |
| BYR | Belarusian Ruble |
| BAM | Bosnia-Herzegovina Convertible Mark |
| BGN | Bulgarian Lev |
| HRK | Croatian Kuna |
| CZK | Czech Koruna |
| DKK | Danish Krone |
| NOK | Norwegian Krone |
| EEK | Estonian Kroon |
| GIP | Gibraltar Pound |
| HUF | Hungarian Forint |
| ISK | Icelandic Krona |
| LVL | Latvian Lats |
| LTL | Lithuanian Litas |
| MKD | Macedonian Denar |
| MDL | Moldovan Leu |
| ANG | Netherlands Antillian Guilder |
| PLN | Polish Zloty |
| RON | Romanian New Leu |
| RUB | Russian Ruble |
| RSD | Serbian Dinar |
| TRY | Turkish Lira |
| UAH | Ukrainian Hryvnia |
| Other | Other |

| Currency Loan Level Swap Legend | |
|---|---|
| OE | Other currency to Euros |
| OS | Other currency to Great British Pound (Sterling) |
| O | Other |

| Financial Information Submission Penalties Legend | |
|---|---|
| M | Monetary |
| N | No Penalties |
| O | Other Penalties |

| ICR / DSCR Indicator Code Legend | |
|---|---|
| P | Partial - Not all properties received financials, servicer to leave empty |
| A | Average - Not all properties received financials, servicer allocates debt service only to properties where financials are received |
| F | Full - All statements collected for all properties |
| W | Worst Case - Not all properties received financials, servicer allocates 100% of debt service to all properties where financials are received |
| N | None Collected - No financials were received |
| C | Consolidated - All properties reported on one "rolled up" financial from the borrower |
| L | Whole loan based on loan agreements |
| WCREFC | Whole loan based on CREFC Europe method |
| TL | Trust Note based on loan agreements |
| TCREFC | Trust Note based on CREFC Europe method |

| Index Code Legend | |
|---|---|
| A | 1 month £LIBOR |
| B | 3 month £LIBOR |
| C | 6 month £LIBOR |
| D | 12 month £LIBOR |
| E | 1 month US$LIBOR |
| F | 3 month US$LIBOR |
| G | 6 month US$LIBOR |
| H | 12 month US$LIBOR |
| I | 1 month Euro LIBOR |
| J | 3 month Euro LIBOR |
| K | 6 month Euro LIBOR |
| L | 12 month Euro LIBOR |
| M | 1 month EURIBOR |
| N | 3 month EURIBOR |
| O | 6 month EURIBOR |
| P | 12 month EURIBOR |
| Q | 1 month STIBOR |
| R | 3 month STIBOR |
| S | 6 month STIBOR |
| T | 1 month Swiss LIBOR |
| U | 3 month Swiss LIBOR |
| V | 6 month Swiss LIBOR |
| X | Fixed Rate |
| Y | All Others Use Short Text Description |

| Liquidation / Prepayment Code Legend | |
|---|---|
| 1 | Partial Liquidation (Curtailment) |
| 2 | Payoff Prior To Maturity |
| 3 | Liquidation / Disposition |
| 4 | Repurchase / Substitution |
| 5 | Full Payoff at Maturity |
| 6 | Discounted Payoff (DPO) |
| 7 | Blank |
| 8 | Payoff w/ penalty |
| 9 | Payoff w / Yield Maintenance |
| 10 | Curtailment w / Penalty |
| 11 | Curtailment w / Yield Maintence |

| Loan Financial Ratio Legend | |
|---|---|
| CP | Current Period |
| PRO_6MF | Projection - 6 month forward calculation |
| PRO_12MF | Projection - 12 month forward calculation |
| COM_CP6MF | Combo 6 - Current period and a 6 month forward calculation |
| COM_CP12MF | Combo 12 - Current period calculation and a 12 month forward calculation |
| HIS_6MB | Historical - 6 month backward calculation |
| HIS_12MB | Historical - 12 month backward calculation |
| MOD | Modified - Includes a reserve injection or a percentage rental income probability calculation |
| MULP | Multiple Period - Consecutive period calculation |
| LTV | LTV - based on outstanding principal balance / current portfolio value |
| LTV_O | LTV - Other |
| CREFC_CP | CREFC-Europe Standard - Current period calculation |
| CREFC_LTV | CREFC-Europe Standard - LTV |

| Loan Level Swap Legend | |
|---|---|
| L | Fixed to LIBOR |
| E | Fixed to Euribor |
| O | Other |

| Loan Level Swap Termination Legend | |
|---|---|
| RD | Swap terminated due to ratings downgrade of loan level swap provider |
| PD | Swap terminated do to payment default to loan swap provider |
| SD | Swap terminated for other default by swap counterparty |
| BD | Swap terminated for other default by Borrower |
| PP | Swap terminated in connection with full or partial prepayment by borrower |

| Loan Structure Code Legend | |
|---|---|
| WL | Whole Loan Structure |
| PP | Participated mortgage loan with pari passu debt outside the issuance vehicle eg. syndicated loan |
| PS | Participated mortgage loan with subordinate debt outside the issuance vehicle |
| A1 | A Loan; A/B participation structure |
| B1 | B Loan; A/B participation structure |
| A2 | A Loan; A/B/C participation structure |
| B2 | B Loan; A/B/C participation structure |
| C2 | C Loan; A/B/C participation structure |
| MZ | Structural mezzanine financing |
| SUB | Subordinate debt with separate loan documentation outside the issuance vehicle |

| Modification Code Legend | |
|---|---|
| 1 | Loan maturity date extension |
| 2 | Amortisation change |
| 3 | Principal write-off |
| 4 | Temporary rate reduction |
| 5 | Capitalisation of interest |
| 6 | Capitalisation of costs advanced (e.g., insurance, ground rent) |
| 7 | Other |
| 8 | Combination |

| Multi Property Indicator Legend | |
|---|---|
| P | Partial - Not all properties received financials; Servicer to leave empty |
| A | Average - Not all properties received financials; Servicer allocates debt service only to properties where financials received |
| F | Full - All statements collected for all properties |
| W | Worst Case - Not all properties received financials; Servicer allocates 100% of debt service to all properties where financials are received. |
| N | None Collected - no financials were received |
| C | Consolidated - All properties reported on one "rolled up" financial from the borrower |

| NOI/NCF Indicator Code Legend | |
|---|---|
| CREFC | Calculated using CREFC-Europe standard |
| PSA | Calculated using a definition given in the issuer vehical documents |
| U/W | Calculated using the loan underwriting method |

| Participation Legend | |
|---|---|
| A | Assignment |
| N | Novation |
| EA | Equitable Assignment |
| FP | Funded Participation (pari passu interest) |
| JP | Junior Participation Interest |
| LA | Legal Assignment |
| NA | Notified Assignment |
| SP | Sub Participation |
| RP | Risk Participation |
| SP | Sale |
| OT | Other |

| Party that carried out the last property Inspection | |
|---|---|
| AM | Asset Manager |
| S | Servicer |
| V | Valuer |
| II | Independent Inspector |

| Property Status Codes | |
|---|---|
| 1 | In Foreclosure |
| 2 | Real Estate Owned (REO) |
| 3 | Defeased |
| 4 | Partial Release |
| 5 | Released |
| 6 | Same as at issue date |

| Property Title | |
|---|---|
| 1 | Freehold |
| 2 | Leasehold |
| 3 | Mixed (Freehold/Leasehold) |

| Property Type Code Legend | |
|---|---|
| CP | Caravan Park |
| CPK | Car Park |
| HC | Health Care |
| HO | Hospitality / Hotel |
| IN | Industrial |
| LA | Land |
| LE | Leisure |
| MF | Multifamily |
| MU | Mixed Use |
| OF | Office |
| OT | Other |
| PUB | Pub |
| RT | Retail |
| SS | Self Storage |
| WH | Warehouse |
| XX | Various |
| ZZ | Missing Information |

| Remedies Upon Breach of Financial Covenants Legend | |
|---|---|
| 1 | Event of Default |
| 2 | Additional Amortisation |
| 3 | Cash Trap Reserve |
| 4 | Terminate Property Manager |
| 5 | Other |

| Rounding Code Legend | |
|---|---|
| 1 | Unrounded |
| 2 | Nearest Percentage Increment |
| 3 | Up To Nearest Percentage Increment |
| 4 | Down to Nearest Percentage Increment |

| Status of Loan Legend | |
|---|---|
| A | Payment Not Received But Still In Grace Period |
| B | Late Payment but Less than 30 Days Delinquent |
| 0 | Current |
| 1 | 90+ Days Delinquent |
| 2 | Performing Matured Balloon Loan |
| 3 | Non Performing Matured Balloon Loan |
| 4 | Enforcement In Process |
| 5 | Property in possession |

| Subordinated Debt Rights Legend | |
|---|---|
| CR | Cure Rights |
| PR | Purchase Rights |

| Swap Breakage Legend | |
|---|---|
| TI | Total Indemnification from Borrower |
| PI | Partial Indemnification from Borrower |
| NI | No Indemnification from Borrower |

| Trigger Event Legend | |
|---|---|
| LTVT | Loan-to-Value Trigger |
| ICRT | Interest Cover Trigger |
| DSCRT | Debt Service Cover Trigger |
| NOIT | Net Operating Income Trigger |
| OT | Other Trigger |

| Workout Strategy Legend | |
|---|---|
| 1 | Modification |
| 2 | Enforcement |
| 3 | Receivership |
| 4 | Insolvency |
| 5 | Extension |
| 6 | Loan Sale |
| 7 | Discounted Pay Off |
| 8 | Property In Possession |
| 9 | Resolved |
| 10 | Pending Return to Servicer |
| 11 | Deed in Lieu of Foreclosure |
| 12 | Full Payoff |
| 13 | Reps and Warranties |
| 14 | Other or TBD |

**CRE Finance Council Europe**
**European Reporting Investor Reporting Package**
**"Loan Setup" File**
(Data Record Layout, Version 2.0) Cross Refenced as "ES"

| Field Grouping | Field Names | Field Number | Field Requirement | Field Definition & Criteria |
|---|---|---|---|---|
| Loan Identifiers | Transaction Pool Identifier | ES1 | Mandatory | The unique transaction or pool identification string. Transaction name |
| Loan Identifiers | Group Identifier | ES2 | Mandatory | The alpha-numeric code assigned to each loan group within an issue. A group identifier may not be applicable for every transaction. |
| Loan Identifiers | Loan Servicer Identifier | ES3 | Mandatory | The loan servicer unique identification string assigned to the loan. |
| Loan Identifiers | Offering Circular Loan Identifier | ES4 | Mandatory | The offering circular or prospectus unique number assigned to each loan within the transaction or pool. |
| Loan Identifiers | Transaction Loan Name | ES5 | Mandatory | The offering circular or prospectus unique name assigned to each loan within the transaction or pool. |
| Loan Identifiers | Loan Sponsor | ES6 | Mandatory | Loan sponsor |
| Loan Identifiers | Loan Origination Date | ES7 | Mandatory | Date of original loan advance. If no data available refer to Overview Document for inputs. |
| Original Loan Terms | Loan Currency | ES8 | Mandatory | The currency currency denomination in which the loan is being reported. Please use the Currency Legend. |
| Original Loan Terms | Whole Loan Balance at Origination | ES9 | Mandatory | Whole loan balance at origination representing 100% full facility i.e. securitised and unsecuritised / owned and un-owned amount (in loan currency). If no data available refer to Overview Document for inputs. |
| Original Loan Terms | Original Term of _oan | ES10 | Mandatory | Original contractual term (number of months). If no data available refer to Overview Document for inputs. |
| Original Loan Terms | Start Date of Amortisation | ES11 | Mandatory | The date that amortisation will commence on the whole loan (this may be a date prior to the issue date). |
| Original Loan Terms | Interest Rate Index Code | ES12 | Mandatory | Refer to the Index Code Legend to select the code describing the interest rate type for the loan. |
| Original Loan Terms | Original Loan Interest Rate | ES13 | Mandatory | Loan all-in interest rate at inception of loan. If multiple tranches with different interest rates then apply a weighted average rate. |
| Original Loan Terms | First Loan Payment Due Date | ES14 | Mandatory | The first payment date of the mortgage loan which is not the first payment date after issuance. The date that the first interest payment was due on the loan following origination ( not first date after securitisation). |
| Original Loan Terms | Pool Cut-off Date | ES15 | Mandatory | Pool or Portfolio cut-off date. All dates take DD-MM-YYYY format. At issuance data. |
| Original Loan Terms | Loan Country | ES16 | Mandatory | Country of permanent establishment. See Overview Document for full list of Countries |
| Original Loan Terms | Loan Purpose | ES17 | Mandatory | Loan purpose, permissible answers:<br>Acquisition for investment (1)<br>Acquisition for liquidation (2)<br>Refinancing (3)<br>Construction (4)<br>Redevelopment (5)<br>Other (6)<br>No Data (0) |

**CRE Finance Council Europe**
**European Reporting Investor Reporting Package**
**"Loan Setup" File**
(Data Record Layout, Version 2.0) Cross Refenced as "ES"

| Field Grouping | Field Names | Field Number | Field Requirement | Field Definition & Criteria |
|---|---|---|---|---|
| Original Loan Terms | Mortgage Security | ES18 | Optional | Is the Loan secured by the mortgages on the properties? If no data available refer to Overview Document for inputs. |
| Original Loan Terms | Blank Field | ES19 | | |
| Collateral Details | Number of Properties At Issue Date | ES20 | Mandatory | The number of properties that serve as security for the loan at the Issue Date. |
| Loan Statistics at Issue Date | CREFC Europe ICR (NOI) at Issue Date | ES21 | Optional | The CREFC-Europe Interest Coverage Ratio for the loan (whole) at the Issue Date is calculated based on the formula described within "Methodology for Analyzing" guide. |
| Loan Statistics at Issue Date | CREFC Europe DSCR (NOI) at Issue Date | ES22 | Optional | The CREFC-Europe Debt Service Coverage Ratio for the loan (whole) at the Issue Date is calculated based on the formula described within "Methodology for Analyzing" guide. |
| Loan Statistics at Issue Date | CREFC Europe LTV at Issue Date | ES23 | Optional | The CREFC-Europe Loan to Value Ratio for the loan (whole) at the Issue Date is calculated based on the formula described within "Methodology for Analyzing" guide. |
| Loan Statistics at Issue Date | Trust ICR at Issue Date | ES24 | Mandatory | At Issue interest coverage ratio calculation for the A-Loan based on the offering documentation. Please refer to Overview Document for inputs. |
| Loan Statistics at Issue Date | Trust DSCR at Issue Date | ES25 | Mandatory | At Issue debt service coverage ratio calculation for the A-Loan based on the offering documentation. Please refer to Overview Document for inputs. |
| Loan Statistics at Issue Date | Trust LTV at Issue Date | ES26 | Mandatory | At Issue Loan to Value ratio (LTV) for the A-Loan based on the the offering documentation. Please refer to Overview Document for inputs. |
| Collateral Details | Blank Field | ES27 | | |
| Collateral Details | Blank Field | ES28 | | |
| Collateral Details | Issue Date Net Square Meter | ES29 | Mandatory | The total net rentable area of the properties in square metres that serve as security for the loan at the Issue Date. For multiple properties, if not all information available, leave blank. Complete either square feet or square metres field (or both if easier). |
| Collateral Details | Issue Date Number of Units/Beds/Rooms | ES30 | Optional | For property type Multifamily enter number of units, for Hospitality/Hotel/Healthcare - beds, for Caravan Parks - units, Lodging=rooms, Self Storage=units. For Multiple properties, if all the same Property Type, sum the values. If no data available refer to Overview Document for inputs. |
| Collateral Details | Year Built | ES31 | Optional | Year the property was built per the valuation report or offering document. For multiple properties, include the earliest date of the property. |
| Collateral Details | Property Form of Title | ES32 | Optional | The relevent form of property title (i.e. Freehold, Leasehold or Mixed). Please utilse the relevant coding within the "Property Title Codes " located in the Data File Legends. A lease on land only, in which the borrower usually owns a building or is required to build as specified in the lease. Such leases are usually long-term net leases; the borrower's rights and obligations continue until the lease expires or is terminated through default. If multiple properties refer to Overview Document for inputs. |

CRE Finance Council Europe
European Reporting Investor Reporting Package
**"Loan Setup" File**
(Data Record Layout, Version 2.0) Cross Refrenced as "ES"

| Field Grouping | Field Names | Field Number | Field Requirement | Field Definition & Criteria |
|---|---|---|---|---|
| Collateral Details | Blank Field | ES33 | | |
| Collateral Details | Blank Field | ES34 | | |
| Collateral Details | Blank Field | ES35 | | |
| Collateral Details | Blank Field | ES36 | | |
| Collateral Details | Blank Field | ES37 | | |
| Loan Covenant Details | Interest Coverage Ratio Method (Whole Loan) | ES38 | Mandatory | Please define calculation of ICR financial covenant requirment at the whole loan level, the inferred method of calculation. Please refer to the Loan Financial Ratio Legend. |
| Loan Covenant Details | Debt Service Coverage Ratio Method (Whole Loan) | ES39 | Mandatory | Please define calculation of DSCR financial covenant requirment at the whole loan level, the inferred method of calculation. Please refer to the Loan Financial Ratio Legend. |
| Loan Covenant Details | Loan to Value Method (Whole) | ES40 | Mandatory | Please define calculation of LTV financial covenant requirment at the whole loan level, the inferred method of calculation. Please refer to the Loan Financial Ratio Legend. |
| Loan Covenant Details | Other Financial Covenant Code | ES41 | Mandatory | If there is another code required for ICR or DSCR financial covenant requirment at the whole loan level. Please refer to the Loan Financial Ratio Legend. |
| Loan Covenant Details | Interest Coverage Ratio Method (ICR Trust) | ES42 | Mandatory | Please define the A- Loan Interest Coverage Ratio method of calculation. Please refer to the Loan Financial Ratio Legend. |
| Loan Covenant Details | Debt Service Coverage Ratio Method (DSCR Trust) | ES43 | Mandatory | Please define the A- Loan Debt Service Coverage Ratio method of calculation. Please refer to the Loan Financial Ratio Legend. |
| Loan Covenant Details | Loan to Value Method (LTV Trust) | ES44 | Mandatory | Please define the A- Loan Loan to Value Method method of calculation. Please refer to the Loan Financial Ratio Legend. |
| Loan Statistics at Issue Date | Revenue At Issue Date | ES45 | Mandatory | The total underwritten revenue from all sources for a property as described in the Offering Circular. If multiple properties, sum the values in the Property File. If missing data or if all received/consolidated, use the DSCR Indicator Legend rule. |
| Loan Statistics at Issue Date | Operating Expenses At Issue Date | ES46 | Mandatory | Total underwritten operating expenses for the properties a described in the offering Circular. These may include real estate taxes, insurance, management, utilities, maintenance and repairs and direct property costs to the landlord; capital expenditures and leasing commissions are excluded. If multiple properties exist, total the operating expenses of the underlying properties. If multiple properties exist and data is not available for all properties or if received/consolidated, refer to the DSCR Indicator Legend rule. |
| Loan Statistics at Issue Date | NOI At Issue Date | ES47 | Mandatory | Revenue less Operating Expenses at Issue Date (Field ES45 minus ES46) If multiple properties, sum the values. If missing data or if all received/consolidated, refer to the DSCR Indicator Legend rule. |
| Loan Statistics at Issue Date | Capital Expenditures at Issue Date | ES48 | Mandatory | Capex at Issue Date (as opposed to repairs and maintenance) if identified in the Offering Circular. If missing date or if all received/consolidated refer to the DSCR Indicator Legend rule |
| Loan Statistics at Issue Date | NCF At Issue Date | ES49 | Mandatory | NOI less Capex at Issue Date (Field ES47 less ES48). If missing data or if all received/consolidated refer to the DSCR indicator Legend rule. |

CRE Finance Council Europe
European Investor Reporting Package
**"Loan Setup" File**
(Data Record Layout, Version 2.0) Cross Refrenced as "ES"

| Field Grouping | Field Names | Field Number | Field Requirement | Field Definition & Criteria |
|---|---|---|---|---|
| Loan Statistics at Issue Date | Whole Loan ICR at Issue Date | ES50 | Mandatory | Interest Coverage Ratio for the loan (Whole Loan) at the issue date as described in the offering circular (if available), and/or reflects the calculated method within the loan documentation (i.e. compliance ratio). If no data available refer to Overview Document for inputs. |
| Loan Statistics at Issue Date | Blank Field | ES51 | | |
| Loan Statistics at Issue Date | Whole Loan DSCR at Issue Date | ES52 | Mandatory | Debt Service Coverage Ratio for the loan (Whole Loan) at the issue date as described in the offering circular (if available), and/or reflects the calculated method within the loan documentation (i.e. compliance ratio). If no data available refer to Overview Document for inputs. |
| Loan Statistics at Issue Date | Blank Field | ES53 | | |
| Loan Statistics at Issue Date | ICR / DSCR Indicator At Issue Date | ES54 | Mandatory | Code describing how the DSCR is calculated/applied when a loan has multiple properties. See DSCR Indicator Legend for codes. |
| Loan Statistics at Issue Date | Loan to Value Ratio at Issue Date (Whole Loan) | ES55 | Mandatory | Original Loan to Value (LTV) at issue date (Whole Loan) as described in the offering circular (if available). If no data available refer to Overview Document for inputs. |
| Loan Statistics at Issue Date | Portfolio Value At Issue Date | ES56 | Mandatory | The valuation of the properties securing the loan at Issue Date as described in the Offering Circular. If multiple properties sum the value in the Property File, otherwise leave blank. |
| Loan Statistics at Issue Date | Valuation Date At Issue Date | ES57 | Mandatory | The date the valuation was prepared for the values disclosed in the Offering Circular. For multiple properties, if several dates, take the most recent date. |
| Loan Statistics at Issue Date | Economic Occupancy At Issue Date | ES58 | Mandatory | The percentage of rentable space with signed leased in place at Issue Date if disclosed in Offering Circular (tenants may not be in occupation but are paying rent). If multiple properties use weighted average by using the calculation (Current Allocated % (Prop)*Occupancy)) for each property. If missing some date leave blank. |
| Loan Statistics at Issue Date | Committed Principal Balance At Issue Date | ES59 | Optional | The committed balance, including any undrawn amounts, of the whole loan at Issue Date. |
| Loan Statistics at Issue Date | Actual Principal Balance At Issue Date (Whole Loan) | ES60 | Mandatory | Actual Principal Balance of the whole loan at the Issue Date as identified in the Offering Circular. |
| Loan Statistics at Issue Date | Periodic Principal &Interest Payment At Issue Date | ES61 | Mandatory | The scheduled principal & interest amount that is due on the next Loan Payment Date as at the Issue Date. |
| Loan Statistics at Issue Date | Loan Rate At Issue Date | ES62 | Mandatory | The total interest rate (eg Libor + Margin) that is being used to calculate interest due on the loan at the Issue Date. |
| Loan Statistics at Issue Date | Ranking of Charge at Issue Date | ES63 | Mandatory | Is the security granted to the Issue a first ranking security, ie does it have priority over all other lenders/parties (enter 1); or is it second ranking, ie subordinated in some way (enter 2). |
| Loan Statistics at Issue Date | Financials reported at issuance as of Date | ES64 | Optional | The end date of the financials used to support the Revenue and Expenses amounts disclosed in the Offering Circular if available, otherwise the Issue Date. If multiple properties and the dates are the same, enter the date, or if different or missing any leave blank. |
| Loan Statistics at Issue Date | Remaining Term At Issue Date | ES65 | Mandatory | Remaining number of months until maturity of loan at issue date. If no data available refer to Overview Document for inputs. |
| Loan Statistics at Issue Date | Remaining Amort Term At Issue Date | ES66 | Mandatory | The number of months remaining to maturity of the loan of the amortisation term. If amortisation has not commenced at the Issue Date this will be less than the Remaining Term at Issue Date. |

561

CRE Finance Council Europe
European Reporting Investor Reporting Package
**"Loan Setup" File**
(Data Record Layout, Version 2.0) Cross Refenced as "ES"

| Field Grouping | Field Names | Field Number | Field Requirement | Field Definition & Criteria |
|---|---|---|---|---|
| Loan Statistics at Issue Date | Loan Maturity Date at Issue Date | ES67 | Mandatory | The maturity date of the loan as defined in the loan agreement. This would not take into account any extended maturity date that may be allowed under the loan agreement, but the initial maturity date. |
| Loan Statistics at Issue Date | Blank Field | ES68 | | |
| Loan Statistics at Issue Date | Actual Principal Balance At Issue Date (Trust) | ES69 | Mandatory | Actual Principal Balance of the A Note loan at the Issue Date as identified in the Offering Circular. |
| Loan Statistics at Issue Date | Extension Option | ES70 | Mandatory | Indicate whether there is an option to extend the term of the loan and push out the maturity date. If no data available refer to Overview Document for inputs. |
| Loan Statistics at Issue Date | Blank Field | ES71 | | |
| Loan Statistics at Issue Date | Blank Field | ES72 | | |
| Loan Escrow & Reserve Details | Amounts Held in Escrow at Issue Date | ES73 | Mandatory | Total balance of the legally charged reserve accounts at the loan level at the Issue Date. |
| Loan Escrow & Reserve Details | Collection Of Escrows | ES74 | Mandatory | Enter Y - (yes) if any payments are held in reserve accounts to cover ground lease payments, insurance or taxes only (not maintenance, improvements, capex, etc) as required under the loan agreement, otherwise N - (No). |
| Loan Escrow & Reserve Details | Collection Of Other Reserves | ES75 | Mandatory | Are any amounts other than round rents taxes or insurance held in reserve accounts as required under the terms of the loan agreement for tenant improvements, leasing commissions and similar items in respect of the related property or for purpose of providing additional collateral for such loan. Y= Yes or N =No |
| Loan Escrow & Reserve Details | Escrow Held Upon Trigger Event | ES76 | Mandatory | Does the loan agreement require reserve amounts to be made upon the occurrence of any trigger events. Y= Yes or N =No |
| Loan Escrow & Reserve Details | Trigger for Escrow to be Held | ES77 | Mandatory | If yes, refer the Trigger Event Legend and describe type of trigger event. |
| Loan Escrow & Reserve Details | Target Escrow Amounts / Reserves | ES78 | Mandatory | Target escrow amounts or reserve amounts |
| Loan Escrow & Reserve Details | Escrow Account Release Conditions | ES79 | Mandatory | Release conditions of the escrow account |
| Loan Escrow & Reserve Details | Conditions of Drawing Cash Reserve | ES80 | Mandatory | When can the Cash Reserve be used: Breach of Financial Covenant (1) Trigger Event (2) Other (3) No Data (0) |
| Loan Escrow & Reserve Details | Blank Field | ES81 | | |
| Loan Grouping & Substitutions Details | Cross-Collateralised Loan Grouping | ES82 | Mandatory | Indicator of loans that are cross collateralised (Example: loans 1 and 44 are cross collateralised as are loans 4 and 47). |
| Loan Grouping & Substitutions Details | Substituted Loan | ES83 | Mandatory | Is this loan a substitute for another loan on a date after the Issue Date? Y=Yes N=No |
| Loan Grouping & Substitutions Details | Date of Substitution | ES84 | Mandatory | If loan was substituted after the Issue Date, the date of such substitution |
| Loan Grouping & Substitutions Details | Grace Days Allowed | ES85 | Mandatory | The number of days after a payment is due in which the lender will not charge a late penalty or report the payment as late. |
| Loan Grouping & Substitutions Details | Additional Financing Indicator | ES86 | Mandatory | Code indicating whether whole loan has additional financing/mezzanine debt present. See Additional Financing Indicator Legend |

CRE Finance Council Europe
European Reporting Investor Reporting Package
**"Loan Setup" File**
(Data Record Layout, Version 2.0) Cross Refrenced as "ES"

| Field Grouping | Field Names | Field Number | Field Requirement | Field Definition & Criteria |
|---|---|---|---|---|
| Loan Grouping & Substitutions Details | Blank Field | ES87 | | |
| Loan Grouping & Substitutions Details | Blank Field | ES88 | | |
| Loan Grouping & Substitutions Details | Blank Field | ES89 | | |
| Loan Grouping & Substitutions Details | Blank Field | ES90 | | |
| Loan Grouping & Substitutions Details | Blank Field | ES91 | | |
| Loan Interest Rate Details | Interest Rate Type | ES92 | Mandatory | Use a code to describe the type of interest rate applied to the loan. 1=Fixed, 2=Floating, 3=Step, 4=Mixed/Fixed Floating, 9=Other |
| Loan Interest Rate Details | Interest Accrual Method Code | ES93 | Mandatory | Code indicating the 'number of days' convention used to calculate interest. 1=30/360, 2=actual/365, 3=actual/360, 4=actual/actual, 5=actual/366, 6=simple, |
| Loan Interest Rate Details | Interest in Arrears (Y/N) | ES94 | Mandatory | Is the interest that accrues on the loan paid in arrears Y(es) or N(o) |
| Loan Interest Rate Details | Blank Field | ES95 | | |
| Loan Interest Rate Details | Blank Field | ES96 | | |
| Loan Interest Rate Details | Blank Field | ES97 | | |
| Loan Interest Rate Details | Trust Loan Amortisation Type (if applicable) | ES98 | Mandatory | Refer to the Amortisation Code legend to describe the type of amortisation that applies to the Trust Loan. Trust-Loan amortisation type:<br>Fully Amortising (1)<br>Amortising Baloon (2)<br>Interest Only Balloon (3)<br>Interest Only / Amortising (Hard/Soft) (4)<br>Interest Only / Amortising (Hard/Soft) / Balloon (5)<br>Principal Only (6)<br>Annuity (7)<br>Linear (8)<br>Cash Sweep (9)<br>Trigger (10)<br>Hyper-Amortisation (11)<br>Other (12)<br>No Data (0) |
| Whole Loan Amortisation Details | Whole Loan Amortisation Type (if applicable) | ES99 | Mandatory | Refer to the Amortisation Code legend to describe the type of amortisation that applies to the loan. Whole loan amortisation type:<br>Fully Amortising (1)<br>Amortising Baloon (2)<br>Interest Only Balloon (3)<br>Interest Only / Amortising (Hard/Soft) (4)<br>Interest Only / Amortising (Hard/Soft) / Balloon (5)<br>Principal Only (6)<br>Annuity (7)<br>Linear (8)<br>Cash Sweep (9)<br>Trigger (10)<br>Hyper-Amortisation (11)<br>Other (12)<br>No Data (0) |

CRE Finance Council Europe
European Reporting Investor Reporting Package
**"Loan Setup" File**
(Data Record Layout, Version 2.0) Cross Refrenced as "ES"

| Field Grouping | Field Names | Field Number | Field Requirement | Field Definition & Criteria |
|---|---|---|---|---|
| Whole Loan Amortisation Details | Original Length of Interest Only Period | ES100 | Optional | Number of months that loan is interest only (from the date of origination not from the Issue Date) |
| Whole Loan Amortisation Details | Amortisation Trigger | ES101 | Optional | Y=Yes N=No . Identify if a trigger event caused the loan to amortise in addition to scheduled amortisation. |
| Whole Loan Amortisation Details | Amortisation Trigger Types | ES102 | Optional | If yes, refer the Trigger Event Legend and describe type of trigger event. |
| Whole Loan Amortisation Details | Amortisation Trigger Levels | ES103 | Optional | What level of amortisation will be required if a trigger event occurs. Describe as a % of the loan balance at origination if possible. If multiple triggers or not easily described leave blank |
| Whole Loan Amortisation Details | Accrual of Interest Allowed | ES104 | Mandatory | Do the loan documents allow for interest to be accrued and capitalised - Y=Yes N=No |
| Whole Loan Amortisation Details | Waterfall A-B Pre Enforcement Scheduled Payments (PRINCIPAL) | ES105 | Optional | Sequential (1)<br>B Loan first (2)<br>Pro-rata (3)<br>Modified pro-rata (4)<br>Other (5)<br>No Data (0) |
| Whole Loan Amortisation Details | Modified Pro Rata A-B Loan (PRINCIPAL) | ES106 | Optional | please insert % of all periodical scheduled payments that go to A loan in A-B Loan structure. If no data available refer to Overview Document for inputs. |
| Whole Loan Amortisation Details | Waterfall Type A-B Loan | ES107 | Optional | IPIP (interest A, principal A, interest B, principal B) (1)<br>IIPP (interest A, interest B, principal A, principal B) (2)<br>Other (3)<br>No Data (0) |
| Loan Prepayment Details | Prepayment Lock-out End Date | ES108 | Mandatory | The date after which the lender allows prepayment of the loan. If there are no restrictions leave blank |
| Loan Prepayment Details | Yield Maintenance End Date | ES109 | Mandatory | The date after which the lender allows prepayment of the loan without requirement for a prepayment fee or yield maintenance to be paid. Date after which loan can be prepaid without yield maintenance |
| Loan Prepayment Details | Prepayment Premium End Date | ES110 | Mandatory | The date after which the lender allows prepayment of the loan without requirement for a prepayment fee to be paid. |
| Loan Prepayment Details | Prepayment Terms Description | ES111 | Mandatory | Should reflect the information in offering circular. For instance, if the prepayment terms are the payment of a 1% fee in year one, 0.5% in year two and 0.25% in year three of the loan this may be shown in the offering circular as: 1%(12), 0.5%(24), 0.25%(36). If no data available refer to Overview Document for inputs. |
| Loan Prepayment Details | Do Non-payments on Prior Ranking Claims Constitute a Default of the Loan? | ES112 | Mandatory | Do Non-payments on Prior Ranking Claims Constitute a Default of the Loan? |
| Loan Prepayment Details | Non-payments on Equal Ranking Loans Constitute Default of Property? | ES113 | Mandatory | Non-payments on Equal Ranking Loans Constitute Default of Property? |
| Loan Prepayment Details | Blank Field | ES114 | | |
| Loan Hedging Details | Loan Margin | ES115 | | The rate added to the index rate used to calculate the interest paid on the loan |

**CRE Finance Council Europe**
**European Reporting Investor Reporting Package**
**"Loan Setup" File**
(Data Record Layout, Version 2.0) Cross Refrenced as "ES"

| Field Grouping | Field Names | Field Number | Field Requirement | Field Definition & Criteria |
|---|---|---|---|---|
| Loan Hedging Details | Lifetime Rate Cap | ES116 | Mandatory | Maximum rate that the borrower must pay on a floating rate loan as required under the terms of the loan agreement |
| Loan Hedging Details | Lifetime Rate Floor | ES117 | Mandatory | Minimum rate that the borrower must pay on a floating rate loan as required under the terms of the loan agreement |
| Loan Hedging Details | Type of Loan Level Swap | ES118 | Mandatory | Describe the type of loan level swap that applies - C = Currency Swap, I = Interest Rate Swap, CI = Currency and Interest Rate Swap. |
| Loan Hedging Details | Loan Swap Provider | ES119 | Mandatory | The name of the swap provider for the loan if the Borrower has the direct contract with the swap counterparty. Leave blank if the loan has been hedged with the lender having the contract with the swap counterparty. |
| Loan Hedging Details | Type of Interest Rate Loan Level Swap | ES120 | Mandatory | Describe the type of interest rate swap that applies to the loan, refer to the Loan Level Swap Legend |
| Loan Hedging Details | Type of Currency Loan Level Swap | ES121 | Mandatory | Describe the type of currency rate swap, refer to the Currency Loan Rate Swap Legend |
| Loan Hedging Details | Payment Obligations by Loan Swap provider | ES122 | Optional | The spread over Index (if any) payable by Loan Swap Provider on an Interest Rate Swap |
| Loan Hedging Details | Swap Rate payable by borrower | ES123 | Optional | The strike price that is payable by the Borrower under the Interest Rate Swap |
| Loan Hedging Details | Exchange Rate for Loan Level Swap | ES124 | Mandatory | The exchange rate that has been set for a currency loan level swap |
| Loan Hedging Details | Start Date of Loan Level Swap | ES125 | Mandatory | |
| Loan Hedging Details | End Date of Loan Level Swap | ES126 | Mandatory | |
| Loan Hedging Details | Required Ratings of Loan Swap Provider | ES127 | Optional | Identify the minimum rating requirements of Loan Swap Provider either as required under the loan or servicing agreement |
| Loan Hedging Details | Actual Ratings of Loan Swap Provider | ES128 | Optional | Identify the ratings of the swap counterparty as of the date of issuance of the notes at issue date |
| Loan Hedging Details | Borrower Obligation to Pay Breakage on Loan Level Swap | ES129 | Mandatory | Extent to which Borrower is obligated to pay breakage costs to loan swap provider (see Swap Breakage Legend). Refer to Swap Breakage Legend for code to describe what level of indemnification is given by the borrower to pay breakage costs on the swap. |
| Loan Hedging Details | Reset Date for Loan Level Swap | ES130 | Mandatory | The reset date for any interest rate swap. What date will the rate on the swap be reset (give the next date that is due) |
| Loan Hedging Details | Blank Field | ES131 | | |
| Loan Hedging Details | Blank Field | ES132 | | |
| Loan Hedging Details | Blank Field | ES133 | | |
| Loan Hedging Details | Blank Field | ES134 | | |
| Loan Rate Adjustment Details | First Rate Adjustment Date | ES135 | Optional | For adjustable rate loans, enter the first date that the interest rate was due to change. For fixed rate loans, enter the first interest payment date (not the first date after securitisation on which it could change). |

**CRE Finance Council Europe**
**European Reporting Investor Reporting Package**
**"Loan Setup" File**
(Data Record Layout, Version 2.0) Cross Refrenced as "ES"

| Field Grouping | Field Names | Field Number | Field Requirement | Field Definition & Criteria |
|---|---|---|---|---|
| Loan Rate Adjustment Details | First Payment Adjustment Date | ES136 | Optional | For adjustable rate loans, the first date that the amount of scheduled principal and/or interest is due to change. For fixed rate loans, enter the first date that the amount of scheduled principal or interest is due (not the first date after securitisation on which it could change). |
| Loan Rate Adjustment Details | Payment Frequency | ES137 | Mandatory | Frequency of interest and amortisation payments on Loan according to original loan documents. 1=Monthly, 3=Quarterly, 6=Semi-Annually, 12=Annually.//Frequency of payments due, i.e. number of months between payments. Monthly (1) Quarterly (2) Semi annually (3) Annual (4) Bullet (5) Amortisation given in template (6) Other (7) No Data (0) |
| Loan Rate Adjustment Details | Rate Reset Frequency | ES138 | Mandatory | Frequency with which the interest rate is reset according to original loan documents. 1=Monthly, 3=Quarterly, 6=Semi-Annually, 12=Annually, 365=Daily |
| Loan Rate Adjustment Details | Pay Reset Frequency | ES139 | Mandatory | Frequency with which the P&I payment is reset according to original loan documents. 1=Monthly, 3=Quarterly, 6=Semi-Annually, 12=Annually, 365=Daily |
| Loan Rate Adjustment Details | Index Look Back In Days | ES140 | Mandatory | The number of days prior to the interest payment date that the interest rate is set (eg Euribor set 2 days prior to interest payment date) |
| Loan Rate Adjustment Details | Index Determination Date | ES141 | Mandatory | If the Loan Agreement states specific dates for the index to be set. |
| Loan Rate Adjustment Details | Waterfall A-B Pre Enforcement Scheduled Payments (INTEREST) | ES142 | Optional | Sequential (1) B Loan first (2) Pro-rata (3) Modified pro-rata (4) Other (5) No Data (0) |
| Loan Rate Adjustment Details | Blank Field | ES143 | | |
| Loan Rate Adjustment Details | Blank Field | ES144 | | |
| Loan Rate Adjustment Details | Blank Field | ES145 | | |
| Loan Rate Adjustment Details | Blank Field | ES146 | | |
| Loan Rate Adjustment Details | Blank Field | ES147 | | |
| Loan Syndication & Participation Details | Loan Structure | ES148 | Mandatory | Refer to the Loan Structure Code to describe what structure applies to this loan eg whole loan, A/B splits, syndicated. Use multiple codes as applicable. Whole Loan (1) A Loan (2) B Loan (3) Other (4) No Data (0) |

**CRE Finance Council Europe**
**European Reporting Investor Reporting Package**
**"Loan Setup" File**
(Data Record Layout, Version 2.0) Cross Refrenced as "ES"

| Field Grouping | Field Names | Field Number | Field Requirement | Field Definition & Criteria |
|---|---|---|---|---|
| Loan Syndication & Participation Details | Syndicated Loan | ES149 | Mandatory | Is the loan part of a syndicated loan? Y= Yes or N =No. If no data available refer to Overview Document for inputs. |
| Loan Syndication & Participation Details | Date of Syndication | ES150 | Optional | Date of Syndication |
| Loan Syndication & Participation Details | Type of Syndication | ES151 | Optional | See Participation Legend. Type of syndication: Assignment (1) Novation (2) Equitable Assignment (3) Funded Participation (pari passu interest) (4) Junior Participation Interest (5) Legal Assignment (6) Notified Assignment (7) Sub Participation (8) Risk Participation (9) Sale (10) Other (11) No Data (0) |
| Loan Syndication & Participation Details | Participation of Issuer in Syndicated Loan | ES152 | Optional | Refer to Participation Legend to describe the method used by the Issuer to acquire ownership in the syndicated loan. |
| Loan Syndication & Participation Details | Syndicated Total Loan Balance | ES153 | Optional | Enter the total balance of the syndicated loan at Issue Date. |
| Loan Syndication & Participation Details | Blank Field | ES154 | | |
| Loan Syndication & Participation Details | Percentage of Total Loan Facility being Securitised | ES155 | Mandatory | Percentage of total loan in securitisation at Issue Date. If no data available refer to Overview Document for inputs. |
| Loan Syndication & Participation Details | Name of Controlling Syndicate Member | ES156 | Optional | Name of the party that controls or is the majority for decision making of the syndication |
| Loan Syndication & Participation Details | Relationship of Controlling Syndicate Member | ES157 | Optional | Describe the relationship of the controlling syndicate member to the Issuer e.g. investor or other syndicate lender. |
| Loan Syndication & Participation Details | Other Material Syndicate Members (>33% interest) | ES158 | Optional | Name of material syndicate members: defined as banks owning 33% or more of the loan |
| Loan Syndication & Participation Details | Rights of Controlling Party for Material Decisions | ES159 | Mandatory | Please see Controlling Party Rights (Material Decisions) Legend. Does owner of any participation other than the issuer have the right to make major decisions? Y=Yes or N=No. |
| Loan Syndication & Participation Details | Rights of Issuer's Loan | ES160 | Optional | Refer to Controlling Party Rights (Material Decisions) Legend to describe the rights the Issuer may have on material decisions. |
| Loan Syndication & Participation Details | Method of Notification for Material Decisions | ES161 | Optional | What method must the facility agent use to advise about matters relating to material decisions eg mail, verbal, electronic. |
| Loan Syndication & Participation Details | Major Decision Notification Period | ES162 | Optional | How many days notice is required to respond on matters relating to material decisions. |
| Loan Syndication & Participation Details | Participant Deadlock Resolutions Methods | ES163 | Optional | What methods can be used to resolve deadlocks on material decisions eg Shot Gun Buy-Sell, Independent Arbitrator, Other Method. |
| Loan Syndication & Participation Details | Method of Notification | ES164 | Optional | What method must the facility agent use to advise about matters relating to deadlocks eg mail, verbal, electronic. |
| Loan Syndication & Participation Details | Deadlock Notification Period | ES165 | Optional | How many days notice is allowed to respond when there is a deadlock. |
| Loan Syndication & Participation Details | Agent Bank of Syndication | ES166 | Mandatory | Agent bank. If no data available refer to Overview Document for inputs. |

**CRE Finance Council Europe**
**European Reporting Investor Reporting Package**
**"Loan Setup" File**
(Data Record Layout, Version 2.0) Cross Refrenced as "ES"

| Field Grouping | Field Names | Field Number | Field Requirement | Field Definition & Criteria |
|---|---|---|---|---|
| Loan Syndication & Participation Details | Blank Field | ES167 | | |
| Loan Syndication & Participation Details | Blank Field | ES168 | | |
| Misc. Loan Details | Last Setup Change Date | ES169 | Mandatory | The Loan Payment Date that any information in the Loan Set Up File was last changed, following any amendments/modifications to the loan agreement. |
| Misc. Loan Details | Remedy for Breach of Financial Covenant | ES170 | Mandatory | Refer to the "Remedies Upon Breach of Financial Covenants' Legend to select the code describing the remedy for the financial covenant breach. |
| Misc. Loan Details | Loan Originator | ES171 | Mandatory | Name of the originator/Lender that sold the loan to the Issuer. Name of entity ultimately responsible for the representations and warranties of the loan. |
| Misc. Loan Details | Blank Field | ES172 | | |
| Misc. Loan Details | Financial Information Submission Penalties | ES173 | Mandatory | Indicator for penalties for borrower's failure to submit required financial information (Op. Stmt, Schedule, etc.) as per loan documents. Refer to the "Information Submission Penalties" Legend |
| Misc. Loan Details | Loan Recourse | ES174 | Mandatory | Is there recourse to another party (eg guarantor) if the event the borrower defaults on an obligation under the loan agreement? Y=Yes, N=No. |
| Misc. Loan Details | Rounding Code | ES175 | Mandatory | Refer to Rounding Code Legend to describe the method for rounding the interest rate. |
| Misc. Loan Details | Rounding Increment | ES176 | Mandatory | The incremental percentage by which an index rate should be rounded in determining the interest rate as set out in the loan agreement. |
| Misc. Loan Details | Blank Field | ES177 | | |
| Misc. Loan Details | Subordinated Debt Rights Code | ES178 | Optional | Refer to Legend to describe the rights/obligations the Lender may have on material decisions. Full enforcement rights (1)<br>Limited enforcement rights (2)<br>No enforcement rights (3)<br>Other (4)<br>No Data (0) |
| Misc. Loan Details | Special Servicer Name | ES179 | Mandatory | Servicing Standard (Choice). Does the servicer of the loan service the Whole Loan (both the A and B components) or just the A or B component?<br>Special Servicer name at issue |
| Misc. Loan Details | Servicing Standard | ES179 | Mandatory | Servicing Standard (Choice). Does the servicer of the loan service the Whole Loan (both the A and B components) or just the A or B component?<br>Whole Loan (1)<br>A Loan (2)<br>B Loan (3)<br>Other (4)<br>No Data (0) |
| Misc. Loan Details | If Restructuring, Noteholder Consent Needed? | ES180 | Mandatory | Is Noteholder consent needed in a restructuring? If no data available refer to Overview Document for inputs. |

**CRE Finance Council Europe**
**European Reporting Investor Reporting Package**
**"Loan Periodic Update" File**
(Data Record Layout, Version 2.0) Cross Refrenced as "EL"

| Field Grouping | Field Names | Field Number | Field Requirement | Field Definition & Criteria |
|---|---|---|---|---|
| Loan Identifiers & Payment Date Details | Transaction_Pool Identifier | EL1 | Mandatory | The unique transaction or pool identification string. Transaction name |
| Loan Identifiers & Payment Date Details | Group Identifier | EL2 | Mandatory | The alpha-numeric code assigned to each loan group within an issue.  A group identifier may not be applicable for every transaction. |
| Loan Identifiers & Payment Date Details | Loan Servicer Identifier | EL3 | Mandatory | The loan servicer unique identification string assigned to the loan. |
| Loan Identifiers & Payment Date Details | Offering Circular Loan Identifier | EL4 | Mandatory | The offering circular or prospectus unique number assigned to each loan within the transaction or pool. |
| Loan Identifiers & Payment Date Details | Number of Properties | EL5 | Mandatory | The number of properties that serve as security for the loan. |
| Loan Identifiers & Payment Date Details | Loan Payment Date | EL6 | Mandatory | The date principal and interest is paid to the Issuer, this would normally be the interest payment date of the loan. |
| Loan Identifiers & Payment Date Details | Paid through Date | EL7 | Mandatory | The date at which all payments have been paid in full with no shortfalls.  On a performing loan this will be the Loan Payment Date immediately prior  to the date in Field EL6. |
| Loan Identifiers & Payment Date Details | Index Rate Reset Date | EL8 | Mandatory | For adjustable rate loans, the next date that the interest rate is due to change. For fixed rate loans, enter the next interest payment date. |
| Loan Identifiers & Payment Date Details | Next Payment Adjustment Date | EL9 | Mandatory | For adjustable rate loans, the next date that the amount of scheduled principal and/or interest is due to change. For fixed rate loans, enter the next payment date. |
| Loan Identifiers & Payment Date Details | Loan Maturity Date | EL10 | Mandatory | The current maturity date of the loan as defined in the loan agreement.  This would not take into account any approved maturity date  extendtensions that may be allowed under the loan agreement. |
| Loan Identifiers & Payment Date Details | Transaction Loan Name | EL11 | Mandatory | The offering circular or prospectus unique name assigned to each loan within the transaction or pool. |
| Loan Identifiers & Payment Date Details | Next Loan Payment Date | EL12 | Mandatory | Date of next loan payment. If no data available refer to Overview Document for inputs. |
| Loan Identifiers & Payment Date Details | Blank Field | EL13 | | |
| Loan Identifiers & Payment Date Details | Blank Field | EL14 | | |
| Loan Identifiers & Payment Date Details | Blank Field | EL15 | | |
| Rate Details | Current Index Rate (Whole Loan) | EL16 | Mandatory | The index rate used to determine the current whole loan interest rate. The interest rate (before margin) used to calculate the interest paid on the (Whole) Loan Payment Date in Field EL6. |
| Rate Details | Current Margin Rate (Whole Loan) | EL17 | Mandatory | Margin used to determine the current whole loan interest rate. The margin being used to calculate the interest paid on the (Whole) Loan Payment Date in Field EL6. |
| Rate Details | Current Interest Rate (Whole Loan) | EL18 | Mandatory | The total interest rate being used to calculate the interest paid on the(Whole) Loan Payment Date in Field EL6 (sum of Field EL16 and EL18). |
| Rate Details | Current Interest Rate (Trust Loan) | EL19 | Mandatory | Gross rate per annum used to calculate the current period scheduled interest on the A portion of the loan.  If no data available refer to Taxonomy for inputs. |

**CRE Finance Council Europe**
**European Reporting Investor Reporting Package**
**"Loan Periodic Update" File**
(Data Record Layout, Version 2.0) Cross Refrenced as "EL"

| Field Grouping | Field Names | Field Number | Field Requirement | Field Definition & Criteria |
|---|---|---|---|---|
| Rate Details | Next Index Rate (Whole Loan) | EL20 | Mandatory | The next period index rate used to determine the current whole loan interest rate. The interest rate (before margin) used to calculate the interest paid on the (Whole) Loan Payment Date in Field EL6. |
| Rate Details | Current Default Rate (Whole Loan) | EL21 | | The total interest rate being used to calculate the default interest paid on the Whole Loan Payment Date in Field EL42. |
| Rate Details | Blank Field | EL22 | | |
| Rate Details | Blank Field | EL23 | | |
| Principal Details | Current Beginning Opening Balance (Whole Loan) | EL24 | Mandatory | Outstanding balance at beginning of current period. The outstanding balance of the loan at the beginning of the interest period used the calculate the interest due on the Loan Payment Date in Field EL6. |
| Principal Details | Scheduled Principal Amount (Whole Loan) | EL25 | Mandatory | Scheduled principal payment due on the loan for the current period. The principal payment due to be paid to the Issuer on the Loan Payment Date in Field EL6 eg amortisation but not prepayments. |
| Principal Details | Current Ending Scheduled Balance (Whole Loan) | EL26 | Mandatory | Outstanding scheduled principal balance of loan at end of current period following amortisation but prior to any prepayments. The principal balance of the loan that would be outstanding following the scheduled principal payment but prior to any prepayments (Field EL24 minus EL25). |
| Principal Details | Unscheduled Principal Collections (Whole Loan) | EL27 | Mandatory | Unscheduled payments of principal received during the current period. Other principal payments received during the interest period that will be used to pay down the loan. This may relate to sales proceeds, voluntary prepayments, or liquidation amounts. |
| Principal Details | Other Principal Adjustments (Whole Loan) | EL28 | Mandatory | Unscheduled principal adjustments for interest period, not associated with movement of cash. Any other amounts that would cause the balance of the loan to be decreased or increased in the current period which are not considered Unscheduled Principal Collections and are not Scheduled Principal. Examples include write offs and adjustments necessary to synchronize the Servicer's records with the value of the bonds. |
| Principal Details | Actual Ending Loan Balance (Whole Loan) | EL29 | Mandatory | Outstanding actual principal balance at the end of the current period. The actual balance of the loan outstanding for the next interest period following all principal payments. |
| Principal Details | Current Beginning Balance (Trust Loan) | EL30 | Mandatory | Outstanding balance (A- Loan) at beginning of current period. The outstanding balance of the A Loan at the beginning of the interest period used the calculate the interest due on the Loan Payment Date. |
| Principal Details | Total Principal Collections (Trust Loan) | EL31 | Mandatory | All payments of principal (A- Loan) received during the current period. The principal payment of the A- Loan due to be paid to the Issuer on the Loan Payment Date in Field EL6 eg amortisation but not prepayments. |
| Principal Details | Actual Ending Loan Balance (Trust Loan) | EL32 | Mandatory | Outstanding actual principal balance (A- Loan) at the end of the current period. The principal balance of the A- Loan that would be outstanding following the scheduled principal payment. |
| Principal Details | Committed Undrawn Facility Loan Balance (Whole Loan) | EL33 | Mandatory | The total whole loan (senior debt) remaining facility/ Undrawn balance at the end of the period. The total whole loan (senior debt) remaining facility at the end of the Interest Payment Date that the borrower can still draw upon |
| Principal Details | Blank Field | EL34 | | |

**CRE Finance Council Europe**
**European Reporting Investor Reporting Package**
**"Loan Periodic Update" File**
(Data Record Layout, Version 2.0) Cross Referenced as "EL"

| Field Grouping | Field Names | Field Number | Field Requirement | Field Definition & Criteria |
|---|---|---|---|---|
| Interest Details | Scheduled Interest Amount Due (Whole Loan) | EL35 | Mandatory | Gross interest for period assuming no repayment in current period for the whole loan. The total interest that is due on the Loan Payment Date, assuming no prepayments are made during the interest period. Interest should be based on the underlying rate as per the loan agreement |
| Interest Details | Prepayment Interest Excess_Shortfall | EL36 | Mandatory | Shortfall or excess of actual interest payment from the scheduled interest payment for the current period that is not related to a loan default. Results from a prepayment received on a date other than a scheduled payment due date: Shortfall – The difference by which the amount of interest paid is less than the scheduled interest that was due on the Loan Payment Date, (this would only apply if there is a shortfall after the borrower has paid any break costs). Excess – Interest collected in excess of the accrued interest due for the loan interest accrual period. A negative number displays shortfall and excess is displayed as a positive number. |
| Interest Details | Other Interest Adjustment | EL37 | Mandatory | Companion field for Other Principal Adjustments (Field EL28) to show unscheduled interest adjustments for the related collection period. |
| Interest Details | Reimbursed Interest on Advances | EL38 | Optional | Indicates any reimbursed interest on property protection advances in the calculation of the reconciliation of funds. Cumulative amount of interest paid to the Servicer for any property protection advances. |
| Interest Details | Negative Amortisation | EL39 | Mandatory | Negative amortisation/deferred interest/capitalised interest without penalty. Negative amortisation occurs when interest accrued during a payment period is greater than the scheduled payment and the excess amount is added to the outstanding loan balance. |
| Interest Details | Actual Interest Paid (Whole Loan) | EL40 | Mandatory | Whole Loan actual interest paid current in period. Total amount of interest paid by the borrower during the interest period or on the Loan Payment Date. |
| Interest Details | Actual Interest Paid (Trust Loan) | EL41 | Mandatory | Total amount of interest paid to the A Loan during the interest period or on the Loan Payment Date. |
| Interest Details | Actual Default Interest | EL42 | Mandatory | Whole Loan actual default interest paid in current period. Total amount of default interest paid by the borrower during the interest period or on the Loan Payment Date. |
| Interest Details | Deferred Interest (Whole Loan) | EL43 | Mandatory | Deferred interest on the whole loan. Deferred interest is the amount by which the interest a borrower is required to pay on a mortgage loan is less than the amount of interest accrued on the outstanding principal balance. Deferred interest is not added to the outstanding loan balance. |
| Interest Details | Capitalised Interest (Whole Loan) | EL44 | Mandatory | Capitalised interest on the whole loan. Capitalised interest is where interest is added to the loan balance at the end of the interest period in accordance with loan agreement. |
| Interest Details | Blank Field | EL45 | | |
| Principal & Interest Details | Total Scheduled Principal & Interest due (Whole Loan) | EL46 | Mandatory | Scheduled principal & interest payment due on the loan for the current period for the Issuer (whole loan). The total scheduled principal and interest due on the Loan Payment Date (sum of Fields EL25 and EL35) - can be used for DSCR calculations. |
| Principal & Interest Details | Total Shortfalls in Principal & Interest Outstanding (Whole Loan) | EL47 | Mandatory | Cumulative outstanding P&I amounts due on loan at the end of the current period. The cumulative amount of any unpaid principal and interest on the Loan Payment Date. |

571

**CRE Finance Council Europe**
**European Reporting Investor Reporting Package**
**"Loan Periodic Update" File**
(Data Record Layout, Version 2.0) Cross Refrenced as "EL"

| Field Grouping | Field Names | Field Number | Field Requirement | Field Definition & Criteria |
|---|---|---|---|---|
| Principal & Interest Details | Total Other Amounts Outstanding | EL48 | Mandatory | Cumulative outstanding amounts on loan (e.g., insurance premium, ground rents, cap ex) at the end of the current period that have been expended by Issuer/Servicer. The cumulative amount of any property protection advances or other sums that have been advanced by the Servicer or Issuer and not yet reimbursed by the borrower. |
| Principal & Interest Details | Cumulative Amount Outstanding | EL49 | Optional | The sum of Field EL47 and EL48 |
| Principal & Interest Details | Amortisation Trigger Reached | EL50 | Mandatory | Y=Yes N=No N/A=Not Applicable If the Loan has an amortisation trigger, has the trigger been met |
| Principal & Interest Details | Current Amortisation Type | EL51 | Optional | The type of amortisation that applies to the Loan. Loan amortisation type |
| Principal & Interest Details | Annuity Full Amortisation Period | EL52 | Optional | If Annuity amortisation, period over which loan would fully amortise if scheduled annuity payment continued to paid until zero balance was achieved |
| Principal & Interest Details | Linear Amortisation per Annum | EL53 | Optional | |
| Principal & Interest Details | Total Scheduled Principal & Interest Paid (Trust Loan) | EL54 | Mandatory | Scheduled Principal & Interest payment due on the A - Loan for the current period for the Issuer. |
| Principal & Interest Details | Blank Field | EL55 | | |
| Principal & Interest Details | Blank Field | EL56 | | |
| Principal & Interest Details | Blank Field | EL57 | | |
| Principal & Interest Details | Blank Field | EL58 | | |
| Most Recent YTD Financial Details | Most Recent Financial As of Start Date | EL59 | Optional | The first day of the financials used for the most recent financial operating statement (e.g. year to date or trailing 12 months) - should be the day after the date for preceding fiscal year end statement Field EL86. If multiple properties and all the same date, print date. If multiple properties and different dates use the earliest date . |
| Most Recent YTD Financial Details | Most Recent Financial As of End Date | EL60 | Optional | The end date of the financials used for the most recent financial operating statement (e.g. year to date or trailing 12 months). If multiple properties and all the same date, print date. If multiple properties and different dates use the latest date. |
| Most Recent YTD Financial Details | Most Recent Financial Indicator | EL61 | Optional | This field is used to describe the period for which the most recent financial data is reflected. Check Start & End Date applies to fields EL65 to EL83.<br>Trailing 12 months actual (1)<br>Trailing 12 months normalized (2)<br>Year to Date actual (3)<br>Year to Date normalized (4)<br>Other (5)<br>No Data (0) |
| Most Recent YTD Financial Details | NOI / NCF Indicator | EL62 | Optional | Refer to the NOI/NCF Indicator Legend to describe which method is being used to calculate the NOI/NCF used in these reports. Applies to methodology used in the Preceding Fiscal Year Financial Details (EL66-EL101) and Second Preceding Fiscal Year Financial Details (EL102-EL117). |

**CRE Finance Council Europe**
**European Reporting Investor Reporting Package**
**"Loan Periodic Update" File**
(Data Record Layout, Version 2.0) Cross Referenced as "EL"

| Field Grouping | Field Names | Field Number | Field Requirement | Field Definition & Criteria |
|---|---|---|---|---|
| Most Recent YTD Financial Details | Loan Covenant Trigger_Breach | EL63 | Mandatory | Refer to Trigger Event Legend for descriptions of the types of financial covenants. Complete if there has been a breach, otherwise leave blank. pe of Covenant Breach / Trigger: Interest Cover Ratio (ICR) (1) Debt Service Cover Ratio (DSCR) (2) Loan to Value (LTV) (3) ICR / DSCR (4) ICR / DSCR / LTV (5) Property Level Breach (6) Borrower Level Breach (7) Tenant / Vacancy Level Breach (8) Other (9) No Data (0) |
| Most Recent YTD Financial Details | Borrower Reporting Breach | EL64 | Mandatory | Is Borrower in breach of its obligation to deliver reports to loan servicer or lender? Y = Yes or N = No |
| Most Recent YTD Financial Details | Most Recent Revenue | EL65 | Optional | If multiple properties then sum the value, if missing any then populate using the "Multi Property Indicator Legend" rule. Total revenues for the period covered by the most recent financial operating statement (i.e year to date or trailing 12 months) for all the properties. If multiple properties then sum the revenue (should match figures for sum of properties in Property File for this loan), if missing any or if all received/consolidated, then populate using the Multi Property Indicator Legend rule. May be normalised if required by the applicable servicing agreement. |
| Most Recent YTD Financial Details | Most Recent Operating Expenses | EL66 | Optional | If multiple properties then sum the value, if missing any then populate using the "Multi Property Indicator Legend" rule. Total operating expenses for the period covered by the most recent financial operating statement (i.e. year to date or trailing 12 months) for all properties. These may include real estate taxes, insurance, management, utilities, maintenance and repairs and direct property costs to the landlord; capital expenditures and leasing commissions are excluded. If multiple properties exist, total the operating expenses of the underlying properties. If multiple properties exist and data is not available for all properties or if received/consolidated, refer to the Multi Property Indicator Legend rule. May be normalised if required by the applicable servicing agreement. |
| Most Recent YTD Financial Details | Most Recent NOI | EL67 | Optional | If multiple properties then sum the value, if missing any then populate using the "Multi Property Indicator Legend" rule. Total revenues less total operating expenses for the period covered by the most recent financial operating statement (Field EL65 minus EL66) If multiple properties exist and not all information available or consolidated refer to the Multi Property Indicator Legend. |
| Most Recent YTD Financial Details | Most Recent Capital Expenditure | EL68 | Optional | Total capex (as opposed to repairs and maintenance) for the period covered by the most recent financial operating statement (ie year to date or trailing 12 months) for all the properties. |

**CRE Finance Council Europe**
**European Reporting Investor Reporting Package**
**"Loan Periodic Update" File**
(Data Record Layout, Version 2.0) Cross Refrenced as "EL"

| Field Grouping | Field Names | Field Number | Field Requirement | Field Definition & Criteria |
|---|---|---|---|---|
| Most Recent YTD Financial Details | Most Recent Net Cash Flow | EL69 | Optional | Most Recent Net Cash Flow related to Financial As of Ending Date EL73. If multiple properties then sum the value, if missing any then populate using the "Multi Property Indicator Legend" rule. Total NOI less total capex for the period covered by the most recent financial operating statement (Field EL67 minus EL68) If multiple properties and not all information is available, refer to the Multi Property Indicator Legend. |
| Most Recent YTD Financial Details | Most Recent Interest Paid | EL70 | Optional | Total interest due for the period covered by the most recent financial operating statement (ie year to date or trailing 12 months). Sum of interest paid in Financial YTD |
| Most Recent YTD Financial Details | Most Recent CREFC-Europe ICR (NOI) | EL71 | Optional | Calculate the CREFC-Europe Interest Coverage Ratio for the loan (whole) based on Net Operating Income for the most recent period. Please refer to the formula described within "Methodology for Analyzing" guide. |
| Most Recent YTD Financial Details | Most Recent Debt Service Amount | EL72 | Optional | Total scheduled payments of principal and Interest  due during the period covered by the  most recent financial operating statement (ie year to date or trailing 12 months). Should equal the sum of the values for properties securing this loan shown in the Property File Field EP67. |
| Most Recent YTD Financial Details | Most Recent CREFC-Europe DSCR (NOI) | EL73 | Optional | Calculate the CREFC-Europe Debt Service Coverage Ratio for the loan (whole) based on Net Operating Income for the most recent period. Please refer to the formula described within "Methodology for Analyzing" guide. |
| Most Recent YTD Financial Details | Most Recent CREFC-Europe DSCR (NCF) | EL74 | Optional | Calculate the CREFC-Europe Debt Service Coverage Ratio for the loan (whole) based on Net Cash Flow for the most recent period. Please refer to the formula described within "Methodology for Analyzing" guide. |
| Most Recent YTD Financial Details | Most Recent DSCR Indicator | EL75 | Optional | Flag used to explain how the DSCR was calculated when there are multiple properties. Please use the Multi Property Indicator Legend |
| Most Recent YTD Financial Details | Most Recent Economic Occupancy | EL76 | Optional | The most recent available percentage of rentable space with signed leases in place (tenants may not be in occupation but are paying rent). Should be derived from a rent roll or other document indicating occupancy consistent with most recent financial year information. |
| Most Recent YTD Financial Details | Most Recent Physical Occupancy | EL77 | Optional | The most recent available percentage of rentable space actually occupied (ie where tenants are actually in occupation and not vacated). Should be derived from a rent roll or other document indicating occupancy consistent with most recent financial year information. |
| Most Recent YTD Financial Details | Most Recent Valuation Date | EL78 | Mandatory | The date the most recent valuation/appraisal was prepared.  If multiple properties and all the same date, print date.  If multiple properties use the earliest valuation date. |
| Most Recent YTD Financial Details | Most Recent Valuation or Internal Value | EL79 | Mandatory | The most recent valuation of all properties securing the loan. If multiple properties, sum the value. Refer to total in Property file. |
| Most Recent YTD Financial Details | Most Recent Loan to Value Ratio (Whole Loan) | EL80 | Mandatory | Most recent Loan to Value (LTV) for the loan (whole) based on the loan documentation |
| Most Recent YTD Financial Details | Most Recent Debt Service Cover Ratio (Whole Loan) | EL81 | Mandatory | Most recent Debt Service Coverage Ratio (DSCR) for the loan (whole) based on the loan documentation |

**CRE Finance Council Europe**
**European Reporting Investor Reporting Package**
**"Loan Periodic Update" File**
(Data Record Layout, Version 2.0) Cross Refrenced as "EL'

| Field Grouping | Field Names | Field Number | Field Requirement | Field Definition & Criteria |
|---|---|---|---|---|
| Most Recent YTD Financial Details | Most Recent CREFC-Europe LTV Ratio (Whole Loan) | EL82 | Optional | Most recent CREFC-Europe Loan to Value (LTV) for the loan (whole) which would include all senior ranking debt positions. Please refer to the formula described within "Methodology for Analyzing" guide. |
| Most Recent YTD Financial Details | Most Recent Interest Cover Ratio (Whole Loan) | EL83 | Mandatory | Most recent Interest Coverage Ratio (ICR) for the loan (whole) based on the loan documentation |
| Most Recent YTD Financial Details | Most Recent Interest Cover Ratio (Trust Loan) | EL84 | Mandatory | Most recent interest coverage ratio calculation for the A-Loan based on the offering documentation. Please refer to Taxonomy for inputs. |
| Most Recent YTD Financial Details | Most Recent Debt Service Cover Ratio (Trust Loan) | EL85 | Mandatory | Most recent debt service coverage ratio calculation for the A-Loan based on the offering documentation. Please refer to Taxonomy for inputs. |
| Most Recent YTD Financial Details | Most Recent Loan to Value Ratio (Trust Loan) | EL86 | Mandatory | Most recent Loan to Value ratio (LTV) for the Trust-Loan based on the he offering documentation. Please refer to Taxonomy for inputs. |
| Preceding Fiscal Year Financial Details | Preceding Financial Year Revenue | EL87 | Optional | If multiple properties then sum the value, if missing any then populate using the "Multi Property Indicator Legend" rule |
| Preceding Fiscal Year Financial Details | Preceding Financial Operating Expenses | EL88 | Optional | If multiple properties then sum the value, if missing any then populate using the "Multi Property Indicator Legend" rule |
| Preceding Fiscal Year Financial Details | Preceding Financial Year NOI | EL89 | Optional | If multiple properties then sum the value, if missing any then populate using the "DSCR Indicator Legend" rule |
| Preceding Fiscal Year Financial Details | Preceding Financial Year NCF | EL90 | Optional | Preceding Fiscal Year Net Cash Flow. If multiple properties then sum the value, if missing any then populate using the "Multi Property Indicator Legend" rule |
| Preceding Fiscal Year Financial Details | Preceding Year CREFC-Europe ICR (NOI) | EL91 | Optional | Preceding year (last period reported) Interest Coverage Ratio for the loan (whole) based on the CREFC-Europe method and utilising NOI |
| Preceding Fiscal Year Financial Details | Preceding Financial Year Debt Svc Amount | EL92 | Optional | If multiple properties then sum the value, if missing any then populate using the "Multi Property Indicator Legend" rule |
| Preceding Fiscal Year Financial Details | Preceding Year CREFC-Europe DSCR (NOI) | EL93 | Optional | Preceding year (last period reported) Debt Service Coverage Ratio for the loan (whole) based on the CREFC-Europe method and utilising NOI |
| Preceding Fiscal Year Financial Details | Blank Field | EL94 | | |
| Preceding Fiscal Year Financial Details | Preceding Year DSCR Indicator | EL95 | Optional | Flag used to explain how the DSCR was calculated when there are multiple properties. See Multi Property Indicator Legend |
| Preceding Fiscal Year Financial Details | Preceding Financial Year Economic Occupancy | EL96 | Optional | If multiple properties, use weighted average by using the calculation [Current Allocated % (Prop) * Occupancy (Oper)] for each Property, if missing any then leave empty |
| Preceding Fiscal Year Financial Details | Preceding Year DSCR (Whole) | EL97 | Optional | Preceding year (last period reported) debt service coverage ratio for the loan (whole) based on the loan documentation |
| Preceding Fiscal Year Financial Details | Blank Field | EL98 | | |
| Preceding Fiscal Year Financial Details | Preceding Year ICR (Whole) | EL99 | Optional | Preceding year (last period reported) interest coverage ratio for the loan (whole) based on the loan documentation |

**CRE Finance Council Europe**
**European Reporting Investor Reporting Package**
**"Loan Periodic Update" File**
(Data Record Layout, Version 2.0) Cross Refrenced as 'EL'

| Field Grouping | Field Names | Field Number | Field Requirement | Field Definition & Criteria |
|---|---|---|---|---|
| Preceding Fiscal Year Financial Details | Blank Field | EL100 | | Blank Field |
| Preceding Fiscal Year Financial Details | Preceding Year ICR (Trust Note) | EL101 | Optional | Preceding year (last period reported) interest coverage ratio for the Trust Note based on the offering documentation |
| Second Preceding Fiscal Year Financial Details | Second Preceding Financial Year Financial As of Date | EL102 | Optional | If multiple properties and all the same then print the date, if missing any then leave empty |
| Second Preceding Fiscal Year Financial Details | Second Preceding Financial Year Revenue | EL103 | Optional | If multiple properties then sum the value, if missing any then populate using the "Multi Property Indicator Legend" rule |
| Second Preceding Fiscal Year Financial Details | Second Preceding Financial Year Operating Expenses | EL104 | Optional | If multiple properties then sum the value, if missing any then populate using the "Multi Property Indicator Legend" rule |
| Second Preceding Fiscal Year Financial Details | Second Preceding Financial Year NOI | EL105 | Optional | If multiple properties then sum the value, if missing any then populate using the "Multi Property Indicator Legend" rule |
| Second Preceding Fiscal Year Financial Details | Second Preceding Financial Year NCF | EL106 | Optional | Second Preceding Fiscal Year Net Cash Flow related to Financial As of Date EL102. If multiple properties then sum the value, if missing any then populate using the "Multi Property Indicator Legend" rule |
| Second Preceding Fiscal Year Financial Details | Second Preceding Year CREFC-Europe ICR (NOI) | EL107 | Optional | Second Preceding year (preceding year reported) Interest Coverage Ratio for the loan (whole) based on the CREFC-Europe method and utilising NOI |
| Second Preceding Fiscal Year Financial Details | Second Preceding Financial Year Debt Service Amount | EL108 | Optional | If multiple properties then sum the value, if missing any then populate using the "Multi Property Indicator Legend" rule |
| Second Preceding Fiscal Year Financial Details | Second Preceding Year CREFC-Europe DSCR (NOI) | EL109 | Optional | Second Preceding year (preceding year reported) Debt Service Coverage Ratio for the loan (whole) based on the CREFC-Europe method and utilising NOI |
| Second Preceding Fiscal Year Financial Details | Second Preceding Year DSCR (Whole) | EL110 | Optional | Second preceding year (preceding year reported) debt service coverage ratio for the loan (whole) based on the loan documentation |
| Second Preceding Fiscal Year Financial Details | Second Preceding Year DSCR Indicator | EL111 | Optional | Flag used to explain how the DSCR was calculated when there are multiple properties. See Multi Property Indicator Legend |
| Second Preceding Fiscal Year Financial Details | Second Preceding Financial Year Economic Occupancy | EL112 | Optional | If multiple properties, use weighted average by using the calculation [Current Allocated % (Prop) * Occupancy (Oper)] for each Property. If missing any then leave empty |
| Second Preceding Fiscal Year Financial Details | Second Preceding Year ICR (Whole) | EL113 | Optional | Second preceding year (preceding year reported) interest coverage ratio for the loan (whole) based on the loan documentation |
| Second Preceding Fiscal Year Financial Details | Blank Field | EL114 | | |
| Second Preceding Fiscal Year Financial Details | Second Preceding Year ICR (Trust Note) | EL115 | Optional | Second preceding year (last period reported) interest coverage ratio for the Trust Note based on the offering documentation |
| Most Recent YTD Financial Details | Most Recent CREFC-Europe ICR (NOI/TFC) | EL116 | Optional | Calculate the CREFC-Europe Interest Coverage Ratio for the loan (whole) based on Net Operating Income divided by the Total Finance Cost which will take into account net hedge payments for the most recent period. Please refer to the formula described within "Methodology for Analyzing" guide. |

**CRE Finance Council Europe**
**European Reporting Investor Reporting Package**
**"Loan Periodic Update" File**
(Data Record Layout, Version 2.0) Cross Referenced as "EL"

| Field Grouping | Field Names | Field Number | Field Requirement | Field Definition & Criteria |
|---|---|---|---|---|
| Most Recent YTD Financial Details | Most Recent CREFC-Europe DSCR (NOI/TFC) | EL117 | Optional | Calculate the CREFC-Europe Debt Service Coverage Ratio for the loan (whole) based on Net Operating Income divided by the Total Finance Cost which will take into account net hedge payments for the most recent period. Please refer to the formula described within "Methodology for Analyzing" guide. |
| Reserve & Escrow Details | Total Reserve Balance | EL118 | Mandatory | Total balance of the reserve accounts at the loan level at the Loan Payment Date. Includes Maintenance, Repairs & Environmental, etc. (excludes Tax & Insurance reserves Includes LC's for reserves. Should be completed if Field ES75 Collection of Other Reserves in Loan Set up is "Y" = Yes. If no reserve accounts then "0" to be used. |
| Reserve & Escrow Details | Escrow Trigger Event Occurred | EL119 | Mandatory | Enter Yes if an event has occurred which has caused reserve amounts to be established . Enter No if payments are built up as a normal condition of the loan agreement). |
| Reserve & Escrow Details | Amounts Added to Escrows in Current Period | EL120 | Mandatory | Amount that has been added to any escrows or reserves during Current Period. |
| Reserve & Escrow Details | Blank Field | EL121 | | |
| Reserve & Escrow Details | Blank Field | EL122 | | |
| Reserve & Escrow Details | Blank Field | EL123 | | |
| Reserve & Escrow Details | Blank Field | EL124 | | |
| Reserve & Escrow Details | Blank Field | EL125 | | |
| Liquidation & Prepayment Details | Liquidation / Prepayment Date | EL126 | Mandatory | The date on which an unscheduled principal payment or liquidation proceeds are received. |
| Liquidation & Prepayment Details | Liquidation / Prepayment Code | EL127 | Mandatory | Code assigned to any unscheduled principal payments or liquidation proceeds received during the collection period. Specific codes apply. See Liquidation/Prepayment Code Legend. Please refer to Taxonomy for inputs. |
| Liquidation & Prepayment Details | Loan Prepayment Fee | EL128 | Optional | Amount collected from the borrower as the fee due for making prepayments as required under the terms of the loan agreement. This is not intended to include any amounts paid as a "break cost" to make up interest payments up to the Loan Payment Date. |
| Liquidation & Prepayment Details | Blank Field | EL129 | | |
| Liquidation & Prepayment Details | Blank Field | EL130 | | |
| Liquidation & Prepayment Details | Blank Field | EL131 | | |
| Liquidation & Prepayment Details | Blank Field | EL132 | | |
| Liquidation & Prepayment Details | Blank Field | EL133 | | |
| Borrower Level Hedging Details | Name of Loan Swap Provider (Borrower Level) | EL134 | Mandatory | The name of the Swap provider for the loan if the Borrower has the direct contract with the swap counterparty. |
| Borrower Level Hedging Details | Actual Ratings of Loan Swap Provider (Borrower Level) | EL135 | Mandatory | Identify the ratings of the Swap Counterparty as of the Loan Payment Date. |
| Borrower Level Hedging Details | Full or Partial Termination Event of Loan Level Swap for Current Period (Borrower Level) | EL136 | Mandatory | If loan swap has been terminated during current period, identify reason. Refer to "Loan Level Swap Termination Legend" for code to reflect the reason for termination. Please refer to Taxonomy for inputs. |
| Borrower Level Hedging Details | Net Periodic Payment due to Loan Swap Provider (Borrower Level) | EL137 | Mandatory | Amount of payment made by the borrower to the swap counterparty on the Loan Payment Date as required by the Swap contract. This does not include any breakage or termination payments. Please refer to Taxonomy for inputs. |

577

**CRE Finance Council Europe**
**European Reporting Investor Reporting Package**
**"Loan Periodic Update" File**
(Data Record Layout, Version 2.0) Cross Refrenced as "EL"

| Field Grouping | Field Names | Field Number | Field Requirement | Field Definition & Criteria |
|---|---|---|---|---|
| Borrower Level Hedging Details | Net Periodic Payment due from Loan Swap Provider (Borrower Level) | EL138 | Mandatory | Amount of payment made by the swap counterparty to the borrower on the Loan Payment Date as required by the Swap contract. This does not include any breakage or termination payments. Please refer to Taxonomy for inputs. |
| Borrower Level Hedging Details | Breakage Costs Due to Loan Swap Provider | EL139 | Mandatory | Amount of any payment due from the borrower to the swap counterparty for partial of full termination of the Swap. |
| Borrower Level Hedging Details | Shortfall in Payment of Breakage Costs on Loan Level Swap | EL140 | Mandatory | Amount of any shortfall, if any, of breakage costs resulting from the full or partial termination of the swap, paid by the borrower. |
| Borrower Level Hedging Details | Breakage Costs Due from Loan Level Swap Countparty | EL141 | Mandatory | Amount of any gains paid by the swap counterparty to the borrower on full or partial termination. |
| Borrower Level Hedging Details | Next Reset Date for the Loan Level Swap | EL142 | Mandatory | Date of next reset date on the loan level swap. |
| Borrower Level Hedging Details | Blank Field | EL143 | | |
| Borrower Level Hedging Details | Blank Field | EL144 | | |
| Borrower Level Hedging Details | Blank Field | EL145 | | |
| Borrower Level Hedging Details | Blank Field | EL146 | | |
| Borrower Level Hedging Details | Blank Field | EL147 | | |
| Delinquent Loan Status Details | Loan Status | EL148 | Mandatory | Refer to the Status of Loan Legend to determine the code used to explain the loan status (ie current, non payment etc ). If a loan has multiple Status Codes triggered, Servicer discretion to determine which codes reported. Please refer to Taxonomy for inputs. |
| Delinquent Loan Status Details | Enforcement Start Date | EL149 | Mandatory | The date on which foreclosure or adminstration proceedings or alternative enforcement procedures were initiated against or agreed by the borrower. |
| Delinquent Loan Status Details | Special Servicing Status | EL150 | Mandatory | As of the Loan Payment Date is the loan currently being specially serviced? Y= Yes or N =No. Please refer to Taxonomy for inputs. |
| Delinquent Loan Status Details | Workout Strategy Code | EL151 | Mandatory | Work-out strategy: Modification (1) Enforcement (2) Receivership (3) Insolvency (4) Extension (5) Loan Sale (6) Discounted Pay Off (7) Property in Possession (8) Resolved (9) Pending Return to Servicer (10) Deed in Lieu of Foreclosure (11) Full Pay Off (12) Reps and Warranties (13) Other (14) No Data (0) |
| Delinquent Loan Status Details | Expected Timing of Recoveries | EL152 | Mandatory | Expected recovery timing in months |

**CRE Finance Council Europe**
**European Reporting Investor Reporting Package**
**"Loan Periodic Update" File**
(Data Record Layout, Version 2.0) Cross Refrenced as "EL"

| Field Grouping | Field Names | Field Number | Field Requirement | Field Definition & Criteria |
|---|---|---|---|---|
| Delinquent Loan Status Details | In Insolvency | EL153 | Mandatory | Insolvency Status of Loan (If In Insolvency "Y", Else "N"). |
| Delinquent Loan Status Details | Insolvency Date | EL154 | Mandatory | Date Of Insolvency |
| Delinquent Loan Status Details | Property Possession Date | EL155 | Mandatory | The date on which title to (or an alternative form of effective control and ability to dispose of) the collateral property were obtained. If multiple properties have the same date then print that date otherwise leave empty |
| Delinquent Loan Status Details | Net Proceeds Received on Liquidation | EL156 | Mandatory | Net proceeds recieved on liquidation used to determine loss to the Issuer per the Transaction Documents. The amount of the net proceeds of sale received, this will determine whether there is a loss or shortfall on the loan. |
| Delinquent Loan Status Details | Liquidation Expense | EL157 | Mandatory | Expenses associated with the liquidation to be netted from the other assets of issuer to determine loss per the Transaction Documents. Amount of any liquidation expenses that will be paid out of the net sales proceeds to determine whether there will be any loss. |
| Delinquent Loan Status Details | Realised Loss to Securitisation | EL158 | Mandatory | Outstanding balance of loan (plus Liquidation Expenses) less net Liquidation Proceeds Received. The amount of any loss to the Issuer after deducting liquidation expenses from the net sales proceeds. |
| Delinquent Loan Status Details | Number of months in Arrears | EL159 | Mandatory | Number of months this loan is in arrears at the end of the current period according to the definition of the issuer. If no data available refer to Overview Document for inputs. |
| Delinquent Loan Status Details | Default Amount | EL160 | Mandatory | Total default amount before the application of sale proceeds and recoveries |
| Delinquent Loan Status Details | Cumulative Recoveries | EL161 | Mandatory | Total recoveries including all sale proceeds. Only relevant for loans that have defaulted/foreclosed |
| Delinquent Loan Status Details | Present Value of Expected Recoveries | EL162 | Optional | Present value of expected recoveries |
| Delinquent Loan Status Details | Blank Field | EL163 | | |
| Loan Modification Details | Last Setup Change Date | EL164 | Mandatory | The Loan Payment Date that any information in the Loan Set Up File was last changed, following any amendments/modifications to the loan agreement. |
| Loan Modification Details | Last Loan Sale Date | EL165 | Mandatory | The date the loan was sold to the Issuer, if the loan was part of the original securitisation, then this will be the Issue Date. |
| Loan Modification Details | Last Property Issue Date | EL166 | Mandatory | Date the latest property or properties were contributed to this securitisation. If any properties have been substituted, enter the date of the last substitution. If the properties was part of the original transaction, this will be the Issue Date. |
| Loan Modification Details | Date of Assumption | EL167 | Mandatory | Date the assignment/novation or assumption was executed by the new borrower (leave blank if original borrower). |
| Loan Modification Details | Appraisal Reduction Amount Date | EL168 | Mandatory | Date the Appraisal Reduction Amount was calculated and approved (initial or updated calculation as of date). The calculation may be performed monthly, annually, etc. and is triggered by an Appraisal Reduction Event. The Appraisal Reduction Amount is then reported as of the loan or note payment date that follows the Appraisal Reduction Amount calculation date. The effective date of the last Appraisal Reduction Amount, not the date of the appraisal used to derive the ARA amount |
| Loan Modification Details | Date of Last Modification | EL169 | Mandatory | Last effective date the loan was modified, leave blank if no changes. |
| Loan Modification Details | Modification Code | EL170 | Mandatory | Refer to Modification Code Legend for code to describe type of modification |

**CRE Finance Council Europe**
**European Reporting Investor Reporting Package**
**"Loan Periodic Update" File**
(Data Record Layout, Version 2.0) Cross Refrenced as "EL"

| Field Grouping | Field Names | Field Number | Field Requirement | Field Definition & Criteria |
|---|---|---|---|---|
| Loan Modification Details | Modified Payment Rate | EL171 | Mandatory | If the loan has been restructured (probably during a workout process), and the new amount, expressed as a percentage of the loan balance, should be entered, otherwise leave blank. |
| Loan Modification Details | Modified Loan Interest Rate | EL172 | Mandatory | If the loan has been restructured (probably during a workout process), and the interest rate/margin has been amended, then the new rate should be entered, otherwise leave blank. |
| Loan Modification Details | Blank Field | EL173 | | |
| Loan Modification Details | Blank Field | EL174 | | |
| Loan Modification Details | Blank Field | EL175 | | |
| Loan Modification Details | Blank Field | EL176 | | |
| Loan Modification Details | Blank Field | EL177 | | |
| Loan Modification Details | Blank Field | EL178 | | |
| Loan Syndication & Participation Details | Percentage of Total Loan which is Securitised | EL179 | Optional | If the loan has been split or in the case of a syndicated loan, the issuer owns a part of the loan, Please give the current percentage of the loan that is sold to the issuer as of the most recent Loan Payment Date. |
| Loan Syndication & Participation Details | Change in Controlling Party | EL180 | Optional | Has there been a change in the Controlling Party since the prior reporting period? Y=Yes or N=No |
| Loan Syndication & Participation Details | Name of Old Controlling Party | EL181 | Optional | Name of Institution |
| Loan Syndication & Participation Details | Name of New Controlling Party | EL182 | Optional | Name of Institution |
| Loan Syndication & Participation Details | Date of Change of Controlling Party | EL183 | Optional | Date that Controlling Party under Syndicated Loan has changed |
| Loan Syndication & Participation Details | Blank Field | EL184 | | |
| Loan Syndication & Participation Details | Blank Field | EL185 | | |
| Loan Syndication & Participation Details | Blank Field | EL186 | | |
| Loan Syndication & Participation Details | Blank Field | EL187 | | |
| Loan Syndication & Participation Details | Blank Field | EL188 | | |
| Special Servicing Details | Servicer Watchlist | EL189 | Mandatory | The first determination date that a loan was placed on the Watchlist. If loan came off the Watchlist in a prior period and is now coming back on, use the new entry date. Please refer to Taxonomy for inputs. |
| Special Servicing Details | Most Recent Special Servicer Transfer Date | EL190 | Mandatory | The date a loan was transferred to the Special Servicer following a servicing transfer event. Note: If the loan has had multiple transfers, this should be the last date transferred to special servicing. |
| Special Servicing Details | Most Recent Primary Servicer Return Date | EL191 | Mandatory | The date a loan becomes a "Corrected Mortgage Loan", which is the date the loan was returned to the Master/Primary Servicer from the Special Servicer. Note: If the loan has had multiple transfers, this should be the last date returned to the Master/Primary Servicer from Special Servicing. |
| Special Servicing Details | Special Servicing Fee Amount plus Adjustments | EL192 | Optional | The total of all amounts paid to the Special Servicer during the current period, this will include the basic fee plus any other amounts paid whether expenses or fees. |

CRE Finance Council Europe
European Reporting Investor Reporting Package
**"Loan Periodic Update" File**
(Data Record Layout, Version 2.0) Cross Refrenced as "EL"

| Field Grouping | Field Names | Field Number | Field Requirement | Field Definition & Criteria |
|---|---|---|---|---|
| Special Servicing Details | Servicer Fee Amount | EL193 | Optional | The amount of the fee paid to the Servicer for the current period as calculated in accordance with the Servicing Agreement. |
| Special Servicing Details | Period Cost | EL194 | Optional | Any other amounts that may be deducted from the interest paid by the borrowerat the loan level that would reduce the amounts payable to the Issuer |
| Special Servicing Details | Workout Fee Amount | EL195 | Optional | The amount of any workout fee being paid to the special Servicer for the current period on a loan that has become a corrected loan. |
| Special Servicing Details | Liquidation Fee Amount | EL196 | Optional | The amount of any liquidation fee paid to the special Servicer for the current period on a specially serviced loan following the liquidation of a property securing the loan. |
| Special Servicing Details | Non Recoverability Determined | EL197 | Mandatory | Indicator (Yes/No) as to whether the Servicer/Special has determined that there will be a shortfall in recovering any advances it has made and the outstanding loan balance and any other amounts owing on the loan from proceeds upon sale or liquidation of the property or Loan. |
| Special Servicing Details | Date of Loan Breach | EL198 | Mandatory | The date the breach occurred. If multipal breaches, the date of the earliest breach. |
| Special Servicing Details | Date of Loan Breach Cure | EL199 | Mandatory | The date the breach cured. If multipal breaches, the date which the last breach cured. |
| Special Servicing Details | Watchlist Criteria Code | EL200 | Mandatory | Servicer Watchlist Code per CMSA-Europe Watchlist Criteria - Portfolio Review Guidelines. If multipal criteria are applicable, please list the most detrimental code |
| Special Servicing Details | Blank Field | EL201 | | |
| Special Servicing Details | Blank Field | EL202 | | |

581

**CRE Finance Council Europe**
**European Reporting Investor Reporting Package**
**"Property" File**
(Data Record Layout, Version 2.0) Cross Refrenced as "EP"

| Field Grouping | Field Names | Field Number | Field Requirement | Field Definition & Criteria |
|---|---|---|---|---|
| Loan Identifiers & Payment Date Details | Transaction_Pool Identifier | EP1 | Mandatory | The unique transaction or pool identification string. Transaction name |
| Loan Identifiers & Payment Date Details | Loan Servicer Identifier | EP2 | Mandatory | The loan servicer unique identification string assigned to the loan. |
| Loan Identifiers & Payment Date Details | Offering Circular Loan Identifier | EP3 | Mandatory | The offering circular or prospectus unique number assigned to each loan within the transaction or pool. |
| Loan Identifiers & Payment Date Details | Property Identifier | EP4 | Mandatory | The loan servicer unique identification string assigned to each property within a loan. |
| Loan Identifiers & Payment Date Details | Distribution Date | EP5 | Mandatory | Note interest and principal payment date corresponding to data within file. |
| Loan Identifiers & Payment Date Details | Property Cross-Collateralised Loan Grouping | EP6 | Mandatory | Please enter relevant Offering Circular Loan Identifiers, if one property secures several loans within the transaction or pool. If no data available refer to Overview Document for inputs. |
| Loan Identifiers & Payment Date Details | Blank Field | EP7 | | |
| Loan Identifiers & Payment Date Details | Blank Field | EP8 | | |
| Loan Identifiers & Payment Date Details | Blank Field | EP9 | | |
| Loan Identifiers & Payment Date Details | Blank Field | EP10 | | |
| Loan Identifiers & Payment Date Details | Blank Field | EP11 | | |
| Collateral Details | Property Name | EP12 | Mandatory | The name of the property that serves as security for the loan. If multiple properties, print "Various." |
| Collateral Details | Property Address | EP13 | Mandatory | The address of the property that serves as security for the loan. If multiple properties, print "Various." |
| Collateral Details | Property City_Town | EP14 | Mandatory | City or town name where the property or properties are located. If multiple properties have the same city then print the same city, otherwise print "Various". Missing information print "Incomplete". |
| Collateral Details | Property Region | EP15 | Optional | The region description of where the property is located based on the Nomenclature of Territorial Units for Statistics (NUTS) using regional coding format (NUTS2). |
| Collateral Details | Property Post Code | EP16 | Mandatory | The primary property postal code. First 2 - 4 characters must be provided at a minimum. |
| Collateral Details | Property Country | EP17 | Mandatory | The country where the property is located. If multiple properties have the same country then print the country, otherwise print "Various." |
| Collateral Details | Property Type Code | EP18 | Mandatory | The property type or use reference defined in the valuation report or offering documentation. Please utilise the relevant coding within the "Property Type Code Legend" located in the Data File Legends. |
| Collateral Details | Year Built | EP19 | Mandatory | Year the property was built per the valuation report or offering document. |
| Collateral Details | Year Last Renovated | EP20 | Mandatory | Year that last major renovation/new construction was completed on the property per the valuation report or offering document. |
| Collateral Details | Net Square Metres At Issue Date | EP21 | Mandatory | The total net rentable area of the properties in square metres that serve as security for the loan per the most recent valuation report. For multiple properties, if not all information available, leave blank. |
| Collateral Details | Net Internal Floor Area Validated | EP22 | Mandatory | Has a Valuer verified the net internal floor area of the property? |

CRE Finance Council Europe
European Reporting Investor Reporting Package
**"Property" File**
(Data Record Layout, Version 2.0) Cross Refrenced as "EP"

| Field Grouping | Field Names | Field Number | Field Requirement | Field Definition & Criteria |
|---|---|---|---|---|
| Collateral Details | Number of Units/Beds/Rooms | EP23 | Mandatory | For property type Multifamily enter number of units, for Hospitality/Hotel/Healthcare - beds, for Caravan Parks - units, Lodging/rooms, Self Storage=units. For Multiple properties, if all the same Property Type, sum the values. If no data available refer to Overview Document for inputs. |
| Collateral Details | Property Status | EP24 | Mandatory | Most recent loan status of property. Please utilise the relevant coding within the "Property Status Codes " located in the Data File Legends. |
| Collateral Details | Property Condition | EP25 | Mandatory | Property condition per loan servicer most recent property inspection or valuation report. Please utilise the following coding (E = Excellent, G = Good, F = Fair, P = Poor) or other method within valuation report |
| Collateral Details | Date of Last Property Inspection | EP26 | Mandatory | Date of last physical site inspection |
| Collateral Details | Property Form on Title | EP27 | Mandatory | The relevant form of property title (i.e. Freehold, Leasehold or Mixed). Please utilise the relevant coding within the "Property Title Codes " located in the Data File Legends. A lease on land only, in which the borrower usually owns a building or is required to build as specified in the lease. Such leases are usually long term net leases; the borrower's rights and obligations continue until the lease expires or is terminated through default. If multiple properties refer to Overview Document for inputs. |
| Collateral Details | Property Leasehold Expiry | EP28 | Mandatory | Provide the earliest date the leasehold interest expires. If no data available refer to Overview Document for inputs. |
| Collateral Details | Ground Rent Payable | EP29 | Mandatory | If property is leasehold, please provide the current annual leasehold rent payable to the lessor. |
| Collateral Details | Date of Most Recent Valuation | EP30 | Mandatory | Date of the last property valuation. For multiple properties, if several dates, enter latest. If no data available refer to Overview Document for inputs. |
| Collateral Details | Most Recent Valuation | EP31 | Mandatory | The most recent valuation of all properties securing the loan. If multiple properties, sum the value. If missing any, leave empty. |
| Collateral Details | Most Recent Valuation Source | EP32 | Mandatory | Name of valuation firm who performed the most recent property valuation. |
| Collateral Details | Total Reserve Balance allocated to Property | EP33 | Mandatory | Total balance of the reserve accounts for the property at the Loan Payment Date. Includes Maintenance, Repairs & Environmental, etc. (excludes Tax & Insurance escrows). Includes leasing commissions for reserves. |
| Collateral Details | Party that carried out the last property inspection | EP34 | Mandatory | The party that carried out the last property inspection. Refer to "Party that carried out the last property inspection" table or add free text field |
| Collateral Details | Most Recent Valuation Basis | EP35 | Mandatory | The most recent Valuation Basis. Please utilise the relevant coding within the "Valuation Basis Legend" located in the Data File Legends. (e.g. open market value, vacant possession etc.) |
| Collateral Details | Next Scheduled Valuation Date | EP36 | Optional | Next scheduled valuation date. If no data available refer to Overview Document for inputs. |
| Collateral Details | Blank Field | EP37 | | |
| Collateral Details | Blank Field | EP38 | | |
| Issue Date Details | Property Issue Date | EP39 | Mandatory | Date the property was contributed to the securitisation. If this property has been substituted, enter the date of the substitution. If the property was part of the original transaction, this will be the Issue Date. |
| Issue Date Details | Allocated Percentage of Loan at Issue Date | EP40 | Mandatory | Allocated loan % attributable to property at Issue Date where there is more than one property securing the loan. This may be set out in the Loan Agreement, otherwise assign by valuation or NOI. |
| Issue Date Details | Date of Financials at Issue Date | EP41 | Mandatory | The end date of the financials for the information used in the Offering Circular (e.g. year to date, annual, Quarterly or Trailing 12 months). If multiple properties, or missing, refer to Overview Document for inputs. |
| Issue Date Details | Property Revenue at Issue Date | EP42 | Optional | The total underwritten revenues from all sources for a property as described in the Offering Circular. If multiple properties, sum the values. If missing data or if all consolidated, refer to Overview Document for inputs. |
| Issue Date Details | Operating Expenses At Issue Date | EP43 | Optional | Total underwritten operating expenses for the properties a described in the Offering Circular. These may include real estate taxes, insurance, management, utilities, maintenance and repairs and direct property costs to the landlord; capital expenditures and leasing commissions are excluded. If multiple properties, exist and data is not available for all properties or consolidated, refer to Overview Document for inputs. |
| Issue Date Details | Net Operating Income at Issue Date | EP44 | Optional | Revenue less Operating Expenses at Issue Date. If multiple properties, sum the values. If missing data or if all consolidated, refer to Overview Document for inputs. |

583

CRE Finance Council Europe
European Reporting Investor Reporting Package
"Property" File
(Data Record Layout, Version 2.0) Cross Referenced as "EP"

| Field Grouping | Field Names | Field Number | Field Requirement | Field Definition & Criteria |
|---|---|---|---|---|
| Issue Date Details | Capital Expenditure at Issue Date | EP45 | Optional | Capital Expenses at Issue Date (as opposed to repairs and maintenance) if identified in the Offering Circular. If missing data or if all consolidated, refer to Overview Document for inputs. |
| Issue Date Details | Net Cash Flow at Issue Date | EP46 | Optional | Net Operating Income less Capital Expenses at Issue Date. If missing data or if all consolidated, refer to Overview Document for inputs. |
| Issue Date Details | DSCR (NOI) at Issue Date | EP47 | Optional | The DSCR at Issue Date. Calculate by using the NOI at Issue Date and applying the Allocated % of Loan at Issue Date to the Periodic Principal and Interest at Issue Date. If multiple properties and not all information available refer to Overview Document for inputs. |
| Issue Date Details | Valuation at Issue Date | EP48 | Optional | The valuation of the properties securing the loan at Issue Date as described in the Offering Circular. If multiple properties sum the value or refer to Overview Document for inputs. |
| Issue Date Details | Date of Valuation at Issue Date | EP49 | Mandatory | The date the valuation was prepared for the values disclosed in the Offering Circular. For multiple properties, if several dates, enter latest or refer to Overview Document for inputs. |
| Issue Date Details | Vacant Possession Value at Date of Issue | EP50 | Optional | Vacant possession value at Date of Issue. If no data available refer to Overview Document for inputs. |
| Issue Date Details | Commercial Area | EP51 | Mandatory | The total net Commercial rentable area of the properties in square metres that serve as security for the loan per the most recent valuation report. For multiple properties, if not all information available, leave blank. |
| Issue Date Details | Residential Area | EP52 | Mandatory | Residential area of property in square meters. The total net Residential rentable area of the properties in square metres that serve as security for the loan per the most recent valuation report. For multiple properties, if not all information available, leave blank. |
| Issue Date Details | Blank Field | EP53 | Mandatory | |
| Issue Date Details | Blank Field | EP54 | Mandatory | |
| Most Recent YTD Financial Details | Current Allocated Loan Percentage | EP55 | Mandatory | Allocated loan % attributable to property at Loan Payment Date where there is more than one property securing the loan, the sum of all % should total 100%. This may be set out in the Loan Agreement, otherwise assign by valuation (NOI) or refer to Overview Document for inputs. |
| Most Recent YTD Financial Details | Current Allocated Ending Loan Amount | EP56 | Mandatory | Apply the Current Allocated % to the Actual Balance outstanding on the Loan. |
| Most Recent YTD Financial Details | Most Recent Financial As of Start Date | EP57 | Mandatory | The first day of the financials used for the most recent financial operating statement (e.g. Monthly, Quarterly, Year to Date or Trailing 12 months). If multiple properties and all the same date, print date. If missing any refer to Overview Document for inputs. |
| Most Recent YTD Financial Details | Most Recent Financial As of End Date | EP58 | Mandatory | The end and date of the financials used for the most recent financial operating statement (e.g. Monthly, Quarterly, Year to Date or Trailing 12 months). If multiple properties and all the same date, print date. If missing any refer to Overview Document for inputs. |
| Most Recent YTD Financial Details | Last Month of Year used for Reporting Financials | EP59 | Mandatory | Enter the month that the financials for each year (most recent, preceding and second preceding) will end. Refer to Overview Document for inputs. |
| Most Recent YTD Financial Details | NOI / NCF Indicator | EP60 | Optional | Refer to the NOI/NCF Indicator Legend to describe which method is being used to calculate the Net Operating Income and Net Cash Flow used in these reports. Refer to Overview Document for inputs. |
| Most Recent YTD Financial Details | Most Recent Financial Indicator | EP61 | Mandatory | This field is used to describe the period for which the most recent financial data is reflected. TA=Trailing 12 months actual. TN=Trailing 12 months normalized, YA=Year to Date actual, YN=Year to Date normalized. Check Start & End Date applies to fields EL66 to EL83. If there are multiple properties that are all the same, print the value. If missing any values or they are not the same, use combination of statements covering the same period with the same value. |
| Most Recent YTD Financial Details | Most Recent Revenue | EP62 | Mandatory | Total revenues for the period covered by the most recent financial operating statement (e.g. Monthly, Quarterly, Year to Date or Trailing 12 months) for all the properties. If multiple properties then sum the revenue (should match figures for sum of properties in Property File for this loan). Refer to Overview Document for inputs. (If missing any of all received/consolidated, then populate using the DSCR Indicator Legend rule. May be normalised if required by the applicable servicing agreement.) |

CRE Finance Council Europe
European Reporting Investor Reporting Package
**"Property" File**
(Data Record Layout, Version 2.0) Cross Refrenced as "EP"

| Field Grouping | Field Names | Field Number | Field Requirement | Field Definition & Criteria |
|---|---|---|---|---|
| Most Recent YTD Financial Details | Most Recent Operating Expenses | EP63 | Mandatory | Total operating expenses for the period covered by the most recent financial operating statement (e.g. Monthly, Quarterly, Year to Date or Trailing 12 months) for all properties. These may include real estate taxes, insurance, management, utilities, maintenance and repairs and direct property costs to the landlord; capital expenditures and leasing commissions are excluded. If multiple properties exist, total the operating expenses of the underlying properties. If multiple properties exist and data is not available for all properties or if received/consolidated, refer to Overview Document for inputs. [refer to the DSCR Indicator Legend rule. May be normalised if required by the applicable servicing agreement.] |
| Most Recent YTD Financial Details | Most Recent Net Operating Income | EP64 | Mandatory | Total revenues less total operating expenses for the period covered by the most recent financial operating statement. If multiple properties exist and not all information available or consolidated refer to Overview Document for inputs. [refer to the DSCR Indicator Legend] |
| Most Recent YTD Financial Details | Most Recent Capital Expenditure | EP65 | Mandatory | Total Capital Expenditures (as opposed to repairs and maintenance) for the period covered by the most recent financial operating statement e.g. Monthly, Quarterly, Year to Date or Trailing 12 months) for all the properties. If multiple properties exist and data is not available for all properties or if received/consolidated, refer to Overview Document for inputs. [refer to the DSCR Indicator Legend rule. May be normalised if required by the applicable servicing agreement.] |
| Most Recent YTD Financial Details | Most Recent Net Cash Flow | EP66 | Mandatory | Total Net Operating Income less Capital Expenses for the period covered by the most recent financial operating statement. If multiple properties and not all information is available, refer to Overview Document for inputs. |
| Most Recent YTD Financial Details | Most Recent Debt Service Amount | EP67 | Mandatory | Total scheduled payments of principal and interest due during the period covered by the most recent financial operating statement (e.g. Monthly, Quarterly, Year to Date or Trailing 12 months). Refer to Overview Document for calculation. [Calculate by applying the EP55 (Current Allocated %) to the Most Recent Loan Debt Service amount in ELT2.] |
| Most Recent YTD Financial Details | Most Recent DSCR (NOI) | EP68 | Mandatory | Calculate the DSCR based on NOI for the period covered by the most recent financial operating statement (e.g. Monthly, Quarterly, Year to Date or Trailing 12 months). If multiple properties exist and not all information available, refer to Overview Document for inputs. |
| Most Recent YTD Financial Details | Blank Field | EP69 | | Blank Field |
| Most Recent YTD Financial Details | Blank Field | EP70 | | Blank Field |
| Most Recent YTD Financial Details | Contractual Annual Rental Income | EP71 | Mandatory | The contractual annual rental income derived from the most recent Borrower tenancy schedule. Refer to EP100 and Overview Document for inputs. |
| Most Recent YTD Financial Details | Blank Field | EP72 | | Blank Field |
| Most Recent YTD Financial Details | Blank Field | EP73 | | Blank Field |
| Preceding Fiscal Year Financial Details | Preceding Financial Reporting Year as of Date | EP74 | Optional | Refers to end date of financial period |
| Preceding Fiscal Year Financial Details | Preceding Financial Reporting Year Revenue | EP75 | Optional | Preceding Financial Reporting year revenue |
| Preceding Fiscal Year Financial Details | Preceding Financial Reporting Year Operating Expenses | EP76 | Optional | Preceding Financial Reporting year operating expenses |
| Preceding Fiscal Year Financial Details | Preceding Financial Reporting Year NOI | EP77 | Optional | Preceding Financial Reporting year NOI |
| Preceding Fiscal Year Financial Details | Preceding Financial Reporting Year Capital Expenditure | EP78 | Optional | Preceding Financial Reporting year Capital Expenses |

CRE Finance Council Europe
European Reporting Investor Reporting Package
**"Property" File**
(Data Record Layout, Version 2.0) Cross Refrenced as "EP"

| Field Grouping | Field Names | Field Number | Field Requirement | Field Definition & Criteria |
|---|---|---|---|---|
| Preceding Fiscal Year Financial Details | Preceding Financial Reporting Year NCF | EP79 | Optional | Preceding Financial Reporting year NCF |
| Preceding Fiscal Year Financial Details | Preceding Financial Reporting Year Debt Service Amount | EP80 | Optional | Preceding Financial Reporting Year Debt Service Amount |
| Preceding Fiscal Year Financial Details | Preceding Financial Reporting Year DSCR (NOI) | EP81 | Optional | Preceding Financial Reporting Year DSCR (NOI) |
| Preceding Fiscal Year Financial Details | Blank Field | EP82 | | |
| Preceding Fiscal Year Financial Details | Blank Field | EP83 | | |
| Preceding Fiscal Year Financial Details | Blank Field | EP84 | | |
| Preceding Fiscal Year Financial Details | Blank Field | EP85 | | |
| Preceding Fiscal Year Financial Details | Blank Field | EP86 | | |
| Second Preceding Fiscal Year Financial Details | Second Preceding Financial Reporting Year Financial As of Date | EP87 | Optional | Second preceding Financial Reporting year financial as of date |
| Second Preceding Fiscal Year Financial Details | Second Preceding Financial Reporting Year Revenue | EP88 | Optional | Second preceding Financial Reporting year revenue |
| Second Preceding Fiscal Year Financial Details | Second Preceding Financial Reporting Year Operating Expenses | EP89 | Optional | Second preceding Financial Reporting year operating expenses |
| Second Preceding Fiscal Year Financial Details | Second Preceding Financial Reporting Year NOI | EP90 | Optional | Second preceding Financial Reporting year NOI |
| Second Preceding Fiscal Year Financial Details | Second Preceding Financial Reporting Year Capital Expenditure | EP91 | Optional | Second Preceding Financial Reporting Year Capital Expenses |
| Second Preceding Fiscal Year Financial Details | Second Preceding Financial Reporting Year NCF | EP92 | Optional | Second preceding Financial Reporting year NCF |
| Second Preceding Fiscal Year Financial Details | Second Preceding Financial Reporting Year Debt Service Amount | EP93 | Optional | Second Preceding Financial Reporting Year Debt Service Amount |
| Second Preceding Fiscal Year Financial Details | Second Preceding Financial Reporting Year DSCR (NOI) | EP94 | Optional | Second Preceding Financial Reporting Year DSCR (NOI) |
| Second Preceding Fiscal Year Financial Details | Blank Field | EP95 | | |
| Second Preceding Fiscal Year Financial Details | Blank Field | EP96 | | |
| Second Preceding Fiscal Year Financial Details | Blank Field | EP97 | | |
| Second Preceding Fiscal Year Financial Details | Blank Field | EP98 | | |

CRE Finance Council Europe
European Reporting Investor Reporting Package
**"Property" File**
(Data Record Layout, Version 2.0) Cross Refrenced as "EP"

| Field Grouping | Field Names | Field Number | Field Requirement | Field Definition & Criteria |
|---|---|---|---|---|
| Second Preceding Fiscal Year Financial Details | Blank Field | EP99 | | |
| Occupancy Details | Occupancy Asof Date | EP100 | Mandatory | Date of most recently received rent roll/ tenancy schedule. Refer to Overview Document for inputs. Refer to Overview Document for inputs. [(for hospitality (hotels), and health care properties use average occupancy for the period for which the financial statements are reported).] |
| Occupancy Details | Physical Occupancy at Issue Date | EP101 | Mandatory | The most recent available percentage of rentable space actually occupied (ie where tenants are actually in occupation and not vacated). Should be derived from a rent roll or other document indicating occupancy consistent with most recent financial year information. If multiple properties, populate with weighted average, using the calculation [Current Allocated % (Prop) * Occupancy (Oper)] for each Property. If missing any or the information is not available, refer to Overview Document for inputs. |
| Occupancy Details | Most Recent Physical Occupancy | EP102 | Mandatory | The most recent available percentage of rentable space actually occupied (ie where tenants are actually in occupation and not vacated). Should be derived from a rent roll or other document indicating occupancy consistent with most recent financial year information. |
| Occupancy Details | Most Recent Economic Occupancy | EP103 | Optional | The most recent available percentage of rentable space with signed leases in place (tenants may not be in occupation but are paying rent). Should be derived from a rent roll or other document indicating occupancy consistent with most recent financial year information. |
| Occupancy Details | Available Tenant by Tenant Data | EP104 | Mandatory | Is the tenant information available on a tenant by tenant basis? If no data available refer to Overview Document for inputs. |
| Occupancy Details | Number of Tenants | EP105 | Optional | Number of tenants. This refers to the number of Tenant's NOT Tenancies. So if the same company has more than 1 lease in the same property this only counts as 1 tenant. If no data available refer to Overview Document for inputs. |
| Occupancy Details | Current Units as of Date | EP106 | Optional | Date of most recent update to current units. |
| Occupancy Details | Current Units | EP107 | Optional | For property type Multifamily Breakup (MFB) enter number of units left to be sold |
| Occupancy Details | Weighted Average Lease Terms | EP108 | Optional | Weighted average lease terms. If no data available refer to Overview Document for inputs. |
| Occupancy Details | Weighted Average Lease Terms (1st Break) | EP109 | Optional | Weighted average lease terms after all 1st Break options. If no data available refer to Overview Document for inputs. |
| Occupancy Details | Blank Field | EP110 | | |
| Top Three Tenant Details | % Income expiring 1-12 months | EP111 | Mandatory | Percentage of income expiring in 1 to 12 months from Occupancy as of Date (Field EP100). |
| Top Three Tenant Details | % Income expiring 13-24 months | EP112 | Mandatory | Percentage of income expiring in 13 to 24 months. |
| Top Three Tenant Details | % Income expiring 25-36 months | EP113 | Mandatory | Percentage of income expiring in 25 to 36 months. |
| Top Three Tenant Details | % Income expiring 37-48 months | EP114 | Mandatory | Percentage of income expiring in 37 to 48 months. |
| Top Three Tenant Details | % Income expiring 49+ months | EP115 | Mandatory | Percentage of income expiring in 49 or more months. |
| Top Three Tenant Details | Largest Tenant: by Income (Net) | EP116 | Mandatory | Name of largest current tenant by net rent. |
| Top Three Tenant Details | Date of Lease Expiration of Largest Tenant | EP117 | Mandatory | Expiration date of lease of largest current tenant (by net rent). |
| Top Three Tenant Details | Rent Payable by Largest Tenant | EP118 | Mandatory | Annual Rent payable by largest current tenant. |

**CRE Finance Council Europe**
**European Reporting Investor Reporting Package**
**"Property" File**
(Data Record Layout, Version 2.0) Cross Refrenced as "EP"

| Field Grouping | Field Names | Field Number | Field Requirement | Field Definition & Criteria |
|---|---|---|---|---|
| Top Three Tenant Details | 2nd Largest Tenant by Income (Net) | EP119 | Mandatory | Name of second largest current tenant (by net rent). |
| Top Three Tenant Details | Date of Lease Expiration of 2nd Largest Tenant | EP120 | Mandatory | Expiration date of lease of second largest current tenant (net annual rent). |
| Top Three Tenant Details | Rent Payable by 2nd Largest Tenant | EP121 | Mandatory | Rent Payable by second largest current tenant. |
| Top Three Tenant Details | 3rd Largest Tenant by Income (Net) | EP122 | Mandatory | Name of third largest current tenant  (by net rent). |
| Top Three Tenant Details | Date of Lease Expiration of 3rd Largest Tenant | EP123 | Mandatory | Expiration date of lease of third largest current tenant (net annual rent). |
| Top Three Tenant Details | Rent Payable by 3rd Largest Tenant | EP124 | Mandatory | Rent Payable by third largest current tenant. |
| Top Three Tenant Details | Rating of Largest Tenant | EP125 | Optional | Rating of largest tenant as of the Distribution Date |
| Top Three Tenant Details | Blank Field | EP126 | | |
| Top Three Tenant Details | Blank Field | EP127 | | |
| Top Three Tenant Details | Blank Field | EP128 | | |
| Top Three Tenant Details | Blank Field | EP129 | | |
| Foreclosure Details | Date Asset Expected to Be Resolved or Foreclosed | EP130 | Mandatory | Estimated date the Special Servicer expects resolution. If multiple properties, print latest date from the affiliated properties. If in foreclosure = Expected Date of Foreclosure and if Property Possession = Expected Sale Date. |
| Foreclosure Details | Possession Proceedings Start Date | EP131 | Mandatory | The date on which foreclosure proceedings or alternative enforcement procedures were initiated against or agreed by the borrower. |
| Foreclosure Details | Date of Receivership | EP132 | Mandatory | The date on which title to (or an alternative form of effective control and ability to dispose of) the collateral property were obtained. |
| Foreclosure Details | Blank Field | EP133 | | |
| Foreclosure Details | Blank Field | EP134 | | |
| Foreclosure Details | Blank Field | EP135 | | |
| Foreclosure Details | Blank Field | EP136 | | |
| Foreclosure Details | Blank Field | EP137 | | |

**CRE Finance Council Europe**
**European Reporting Investor Reporting Package**
**"Bond Level" File**
(Data Record Layout, Version 2.0) Cross Referenced as "EB"

| Field Grouping | Field Names | Field Number | Field Requirement | Field Definition & Criteria |
|---|---|---|---|---|
| General | Transaction_Pool Identifier | EB1 | Mandatory | The unique transaction or pool identification string. Transaction name |
| General | Distribution Date | EB2 | Mandatory | Note interest and principal payment date corresponding to data within file. |
| General | Record Date | EB3 | Mandatory | Date note class must be held as of to be considered holder of record |
| General | Class Name / Class Identifier | EB4 | Mandatory | Note class / tranche name or identifier |
| General | CUSIP (Rule 144A) | EB5 | Mandatory | The security identification code assigned to each note class or tranche pursuant to standards established by the Committee on Uniform Security Identification Procedures number for Rule 144A requirments or other securities code established by an exchange or other entity |
| General | International Securities Identification Number | EB6 | Mandatory | The security identification code assigned to each note class or tranche pursuant to standards established by the International Standards Organisation (ISIN) or other securities code established by an exchange or other entity |
| General | Common Code (Rule 144A) | EB7 | Mandatory | Nine-digit identification code issued for each note class or tranche jointly by CEDEL and Euroclear |
| General | International Securities Identification Number (Reg. S) | EB8 | Mandatory | The security identification code assigned to each note class or tranche pursuant to standards established by the International Standards Organisation (ISIN) for Regulation S requirments or other securities code established by an exchange or other entity |
| General | Common Code (Reg. S) | EB9 | Mandatory | The security identification code assigned to each note class or tranche pursuant to standards established by the Committee on Uniform Security Identification Procedures number for Regulation S requirments or other securities code established by an exchange or other entity |
| General | Issuance Date | EB10 | Mandatory | Date of note issuance |

**CRE Finance Council Europe**
**European Reporting Investor Reporting Package**
**"Bond Level" File**
(Data Record Layout, Version 2.0) Cross Referenced as "EB"

| Field Grouping | Field Names | Field Number | Field Requirement | Field Definition & Criteria |
|---|---|---|---|---|
| General | Legal Maturity Date | EB11 | Mandatory | The date which anote class specific or tranche of must be repaid in order not to be in default |
| General | Currency | EB12 | Mandatory | Type of currency in which the note class or tranche monetary value is expressed. Please utilise the relevent coding within the "Currency Legend" located in the Data File Legends. |
| General | Blank Field | EB13 | | |
| Principal | Original Principal Balance | EB14 | Mandatory | The original principal balance of the specific note class or tranche at the issuance date |
| Principal | Notional Flag | EB15 | Mandatory | "Y" for Notional, "N" if this note class or tranche is interest only i.e. an IO strip |
| Principal | Beginning Principal Balance | EB16 | Mandatory | The outstanding principal balance of the note class or tranche at the beginning of the current period. |
| Principal | Scheduled Principal | EB17 | Mandatory | The scheduled principal paid to the note class or tranche during the period. |
| Principal | Unscheduled Principal | EB18 | Mandatory | The unscheduled principal paid to the note class or tranche during the period. |
| Principal | Total Principal Distribution | EB19 | Mandatory | The total principal (scheduled and unscheduled) paid to the note class or tranche during the period. |
| Principal | Amortisation Type | EB20 | Mandatory | The amortisation method in which the note class or tranche is paid periodically. Please utilise the relevant coding within the "Amortisation Type Code Legend" located in the Data File Legends. |
| Principal | Date Interest Only Period Ends | EB21 | Mandatory | Length of interest only period |
| Principal | Capitalised Interest | EB22 | Mandatory | Any interest added to the class balance including negative amortisation |
| Principal | Principal Loss | EB23 | Mandatory | The total principal loss for the reporting period |

CRE Finance Council Europe
European Reporting Investor Reporting Package
**"Bond Level" File**
(Data Record Layout, Version 2.0) Cross Referenced as "EB"

| Field Grouping | Field Names | Field Number | Field Requirement | Field Definition & Criteria |
|---|---|---|---|---|
| Principal | Cumulative Principal Losses | EB24 | Mandatory | Principal losses allocated cumulative-to-date |
| Principal | Ending Principal Balance | EB25 | Mandatory | The outstanding principal balance of the note class or tranche at the end of the current period. |
| Principal | Payment Note factor | EB26 | Mandatory | Principal paid on the note class or tranche in the reporting period as a fraction of the note or tranche original (initial) balance (0<x<1), up to 5 decimal points. |
| Principal | Ending Note factor | EB27 | Mandatory | Ending note class or tranche principal after the payments of the current reporting period as a fraction of the note or tranche original (initial) balance (0<x<1), up to 5 decimal points. |
| Principal | Next Note Payment Date | EB28 | Mandatory | The next period note class or tranche payment/distribution date. |
| Principal | Blank Field | EB29 | | |
| Interest | Index Rate Type | EB30 | Mandatory | The base reference interest index as defined in the offering document applicable to the specific note class or tranche. Please utilise the relevant coding within the " Index Code Legend " located in the Data File Legends. |
| Interest | Current Index Rate | EB31 | Mandatory | The current value of the index rate applied to the specific note class or tranche during the current accrual period, to a minimum of 5 decimal places. |
| Interest | Margin Note Rate | EB32 | Mandatory | The amortisation method in which the note class or tranche is paid periodically. Please utilise the relevant coding within the "Amortisation Type Code Legend" located in the Data File Legends. |
| Interest | Accrual Method | EB33 | Mandatory | The accrual method in which the note class or tranche is calculated periodically. Please utilise the relevant coding within the "Accrual Method Legend" located in the Data File Legends. |
| Interest | Current Accrual Days | EB34 | Mandatory | The number of accrual days applicable to the calculation of current period remittance interest |
| Interest | Interest Accrued | EB35 | Mandatory | The amount of accrued interest |
| Interest | Step Up / Step Down Dates | EB36 | Optional | The applicable dates of any step up or step down in interest rate |

CRE Finance Council Europe
European Reporting Investor Reporting Package
**"Bond Level" File**
(Data Record Layout, Version 2.0) Cross Referenced as "EB"

| Field Grouping | Field Names | Field Number | Field Requirement | Field Definition & Criteria |
|---|---|---|---|---|
| Interest | Step Up / Step Down Formula | EB37 | Optional | The details of the applicable step up/step down |
| Interest | Available Funds Cap Applicable | EB38 | Mandatory | Does the Note class benefit an Available Funds Cap (AFC) mechanism? Yes (Y) or No (N) |
| Interest | Prepayment Penalty Allocation | EB39 | Optional | Amount of prepayment penalties allocated to this Class |
| Interest | Cumulative Prepayment Penalty Allocation | EB40 | Optional | Total amount of prepayment penalties allocated to date |
| Interest | Yield Maintenance Allocation | EB41 | Optional | Amount of yield maintenance penalties allocated to this class |
| Interest | Cumulative Yield Maintenance Allocation | EB42 | Optional | Total amount of yield maintenance penalties allocated to date |
| Interest | Prepayment Interest Shortfall | EB43 | Optional | Interest adjustments for PPIS for this class |
| Interest | Appraisal Reduction Amount | EB44 | Mandatory | Current appraisal reduction allocated to this class |
| Interest | Cumulative Appraisal Reduction | EB45 | Mandatory | Total cumulative appraisal reduction allocated |
| Interest | Other Interest Distribution | EB46 | Mandatory | Other specific additions to interest |
| Interest | Current Interest Shortfall | EB47 | Mandatory | Interest shortfall amount for this reporting period for this class |
| Interest | Cumulative Interest Shortfall | EB48 | Mandatory | Cumulative Interest Shortfall to date |
| Interest | Total Interest Distribution | EB49 | Mandatory | The total interest payment made |

**CRE Finance Council Europe**
**European Reporting Investor Reporting Package**
**"Bond Level" File**
(Data Record Layout, Version 2.0) Cross Referenced as "EB"

| Field Grouping | Field Names | Field Number | Field Requirement | Field Definition & Criteria |
|---|---|---|---|---|
| Interest | Beginning Unpaid Interest Balance | EB50 | Mandatory | Outstanding interest shortfall at the beginning of the current period |
| Interest | Short-Term Unpaid Interest | EB51 | Mandatory | Any interest deferred in the current period and payable on the next Payment Date |
| Interest | Long-Term Unpaid Interest | EB52 | Mandatory | Any interest deferred in the current period and payable on the Maturity Date |
| Interest | Ending Unpaid Interest Balance | EB53 | Optional | Outstanding interest shortfall at the end of the current period |
| Interest | Blank Field | EB54 | | Blank Field |
| Interest | Available Funds Cap Trigger Event | EB55 | Mandatory | Has an Available Funds Cap (AFC) event been triggered? Yes (Y) or No (N) |
| Interest | Next Period Index Rate | EB56 | Mandatory | The next period value of the Index rate |
| Interest | Next Index Reset Date | EB57 | Mandatory | The next period Index Rate reset date |
| Bond Ratings | Fitch - Original Rating | EB58 | Mandatory | Original Fitch rating (includes original Duff and Phelps ratings) |
| Bond Ratings | Fitch - Most Recent Rating | EB59 | Mandatory | Current Fitch rating |
| Bond Ratings | Fitch - Date of Recent rating from Rating Agency | EB60 | Mandatory | This represents the latest date that Fitch re-affirmed the rating |
| Bond Ratings | Moody's - Original Rating | EB61 | Mandatory | Original Moody's rating |

593

CRE Finance Council Europe
European Reporting Investor Reporting Package
**"Bond Level" File**
(Data Record Layout, Version 2.0) Cross Referenced as "EB"

| Field Grouping | Field Names | Field Number | Field Requirement | Field Definition & Criteria |
|---|---|---|---|---|
| Bond Ratings | Moody's - Most Recent Rating | EB62 | Mandatory | Current Moody's rating |
| Bond Ratings | Moody's - Date of Recent Rating from Rating Agency | EB63 | Mandatory | This represents the latest date that Moody's re-affirmed the rating |
| Bond Ratings | Standard and Poors - Original Rating | EB64 | Mandatory | Original S&P rating |
| Bond Ratings | Standard and Poors - Most Recent Rating | EB65 | Mandatory | Current S&P rating |
| Bond Ratings | Standard and Poors - Date of Recent Rating from Rating Agency | EB66 | Mandatory | This represents the latest date that Standard and Poors re-affirmed the rating |
| Liquidity Facility | Liquidity Facility - Beginning Balance | EB67 | Mandatory | The beginning balance of the liquidity facility.  If no data available refer to Taxonomy for inputs. |
| Liquidity Facility | Adjustments To The Liquidity Facility | EB68 | Mandatory | Any adjustments to the liquidity facility.  If no data available refer to Taxonomy for inputs. |
| Liquidity Facility | Drawdowns On The Liquidity Facility | EB69 | Mandatory | Amount of drawdown on the liquidity facility.  If no data available refer to Taxonomy for inputs. |
| Liquidity Facility | Repayments To The Liquidity Facility | EB70 | Mandatory | Repayment amounts to the liquidity facility.  If no data available refer to Taxonomy for inputs. |
| Liquidity Facility | Closing Liquidity Facility Balance | EB71 | Mandatory | The closing balance.  If no data available refer to Taxonomy for inputs. |

594

# Glossary

## A

**A Lender or A Loan Holder or A Note Holder**
  The Lender which holds the A Loan in an AB Structure.

**A Loan** or **A Note**
  The senior tranche in an AB Structure typically securitised or placed within a CMBS.

**A Loan Holder**
  See A Lender.

**A Note**
  See A Loan.

**A Note Holder**
  See A Lender.

**AAOIFI**
  Accounting and Auditing Organisation for Islamic Financial Institutions.

**ABCDS**
  Credit Derivatives referencing CMBS, MBS, ABS or CDO Securities. ABCDS are typically drafted using the CPS Template or the PAUG Template.

**AB Structure**
  A senior-subordinate debt structure whereby the ownership of a single mortgage loan is tranched into one or more senior tranches and one or more subordinate tranches.

**ABS**
  See Asset Backed Securitisation/Securities.

**Abandonment**
  The voluntary relinquishment of a property or an interest in a property where there is no intention of resuming possession of the property or of keeping rights therein.

**Acceleration**
  The process whereby a Loan is declared due and payable prior to its scheduled repayment date, usually following the occurrence of an Event of Default.

**Accounting Records**
  The manual or computerised records of assets and liabilities, monetary transactions, various journals, ledgers, and supporting documents (such as agreements, cheques, invoices and vouchers), which certain organisations are required to keep for a certain number of years.

**Accrued Interest**

Interest charged or due on a loan which is unpaid. This is often added to the outstanding principal balance and must be paid before any reduction in the principal balance is allowed.

**Accrued Rate**

The rate at which interest is charged or is due on a loan.

**Adjustable Rate Mortgage**

A mortgage loan whereby the interest rate changes on specific dates.

**Administration**

The procedure under the Insolvency Act 1986 where a company may be reorganised or its assets realised under the protection of a statutory moratorium. At the end of the administration, the company will usually have been restructured or the business and/or assets will have been sold by the Administrator. Administration can be commenced by obtaining a court order or the company, its directors or the holder of a Qualifying Floating Charge may use the out-of-court appointment route.

**Administration Rate**

The annual servicing fee as a percentage of the outstanding principal balance of each loan.

**Administrative Receivership**

The remedy by which a secured Creditor may realise assets subject to its Security. Creditors with a Floating Charge (created prior to 15 September 2003) over the whole (or substantially the whole) of the assets of the company can appoint an administrative receiver. For Floating Charges created on or after 15 September 2003, Administrative Receivership is only available in a limited number of exceptional circumstances. The holder of a Qualifying Floating Charge created on or after 15 September 2003 can appoint an Administrator.

**Administrator**

An insolvency practitioner appointed by the court or by a company, its directors or the holder of a Qualifying Floating Charge using the out-of-court appointment route, to carry out the Administration. An Administrator is given wide powers to manage the company's affairs, business and property and at the end of the Administration the company is usually either returned to the directors or liquidated.

**ADR**

See American Depository Receipts.

**Advance**

In the context of a Mortgage Loan, an advance made by a Lender to a Borrower. In the context of a CMBS transaction, a payment by the Special Servicer (in respect of Non-Performing Loans) or the Master Servicer (in respect of Performing Loans) so that payments due on the CMBS can continue as scheduled.

**Advances**

Payments by the Special Servicer (in respect of delinquent loans) or the Master Servicer (in respect of performing loans) so that note payments can continue as scheduled. These can be required for a variety of payments alongside principal and interest payments (for example taxes and insurance) but do not include fees which the trustee or an officer of the trustee deems non-recoverable.

**Adverse Selection**

The process by which the risk profile of an asset pool is assumed to worsen over time due to a presumption that more creditworthy borrowers are more likely to prepay their loans resulting over time in less creditworthy borrowers predominating.

**Advisory Committee**

A committee consisting of representatives of a private equity fund's larger investors established to review and approve conflict items and certain major decisions relating to the fund.

**Agent**

See Facility Agent.

**Aggregation Risk**

The risk assumed while mortgages are being warehoused during the process of pooling them for ultimate securitisation. The mortgage holder faces the risk that the value of the mortgages will decline before the securitisation can be executed due to factors such as adverse interest rate movements or credit losses.

**AIF**

See Authorised Investment Funds.

**AIM**

The Alternate Investment Market of the London Stock Exchange.

**All in Cost**

The total cost of a securitisation to the issuer or sponsor (including the interest rate paid to investors' underwriting expenses and various other expenses such as legal and documentation fees) amortised over the expected average life of the issue. This is often quoted in basis points to indicate what would have been added to the yield had these expenses not been incurred in the creation of the security.

**Allocated Percentage**

The proportion of the principal amount of a mortgage loan secured by multiple properties which is associated with each individual property. The proportion is usually calculated by dividing the net operating income or net cash flow produced by the one property by the cumulative net operating income or net cash flow produced by all of the properties that secure the loan. Consequently the sum of all of the allocated percentages should be 100 per cent.

**Allocation of Realised CMBS Losses**

A CMBS provision that defines how realised losses will be allocated to each class of certificate holders.

**A Loan**

The senior tranche in an AB Structure.

**Al-Musharaka**

An Islamic financing method derived from a partnership contract in which a bank participates with one or more clients.

**Alpha**

The return delivered when the manager uses skill to out-perform the market competition at the relevant risk level.

**Al-Sharika**

An Islamic finance term meaning a partnership for profit.

**Alternative A Loan**

A first ranking residential mortgage loan that generally conforms to traditional prime credit guidelines, although the LTV ratio, loan documentation, occupancy status, property type, or other factors cause the loan not to qualify under standard underwriting programs. Less than full documentation is typically the reason for classifying a loan as Alternative A.

**American Depository Receipts**

A mechanism designed to facilitate trading in shares of non-US companies in the US stock markets. The main purpose is to create an instrument which can easily be settled through US stock market clearing systems.

**Amortisation**

The scheduled repayment of debt in regular instalments over a period of time until repaid in full. For non-scheduled repayment, see Prepayment.

**Amortisation Polled**

A period during which the outstanding balance of any related securities of a transaction are partially repaid. This may follow the revolving period of a transaction.

**Anchor Tenant(s)**

One or more large shops or supermarkets introduced to a shopping centre in key positions to attract shoppers into the centre in order to encourage other retailers to Lease units.

**Annual Payment Cap**

In relation to an adjustable rate mortgage loan, the maximum percentage in any one year by which the due payments of principal and interest can be increased.

**Annualised Net Rents**

In any year, the sum of all gross rent proceeds received by a Landlord plus, where any rent reviews are outstanding, the estimated increase in gross rents (as determined by external valuers) for that year, less any ground rents payable under the head Leases.

**A Notes**

The most senior tranche of an ABS or MBS issue. These rank senior to other tranches both in priority of repayment of principal and credit terms. A Notes are rated as Investment Grade and are thus appropriate for regulated institutional investors.

**Appraisal**

The assessment of the likely future performance of an investment, which can be used to determine value or to assess risk. In the context of a US real estate financing, a term used to mean a Valuation.

**Appraisal Reduction**

Following certain events based on loan delinquency, an appraisal will be performed to determine if the property value justifies any further advances by the Servicer. If the value is reduced below the loan balance plus authorised advances, the Servicer will stop or reduce principal and interest payments on the loan to the Trustee. The Trustee will then reduce principal and interest payments to the certificate holders in order of their priority, beginning with the first-loss security.

**Arbitrage**

The simultaneous purchase and sale of an asset in order to profit from a difference in its price, usually on different exchanges or market-places. An example of this is where a domestic stock also trades on a foreign exchange in another country, where its price has not adjusted in line with the exchange rate. A trader purchases the stock where it is undervalued and short sells the stock where it is overvalued, thus profiting from the difference.

**Arbitrage CDO**

A CDO transaction which is based on assets the aggregate yield of which is less than the aggregate yield for which the securities issued in connection with the transaction can be sold or funded.

**AREA**

The Asian Real Estate Association.

**Arrangement Fee**

The fee payable by a Borrower to the Arranger of a Loan.

**Arranger**

The bank which arranges a Loan involving more than one Lender.

**Asking Rent**

A prospective rent offered by the landlord to a prospective tenant. The actual rent paid will often be less than this following negotiations and concessions.

**Asset-Backed Securities (ABS)**

Bonds or notes collateralised (or "backed") by a specific pool of financial assets. Such financial assets will generally have predictable income flows (for example credit card receivables or vehicle loans) and are originated by banks and other credit providers.

**Asset-Backed Commercial Paper**

A short-term investment vehicle with a maturity that is typically between 90 and 180 days issued by a bank or other financial institution. The notes are backed by physical assets and used for short-term financing needs.

**Asset-Independent Approach**

An approach to rating synthetic securities which is not based on a credit evaluation of the SPE's assets. Instead the credit rating is in accordance with the creditworthiness of the swap counterparty or its guarantor.

**Asset Liquidity**

The quality of a real estate asset assessed in terms of the ease with which ownership and/or the financial structure of the asset can be changed.

**Asset Manager**

An entity appointed by a real property holding vehicle to provide investment advisory services and/or discretionary investment management services in respect of real property or a beneficial interest in real property held by such vehicle. The services of the asset manager will be particularly necessary where the holding vehicle is a SPV with independent directors unfamiliar with the management of real property. The regulatory status of the manager can differ depending on whether the manager makes investment decisions on behalf of the vehicle, and therefore provides discretionary investment management services, or the manager does not make investment decisions on behalf of the vehicle, and therefore provides only investment advisory services. See also Investment Manager and Property Manager.

**Asset Originator**

The party that has originated an asset or group of assets by extending credit to one or more creditors.

**Asset Protection Scheme**

A UK Government scheme announced in June 2009 to enable the UK Government to provide participating institutions with protection against future credit losses on defined portfolios of assets in exchange for a fee.

**Asset Reliability**

The quality of a real estate asset assessed in terms of criteria relating to ownership and/or use.

**Assignment**

The transfer of an interest, right, claim or property from one party to another.

**Attachment**

The point in time at which a Lender's Security is deemed to attach to the asset in question. Attachment occurs, in the case of a legal Mortgage, when legal title is conveyed to the Mortgagee and, in the case of a charge or equitable Mortgage, when the Security interest is created.

**Attribution Analysis**

The method for explaining returns on the basis of stock selection, sector allocation, active management and target style, such as core real estate investment, core plus real estate investment or opportunistic.

**Ausbietungsgarantie**

A German term for a guarantee from a secured lender to a bidder to release its security if a reserve price is met.

**Authorised Investment Funds (AIF)**

Tax-exempt unlisted UK funds.

**Authorised Unit Trust**

A UK based unit trust that has been authorised by the FSA to market its units to the general public (often referred to as retail investors). See also Unauthorised Unit Trust.

**Automated Valuation Models or AVMs**

Computer based valuation packages, designed to provide a basic valuation of assets based on standard information inputted into the program. They are used mainly for large scale valuations, such as residential apartment blocks.

**Available Funds**

All funds available or collected from the borrower or borrowers (for example principal and interest payments, prepayments) to make payment obligations under a loan.

**Available Funds Cap**

A ceiling applied to the amount of interest payable to noteholders being the extent of interest accrued on a pool of loans.

**Average Life**

A measure of the anticipated life span of an investment based on the average length of time required before all principal invested in repaid.

**AVM**

See Automated Valuation Models.

## B

**B Lender** or **B Loan Holder** or **B Note Holder**

The Lender which holds the B Loan in an AB Structure.

**B Loan** or **B Note**

The subordinate tranche in an AB Structure, held outside a CMBS, but can be held in a CRE CDO.

**B Loan Holder**

See B Lender.

**B Note**

See B Loan.

**B Note Holder**

See B Lender.

**B Piece**

The most subordinated tranche in a CMBS issuance and represents the First Loss Piece. These are often confused with B Loan.

**B Piece Holder**

The holder of a B Piece. The term is often confused with B Lender.

**Backstop Facility**

A facility provided by a highly rated entity which can be drawn on should the entity with the primary obligation to make the payment be unable to do so.

**Balance Sheet**

A condensed statement that shows the financial position of an entity on a specified date (usually the last day of an accounting period) and will, amongst other things, contain details as to the assets and liabilities of the entity. It is often part of the Accounting Records.

**Balance-Sheet CDO**

A CDO transaction in which the sponsor securitises assets which it already owns.

**Balance Sheet Lender**

A bank or other financial institution that originates Loans for the purpose of holding those Loans on its balance sheet until such time as they are repaid. By comparison, a bank may originate Loans for the purpose of selling those Loans into a CMBS transaction via the OTD model and therefore removing such Loans from its balance sheet.

**Balloon Loan**

A Loan that requires the Borrower to make relatively small principal and/or interest repayments during the life of the Loan and a much larger principal repayment at maturity. The final payment is often referred to as the balloon repayment.

**Bank for International Settlements (BIS)**

An international bank based in Basel, Switzerland, which monitors and collects data on international banking activity and circulates rules concerning international bank regulation.

**Bankruptcy-Remote**

A description of an entity which is protected from or is unlikely to be the subject of insolvency, bankruptcy or similar proceedings from third party Creditors. A Bankruptcy Remote entity is typically used in Securitisation and many commercial Mortgage Loan transactions to provide comfort to the transaction parties that the credit risk of the Bankruptcy Remote entity is isolated.

**Basel I, II, III**

Basel Accords are recommendations on banking laws and regulations issued by the Basel Committee on Banking Supervision. Basel guidelines aim to provide the national regulators with a set of requirements to ensure that banks have adequate capital for the risk they expose themselves to through their lending and investment practices. The number (I, II, III) refers to revised version of the Basel Accords.

**Basel I** or **Basel Accord**

A set of international banking regulations introduced in 1988 by the Basel Committee, which set out the minimum capital requirements of financial institutions with the goal of minimising credit risk.

**Basel II**

A revision of Basel I designed to make the framework more risk sensitive and representative of modern banks' risk management practices. Basel II was implemented in the European Union via the Capital Requirements Directive (Directive 2006/48/EC and Directive 2006/49/EC).

**Basel III**

A revision of Basel II which is designed to strengthen both capital requirements and introduce new regulatory requirements on both liquidity and bank leverage.

**Basel Committee**

The Basel Committee on Banking Supervision. The organisation which carries out consultation and aims to develop capital requirements which reflect the risks faced by the banking industry.

**Basis Point (bp)**

One-hundredth of one percentage point. One basis point is the smallest measure used to quote yields on bills, notes and bonds.

**Basis Risk**

The risk that payments received from the underlying mortgage loans do not match the necessary payments out to bondholders. This arises from discrepancy between the indices to which the mortgage and the bonds are linked. For example, if mortgages are at fixed rates but bonds are at floating rates the bonds could accrue interest at a higher rate than the underlying mortgage loans. The resulting shortfall is known as the basis risk shortfall.

**BBA**

See British Banking Association.

**BCO**

British Council for Offices. An organisation which researches, develops and communicates best practice in all aspects of the office sector.

**Beta**

The return delivered when the manager exposes the client's capital to the market taking a particular amount of market risk.

**Bifurcation**

The process of splitting a loan into a senior and a junior tranche.

**BIPRU**

The FSA's Prudential Sourcebook for Banks, Building Societies and Investment Firms.

**BIS**

See Bank for International Settlements.

**Blind-Pool Funds**

The assets of Private Equity Real Estate Funds or other investment vehicles which are not determined and/or communicated to investors at the time of investment.

**Blockers**

Entities used to block a certain action (such as certain tax effects) from flowing from a fund through to particular investors (often special types of feeders) or another fund as a whole (often special subsidiary entities).

**Boilerplate**

The collective name given to provisions, often of a standard nature, which are typically included in most agreements and which do not relate to the substantive provisions of an agreement. Governing law, assignment, notices and amendment provisions are examples of boilerplate clauses.

**Bond**

A certificate of debt issued by a government or corporate entity promising payment of the original investment plus interest by a specified future date. Bonds typically have a longer maturity than Notes. See also Notes and Securities.

**Borrower**

The entity borrowing money from a Lender.

**BPF**

British Property Federation. This is a membership organisation which represents the interests of those involved in property ownership and investment.

**B Loan**

The subordinate tranche in an AB Structure.

**B Notes**

A subordinated tranche in a CMBS structure.

**B Pieces**

Tranches of a CMBS issuance which are rated BB or lower and are therefore below investment grade.

**Bracket**

Categorising loans according to a sole shared attribute. For example in a term bracket all loans will have the same average life.

**Break Clause**

See Break Option.

**Break Option** or **Break Clause**

An option incorporated in a Lease, which allows the Landlord, Tenant, or in some cases, both, to terminate the Lease before its contractual expiry date. It is usually subject to a notice period and is sometimes subject to a premium payment in the case of a Tenant. In some Leases, there is a provision for a rolling break option, whereby it can be exercised at any point after a certain date, subject to notice.

**Bridge Finance**

Short-term interim funding made available to a Borrower until funding of a more permanent nature is put in place.

**British Banking Association or BBA**

An association for the United Kingdom banking and financial services sector that speaks for over 200 banking members from 60 countries on a full range of UK and international banking issues, which is responsible for, amongst other things, publishing the daily LIBOR rate.

**Broker's Opinion of Vaule (BOV)**

An assessment of what an asset will trade for in the market.

**Brownfield Site**

A site that has previously been developed and is available for redevelopment. Such sites may be contaminated.

**Building Society**

A financial institution, owned by its members, that offers banking and other financial services. Building Societies are authorised under the Building Societies Act 1986.

**Bull Run**

A sustained period of strong performance. This term may be applied to a market, a sector, or a single Security.

**Bullet Loan**
> A loan whereby principal is repaid in its entirety through a single payment at maturity.

**Buy To Let**
> Real estate that is purchased with the intention of letting to Tenants for profit.

# C

**Callable**
> A loan or securities over which the borrower has the option to require repayment ahead of schedule.

**Call Protection**
> Protection against the risk that loans will be prepaid early, or protection against prepayment risk.

**Capital Adequacy**
> The obligation on a regulated entity (such as a bank or building society) to maintain a certain minimum level of capital in proportion to the risk profile of its assets. Such regulated entities may be able to meet the capital adequacy requirement by securitising their assets and removing them from their balance sheet without recourse, thereby negating the obligation to maintain capital with respect to the securitised assets.

**Capital Allowances**
> One of several kinds of benefit available to an owner against income tax or Corporation Tax for capital expenditure on certain qualifying buildings.

**Capital Calls**
> Notifications by a private equity fund to its investors made at any time during the investment period (and often on a limited basis for certain specific items after the investment period) requiring the investors to make payments to the fund in lieu of their Capital Commitments.

**Capital Commitments**
> Contractual commitments to make a capital contribution to a private equity fund by the fund investors, which are drawn down through a series of Capital Calls, primarily during the investment period.

**Capital Gain**
> A gain that arises when an investment is sold at a higher price than originally paid.

**Capital Gains Tax** or **CGT**
> Tax payable on a Capital Gain.

**Capital Markets**
> A financial market in which long-term debt and equity Securities are bought and sold.

**Capital Requirements Directive (CRD)**

The CRD aligns European legislation with international standards on capital by implementing the Basel Accords in the European Union. CRD 2 and CRD 3 update and refine the CRD and strengthens the EU regulatory framework.

## Capitalisation

In a Loan context, the process of adding interest to the principal amount of the Loan rather than the interest being paid periodically during the term of the Loan. In a corporate context, see Market Capitalisation.

## Capitalisation Rate or Cap Rate

A measure of a property's value based on current performance and also a measure of investor's expectations. Calculated by dividing the net operating income for the year by the value of the property.

## Capped Floating-Rate Note

A floating rate note with an upper limit or cap on the coupon rate. This prevents the investor from benefiting from interest rate movements which would take the coupon above the cap.

## Carried Interest

An allocation of a private equity fund's profits made from the capital accounts of the fund's limited partners to the capital account of the fund's general partner or manager. Carried interest is often equal to 20% of the realised gains actually distributed to the investors. Carried interest may be calculated on a Portfolio-wide basis or on a modified deal-by-deal level.

## Cash Collateral

A reserve fund that can be accessed in the event of credit losses and subsequent claims by investors. A type of credit enhancement. The account in which the funds are held is the Cash Collateral Account (CCA) and lent to the issuer by a third party under a loan agreement.

## Cash Collateral Account

A bank account that serves to secure and service a loan. It is essentially a zero-balance account and no sums may be withdrawn.

## Cash Flow Note

A note which is not based on an interest rate but repaid periodically based on a portion of cash flow derived by the secured property.

## Cash Flow Waterfall

The order in which the cash flow available to an Issuer, after covering all expenses, is allocated to the debt service owed to holders of the various classes of issued securities.

## Cash-on-Cash return

A measure of the short term return on property investment calculated by dividing cash flow received from the property by the equity invested in the property.

## Cash-Out Refinance Mortgage Loan

A mortgage loan taken in order to refinance an existing mortgage loan in a situation where the amount of the new loan exceeds (by more than 1%) the amount required to cover repayment of the existing loan, closing costs and repayment of any outstanding subordinate mortgage loans. The borrower can put the additional cash to whatever use it pleases.

**Cash Trap**

A provision often seen in intercreditor agreements whereby all amounts that would be distributable to a junior lender commencing immediately on a payment default or borrower insolvency are held in escrow (trapped) pending the senior lender's decision to enforce or the junior leader's decision to cure the borrower default.

**Casualty**

Unexpected damage or destruction to a property.

**CBO**

See Collateralised Bond Obligation.

**CDO**

See Collateralised Debt Obligation.

**CDO²**

See Collateralised Debt Obligation Squared.

**CDS**

See Credit Default Swap.

**Cédulas**

Cédula hipotecaria (Spanish covered bonds) are notes issued by financial institutions which pay a fixed interest rate and which are guaranteed by mortgage loans granted by the issuing entity. Such cédula hipotecaria can only be issued by Spanish credit institutions (*entidades de crédito oficial*), Spanish savings banks (*cajas de ahorro*) or specialised companies formed with the sole object of, among other things, granting loans or mortgage guarantees (*sociedades de crédio hipotecario*).

**CGT**

See Capital Gains Tax.

**Centre of Main Interest (COMI)**

The term relevant with respect to insolvency. An entity's centre of main interests is generally (in an EU context) where the main insolvency proceedings against that entity will be taken.

**Certificate**

A formal certificate evidencing beneficial ownership in a trust fund. Owned by a certificate holder.

**Charge**

Security over a particular asset or class of assets that gives the chargee the right to have the particular asset or class of assets (and all proceeds from the sale of such asset or class of assets) appropriated to the discharge of the debt in question. A charge does not transfer legal ownership. It is merely an encumbrance on the asset.

**Cherry-Picking**

The practice of applying specific criteria to select assets from a portfolio; the opposite of a sample selected at random.

**Civil Law**

Legal systems (codified and uncodified) based mainly on concepts and principles of Roman law.

**Clawback**

A repayment by a private equity fund's general partner or manager of all or a portion of Carried Interest previously received from the fund to the extent required by the fund's investors to ensure that the Carried Interest is not paid on previous successful deals to protect investors against any losses sustained on any subsequent failed deals. A mechanism for investors to protect their capital and preferred return.

**Clean-Up Call**

An optional redemption of securities at a point when there is 15% or less of the original principal balance of the underlying collateral pool outstanding and the cost of servicing the remaining pool of assets has become uneconomic. The issuing SPE will sell the remaining assets (usually at par) to the senior or the originator/sponsor of the assets and use the proceeds to effect the redemption. The benefit to investors of such a redemption is that it provides assurance that they will not be left with a tiny, illiquid fraction of their original investment.

**Clearstream International**

A subsidiary of Deutsche Borse AG that provides clearing, settlement and custody services for stocks and bonds traded in European domestic and cross-border markets.

**Clearing House**

A financial institution that provides clearing, settlement and custody services for stocks and Bonds traded in domestic and cross-border markets. Clearstream International, Euroclear and the Depository Trust Company (DTC) are examples of clearing houses.

**Clearing System**

The trading system used for trading publicly traded Securities designed to promote world trade and market efficiency. Most international clearing transactions are administered by an international clearing house.

**CLO**

See Collateralised Loan Obligations.

**CLN**

See Credit-Linked Note.

**Close Company**

A company in which the directors control more than half the voting shares, or where such control is exercised by five or fewer people and their associates.

**Closed-Ended Fund**

A Real Estate Fund from which investors cannot demand to have their capital redeemed or paid back, and which are not normally open to new investors to subscribe for new units for cash other than when the fund is formally raising additional capital. Closed-ended funds are normally limited life structures, but the term 'closed-ended' means that a finite number of units will be in issue for long periods of time. Compare with Open-Ended Fund.

**CMBS**

See Commercial Mortgage Backed Securities/Securitisation.

**Co-Insurance**

The sharing of risk by insurer and insured or by two or more insurers each taking liability for an agreed proportion of the whole amount at risk either immediately or in sequential layers.

**Collar**

The lowest rate acceptable to a note purchaser or the lowest price acceptable to the issuer.

**Collateral**

Those assets belonging to a Borrower or Issuer which are secured in favour of the Lender or Noteholders, respectively. Should the Borrower or Issuer default on its obligations under the Loan Agreement or conditions of the Notes, the Lender or the Noteholders can apply the secured or pledged assets to make good any amounts owed to them (in the case of Securitisation, subject to any priority of payments).

**Collateralised Bond Obligation (CBO)**

A security backed by a pool of corporate bonds.

**Collateralised Debt Obligation (CDO)**

A security backed by a pool of various types of debt, which may include corporate bonds sold in the capital markets, loans made to corporations by institutional lenders and tranches of securitisations.

**Collateralised Debt Obligation Squared (CDO$^2$)**

A CDO backed by a Portfolio of Securities issued by other CDOs.

**Collateral Debt Security**

The underlying debt obligations (or Collateral) that comprise the Portfolio of a CDO or a CLO.

**Collateralised Loan Obligation (CLO)**

CLO can be used in two contexts. First, it can refer to the Debt Securities backed by a Portfolio of Loans made to corporations by institutional Lenders, usually commercial banks. Second, to the overall transaction by which the Securities are issued and sold in the Capital Markets.

**Collateralised Mortgage Obligation (CMO)**

A security backed by a pool of mortgage loans or some combination of residential mortgage loans and agency securities. CMO issuances usually involves multiple classes of securities with varying maturities and coupons.

**Collection Account**

The account into which (generally) all payments and collectables received on mortgages are deposited.

**Combined LTV Ratio**

An LTV ratio calculated in situations where a property secures more than one mortgage loan.

**Comfort Letter**

Either: (a) a letter from one party to an agreement to the other that certain actions which are not contemplated by the agreement will not taken; or (b) an independent auditor's letter providing assurance that information in the registration statement and prospectus is correct and that no material changes have occurred since its preparation. This does not positively state the information is correct, only that the accountants are not aware of anything to indicate it is not correct. This is therefore sometimes called a cold comfort letter.

**COMI**

See Centre of Main Interest.

**Commercial Mortgage Backed Securities or Commercial Mortgage Backed Securitisations (CMBS)**

The CMBS abbreviation is used in two contexts. The former refers to securities that are backed by one or more pools of mortgages secured by commercial real estate, such as shopping centres, industrial parks, office buildings and hotels. All principal and interest from the mortgages flow to the noteholders in a pre-determined sequence. The latter refers to the overall transaction by which the securities are issued and sold in the capital markets.

**CMBS 2.0**

A term used to describe the new self-imposed industry standards, and regulatory and legislative changes to the CMBS market.

**CMBS Noteholder Forum**

A method used by CMBS noteholders to identify and communication with each other, managed by a forum co-ordinatior

**Commercial Real Estate Collateralised Debt Obligations (CRE CDOs)**

CRE CDO can be used in two contexts. First, it can refer to Debt Securities that are backed by a Portfolio of Mortgage Loans, Securities, B Loans or other debt interests related to commercial real estate. Second, it can refer to the overall transaction by which the Securities are issued and sold in the Capital Markets.

**Commonhold**

A form of land ownership in England and Wales, established by the Commonhold and Leasehold Reform Act 2002. It combines Freehold ownership of a single property within a larger development, with membership of a limited company that will own and manage the common parts of the development. Although most likely to be used in relation to residential flats, Commonhold is also suitable for houses, mixed use and commercial developments.

**Commercial Paper (CP)**

Short-term promissory Notes with a maturity of generally less than 270 days and most commonly between 30 and 50 days or less.

**Commercial Real Estate Finance Council Europe**

A trade association which promotes the strength and liquidity of commercial real estate finance. Formerly the Commercial Mortgage Securities Association.

**Commingling Risk**

The risk that cash belonging to an issuing SPE is mixed with cash belonging to a third party (for example, the originator or Servicer) with the result that, should the third party become insolvent/bankrupt, such cash cannot be separately identified or such cash is frozen in the accounts of the third party.

**Company Voluntary Arrangement (CVA)**

A compromise or other arrangement with Creditors under the Insolvency Act 1986, which is implemented under the supervision of an insolvency practitioner (known as the nominee before the proposals are implemented, who then becomes known as the supervisor). The arrangement will be binding on Creditors if the relevant majorities vote in favour of the proposals at properly convened meetings of Creditors and Shareholders of the company. The arrangement does not affect the rights of secured or preferential Creditors unless they agree to the proposals. Small companies have an optional *moratorium* before any CVA is put into place.

**Compliance Certificate**

A certificate typically signed by a director of a Borrower confirming that the Borrower is in compliance with the financial covenants and certain other obligations set out in the Loan Agreement.

**Compulsory Purchase Order**

An order issued by the government, or local authority, which enables the local authority to compulsorily purchase land in order to enable development, whether it be for highways purposes, or for building construction.

**Concentration Risk**

A risk that a pool which is not particularly diverse will suffer disproportionately from certain economic or market developments or changes. Having a diverse pool of loans mitigates this risk.

**Concessions**

An incentive offered to attract and retain tenants whereby payments under a lease are reduced, most often through a rent free period. These make the calculation of net cash flow (and correspondingly debt service coverage ratios) difficult to calculate.

**Conciliateur**

French term for an insolvency administrator.

**Conditions Precedent**

Those conditions which must be satisfied before a Lender is prepared to advance funds to a Borrower. The conditions precedent required by a Lender will be listed in the Loan Agreement and include, amongst other things, board resolutions of the Obligors, valuations of the property and a legal report on title. Sometimes referred to as "closing conditions".

**Conduit**

The legal entity which provides the link between the lender(s) originating loans and the ultimate investor(s). The conduit purchases loans from third parties and once sufficient volume has been accumulated, pools these loans to sell in the CMBS market. In the

European CMBS market the pool is generally of less than twenty loans with a wide or narrow range of properties. On the other hand, in the US market the pool may consist of anything between 50 to 100 loans secured on a wide range of properties.

## Confirmation

A document that evidences the economics of a Derivative trade and governs the performance of the dealer and end user upon the occurrence of certain contemplated events that may occur during the term of the trade. A Confirmation may be either a short-form or long-form. The short form version is executed in connection with an existing ISDA Master Agreement and a long-form Confirmation is typically executed in anticipation of the dealer and counterparty entering into an ISDA Master Agreement, which is the best practice.

## Control Valuation Event or CVE

A term relevant to AB Structure as being the point in time when the value of the property serving as Collateral for the whole Loan has decreased to such an extent that the B Lender is not likely to get a meaningful economic recovery on their investment (i.e. repayment of the B Loan). Following the occurrence of a Control Valuation Event the relevant B Lender can no longer exercise its Cure Rights.

## Controlling Class

The class of Noteholders in a Securitisation that has the contractual right to control the occurrence of certain events, such as forced redemptions, following an Event of Default or certain tax related events. In CMBS transactions the Controlling Class is normally the most subordinate class of Notes, while in CDO transactions the Controlling Class is normally the most Senior Class of Notes. In order to address conflicts of interest among different parts of the capital structure, other classes or parties (including the Controlling Party) may have a right to vote on or to veto certain actions of or with respect to the issuing entity.

## Controlling Class Representative (CCR)

Appointed by the Controlling Class, the Controlling Class Representative has contractual consent or consultation rights in connection with the proposed actions of the Servicer/Special Servicer in connection with a serviced loan.

## Controlling Party

The party with the contractual right to approve and direct certain acts of the Servicer or Special Servicer. In the context of AB Structures, the Controlling Party is typically the holder of the B Loan pending the occurrence of a Control Valuation Event and thereafter the Controlling Class in a CMBS. See also Operating Advisor.

## Constant Prepayment Rate

The percentage of the outstanding principal which will theoretically be prepaid in one year, estimated based on a constant (rather than variable) rate of prepayment.

## Controlled Amortisation

A period that may follow the revolving period of a transaction, during which the outstanding balance of the related securities is partially repaid. A controlled amortisation period is usually 12 months in length.

**Core Real Estate Investments**

Property investments that have the following defining characteristics: they are substantially rented, they have an orderly Lease expiration schedule, they are of high quality and are from the four basic property types – offices, industrial, retail and multi-family. Core Real Estate Investments must also be well maintained in a major city, carry no more than 50% debt, have an internal rate of return of approximately 6-8%, have low roll-over and an investment structure with significant control.

**Core-Plus Real Estate Investments**

Property investments that are relatively safe but are riskier than Core Real Estate investments. Core-Plus Real Estate Investments generally have an internal rate of return from 8% to 11% and involve debt at 50% to 60% of the property's value.

**Corporate Guarantee**

A form of credit enhancement whereby the issuer or a third party provides a guarantee in respect of certain losses up to a specified sum. The guarantor will be subject to minimum rating requirements.

**Corporation Tax**

Tax payable by a company on its profits.

**Corrected Loan**

A loan which, after being transferred to the Special Servicer for handling has been corrected and is now reperforming.

**Cost of Funds**

The cost of borrowing money. For a Borrower, it is the effective rate it pays on its current debt, namely interest and fee charges. Cost of funds can be measured before and after tax however, because interest expense is deductible, the after-tax cost is seen most often.

**Counterparty**

A party to a Derivatives or Hedging contract that may be, in the case of a Derivatives trade, either the dealer or the end user and, in the case of Hedging transaction, the Hedge Counterparty.

**Covenant**

In a legal context, a promise to do or not to do something. In a financial context, the term used to describe the financial worth of a company and is normally ascertained by reference to trading figures or other financial assessments. In a contractual context, the term refers to the contractual obligations contained in a Lease or Loan Agreement. Contractual covenants can be positive (requiring the covenantor to take action) or negative (requiring the covenantor to refrain from taking action).

**Core Capital**

Core Capital or Tier 1 Capital is a term used to describe the capital adequacy of a bank and includes equity capital and disclosed reserves.

**Cost of Equity**

The return a company theoretically pays to its shareholders.

**Covered Bonds**

Debt Securities backed by a Portfolio of Mortgages or other public sector Loans. Covered Bonds are issued by banks and remain on the issuing bank's balance sheet and provide the holders of the Covered Bonds will full recourse to the assets of the originator. Covered Bonds can be contrasted to CMBS, which are off-balance sheet debt obligations entitling the holders of the CMBS recourse only to the assets securitised.

**CP**

See Commercial Paper.

**CPS Template**

The template for Credit Derivative Transaction on Asset Backed Security With Cash or Physical Settlement published by ISDA in 2005, as amended. This template adopts the Credit Derivatives Definitions to address trading of ABCDS in European markets.

**CRA Regulation**

See European Communities Regulation on Credit Rating Agencies.

**CRD**

See Capital Requirements Directive.

**CRD 2**

A 2007 European directive which makes changes to CRD by improving the quality of firms' capital by establishing a clear EU-wide criteria for assessing the eligibility of hybrid capital to be considered as part of a firm's overall capital, risk management of securities, supervision of cross-border banking groups and amending certain technical provisions of CRD to correct unintentional errors.

**CRD 3**

A 2009 European directive which makes further changes to CRD to complement CRD 2 which includes higher capitalisation requirements for re-securitisations, updating disclosure standards for securitisation exposures to increase market confidence and strengthening trading book capital requirements.

**Credit Committee**

The committee within a bank, building society or other financial institution that assesses the credit risk to the bank of it making a Loan to a Borrower. The credit committee ultimately approves the terms on which a Loan is made to that Borrower and the Security it requires from the Borrower.

**Credit Default Swap**

A credit default swap is a contract whereby the protection seller agrees to pay to the protection buyer the settlement amount should certain credit events occur. This gives protection to the protection buyer, in return for which the protection buyer will pay the protection seller a premium.

**Credit Derivatives**

Instruments used in the capital markets to re-allocate credit risk from one party to another, such as credit default swaps, total return swaps and credit-linked notes.

**Credit Derivatives Definitions**

The ISDA 2003 Credit Derivatives Definitions. These were published by ISDA in order to facilitate the trading of credit risk of operating companies with a large public float of Debt Securities.

**Credit Enhancement**

An instrument or mechanism which operates alongside the mortgage collateral to enhance the credit quality of the mortgage backed securities and thereby support the desired credit rating of the securities. Basically these are elements within the structure of a securitisation which are designed to ensure that investors do not suffer from decreases in the value of the underlying assets.

**Credit Enhancer**

A party that agrees to provide credit enhancement for a pool of assets by making payments, usually up to a specified amount, should the cash flow produced by the underlying pool of assets be less than the amounts contractually required due to defaults by the underlying obligors.

**Credit Guarantee Scheme**

A UK Government scheme launched in October 2008 and closed to new issuance in February 2010 that was intended to provide sufficient liquidity in the short term, make available new capital to UK banks and building societies to strengthen their resources, and ensure that the banking system has the funds necessary to maintain lending in the medium term.

**Credit-Linked Note**

A note, payment of which is dependant on a credit event occurring or credit measure existing with respect to a reference entity or pool of assets.

**Credit Rating Agency (CRA)**

See Rating Agency.

**Credit Risk**

The risk that the lender will be either (1) repaid less than the amount owed to it, (2) repaid over a longer period than originally agreed or, in the worst case, (3) not be repaid at all.

**Credit Support Annex (CSA)**

A document often entered into in connection with a Credit Derivative transaction that states the parties' duties to deliver and return Collateral as a method of credit protection for the parties to the Credit Derivative transaction.

**Credit Tenant**

A tenant which is rated as investment grade.

**Credit Tenant Lease**

A lease of part or all of a commercial property to a credit tenant.

**Credit Tenant Lease Loans**

Mortgage loan secured by commercial properties occupied by investment-grade credit tenants. The loans are underwritten and structured based on the anticipated cash flow from the leases rather than on the value of the underlying real estate.

**Creditor**

An entity to whom money is owned.

**Cross-Collateralisation**

A provision by which collateral for one mortgage also serves as collateral for other mortgage(s) in the structure. This is a technique for enhancing the protection provided to a lender which adds value to the structure and therefore is a form of credit enhancement. Generally seen in connection with commercial mortgage loans.

**Crystallisation**

The point in time following a default or similar event when a Floating Charge is converted into a Fixed Charge over the assets to which it attaches.

**CSA**

See Credit Support Annex.

**Cure Payments**

Payments made by a B Lender when exercising its Cure Rights. Cure Payments can comprise: (a) Prepayment of the A Loan in an amount necessary to ensure compliance with the underlying remediable default, together with all other related payments in respect of the A Loan which the Borrower would have had to make as a result of such Prepayment had the Borrower made the Prepayment itself; (b) placing on deposit or posting of Collateral or a Letter of Credit in an amount equal to any shortfall that triggered a remediable default; and (c) placing on deposit on behalf of the A Lenders in an amount equal to the Prepayment of the A Loan which would have been required to have been received from the Borrower to ensure that the Borrower could have remedied the remediable default.

**Cure Rights**

Rights given to a subordinated lender which enables it to cure certain remediable Loan level defaults within a certain time period and include, amongst others, the right to make Cure Payments.

**Current Delinquency Status**

The delinquency status of a loan as of the current date.

**Custodian**

A bank or other financial institution that holds Securities and other financial assets for safe custody and record keeping on behalf of investors. A Custodian will usually be required to hold Securities on behalf of those entities which are not participants in the clearing systems.

**Customary Laws**

Traditional common rule or practice that has become an intrinsic part of the accepted and expected conduct in a community, profession or trade and is treated as a legal requirement.

**Cut off date**

The date the underlying pool of assets which secures a CMBS issuance is identified, calculations are based on this before issuing the securities.

**CVA**

See Company Voluntary Arrangement.

**CVE**

See Control Valuation Event.

# D

**Dark Space**

Empty space in a property for which the tenant continues to pay rent. Tenants in large properties may exercise break rights in leases should any other tenant go dark.

**DCF**

See Discounted Cash Flow.

**Dealer**

An entity, usually a bank or broker, whose economic function is to make a market so that buyers and sellers can readily transact in that market.

**Debenture**

A document evidencing the indebtedness of one party to another and the terms and conditions governing the relationship between the creditor who lends funds to the debtor who in turn repays the principal amount lent to it with or without interest.

**Debenture (UK)**

An instrument executed by a Borrower as a deed in favour of a Lender, providing the Lender with Security over the whole or substantially the whole of the Borrower's assets and undertaking. A Debenture typically creates a Fixed Charge over the assets of the Borrower which are not disposed of in the ordinary course of business of the company and a Floating Charge over the rest of the company's undertaking and reserving to the Lender the power to appoint an Administrator or a Receiver with extensive authority to get in the assets, run the Borrower's business and dispose of the assets either piecemeal or as part of a sale of the business as a going concern.

**Debenture (US)**

A document evidencing the indebtedness of one party to another and the terms and conditions governing the relationship between the Creditor who lends funds to the Debtor who in turn repays the principal amount lent to it with or without interest.

**Debt Service Payments**

Payments which the borrower is required to make under the relevant credit agreement.

**Debt Securities**

Debt obligations issued in the form of a Bond or Note representing a promise from the Issuer to repay at some future date. In Securitisation transactions, Issuers will issue various classes of Debt Securities with varying risk and return profiles.

**Debtor**

An entity who owes money.

**Deed of Trust**

A US real estate Security instrument pursuant to which a grantor (the Borrower) grants a Lien on real property to the Trustee for the benefit of the beneficiary (the Lender) to secure a debt. A deed of trust usually also includes an assignment of Leases and rents and a Security interest in fixtures and personal property.

**Debt Service**

The scheduled payments on a loan, including principal, interest and other fees stipulated in the credit agreement.

**Debt Service Coverage Ratio (DSCR)**

The net cash flow generated by an income-generating property on an annual basis divided by the annual debt service payments required under the terms of the mortgage loan or loans entered into for the purpose of financing the property. This is generally expressed as a multiple and gives a measure of a property's ability to cover debt service payments. Should this ratio drop below 1.0, there will be insufficient cash flow from the property to cover debt payments.

**Default**

A violation of the terms and conditions set out in the relevant credit agreement.

**Default**

An event which with the passing of time or the giving of notice would constitute an Event of Default. Default is often used loosely to refer to an Event of Default.

**Defeasance**

The setting aside of cash or a portfolio of high-quality assets to cover the remaining interest and principal payments due with respect to a debt.

**Defective Title**

A title to land affected by a matter which leaves the ownership or use of the land open to challenge or otherwise unmarketable.

**Deferred Consideration**

A term used by practitioners to refer to consideration that will or may be payable sometime in the future rather than at completion. Deferred Consideration may be payable in a number of different ways including cash, loan notes and shares.

**Deferred Interest**

The amount of interest that is added to the principal balance of a debt obligation (whether a Loan or Bond) when the contractual terms of that debt obligation allow for a payment of interest to be made in an amount that is less than the scheduled amount of interest due.

**Deferred Maintenance Account**

An account set up by a borrower to cover the cost of any repairs or future maintenance of a property.

**Delinquency**

Failure to comply with a debt obligation by the specified due date.

**Demand Notes**

Short term loans or notes which include a provision that repayment can be demanded or the note called should the lender choose. Such notes often require all cash flows net of debt service to be applied to amortise a loan should the borrower fail to demonstrate progress towards refinancing. These can be fast pay whereby if the balloon payment of a balloon mortgage is not met, the borrower must apply excess cash flows to pay down the loan balance.

**Derivative**

A financial instrument whose value depends on the characteristics and value of an underlying asset, typically a commodity, Bond, Interest Rate, equity or currency.

**Determination Date**

The date of the month used as a set off date for calculations of the payments due on securities.

**Development**

The making of any material change in the use of any buildings or other land, not including internal alterations that do not materially affect its appearance.

**Development Construction Cost**

The total cost of construction of a project to completion, excluding site values and finance costs.

**Development Finance**

A Loan made to a Borrower to fund the Development Construction Costs in respect of a Development.

**Development Pipeline**

Typically the combination of a development programme, together with proposed schemes that are not yet included in the Development programme but are more likely to proceed than not.

**Direct Property Fund**

A fund that invests 100% in Direct Property Investment and holds no property shares, REITs, other equities or other indirect holdings.

**Direct Property Investment**

The acquisition of legal and/or beneficial title to real estate.

**Discounted Cash Flow or DCF**

A financial appraisal based on analysis of future income flow on an asset, allowing for a discount back to present day values.

**Discount Margin**

The difference between the price and the face value of a security.

**Discount to NAV**

The percentage difference between the Net Asset Value of the assets of the company (subject to certain adjustments for debt etc) and the market capitalisation of the company.

**Distressed Mortgage Loan**

Another term for a non performing loan.

**Distribution Date**

The date of the month when payments on securities are made to investors. Necessarily this falls a few days after the Determination Date.

**Dodd–Frank Wall Street Reform and Consumer Protection Act**

This is a US Act which changes the regulatory structure through creating new agencies and merging or removing others in an effort to streamline the regulatory process, increasing oversight of specific institutions regarded as a systemic risk, amending the Federal Reserve Act and promoting transparency.

**Dominant Tenement**

See Easement.

**Double Net Lease**

See Net Net Lease.

**Double Taxation Avoidance Agreements**

The Double Tax Avoidance Agreements (DTAA) is a bilateral agreement entered into between two countries. The basic objective is to avoid taxation of income in both the countries (i.e. Double taxation of same income) and to promote and foster economic trade and investment between the two countries.

**Dow Jones US Real Estate Index**

An index that is designed to provide measures of real estate Securities and is composed primarily of REITs.

**downREIT**

A REIT structure similar to that of an UPREIT, except that the downREIT may own property directly as well as property being held by one or more Limited Partnerships of which the REIT is general partner and a limited partner.

**DSCR**

See Debt Service Coverage Ratio.

**DTAA**

See Double Taxation Avoidance Agreements.

**Due Diligence**

In practical terms this is the investigation and fact finding exercise carried out by a potential purchaser to allow him to make a more well-informed decision about whether to purchase or invest. In legal terms this is a measure of prudence as can be expected from a reasonable and prudent person in the circumstances of the particular deal. The degree of prudence depends on the facts of the case and is judged on industry standards. In a CMBS transaction, investors rely on the expertise of the professionals involved as it is impossible for them to inspect properties, financial records and the due diligence such professionals have carried out.

# E

**Earn Out Loans**

A credit agreement under which the original principal balance can be resized for further advances should the operating performance of a property be able to service the additional debt.

**Easement**

A right benefiting a piece of land (known as the dominant tenement) that is enjoyed over land owned by someone else (known as the servient tenement).

**EBA**

European Banking Authority. Established in January 2011 by the European Parliament; it has taken over all existing and ongoing tasks and responsibilities from the Committee of European Banking Supervisors (CEBS). It is responsible for EU-wide stress testing and recapitalisation needs.

**EBITA**

Accounting term to mean the earnings of a company (or group of companies) before the deduction of interest, tax and amortisation.

**EC**

European Community (often used interchangeably with EU).

**EEA**

The European Economic Area, a common market (established in 1994) among members of the EU and EFTA.

**EFTA**

The European Free Trade Association.

**EMEA**

Regional designation for Europe, the Middle East and Africa.

**Encumbrance**

A claim or a right to property by a party that is not the property owner. Typical encumbrances include issues such as Leases, Mortgages and restrictive covenants.

**End User**

An entity that enters a Derivatives contract in order to hold the position whether for Hedging, speculative or arbitrage purposes and not for the purpose of market making.

**Enforceability Opinion**

A legal opinion stating that the obligations imposed on a party by an agreement will be legal, valid and binding on that party in accordance with its terms, subject to certain standard assumptions and qualifications.

**Enforcement**

The process whereby the lender takes control of the collateral including the cash flow from the mortgaged property.

**Environmental Risk**

The risk of the value of a property being decreased by the presence of hazardous materials (for example asbestos). Rating agencies may include the possibility of non-compliance with future environmental standards in their analysis even if a property complies with current environmental standards.

**EPF**

The European Property Federation.

**EPRA**

European Public Real Estate Association; an industry body for quoted property companies and investors in quoted property stocks.

**Equitable Mortgage**

See Mortgage.

**Equitable Transfer**

The transfer of the beneficial ownership, as opposed to legal ownership, of property. This is often seen in European RMBS.

**Equitable Transfer**

The transfer of the beneficial ownership, as opposed to legal ownership, of property. This is often seen in European securitisation transactions as it is often significantly cheaper to arrange than a legal transfer.

**Equity**

A provision allowing a lender or an investor to receive an equity based return in addition to normal rates upon the occurrence of certain events.

**Equity Finance**

Money in the form of share capital made available to a company, generally for a specific venture such as a development where the subscriber, as part of the bargain, becomes entitled to a share of any profit, whether or not in receipt of dividends.

**Equity Release**

Retail financial product, usually in the form of a lifetime Mortgage or home reversion plan, that allows residential property owners to realise some or all of the equity and remain living in their house.

**Equivalent Yield**

The return on an investment calculated by dividing the mean income by the value/purchase price and expressed in terms of a percentage.

**ERISA (or Employee Retirement Income Security Act of 1974)**

US legislation which stipulates the standard of risk suitable and acceptable for private pension plan investments.

**ERV**

See Estimated Rental Value.

**Escrow Account**

An account jointly held by the Borrower and Lender containing funds for capital expenses, such as improvement or insurance.

**Establishment**

In the context of cross-border insolvencies any place of operations where the Debtor carries out a non-transitory economic activity.

**Estate**

A term used in common law to signify all the property belonging to a person.

**Estimated Rental Value**

The rent that a property might reasonably be able to command in the open market at a given time, subject to the terms of the relevant Lease.

**ETF**

See Exchange Traded Fund.

**EU**

The European Union (established in 1993), a political and economic union of sovereign states aimed at maintaining freedom of trade and developing community of legal and economic structures.

**EU Insolvency Regulation**

The EU Insolvency Regulation (1346/2000) came into effect on May 31 2002. The primary function of the regulation is to codify the manner in which a member state determines whether it has jurisdiction to open insolvency proceedings.

**European Communities Regulation on CRAs**

This came into force in 2009 and introduced a harmonised approach to the regulation of credit rating activities in the European Union and established a registration system for CRAs.

**Euro Interbank Offered Rate (EURIBOR)**

The interest rate at which interbank term deposits denominated in Euros are offered by one prime bank in the euro zone to another prime bank in the euro zone. EURIBOR is established by a panel of about 60 European banks. As with LIBOR, there are EURIBOR rates for deposits of various maturities.

**Euroclear**

One of two principal clearing systems in the Eurobond Market, functioning much like the Depository Trust Company in the US market. Euroclear began operations in 1968, is located in Brussels and is managed by Morgan Guaranty Bank.

**European Insurance and Occupational Pension Authority (EIOPA)**

An independent advisory body to the European Parliament, European Council and European Commission which monitors and identifies trends as well as potential risks and vulnerabilities stemming from the micro-prudential level across borders and sectors.

**European Investor Reporting Package**

A product designed by CREFC-Europe which provides relevant data that loan and securities investors can use to compare loans and bonds across multiple European transactions.

**Event of Default**

An event specified in a commercial agreement where a non-defaulting party can terminate the agreement. In the context of debt finance and Securitisation transactions, an Event of Default will entitle the Lender or Noteholders (respectively) to declare all amounts owing by the Borrower or Issuer (as applicable) to accelerate the debt obligations as being immediately due and payable thereby enabling Enforcement. Typical events of default include non-payment of interest or principal, breach of representation, breach of covenant, cross-default, material adverse change and insolvency. See also Default.

**Event Risk**

Certain events (for example natural disaster, industrial accident and takeover) cannot be predicted via a standard method of credit analysis. The risk that such events pose to an issuer's ability to make its debt service payments is the Event Risk.

**Excess Interest/Excess Spread**

Interest or other income received by a Securitisation Issuer which exceeds the stated amount of interest required to be paid on the various classes of Securities.

**Excess Servicing Fee**

The portion of the interest charged to underlying obligors in a securitisation structure that is in excess of the interest portion of debt service payments or the regular servicing fee.

**Excess Spread**

Interest or other income received by a Securitisation Issuer which exceeds the stated amount of interest required to be paid on the various classes of Securities.

**Exchange**

The exchange of contracts in a real estate acquisition.

**Exchange Controls**

Restrictions on conversion of a country's currency for another imposed by its government in an attempt to improve its balance of payments position.

**Exchange Traded Fund (ETF)**

Funds traded like normal shares which allow investors to spread investments by tracking the performance of an entire index.

**Exit Value**

The value of a property on a particular date, either at the end of an agreed Loan term, or applied to a date an investor has targeted to sell an investment in the future.

**Expected Maturity**

The date as of which securities are expected to be repaid in full based on a specified assumption regarding the rate of repayment of the underlying assets.

**Expense Ratio**

The ratio of operating expenses and operating revenues.

**Expense Stops**

Lease clauses which limit the amount of a landlords obligation for expense on a property, with expenses in excess of this amount being met by the tenant.

**Exposure at Default**

A lender's exposure at the time of default and is equal to the outstanding amount of loan principal and interest accruing at that time.

**Extend and Amend**

This is an extension to the loan maturity date usually in exchange for an uplift in margin or a more punitive amortisation profile.

**Extend and Pretend**

See Extend and Amend.

**Extension Adviser**

A third party with the right or obligation to approve loan extensions or notifications recommended by the Master or Special Servicer.

**Extension/Extension Option**

A grace period following the contractual termination date given to a borrower to repay a loan (through refinancing or sale). Used to prevent foreclosing on the property and the additional cost this incurs.

**Extension Risk**

The potential inability to refinance balloon mortgages in a timely manner, with the result that the life of the security may be extended beyond the expected life.

**External Credit Enhancement**

Credit support provided by a highly rated third-party to enhance the rating of the securitisation structure.

**Extraordinary General Meeting ("EGM")**

An unscheduled meeting of shareholders called to approve non-routine matters. Under the Companies Act 2006, the term "extraordinary general meeting" is no longer applicable and instead the term "general meeting" is used to describe a meeting of company members.

# F

**Face Rent**

Rental payments without adjustments for any lease concessions (for example rent-free periods).

**Facility Agent**

The entity that deals with the day-to-day administration of a Loan on behalf of the Lenders.

**Facility Office**

The office or branch of a Lender through which it performs its obligations under a Loan Agreement.

**Fast Pay**

A descriptive term applied to a security or a transaction structure aimed at ensuring repayment of principal on an accelerated schedule.

**Fannie Mae (or Federal National Mortgage Association or FNMA)**

A quasi private US corporation which purchases and pools conventional mortgages then issues securities using these as collateral. Holders of Fannie Mae certificates are guaranteed full and timely payment of principal and interest.

**Fatwa/Fatawah**

A written confirmation of a Sharia'a scholar or board. This has no binding effect under secular law. Historically this was a short summary of the decision, and more recently these have been structured like Anglo–American legal opinions.

**FDI**

See Foreign Direct Investment.

**FDIC**

See Federal Deposit Insurance Corporation.

**Federal Deposit Insurance Corporation (FDIC)**

A US government agency that insures deposits of depository institutions.

**Feeders**

Entities created above the fund to accommodate the special (often tax-related) requirements of one or more investors.

**Feuhold**

The Scottish equivalent of Freehold.

**FHCMC**

See Freddie Mac.

**Fiduciary**

A person to whom power or property is entrusted for the benefit of another (e.g. a director owes fiduciary duties to the company of which he is a director).

**Final Maturity**

See Legal Maturity.

**Finance Documents**

A collective term used to refer to those documents entered into between the Lender, the Borrower and any Obligors. A Lender will require all Finance Documents to be entered into before the Lender will advance funds to the Borrower. Typically, the Finance Documents will include the Loan Agreement, Security Documents, Hedging Documents, Intercreditor Agreement and fee letters. A breach of any Finance Document will typically constitute an Event of Default under the Loan Agreement.

**Finance Lease**

A Lease that transfers the risks and rewards of a fixed asset without transferring legal ownership. The Lender (often a finance house) buys the asset and then Leases it to the Borrower (lessee). The lessee is required to make Lease payments over the life of the Lease equivalent to the full value of the fixed asset and will also pay a return on capital to the Lender. At the end of the Lease, provided the lessee has paid the Lender all amounts due to it, the asset is transferred to the lessee.

**Finance Parties**

A collective term used in syndicated or securitised Loans to refer to those entities within the Lender group and includes the current Lenders, the Facility Agent, the Arranger, the Security Trustee and any Hedge Counterparty. Obligors owe obligations to all the Finance Parties and so the Security is held on trust by the Security Trustee for the benefit of all Finance Parties. Also referred to as the Secured Parties.

**Financial Covenants**

Positive or negative obligations on the borrower relating purely to financial matters, for example to maintain LTV to a certain percentage.

**Financial Institutions and Reform, Recovery and Enforcement Act 1989 (FIRREA)**

A US federal act that revamped the regulation and insurance of depositary financial institutions. The Act created several new institutions including the Resolution Trust Corporation.

**Financial Services Authority (FSA)**

A body that oversees the regulation of all providers of financial services in the UK.

**Financial Stability Board (FSB)**

Established in 2009 at the London G-20 summit, the FSB is an international body that monitors and makes recommendations about the global financial system.

**Financial Stability Forum (FSF)**

Established in 1999 at the behest of G7 finance ministers and central bank governors, the purpose of the FSF was to identify and over see action to remove threats and vulnerabilities to the international financial system. The FSF was succeeded by the FSB in 2009.

**First Loss Piece**

The most junior class of a CMBS which suffers losses from a mortgage pool before any other classes suffer.

**Fixed Charge**

A form of Security by which an asset or group of assets owned by a company are charged as Security for borrowings or other indebtedness. The chargor remains the legal owner of the asset subject to the Fixed Charge but is prohibited from dealing with such assets without the Lender's consent. A Fixed Charge will rank ahead of any Floating Charge in the order of repayment on insolvency. See also Floating Charge.

**Fixed Charge Receiver**

A Receiver appointed to deal with assets which are the subject of a Fixed Charge. See also Receiver.

**Fixed Income Investor**

An investor seeking a fixed (and therefore certain) rate of return on their investments.

**Fixed Rate Interest**

An Interest Rate that will not change during the term of a Loan.

**Floating Charge**

A form of Security by which an asset or group of assets owned by a company are charged as Security for borrowings or other indebted ness. The Lender's interest attaches to a changing Pool of assets until Crystallisation. The advantage of a Floating Charge is that, before insolvency, it allows the chargor to deal with charged assets during the course of a company's business without the consent of the Lender (e.g. by transferring or selling the assets). See also Fixed Charge, Crystallisation and Qualifying Floating Charge.

**Floating Rate Interest**

An Interest Rate which may vary during the term of the Loan. Typical Floating Rate Interest include LIBOR and EURIBOR.

**Floating-Rate Notes**

A class of securities having a variable (or floating), rather than fixed interest rate, but typically a margin above a market index.

**FNMA**

See Fannie Mae.

**Fonds Commun de Créance (FCC)**

A type of closed-end mutual debt fund used as a funding vehicle in French securitisations.

**Foreclosure**

A proceeding, in or out of court, brought a lender holding a mortgage on real property seeking to enable the lender to sell the property and apply the sale proceeds to satisfy amounts owned by the owner under the related loan.

**Foreign Account Tax Compliant Act (FACTA)**

FACTA is a US act that aims to improve tax compliance involving foreign financial assets and offshore accounts. Under FATCA, U.S. taxpayers with specified foreign financial assets that exceed certain thresholds must report those assets to the IRS. FATCA will require foreign financial institutions to report directly to the IRS information about financial accounts held by U.S. taxpayers, or held by foreign entities in which U.S. taxpayers hold a substantial ownership interest.

**Foreign Court**

A judicial or other authority competent to control or supervise a Foreign Proceeding.

**Foreign Direct Investment or FDI**

A company from one country making a physical investment into real estate in another country.

**Foreign Main Proceeding**

A Foreign Proceeding pending in the country where the Debtor has its COMI.

**Foreign Nonmain Proceeding**

A Foreign Proceeding, other than a Foreign Main Proceeding, pending in a country where the Debtor has an establishment.

**Foreign Proceeding**

A judicial or administrative proceeding in a foreign country, including an interim proceeding, under a law relating to insolvency or adjustment of debt in which proceeding the assets and affairs of the Debtor are subject to control or supervision by a foreign court, for the purpose of reorganisation or liquidation.

**Foreign Representative**

A person or body, including a person or body appointed on an interim basis, authorised in a foreign proceeding to administer the reorganisation of the liquidation of the Debtor's assets or affairs or to act as a representative of such foreign proceeding.

**Forwards**

A contract that calls for the sale, in the future, of an asset. The price and quantity (as well as other terms) are agreed upon by the parties to a forward at the outset.

**Freddie Mac (or Federal Home Loan Mortgage Corporation or FHCMC)**

A quasi private US corporation. This entity is charged with providing liquidity to the secondary market for single family mortgages and issues securities using these mortgages as the underlying collateral. Holders of Freddie Mac certificates are assured of timely payment of interest and eventual payment of principal.

**Freehold**

An estate in land which provides the holder of the estate with rights of ownership. There are several different types of Freehold estate. The most common are 'Fee simple' that is effectively absolute ownership of the land and 'Life estate' which effectively means ownership for the duration of the holder's life.

**Freeholder**

The owner of a Freehold.

**FSA**

See Financial Services Authority.

**FTSE 100**

The benchmark index of the London Stock Exchange. It is a market value weighted index of the 100 largest UK stocks by market capitalisation.

**FTSE NAREIT All REITs Index**

A stock market index containing all qualified REITs with common stock traded on the New York Stock Exchange of NASDAQ National Market, without regard to any minimum size, liquidity criteria or free float adjustments. The index is maintained by FTSE Group, an independent company that began as a joint venture between the Financial Times and the London Stock Exchange.

**Full Service Lease**

A Lease which provides that the Landlord pays all building expenses. Also called a Gross Full Service Lease or a Gross Rent Lease.

**Funds of Funds**

An investment fund that invests in other investment funds rather than investing directly in shares, Bonds or other Securities.

**Fusion Deals**

A CMBS which features a combination of conduit loans, small loans and large loans.

**Futures**

Highly standardised Forwards that are traded on an exchange.


# G


**G-7**

Abbreviation for the Group of Seven, a forum of the world's leading industrial nations to meet and discuss global economic matters. G-7 members are: Canada, France, Germany, Italy, Japan, the UK and the US.

**G-8**

The G-7 plus Russia.

**G-20**

Established in 1999, the group of 20 finance ministers and central bank governors is a forum for discussion between industrial and emerging market countries on issues of global economic stability. The G-20 is comprised of 19 countries and the European Union. The 19 countries are: Argentina, Australia, Brazil, Canada, China, France, Germany, India, Indonesia, Italy, Japan, Mexico, Russia, Saudi Arabia, South Africa, South Korea, Turkey, the UK and the US.

**GAAP**

Acronym for generally accepted accounting principals. A standardised framework of guidelines for the preparation of financial statements. There are various sets of generally accepted accounting principals worldwide, such as US, UK and German.

**Gearing**

An accounting term used to define the debt-to-equity ratio of a company. SPEs will typically be more highly geared than operating companies.

**General/Multiline Insurer**

An insurer which transacts business over a range of classes of insurance. Contrast with Monoline Insurer.

**Generally Accepted Accounting Principals**

See GAAP.

**General Meeting**

Formerly known as an extraordinary general meeting. A general meeting can be either a non-routine meeting of a company called for a specific purpose or an annual general meeting.

**GIC**

See Guaranteed Investment Contract.

**Ginnie Mae** or **Governmental National Mortgage Association** or **GNMA**

A wholly-owned government corporation within the US Department of Housing and Urban Development. This entity is charged with providing liquidity to the secondary market for single family Mortgages by guaranteeing that investors will receive the timely payment of principal of and interest on Mortgage-backed Securities that are backed by federally insured or guaranteed Loans.

**Globally Systematically Important Financial Institutions (GSIFIs)**

A list of financial institutions produced by the Financial Stability Board whose failure in the Financial Stability Board's view could trigger a global financial crisis.

**GNMA**

See Ginnie Mae.

**GOEF**

German Open-Ended Funds; indirect real estate investment vehicles that are of particular importance in Germany. Shares are directly backed by properties and liquid assets held by the fund; as an open-ended vehicle, a fund can create new shares on demand, and investors buy shares at net asset value.

**Government National Mortgage Association (Ginnie Mae or GNMA)**

This is a US government related agency which guarantees securities which use mortgages initially issued by approved lenders as their underlying collateral.

**Government Sponsored Enterprise (GSE)**

The collective description for the US government agencies formed to provide a secondary market for residential real estate loans. Includes Fannie Mae, Freddie Mac and Ginnie Mae.

**Grace Period**

The period of time during which a party, typically a Debtor, has to pay overdue amounts or remedy any other defaults before it incurs further interest and/or the relevant Creditor initiates enforcement proceedings.

**Graduated Payment Mortgage**

A mortgage where the individual loan payments are graduated on the basis of pre-defined schedules.

**Granularity**

This is achieved where an underlying pool of loans is made up of smaller loans. Pools which contain a small number of higher value loans are said to be less granular, or more lumpy.

**Green Property Funds**

Socially responsible property funds which invest in sustainable and/or carbon-neutral property investments and developments.

**Greenfield Site**

Previously undeveloped land which is, or is potentially, available for development, e.g. agricultural land.

**Gross Asset Value**

The appraised value of the properties in a REIT or Real Estate Fund.

**Gross Development Value**

The value of a development based on the assumption that such development has been completed and the building is fully let.

**Gross Full Service Lease**

A lease which provides that the landlord pays all building expenses. Also called a full service lease or a gross rent lease.

**Gross Rent Lease**

See Full Service Lease.

**Ground Lease**

A long Lease granted at a ground rent, i.e. a rent disregarding the value of any buildings or other improvements of the land but reflecting any right to develop the land.

**Ground Rent**

Rent paid for vacant land which is suitable for development.

**GSE**

See Government Sponsored Enterprise.

**Guarantee**

A promise from a third party to repay a debt if the original Borrower fails to do so. The Guarantee may extend beyond the payment obligations.

**Guaranteed Investment Contract (GIC)**

A deposit account provided by a financial institution that guarantees a minimum rate of return, thereby mitigating interest rate risk.

**Guarantor**

An entity which provides a Guarantee.


# H

**Haircut**

The expression given to the reduction in the value attributed to an asset or the income or cash flow anticipated to be received from a property, usually by applying a percentage to this value.

**Hard Costs**

The element of the building cost or purchase cost of real estate which includes the land, building material, plant, machinery and inventory.

**Head Lease**

A Lease of property between the Freeholder and a Tenant which grants overall contractual responsibility of the property to one particular Tenant. The head lessee will usually sublet the property or part of the property to occupational Tenants pursuant to an Occupational Lease.

**Head Rent**

The rent paid by a head lessee to the Freeholder under a Head Lease.

**Heads of Terms**

A document which sets out the main commercial terms of a transaction. In a real estate Loan transaction the Heads of Terms would typically include the Interest Rate, the term of the Loan, the repayment schedule, fees, Events of Default, Financial Covenants and Conditions Precedent. Sometimes called a Term Sheet.

**Hedge Counterparty**

The entity which enters into Hedging transaction with a Borrower.

**Hedge Fund**

An investment fund that buys and sells assets on a speculative basis in order to out perform the market or index in which it is invested.

**Hedging**

A general term used to refer to strategies adopted to offset investment risks. Examples of hedging include the use of derivative instruments to protect against fluctuations in interest rates or currency exchange rates, or investment in assets whose value is expected to rise faster than inflation to protect against inflation (interest rate hedging, currency hedging and inflation rate hedging respectively).

**Hedging Documents**

The documents that document the Hedging arrangements entered into between the Borrower and the Hedge Counterparty and will usually include and ISDA Master Agreement and Schedule, a Confirmation and possibly a CSA.

**Hissas**

An Islamic finance term referring to the sale and purchase of partnership interests from one partner to another.

**HMRC (UK)**

HM Revenue & Customs. A UK Government department formed on 18 April 2005 from a merger between the Inland Revenue and HM Customs & Excise. The Government department responsible for the collection of taxes and the payment of some forms of state support.

**Hot Desking**

Relatively recent innovation in open space occupation, whereby employees share a desk, rather than have a desk individually allocated. It is becoming increasingly popular in companies where a significant number of staff are out of the office at any one time.

**Housing Associations**

Independent not-for-profit UK bodies that principally provide low-cost social housing.

**Hurdle Rate**

A break-even debt service calculation which establishes the maximum interest rate a mortgaged property can handle at maturity if the property must be refinanced. Also called break even debt service analysis.

**Hybrid**

A term used to refer to a whole-business securitisation. Such a transaction entails risks that are a hybrid of pure corporate risk and the risks associated with traditional securitisations backed by financial assets or diversified pools of corporate credits.

**Hybrid Debt**

Investments that have equity and debt features such as participating Mortgages, convertible Mortgages and convertible participating Mortgages.

**Hyper-Amortisation**

The accelerated paydown of a CMBS class achieved through the allocation of all principal and interest to that class.

**Hypothekenpfandbriefe**

See Pfandbriefe.

# I

**ICR**

See Interest Cover Ratio.

**IDB**

Islamic Development Bank.

**IFSB**

The Islamic Financial Services Board.

**Ijara**

An Islamic finance term meaning a lease. A predominant structure in Islamic real estate finance. Securitisations which use this structure are termed Ijara al Sukuk.

**Illiquid**

An asset which is not easily tradable, the opposite of liquid.

**Impound or Escrow Account**

An account jointly held by the borrower and lender containing funds for capital expenses, such as improvement or insurance.

**In the Money**

An option is described as being in the money when the price of the underlying instrument is above the strike or exercise price for a call option and below the strike price for a put option. The more an option is in the money the more expensive it becomes. Options are described as being deep in the money when they are likely to expire in the money.

**Income**

The excess of revenue over expenses for an accounting period.

**Income-to-interest cover**

See Interest Cover Ratio.

**Indemnity**

An obligation undertaken by one party (rather than one imposed by force of law) to pay another party in the event that the second party suffers a specified loss.

**Independent Commission on Banking**

A commission established by the UK Government in June 2010 to consider structural and non related structural reforms to the UK banking sector to promote stability and competition.

**Independent Director**

A key component of SPEs. This is a member of the board of directors of the borrowing or issuing entity where a vote is required for certain important acts of the entity such as declaration of bankruptcy. This removes control of the entity from the hands of affiliated principals.

**Indirect Property Fund**

A fund that invests 100% in Indirect Property Investment.

**Indirect Property Investment**

Ownership of shares or units in a company or Partnership which holds legal and/or beneficial title to real estate, such as REITs and PUTs.

**Initial Yield**

The return on an investment calculated by dividing the current income by the purchase price of the investment.

**INREV**

Investors in Non-listed Real Estate Vehicles; the European industry association for investors in non-listed real estate funds.

**Insolvency**

The inability to pay debts when they fall due. Although not specifically defined in the Insolvency Act 1986, a company is deemed unable to pay its debts if: (i) a statutory demand as been served on it and not paid on time, (ii) it has failed to pay a judgement debt, (iii) the court is satisfied that it is unable to pay their debts as they fall due (the cash-flow test) or (iv) the court is satisfied that the value of its assets is less than the amount of its liabilities taking into account contingent and prospective liabilities (the balance sheet test). If a company is unable to pay its debts a Creditor may petition the court for it to be placed into compulsory liquidation.

**Insuring Capacity**

The financial amount which an insurer wishes and/or is able within its capital structure to commit to a particular risk or class of risks.

**Intercreditor Agreement**

An agreement which governs the relationship between the holders of senior and junior loans. Whilst this is expressed as an agreement, this document will usually be executed as a deed.

**Interest Cover Ratio (ICR)**

A ratio used to determine how easily a Borrower or Securitisation Issuer can pay interest due on a Loan or class of Securities. Generally calculated by dividing the amount of income a Borrower or Issuer receives by the amount of interest the Borrower or Issuer is required to pay in any given period.

**Interest Only Strip (IO Strip)**

Should the interest rate on the underlying loans exceed the interest paid on the issued securities backed by the same, the surplus is removed and added as a further class, the IO strip. Usually sold for a small percentage of the price of the whole security, these can be very volatile, for example if there is a large amount of pre-payment this could remove the interest stream to pay the IO strip, usually curtailing the life span of the IO strip.

**Interest Paid versus Interest Impacted**

This clause in the CMBS structure determines how and when losses are allocated, for example before or after principal is paid. This has a major impact on the yield of the most junior noteholders.

**Interest Payment Date**

The date on which interest on the Loan is paid. Often shortened to IPD.

**Interest Period**

The period between two successive Interest Payment Dates. Interest on a Loan accrues during an Interest Period and is paid on the Interest Payment Date falling at the end of Interest Period.

**Interest Proceeds**

Collections received from underlying debt instruments that consist of interest payments and other non-principal receipts, such as finance charges.

**Interest Rate**

The rate at which interest is charged or is due on a debt obligation and typically consists of a Margin, an interest basis (such as LIBOR) and, in Loans, mandatory costs. See also Fixed Rate Interest and Floating Rate Interest.

**Interest Rate Cap**

Limits the rate to a maximum or cap thereby protecting the borrower from rising rates. Often purchased by the borrower.

**Interest Rate Hedge**

A Derivative instruments that protects the Protection Buyer against Interest Rate Risk. Typically, the Protection Buyer will pay interest at a fixed rate to the Protection Seller and in return receive interest at a variable rate from the Protection Seller.

**Interest Rate Risk**

A change in interest rates may mean that interest earned on assets in a low interest rate environment will not be sufficient to service payments required in respect of liabilities incurred in a higher interest rate environment, thereby leading to shortfall. The risk of such shortfall (and the corresponding change in a security's value), is the interest rate risk.

**Interest Rate Swap**

A binding agreement between two counterparties to exchange periodic interest payments on a predetermined principal amount, which is referred to as the notional amount. Typically, one counterparty will pay interest at a fixed rate and in return receive interest at a variable rate, with the opposite applying to the other counterparty.

**Interest Shortfall**

The difference between the aggregate amount of interest payments received from the borrowers and the accrued interest on the certificates.

**Internal Approach**

A method of calculating credit risk under Basel II which allows banks to use their internal methods and procedures to model, assess and regulate risk, rather than relying on external assessments. See also Standardised Approach.

**Internal Credit Enhancement**

Mechanisms inherent within the securitisation structure designed to improve the credit quality of the senior classes of securities, most commonly involving the channelling of asset cash flow in ways that protect those senior classes from experiencing shortfalls.

**Internal Rate of Return (IRR)**

A compounded rate of return on an investment, calculated to show the rate at which the present values of future cash flows from an investment is equal to the cost of the investment.

**Internal Rating Based Approach**

Established by the Basel Accords, this provides a single framework by which a given set of risk components or inputs are translated into minimum capital requirements. The framework allows for a foundation method and more advanced methodologies. In the foundation method, banks estimate the probability of default associated with each borrower and the bank supervisors supply other inputs. In the advanced methodology, a bank with a sufficiently developed internal capital allocation process is permitted to supply other necessary inputs as well.

**In The Pool**

A tranche of a loan which is included in the pool of loans which is to be securitised.

**Investment Grade**

A term used to describe Securities rated in one of the top four rating categories (AAA, AA, A and BBB or equivalent) by one or more Rating Agencies.

**Investment Manager**

The party responsible for managing a Portfolio of assets on behalf of the owner of that Portfolio. An Investment Manager will typically be responsible for actively managing the Portfolio and making investment related decisions. In the context of a Portfolio of real property this may also include carrying out the function of Property Manager. See also Asset Manager.

**Investment Period**

The period that commences on a private equity fund's initial closing date (when capital contributions are first accepted) and runs for the period (typically two to three years) negotiated with the fund's investors (often with some provisions for transactions in process at the end of the period).

**Investment Property**

Any property purchased with the primary intention of retaining it and enjoying the total return (rental income and appreciation in capital value) over the life of the interest acquired.

**Investment Property Databank**

A provider of performance data and analysis for owners, investors and manager of real estate.

**Involuntary Repayment**

Pre-payment on a mortgage loan due to default.

**IO Strip**

See Interest Only Strip.

**IPD**

The Investment Property Databank. The term IPD is also used to refer to an Interest Payment Date.

**IPF**

The Investment Property Forum.

**IRR**

Internal Rate of Return; a rate of return used in capital budgeting to measure or compare profitability. It is the discount rate that makes the net present value of all cashflows from a particular project equal to zero.

**Irrational Exuberance**

A term coined by former Federal Reserve chairman, Alan Greenspan to describe unsustainable investor enthusiasm that drives asset prices up to levels that are not supported by the fundamentals.

**ISDA**

International Swaps and Derivatives Association, a global trade association for privately negotiated derivates and the leading organisation that promulgates industry-standard Swaps and Derivatives documentation.

**ISDA Master Agreement**

An umbrella agreement that documents Derivative transactions which is amended and supplemented by a Schedule.

**Issue Credit Rating**

A rating agency opinion of the creditworthiness of an obligor with respect to a specific financial obligation, a specific class of financial obligations, or a specific financial program (including MTN programs and CP programs). Relevant factors in determining the issue credit rating are the creditworthiness of guarantors, insurers, the currency of the obligation as well as other forms of credit enhancement.

**Issuer**

A party that has authorised the creation and sale of securities to investors. In a securitisation structure, the issuer is usually established as an SPE in a jurisdiction that offers a favourable legal regime in terms of the ability to achieve bankruptcy-remote status for the issuer and the security arrangements provided for the investors and which affords favourable the tax treatment. Common jurisdictions used for establishing SPEs are England, Italy, Ireland, The Netherlands, Luxemburg and Jersey.

**Issuer Collection Account**

An account opened in the name of the Issuer at the Issuer's cash management bank into which the Servicer deposits payments from the borrower.

**Issuing Bank**

A bank that issues a Letter of Credit.

**Issuer Credit Rating (ICR)**

A rating agency opinion of an obligor's overall financial capacity to pay its financial obligations. This is basically an opinion of creditworthiness. An ICR focuses on the obligor's general capacity and willingness to meet its financial commitments as they fall due. Unlike the issue credit rating, this does not apply to any specific financial obligations.

**Istisna'a**

An Islamic finance term meaning construction contract. One of the 14 categories of permissible sukuk specified by the AAOIFI.

**Istisna' –Ijara Structure**

An Islamic finance term meaning a construction-lease financing structure.

# J

**J-curve**
> The time-variant profile of the performance of an unlisted fund which expends fees and taxes as it acquires assets.

**Junior Class** or **Junior Notes**
> See Subordinated Class or Subordinated Notes.

**Junior Debt**
> See Subordinated Debt.

**Junior Notes**
> See Junior Class.

**Junior Tranche**
> See Tranche.

**Junk Bonds**
> A colloquial term applied to below investment grade securities.

# K

**Kalte Zwangsverwaltung**
> German term for cold forced administration.

**Key Persons**
> One or more persons designated by a private equity fund or a Lender as key to the expected success of the fund or a Borrower. Key persons must often devote a certain amount of time to the business, and a violation of the key person provisions usually allows the investors to either stop funding new transactions or to remove the general partner or manager or call an Event of Default of the Loan (as appropriate).

**Kick off**
> The point at which the process of creating and issuing the CMBS commences.

# L

**Landlord:** The owner of an interest in land who, in consideration of rents, grants the right to exclusive possession of that land to another person for a specific period by way of a Lease.

**Land Registration**
> The process by which a state body records transfers of ownership of interests in real estate for the purpose of making the transfer conclusively effective and/or a matter of public knowledge.

**LC**
> See Letter of Credit.

**Lead Manager**

An investment bank or securities dealer that manages a syndicate of dealer banks and agrees to place a securities issuance. It is usually allocated a larger share of the issuance and therefore has more at stake in terms of the success of the effort to market and place the securities. As a result, the lead manager often takes on the role of chief advisor to the issuer or, in a securitisation structure, to the seller of the assets that are being securitised and is responsible for structuring the securities to be issued and liaising with other parties such as rating agencies, lawyers and credit enhancers. The lead manager is also closely involved in the preparation of the offering circular and advises its client on the pricing of the related securities. The lead manager may have legal liability as to the compliance of the issuance with relevant securities laws and regulations.

**Leakage**
Cash which escapes or is lost during its movement through a securitisation structure from underlying tenants to the issuer which has not been built into the structure and is unexpected.

**Lease**
The grant of a right to the exclusive possession of land for a definite period (which is less than that held by the grantor), or the document granting the right.

**Lease Assignment**
A form of credit enhancement whereby lease payments are made directly to the Servicer.

**Leasehold**
An estate in land which provides the holder of the estate with rights of possession and use of the land but not ownership. The Freehold is retained by the Freeholder who grants the Lease (also referred to as a tenancy) as the Landlord (also referred to as the lessor) to the holder of the estate, who is referred to as the Tenant or lessee.

**Legal Final Maturity**
The date by which the principal balance of securities must be repaid.

**Legal Mortgage**
See Mortgage.

**Lender**
An individual, bank, building society or other financial institution who/that lends money to a Borrower.

**Letter of Credit (LOC or LC)**
A form of credit enhancement whereby a third party agrees to make funds available. The third party rating is generally required to be at least equal to the highest rating of the securities. to or upon the order of a third party Creditor of a Borrower upon receiving a demand for payment.

**Leverage**
The use of debt in addition to the investment of equity as a means to finance an acquisition. The greater (lesser) the level of debt in proportion to equity the greater (lesser) the Leverage.

**LIBOR or London Interbank Offered Rate**

The rate of interest at which interbank term deposits are offered by one prime bank in the London interbank market to another prime bank in the London Interbank Market. There are LIBOR rates for deposits of various maturities.

**Licence**

The lawful grant of a permission to do something that would otherwise not be legal or allowed, for example, to occupy a property, or to assign a Lease where the Landlord's consent is required.

**Lien**

An encumbrance against a property which may be voluntary (as in the case of a mortgage) or involuntary (as in the case of a lien for unpaid property taxes), and acts as security for amounts owed to the holder of the lien.

**Limited Partnership (LP)**

A Partnership structure which enables a pool of investors to invest together in one or more assets. The general partner (GP) must have unlimited liability while the other partners have limited liability. The investment vehicle is tax transparent.

**Limited Purpose Entity (LPE)**

A corporate vehicle (whether in the form of a limited company, partnership, trust, limited partnership or other form) which complies with rating agency LPE criteria. An LPE is usually the property owner. Due to inherent risks which stem from property ownership, LPEs are not fully insolvency remote but instead are structured so that insolvency risks are mitigated to the fullest possible extent. Characteristics which mitigate insolvency risk include: use of newly formed entities, contractual restrictions on activities and powers, non-petition covenants, separateness covenants and no employees.

**Line-of-Credit Mortgage Loan**

A mortgage loan that is linked to a revolving line of credit upon which the borrower can draw at any time during the life of the loan. The interest rate charged on the loan is usually variable and accrues on the basis of the outstanding balance only, while the undrawn principal limit grows at an annual rate.

**Liquidation**

Either a voluntary liquidation or a compulsory liquidation. Voluntary liquidation is a non-court based procedure to wind up a company commenced by the company's Shareholders. There are two types of voluntary liquidation: (i) members' voluntary liquidation which can be commenced if the directors of the company are able to swear a declaration that the company is solvent and 75% of the company's members have agreed to place the company into liquidation and (ii) creditors' voluntary liquidation where the directors cannot swear that the company is solvent. A compulsory liquidation is commenced by a petition to the court, usually presented by a Creditor who is owed money by the company.

**Liquidation Fee**

The fee ordinarily payable to a Special Servicer in respect of a specially serviced loan as percentage of the proceeds of sale (net of costs and expenses of sale) arising form the sale of a loan, any obligor of such loan or any part of any property or properties securing such loan.

**Liquidator**

Insolvency practitioner appointed by a company's Shareholders or unsecured Creditors, or on a court order, to manage the winding up of an entity.

**Liquidity**

A measure of the ease and frequency with which assets can be traded. It is a function of both the time it takes to close a particular action and the ability to trade the asset at market prices. Those traded more readily are said to be more liquid.

**Liquidity Facility**

A facility, such as an LOC, used to enhance the liquidity (but not the creditworthiness) of securitised assets. This facility provides cash to make the necessary payments of principal and interest on securities in the event of a shortfall in the cash available to the Issuer to make these payments. Amounts drawn on this facility become a senior obligation of the Issuer and will rank at least pari passu with the related securities.

**Liquidity Provider**

The provider of a liquidity facility.

**Liquidity Risk**

The risk that there will only be a limited number of buyers interested in buying an asset if and when the current owner of the asset wishes to sell it. Basically the risk that an owner of an asset will not be able to dispose of that asset.

**Listed**

Listed (quoted) on a stock exchange for public trading.

**Listed Building**

A building of special architectural or historical interest which the owner may not alter, extend or demolish without listed building consent.

**Listed Real Estate Investments**

Property investments that are traded on exchanges and priced on the basis of supply and demand for shares in the companies.

**Listing Agent**

The agent responsible for carrying out the procedures required to have securities listed on the appropriate stock exchange.

**Loan**

The advance of monies from one party (the Lender) to another party (the Borrower) which must be repaid on some future date.

**Loan Agreement**

The document which sets out the terms and conditions on which the Lender is prepared to lend monies to the Borrower. The Loan

Agreement will contain the commercial terms of the Loan as well as, amongst other things, representations, covenants, undertakings and Events of Default.

**Loan to Cost Ratio**

This is the proportion of the cost of a development project that a lending institution will be prepared to lend.

**Loan Files**

A record maintained by the Servicer of, amongst other things, debt service payments, property protection advances, property inspection reports, financial statements, property level intelligence, modifications to any loan documents and records of special servicing transfer events.

**Loan Loss Provisions**

An expense set-aside as an allowance for bad loans (when a customer defaults or terms of a loan have to be renegotiated, for example).

**Loan to Value Covenant**

A covenant by the Borrower that the Loan will not exceed a certain LTV threshold.

**Loan-to-Value (LTV) Ratio**

The balance of a mortgage loan over either the value of the property financed by the loan or the price paid by the borrower to acquire the property and provides a measure of the equity the borrower has in the asset that secures the loan. The greater the LTV ratio, the less equity the borrower has at stake and the less protection is available to the lender by virtue of the security arrangement.

**Loan Warranties**

An assurance or promise in relation to a loan, the breach of which may give rise to a claim for damages.

**LOC**

See Letter of Credit.

**Lock Box Provision**

A provision giving trustees the control of the underlying properties in a CMBS so that property owners only have a claim to cash flows net of expenses.

**Lock-Out Period**

The time period following origination during which the borrower cannot prepay the mortgage loan.

**London Interbank Offered Rate (LIBOR)**

The rate of interest that major international banks in London charge each other for borrowings. There are LIBOR rates for deposits of various maturities.

**Loss Curve**

A graphical representation of the pattern of losses experienced over time regarding a sample of loans or receivables, based on plotting the defaults or losses that occur over the life of all loans or receivables in the sample.

**Loss Given Default**

This represents the loss as a percentage of Exposure at Default.

**Loss Ratio**

The proportion of an insurer's premium income in any one year expended on paying and/or adjusting claims expressed as a percentage of the premium revenue.

**Loss Security**

The ratio of the outstanding principal paid on the loans minus the realised loss to the outstanding principal on the mortgage loans. Gives a rate of loss on a liquidated mortgage.

**Loss to Lease**

The difference between the rent being paid for property and the market rental rate for such a property.

**Long Term Refinancing Operation (LTRO)**

The ECB controls liquidity in the banking system via Refinancing Operations, which are basically repurchase agreements. Banks put up acceptable collateral with the ECB and receive a cash loan in return. In December 2011, the ECB extended the time frame to borrow to allow banks access to relatively inexpensive funding for up to 3 years.

**LP**

See Limited Partnership.

**LPA Receiver**

A person (not necessarily an insolvency practitioner) appointed under the Law of Property Act 1925 by a Lender holding a Fixed Charge over property in order to enforce the Lender's Security. A LPA Receiver has the powers and duties specified in the Law of Property Act 1925 but these can be modified by express provisions in the Security Document. An LPA Receiver is usually appointed with a view to selling the charged property or collecting the rental income from it for the Lender.

**LPE**

See Limited Purpose Entity.

**LTV**

See Loan to Value.

**LTV Covenant**

See Loan to Value Covenant.


# M


**MAD**

See Market Abuse Directive.

**Main Proceedings**

Insolvency proceedings which are brought in the member state in which the Debtor has its COMI. Once these proceedings are commenced all the assets of the Debtor are subject to the main proceedings, regardless of the member state where they are situated, unless Secondary/Territorial Proceedings are opened or already in place.

**Majority Lenders**

A term used in a syndicated or securitisable Loan Agreement to refer to that percentage (typically set at 66 2/3%) of Lenders (by size of commitment) that are required to approve certain decisions in respect of the Loan and related documentation.

**Management Fee**

In a private equity context, a fee paid by investors in a Private Equity Real Estate Fund to the general partner or an Investment Manager of the fund. The management fee is typically calculated as a percentage of the total capital commitments to the fund during the investment period, and as a percentage of the invested capital thereafter.

**Mandatory Cost**

The cost to a Lender incurred by complying with its regulatory funding requirements. This is not to be confused with Capital Adequacy requirements. The cost is paid by way of deposit to the Bank of England and the interest earned on that deposit helps fund the Bank of England's supervisory role. This cost is typically passed on to the Borrower and calculated as a percentage of that Lender's commitment in the Loan.

**Mandatory Prepayment**

A Prepayment following the occurrence of certain events, for example, on disposal of an asset, a change in control of the Borrower, or on receipt of insurance proceeds.

**Margin**

(i) In a Loan context, the percentage rate above a Lender's Cost of Funds that a Borrower has to pay on a Loan. The Margin reflects both the Lender's profit element for making the Loan as well as its pricing of the risk in advancing funds to a Borrower. (ii) In a Securitisation context, the percentage rate paid on each class of Securities above a particular interest basis (such as EURIBOR). The Margin paid on the Senior Class will be less than the Margin paid on the more Subordinated Classes.

**Mark to Market**

To re-state the value of an asset based on its current market price.

**Market Abuse Directive (MAD)**

EU Directive 2003/6/EC. The Market Abuse Directive sets a common framework for tackling insider dealing and market manipulation in the EU and the proper disclosure of information to the market.

**Market Capitalisation**

The value of a company determined by reference to the market price of its shares and the total number of shares in issue.

**Market to Market**

The act of recording the value of a position or portfolio based on the day's closing price. Instead of being valued at the original purchase price, the portfolio is valued at its current worth, reflecting any profit or loss which is not yet realised but which would be if the position was sold immediately.

**Market Value**

The estimated amount which a property should be exchanged on the date of valuation between a willing buyer and willing seller in an arm's length transaction.

**Master Servicer**

The party responsible for servicing mortgage loans.

**Master Servicing Fee**

The main fee paid to the Master Servicer for the servicing services it provides. Generally payable monthly from interest on the loan.

**Master Trust**

An SPE that issues multiple series of securities backed by a single pool of assets, with the cash flow generated by the assets being allocated between the series according to a predetermined formula.

**Maturity Date**

The date on which a bond or other security becomes due and payable in full.

**Mayfair**

The term used to describe the most valuable property in the underlying pool of assets. If the Mayfair amounts to a very high percentage of the value of the entire pool, the pool is said to be Mayfair heavy.

**MBS**

See Mortgage Backed Securities.

**Medium-Term Note (MTN)**

A corporate debt instrument that is continuously offered over a period of time by an agent of the Issuer. Investors can select from maturity bands of nine months to one year, more than one year to 18 months, more than 18 months to two years, etc., up to 30 years.

**Mezzanine Debt**

Debt (often more expensive, highly leveraged) which is subordinated to the Senior Debt.

**Mezzanine Pieces**

Classes or tranches rated in the middle range of a multi-class security. These are more secure than the first loss piece but less secure than senior classes.

**Mezzanine Investor**

A party who actively invests in mezzanine debt.

**Modelling/Cash Flow Modelling**

When converted into securities, all payments are chronologically collated to the class created in the issuance. Cash flows are estimated in a variety of circumstances using multiple variables (or models).

**Money Laundering**

Legitimisation of illegally obtained money to hide its true nature or source.

**Moratorium**

A period of time during which a certain activity is not allowed or required. In the context of a workout, an agreed period during which the Creditors cannot enforce their rights to enable a restructuring plan to be agreed. In the context of an Administration, the period during which a Creditor may not commence or continue any legal action against the company or enforce its Security without the consent of the court or the Administrator.

**Monoline Insurer**

An insurance company which may only write insurance policies relating to a single type of risk. In a financial context, the monoline insurer unconditionally guarantees the repayment of certain securities issued in connection with specified types of transactions (usually a securitisation) in return for the payment of a fee or premium.

The financial guarantee provided by a monoline insurer will generally allow the insured class or classes of a securitisation to be rated based on the financial guarantee rating of the insurer, with the result that the classes are rated higher than they would be were the financial guarantee not in place.

**Monte Carlo Approach or Method**

Monte Carlo methods are used in finance and mathematical finance to value and analyze instruments, portfolios and investments by simulating the various sources of uncertainty affecting their value, and then determining their average value over the range of resultant outcomes

**MoRE Analysis**

Moody's ratings approach to real estate analysis in EMEA.

**Mortgage**

A security interest in real property given as security for the repayment of a loan.

**Mortgage (UK)**

The transfer of the ownership in real property by way of Security for repayment of a Loan on the express or implied condition that it will be re-transferred on the discharge of the secured obligations. A Legal Mortgage transfers legal title to the Mortgagee and prevents the Mortgagor from dealing with the mortgaged asset while it is subject to the Mortgage. An Equitable Mortgage arises where the formalities to create a Legal Mortgage have not been completed or where the asset subject to the Mortgage is only an equitable interest. An Equitable Mortgage only transfers a beneficial interest in the asset to the Mortgagee with legal title remaining with the Mortgagor.

**Mortgage (US)**

A two party real property Security instrument in which the Mortgagor grants a Lien on real property to the Mortgagee to secure a debt. The Mortgage usually also includes an assignment of Leases and rents as well as a Security interest in personal property.

**Mortgage-Backed Securities (MBS)**

MBS include all securities whose security for repayment consists of a mortgage loan (or a pool of mortgage loans) secured on real property. Payments of interest and principal to investors are derived from payments received on the underlying mortgage loans.

**Mortgage Loan**

A Loan for the financing or refinancing of real estate whereby the Loan is secured by way of Mortgage over the real estate.

**Mortgagee**

The party taking the benefit of the Mortgage, usually a Lender.

**Mortgagor**

The borrower with respect to a Mortgage Loan.

**MTN**

See Medium Term Note.

**Mudaraba**

An Islamic finance term meaning a partnership whereby one party contributes services and another party capital. Securitisations which use this structure are termed Sukuk al-Mudaraba.

**Mudarib**

An Islamic finance term meaning the partner in a mudaraba structure which provides services and capital and usually no cash.

**Multi-family Property**

A building with at least five residential units, often classed as high rise, low rise or garden apartments. The quality of such properties is distinguished as:

Class A – command the highest rental rates in the market due to design/construction/location. Usually managed by large management companies.

Class B – command average rental rates in the market due to outdated design and finish but still which are of adequate construction quality and are well maintained. Again usually managed by large management companies. This class compiles the majority of properties collateralising up RMBS.

Class C – command below average rental rates due to poor maintenance/build in less desirable areas/occupied by tenants in less stable income streams. Generally managed by smaller, local property management companies.

**Murabaha**

Islamic finance term meaning sale at a mark-up. A prevalent structure in Islamic financing. Securitisations which use this structure are termed Sukuk al-Murabaha.

**Murubaha**

Islamic finance term meaning a partnership. Securitisations which use this structure are termed Sukuk al-Murubaha.

**Musharaka**

An Islamic finance term meaning a capital provider structure. Here each partner contributes capital and there is a much greater flexibility in allocating management responsibilities among partners, with joint rights of management being frequent and usual.

**Mutual Fund**

A professionally managed collective investment fund that distributes its shares to both retail and professional investors and that invests in stocks, Bonds, short-term money market instruments, and/or other Securities. The term is used as a generic descriptive identifier for various types of collection investment vehicles, such as unit trusts, open-ended investment companies, unitized insurance funds and UCITs.

# N

**NAREIT**

The National Association of Real Estate Investment Trusts, a US organisation.

**National Asset Management Agency (NAMA)**

A body created by the Irish Government in 2009, to function as a 'bad bank', acquiring property developments loans from Irish banks in response to the Irish financial crisis.

**NAV**

See Net Asset Value.

**NCREIF**

The National Council of Real Estate Investment Fiduciaries, a US member-supported non-profit association that publishes various real estate returns including total return, income and capital appreciation returns varying by property type and region.

**Negative Amortisation**

This occurs when the principal balance of a loan based on the amount paid periodically by the borrower is less than the amount required to cover the amount of interest due. The unpaid interest is generally added to the outstanding principal balance.

**Negative Amortisation Limit**

The maximum amount by which the balance of a negatively amortising loan can increase before the LTV ratio exceeds a pre-defined limit. When this limit is reached, the repayment schedule for the loan is revised to ensure that the full balance will be repaid by maturity.

**Negative Pledge**

An undertaking by a Borrower or other Obligor not to create, or permit to subsist, Security over its assets without the prior consent of the Lender.

**Net Asset Value (NAV)**

The appraised value of an entity's assets less the value of its liabilities.

**Net Effective Rent**

The gross rent less all operating expenses, rental concessions, tenant improvements etc. This can be a negative figure.

**Net Net Lease (or double net lease)**

A lease which requires the tenant to pay for property taxes and insurance in addition to the rent.

**Net Net Net Lease (or triple net lease)**

A lease which requires the tenant to pay for property taxes, insurance and maintenance in addition to the rent.

**Net Operating Cash Flow (NOCF)**
Total income less operating expenses and adjustments but before mortgage payments, tenant improvements, replacement revenues and leasing commissions. This is used as the basis for many financial calculations (for example debt service coverage ratios).

**Net Receivables**
The principal balance of receivables minus any portion of the interest due with respect to those receivables.

**Net Rent**
The income from a property after deduction of all outgoings, including repairs, insurance and management costs, but excluding taxes payable by the recipient.

**Net Stable Funding Ratio (NSFR)**
A measurement of the amount of long-term, stable sources of funding employed by an institution relative to the liquidity profiles of the assets it has funded and the potential for contingent calls on funding liquidity arising from off-balance sheet commitments and obligations, which has been proposed within the Basel III Accord.

**Netting**
The process of terminating or cancelling reciprocal obligations enjoyed by two parties to an agreement or contract, where those terminated or cancelled obligations are replacement by a single payment obligation from one party to the other.

**NICE**
A term used to describe a period of non inflationary consistent expansion that followed the UK Government's move to give the Bank of England the freedom to set interest rates soon after the 1997 General Election.

**NOCF**
See Net Operating Cash Flow.

**Non Consolidation Opinion**
A key feature of an SPE or bankruptcy remote entity. This is a legal opinion which confirms that the assets of an entity would not be substantially consolidated with those of its affiliates.

**Non-Performing Loan**
A Mortgage Loan or other debt instrument with respect to which the Borrower or Obligor has failed to make at least three scheduled payments.

**Non-Recourse**
Whereby a Borrower does not have any liability for a Loan beyond the assets it has granted as Security to a Lender. The Lender will have no right of recourse to a Borrower if those secured assets are insufficient to satisfy its liability to the Lender.

**Note**
A certificate of debt issued by a government or corporate entity promising payment of the original investment plus interest by a specified future date. Notes typically have a shorter maturity than Bonds. See also Bonds and Securities.

**Noteholder**
The holder of a Note or other Security.

**Notice Rights**
Rights often given to subordinated lenders allowing them notice that the loan is non-performing, or that a special servicing transfer event has occurred. Twinned with Cure Rights.

**Notional Amount**
The figure used as the basis for calculating the interest due with respect to an obligation that either has no principal balance or has a principal balance that is not the balance used for calculating interest.

**Novation**
The transfer of contractual obligations from one party to another and which requires the consent of the counterparty.

# O

**Obligor**
The party that has taken on the responsibility for taking certain actions under the terms of a contractual agreement. These actions often include making payments to parties. In a securitisation structure, the term generally refers to the parties making payments on the assets being securitised; these payments are the source of cash flows from which investors are repaid.

**OECD**
The Organisation for Economic Co-operation and Development.

**OEIC**
See Open-Ended Investment Company.

**Off-Balance Sheet Pass Through Securitisation**
Where assets are transferred to a trustee for the sole purpose of issuing asset-back securities.

**Off-Balance Sheet Pay Through Securitisation**
A development of Off-Balance Sheet Pass Through Securitisation due to the diversity of the European market in terms of types of underlying assets, types of security and applicable taxes, regulations and laws.

**Öffentliche Pfandbriefe**
See Pfandbriefe.

**Offering Circular**
A document used to promote a new securities issuance to prospective investors. This describes the transaction, including the features of each class of securities to be issued (such as the basis for interest payments, credit rating, expected average life and priority with respect to other classes). In a securitisation structure, the offering circular also gives details of the underlying assets, for example the type of assets and their credit quality. The offering circular is usually prepared by the lead manager of the securities issuance and its legal advisors.

**Official List**

The FSA's list of securities that have been admitted to listing. As the competent authority, the FSA must maintain the official list in accordance with Part VI of the Financial Services and Markets Act 2000.

**Official Receiver**

An officer of the court and civil servant who deals with bankruptcies and compulsory company liquidations. Such person has various functions which include becoming the first liquidator when the court makes a winding up order against the company, being appointed by the court as interim Receiver or provisional liquidator once the winding-up order has been presented and investigating the conduct of the company and directors.

**OIC**

The Organisation of the Islamic Conference.

**On-Balance Sheet securitisation**

Examples include covered mortgage bonds and Pfandbriefe style products.

**One-Tier Transaction**

A securitisation in which the transferor sells or pledges assets directly to the issuing SPE and/or the bond trustee or custodian and in doing so does not involve multiple transfers of the assets and one or more intermediate SPEs (thereby reducing transaction costs).

**OpCo – PropCo Structure**

This arises where an operating borrower with significant property assets (such as pubs and care homes) is acquired and restructured into two separate companies. OpCo is the operating company and operates the business, PropCo holds all the property assets. OpCo then takes a lease from PropCo on all of the operating properties.

**Open-Ended Commingled Investment Funds**

Investment funds where the number of shares outstanding changes when new shares are sold or old shares are redeemed and pricing is Net Asset Value.

**Open-Ended Fund**

A Real Estate Fund from which investors can demand to have their capital redeemed or paid back. These are usually also open to new investors who can subscribe for new units for cash. Compare with Closed-Ended Fund.

**Open-Ended Investment Company (OEIC)**

UK open-ended collective investment scheme of variable size that is structured as a company (rather than a trust) which invests in a broad range of assets.

**Open Pre-Payment**

A clause permitting prepayment of all or a portion of a loan without incurring a fee or penalty often restricted to a specified period.

**Open Standards Consortium for Real Estate (OSCRE)**

A Non-profit organization dedicated to the development of industry standards for data exchange.

**Operating Advisor**

A party appointed by the Controlling Class whom the Servicer or Special Servicer must consult with before making certain decisions with respect to the loans.

**Opportunistic Real Estate Investments**

Investments that are the most risky, are in non-traditional property types, including speculative development, seek internal rates of return of 15+% or more and have debt levels at more than 70% of the property value. They are characterised by property assets that have low economic occupancy, high tenant roll-over, are in secondary or tertiary markets and have investment structures with minimal control.

**Option**

Contracts that entitle the holder to the right to purchase or sell an asset for a specific price at a specific time in the future.

**Option Adjusted Spreads**

A representation of incremental return incorporating interest rate volatility and variations in cash flow due to changes in rates. Used in RMBS to price the prepayment risk to an investor. Less relevant to CMBS given the prevalence of prepayment penalties.

**Option Pledge**

The right but not the obligation to deliver goods or personal property as Security for a debt or obligation.

**Optional Termination**

A right granted to certain classes of Noteholders in a Securitisation defining when and under what circumstances a Securitisation can be redeemed ahead of its Expected Maturity or Final Maturity.

**Original Issue Discount**

A bond which is sold below, or at a discount to, par.

**Original Lender**

See Lender.

**Original LTV Ratio**

The original amount owed with respect to a mortgage loan divided by the value of the property on which the loan is secured. In the case of commercial mortgage loans, value is generally taken to mean the current appraised value of the property.

**Original Valuation**

The initial amount the asset was considered to be worth.

**Originate-to-Distribute (OTD)**

The process of originating Loans for the purpose of securitising or syndicating where the Originator intends to retain no, or only a small, interest in that Loan. By using the OTD model, an Originator is able to remove an asset from its balance sheet relatively quickly which allows it to originate more assets.

**Origination**

The process of making loans.

**Originator**

An entity that underwrites and makes loans; the obligations arising with respect to such loans are originally owed to this entity before the transfer to the SPE. See also Origination.

**OTC**

See Over the Counter.

**OTD**

See Originate-to-Distribute

**Out of the Money**

An option is described as being out of the money when the price of the underlying instrument is below the strike or exercise price for a call option (an option to buy) and above the strike price for a put option (an option to sell). The more an option is out of the money the cheaper it becomes as the likelihood that it will be exercised becomes smaller. Options can also be described as being deeply out of the money when they are likely to expire out of the money.

**Out of The Pool**

A tranche of a loan which is not included in the pool of loans which are to be securitised.

**Outstanding Principal Amount**

The primary amount left unpaid.

**Over Collateralisation**

A capital structure in which the value of assets exceed liabilities and thereafter a form of credit enhancement (used most regularly in certain asset-backed transactions). For example, an issuance of £100 million of senior securities might be secured by a pool of assets valued at £150 million, in which case the overcollateralisation for the senior securities would be 33%.

**Over-Rented**

A property is over-rented when it is subject to a Lease, or Leases, where the current rent passing is greater than could be achieved in the open market at the current time.

**Over-the-Counter (OTC)**

A description for Derivatives that are not traded over an organised exchange. Derivative contracts are entered into directly between the parties, enabling them to tailor the contract to match the terms of a particular transaction.

# P

**PAIF**

See Property Authorised Investment Fund.

**Partnership**

A type of business organisation in which persons pool money, skills and other resources, and share profit and loss in accordance with the terms of a Partnership Agreement.

**Partnership Agreement**

A written agreement between partners to a Partnership who join as partners to form and carry on a business.

**Passing Rent**

The rent which is currently payable under the terms of a Lease or tenancy agreement.

**PAUG Template**

The template for Credit Derivative Transaction on Mortgage-Backed Securities with Pay-As-You-Go or Physical Settlement published by ISDA in 2005, as amended. The PAUG Template adopts the Credit Derivatives Definitions to address trading of ABCDS in North American markets. This template addresses the settlement and credit issues associated with CDS referencing MBS and certain types of ABS more specifically than does the CPS Template through the innovation of so-called pay-as-you-go settlement of floating amount events.

**Pay Rate**

The periodic rate at which interest is paid on a mortgage. May differ from the accrual rate.

**Paying Agent**

A bank of international standing and reputation that is responsible for making payments on commercial mortgage loans. In general, payment is made via a clearing system (in Europe usually through Euroclear or Clearstream International). In Europe, this role is often assumed by an entity affiliated with the trustee or the administrator; by contrast, in the US, the trustee itself is generally responsible for making payments to investors.

**Payment History**

A record of a borrower's payments.

**Payment in Kind**

See PIK or PIK able.

**Payout Event**

An early amortisation event.

**Percentage Lease**

Rent payments which include overage as a percentage of gross expenses which exceed a certain amount as well as minimum of base rent. Common in large rental stores.

**Perfection**

A generic term used to describe the process that must be taken in order that a charge holder's Security has the intended priority over the chargor's other Creditors.

**Performing**

Term used to describe a loan or other receivable with respect to which the borrower has made all scheduled interest and principal payments under the terms of the loan.

**Performing Loan**

A Mortgage Loan or other receivable in respect of which the Borrower has made all scheduled interest and principal payments on the due date for payment.

**Pfandbriefe**

A debt instrument issued by German mortgage banks and certain German financial institutions. There are two types of Pfandbriefe: "Hypothekenpfandbriefe" that banks use to finance their lending activities and "Offentliche Pfandbriefe" that they use to finance their lending to public sector entities.

**Phase Rent**

Rental payments without adjustments for any lease concessions (for example rent free periods).

**PIA**

See Property Industry Alliance.

**PIC**

See Property Investment Certificate.

**PID**

See Property Income Distribution.

**PIK** or **PIK-able**

Payment in Kind. CDO Bonds (typically Mezzanine Pieces) that provide for the deferral of interest if funds available to the Issuer from the underlying Portfolio of assets are insufficient to pay interest in full and on time on those CDO Bonds.

**Pledge (US)**

A Security interest in property of the Debtor or third party which includes the right of the Creditor to enforce it in case of the Debtor's default by way of public sale. The Creditor's right to levy on pledged property is senior to the rights of subsequent pledge Creditors and unsecured Creditors. Whilst a pledge is a type of possessory Security where the Creditor takes possession of the pledged property, title to the pledged property does not pass to the Creditor.

**PLN**

See Property Linked Note.

**Plumbing**

To remedy or cure any leakage from a securitisation structure.

**Pool**

See Portfolio.

**Pool Factor**

The percentage of the original aggregate principal balance of a pool of assets which is still outstanding as of a particular date.

**Pooling and Servicing Agreement**

A contract that documents a transaction in which a defined group of financial assets are aggregated and details how the future cash flows to be generated by those assets will be divided between the parties to the contract. This also details the responsibilities of the Master Servicer and the Special Servicer for managing a CMBS.

**Portfolio**

The combination or spread of investments or assets held by an investor, fund or Issuer.

**Portfolio Lender**

A company that not only originates mortgage loans, but also holds a portfolio of their loans instead of selling them off in a secondary market.

**Portfolio Manager**

An individual or institution that manages a portfolio of investments.

**Preferred Equity**

Financing that is similar to mezzanine loan but structured to a senior equity position rather than as a loan. A preferred equity interest will typically have a stated preferred return and control rights similar to or greater than those of a mezzanine lender.

**Pre-Let**

A legally enforceable agreement for letting to take effect at a future date, upon completion of a development that is proposed or under construction at the time of the agreement.

**Preliminary Prospectus**

A prospectus which includes all or nearly all the information which will be included in the final version, identified by red printing on the front cover. This is essentially a marketing tool allowing investors to assess the utility of the security for meeting their investment objectors and allows the issuer to gauge interest in the proposed issues.

**Premium**

An amount in excess of the regular price paid for an asset (or the par value of a security), usually as an inducement or incentive.

**Prepayment**

A payment by the borrower which is greater than and/or earlier than the scheduled repayments.

**Prepayment Interest Shortfall**

The shortfall between the interest accrued on the corresponding mortgages and that accrued from a prepayment, generally when interest received from the prepayment is less than the interest on notes. Such shortfall may be allocated to certain classes of notes and, if so, that class will be adversely affected.

**Prepayment Penalty or Prepayment Premium**

A levy imposed on prepayments made on a mortgaged loan to discourage prepayment.

**Prepayment Rate**

The rate at which the mortgage loans (or other receivables in discrete pools) are reported to have been prepaid, expressed as a percentage of the remaining principal balance of the pool. Prepayment rates are often sensitive to market rates of interest.

**Prepayment Risk**

The risk that the yield on an investment will be adversely affected if some or all of the principal amount invested is repaid ahead of schedule. Commercial mortgages often reduce this risk through lockout periods, prepayment premiums and/or yield maintenance. Prepayment risk can also be taken to include extension risk, which is related to the repayment of principal more slowly than expected.

**Prescribed Part**

657

The fund required under section 176A of the Insolvency Act 1986 to be set aside out of the net realisations of property subject to a Floating Charge and made available to unsecured Creditors. The prescribed part was introduced by the Enterprise Act 2002.

**Pricing**

The process of determining the coupon and the price for securities prior to their issuance. The price of any financial instrument should be equal to the present value of the cost flow that it is expected to produce. In a securitisation structure, due to the effect of prepayment on the timing of the cash flows, the pricing process generates expected-case cash flows using a prepayment scenario.

**Prime Property**

A property investment regarded as the best in its class and location.

**Principal Only Notes**

Classes of Notes that are only entitled to principal distribution but not distribution of interest. See also Interest Only Strips.

**Principal Proceeds**

Collections received from underlying debt instruments that consist of principal payments, whether scheduled or unscheduled.

**Priority**

The right of a secured creditor to take enforcement action and to receive payment in priority to other competing interests.

**Priority of Distributions**

Provisions which dictate how, when and to whom available funds will be distributed.

**Priority of Payments**

The provisions in a Securitisation (or any other transaction involving structural subordination) which dictate how, when and to whom available funds will be distributed. Generally, available funds will be distributed to each class of Securities in accordance with their respective seniority. Once interest and principal due on the most Senior Class of Securities has been paid, interest and principal due on the next most Senior Class of Securities will be paid and so on. Also known as the Waterfall.

**Private Equity**

Money invested in entities which are not listed on any stock exchange.

**Private Equity Real Estate Funds**

Pooled investment vehicles formed to allow multiple investors to collectively invest in a series of real estate projects to achieve certain economic goals within certain risk tolerances.

**Private Label Securitisation**

Privately sponsored MBS and CMBS Securitisations using investment bank and commercial bank lending conduits.

**Private Placement**

The sale of securities to investors who meet certain criteria who are deemed to be sophisticated investors (for example insurance companies, pension funds).

**Private Real Estate Investments**

Direct real estate investments and indirect real estate investments, such as open-ended and closed-ended funds, that directly invest in real estate that are not traded on the exchanges.

**Probability of Default**

A borrower's likelihood of defaulting under a set of economic conditions.

**Procédure de Sauvegarde**

French safeguarding procedure akin to Administration.

**Professional Indemnity Insurance**

Insurance purchased by a provider of professional services to protect the provider against claims made by the person to whom the services are provided alleging loss caused by the provider's negligence.

**Profit Share**

A loan or investment provision that allows the lender/investor to receive an equity-based return in addition to normal rates upon some event. Typically this involves a lender/investor receiving a disproportionate percentage share of the proceeds in refinancing or sale.

**Profit Stripping**

The process whereby a company that has sold its assets in a securitisation continues to extract value from those assets by siphoning off the profits earned by the securitisation vehicle. The company therefore retains the economic benefits of ownership of the securitised assets.

**Prohibited Business Activities**

In an Islamic finance context, the conduct of business whose core activities (a) include manufacture or distribution of alcohol beverages or pork products for human consumption (or in some cases firearms); (b) have a significant involvement in gaming, brokerage, interest based banking or impermissible insurance; (c) accrue certain types of entertainment elements (especially pornography); or (d) have impermissible amounts of interest based indebtedness or interest income. Activities (a) through (c) are prohibited under the Sharia'a.

**Property Authorised Investment Fund**

An AIF that invests in real estate.

**Property Derivative**

A Derivative which has a price and value derived from a published commercial or residential property index. A Property Derivative presents the opportunity to hedge or speculate with respect to property values for a period of time.

**Property Income Distribution (PID)**

Dividends paid by UK REITs from the profits of its Property Investment Business.

**Property Industry Alliance (PIA)**

Alliance of four UK property trade bodies – the British Property Federation (BPF), British Council for Offices (BCO), Investment Property Forum (IPF) and the Royal Institution of Chartered surveyors (RICS) – that work together on issues of mutual concern.

**Property Investment Certificate (PIC)**

A British, publicly-traded Debt Security representing a holding in a special purpose vehicle that owns real estate. PIC coupons and redemption value depend on the performance of a real estate index such as an index published by the IPD.

**Property Linked Notes (PLN)**

A Debt Security with a return that is based on the performance of property. A PLN may be structured to give its holder control rights with respect to the underlying property. PLNs have been issued by owners of real property in order to divest themselves of the income stream, expenses and responsibilities relating to the ownership of property. The holder of the PLN in essence steps into the shoes of the real property owner for the term of the PLN.

**Property Manager**

The party responsible for the management of a property.

**Property Protection Advance**

A mechanism by which the Servicer or Special Servicer can provide amounts required to protect the property serving as collateral for the loan, for example payment of insurance premiums. In the event that a property protection payment is not made by the borrower, the Servicer or Special Servicer can require a property protection advance to be made either by the borrower drawing on a liquidity facility or the Servicer or Special Servicer making the payment out of its own funds then being reimbursed by the Issuer.

**Property Protection Payment**

A payment required to be made by the borrower in respect of the property serving as collateral such as insurance, real estate taxes or rent due under a headlease.

**Property Unit Trust**

An unincorporated fund established under a trust structure for the purpose of investing in real estate. The investors in PUTs are the beneficiaries under the trust. See also Authorised Unit Trust and Unauthorised Unit Trust.

**Prospectus**

The document which contains all the material information about a security. Termed the black as opposed to the red. In a CMBS this includes details of the properties, the payment sequence amongst classes and the treatment of defaults and prepayments. All relevant information about a security must be included in the prospectus. In connection with European deals, an Offering Circular ("OC") issued in accordance with the Prospectus Directive. See also Offering Circular.

**Prospectus Directive**

EC Directive 2003/71/EC. The Prospectus Directive sets out the disclosure obligations for Issuers of Securities that are to be offered to the public or admitting to trading on any regulated market within the EU. The European Commission issued a further amending directive designed to simplify and improve the application of the Prospectus Directive which came into force on 1 July 2012 across the EU.

**Protection Buyer**

The party transferring the credit risk associated with certain assets to another party in return for payment often seen in transactions such as credit default swaps. Payment is typically an up-front premium.

**Protection Seller**

The party that accepts the credit risk associated with certain assets (often seen in transactions such as credit default swaps, as mentioned above). Should losses on the assets exceed a specified amount, the protection seller makes credit protection payments to the protection buyer.

**100% PSA**

The benchmark mortgage prepayment scenario. Under this scenario, the monthly prepayment rate is assumed to be 0.2% per annum in the first month after issuance and to increase by 20 bps per year each month for the next 28 months. Beginning in the 30th month after issuance, the monthly prepayment rate is assumed to level off at 6% per annum and to remain at that level for the life of the mortgage pool to which the scenario is being applied.

**200% PSA**

A prepayment scenario in which prepayments are assumed to be made twice as fast as under the benchmark mortgage prepayment scenario. Under the 200% PSA scenario, the monthly prepayment rate is assumed to be 0.4% per year in the first month after issuance and to increase by 40 bps per year each month for the next 28 months. Beginning in the 30th month after issuance, the monthly prepayment rate is assumed to level off at 12% per year and to remain at that level for the life of the mortgage pool to which the scenario is being applied.

**Public Real Estate Investments**

Indirect Property Investments in exchange traded companies that invest in real estate.

**Purchase Event of Default**

A right given to subordinated lenders to purchase the senior portion of a loan which has gone into default.

**PUT**

See Property Unit Trust.

# Q

**QFC**

See Qualifying Floating Charge.

**QIS**

See Qualified Investor Scheme.

**QRS**

See Qualified REIT Subsidiary.

**Qualified Investor Scheme (QIS)**

A type of Authorised Investment Fund (AIF) which has wider investment powers and is subject to lighter regulation than other types of AIF. Investment in a QIS is open only to 'qualified investors', who will either be corporates or sophisticated individual investors who are expected to understand the risks involved in a wide range of investments.

**Qualified Mortgage**

A mortgage which can appropriately be included in a CMBS.

**Qualified REIT Subsidiary (QRS)**

A wholly-owned subsidiary of a REIT that is disregarded for tax purposes. A QRS may only own REIT qualified assets and generate REIT qualified income.

**Qualifying Floating Charge (QFC)**

A Floating Charge over the whole or substantially the whole of the company's property created by an instrument which (i) states that paragraph 14 of Schedule B1 to the Insolvency Act 1986 applies to it, (ii) purports to empower the holder of the Floating Charge to appoint an Administrator of the company or (iii) purports to empower the holder of the Floating Charge to make an appointment of an administrative receiver within the meaning given by section 29(2) of the Insolvency Act 1986.

**Qualifying Lender**

A party to whom a Lender can assign all or part of its interest in a Loan. Generally, a Qualifying Lender must be a bank or other financial institution which, were it to acquire an interest in the Loan, would not cause an increase in tax liability to the Borrower.

# R

**Rabb ul-Maal**

An Islamic finance term meaning partners in a mudaraba structure which provide capital in cash or in kind and generally do not interfere with the management or service component.

**Rack Rent**

Rent that represents the full open market annual value of a holding.

**Rake Bonds**

Loan specific securities backed by a B Note, or the junior component of a single commercial mortgage loan.

**Ramp Up**

The period of time following closing of a Securitisation (typically found in CDOs) during which the Issuer may acquire additional Collateral in order to "ramp up" a Portfolio at least equal in principal value to the amount of Securities issued by the Issuer.

**Ramp Up Period**

The period in a CDO during which the Issuer can "Ramp Up" the Portfolio. During the Ramp Up Period certain collateral tests are disapplied.

**Rate Creep**

This arises where the principal amount allocated sequentially (to the senior loan in priority to the junior) causes the weighted average rate on the senior and junior loans set out in the intercreditor agreement to creep above the weighted coverage whole loan rate that the tenant pays, with the result that there is an available funds shortfall with an increasing portion of junior loan interest becoming non-recoverable.

**Rate Step-Ups**

Agreed increases in interest rates. These can occur at certain specified times or upon the occurrence of certain events, for example if the borrower is unable to obtain a signed sales contract on the underlying property.

**Rated Obligations**

The obligation on an issuer to pay principal and interest which has been assigned a rating by a rating agency according to the likelihood they would be able to comply with those obligations.

**Rated Securities**

Securities of an Issuer which have been assigned a credit rating by a Rating Agency.

**Rating Agency**

Organisations which examine the likelihood of timely receipt of interest and ultimate repayment of principal on Securities issued by, amongst others, Securitisation Issuers. The process involves examining the credit strength of the underlying Portfolio, the cashflows of the transaction and the levels of subordination at each level of the capital structure. Ratings range from AAA (highest) to CCC (lowest).

**Rating Agency Confirmation**

A written statement issued by a rating agency that confirms, post-closing, that a proposed action in respect of the relevant transaction will not result in a downgrade or the withdrawal of current ratings of notes.

**RBC**

See Risk Based Capital.

**Real Estate Derivatives Special Interest Group** or **RED-SIG**

A US industry alliance established to offer insight and perspective on the use and implementation of US commercial property Derivative products and to facilitate the exchange of information on the use and implementation of commercial property directives.

**Real Estate Fund**

A legal entity which acts as a wrapper or vehicle into which investors place capital and which then invests in property.

**Real Estate Investment Trust (REIT)**

A tax election option which allows a specially formed vehicle to invest in real estate and/or securities backed by real estate. Such entities receive favourable tax breaks.

**Real Estate Mortgage Investment Conduit (REMIC)**

A legislation financial vehicle which allows for the issuance of multi-class securities with no adverse tax consequences. A REMIC is a pass-through entity that can hold loans secured by real property without the regulatory, accounting and economic obstacles inherent in other forms of mortgage-backed securities. A REMIC is a bankruptcy-remote legal entity which distributes the cash flow to bondholders of various classes or tranches of securities without being taxed at the entity level.

**Realised Loss**

The amount unrecovered when a foreclosed loan is sold, equal to (i) the unpaid balance of the loan; plus (ii) all unpaid scheduled interest; plus (iii) all fees applied to the sale of the property; minus (iv) the amount received from the sale.

**Receivables**

General term referring to principal and interest related cash flows generated by an asset and are payable to (or receivable by) the owner of the asset.

**Receiver**

A person appointed by the holder of a charge to enforce its Security. The appointment of a Receiver by a secured Creditor is a contractual remedy without recourse to the courts. A Receiver can be a Fixed Charge Receiver, LPA Receiver or administrative receiver. The Receiver's primary duty is to the appointing secured Creditor.

**Recognised Investment Exchange**

A Securities market which has been recognised as meeting the requirements stipulated by the UK Financial Services Authority.

**Red Book Valuation**

A new independent vaulation commissioned by a loan servicer.

**RED-SIG**

See Real Estate Derivatives Special Interest Group.

**Redemption**

The process of repaying all amounts due on Securities in a Securitisation. Redemption can occur on final maturity, following the occurrence of an Event of Default, on prepayment of the underlying assets, at the option of certain classes of Noteholders following the occurrence of certain events, and following the occurrence of certain tax events.

**Redevelopment**

Development of land which entails or follows the removal of all or most of the already existing buildings or structures.

**Refinancing Risk**

The risk that a borrower will not be able to refinance the mortgage on maturity thus extending the life of a security which uses this mortgage as collateral. See also Balloon Risk.

**Reinsurance**

Where an insurer relieves itself of all or part of an insurance risk by passing that risk on to another insurance company.

**Reinvestment Period**

The period in a CDO during which the Issuer may acquire new assets and substitute existing assets.

**Reinvestment Risk**

The risk that income from an investment can not be reinvested at the same rate of return as the investment that generated such income.

**REIT**

See Real Estate Investment Trust.

**REIT debt securities**

Securities issued by a real estate investment trust which are generally unsecured and may be subordinated to other obligations of the issuer.

**Release provision**

Either (a) a provision to release collateral under a mortgage for a pre-agreed amount or (b) a provision which requires the borrower, if it prepays the loan associated with one property in the pool which is consolidated and cross collaterised, to prepay a portion of all other loans in the pool (thereby stopping the borrower cherry picking properties in a pool).

**Relevant Information Summary or RIS**

RIS refers to a summary of any information relating to a loan or any property that the Servicer or the Special Servicer reasonably determines is likely to have a material impact on the value of the loan (or whole loan as applicable).

**REMIC**

See Real Estate Mortgage Investment Conduit.

**Remittance Report**

A report sent to noteholders on each distribution date by the Servicer containing information about the current distribution.

**Rent Free Period**

A defined period of time commencing from the start of the Lease during which the Tenant does not pay any rent.

**Rent Step-Up**

A lease whereby the rent increases at set intervals for a certain pre-agreed period or for the life of the lease.

**Rental Growth**

The rate of growth over a specified period of the Estimated Rental Value of a property.

**Rental Income Yield**

Rental income expressed as a percentage of the value of a real estate investment.

**REOC**

A real estate operating company.

**Repatriation**

Return of a financial asset (such as earnings) from a foreign country to an entity's home country.

**Representations and Warranties**

Clauses in an agreement in which various parties to the agreement confirm certain factual matters and agree that, should those statements of fact be untrue or incorrect, they will take steps to ensure that the statements are corrected or otherwise compensate the other parties to the agreement because the statements are not correct. In the context of a securitisation, the representations and warranties usually cover the condition and quality of the assets at the time of their transfer from the originator to the SPE or an intermediate transferor. They generally also specify the remedies available to the SPE or the intermediate transferor in the event that any of the representations are subsequently found to have been untrue. These may still be enforceable once the asset has been included in a securitised pool of assets.

**Reserve Account**

A funded account available for use by an SPE for certain specified purposes and often used as a form of credit enhancement. Virtually all reserve accounts are at least partially funded at the start of the related transactions, but many are structured to be built up over time using the excess cash flow that is available after making payments to investors.

**Reserving**

An amount maintained by an insurer in liquid form from its premium revenue against future claims, whether imposed by an insurance regulator or which the insurer itself chooses to maintain.

**Residential Mortgage-Backed Securities (RMBS)**

The RMBS abbreviation is used in two contexts. Residential Mortgage Backed Securities refers to Debt Securities that are backed by one or more Pools of Mortgages secured by residential real estate. All principal and interest from the Mortgages flow to the Noteholders in a pre-determined sequence. Residential Mortgage Backed Securitisation also refers to the overall transaction by which the Securities are issued and sold in the Capital Markets.

**Residual**

The term applied to any cash flow remaining after the liquidation of all security classes in a CMBS.

**Resolution Trust Company (US)**

A US Government owned asset management company that was responsible for liquidating assets (primarily real estate assets) that had been assets of saving and loan associations declared insolvent.

**Retail Sector**

A sector of commercial property types that includes high street shops, shopping centres and retail warehouses.

**Retention of Title**

A contractual provision by which the passing of title in goods supplied under the contract is made conditional on payment of the full purchase price by the buyer.

**Return on Equity**

The ratio of a company's profits to its shareholder equity expressed as a percentage.

**Reverse Earn-Out Loans**

Loans in respect of which provisions concerning resizing are made at origination on the basis of criteria not yet met, or not yet achieved consistently. Criteria will be specified and, if these are not met by specified dates, the loan will be resized downwards. The difference between the original balance of the loan and the resized balance must be paid down by the borrower.

**Reversion**

The ultimate sale of a property after a holding period (can be a theoretical sale).

**Reversionary Cap Rate**

The capitalisation rate applied to the expected sale price of a property after a holding period. This will be higher than the going-in cap rate.

**Reversionary Estate**

Where a property owner makes an effective transfer of a property to another but retains some future right to the property.

**Reversionary Rent/Income**

A change in income that will arise following a rent review or renewal of a Lease or re-letting of a property.

**Reversionary Value**

The expected value of a property upon reversion.

**Reversionary Yield**

The return on an investment calculated by dividing the reversionary income by the value/purchase price and expressed in terms of a percentage.

**Revolving Period**

The period during which newly originated loans or other receivables may be added to the asset pool of a revolving transaction.

**Riba**

An Islamic finance term meaning interest. The payment or receipt of riba is prohibited under Sharia'a law.

**RICS**

The UK Royal Institution of Chartered Surveyors.

**RIE**

See Recognised Investment Exchange.

**Right in Personam**

A right which is only enforceable against the person originally bound. Personal or contractual Security is a promise by the Borrower to pay the underlying debt and is usually augmented by a Right in Rem and real Security.

**Right in Rem**

A right available against the world at large (i.e. a right of property) save for a purchaser without notice, in contrast to a Right in Personam. Real Security gives the Lender a right in rem enforceable against a specific asset of the Borrower.

**Right to Cure**

The right for a specified interested third party to assume the responsibilities of a party who has breached a contractual obligation with a view to remedying the breach and preserving their interests.

**Right of Substitution**

The right to replace collateral, parties or other components in a contractual obligation.

**Risk Based Capital (RBC)**

An amount of capital or net worth an investor must identify and allocate to absorb a potential loss on an instrument. The amount of RBC varies amongst asset classes and is usually expressed as a percentage of the amount at risk.

**Risk Diversity**

The pooling of diverse loans to avoid and reduce concentration risk.

**Risk-Weighting**

The practice of classifying assets on the basis of the degree of risk that they entail.

**Risk-Weighting Bucket**

A risk-weighting category that is defined as including assets that involve a similar degree of risk.

**RMBS**

See Residential Mortgage Backed Securitisation.

**ROE**

See Return on Equity.

**Russell NCREIF Index**

Numerous indexes complied by the Frank Russell Company and the National Council and Real Estate Investment Fiduciaries on commercial real estate performance. Often used in the US as a benchmark for real estate investment performance.

**Russell 2000 Index**

A stock market index compiled by the Tacoma, Washington-based Russell Investment Group. Using a rules-based and transparent process, Russell forms its indexes by listing all companies in descending order by market capitalisation adjusted for float, which is the actual number of shares available for trading. In the US, the top 3,000 stocks (those of the 3,000 largest companies) make up the broad-cap Russell 1000 Index, and the bottom 2,000 (the smallest companies) make up the small-cap Russell 2000 Index.

# S

**S&P 500**

An index of the 500 largest publically traded companies in the United States. It is a market value weighted index which is also float adjusted.

**Sakk**

An Islamic finance term which is the singular of Sukuk.

**Salam**

An Islamic finance term meaning forward sale. One of the 14 categories of permissible Sukuk specified by the AAOIFI.

**Sale and Lease Back**

A transaction where the seller sells real property to the purchaser and the purchaser Leases the real property back to the seller.

**Sanierungsgutachten**

German term for a restructuring opinion.

**Schedule**

An agreement that supplements, amends and customises an executed ISDA Master Agreement to fit the particular contractual needs of the counterparties.

**Scheduled Interest**

The amount of interest owed at the end of the current period.

**Scheduled Principal**

The amount of principal scheduled to be repaid at the end of the current period.

**Schuldschein or Schuldscheindarlehen**

Loans made in the domestic German market that are evidenced by a promissory note.

**Schützschreiben**

Preventative declaration made by creditors under German law.

**SDLT**

See Stamp Duty Land Tax.

**Seasoning**

Descriptive term used to refer to the age of an asset being securitised. This gives an indication of how long the obligor has been making payments and satisfying its other obligations with respect to the asset prior to its securitisation. An asset becomes more seasoned as the period it has been performing to its terms increases. It is presumed that more seasoned assets have a lower likelihood of default.

**SEC**

See Securities and Exchange Commission.

**Second-Lien Mortgage Loan**

A loan secured by a mortgage or trust deed, the security of which is junior to the security of another mortgage or trust deed.

**Secondary Market**

A market in which existing securities are re-traded (as opposed to a primary market in which assets are originally sold by the entity that made those assets).

**Secondary Mortgage Market**

The market for the buying, selling and trading of individual mortgage loans and MBS.

**Secondary/Territorial Proceedings**

In the context of the EC Regulation, insolvency proceedings which are brought in any place where the debtor carries out a non-transitory economic activity with human means and goods but which is not the member state where the Debtor has its Centre of Main Interests or COMI.

**Section 106 Agreement**

Section 106 agreements (Town and Country Planning Act 1990) are signed subsequent to a planning consent being granted, that impose upon the developer obligations financially, or otherwise, that are conditions precedent to the implementation of any planning consent.

**Secured Debt**

Borrowing that is made, in part, on the basis of security pledged by the borrower to the lender.

**Secured Parties**

See Finance Parties.

**Securities**

See Debt Securities.

**Securities and Exchange Commission (SEC)**

A US government agency which issues regulations and enforces provisions of federal securities laws and its own regulations, including regulations governing the disclosure of information provided in connection with offering securities for sale to the public. The SEC is also responsible for regulating the trading of these securities.

**Securitisation**

A means of raising finance secured on the back of identifiable and predictable cash flows derived from a particular class of assets (such as rents, receivables, mortgages or operating properties).

**Security**

Assets that one party pledges to another party to safeguard amounts lent to that party. Following the occurrence of certain events, the party benefiting from the grant of Security can use the secured assets towards recovering the amounts owed to it. See also Legal Mortgage, Fixed Charge, Floating Charge, Perfection and Enforcement.

**Security Documents**

The collective name for those Finance Documents granting Security in favour of the Secured Parties/Finance Parties.

**Security Interest**

An interest that makes the enforcement of a Lender's rights more secure or certain, for example, by granting the Lender recourse to particular property in Priority to other Creditors.

**Security Package**

The name given to the overall Security granted by the Obligors and documented in the Security Documents.

**Security Trustee**

The entity which holds the Security Package on trust for all Secured Parties.

**Self-Amortising Loans**

A loan whereby the full amount of principal will be paid off at termination.

**Senior/Junior**

A common structure of securitisations that provides credit enhancement to one or more classes of securities by ranking them ahead of (or senior to) other classes of securities (junior classes). In a basic two-class senior/junior relationship, the senior classes are often called the class A notes and the junior (or subordinated) classes are called the class B notes. The class A notes will receive all cash flow up to the required scheduled interest and principal payments. The class B notes provide credit enhancement to the class A notes and experience 100%

of losses on the security until the amount of the class B notes is exceeded, when class A will experience all future losses.

**Senior Class** or **Senior Notes**

A class of Investment Grade Securities issued in a Securitisation that rank senior in priority to the Subordinated Classes issued in the same transaction.

**Senior Debt**

A debt obligation that is paid in priority to all other debts pursuant to the terms of an Intercreditor Agreement. The Senior Debt is typically repaid in full before the Subordinated Debt is repaid.

**Senior Notes**

See Senior Class.

**Senior Pieces**

Classes or tranches rated above BBB (or an investment grade) which are appropriate for regulated institutional investors.

**Senior Tranche**

See Tranche.

**Serviced Offices**

A general term used to describe offices which are let on an inclusive basis. They are normally subject to relatively short term licences. The rent is usually calculated on a per desk/room basis and is inclusive of all rates and service charges, as well as power and communication costs.

**Servicer**

The organisation that is responsible for collecting loan payments from individual borrowers and for remitting the aggregate amounts received to the owner or owners of the loans.

**Servicer Event of Defaults**

An event allowing the issuer to terminate the appointment of the Servicer or Special Servicer.

**Servicers Watch List**

A list of Loans maintained and published by a Servicer which indicates those Loans that should be elevated to a higher level of monitoring because, for example, the Borrower may have breached covenants or the Sponsor faces financial trouble.

**Servicing Advances**

The customary, necessary and reasonable out-of-pocket expenses incurred by the Master Servicer or Special Servicer in performing their duties. These are generally paid directly and then reimbursed from future payments.

**Servicing Agreement**

The contract that governs the responsibilities of the Master Servicer and the Special Servicer for managing and collecting payments on a Portfolio of Mortgage Loans that are held in a CMBS.

**Servicing Override**

The rights of the Controlling Class (in particular in any concert rights they may have) can be overridden by the servicer if it determines that following the course of action proposed by the Operating Advisor or the Controlling Class would violate the Servicing Standard.

**Servicing Standard**

The standard that the Servicer and Special Servicer must adhere to when performing their respective functions. The wording of the standard will be set out in the Servicing Agreement.

**Servicing Standard Override**

A right given to the Servicer and Special Servicer to override a course of action proposed by the Controlling Class or Operating Advisor in the exercise of their rights if the Servicer or Special Servicer determines that the proposed course of action would violate the Servicing Standard.

**Servicing Tape**

A record maintained by the Servicer of the current and historical loan payment profile of a loan.

**Servicing Transfer Event**

An event that triggers the transfer of the management of a mortgage loan from the Servicer to Special Servicer. A Servicing Transfer Event occurs when a borrower has defaulted or, in the reasonable adjustment of the Servicer, is likely to default and not be cured/corrected within a reasonable time. In this event the Servicer can transfer the day-today handling of the account to the Special Servicer until such time as the Special Servicer determines that the default has been cured/corrected.

**Servicing Power of Attorney**

A power of attorney (usually in a prescribed form in the Servicing Agreement) in favour of the Servicer and Special Servicer enabling the Special Servicer and Servicer to act on behalf of the relevant Finance Parties under the Finance Documents.

**Servient Tenement**

See Easement.

**Set-Off**

Where a Debtor has a cross-claim against a Creditor to the reduction or extinguishment of the Creditor's claim by the amount of his cross-claim.

**Share Capital**

Invested money that is not repaid to the investors in the normal course of business.

**Shareholder**

An individual, group or organisation that holds one or more shares in a company and in whose name a share certificate is issued.

**Shareholders Agreement**

A contract entered into between the Shareholders of a company which defines the Shareholders mutual obligations, privileges, protections and rights.

**Sharia'a Board or Sharia'a Supervisory Board**

The panel of Islamic scholars who determine whether an Islamic financial structure is sharia'a compliant.

**Sharikat**

An Islamic finance term meaning a partnership whereby work and capital may be allocated over all persons with correlative loss sharing.

**Sharkat ul-amwaal**

An Islamic finance term meaning a musharaka which is a property partnership.

**Sharpe Ratio**

An investment ratio used to measure the risk-adjusted performance in respect of a financial asset. The Sharpe Ratio provides an indication as to whether an asset's return is due to a smart investment choice or excessive risk.

**Shell Rent**

A portion of rental rates intended to amortise the cost of extraordinary tenant improvements.

**SIV**

See Structured Investment Vehicle.

**Slotting**

The methods set out in BIPRU Regulation 4.5.8 R for assigning risk weights for specialised commercial real estate lending exposures.

**Small and Medium Sized Enterprises (or SME)**

A company which by virtue of its number of employees, turnover or balance sheet total is classed as a small or medium enterprise.

**Soft Costs**

The element of the building cost or purchase cost of real estate which includes the due diligence fees, legal fees, accounting fees, surveyor fees and architect fees.

**Solvency 2**

A review of the capital adequacy regime for the European insurance industry. It aims to establish a revised set of EU-wide capital requirements and risk management standards that will replace the current solvency requirements.

**Sovereign Wealth Fund (SWF)**

A state-owned investment fund composed of financial assets derived from a country's reserves that have accumulated from budget and trade surpluses, often from revenue from generated from the export of natural resources.

**Special Liquidity Scheme**

A Bank of England scheme introduced in April 2008 which closed in January 2012 that was designed to improve the liquidity position of the banking system by allowing banks and building societies to swap their high quality mortgage backed and other securities for UK Treasury Bills for up to 3 years.

**Special-Purpose Entity (SPE)**

A Bankruptcy Remote corporate vehicle (whether in the form of a limited company, Partnership, trust, Limited Partnership or other form) often used in debt finance and Securitisation transactions. The

Bankruptcy Remoteness protects Lenders or Noteholders from having the underlying assets involved in insolvency proceedings against the Borrower or Issuer.

**Special Purpose Vehicle (SPV)**

See Special Purpose Entity.

**Special Servicer**

This can be the same or a different party to the Master Servicer, but is responsible for managing loans which have defaulted and carrying out the work of process.

**Special Servicing**

A term used to describe when a Mortgage Loan is being serviced by a Special Servicer following the occurrence of a Special Servicing Transfer Event.

**Special Servicing Fee**

The portion of the Special Servicer's fee which accrues with each specially serviced mortgaged loan.

**Special Servicing Transfer Event**

An event triggering the transfer of the servicing responsibilities from the Master Servicer to the Special Servicer. The trigger event is generally when the borrower has defaulted or, in the Master Servicer's reasonable opinion, is likely to default and be unable to cure the same within a reasonable time.

**Specially Serviced Loan**

A Mortgage Loan serviced by a Special Servicer.

**Sponsor**

Either (i) the entity that sponsors a Securitisation; or (ii) the entity that provides equity to a Borrower in a real estate finance transaction.

**Spread Accounts**

A revenue account into which is paid any collateral interest which is in excess of note interest which is not directed at any particular class. This provides credit enhancement in that it absorbs mortgage losses up to a structured cap.

**S&P 500 Index**

A stock market index containing the stocks of 500 large capitalisation corporations, most of which are American. The index is float weighted; that is, movements in price of companies that have higher float-based market values (share price multiplied by the number of shares which Standard & Poors determines are available for public trading) have a greater effect on the index than companies with smaller market values. The index is owned and maintained by Standard & Poors, a division of McGraw-Hill. S&P 500 is used in reference not only to the index but also to the 500 companies that have their common stock included in the index.

**SPV**

See Special Purpose Vehicle.

**Stamp Duty Land Tax**

Tax on transactions involving the acquisition of interests in UK land.

**Stand Alone Securitisation**

A securitisation based on a single loan. This has a very high concentration risk.

**Standard Prepayment Assumption**

This is a measure of prepayment rates on loans based on a variable rate of prepayments each month relative to the outstanding principal balance of the loans. Contrast with the Constant Prepayment Rate which assumes a constant rate of prepayment each month.

**Standardised Approach**

A method of calculating credit risk under Basel II involving the categorisation of banking book exposures.

**Static Pool**

A pool of assets made up solely of assets originated during a finite period of time, such as a month or a quarter.

**Statutory Declaration of Solvency**

A written statement by the directors of a UK company that they have made a full inquiry into the company's affairs and that, having done so, they believe that the company will be able to pay its debts in full within 12 months from the start of the winding up. The declaration is signed by the directors and declared to be true before a solicitor or person authorised to take oaths. The declaration will include a statement of the company's assets and liabilities as at the latest practicable date before making the declaration.

**Strategic Land**

A general reference to land holdings which are purchased or held with a view to add value by development at some future stage. Typically this only includes land which does not yet have consent for alternative and more valuable uses, and is principally applied to residential land, such as land banks, held by house buildings.

**Stress Testing**

The process used to evaluate whether the assets that will form the collateral for a securitisation are likely to produce sufficient cash flows in a variety of economic scenarios to be able to continue to make the principal and interest payments due on the related securities. The scenarios generally include a worst case and provide an indication of whether the proposed structure and level of credit enhancement is sufficient to achieve a particular credit rating for some or all of the various tranches issued in connection with the transaction. (See also WAFF and VIALS.)

**Stripped Interest Notes**

Note classes entitled to interest distributions but no (or a nominal) distribution of principal.

**Stripped Principal Notes**

Note classes entitled to principal distribution but no (or a nominal) distribution of interest.

**Structured Finance**

A type of financing in which the credit quality of the debt is assumed to be based not on the financial strength of the debtor itself, but on a direct guarantee from a creditworthy entity or on the credit quality of the debtor's assets, with or without credit enhancement.

**Structured Investment Vehicle (SIV)**

A type of SPE that funds the purchase of its assets, which consist primarily of highly rated securities, through the issuance of both CP and MTNs. Should an SIV default, its pool of assets may need to be liquidated; therefore, the rating on an SIV reflects the risks associated with potential credit deterioration in the portfolio and market value risks associated with selling the assets.

**Structuring**

The process by which combinations of mortgages and security classes are put together to achieve the highest price for a CMBS based on the current market position.

**Structuring Bank**

The investment bank responsible for co-ordinating the execution of a securitisation with respect to the originator/client, law firms, rating agencies, and other third parties. Typically, the structuring bank performs a due diligence exercise with respect to the assets to be securitised and the capacity of the Servicer including an identification of historical information and often an asset audit. The structuring bank is also responsible for developing and documenting the legal structure of the transaction and for identifying and resolving accounting and tax issues. In the case of a public issue, the structuring bank oversees the preparation of an information memorandum or offering circular to be used for the offering and listing of the related securities. The structuring bank ensures that the transaction complies with local regulatory requirements.

**Subordinated Class**

A class of securities with rights that are subordinate to the rights of other classes of securities issued in connection with the same transaction. Subordination usually relates to the rights of holders of the securities to receive promised debt service payments, particularly where there is a shortfall in cash flow to pay promised amounts to the holders of all classes of securities, although this could be related to the voting rights of noteholders.

**Subordinated Debt**

Debt which ranks junior to other debt. Such debt is usually paid after amounts currently due (or previously due) to holders of senior debt before paying amounts currently due (or previously due) to holders of the subordinated debt.

**Subordinated Notes**

See Subordinated Class.

**Subordination**

Where one Creditor (or group of Creditors) agrees not to be paid by a Borrower or other common Debtor (such as an Issuer) until another Creditor (or group of Creditors) have been paid. A form of Credit Enhancement where the risk of credit losses is disproportionately allocated amongst the Creditors. See also Senior Debt, Subordinated Debt, Senior Class and Subordinated Class.

**Subordination Agreement**

Formal document acknowledging that one party's claim or interest is inferior (junior) to that of the other party of parties. See also Intercreditor Agreement.

**Sub-Performing Loan**

A loan which is producing payments (even the full principal and interest payments required) but with an unacceptable debt coverage ratio. Some investors also apply this term to loans making all necessary payments but the LTV ratio (or other indicatory value) suggest it is unlikely to be fully paid off at maturity.

**Sub-Prime**

Residential Mortgage Borrowers with a tarnished or limited credit history. Loans made to sub-prime Borrowers carry a greater credit risk than Loans made to non sub-prime Borrowers.

**Subrogation**

The succession by one party, often an insurer, to another party's legal right to collect a debt from or enforce a claim against a third partly.

**Subscription Facility**

A Loan advanced to a Private Equity Real Estate Fund secured by unfunded commitments of the fund's investors that allow the fund to minimise the number of capital calls on its investors by serving as working capital and for bridge financing and giving the fund a way to quickly finance the day to day needs of its operations.

**Sub-Servicing**

This is when the Servicer and/or the Special Servicer sub-contracts some or all of their obligations. This is generally prohibited if it would result in the downgrade in the rating of the notes. The Servicer and Special Servicer would remain liable for any breach by the sub-servicer of their obligations under the servicing agreement.

**Sukuk**

An Islamic finance term which refers to both Islamic bonds and Islamic securitisations.

**Survivability**

A term applied to contractual terms which are still enforceable once the loan has been included in a security. Often the case with representations and warranties.

**Swap**

An agreement pursuant to which two counterparties agree to exchange one cash flow stream for another, for example fixed-to-floating interest-rate swaps, currency swaps, or swaps to change the maturities or yields of a bond portfolio.

**Swap Provider**

The party that writes a swap contract.

**Syndicate**

A group of Lenders that together make a Loan available to a Borrower.

**Syndicated Loan**

A large loan arranged by a group of international banks that form a syndicate, headed by a lead manager. The borrower pays the lead manager a fee whose size depends of the complexity of the loan and the risk involved.

**Synthetic CDO**

A CDO transaction in which the transfer of risk is effected through the use of a Credit Derivative as opposed to a True Sale of the assets. See also Synthetic Securitisation.

**Synthetic CMBS**

A CMBS transaction in which the transfer of risk is effected through the use of a Credit Derivative as opposed to a True Sale of the assets. See also Synthetic Securitisation.

**Synthetic Securities**

Securities designed to modify the cash flows generated by underlying asset securities that are rated primarily on the creditworthiness of the asset securities and currency or interest rate swaps or other similar agreements.

**Synthetic Securitisation**

A Synthetic Securitisation achieves the same economic result as in a True Sale Securitisation of physical assets, but relies on the transfer of credit risk through Derivative contracts in respect of the Portfolio. The Issuer (as Protection Seller) agrees to pay the legal owner of those assets (the Protection Buyer) an amount equal to the losses it suffers as a result of certain credit events occurring on the underlying Portfolio (such as an underlying obligor payment default). These payments are funded from the proceeds of issuing CLNs to Capital Market investors. Until such time as a credit event occurs, the proceeds from the issuance of the CLNs are invested by the Issuer in risk-free investments such as government Securities. The principal amount of each class of CLNs is written down in line with a principal reduction in the market value of the reference Portfolio resulting from a credit event.

# T

**Taxable REIT Subsidiary**

A wholly-owned subsidiary of a REIT that is taxed as a corporation. Dividends from a Taxable REIT Subsidiary are good REIT income which means a REIT can conduct operations through a Taxable REIT Subsidiary that benefit the REIT even though those operations generate non-qualifying REIT income.

**Tenant**

An individual or corporate body holding a tenancy.

**Tenant Improvements**

The expense, generally met by the tenant, of physically improving the leased property or space.

**Term**

The lifespan of a Loan being the period of time from the borrowing of the Loan to the repayment of the Loan.

**Term Asset-Backed Securities Loan Facility (TALF)**

A program created by the United States Federal Reserve to help market participants meet the credit needs of households and small businesses by supporting the issuance of ABS. Closed for loan extensions against newly issued CMBS on June 30, 2010 and for new loan extensions against all other types of collateral on March 31, 2010.

**Term Sheet**

See Heads of Terms.

**Third Party Pool Insurance**

A form of credit enhancement whereby the issuer pays a bond issuer an annual premium, in return for which the issuer will absorb the loss on mortgaged loans. This therefore protects investors from any losses on the mortgage loans. The CMBS is usually never rated higher than the credit rating of the third party insurer. See also monoline insurer.

**Tier 1 Capital**

See Core Capital.

**Title Insurance**

The application of insurance to the ownership and/or use of interests in real estate.

**TOGC**

A term indicating the transfer of a business as a going concern.

**Top-Down Approach to Investing**

A strategy adopted by an investor whereby large scale trends in the general economy are examined and industries and companies to invest in selected which are likely to benefit from those trends, contrast with a bottom-up approach to investing.

**Torrens Systems**

An approach to transfers of interests in real estate which creates a real right through the act of registration carried out by a state body and which typically provides both a plan-based record and an indemnity from the state.

**Total Return Swap (TRS)**

A Derivative trade between a dealer and end user whereby one of the two parties exchanges the total return of an asset (including, for example, appreciation and dividends or other distributions relating to that asset) for a fixed or floating amount plus a spread that reflects the credit profile of a counterparty and other factors, plus any depreciation with respect to the underlying asset. A TRS may be structured as a Property Derivative, a Credit Derivative or as other Derivatives.

**Tranche**

A term used to refer to a class of Securities and the collective description of the discreetly rated classes of CMBS securities. Each class is paid a pre-determined coupon and principal based on a payment sequence. The lower rated tranches generally have higher coupons (to compensate for increased risk) and longer life spans as they do not receive principal payments until higher rated tranches have been paid off.. See also Subordination, Senior Class, Mezzanine Piece and Subordinated Class.

**Tranching Account**

An account opened by the security trustee pursuant to the terms of the intercreditor agreement pursuant to which it agrees to hold all amounts received on the whole mortgage loan in its entirety on trust for the holders of each tranche and to disburse such amounts pursuant to the terms of the intercreditor agreement.

**Treasuries**

Negotiable debt obligations of the US government issued with varying maturities and backed by the credit of the US government.

**Trigger Event**

In a securitisation structure, the occurrence of an event which indicates that the financial condition of the issuer or some other party associated with the transaction is deteriorating. Such events will often be defined in the transaction documents, as are the changes to the transaction structure and/or priority of payments that are to be made following the occurrence of such an event.

**Triple Net Lease**

See Net Net Net Lease.

**Trophy Asset**

A large commercial property that enjoys a high profile as a result of some combination of prestigious location, highly visible owners, prominent tenants and often striking design.

**Troubled Asset Relief Program (TARP)**

A United States Government program to purchase assets and equity from financial institutions to strengthen the financial sector.

**TRS**

See Total Return Swap.

**True Sale**

A sale transaction which is recognised by the courts as a sale, not a grant of Security interest by the seller. Recognition as a True Sale is necessary to ensure that the title to the underlying real property, and not merely a Security interest on the real property, is effectively transferred to the purchaser. Although there is no court precedent defining the requirements of a True Sale, it is generally understood that various factors, including the parties' intention, need to be taken into consideration when determining whether the sale transaction is recognised as a True Sale.

**True Sale Opinion**

With respect to a securitisation, a legal opinion to the effect that the assets that are being securitised have been transferred from the originator to the issuing SPE that these assets will not form part of the bankruptcy estate of the originator or be subject to any applicable automatic stay or moratorium provisions.

**Truro**

The true value of a redenominated Euro following a eurozone breakup.

**Trustee**

A third party, often a specialist trust corporation or part of a bank, appointed to act on behalf of investors. In the case of a securitisation, the trustee is given responsibility for making certain key decisions that may arise during the life of the transaction. The role of the trustee may also include holding security over the securitised assets and control over cash flows. It is often a requirement of listing ABS that an independent trustee be appointed. The trustee receives regular reports on the performance of the underlying assets in order to check whether, for instance, cash flow procedures are being followed. Subject to appropriate indemnity and other protections, the trustee is also typically responsible for finding a replacement servicer when necessary, taking up legal proceedings on behalf of the investors, and, as the case may be, selling the assets in order to repay investors. To enable the trustee to perform its duties and to provide adequate remuneration, it receives a fee paid senior to all other expenses and a senior ranking indemnity to cover all unexpected costs and expenses.

**Turner Review**

A review carried out by Lord Turner, the chairman of the FSA, of the UK's approach to bank regulation with recommendations for reforming the ways banks are regulated. This review was commissioned by the British Chancellor of the Exchequer.

# U

**UBTI**

Unrelated Business Taxable Income. A tax placed on the income of otherwise non-taxable entities with respect to certain specified types of income.

**UCC**

The US Uniform Commercial Code, the uniform law adopted in all 50 US States and the District of Columbia (with minor local variations), which, amongst other things, governs the creation, perfection, priority and enforcement of Security interest in most types of US personal property.

**UCIT**

See Undertakings for Collective Investment in Transferable Securities.

**Umbrella Partnership REIT or UPREIT**

A REIT structured to be the general partner and a limited partner of an operating Limited Partnership that holds all of the real estate assets. The UPREIT structure allows owners of property to exchange their property for interest in the Limited Partnership in a tax-free exchange while diversifying their holdings. The Limited Partnership interests can be exchanged for REIT shares at a later time giving the holder of

Limited Partnership interests liquidity, but such conversion will result in a realisation of the deferred tax on the gain of the contributed property.

**Unauthorised Unit Trust**

An unregulated unit trust which may only be offered to institutional investors. See also Authorised Unit Trust.

**Undertakings for Collective Investment in Transferable Securities** or **UCIT**

Retail collective investment funds established in accordance with European Union directives that are permitted to operate freely throughout the EU on the basis of a single authorisation from one member state. In practice many EU member nations have imposed additional regulatory requirements that have impeded free operation with the effect of protecting local asset managers. These are similar in many respects to Mutual Funds.

**Underwriter**

Any party that takes on risk. In the context of the capital markets, a securities dealer will act as underwriter to an issuance and commit to purchasing all or part of the securities at a specified price thereby giving the issuer certainty that the securities will be placed and at what price and eliminating the market risk. In return for assuming this risk, the underwriter will charge a fee.

**Unlisted Real Estate Investments**

Property investments that are not traded on exchanges.

**UPREIT**

See Umbrella Partnership REIT.

**Upward Only Rent Review**

A clause in a Lease that specifically states that the rent can only be reviewed to the greater of the previous rent or the current market rent. The rent can never go down but can stay the same. This is a standard clause in most UK Leases.


# V


**Vacant Possession**

A term used to describe a property which is not subject to an occupational Lease or licence that may produce income. It does not, however, refer to a property that is occupied by the owner.

**Valuation**

An appraisal of a property carried out by independent valuers in order to establish the approximate value of the property.

**Valuation Report**

A report prepared by valuation surveyors attributing a value to a property usually for financing purposes.

**Valuation Shopping**

A process whereby borrowers select and present their choice of valuer from the outset of a transaction based on who they know will give them the highest potential value.

**Value**

Unless specified to the contrary the fair market value of a property determined in an appraisal made by the originator when the loan is first made.

**Value-Added Real Estate Investments**

Property investments that are slightly more risky than Core-Plus and generally seek internal rates of 11% to 15%. Value-Added Real Estate Investments carry debt of between 50% to 75% of the property's value, and rely more on local knowledge than Core or Core-Plus Investment.

**VAT**

Value Added Tax.

**VATA 1994**

Value Added Tax Act 1994.

**Vickers Report**

This is the final report of the Independent Commission on Banking, chaired by Sir John Vickers. The Commission was asked to consider structural and related non-structural reforms to the UK banking sector to promote financial stability and competition.

**Void Periods**

A period of time during which a property, or part of a property, does not generate any income, either where there is no Lease in place, or where there is a Lease in place but there is a Rent Free Period that has not yet expired.

**Voluntary Prepayments**

Prepayments by the borrower so to reduce or pay off the outstanding principal, often due to the borrower refinancing at lower interest rates.

**Voting Rights Enforcement**

A type of Enforcement action whereby the rights attaching to pledged shares are exercised by the Secured Parties/Finance Parties. A Voting Rights Enforcement is often used to replace the board of directors of the Borrower vehicle.

# W

**Wakala**

An Islamic finance term meaning agency. One of the 14 categories of permissible Sukuk specified by the AAOIFI.

**Waterfall**

The term applied to the cash flow pay-out priority in a CMBS. Generally, cash flow pays principal and interest to the highest rated tranche but interest only to lower rated tranches. Once the notes from the highest rated tranche are paid down, cash flow then pays principal and interest on next highest rated tranche and so on. The sequence will be stipulated in the prospectus at the time of issue. See Priority of Payments.

**Weighted-Average Cost of Funds**

The weighted-average rate of return that an issuer must offer to investors in the event of a combination of borrowed funds and equity investments. Also referred to as the weighted-average cost of capital.

**Weighted-Average Coupon (WAC)**

The average interest rate for a group of loans or securities, calculated by multiplying the coupon applicable to each loan or security in the group by the proportion of the outstanding principal balance of the entire pool made up by the loan or security to which the coupon relates.

**Weighted-Average Foreclosure Frequency (WAFF)**

The estimated percentage of assets in the securitisation pool that will go into default under an economic scenario designed to test whether the cash flow that is expected to be generated by the pool plus available credit enhancement will be sufficient to repay all securities rated at a certain rating category or higher. The WAFF is used in conjunction with the WALS to determine the expected level of losses at different rating categories.

**Weighted Average Life**

The average time until all scheduled principal payments are expected to have been made, weighted by the size of each mortgage in the pool.

**Weighted-Average Loss Severity (WALS)**

The average loss that is expected to be incurred in the event that any one asset in a securitisation pool goes into default, expressed as a percentage of outstanding principal balance of such asset as of the date of the default. The expected loss is predicted by making various assumptions about the potential decline in the market value of collateral that may secure the asset. The WALS is used in conjunction with the WAFF to determine the expected level of losses at different rating categories.

**Weighted–Average Maturity (WAM)**

A measure of the remaining term to maturity of a group of loans, calculated by multiplying the remaining months to maturity of each loan in the group by the proportion of the outstanding principal balance of the entire pool made up by the loan or security to which the coupon relates.

**Weighted Average Unexpired Lease Term (WAULT)**

The average lease term remaining to expiry or lease break across the investment portfolio, weighted by rental income. Excludes short-term lettings such as car parks and advertising hoardings, residential leases and long ground leases.

**Whole Business Securitisation**

A whole-business or corporate securitisation refers to the issuance of bonds backed by a company's cash flow generating assets and/or its inventory. The security may have been legally isolated in favour of the holders of the notes and might be managed by a backup operator, thereby prolonging the security's cash flow generating capacity in favour of the noteholders should bankruptcy proceedings be brought against the company or the company become insolvent. With appropriate enhancements to the securitised debt structure in place, securitisation can achieve a higher rating on (and longer term of) the securitised debt than a company's secured or unsecured corporate debt.

**Whole Loan**

A whole Mortgage Loan and the term used in AB Structures to refer to a Mortgage Loan before it is bifurcated into an A Loan and B Loan.

**Withholding Tax**

A tax levied on income (interest and dividends) from debt obligations owned by foreign investors. This can be claimed back if there is a double tax treaty in place between the relevant countries.

**Workout Fee**

The fee the Special Servicer is entitled to for any specialist serviced loan which becomes corrected. It provides an incentive for the Special Servicer to correct a non-performing loan as soon as possible. This fee is paid only whilst the loan remains a corrected mortgaged loan.

# X

**X-Class Coupon**

This is a deal's profit taken by the issuing bank.

**X-Notes**

The term usually given to the notes which form the IO strip in a CMBS.

# Y

**Yield**

The return on an investment, calculated by dividing the income at any particular moment, divided by the value/purchase price and expressed in terms of a percentage.

**Yield Maintenance**

A prepayment provision to ensure investors attain the same yield as if the borrower had made all scheduled payments until maturity, therefore removing the prepayment risk.

**Yield Shift**

The movement in the yield of an investment, whether upwards of downwards.

**Yield Spread**

The difference in yield between a security and a separate benchmark (for example UK treasuries of the same maturity).

### Yield to Average Life

A calculation based on the expected term of the class rather than its final stated maturity. Used in lieu of yield to maturity.

### Yield to Maturity

The calculation of the return an investor will receive if a note is held to its maturity date. This takes into account purchase price, redemption value, time to maturity, coupon and the time between interest payments.

# Z

### Zero Coupon Note

A note that does not pay interest and therefore does not have a coupon but is traded at a deep discount, rendering profit at maturity when the bond is redeemed for its full face value. Another name for a stripped interest note.

### Zscore

A score used by Lenders indicating their assessment of the financial strength of the Borrower, taking into account factors such as experiences of the Sponsor/Borrower, reliability and payment history.

### Zwangsverwaltung

German term for a forced administration where the court appoints a receiver to take over management of a property from its owners.

### Zwangsversteigerung

German term for where a court forces an auction process over a property.

# Index

All indexing is to heading number

- who are the investors of CMBS?

- Mostly 5-7 yr loans so loan maturities peaking → p.607

- banks being forced to meet more restrictive capital requirements,
     might sell assets to correct ratio.        p. lest

- what's happening to loans at maturity?

- what's the participant attitude on round of th CMBS mkt?

CRD   Central Requirements Directive
       is the implementing measure for the Basel Accord

Basel I → p. 378

FSB     Financial Stability Board

Solvency II